Science

Library of Congress Classification
2012

Prepared by the Policy and Standards Division
Library Services

LIBRARY OF CONGRESS
Cataloging Distribution Service
Washington, D.C.

This edition cumulates all additions and changes to class Q through List 2012/04, dated April 16, 2012. Additions and changes made subsequent to that date are published in lists posted on the World Wide Web at

<http://www.loc.gov/aba/cataloging/classification/weeklylists/>

and are also available in *Classification Web*, the online Web-based edition of the Library of Congress Classification.

Library of Congress Cataloging-in-Publication Data

Library of Congress.
Library of Congress classification. Q. Science / prepared by the Policy and Standards Division, Library Services.
pages cm
"This edition cumulates all additions and changes to class Q through List 2012/04, dated April 16, 2012. Additions and changes made subsequent to that date are published in lists posted on the World Wide Web ... and are also available in Classification Web, the online Web-based edition of the Library of Congress Classification"--Title page verso.
Includes index.
ISBN 978-0-8444-9543-9
1. Classification, Library of Congress. 2. Classification--Books--Science. I. Library of Congress. Policy and Standards Division. II. Title. III. Title: Science.

Z696.U5Q 2012
025.4'65--dc23

2012020259

For sale by the Library of Congress Cataloging Distribution Service,
101 Independence Avenue, S.E., Washington, DC 20541-4912.
Product catalog available on the Web at **www.loc.gov/cds**.

PREFACE

The first edition of Class Q, Science, was published in 1905. Subsequent editions appeared in 1913, 1921, 1948, 1950, 1973, 1989, 1996, 2004, 2007, and 2009. This 2012 edition cumulates changes that have been made since the 2009 edition was published.

Classification numbers or spans of numbers that appear in parentheses are formerly valid numbers that are now obsolete. Numbers or spans that appear in angle brackets are optional numbers that have never been used at the Library of Congress but are provided for other libraries that wish to use them. In most cases, a parenthesized or angle-bracketed number is accompanied by a "see" reference directing the user to the actual number that the Library of Congress currently uses, or a note explaining Library of Congress practice.

Access to the online version of the full Library of Congress Classification is available on the World Wide Web by subscription to Classification Web. Details about ordering and pricing may be obtained from the Cataloging Distribution Service at:

<http://www.loc.gov/cds/>

New or revised numbers and captions are added to the Library of Congress Classification schedules as a result of development proposals made by the cataloging staff of the Library of Congress and cooperating institutions. Upon approval of these proposals by the editorial meeting of the Policy and Standards Division of the Acquisitions and Bibliographic Access Directorate, new classification records are created or existing records are revised in the master classification database. Lists of newly approved or revised classification numbers and captions are posted on the World Wide Web at:

<http://www.loc.gov/aba/cataloging/classification/weeklylists/>

Libby Dechman, cataloging policy specialist in the Policy and Standards Division, is responsible for coordinating the overall intellectual and editorial content of class Q. Kent Griffiths, assistant editor of classification schedules, creates new classification records and their associated index terms, and maintains the master database.

Barbara B. Tillett, Chief
Policy and Standards Division

May 2012

OUTLINE

Q1-390	Science (General)
Q1-295	General
Q300-390	Cybernetics
Q350-390	Information theory
QA1-939	Mathematics
QA1-43	General
QA47-59	Tables
QA71-90	Instruments and machines
QA75-76.95	Calculating machines
QA75.5-76.95	Electronic computers. Computer science
QA76.75-76.765	Computer software
QA101-(145)	Elementary mathematics. Arithmetic
QA150-272.5	Algebra
QA273-280	Probabilities. Mathematical statistics
QA299.6-433	Analysis
QA440-699	Geometry. Trigonometry. Topology
QA801-939	Analytic mechanics
QB1-991	Astronomy
QB1-139	General
QB140-237	Practical and spherical astronomy
QB275-343	Geodesy
QB349-421	Theoretical astronomy and celestial mechanics
QB455-456	Astrogeology
QB460-466	Astrophysics
QB468-480	Non-optical methods of astronomy
QB495-903	Descriptive astronomy
QB500.5-785	Solar system
QB799-903	Stars
QB980-991	Cosmogony. Cosmology
QC1-999	Physics
QC 1-75	General
QC81-114	Weights and measures
QC120-168.85	Descriptive and experimental mechanics
QC170-197	Atomic physics. Constitution and properties of matter Including molecular physics, relativity, quantum theory, and solid state physics
QC221-246	Acoustics. Sound
QC251-338.5	Heat
QC310.15-319	Thermodynamics

	Physics - Continued
QC350-467	Optics. Light
QC450-467	Spectroscopy
QC474-496.9	Radiation physics (General)
QC501-766	Electricity and magnetism
QC501-(721)	Electricity
QC669-675.8	Electromagnetic theory
QC676-678.6	Radio waves (Theory)
QC701-715.4	Electric discharge
QC717.6-718.8	Plasma physics. Ionized gases
QC750-766	Magnetism
QC770-798	Nuclear and particle physics. Atomic energy. Radioactivity
QC793-793.5	Elementary particle physics
QC794.95-798	Radioactivity and radioactive substances
QC801-809	Geophysics. Cosmic physics
QC811-849	Geomagnetism
QC851-999	Meteorology. Climatology
	Including the earth's atmosphere
QC974.5-976	Meteorological optics
QC980-999	Climatology and weather
QC994.95-999	Weather forecasting
QD1-999	Chemistry
QD1-65	General
	Including alchemy
QD71-142	Analytical chemistry
QD146-197	Inorganic chemistry
QD241-441	Organic chemistry
QD415-436	Biochemistry
QD450-801	Physical and theoretical chemistry
QD625-655	Radiation chemistry
QD701-731	Photochemistry
QD901-999	Crystallography
QE1-996.5	Geology
QE1-350.62	General
	Including geographical divisions
QE351-399.2	Mineralogy
QE420-499	Petrology
QE500-639.5	Dynamic and structural geology
QE521-545	Volcanoes and earthquakes
QE601-613.5	Structural geology
QE640-699	Stratigraphy

OUTLINE

	Geology - Continued
QE701-760	Paleontology
QE760.8-899.2	Paleozoology
QE901-996.5	Paleobotany
QH1-278.5	Natural history (General)
QH1-(199.5)	General
	Including nature conservation, geographical distribution
QH201-278.5	Microscopy
QH301-705.5	Biology (General)
QH359-425	Evolution
QH426-470	Genetics
QH471-489	Reproduction
QH501-531	Life
QH540-549.5	Ecology
QH573-671	Cytology
QH705-705.5	Economic biology
QK1-989	Botany
QK1-474.5	General
	Including geographical distribution
QK474.8-495	Spermatophyta. Phanerogams
QK494-494.5	Gymnosperms
QK495	Angiosperms
QK504-(638)	Cryptogams
QK640-(707)	Plant anatomy
QK710-899	Plant physiology
QK900-989	Plant ecology
QL1-991	Zoology
QL1-355	General
	Including geographical distribution
QL360-599.82	Invertebrates
QL461-599.82	Insects
QL605-739.8	Chordates. Vertebrates
QL614-639.8	Fishes
QL640-669.3	Reptiles and amphibians
QL671-699	Birds
QL700-739.8	Mammals
QL750-795	Animal behavior
QL791-795	Stories and anecdotes
QL799-799.5	Morphology

OUTLINE

	Zoology - Continued
QL801-950.9	Anatomy
QL951-991	Embryology
QM1-695	Human anatomy
QM1-511	General
QM531-549	Regional anatomy
QM550-577.8	Human and comparative histology
QM601-695	Human embryology
QP1-(981)	Physiology
QP1-345	General Including influence of the environment
QP351-495	Neurophysiology and neuropsychology
QP501-801	Animal biochemistry
QP(901)-(981)	Experimental pharmacology
QR1-502	Microbiology
QR1-74.5	General
QR75-99.5	Bacteria
QR99.6-99.8	Cyanobacteria
QR100-130	Microbial ecology
QR171	Microorganisms in the animal body
QR180-189.5	Immunology
QR355-502	Virology

Science (General)
For applied science and technology, see Class T
Periodicals. By language of publication
1.A1 Polyglot
1.A3-Z English
2 French
3 German
4 Other languages (not A-Z)
(9) Yearbooks
see Q1+
Collected works (nonserial) see Q111+
Societies
Including works about societies, serial publications of societies
10 International
America
11 United States
21 Canada
22 Latin America
23 Mexico
25 Central America
29 West Indies
33 South America
Europe
41 Great Britain
44 Czechoslovakia
44.2 Hungary
44.4 Austria
46 France
49 Germany
52 Greece
54 Italy
55 Vatican City
56 Belgium
56.2 Luxembourg
57 Netherlands
60 Soviet Union
60.18 Ukraine
60.2 Finland
60.4 Poland
Baltic States
60.6 Estonia
60.7 Latvia
60.8 Lithuania
61 Scandinavia (General)
62 Denmark. Iceland
63 Norway
64 Sweden

Societies
Europe -- Continued
65 Spain. Portugal
67 Switzerland
69 Romania
69.2 Yugoslavia
69.3 Slovenia
69.4 Bulgaria
Turkey see Q80.T8
Asia
72 China
72.5 Taiwan
73 India
74 Indochina
75 Indonesia
76 Philippines
77 Japan
80.A-Z Other regions or countries, A-Z
e.g.
80.C4 Ceylon. Sri Lanka
80.I67 Iran
80.I7 Israel
80.J67 Jordan
80.K6 Korea
80.P3 Pakistan
80.Q38 Qatar
80.R8 Russia in Asia. Siberia
80.S2 Saudi Arabia
80.S5 Singapore
80.S64 Southeast Asia
Sri Lanka see Q80.C4
80.S9 Syria
80.T5 Thailand
80.T8 Turkey
82 Arab countries
83 Islamic countries
Africa
85 South Africa
85.2 Kenya
85.4 Nigeria
85.6 Zimbabwe
85.8 Namibia. South-West Africa
87 Egypt
89 Senegal
89.2 Mauritius
89.5 Sudan
91.A-Z Other regions or countries, A-Z

	Societies
	Africa
	Other regions or countries, A-Z -- Continued
91.A47	Algeria
91.A5	Angola
91.B45	Benin
91.B85	Burkina Faso
91.B87	Burundi
91.C17	Cameroon
91.C4	Central Africa
91.C48	Chad
91.C6	Congo (Democratic Republic). Zaire
91.E84	Ethiopia
91.G5	Ghana
91.M27	Madagascar
91.M3	Malawi
91.M55	Morocco
91.M6	Mozambique
(91.N28)	Namibia see Q85.8
91.S9	Sub-Saharan Africa
91.S95	Swaziland
91.T8	Tunisia
91.Z33	Zambia
93	Australia
94	New Zealand
99	Pacific islands
101	Congresses
	Museums. Exhibitions Cf. Q182.4 Science fairs
105.A1	General works
105.A2-Z	By region or country, A-Z Subarrange each country by Table Q5
	Collected works
111	Series of monographs. Serial collections (nonperiodical) For serial publications of universities or other serial publications not issued by societies see Q1+ For serial publications of societies see Q10+
113	Collected works of individual authors
	Scientific voyages and expeditions (General) For expeditions of special fields, see the field, e.g. G145+ Geographical exploration; QH11 Naturalists' expeditions; TL799 Flights to special planets; etc.
115	General works
116	Handbooks for scientific expeditions
121	Encyclopedias
123	Dictionaries

124 Translating services. Translating
Cf. T11.5 Technical translating
History
Including science and state
124.6 Periodicals, societies, congresses, serial publications
124.7 Collected works (nonserial)
124.8 Dictionaries and encyclopedias
124.85 Nomenclature, terminology, notation, abbreviations
General works see Q125+
124.95 Ancient
124.97 Medieval
Modern
125 General works
125.2 Renaissance through 1700
125.4 Outlines, syllabi
125.6 Pictorial works and atlases
126 Popular works
126.4 Juvenile works
126.8 Addresses, essays, lectures
126.9 Study and teaching. Research
127.A-Z By region or country, A-Z
e. g.
127.G4 Great Britain
127.G7 Greece
127.2 Developing countries
128 Contributions to science. By religious or ethnic groups
130 Women in science. Women scientists
For biography see Q141+
Cf. HQ1397 Women in science and the arts
Biography
141 Collective
143.A-Z Individual, A-Z
e.g.
143.G4 Galvani, Luigi
143.H5 Helmholtz, Hermann von
143.P2 Pasteur, Louis
143.S8 Swedenborg, Emanuel
145 Directories
Science as a profession. Vocational guidance
Cf. Q130 Women in science
147 General works
148 Employment surveys, manpower requirements, statistics, etc.
149.A-Z By region or country, A-Z
Brain drain
150 General works
150.2.A-Z By region or country, A-Z

	Early works through 1800
	Including textbooks
151	Ancient
153	Medieval
155	1500-1700
157	1701-1800
	General works and treatises
158	1801-1969
158.5	1970-
	Textbooks
	Advanced
160	1801-1969
160.2	1970-
	Elementary
161	1801-1969
161.2	1970-
161.7	Pictorial works and atlases
	Cf. Q222 Scientific illustration
162	Popular works
163	Juvenile works
164	Recreations, home experiments, etc.
	Including experiments for children
	Cf. Q182.3 Science projects
167	Anecdotes, facetiae, satire, etc.
171	Addresses, essays, lectures
172	Special aspects of the subject as a whole
172.5.A-Z	Special topics, A-Z
172.5.C45	Chaotic behavior in systems
	Including pattern formation
	Cf. QC174.17.C45 Quantum theory
172.5.C74	Creative ability in science
172.5.E77	Errors
(172.5.F7)	Fraud
	see Q175.37
172.5.H47	Heresy in science
172.5.I5	International cooperation
	Parapsychology and science see BF1045.S33
	Pattern formation see Q172.5.C45
172.5.P65	Popular culture
172.5.P77	Pseudoscience
172.5.P82	Public opinion
172.5.S34	Science indicators
172.5.S47	Serendipity in science
172.5.S95	Symmetry
172.5.S96	Synchronization
172.5.V37	Variational principles
	Cf. QC174.17.V35 Quantum theory

173 Miscellany and curiosa
Philosophy. Methodology
Cf. B67 Philosophy in relation to science
Cf. BF1275.S3 Spiritualism and science
Cf. BJ57 Ethics and science
Cf. BL239+ Religion and science
Cf. BT590.S4 Christ and science
174 Periodicals, societies, congresses, serial publications
174.6 Collected works (nonserial)
174.7 Dictionaries and encyclopedias
174.8 History
175 General works, treatises, and advanced textbooks
175.2 Juvenile works
175.3 Addresses, essays, lectures
175.32.A-Z Special topics, A-Z
175.32.A24 Abduction (Logic)
175.32.A47 Aesthetics
175.32.C38 Causation
175.32.C65 Complexity (Philosophy)
175.32.C66 Constructive realism
175.32.D52 Dialectical materialism
175.32.D53 Dialogue
175.32.E44 Emergence (Philosophy)
Epistemology, Virtue see Q175.32.V57
175.32.E85 Evolution
175.32.E97 Explanation
175.32.I34 Idéologues (French philosophers)
175.32.I54 Inference
175.32.K45 Knowledge, Theory of
Logic see Q175.32.R45
175.32.M38 Mathematical models
175.32.M43 Meaning (Philosophy)
175.32.N38 Naturalism
175.32.O58 Ontology
175.32.R42 Realism
175.32.R45 Reasoning. Logic
175.32.R47 Reductionism
175.32.S78 Structuralism
175.32.S83 Subjectivity
175.32.T56 Time
175.32.T78 Truth
175.32.V35 Values
175.32.V57 Virtue epistemology
175.32.V65 Vitalism
Scientific ethics
Cf. Q180.55.M67 Moral and ethical aspects of research
175.35 General works, treatises, and textbooks

	Scientific ethics -- Continued
175.37	Fraud
	Social aspects
	Class here works that discuss the impact of science on modern society and the sociology of science.
	For works on the role of science in the history and development of civilization see CB478
175.4	Periodicals, societies, congresses, serial publications
175.46	History
175.5	General works, treatises, and textbooks
175.52.A-Z	By region or country, A-Z
175.54	Developing countries
175.55	Addresses, essays, lectures
176	Periodicity. Cycles
177	Classification of the sciences
	Cf. BD239.2+ Speculative philosophy
179	Nomenclature, terminology, notation, abbreviations
	Research
179.9	Periodicals, societies, congresses, serial publications
179.92	Collected works (nonserial)
	Communication of information
179.94	General works
179.96	Information services
179.97	Computer network resources
	Including the Internet
179.98	Directories
180.A1	General works, treatises, and advanced textbooks
	History
180.A3	General works
180.A5-Z	By region or country, A-Z
180.2	Juvenile works
180.3	Handbooks, tables, formulas, etc.
180.4	Anecdotes, facetiae, satire, etc.
180.5	Addresses, essays, lectures
180.55.A-Z	Special topics, A-Z
	Prefer classification by country
180.55.A83	Audiovisual aids
180.55.C55	Classification
180.55.C6	Cost
180.55.D57	Discoveries
180.55.E25	Economic aspects
	For works on the impact of research on the economy see HC79.R4
180.55.E4	Electronic data processing
180.55.E58	Environmental aspects
180.55.E65	Equipment and supplies
180.55.E9	Evaluation

Research
Special topics, A-Z -- Continued
180.55.F5 Finance
180.55.G6 Government support
180.55.G7 Private grants. Foundations. Endowments
180.55.G77 Group work
180.55.I45 Information technology
180.55.I48 Interdisciplinary research
International cooperation see Q172.5.I5
180.55.M3 Management
180.55.M38 Mathematical models
180.55.M4 Methodology
180.55.M67 Moral and ethical aspects
180.55.P7 Proposal writing
180.55.P75 Psychological aspects
180.55.R43 Reduced gravity environments
180.55.S62 Social aspects
180.55.S7 Statistical methods
180.55.V6 Vocational guidance
Laboratories
180.56 General works
180.57 Management
180.58 Records. Laboratory notebooks
180.6.A-Z By region or country, A-Z
Subarrange each country by Table Q6
180.7 Astronautics in science
Cf. TL798.S3 Scientific satellites
Study and teaching
Class here works on the study and teaching of general science at all levels or at the secondary level and higher.
For works on the study and teaching of general science in elementary schools or in both elementary and secondary schools see LB1585+
For programmed texts see Q160+
Cf. Q190+ Audiovisual aids in science teaching
181.A1 Periodicals, societies, congresses, serial publications
181.A2-Z General works, treatises, and textbooks
181.3 Addresses, essays, lectures
181.5 Outlines, syllabi
182 Problems, exercises, examinations
182.3 Experiments
Including science projects
Cf. Q164 Recreations, home experiments, etc.
182.4 Science fairs
182.5 Laboratory manuals

Study and teaching -- Continued
182.7 Electronic information resources
Including computer network resources, the Internet, digital libraries, etc.
Laboratories
183.A1 General works
183.A3-Z By region or country, A-Z
Subarrange each country by Table Q6
By region or country
United States
183.3.A1 General works
183.3.A2-Z By region or state, A-Z
Subarrange each state by Table Q7
183.4.A-Z Other regions or countries, A-Z
Subarrange each country by Table Q7
183.9 Data processing
Instruments and apparatus (General)
184 Periodicals, societies, congresses, serial publications
184.5 Dictionaries and encyclopedias
185 General works, treatises, and textbooks
185.3 Juvenile works
185.7 Catalogs
Audiovisual aids in science teaching
190 General works, treatises, and textbooks
192 Films
194 Radio
196 Television
197 Other (not A-Z)
199 Handbooks, tables, formulas, etc.
209 Science readers in English
Science readers for the study of foreign languages
see PA-PM
(211) Science readers in French
see PC2127.S4
(213) Science readers in German
see PF3127.S3
(215) Science readers in Italian
see PC1127.S3
(219) Science readers in other languages, see PA-PM
222 Scientific illustration
Cf. T11.8 Technical illustration
Communication in science
Cf. Q124 Translating services. Translating
Cf. R118+ Communication in medicine
Cf. T10.5+ Communication of technical information
223 General works

Communication in science -- Continued
Information services
Including information centers
223.2 Periodicals, societies, congresses, serial publications
223.5 Directories
224 General works
224.3.A-Z By region or country, A-Z
Subarrange each country by Table Q5
224.5 Electronic information resources
Including computer network resources, the Internet, digital libraries
Science news. Science and the public
225 General works
225.2.A-Z By region or country, A-Z
225.5 Scientific literature
226 Scientific language
Cf. T11+ Scientific writing
227 Science secretaries. Scientific correspondence
295 System theory
Cf. T57.6+ Operations research. Systems analysis
Cf. TA168 Systems engineering
Cybernetics
Cf. QA75+ Computer science
Cf. QA267+ Machine theory
Cf. QA402.3+ Control theory (Mathematics)
Cf. QP351+ Nervous system and the senses
Cf. TJ212+ Control engineering
Cf. TK7885+ Computer engineering
300 Periodicals, societies, congresses, serial publications
303 Collected works (nonserial)
304 Dictionaries and encyclopedias
305 History
310 General works, treatises, and textbooks
315 Popular works
315.5 Addresses, essays, lectures
316 Study and teaching. Research
Bionics
317 Periodicals, societies, congresses, serial publications
317.5 Collected works (nonserial)
320 General works, treatises, and textbooks
320.5 Juvenile works
321 Addresses, essays, lectures
Self-organizing systems. Conscious automata
325 General works
Machine learning
325.5 General works
325.6 Reinforcement learning

Cybernetics
Self-organizing systems. Conscious automata
Machine learning -- Continued
325.7 Computational learning theory
325.75 Supervised learning
325.78 Back propagation
327 Perceptron theory
Cf. TK7882.P3 Pattern recognition systems
Artificial intelligence
334 Periodicals, societies, congresses, serial publications
334.2 Dictionaries and encyclopedias
334.5 Collected works (nonserial)
335 General works, treatises, and textbooks
335.4 Juvenile works
335.5 Addresses, essays, lectures
335.7 Study and teaching. Research
336 Data processing
Distributed artificial intelligence
337 General works
337.3 Swarm intelligence
337.5 Pattern recognition systems
338 Truth maintenance systems
338.8 Case-based reasoning
338.85 Commonsense reasoning
339 Default reasoning
339.19 Model-based reasoning
339.2 Nonmonotonic reasoning
339.25 Qualitative reasoning
340 Constraints
341 Turing test
342 Computational intelligence
Information theory
Cf. P87+ Communication
Cf. QA268 Coding theory (Mathematics)
Cf. TK5101+ Telecommunication (General)
Cf. ZA3038+ Information resources
350 Periodicals, societies, congresses, serial publications
352 Dictionaries and encyclopedias
355 History
360 General works, treatises, and textbooks
365 Popular works
367 Addresses, essays, lectures
370 Measurements. Tables, calculations, etc.
375 Uncertainty theory
380 Noise
385 Rate distortion theory
386 Statistical methods

Cybernetics
  Information theory -- Continued
    Knowledge representation
387 General works
387.2 Conceptual structures
387.3 Description logics
387.5 Semantic networks
390 Frames
(500-510) Operations research
  see T57.6+

Mathematics
1 Periodicals, societies, congresses, serial publications
3 Collected works (nonserial)
5 Dictionaries and encyclopedias
7 Addresses, essays, lectures
Philosophy
Cf. QA9.615 Recursive functions. Recursive arithmetic
Cf. QA248+ Foundations of arithmetic. Set theory
Cf. QA267+ Machine theory
Cf. QA681 Foundations of geometry
8 Periodicals, societies, congresses, serial publications
8.4 General works, treatises, and textbooks
8.6 Addresses, essays, lectures
8.7 Study and teaching. Research
Mathematical logic
9.A1 Periodicals, societies, congresses, serial publications
9.A5-Z General works, treatises, and textbooks
9.2 Addresses, essays, lectures
Study and teaching. Research see QA8.7
Classical logical systems
Including reverse mathematics
9.25 General works
9.3 Propositional calculus
9.35 Predicate calculus
9.37 Infinitary languages
Nonclassical formal systems
9.4 General works
9.45 Many-valued logic
9.46 Modal logic
Cf. BC199.M6 Logic
9.47 Intuitionistic mathematics
9.5 Combinatory logic and lambda calculus
9.54 Proof systems
Constructive mathematics
9.56 General works
9.58 Algorithms
9.59 Computable functions. Computability theory
Recursion theory
Cf. QA267+ Machine theory
9.6 General works
9.615 Recursive functions. Recursive arithmetic
9.62 Hierarchies
9.63 Unsolvability
9.64 Fuzzy logic
Methodology of deductive systems
9.65 Decidability. Gödel's theorem. Gödel numbers
9.67 Completeness

Philosophy
Mathematical logic -- Continued
9.7 Model theory
9.8 Metamathematics
9.9 Matrix logic
Algebraic logic
10 General works
10.3 Boolean algebra
Cf. QA268.5 Switching theory
10.35 Quantum logic
10.4 Information theory in mathematics
10.5 Mathematics as a profession. Vocational guidance
10.7 Social aspects
10.8 War and mathematics
Study and teaching. Research
Cf. QA135+ Elementary mathematics
11.A1 Periodicals, societies, congresses, serial publications
General works, treatises, and textbooks
11.A2-Z To 2000
11.2 2001-
11.5 Computer network resources
Including the Internet
12 Addresses, essays, lectures
By region or country
United States
13 General works
13.5.A-Z By region or state, A-Z
Subarrange each state by Table Q7
14.A-Z Other regions or countries, A-Z
Subarrange each country by Table Q7
Special teaching methods and aids
16 General works
Audiovisual aids
18 General works, treatises, and textbooks
19.A-Z Special types, A-Z
19.A78 Art
19.B55 Blocks (Toys)
19.B8 Bulletin boards
19.C45 Charts, diagrams, etc.
19.C8 Cuisenaire rods
19.L58 Literature
19.M34 Manipulatives
19.M6 Motion pictures
19.M87 Music
19.O9 Overhead projectors
19.P34 Paper work
Including folding, cutting, etc.

Study and teaching. Research
Special teaching methods and aids
Audiovisual aids
Special types, A-Z -- Continued
19.P53 Picture books
19.T4 Television
20.A-Z Other methods, A-Z
20.C34 Calculators
20.C65 Computer-assisted instruction
Including computer-based experiments
20.E43 Electronic spreadsheets
20.G35 Games
20.G76 Group guidance
20.H54 Hieroglyphics
20.I53 Individualized instruction
20.M33 Magic tricks
20.P67 Portfolios
20.P7 Programmed instruction
For programmed texts, see QA36.5+ QA101+
20.P73 Project method
20.R43 Reading comprehension
20.T43 Teaching teams
20.U55 Unit method of teaching
20.W46 Whole brain learning
20.3 Awards, prizes, etc. Competitions
History
21 General
22 Ancient
23 Medieval
Modern
General see QA21
24 16th-18th centuries
26 19th-20th centuries
27.A-Z By region or country, A-Z
27.5 Women in mathematics. Women mathematicians
For biography see QA28+
Biography
28 Collective
29.A-Z Individual, A-Z
e.g.
29.G3 Gauss
29.J2 Jacobi
29.N2 Napier
30 Directories
Early works through 1800
30.3 Egyptian

Early works through 1800 -- Continued

31 Greek

Including translations and commentaries

For Euclid's Elements for use in schools see QA451

32 Medieval

33 1501-1700

35 1701-1800

General works

36 Comprehensive treatises

Textbooks

36.5 Series of textbooks

Advanced

37 1801-1969

37.2 1970-2000

37.3 2001-

Intermediate (without calculus)

39 1801-1969

39.2 1970-2000

39.3 2001-

Elementary see QA101+

40 Handbooks, manuals, etc.

Popular works see QA93

40.5 Juvenile works

41 Formulas, notation, abbreviations

41.3 Nomenclature, terminology

Communication of mathematical information

41.4 General works

41.5 Information services

41.6 Computer network resources

Including the Internet

41.7 Mathematical literature

42 Language. Authorship

43 Problems, exercises, examinations

Tables

Cf. QA281 Interpolation. Extrapolation

47 General tables

49 Multiplication tables

Including squares and cubes, square roots and cube roots, reciprocals

51 Factor tables

Logarithms. Tables of mathematical functions

Including trigonometric, hyperbolic, etc.

55 General works

59 Theory and use of logarithms

63 Problem solving

Instruments and machines
Including practical mathematics, graphical and numerical calculating
71 General works, treatises, and textbooks
73 Slide rules
74 Computation laboratories
Calculating machines
For works on the use of calculators in mathematic instruction see QA20.C34
75 General works
Electronic computers. Computer science
Including electronic data processing and computer systems
For applications in special fields, see the field, e.g. QD39.3.E46, Electronic data processing in chemistry
Cf. QA267+ Machine theory
Cf. TK7885+ Computer engineering
75.5 Periodicals, societies, congresses, serial publications
76 General works, treatises, and textbooks
76.15 Dictionaries and encyclopedias
Communication of computer science information
76.16 General works
76.162 Information services
76.165 Language. Authorship
76.167 Philosophy
76.17 History
Biography
76.2.A2 Collective
76.2.A3-Z Individual, A-Z
76.215 Directories
76.23 Juvenile works
76.24 Addresses, essays, lectures
76.25 Computer science as a profession. Vocational guidance
Study and teaching. Research
76.27 General works
76.28 Problems, exercises, examinations
76.3 Certification of electronic data processing personnel
76.33 Computer camps
Laboratories
76.35 General works
76.36.A-Z Individual laboratories, A-Z
76.38 Hybrid computers
76.4 Analog computers
Digital computers
76.5 General works
76.52 Juvenile works
76.525 Microcomputer workstations
76.527 Network computers

Instruments and machines
Calculating machines
Electronic computers. Computer science
Digital computers -- Continued

76.53 Time-sharing data processing
Real-time data processing
76.54 General works
76.545 Transaction systems
Online data processing
Including general online information services and general videotex systems
76.55 General works
76.57.A-Z Special systems, A-Z
76.57.A43 America Online
76.57.A77 AT&T WorldNet
76.57.C65 CompuServe
76.57.D44 DELPHI
76.57.E88 eWorld (Online service)
76.57.G45 GEnie (Videotex system)
76.57.G48 GNN
76.57.M52 Microsoft Network
76.57.M55 Minitel
76.57.P75 Prodigy (Online service)
76.57.P77 ProfNet
76.57.S68 SOURCE (Videotex system)
76.57.T44 TÉLÉTEL (Videotex system)
76.57.U43 UMI Online (Videotex system)
76.575 Multimedia systems
Cf. QA76.76.I59 Interactive multimedia
76.58 Parallel processing. Parallel computers
76.585 Cloud computing
76.59 Mobile computing
76.5913 Semantic computing
76.5915 Ubiquitous computing
76.592 Wearable computers
Programming
For computer programs and other software see QA76.75+
76.6 General works
76.612 Constraint programming
76.615 Declarative programming
76.618 Evolutionary programming
76.62 Functional programming
Including functional programming languages
76.623 Genetic programming
76.624 Generative programming
76.6245 Generic programming

Instruments and machines

Calculating machines

Electronic computers. Computer science

Digital computers

Programming -- Continued

76.625 Internet programming. Intranet programming

76.63 Logic programming

76.635 Microprogramming

76.64 Object-oriented programming

Including OPEN method

76.642 Parallel programming

76.65 Visual programming

76.66 Systems programming

Programming languages

76.7 General works

76.73.A-Z Individual languages, A-Z

76.73.A24 ALGOL

76.73.A27 APL

76.73.B3 BASIC

76.73.B78 BSV 753

76.73.C15 C

76.73.C153 C++

76.73.C154 C#

76.73.C25 COBOL

76.73.D25 DRL

76.73.F25 FORTRAN

76.73.J38 Java

76.73.M53 Microsoft Visual Basic

Including Microsoft Visual Basic for applications

MySQL see QA76.73.S67

76.73.O213 OpenCL

76.73.P25 PL/1

76.73.P67 PostScript

Class here works on designing or writing compilers for PostScript

For works on using PostScript to control the page appearance of paper documents, see Z52.5 or Z250.8.P68

76.73.P98 Python

76.73.R3 R (Computer program language)

76.73.S27 SAS (Computer program language)

76.73.S28 Scala

76.73.S67 SQL. MySQL

76.73.Z2 Z

Instruments and machines
Calculating machines
Electronic computers. Computer science -- Continued
Computer software
For individual programs, see the type of program, e.g. QA76.76.T49 Text editors
For application programs, see the field, e.g. HF5548.4.L67 Lotus 1-2-3

76.75 Periodicals. Societies. Serials
76.751 Congresses
76.752 Dictionaries
76.753 Catalogs
76.754 General works
76.755 Handbooks, tables, etc.
76.756 Addresses, essays, lectures
76.758 Software engineering
Including software reengineering
76.76.A-Z Special topics, A-Z
76.76.A63 Application program interfaces
76.76.A65 Application software
76.76.A87 Assemblers
76.76.A98 Automatic differentiations
76.76.C47 Certification of software
76.76.C54 Children's software
76.76.C64 Compatibility of software
76.76.C65 Compilers
Including compilers of individual computer programming languages
76.76.C66 Component software
76.76.C672 Computer games
Class here works on programming computer games
For general works on computer games as well as works on specific computer games and actual software see GV1469.15+
76.76.C68 Computer viruses
76.76.C69 Configuration management
76.76.C73 Costs
76.76.D47 Development
76.76.D49 Device drivers
Including individual device drivers
76.76.D57 Disassemblers
Including decompilers
76.76.D63 Documentation of software
76.76.E93 Evaluation of software
76.76.E95 Expert systems
76.76.F34 Failures of software
File conversion software see QA76.9.F48

Instruments and machines
Calculating machines
Electronic computers. Computer science
Computer software
Special topics, A-Z -- Continued

76.76.F75 Free computer software
Cf. QA76.76.O62 Open source software
76.76.G46 Generators
76.76.H85 Human factors
(76.76.H92) Hypermedia systems
see QA76.76.I59
76.76.H94 Hypertext systems
Including hypertext document markup languages, e. g. HTML (Document markup language), etc.
76.76.I55 Install programs
76.76.I57 Integrated software
76.76.I58 Intelligent agents
76.76.I59 Interactive media. Hypermedia
Cf. QA76.575 Multimedia systems
Measurement, Software see QA76.76.S65
76.76.M52 Microsoft .NET
76.76.M54 Middleware
Including object monitors
76.76.O62 Open source software
(76.76.O63) Operating systems
see QA76.77+
76.76.P37 Patterns, Software
76.76.P74 Productivity
76.76.P76 Protection of software
76.76.Q35 Quality control
76.76.R42 Refactoring of software
76.76.R44 Reliability
76.76.R47 Reusability
76.76.S37 Screen savers
76.76.S375 Self-adaptive software
76.76.S46 Shareware
Software failures see QA76.76.F34
76.76.S64 Software maintenance
Including Year 2000 date conversion
76.76.S65 Software measurement
76.76.S66 Software support
76.76.S69 Spyware
76.76.S73 Standards for software
76.76.S95 Systems software
76.76.T45 Teleprocessing monitors
76.76.T47 Termination
76.76.T48 Testing of software

Instruments and machines
Calculating machines
Electronic computers. Computer science
Computer software
Special topics, A-Z -- Continued

76.76.T49 Text editors
For works on how to use text editors to produce paper documents, see Z52, Z253.3+, or Z253.53+
76.76.T55 Threads
76.76.T83 Translators
76.76.U84 Utilities
76.76.V47 Verification and validation of software
Viruses see QA76.76.C68
76.76.W56 Windows
Class here works on window functionality
For works on individual Microsoft Windows operating systems see QA76.774.A+
Year 2000 date conversion see QA76.76.S64
76.765 Firm-ware
Operating systems
76.77 General works
76.774.A-Z Individual operating systems. By system, A-Z
76.774.B47 Berkeley BSD
76.774.D67 DOS
76.774.I67 iOS
76.774.L46 Linux
76.774.M33 Mac OS
Macintosh OS see QA76.774.M33
76.774.M43 Microsoft Windows 7
76.774.M48 Microsoft Windows Me
76.774.M53 Microsoft Windows NT
76.774.M56 Microsoft Windows Vista
76.774.M58 Microsoft Windows XP
76.774.S65 Solaris
76.774.U64 UNIX
Vista see QA76.774.M56
Windows 7 see QA76.774.M43
Windows ME see QA76.774.M48
Windows NT see QA76.774.M53
Windows Vista see QA76.774.M56
Windows XP see QA76.774.M58
76.8.A-Z Special computers, computer systems, and microprocessors. By name, A-Z
76.8.I12 IBM 360
76.8.I63 iPad
76.8.I64 iPhone
76.8.U6 Univac

Instruments and machines
Calculating machines
Electronic computers. Computer science
Special computers, computer systems, and microprocessors. By name, A-Z -- Continued

76.8.U7 Ural
76.84 Fourth generation computers
76.85 Fifth generation computers
76.87 Neural computers. Neural networks
76.875 Immunocomputers
76.88 Supercomputers. High performance computing
Including heterogeneous computing
76.884 Biocomputers
76.885 Petaflops computers
76.887 Molecular computers. DNA computers
76.889 Quantum computers
76.89 Pen-based computers
76.893 Tablet computers
76.9.A-Z Other topics, A-Z
76.9.A23 Abstract data types
76.9.A25 Access control. Computer security
Cf. HF5548.37 Security measures in electronic data processing departments
76.9.A3 Adaptive computing
76.9.A43 Algorithms
76.9.A48 Ambient intelligence
76.9.A73 Architecture, Computer
76.9.A93 Auditing
Class here works on the auditing of electronic data processing systems and activities
For works dealing with the auditing of electronic data processing departments see HF5548.35
76.9.A955 Automatic hypothesis formation
76.9.A96 Automatic theorem proving
76.9.A97 Autonomic computing
76.9.B22 B method
76.9.B32 Backup processing
76.9.B38 Batch processing
76.9.B84 Bulletin boards
Camps, Computer see QA76.33
Children and computers see QA76.9.C659
Civilization and computers see QA76.9.C66
76.9.C55 Client/server computing
76.9.C58 Computational grids
Computer algorithms see QA76.9.A43
Computer architecture see QA76.9.A73
76.9.C62 Computer arithmetic

Instruments and machines
Calculating machines
Electronic computers. Computer science
Other topics, A-Z -- Continued
Computer camps see QA76.33
76.9.C63 Computer capacity
76.9.C64 Computer literacy
Computer logic see QA76.9.L63
Computer mathematics see QA76.9.M35
76.9.C643 Computer organization
76.9.C65 Computer simulation
Cf. T57.62+ Industrial engineering
Cf. TA343 Engineering mathematics
Computer system failures see QA76.9.F34
76.9.C659 Computers and children
Cf. LC40.5.C66 Computer-assisted home schooling
76.9.C66 Computers and civilization. Social aspects of computers
Computers and family see QA76.9.F35
Computers and older people see QA76.9.O43
Computers and women see QA76.9.W65
76.9.C67 Constraint databases
Conversion of computer files see QA76.9.F48
76.9.C68 Conversion of computer systems
76.9.C72 Cookies (Computer science)
Crowdsourcing see QA76.9.H84
76.9.C92 Cyberinfrastructure
76.9.D26 Database design
76.9.D3 Database management
Cf. QA76.9.D37 Data warehousing
76.9.D314 Database security
76.9.D32 Databases
Including online databases
Cf. QA76.9.W43 Web databases
76.9.D33 Data compression
76.9.D337 Data entry
76.9.D338 Data integration
76.9.D34 Data marts
76.9.D343 Data mining
Including OLAP technology
76.9.D345 Data preparation
76.9.D348 Data recovery
76.9.D35 Data structures
Cf. QA76.9.C72 Cookies (Computer science)
76.9.D37 Data warehousing
76.9.D43 Debugging in computer science
Including structured walkthrough

Instruments and machines
Calculating machines
Electronic computers. Computer science
Other topics, A-Z -- Continued

76.9.D5 Distributed processing
76.9.D6 Documentation
Cf. QA76.76.D63 Software documentation
76.9.E25 Economic aspects
76.9.E53 End-user computing
76.9.E57 Entertainment computing
76.9.E77 Error messages
Ethical aspects see QA76.9.M65
76.9.E94 Evaluation of computer performance
76.9.E95 Evaluation of data processing activities
Expert systems see QA76.76.E95
76.9.F34 Failures of computer systems
Cf. QA76.76.F34 Software failures
76.9.F35 Computers and family
76.9.F38 Fault-tolerant computing
76.9.F48 File conversion
Including individual file conversion software, e.g. Adobe Acrobat
76.9.F5 File organization
76.9.F53 File processing
76.9.F67 Formal methods
76.9.G37 Garbage collection
76.9.G68 Government policy
Granular computing see QA76.9.S63
Graphical user interfaces see QA76.9.U83
Grids, Computational see QA76.9.C58
76.9.H35 Hard disk management
76.9.H36 Hashing
76.9.H84 Human computation. Crowdsourcing
Cf. Q337+ Distributed artificial intelligence
76.9.H85 Human-computer interaction
76.9.I52 Information visualization
76.9.I55 Input design
76.9.I58 Interactive computer systems
76.9.K48 Keyboarding
Class here works on keyboarding computer formats, such as punched cards or punched tape
For works on keyboarding eye-readable reports and displays see Z49+
76.9.L63 Logic, Computer
76.9.M3 Management
76.9.M35 Mathematics, Computer
76.9.M45 Memory management

Instruments and machines
Calculating machines
Electronic computers. Computer science
Other topics, A-Z -- Continued

76.9.M65 Moral and ethical aspects
76.9.M68 Multilingual computing
76.9.N37 Natural computation
76.9.N38 Natural language processing
Cf. P98+ Linguistics
76.9.N47 Netcentric computing
76.9.O35 Object-oriented methods
Cf. QA76.64 Object-oriented programming
OLAP technology see QA76.9.D343
76.9.O43 Computers and older people
76.9.O59 Olympiads
Online databases see QA76.9.D32
Organization, Computer see QA76.9.C643
76.9.P75 Psychological aspects
76.9.Q4 Question-answering systems
Religious aspects see BL255.5
76.9.R45 Remote job entry
Security, Computer see QA76.9.A25
Security, Data base see QA76.9.D314
76.9.S54 Self-stabilization
Social aspects of computers see QA76.9.C66
76.9.S63 Soft computing
Including granular computing
Software maintenance see QA76.76.S64
76.9.S8 Standards
Cf. QA76.76.S73 Standards for software
76.9.S84 Structured techniques
Structured walkthrough see QA76.9.D43
76.9.S88 System design
System failures see QA76.9.F34
76.9.S9 Systems migration
76.9.T43 Technical support
Cf. QA76.76.S66 Software support
76.9.T48 Text processing
76.9.T7 Transborder data flow
76.9.U83 User interfaces
Including graphical user interfaces
76.9.V5 Virtual computer systems
Visualization, Information see QA76.9.I52
76.9.W43 Web databases
76.9.W65 Computers and women

Instruments and machines
Calculating machines
Electronic computers. Computer science -- Continued
76.95 Use of electronic computers in mathematics
For works on the use of calculators in mathematics instruction see QA20.C34
For works on computer-assisted instruction in mathematics see QA20.C65
Miscellaneous geometrical instruments
Cf. T375+ Drawing instruments
77 General works
81 Planimeters
Mechanical aids in higher analysis
85 General works
90 Graphic methods (General). Nomography
93 Popular works
95 Mathematical recreations
For Rubik's Cube, Rubik's Revenge, Rubik's Snake, etc. see QA491
99 Miscellany and curiosa
Elementary mathematics. Arithmetic
Including basic mathematical concepts for the elementary grades
Cf. QA248+ Foundations of arithmetic
Textbooks
101 Through 1845
103 1846-1900
106 1901-1960
107 1961-2000
107.2 2001-
109 Special aspects of the subject as a whole
111 Rapid calculators and short cuts
113 Counting
Class here works dealing with counting, including counting books and other forms of materials
For works dealing with numeration, the concept of numbers, and numeration systems see QA141+
115 Elementary operations
e.g. addition, subtraction, multiplication, division
117 Fractions
Including proportion, ratio
119 Roots
Including square root, cube root
Study and teaching
Cf. LC4621 Education of children with mental disabilities
General works, treatises, and textbooks
135 Through 1960
135.5 1961-2000

	Elementary mathematics. Arithmetic
	Study and teaching
	General works, treatises, and textbooks -- Continued
135.6	2001-
137	Teaching fractions
139	Problems, exercises, examinations
	Numeration, number concept, numeration systems
	Cf. QA241+ Theory of numbers
	Cf. QA297+ Numerical analysis
141	General works, treatises, and textbooks
141.15	Number concept (Elementary)
	Cf. BF456.N7 Numbers. Mathematics (Psychology)
141.2	History
	Cf. GN476.15 Primitive numeration
	Cf. P211+ History of writing
141.3	Juvenile works
141.35	Decimal system
	Class here expository and historical works on the decimal system
	For tables, arithmetic, and other works with values expressed mainly in the decimal system, see the special class numbers that are provided for particular fields, e. g. QA101 Arithmetic. For tables, arithmetic, etc., for other special systems, see QA141.4+
141.4	Binary system
	Duodecimal system
141.5.A1	Periodicals, societies, congresses, serial publications
141.5.A2-Z	General works, treatises, and textbooks
141.6	Octal system
141.8.A-Z	Other special systems, A-Z
141.8.Q5	Quinary system
141.8.S4	Sexadecimal system
141.8.S5	Sexagesimal system
141.8.T45	Ternary system
(145)	Algebra and arithmetic
	see QA101+
	Algebra
150	Periodicals, societies, congresses, serial publications
151	History
	Textbooks
	Elementary
152	Through 1970
152.2	1971-2000
152.3	2001-
	Advanced
154	Through 1970
154.2	1971-2000

	Algebra
	Textbooks
	Advanced -- Continued
154.3	2001-
154.8	Early works to 1800
155	General works and treatises
	Including higher algebra
155.15	Juvenile works
155.2	Addresses, essays, lectures
155.5	Special aspects of the subject as a whole
155.7.A-Z	Special topics, A-Z
155.7.E4	Electronic data processing
157	Problems, exercises, examinations
	Study and teaching. Research
159	General works
159.2	Outlines, syllabi, etc.
161.A-Z	Miscellaneous elementary topics, A-Z
161.B48	Binomial coefficients
161.B5	Binomial theorem
161.E95	Exponents
161.F3	Factors
	Logarithms see QA59
161.P59	Polynomials
162	Abstract algebra
	Cf. QA10.3 Boolean algebra
	Combinatorics. Combinatorial analysis
164	General works
164.8	Enumeration problems. Generating functions
	Cf. QA353.G44 Special functions
164.9	Identities
165	Permutations. Combinations. Partitions
	Including magic squares and magic cubes
	Graph theory
	Cf. QA612.18 Map-coloring problem
166	General works
166.14	Bipartite graphs
166.145	Cayley graphs
166.15	Directed graphs
166.16	Perfect graphs
166.165	Quantum graphs
166.17	Random graphs
166.175	Fuzzy graphs
166.18	Hamiltonian graph theory
166.185	Intersection graph theory
166.19	Eulerian graph theory
166.195	Topological graph theory

Algebra
Combinatorics. Combinatorial analysis
Graph theory -- Continued
166.197 Graph labelings
Including magic labelings
166.2 Trees
166.22 Paths and cycles
166.23 Hypergraphs
166.24 Reconstruction
166.242 Representations of graphs
166.243 Graph connectivity
166.245 Graph algorithms
166.247 Graph coloring
Design and configurations
166.25 General works
166.3 Block designs
166.4 Hadamard matrices
166.6 Matroids. Greedoids
166.7 Packing and covering
166.75 Polyominoes
166.8 Tessellation and tiling
Combinatorial geometry
167 General works
167.2 Finite geometries
169 Homological algebra
Including functors, categories
(171) Group theory
see QA174+
Ordered sets
171.48 General works
171.485 Partially ordered sets
171.49 Semilattices
171.5 Lattice theory
Cf. QD921+ Crystal lattices
Ordered algebraic structures
172 General works
172.4 Ordered groups
Group theory
Cf. QA172.4 Ordered groups
Cf. QA385+ Continuous groups
Cf. QA387 Topological groups. Lie groups
Cf. QA613.7 Topological transformation groups
Cf. QA614.97 Pseudogroups and deformations of structures
Cf. QC174.17.G7 Quantum theory
Cf. QD455.3.G75 Physical chemistry
174 Periodicals, societies, congresses, serial publications

Algebra
Group theory -- Continued
174.2 General works
174.5 Juvenile works
Study and teaching. Research
174.6 General works
174.62.A-Z Special topics, A-Z
174.62.C65 Computer-assisted instruction
174.7.A-Z Special topics, A-Z
174.7.D36 Data processing
174.7.S96 Symmetry
175 Permutation groups
176 Representations of groups
177 Finite groups
178 Infinite groups
179 Linear algebraic groups
180 Abelian groups
181 Groupoids
181.5 Quasigroups
182 Semigroups
182.5 Combinatorial group theory
183 Geometric group theory
Linear and multilinear algebra. Matrices
Cf. QA243 Bilinear forms
General works, treatises, and textbooks
184 To 2000
184.2 2001-
184.5 Problems, exercises, examinations
185.A-Z Special topics, A-Z
185.C65 Computer-assisted instruction
185.D37 Data processing
186 Vector spaces
187 Linear dependence
Matrices
188 General works
191 Determinants
192 Elimination
193 Eigenvalues and eigenvectors
195 Proximity matrices
196 Quaternions
196.5 Random matrices
197 Triangularization
199 Clifford algebras
199.5 Multilinear algebra. Tensor products
Vector and tensor algebra
Cf. QA433 Vector and tensor analysis
200 General works

Algebra
Linear and multilinear algebra. Matrices
Vector and tensor algebra -- Continued
201 Invariants
205 Exterior algebra. Ausdehnungslehre
Theory of equations
211 General works, treatises, and textbooks
212 Roots. Symmetric functions
Cf. QA119 Elementary mathematics
214 General resolution of equations
Including simultaneous equations
215 Cubic, quadratic, biquadratic, and other particular equations
218 Numerical solutions
219 Graphic algebra
Approximation theory
Cf. QA297+ Numerical analysis
221 General works
223 Radial basis functions
224 Spline theory
Number theory
241 General works, treatises, and textbooks
241.5 Geometry of numbers
241.7 Probabilistic number theory
242 Divisibility. Linear congruences. Factorization. Quadratic residues. Diophantine analysis
Arithmetical algebraic geometry
242.5 General works
242.6 Arakelov theory
243 Forms
Including quadratic, bilinear forms
244 Higher congruences, residues. Fermat's theorem
245 Cyclotomy. Application of functions to arithmetic
246 Distribution of primes. Special numerical functions, etc.
246.5 Sequences of integers
Exponential and character sums
246.7 General works
246.8.A-Z Special sums, A-Z
246.8.G38 Gaussian
246.8.K58 Kloosterman
246.8.T75 Trigonometric
Algebraic fields. Algebraic numbers
247 General works
Modular fields. Finite fields
247.3 General works
247.35 Modular arithmetic
247.4 Differential and difference algebra

Algebra
Number theory
Algebraic fields. Algebraic numbers -- Continued
247.45 Division algebras
247.5 Transcendental numbers. Irrational numbers
Foundations of arithmetic. Set theory. Transfinite numbers
248 General works
248.3 Elementary textbooks
248.5 Fuzzy sets
Recursive functions. Recursive arithmetic see QA9.6+
251 Universal algebra
Cf. QA184+ Linear and multilinear algebra
251.3 Commutative rings and algebras
251.35 Group rings
251.38 Local rings
251.4 Noncommutative rings and algebras
251.5 Associative rings and algebras
Nonassociative rings and algebras
252 General works
252.3 Lie algebras. Lie superalgebras
Cf. QA387 Lie groups
252.5 Jordan algebras
255 Complex numbers
(263) Matrices
see QA188+
Machine theory. Abstract machines. Abstract automata
Cf. QA9.6+ Recursive functions
Cf. QA75.5+ Electronic computers
Cf. QA402.3+ Control theory
267 General works, treatises, and textbooks
267.3 Formal languages
Cf. P98+ Language data processing
267.5.A-Z Special types of machines, A-Z
267.5.C45 Cellular automata
267.5.F89 Fuzzy automata
267.5.P7 Probabilistic automata
267.5.S4 Sequential machines
267.5.T45 Temporal automata
267.7 Computational complexity. Kolmogorov complexity
268 Coding theory
268.5 Switching theory
Cf. QA10.3 Boolean algebra
Cf. TK7868.S9 Switching circuits
Game theory
269 General works
Cf. T57.92 Industrial engineering
270 Games of strategy

	Algebra
	Game theory -- Continued
271	Games of chance
272	Differential games
272.4	Cooperative games
272.5	Noncooperative games
	Probabilities
	Cf. T57.3+ Industrial engineering
	Cf. TA340 Engineering mathematics
273.A1	Periodicals, societies, congresses, serial publications
273.A3	Dictionaries and encyclopedias
273.A35	Philosophy
273.A4	History
273.A5-Z	General works, treatises, and textbooks
273.15	Popular works
273.16	Juvenile works
273.18	Addresses, essays, lectures
273.19.A-Z	Special topics, A-Z
273.19.E4	Electronic data processing
	Study and teaching. Research
273.2	General works
273.25	Problems, exercises, examinations
273.26	Computer-assisted instruction
273.27	Programmed instruction
273.3	Handbooks, tables, formulas, etc.
273.4	Axioms and foundations
273.43	Probability theory on algebraic and topological structures
273.45	Combinatorial probabilities
273.5	Geometric probability. Stochastic geometry. Random sets
273.6	Distributions. Characteristic functions
273.67	Limit theorems
	Stochastic processes
	Cf. T57.33 Renewal theory
	Cf. T57.35+ Renewal theory
	Cf. T57.9 Queuing theory
274.A1	Periodicals, societies, congresses, serial publications
274.A5-Z	General works, treatises, and textbooks
274.12	Problems, exercises, etc.
274.13	Axioms and foundations
	Stochastic analysis
274.2	General works
274.22	Stochastic integrals
274.223	Stochastic inequalities
274.225	Stochastic sequences
274.23	Stochastic differential equations
274.25	Stochastic partial differential equations
274.27	Stochastic integral equations

Probabilities
Stochastic processes
Stochastic analysis -- Continued
274.28 Random operators
274.29 White noise theory
274.3 Stationary processes
274.4 Gaussian processes
274.42 Point processes
274.45 Random fields
274.46 Random measures
274.5 Martingales. Semimartingales
274.6 Learning models
Markov processes. Markov chains
274.7 General works
274.73 Random walks
274.75 Diffusion processes. Brownian motion processes
Cf. QC183 Constitution and properties of matter and anti-matter
274.755 Jump processes
274.76 Branching processes
274.8 Queuing theory
274.9 Self-similar processes
275 Theory of errors. Least squares
Mathematical statistics
Including statistical inference and fundamental concepts of statistics
For special applications of statistics, see the field of application, e.g. HD1421+ Agricultural statistics; LB2846 Educational statistics; TA340 Statistical methods in engineering
276.A1 Periodicals, societies, congresses, serial publications
276.A12 Collected works (nonserial)
276.A2-Z General works
276.12 Elementary texts
Including descriptive statistics
276.13 Juvenile works
276.14 Dictionaries and encyclopedias
276.15 History
Biography
276.156 Collective
276.157.A-Z Individual, A-Z
276.16 Addresses, essays, lectures
276.17 Statistics as a profession. Vocational guidance
Study and teaching. Research
276.18 General works
276.19 Outlines, syllabi
276.2 Problems, exercises, examinations
276.22 Computer-assisted instruction

Mathematical statistics
Study and teaching. Research -- Continued
276.23 Geometrical models
276.25 Handbooks, tables, formulas, etc.
Including tables of random numbers
276.3 Graphic methods
Data processing
Class here works on the use of data processing and computers in mathematical statistics in general
For the application of statistical data processing and statistical analysis programs in special fields see the field, e. g. HF5415.125, Marketing; T57.5, Industrial engineering
276.4 General works
276.45.A-Z Special programs or languages, A-Z
276.45.M53 Microsoft Excel
276.45.M56 Minitab
276.45.R3 R (Computer program language)
276.45.S27 SAS (Computer program language)
276.45.S28 SCA statistical system
276.45.S83 Statistica
276.5 Fuzzy statistics
276.6 Sampling theory and methods
276.7 Sampling distribution
276.74 Tolerance regions. Confidence intervals
276.8 Estimation theory
276.9 Minimum message length. Minimum description length
Testing of hypotheses
277 General works
277.3 Chi-square test
277.5 Observed confidence levels
Multivariate analysis
278 General works
278.2 Regression analysis. Correlation analysis
278.3 Path analysis. Structural equation modeling
278.4 Paired and multiple comparisons
278.5 Factor analysis. Principal components analysis. Correspondence analysis
278.6 Latent structure analysis
278.65 Discriminant analysis
278.7 Order statistics
278.75 Ranking and selection
278.8 Nonparametric methods
Analysis of variance and covariance. Analysis of means. Experimental design
279 General works
279.2 Prediction analysis
Decision theory

Mathematical statistics
Decision theory -- Continued
279.4 General works
279.5 Bayesian statistics
279.6 Fuzzy decision making
279.7 Multistage decision procedures. Sequential analysis
280 Time series analysis
281 Interpolation. Extrapolation
Cf. QA47+ Mathematical tables
Cf. QA221+ Approximation theory
Cf. QA273.A1+ Probabilities. Theory of errors. Least squares
Cf. QA297+ Numerical analysis
292 Sequences
Cf. QA246.5 Sequences of integers
295 Series
Including infinite products and other infinite processes
Numerical analysis
Cf. QA221+ Approximation theory
297 General works, treatises, and textbooks
297.3 Problems, exercises, etc.
297.5 Numerical approximation
For numerical solution to differential equations, including initial value problems and boundary value problems see QA370+
Cf. QA71+ Instruments and machines
Cf. QA90 Graphic methods. Nomography
Cf. QA218 Numerical solutions of algebraic equations
Cf. QA275 Least squares
Cf. QA281 Interpolation. Extrapolation
297.55 Relaxation methods
297.6 Smoothing. Curve fitting
297.65 Rounding
297.7 Roundoff errors
297.75 Interval analysis
297.8 Iterative methods
298 Numerical simulation. Monte Carlo method
Cf. T57.62+ Industrial engineering
299 Numerical differentiation
Numerical integration
299.3 General works
299.4.A-Z Special formulas, A-Z
299.4.C83 Cubature formulas
299.4.G3 Gaussian quadrature formulas
Analysis
Including calculus, functional analysis, functions, differential equations

Analysis -- Continued
299.6 Periodicals, societies, congresses, serial publications
Foundations
299.8 General works
299.82 Nonstandard analysis
300 General works, treatises, and textbooks
300.5 Addresses, essays, lectures
301 Problems, exercises, examinations
302 Early works through 1800
Calculus
Cf. QA431 Calculus of differences
General works, treatises, and textbooks
303 Through 2000
303.2 2001-
303.3 Study and teaching. Research
303.5.A-Z Special topics, A-Z
303.5.C65 Computer-assisted instruction
303.5.D37 Data processing
Differential calculus
304 General works
305 Problems, exercises, examinations
306 Miscellaneous special topics
Integral calculus
308 General works
309 Problems, exercises, examinations
310 Tables of integrals
311 Miscellaneous special topics
Measure and integration
Including Lebesgue integrals
312 General works
312.5 Fuzzy measure theory
313 Ergodic theory
Cf. QA329.2 Linear operators
Cf. QA611.5 Topology
314 Fractional calculus
Calculus of variations
Cf. QA402.3+ Control theory
315 General works
316 Miscellaneous special topics
Functional analysis
319 Periodicals, societies, congresses, serial publications
320 General works
321 Addresses, essays, lectures
321.5 Nonlinear functional analysis
322 Topological linear spaces
322.2 Normed linear spaces. Banach spaces
322.4 Inner product spaces. Hilbert spaces

Analysis
Functional analysis -- Continued
322.5 Indefinite inner product spaces
323 Function spaces
324 Theory of distributions
325 Measures, integration, derivatives
326 Topological algebras. Banach algebras
Operator theory
329 General works
329.2 Linear operators
Differential operators
329.4 General works
329.42 Partial differential operators
329.6 Integral operators
329.7 Pseudodifferential operators
Nonlinear operators
329.8 General works
329.9 Fixed point theory
Cf. QA612.24 Fixed points and coincidences
Theory of functions
331 General works, treatises, and advanced textbooks
331.3 Elementary textbooks
331.5 Functions of real variables
331.7 Functions of complex variables
Riemann surfaces
Including multiform, uniform functions
333 General works
335 Fuchsian groups
337 Teichmüller spaces
341 Algebraic functions
342 Logarithmic, circular, and exponential functions
343 Elliptic functions. Elliptic integrals. Modular functions
345 Abelian functions. Theta functions
Including hyperelliptic functions
Special functions
Cf. QA406 Spherical harmonics
Cf. QA408 Bessel functions
Cf. QA409 Lamé functions
351 General
353.A-Z Other special functions, A-Z
353.A9 Automorphic. Fuchsian
353.C17 C-functions
353.C64 Concave functions
353.E5 Entire functions
Fuchsian see QA353.A9
353.G3 Gamma

Analysis
Theory of functions
Special functions
Other special functions, A-Z -- Continued
353.G44 Generating functions
Cf. QA164.8 Combinatorial analysis
353.H9 Hypergeometric
353.P4 Periodic functions
353.T7 Transcendental functions
355 Miscellaneous special topics
360 Geometric principles of analysis. Mapping of regions. Conformal representation
Cf. QA646 Differential geometry
Differential equations
370 Periodicals, societies, congresses, serial publications
371 General works, treatises, and textbooks
Study and teaching. Research
371.3 General works
371.32 Outlines, syllabi, etc.
371.35 Computer-assisted instruction
371.5.A-Z Special topics, A-Z
371.5.D37 Data processing
372 Ordinary differential equations (linear and nonlinear)
372.5 Differential-algebraic equations
373 Differential-difference equations
374 Partial differential equations (first order)
377 Partial differential equations (second and higher orders)
377.3 Evolution equations
Cf. QC20.7.E88 Mathematical physics
377.5 Degenerate differential equations
378 Initial value problems
378.5 Inverse problems
379 Boundary value problems
380 Bifurcation theory
381 Differential forms and invariants
Cf. QA614.46 Pfaffian systems
Continuous groups (of transformations). Infinitesimal transformations
385 General works
387 Topological groups. Lie groups
Cf. QA613.7 Topological transformation groups
Cf. QA613.8 Hopf algebras
Cf. QA614.97 Pseudogroups and deformations of structures

Analysis -- Continued
Analytical methods used in the solution of physical problems
Including mathematical physics (mathematical theory only)
Cf. QC19.2+ Mathematical physics
Cf. TA329+ Engineering mathematics and engineering analysis

401 General works, treatises, and textbooks
System analysis
Cf. T57.6+ Industrial engineering
Cf. TA168 Systems engineering
402 General works
402.2 Decomposition method
Control theory (General and linear)
Cf. TJ212+ Automatic control
402.3 General works
402.35 Nonlinear control theory
402.37 Stochastic control theory
Mathematical optimization. Programming
Cf. T57.7+ Industrial engineering
402.5 General works
402.6 Transportation problems
Including assignment and location problems
Harmonic analysis (General)
Including abstract harmonic analysis
403 General works
403.3 Wavelets
Fourier analysis
403.5 General works
404 Fourier series
404.5 Orthogonal series. Orthogonal functions and polynomials
Potential theory. Pluripotential theory
Cf. QA825+ Analytic mechanics
404.7 General works
405 Harmonic functions
406 Laplace and Legendre functions (Spherical harmonics)
408 Bessel functions (Cylindrical harmonics)
409 Lamé functions (Ellipsoidal harmonics)
411 Toroidal and other harmonics
425 Dirichlet's problem and analogous problems
427 Nonlinear theories. Nonlinearity
431 Difference equations and functional equations. Integral equations. Calculus of differences
432 Operational calculus. Laplace transformation
433 Vector and tensor analysis. Spinor analysis. Scalar field theory
Geometry
Cf. QA681 Foundations of geometry

Geometry -- Continued
440 Periodicals, societies, congresses, serial publications
441 Dictionaries and encyclopedias
442 Philosophy
443 Collected works (nonserial)
443.5 History
444 Early works through 1800
445 General works, treatises, and textbooks
445.5 Juvenile works
446 Addresses, essays, lectures
447 Special aspects of the subject as a whole
448.A-Z Special topics, A-Z
448.D38 Data processing
Elementary geometry
451 Euclid's Elements for use in schools
For commentaries, Greek texts, and translations see QA31
Other textbooks (Plane and solid)
453 General works
455 Plane
457 Solid
459 Problems, exercises, examinations
460.A-Z Special propositions, A-Z
460.P8 Pythagorean theorem
Study and teaching. Research
461 General works, treatises, and textbooks
Special teaching methods and aids
462 General works
462.2.A-Z Special types, A-Z
462.2.C65 Computer-assisted instruction
462.2.G34 Games
463 Laboratory manuals
464 Practical geometry. Geometrical drawing
Cf. QA497 Higher geometrical drawing (Plane)
Cf. QA501+ Descriptive geometry
465 Measurement
Famous problems
466 General works
467 Circle squaring
468 Trisection of the angle
469 Duplication of the cube
471 Projective geometry
Cf. QA554 Projective methods (Analytic geometry)
Modern geometry. Inversions
473 General works
474 Plane
475 Solid

Geometry -- Continued
477 Affine geometry
Special topics in plane geometry
481 Axioms. Postulates. Logic
Cf. QA681 Foundations of geometry
482 Straight lines, angles, triangles, etc.
483 Curves. Ovals
484 Circle
485 Conics
491 Special topics in solid geometry
Including Rubik's Cube, Rubik's Revenge, Rubik's Snake, etc.
497 Higher geometrical drawing (Plane)
Descriptive geometry
Cf. T351+ Mechanical drawing
501 General works, treatises, and textbooks
501.5 Problems, exercises, examinations
Parallel projection
502 General works
Orthogonal projection on two planes
503 General works
505 Isometric projection
507 Oblique projection
Central projection
511 General works
515 Perspective
Class here geometrical works only
Cf. NA2710 Architecture
Cf. NC748+ Drawing
Cf. T369 Mechanical drawing
519 Shades and shadows
Class here geometrical works only
Cf. NC755 Drawing
520 Spherical projection
Cf. GA110+ Map projection
521 Miscellaneous special topics
529 Geometry and trigonometry (combined)
Trigonometry
531 General works, treatises, and textbooks
533 Plane
535 Spherical
537 Problems, exercises, examinations
538 Miscellaneous special topics
Analytic geometry
551 General works, treatises, and textbooks
551.5 Data processing
552 Plane. Conic sections
553 Solid

Geometry
Analytic geometry -- Continued

554	Projective methods
555	Problems, exercises, examinations
556	Coordinates
556.5	Equipollence
557	Straight line and circle. Triangle
559	Conics
559.5	Curves
561	Quadric surfaces
563	Maxima and minima
	Algebraic geometry
564	General works, treatises, and textbooks
	Higher algebraic curves
565	General works, treatises, and textbooks
567	Plane curves
567.2.A-Z	Special curves, A-Z
567.2.C82	Cubic
567.2.E44	Elliptic
567.2.I84	Isothermic
567.2.M63	Modular
567.2.O76	Orthogonal
567.2.Q35	Quartic
567.2.Q54	Quintic
567.2.S56	Smooth affine
	Higher algebraic surfaces
571	General works, treatises, and textbooks
573	Special surfaces Including cubic, quartic surfaces
581	Skew algebraic curves Including twisted cubics, curves of double curvature
582	Tropical geometry
	Transformations, correspondences, and general methods for algebraic configurations Including collineation, correlation
601	General works, treatises, and textbooks
602	Cremona transformations. Quadratic transformations
603	Classification of curves and surfaces. Groups of points and curves
605	Applications of transcendental functions to curves and surfaces
607	Enumerative geometry. Systems of curves and surfaces
608	Connexes, complexes, congruences. Line geometry For algebraic configurations in hyperspace see QA691+
609	Conformal geometry
	Topology

Geometry
Topology -- Continued

611.A1	Periodicals, societies, congresses, serial publications
611.A3	History
611.A34-Z	General works, treatises, and textbooks
611.13	Juvenile works
611.15	Addresses, essays, lectures
	Study and teaching. Research
611.17	General works
611.19	Problems, exercises, examinations
611.2	Fuzzy topology
611.21	Imbeddings
611.23	Compactifications. Compact spaces
611.234	Realcompactness. Realcompactification. Realcompact spaces
611.24	Proximity spaces
611.25	Uniform spaces. Quasi-uniform spaces
611.28	Metric spaces
611.29	Isometries, contractions, expansions
611.3	Other miscellaneous topological spaces For linear topological spaces see QA322
611.35	CW complexes
611.5	Topological dynamics Including those special aspects relating to ergodic theory Cf. QA614.8+ Differentiable dynamical systems
611.7	Fixed point theorems Cf. QA329.9 Nonlinear operators
	Algebraic topology. Combinatorial topology Cf. QA166+ Graph theory
612	General works
	Low-dimensional topology Cf. QA613.2 Manifolds and cell complexes
612.14	General works
612.18	Map-coloring problem
612.19	Four-color problem
	Knot theory. Link theory
612.2	General works
612.23	Braid theory
612.24	Fixed points and coincidences Cf. QA329.9 Fixed point theory
	Homology and cohomology theories Cf. QA169 Homological algebra
612.3	General works
612.32	Intersection homology theory
612.33	K-theory. KK-theory
612.36	Sheaves
612.5	Retracts

	Geometry
	Topology
	Algebraic topology. Combinatorial topology -- Continued
	Fiber spaces. Fiber bundles. Fiberings
612.6	General works
612.63	Vector bundles
	Homotopy theory
612.7	General works
612.72	Homotopy equivalences
612.76	Loop spaces
612.77	H-spaces
612.78	Homotopy groups
612.782	Steenrod algebra
612.79	Obstruction theory
612.8	Spectral sequences
	Manifolds and cell complexes
	Including distance geometry
613	General works
613.2	Topological manifolds
613.4	PL-topology
	Differential topology
613.6	General works
613.618	Characteristic classes
613.619	Vector fields
613.62	Foliations
613.64	Differentiable mappings
613.65	Diffeomorphisms
613.658	Surgery. Handlebodies
613.659	Symplectic and contact topology
613.66	Cobordism
613.7	Topological transformation groups
	Cf. QA387 Topological groups
613.8	Hopf algebras
	Cf. QA387 Topological groups
	Global analysis. Analysis on manifolds
614	General works
	Differentiable manifolds
614.3	General works
614.4	Jets
614.42	Stratified sets
614.44	Supermanifolds
614.46	Pfaffian systems. Pfaffian problem
	Calculus on manifolds
614.5	General works
614.58	Differentiable mappings and singularities. Catastrophes
614.7	Critical point theory
614.73	Harmonic maps

Geometry
Topology
Global analysis. Analysis on manifolds -- Continued
Differentiable dynamical systems
Cf. QA611.5 Topological dynamics
Cf. QA871 Analytic mechanicals

614.8 General works
614.813 Attractors
614.82 Flows
614.83 Hamiltonian systems
614.833 Nonholonomic dynamical systems
614.835 Random dynamical systems
614.84 Shadowing systems
614.85 Symbolic dynamics
614.86 Fractals

Partial differential equations and differential operators on manifolds

614.9 General works
614.92 Index theorems
614.95 Spectral geometry
614.97 Pseudogroups and deformations of structures
Cf. QA387 Lie groups

Infinitesimal geometry

615 General works, treatises, and textbooks

Of curves

621 General works
623 Kinematic geometry. Roulettes
624 Curvature
626 Rectification and quadrature
628 Transcendental curves

Of surfaces

631 General works
634 Curvature
636 Areas and volumes
638 Transcendental surfaces
639 Differential geometry of congruences, etc.

Convex geometry

639.5 General works
640 Convex sets and geometric inequalities
640.3 Convex polyhedra. Convex polytopes
640.5 Convexity spaces

Discrete geometry

640.7 General works
640.72 Aperiodic tilings
640.77 Rigidity

Differential geometry
Including general theory of surfaces

Geometry
Differential geometry -- Continued
641 General works, treatises, and textbooks
642 Problems, exercises, examinations
643 Curves on surfaces
644 Minimal surfaces. Nets of plane curves
645 Surfaces determined by relations of curvature, etc.
646 Conformal and other representations of surfaces
Cf. GA110+ Map projection
Cf. QA360 Mapping of regions, conformal representation
648 Deformation of surfaces
648.5 Web geometry
649 Miscellaneous special topics
660 Projective differential geometry
665 Symplectic geometry. Contact geometry
Global differential geometry
Cf. QA614+ Global analysis. Analysis on manifolds
670 General works
671 Global Riemannian geometry
671.5 Spin geometry
672 Integral geometry
681 Foundations of geometry
685 Non-Euclidean geometry
689 Generalized spaces
Hyperspace
691 General works
699 Popular works. Fiction
Including Flatland, fourth dimension
Analytic mechanics
Class here mathematical works only
Cf. QC120+ Descriptive and experimental mechanics
Cf. TA349+ Applied mechanics
801 Periodicals, societies, congresses, serial publications
801.2 Collected works (nonserial)
801.5 Dictionaries and encyclopedias
801.6 Philosophy
802 History
Including general history of mechanics
803 Newton's Principia and commentaries
804 Early works through 1800
805 General works, treatises, and advanced textbooks
807 Elementary textbooks
807.5 Addresses, essays, lectures
808 Special aspects of the subject as a whole
808.2 Continuum mechanics
Cf. QC155.7 Fluid dynamics

Analytic mechanics -- Continued
808.5 Relativistic mechanics
808.8 Study and teaching
809 Problems, exercises, examinations
810 Handbooks, tables, formulas, etc.
Statics
Cf. TA351 Engineering
821 General works, treatises, and textbooks
823 Composition and resolution of forces at a point
Attractions and potential
Cf. QA404.7+ Potential theory
Cf. QC570+ Electrostatics
825 General works, treatises, and textbooks
827 Ellipsoids and other special systems
831 Rigid bodies. Forces and couples in three dimensions. Equilibrium
835 Chains and flexible surfaces. Catenary
839 Geometry of masses. Center of mass. Moments of inertia
Kinematics
Including composition of motions and displacements, relative motions, moving axes, theory of screws
Cf. QA623 Roulettes
Cf. QC231 Kinematics (Physics)
Cf. TJ175 Kinematics of machinery
841 General works
842 Relativistic kinematics
Dynamics
Cf. QC133+ Descriptive and experimental mechanics
Cf. UF820+ Motion of projectiles (Ballistics)
843 Periodicals, societies, congresses, serial publications
845 General works, treatises, and advanced textbooks
846 Elementary textbooks
Dynamics of a particle
Cf. QB349+ Celestial mechanics
Cf. QC174.17.P7 Problem of many bodies (Quantum theory)
851 General works, treatises, and textbooks
852 Special aspects of the subject as a whole
Including resistance, friction
853 Orbital and constrained motion
855 Motion of surfaces
Rigid dynamics
861 General works, treatises, and textbooks
862.A-Z Special systems, A-Z
862.G9 Gyroscope
862.P4 Pendulum
862.P5 Pistons

Analytic mechanics
Dynamics
Rigid dynamics
Special systems, A-Z -- Continued
862.P76 Projectiles
862.T7 Top
863 Miscellaneous special topics
Theory of vibrations. Oscillations
Cf. QA935+ Vibrations of elastic bodies
865 General works
867 Harmonic motion
867.5 Nonlinear oscillations
871 General methods in dynamics
Including Lagrange's equations, Hamilton's equations, least action, stability of systems
Mechanics of deformable bodies
Fluid mechanics
Cf. QC120+ Descriptive and experimental mechanics
Cf. TA357+ Applied fluid mechanics
901 General works, treatises, and textbooks
903 Problems, exercises, examinations
Hydrostatics
905 General works, treatises, and textbooks
907 Miscellaneous special topics
Including floating bodies, etc.
Cf. VM761+ Stability of ships
Fluid dynamics. Hydrodynamics
Cf. TC160+ Hydraulics
911 General works, treatises, and textbooks
912 Relativistic fluid dynamics
913 Kinematics of fluids. Irrotational motions
920 Magnetohydrodynamics. Magnetofluid dynamics
Cf. QC717+ Ion flow dynamics
Cf. QC718.5.M36 Plasma physics
Cf. QC809.M3 Cosmic physics
922 Two-phase flow. Multiphase flow
924 Jets and cavities
925 Rotating fluids. Vortex motion
Cf. QB410 Rotating masses of gravitating fluid
927 Wave propagation in fluids. Theory of wave motion
Cf. QC223 Mathematical theory of sound
929 Viscous fluids
929.5 Non-Newtonian fluids
Cf. QC189.5.A1+ Rheology

Analytic mechanics
Mechanics of deformable bodies
Fluid mechanics
Fluid dynamics. Hydrodynamics -- Continued
930 Gas dynamics. Aerodynamics
Cf. QC120+ Descriptive and experimental mechanics
Cf. TL570+ Aeronautics
Elasticity. Plasticity
Cf. QC191 Special properties of matter
Cf. TA418+ Mechanical properties of materials
931 General works, treatises, and textbooks
932 Micropolar elasticity
933 Thermoelasticity
Cf. TA418.24+ Temperature dependent properties of materials
934 Torsion
Vibrations of elastic bodies. Wave propagation in elastic solids
935 General works
937 Impact
939 Surface waves

Astronomy
1 Periodicals, societies, congresses, serial publications
Museums. Exhibitions
2.A1 General works
2.A2-Z By region or country, A-Z
Subarrange each country by Table Q5
3 Collected works (nonserial)
Observations
Including serial collections issued by individual observatories.
For annual reports see QB82.A+
4.A-Z By name of issuing observatory, A-Z
4.9.A-Z By region or country, A-Z
6 Star catalogs
Including zone observations, etc.
For catalogs of double stars, multiple stars, binary systems see QB821
For catalogs of variable stars see QB835
Ephemerides
For ephemerides of individual planets, see QB611 QB621 etc.
For ephemerides of planets collectively see QB603.E6
7 Early through 1800
1801-
8.A-Z Nautical and air (or aeronautical) almanacs. By country, A-Z
9 Other yearbooks
General tables
11 Early through 1800
12 1801-
14 Dictionaries and encyclopedias
Communication in astronomy
14.2 General works
14.25 Information services
14.3 Computer network resources
Including the Internet
14.5 Philosophy
History
15 General works
Ancient
16 General works
Cf. CE21+ Ancient chronology
Cf. GN799.A8 Astronomy (Prehistoric archaeology)
17 Chinese
18 Hindu
19 Assyro-Babylonian, etc.
Jewish see QB34
20 Egyptian
21 Greek

	History
	Ancient -- Continued
22	Roman
22.2	Celtic
22.3	Etruscan
	Medieval
	Including Arabic astronomy
23	General works
	Astrology
25	History
	Cf. BF1671+ Occult sciences
26	Medieval works
	Cf. BF1680+ Occult sciences
	Modern astrology see BF1651+
	Modern
28	General works
29	Renaissance through 1700
31	18th century
32	19th-20th centuries
33.A-Z	By region or country, A-Z
34	Jewish astronomy
	Maori astronomy see DU423.A85
34.5	Women in astronomy. Women astronomers
	Biography
35	Collective
36.A-Z	Individual, A-Z
	e.g.
36.B8	Brahe
36.C8	Copernicus
36.G2	Galileo
40	Directories
41	Early works through 1700
	Cf. GA6 Cosmography
	Cf. VK551 Navigation (Early works)
	General works, treatises, and advanced textbooks
	Cf. QB500 Descriptive astronomy
42	1701-1800
43	1801-1969
43.2	1970-2000
43.3	2001-
	Popular works
44	Through 1969
44.2	1970-2000
44.3	2001-
	Elementary textbooks
45	To 2000
45.2	2001-

46	Juvenile works
	Cf. QB63 Stargazers' guides
47	Special aspects of the subject as a whole
51	Addresses, essays, lectures
51.3.A-Z	Special topics, A-Z
51.3.E43	Electronic data processing
51.3.I45	Imaging systems
51.3.L53	Light pollution
	Statistical methods see QB149
51.5	Astronomy as a profession. Vocational guidance
52	Miscellany and curiosa
54	Extraterrestrial life
	Cf. CB156 Terrestrial, evidence of interplanetary voyages
(55)	Astronomical myths, legends, and superstitions
	see GR625
	Study and teaching. Research
61	General works
62	Outlines, syllabi
62.5	Problems, exercises, examinations
62.7	Laboratory manuals
63	Stargazers' guides
64	Observers' handbooks
	Cf. TL796.8 Artificial satellites
65	Atlases and charts
66	Astronomical globes
	Cf. GA12 Manual for globes
67	Miscellaneous models
68	Pictorial works and atlases
	Planetariums
	Including orreries
70	General works
71.A-Z	By region or country, A-Z
	Under each country:
	.x — *General works*
	.x2A-.x2Z — *Individual planetariums. By city, A-Z*
	Observatories
	Cf. QB479.A2+ Radio observatories
	Cf. QB500.267+ Orbiting astronomical observatories
81	General works
82.A-Z	By region or country, A-Z
	Under each country:
	.x — *General works*
	.x2A-.x2Z — *Individual observatories. By place, A-Z*
	Including description, history, annual reports, individual named telescopes, etc.

Observatories -- Continued
84 Observatory buildings
Including domes, piers, rising floors, chairs
Astronomical instruments
Including description, theory, adjustment
84.5 Periodicals, societies, congresses, serial publications
Biography of instrument makers
84.7 Collective
84.75.A-Z Individual, A-Z
85 Early. Astrolabes, etc.
Including descriptions of early observatories
Modern
85.8 History
86 General works, treatises, and textbooks
86.4 Catalogs
Telescopes. Objectives. Mirrors
Including homemade telescopes, optics, accessories
For individual named telescopes in observatories see QB82.A+
Cf. QB479.2 Radio telescopes
Cf. QB500.268 Hubble Space Telescope
88 General works
90 Large astronomical telescopes
97 Equatorial mountings. Driving clocks. Siderostats. Heliostats. Coelostats
101 Meridian instruments
Including transit circle, zenith telescope, visual and photographic
103 Extra-meridian instruments
Including altazimuth, almucantar, transit out of meridian, vertical circle
105 Portable instruments
Including transit, solar compass
Cf. VK583 Sextant
107 Clocks. Chronometers. Chronographs
For use of chronograph in ballistics see UF830.C4
111 Eyepieces
113 Micrometers
115 Levels. Artificial horizons. Illumination, etc.
117 Optical interferometers
Astronomical photography
121 General works
121.5 Equipment and supplies
125 Television in astronomy
126 Video astronomy
Electronics in astronomy
127 General works

Electronics in astronomy -- Continued
Equipment and supplies
127.2 General works
127.4 Charge coupled devices
135 Astronomical photometry
Astronomical spectroscopy see QB465
135.5 Aeronautics in astronomy
Including balloons, etc.
136 Space astronomy
Including astronautics in astronomy
139 Telegraphic codes for transmission of astronomical data
Practical and spherical astronomy
Cf. QB66 Use of globes
Cf. VK551+ Nautical astronomy
140 Periodicals, societies, congresses, serial publications
143 Dictionaries and encyclopedias
144 Early works through 1800
145 General works, treatises, and textbooks
147 Celestial sphere and coordinates
149 Statistical astronomy
Correction and reduction of observations
151 General works, treatises, and textbooks
153 Personal equation
Involving apparatus for its determination
154 Errors of adjustment, etc.
Reduction to center of earth
Refraction
155 Theory and determination of constant
156 Tables
159 Parallax
Correction for movement of earth and equinoxes
Including determination of constants by observation
161 General works, treatises, and textbooks
163 Aberration
Cf. QC671 Electromagnetic theory
165 Precession and nutation
167 Annual parallax
168 Star reduction (from mean to apparent place)
169 Position of pole
171 Determination of the ecliptic
Prediction of eclipses, occultations and transits
175 General works
185 Miscellaneous phenomena at occultations and transits
Geodetic astronomy
Including determination of geographical positions
201 General works, treatises, and textbooks

Practical and spherical astronomy
Geodetic astronomy -- Continued
Observations
Cf. QB296.A1+ Observations (Geodesy)
205.A1 Periodicals, societies, congresses, serial publications
205.A2 General works, treatises, and textbooks
205.A3-Z By region or country, A-Z
e.g.
Mexico
205.M6 General works
205.M7A-.M7Z Local, A-Z
United States
205.U4-.U5 General works
205.U6A-.U6Z By region or state, A-Z
205.U7A-.U7Z By city, A-Z
207 Azimuth. Determination of meridian
Time
For historical chronology, calendar, etc. see CE1+
Cf. BD638 Cosmology
Cf. BF468 Psychology
Cf. GN476.3 Anthropology
Cf. QC173.59.T5 Time dilatation
209 General works
209.5 Juvenile works
Time service
210.A1 General works, treatises, and textbooks
210.A3-Z By region or country, A-Z
211 Sidereal and solar, and their conversion
213 Methods of finding the time
214 Instruments for measuring the time
Including hourglasses
Cf. TS540+ Watches and clocks
215 Sundials and dialing
216 Sunrise and sunset
217 Equation of time
221 Time signals, etc.
223 Systems and standards
224 Prime meridians
Longitude and latitude
224.5 General works, treatises, and textbooks
224.7.A-Z By region or country, A-Z
Longitude
225 Methods of determination
228 Tables and ephemerides
Observations
229 General works, treatises, and textbooks
229.5.A-Z By region or country, A-Z

	Practical and spherical astronomy
	Longitude and latitude -- Continued
	Latitude
231	Methods of determination
233	Tables and ephemerides
	Observations
235	General works, treatises, and textbooks
235.5.A-Z	By region or country, A-Z
237	Variation of latitude
	Geodesy
275	Periodicals, societies, congresses, serial publications
279	Dictionaries and encyclopedias
280	Collected works (nonserial)
280.5	History
281	General works, treatises, and textbooks
281.5	Geodesy as a profession. Vocational guidance
283	Mathematical theory of the figure of the earth
	Cf. QA827 Attractions of ellipsoids
	Cf. QB331 Isostasy
	Cf. QB410 Rotating masses of fluid
285	Popular works
286	Juvenile works
287	Addresses, essays, lectures
291	Special arc measures
	Observations
296.A1	General works, treatises, and textbooks
296.A3-Z	By region or country, A-Z
297	Data processing
	Biography
297.9	Collective
298.A-Z	Individual, A-Z
	e.g.
298.H4	Hassler
298.R8	Rylke
	Study and teaching. Research
299	General works
299.5.A-Z	By region or country, A-Z
	Geodetic surveying
	Cf. TA501+ Plane surveying
	Cf. VK588+ Hydrographic surveying
301	General works
303	Base measuring
	Including apparatus
	Cf. QC101 Standards of length
311	Triangulation
	Cf. TA583 Plane surveying

Geodesy
Geodetic surveying -- Continued
321 Theory and computation. Tables, etc.
Cf. QA275 Least squares
325 Traverse surveying
Cf. TA585 Plane surveying
Instruments
Cf. TA562+ Surveying instruments, methods, etc.
328.A1 General works, treatises, and textbooks
328.A2-Z Special, A-Z
328.G4 Geodimeter
328.P7 Prismatic astrolabe
328.T4 Tellurometer
Gravity determinations
330 Periodicals, societies, congresses, serial publications
331 Theory and description of apparatus. Isostasy
Cf. QA862.P4 Dynamics of pendulum
Observations
Including length of seconds, pendulum, etc.
334 General works, treatises, and textbooks
335.A-Z By region or country, A-Z
336 Data processing
Gravity anomalies
337 General works, treatises, and textbooks
337.5.A-Z By region or country, A-Z
338 Plumbline deflections
339 Disturbances
Including lunar, solar, earth movements
341 Constant of gravitation. Mean density of the earth
343 Satellite geodesy. Artificial satellites in geodesy
Cf. TL798.G4 Geodetic satellites
Theoretical astronomy and celestial mechanics
Cf. TL1050+ Astrodynamics
349 Periodicals, societies, congresses, serial publications
350 Collected works
350.5 History
351 General works, treatises, and textbooks
353 Addresses, essays, lectures
Calculation of orbits. Orbit determination
For orbits of individual planets see QB371+
For planetary orbits in general see QB603.M6
355 General works, treatises, and textbooks
355.3 Kepler's laws
355.5 Kepler's equation
357 Comets (General)
For orbits of individual comets see QB723.A+
Perturbations

Theoretical astronomy and celestial mechanics
Perturbations -- Continued
Planetary theory
361 General works, treatises, and textbooks
361.9 Special aspects of the subject as a whole
362.A-Z Special topics, A-Z
362.F47 Few-body problem
362.M3 Many body problem
362.T5 Three body problem
362.T9 Two body problem
369 Tables and observations
Individual planets
Including tables and orbits
371 Mercury
372 Venus
374 Sun's apparent motion
376 Mars
Asteroids. Minor planets
377 General works, treatises, and textbooks
Individual
378.A-Z By name, A-Z
379 By number, if unnamed
384 Jupiter and Saturn
387 Uranus
388 Neptune
389 Ultra-Neptunian planets
Lunar theory
391 General works, treatises, and textbooks
391.9 Special aspects of the subject as a whole
392.A-Z Special topics, A-Z
392.C3 Capture of the moon by the earth
392.I5 Inequalities of the moon's motion
392.O3 Occultations of stars
397 Observations
399 Tables, charts, diagrams, etc.
Satellites
Including individual planetary satellites
Cf. QB603.R55 Planetary rings
Cf. TL796+ Artificial satellites
401 General works, treatises, and textbooks
401.5 Juvenile works
403 Satellites of Mars
404 Satellites of Jupiter
405 Satellites and ring system of Saturn
406 Satellites of Uranus
407 Satellites and ring system of Neptune
408 Satellites of Pluto

Theoretical astronomy and celestial mechanics -- Continued
410 Figures of equilibrium of rotating masses of fluid
Theory of tides
Cf. GC300+ Oceanography
Cf. QC809.E2 Earth tides
Cf. VK600+ Tidetables
414 Early works through 1800
General works, treatises, and textbooks
415 1801-1969
415.2 1970-
416 Special aspects of the subject as a whole
418 Dictionaries and encyclopedias
419 Miscellany and curiosa
Instruments see GC306
421 Theory of double star systems
Cosmochemistry
450 General works
450.5 Cosmic abundance
Astrogeology
Cf. QB592 Lunar geology
Cf. QB603.G46 Planetary geology
Biography
454 Collective
454.2.A-Z Individual, A-Z
455 General works
455.2 Astromineralogy
455.5 Extraterrestrial seismology
Cf. QB539.I5 Helioseismology
Cf. QB812 Astroseismology
456 Multiring basins
Astrophysics (General)
460 Periodicals, societies, congresses, serial publications
460.15 Collected works (nonserial)
Biography
460.7 Collective
460.72.A-Z Individual, A-Z
461 General works, treatises, and textbooks
461.3 Popular works
461.5 Addresses, essays, lectures
462.2 Data processing
462.3 Mathematics
462.5 Radio astrophysics
462.6 Molecular astrophysics
462.65 Relativistic astrophysics
Plasma astrophysics
462.7 General works
462.72 Double layers

	Astrophysics (General) -- Continued
462.8	Cosmic magnetic fields
	Nuclear astrophysics
463	Periodicals, societies, congresses, serial publications
463.15	Collected works (nonserial)
464	General works, treatises, and textbooks
464.15	Particle acceleration
464.2	Neutrino astrophysics
464.3	Nucleosynthesis
464.4	Radiative capture
465	Astronomical spectroscopy Cf. QB551 Spectroscopy of sun and eclipses Cf. QB870+ Stellar spectroscopy
466.A-Z	Other topics, A-Z
466.A25	Accretion
466.C45	Chaotic behavior in systems
466.C64	Collisions
466.C65	Compact objects
466.C66	Controlled fusion
466.C67	Cosmochronology
466.D58	Disks
466.E65	Equations of state
466.F58	Fluid dynamics
466.G38	Gas dynamics
466.J46	Jets
466.M37	Mass loss
466.P67	Positronium
	Non-optical methods of astronomy
468	General works
	Infrared astronomy
470.A1	Periodicals, societies, congresses, serial publications
470.A5-Z	General works, treatises, and textbooks
	Gamma ray astronomy
471.A1	Periodicals, societies, congresses, serial publications
471.A5-Z	General works, treatises, and textbooks
471.7.A-Z	Special topics, A-Z
471.7.B85	Bursts
	X-ray astronomy
472.A1	Periodicals, societies, congresses, serial publications
472.A5-Z	General works, treatises, and textbooks
472.5	Juvenile works
473	Addresses, essays, lectures
474	Ultraviolet astronomy
	Radio astronomy Cf. QB860 Quasars
475.A1	Periodicals, societies, congresses, serial publications
475.A15	Collected works (nonserial)

Non-optical methods of astronomy
Radio astronomy -- Continued

475.A2 Dictionaries and encyclopedias
History
475.A25 General works
475.A28A-.A28Z By region or country, A-Z
476.5 General works, treatises, and advanced textbooks
477 Popular works
478 Juvenile works
478.5 Addresses, essays, lectures
Observatories
479.A2 General works
479.A5-Z By region or country, A-Z
Under each country:
.x General works
.x2A-.x2Z Individual observatories. By name, A-Z
479.2 Radio telescopes
479.3 Radio interferometers
479.4 Millimeter astronomy
Radio sources
479.5 General works
479.55.A-Z Individual radio sources or types of radio sources, A-Z
479.55.C93 Cygnus A
479.55.H68 Hot spots
479.55.M18 M87 (Galaxy)
479.55.R34 Radio Galaxies
479.55.S88 Superluminal
480 Radar in astronomy

Descriptive astronomy
Periodicals, societies, congresses, serial publications see QB1
General works, treatises, and textbooks see QB42+
Universe. Space. Space sciences
Cf. QB980+ Cosmology
Cf. TL787+ Astronautics. Space travel
495 Periodicals, societies, congresses, serial publications
496 Collected works
497 Dictionaries and encyclopedias
497.2 Communication in space sciences
History
498 General works
498.2.A-Z By region or country, A-Z
500 General works, treatises, and advanced textbooks
500.22 Juvenile works
500.24 Addresses, essays, lectures
500.25 Special aspects of the subject as a whole

	Descriptive astronomy
	Universe. Space. Space sciences -- Continued
500.26.A-Z	Special topics, A-Z
500.26.D38	Data processing
500.26.I58	International cooperation
500.26.S67	Space optics
	Study and teaching. Research
	Including exploration of outer space
500.262	General works
500.264	Experiments
500.266.A-Z	By region or country, A-Z
	Orbiting astronomical observatories
500.267	General works
500.268	Hubble Space Telescope
500.269	Next Generation Space Telescope
500.28	Northern sky
500.3	Southern sky
	Solar system
500.5	Periodicals, societies, congresses, serial publications
501	General works, treatises, and textbooks
501.2	Popular works
501.3	Juvenile works
501.5	Study and teaching. Research
502	Miscellany and curiosa
503	Age of solar system. Origin of solar system
505	Physical conditions
	Including atmospheres, resisting medium, etc.
507	Proper motion in space
	Solar parallax and related constants
508	General works
	Transit of Venus
509	General works, treatises, and textbooks
509.5	1639 transit
511	1761 and 1769 transits
512	1874 transit
513	1882 transit
513.2	2004 transit
515	Transit of Mercury
516	Observations of Mars and asteroids
518	Other methods
	Sun
520	Periodicals, societies, congresses, serial publications
521	General works, treatises, and textbooks
521.4	Popular works
521.5	Juvenile works
521.6	Addresses, essays, lectures

Descriptive astronomy
Solar system
Sun -- Continued

522 Tables, etc.
Cf. QB374 Perturbations
523 Mass, diameter, rotation, etc.
Solar activity
524 General works
525 Sunspots
Cf. BF1729.S92 Astrology
526.A-Z Other special topics, A-Z
526.A37 Active regions
526.C9 Cycles
Energetic particles see QB526.S65
526.F3 Faculae
526.F6 Flares
526.F64 Flocculi. Plages
Plages see QB526.F64
526.P7 Prominences
526.S65 Solar energetic particles
528 Atmosphere, chromosphere
Corona. Solar wind. Heliosphere
529 General works
529.5 Coronal holes
529.6 Corotating interaction regions
531 Radiation, temperature, etc.
Cf. QC910.2+ Solar radiation in meteorology
539.A-Z Other special topics, A-Z
539.C6 Composition
539.E4 Electric field
539.E8 Evolution
539.G7 Granulation
Helioseismology see QB539.I5
539.I5 Interior
Including helioseismology
539.M23 Magnetic fields
539.N6 Noise storms
539.N8 Nuclear reactions
539.O83 Oscillations
539.P58 Polarimetry
539.R3 Radio effects
Seismology see QB539.I5
539.S5 Size
539.S65 Solar neutrinos
539.S655 Solar x-rays
539.T4 Terrestrial-solar relations
540 Miscellany and curiosa

Descriptive astronomy
  Solar system
    Sun -- Continued
      Solar eclipses
          Including works on solar and lunar eclipses combined
          Cf. BL325.E35 Eclipses (Mythology)
541 General works, treatises, and textbooks
541.5 Juvenile works
542 Through 1799
          Class here works on individual solar eclipses occurring through 1799, as well as works discussing collectively eclipses in that time period
        1800-
542.5 Collective
          Individual
543 1800-1899
              Complete by appending a decimal point and the last two digits of the year of the eclipse to QB543 followed by author number and date of publication, e. g. QB543.98.I53 1899, Indian eclipse, 1898; report of the expeditions, c1899
544 1900-1999
              Complete by appending a decimal point and the last two digits of the year of the eclipse to QB544 followed by author number and date of publication, e. g. QB544.91.R36 1989, Rao Joe. Your guide to the great solar eclipse of 1991, c1989
545 2000-2099
              Complete by appending a decimal point and the last two digits of the year of the eclipse to QB545 followed by author number and date of publication
551 Spectroscopy of sun and eclipses
579 Lunar eclipses
    Moon
580 Periodicals, societies, congresses, serial publications
581 General works, treatises, and textbooks
581.9 Popular works
582 Juvenile works
582.3 Study and teaching. Research
582.5 Exploration
        Cf. TL799.M6 Space flights to the moon
583 Distance, parallax
585 Rotation, libration, and shape
588 Temperature, radiation, brightness, phases
591 Surface, physical condition, meteorology

Descriptive astronomy
Solar system
Moon -- Continued
592 Lunar geology. Lunar petrology
Cf. TN291.35 Lunar mining
595 Photographs, maps, drawings
Planets. Planetology
Cf. QB54 Extraterrestrial life
Cf. QB401+ Satellites
Cf. QB500.5+ Solar system
Cf. QB820 Extrasolar planets
Cf. TL799.A+ Flights to special planets
600 Periodicals, societies, congresses, serial publications
600.2 Dictionaries and encyclopedias
Communication of planetological information
600.3 General works
600.32 Information services
600.33 Geographic information systems
600.34 Computer network resources
Including the Internet
600.35 Planetological literature
600.5 Nomenclature, terminology, names
601 General works, treatises, and textbooks
601.9 Popular works
602 Juvenile works
602.9 Special aspects of the subject as a whole
602.95 Data processing
603.A-Z Special topics, A-Z
603.A85 Atmospheres
Including meteorology
603.C6 Composition
603.C7 Cratering
603.C78 Crust
603.E6 Ephemerides
603.F5 Figures
603.G46 Geology
Cf. TN291.3+ Space mining
603.I52 Infrared radiation
603.I53 Internal structure
603.I55 Interplanetary medium
Including interplanetary dust
603.I57 Ionospheres
603.M26 Magnetic fields
603.M3 Mass
Meteorology see QB603.A85

Descriptive astronomy
Solar system
Planets. Planetology
Special topics, A-Z -- Continued
603.M6 Motion
Including orbits
For orbits of individual planets see QB371+
603.O74 Origin
603.R3 Radiation
603.R55 Rings
Cf. QB405 Ring system of Saturn
Cf. QB407 Ring system of Neptune
603.S6 Spectroscopy
603.S95 Surfaces
603.V65 Volcanism
604 Tables, etc.
605 Photographs, maps, drawings
605.2 Miscellany and curiosa
Inferior planets
606 General works
607 Intramercurial planets
Mercury
611 General works
613.A-Z Special topics, A-Z
613.G46 Geology
Transit of Mercury see QB515
Venus
621 General works
623.A-Z Special topics, A-Z
623.A86 Atmosphere
623.G46 Geology
623.M48 Meteorology
Transit of Venus see QB509+
623.V65 Volcanism. Volcanoes
623.W56 Winds
Earth as a planet. Astronomical geography
Cf. QE500+ Geology
630 Periodicals, societies, congresses, serial collections
631 General works, treatises, and textbooks
631.2 Popular works
631.4 Juvenile works
632 Origin
633 Rotation
637 Photographs from space
Seasons
Cf. GR930 Folklore
637.2 General works, treatises, and textbooks

Descriptive astronomy
Solar system
Planets. Planetology
Earth as a planet. Astronomical geography
Seasons -- Continued

637.4 Juvenile literature
637.5 Spring
637.6 Summer
637.7 Autumn
637.8 Winter
638 Miscellany and curiosa
638.8 End of the world

Superior planets
Including other objects beyond Earth
For their satellites, see QB403+

639 General works

Mars

641 General works
643.A-Z Special topics, A-Z
643.A86 Atmosphere
643.C55 Climate
643.D87 Dust storms
643.G46 Geology
643.G73 Gravity
643.M48 Meteorology
Satellites see QB403
643.S42 Seasons
643.V65 Volcanism. Volcanoes
643.W38 Water
643.W56 Wind erosion

Asteroids

651 General works
653.A-Z Individual asteroids, A-Z

Outer planets

659 General works

Jupiter

661 General works
663.A-Z Special topics, A-Z
663.A86 Atmosphere
Satellites see QB404

Saturn

671 General works
673.A-Z Special topics, A-Z
Ring system see QB405
Satellites see QB405

Uranus

681 General works

Descriptive astronomy
Solar system
Planets. Planetology
Superior planets
Outer planets
Uranus -- Continued
683.A-Z Special topics, A-Z
Satellites see QB406
Neptune
691 General works
693.A-Z Special topics, A-Z
Ring system see QB407
Satellites see QB407
Trans-Neptunian objects
Cf. QB701+ Pluto
694 General works
695 Kuiper Belt
Dwarf planets
698 General works
Pluto
701 General works
703.A-Z Special topics, A-Z
Satellites see QB408
705 Ceres
Comets
Cf. QB357 Calculation of orbits
717 Periodicals, societies, congresses, serial publications
721 General works, treatises, and textbooks
721.4 Popular works
721.5 Juvenile works
721.6 Addresses, essays, lectures
722 Catalogs
723.A-Z Periodic comets. By name, A-Z
(723.A7) Arrest's comet
see QB723.D37
723.B5 Biela comet
723.B7 Brooks comet
723.B8 Brorsen comet (I)
723.C6 Comas Sola comet
723.D37 D'Arrest comet
723.D45 Delavan comet
723.D5 Denning comet
723.E3 Encke comet
723.F2 Faye comet
723.G43 Geddes comet
723.H17 Hale-Bopp comet
723.H2 Halley's comet

Descriptive astronomy
Solar system
Comets
Periodic comets. By name, A-Z -- Continued

723.H7 Holmes comet
723.L6 Lexell comet
723.M67 Morehouse comet
723.S56 Shoemaker-Levy 9 comet
723.T3 Tempel 1 comet
723.T8 Tuttle comet
723.V35 Van Biesbroeck comet
724 Comets before 1700
725 1700-1799
Complete by appending a decimal point and the last two digits of the year of the appearance of the comet to QB725 followed by author number and date of publication
726 1800-1899
Complete by appending a decimal point and the last two digits of the year of the appearance of the comet to QB726 followed by author number and date of publication, e.g. QB726.61.K8, Kreutz, Heinrich, Untersuchungen über die Bahn des grossen Kometen von 1861
727 1900-1999
Complete by appending a decimal point and the last two digits of the year of the appearance of the comet to QB727 followed by author number and date of publication
728 2000-2099
Complete by appending a decimal point and the last two digits of the year of the appearance of the comet to QB728 followed by author number and date of publication
729 Distribution of comets
731 Nature and constitution (before the spectroscope)
732 Nature and constitution (modern views)
738 Meteoroids
Meteors
740 Periodicals, societies, congresses, serial publications
741 General works, treatises, and textbooks
741.5 Juvenile works
743 Methods of observation and geometrical topics
Including radiants, altitude, etc.
Periodic showers
745 November
746 August

	Descriptive astronomy
	Solar system
	Meteors -- Continued
748	Orbits
748.2	Streams
	Relation between meteors and comets
749	General works
751	Other theories of the origin of meteors
753	Remarkable meteors, fireballs
	Meteorites Including craters Cf. QE399 Tektites
754.8	Periodicals, societies, congresses, serial publications
755	General works, treatises, and textbooks
755.2	Juvenile literature
755.3	Addresses, essays, lectures
755.5.A-Z	By region or country, A-Z
756.A-Z	Individual meteorites and craters, A-Z
756.A44	Allende meteorite
756.C45	Chinguetti meteorite
756.F47	Fermo meteorite
756.K87	Kurinelli meteorite
756.M4	Meteor Crater (Ariz.)
756.O74	Orgueil meteorite
756.P67	Port Orford meteorite
756.S5	Sikhote-Alin meteorite
756.T58	Thuathe meteorite
756.T8	Tunguska meteorite
756.V74	Vredefort Dome (South Africa)
	Meteorite types or classes
	Iron meteorites. Siderites
757	General works, treatises, and textbooks
757.5.A-Z	Special, A-Z
757.5.A73	Ataxites
757.5.H49	Hexahedrites
757.5.O37	Octahedrites
	Stony meteorites. Aerolites
758	General works, treatises, and textbooks
758.5.A-Z	Special, A-Z
758.5.A47	Achondrites
758.5.C46	Chondrites
759	Stony-iron meteorites. Siderolites. Intermediates
761	Zodiacal light. Counterglow. Gegenschein
	Spectroscopy of moon, planets, comets, etc.
770	Moon
775	Planets
780	Comets

Descriptive astronomy
Solar system
Spectroscopy of moon, planets, comets, etc. -- Continued

785 Meteors

Interstellar matter

790 General works
791 Cosmic dust
791.2 Cosmic grains
791.3 Dark matter
791.35 Missing mass
791.4 Molecular clouds
791.5 Interstellar hydrogen
791.7 Interstellar magnetic fields
792 Circumstellar matter

Stars
Cf. QB6 Star catalogs
Cf. QB870+ Stellar spectroscopy

799 Periodicals, societies, congresses, serial publications
801 General works, treatises, and textbooks
801.6 Popular works
801.7 Juvenile works
801.8 Addresses, essays, lectures
802 Constellation figures. Star names
Cf. QB63 Stargazers' guides
803 Zodiac
Including individual constellations of the zodiac
805 Particular stars (not A-Z)
Cf. QB823 Particular double and multiple stars
Cf. QB837 Particular variable stars
Cf. QB883 Spectra of special stars
806 Stellar evolution
806.5 Starbursts
807 Astrometry
Cf. QB135 Astronomical photometry
808 Structure
809 Atmospheres

Motion
Including orbits, velocities, dynamics

810 General works
811 Proper motion
812 Stellar oscillations. Astroseismology
813 Parallax and distance
814 Masses
815 Magnitudes. Photometric catalogs
816 Color
Cf. QB829 Color of double stars
817 Radiation. Bolometry

	Descriptive astronomy
	Stars -- Continued
817.5	Magnetic fields
818	Stellar diameters
818.5	Stellar collisions Including stellar mergers
819	Distribution Including stellar populations
820	Extrasolar planets
	Double and multiple stars. Binary systems Cf. QB421 Theory Cf. QB903 Spectroscopy
821	General works, treatises, and textbooks Including observations, catalogs
823	Particular stars (not A-Z)
829	Colors of double stars
830	X-ray binaries
	Variable stars. Algol systems Cf. QB895 Spectroscopy
833	Periodicals, societies, congresses, serial publications
835	General works, treatises, and textbooks Including observations, catalogs
835.2	Addresses, essays, lectures
836	Magnitude. Photometric catalogs
837	Particular stars or clusters (not A-Z)
837.5	Cataclysmic variable stars
838	Pulsating stars
841	Temporary or new stars
843.A-Z	Other particular types of stars, A-Z
843.A12	A stars
843.A89	Asymptotic giant branch stars
843.B12	B stars
843.B25	Be stars
843.B55	Black holes
843.B57	Blue stragglers
843.B75	Brightest stars
843.B77	Brown dwarfs
843.C6	Cool stars
	Coronae Borealis stars R see QB843.R12
843.D44	Delta Scuti stars
843.D85	Dwarf novae
843.D9	Dwarf stars
843.E2	Early stars
843.F55	Flare stars
843.L85	Luminous blue variables
843.M16	M stars
843.M3	Magnetic stars

Descriptive astronomy
Stars
Other particular types of stars, A-Z -- Continued
843.N12 N stars
843.N4 Neutron stars
843.O12 O stars
843.P42 Peculiar stars
843.P8 Pulsars
843.R12 R Coronae Borealis stars
843.R17 R Scuti stars
843.R4 Red dwarfs
843.R42 Red giants
843.R72 RR Lyrae stars
843.S53 Shell stars
843.S85 Subgiant stars
843.S9 Supergiant stars
843.S94 Supermassive stars
843.S95 Supernovae
843.S96 Symbiotic stars
843.T12 T Tauri stars
843.W5 White dwarfs
843.W6 Wolf-Rayet stars
Clusters and nebulae
Cf. QB891 Spectroscopy
851 General works, treatises, and textbooks
Including observations, catalogs
Clusters
853 General works
853.5 Globular clusters
Nebulae
855 General works
855.2 Juvenile works
855.5 Planetary nebulae
Including proto-planetary nebulae
855.55 Gaseous nebulae
Including Herbig-Haro objects
855.9.A-Z Individual. By name, A-Z
855.9.C7 Crab Nebula
855.9.H67 Horsehead Nebula
855.9.O75 Orion Nebula
Galaxies
856 Periodicals, societies, congresses, serial publications
857 General works
857.3 Juvenile works
857.5.A-Z Special topics, A-Z
857.5.B84 Bulges
857.5.D37 Data processing

	Descriptive astronomy
	Stars
	Galaxies
	Special topics, A-Z -- Continued
857.5.E96	Evolution
857.5.E97	Extragalactic distances
857.5.G7	Gravitational lenses
	Including microlensing
857.5.H34	Halos
857.5.M34	Magnetic fields
857.5.M67	Motion in the line of sight
	Radio galaxies see QB479.55.R34
857.5.S87	Surface brightness
	Milky Way galaxy
857.7	General works
857.72	Galactic center
858	Dwarf galaxies
	Active galaxies
	Including active galactic nuclei
858.3	General works
858.35	BL Lacertae objects
858.4	Elliptical galaxies
858.42	Spiral galaxies
858.5.A-Z	Other galaxies. By name, A-Z
858.5.M33	Magellanic Clouds
	Clusters of galaxies
858.7	General works
858.8.A-Z	Individual. By name, A-Z
858.8.L63	Local Group
	Cf. QB857.7+ Milky Way
858.8.V57	Virgo Cluster
860	Quasars
	Stellar spectroscopy
870	Periodicals, societies, congresses, serial collections
871	General works, treatises, and textbooks
873	Instruments and apparatus
875	Chemical and physical constitution
881	Classification of stars
	Including classed catalogs
883	Study of special types of spectra
	Including the spectra of special stars
891	Nebulae and clusters
895	Variables and new stars
901	Motion in the line of sight. Radial velocities
903	Spectroscopic observations on double stars

Cosmogony. Cosmology
Including nebular hypothesis, meteoritic hypothesis, glacial cosmogony
Cf. BD493+ Speculative philosophy
Cf. QB503 Origin of solar system

980 Periodicals, societies, congresses, serial publications
980.5 Dictionaries and encyclopedias
981 General works, treatises, and textbooks
982 Popular works
983 Juvenile works
985 Addresses, essays, lectures
991.A-Z Special topics, A-Z
991.B54 Big bang theory
991.C64 Cosmic background radiation
Including cosmic ripples
991.C65 Cosmic rotation
991.C658 Cosmological constants
991.C66 Cosmological distances
991.C87 Curvature cosmology
991.C92 Cyclic universe theory
991.E53 End of the universe
991.E94 Expanding universe
991.G73 Great Attractor
991.I54 Inflationary universe
991.L37 Large scale structure
991.N34 Naked singularities
991.P45 Phase transformations
991.Q36 Quantum cosmology
991.S73 Statistical methods
991.T67 Topological defects

Physics
Cf. QH505 Biophysics
Cf. R895+ Medical physics
Cf. S588.4+ Agricultural physics

1 Periodicals, societies, congresses, serial publications
3 Collected works (nonserial)
5 Dictionaries and encyclopedias
Communication in physics
5.3 General works
5.35 Information services
5.4 Computer network resources
Including the Internet
5.45 Physics literature
5.5 Abstracting and indexing
5.52 Language. Authorship
Philosophy. Methodology
For relativity physics see QC173.5+
For unified field theories see QC173.68+
5.56 Periodicals, societies, congresses, serial publications
5.58 Collected works (nonserial)
6 General works, treatises, and textbooks
6.2 Addresses, essays, lectures
6.4.A-Z Special topics, A-Z
6.4.A27 Absolute, The
6.4.A85 Asian philosophy
6.4.C3 Causality
6.4.C56 Coherent state
6.4.C57 Consciousness
6.4.C58 Constraints
6.4.C6 Continuity. Continuum
6.4.D46 Determinism
Cf. QC174.17.H4 Heisenberg principle
6.4.D5 Dialectical materialism
6.4.D8 Dualism
6.4.F58 Fluctuations
6.4.I34 Identity (Philosophical concept)
6.4.P37 Paradox
6.4.R42 Reality
6.4.R43 Reductionism
6.8 Nomenclature, terminology, notation, abbreviations
History
6.9 Periodicals, societies, congresses, serial publications
7 General works
7.5 Addresses, essays, lectures
9.A-Z By region or country, A-Z
14 Women in physics. Women physicists
For biography see QC15+

	Biography
15	Collective
16.A-Z	Individual, A-Z
	e.g.
	Curie, Marie and Pierre see QD22.C8
16.E5	Einstein
16.N7	Newton
16.2	Directories
	Early works
17	1501-1700
19	1701-1800
	Mathematical physics
	For mathematical theory without practical applications see QA401+
	Cf. QC173.96+ Quantum theory
	Cf. TA329+ Engineering mathematics
19.2	Periodicals, societies, congresses, serial publications
19.3	Collected works (nonserial)
	History
19.6	General works
19.7.A-Z	By region or country, A-Z
20	General works, treatises, and textbooks
20.5	Addresses, essays, lectures
20.6	Special aspects of the subject as a whole
20.7.A-Z	Special topics, A-Z
20.7.A34	Adiabatic invariants
20.7.A37	Algebraic geometry
20.7.A4	Algebraic logic
20.7.A5	Analysis
	Cf. QA401+ Analytical methods for physical problems
20.7.A85	Asymptotic theory
20.7.B38	Bayesian statistical decision theory
20.7.B47	Bethe-ansatz technique
20.7.B54	Bifurcation theory
20.7.B58	Bose algebras
20.7.B6	Boundary value problems
20.7.C14	C*-algebras
20.7.C28	Calculus of tensors
20.7.C3	Calculus of variations
20.7.C36	Catastrophes
20.7.C55	Clifford algebras
20.7.C58	Combinatorial analysis
20.7.C6	Correlation
20.7.C63	Coupled problems
20.7.D4	Decomposition method
20.7.D43	Density functionals
20.7.D45	Determinants

Mathematical physics
Special topics, A-Z -- Continued

20.7.D47 Difference equations
20.7.D5 Differential equations
20.7.D516 Differential games
20.7.D52 Differential geometry
Including noncommutative differential geometry
20.7.D55 Dimensional analysis
20.7.E4 Electronic data processing
20.7.E48 Embedding theorems
20.7.E88 Evolution equations
Cf. QA377.3 Differential equations
20.7.F56 Finite element method
20.7.F67 Fourier transformations
20.7.F73 Fractals
20.7.F84 Functional analysis
20.7.F85 Functional integration
20.7.F87 Functions, Special
20.7.G44 Geometry
20.7.G55 Global analysis
20.7.G7 Graph theory
20.7.G76 Group theory
Cf. QC174.17.G7 Group theoretical methods for quantum mechanical problems
20.7.H35 Hamiltonian systems
20.7.H63 Homogeneous spaces
20.7.H65 Homology and cohomology theories
20.7.I33 Idempotents
20.7.I58 Integral equations
20.7.K47 Kernel functions
20.7.K56 Knot polynomials
20.7.L54 Lie algebras. Lie-admissible algebras
20.7.M24 Manifolds
20.7.M27 Mathematical optimization
20.7.M3 Matrix theory
Cf. QC174.3+ Matrix mechanics
Cf. QC793.3.M36 Elementary particle physics
20.7.M43 Measure theory
Cf. QC174.17.M4 Quantum theory
20.7.M53 Microlocal analysis
20.7.M65 Monte Carlo method
20.7.N58 Nonassociative algebras
Noncommutative differential geometry see QC20.7.D52
20.7.N6 Nonlinear theories
20.7.O65 Operator algebras
20.7.O66 Operator theory
20.7.O75 Orthogonal functions and polynomials

Mathematical physics
Special topics, A-Z -- Continued
20.7.P23 p-adic analysis
20.7.P3 Padé approximant
20.7.P47 Perturbation
20.7.P67 Potential theory
20.7.P7 Probabilities
20.7.R38 Relational calculus
20.7.R4 Relaxation methods
20.7.R43 Renormalization
20.7.S3 Scattering theory
20.7.S54 Singularities
Special functions see QC20.7.F87
20.7.S64 Spectral theory
20.7.S645 Spherical harmonics
20.7.S65 Spinor analysis
20.7.S68 Stability
20.7.S73 Standards
20.7.S8 Stochastic processes
Tensor analysis see QC20.7.C28
20.7.T45 Theory of distributions
20.7.T65 Topology
20.7.T73 Transport theory
20.7.V4 Vector analysis
20.7.W38 Wavelets
20.7.W53 WKB approximation
20.7.Z47 Zeta functions
Study and teaching. Research
20.8 General works
20.815.A-Z By region or country, A-Z
20.82 Problems, exercises, examinations
20.85 Handbooks, tables, formulas, etc.
General works, treatises, and advanced textbooks
21 1801-1969
21.2 1970-2000
21.3 2001-
Elementary textbooks
23 To 2000
23.2 2001-
24 Pictorial works and atlases
24.5 Popular works
25 Juvenile works
26 Recreations, home experiments, etc.
27 Anecdotes, facetiae, satire, etc.
Addresses, essays, lectures see QC71
28 Special aspects of the subject as a whole
29 Physics as a profession. Vocational guidance

Study and teaching. Research
For programmed texts see QC21+
30 General works
31 Outlines, syllabi
32 Problems, exercises, examinations
33 Experiments
Cf. QC26 Home experiments
Laboratory manuals
Elementary
35 General works
36 Laboratory blanks
37 Advanced
39 Physical measurements (General)
Including theory and methods
Cf. QC81+ Weights and measures
Cf. T50 Technical measurement
39.5 Juvenile works
41 Laboratory technique
By region or country
United States
44 General works
45.A-Z By region or state, A-Z
Subarrange each state by Table Q7
47.A-Z Other regions or countries, A-Z
Subarrange each country by Table Q7
48 Developing countries
Laboratories
Cf. QC100.A2+ Standardizing bureaus
Cf. QC541.A1+ Electric laboratories
51.A1 General works
51.A3-Z By region or country, A-Z
Subarrange each country by Table Q6
52 Data processing
Instruments and apparatus (General)
For instruments of special fields, see the field
Cf. QC100.5+ Weights and measures
Cf. QC101+ Instruments for measurement of length, area, weight, etc.
Cf. QC370.5+ Optical instruments
Cf. QC875.5+ Meteorological instruments
53 General works
55 Juvenile works
Museums. Exhibitions
60.A1 General works
60.A2-Z By region or country, A-Z
Subarrange each country by Table Q5
61 Handbooks, tables, formulas, etc.

71	Addresses, essays, lectures
	Force and energy (General)
	Cf. QC310.15+ Thermodynamics
	Philosophy see QA843+
72	History
73	General works, treatises, and textbooks
73.4	Juvenile works
73.6	Study and teaching. Research
73.8.A-Z	Special topics, A-Z
73.8.C6	Conservation of energy
73.8.C65	Correlation of forces
73.8.E53	Energy transfer
73.8.M4	Mechanical advantage
73.8.W65	Work
75	Miscellany and curiosa
	Weights and measures. Units of measurement
	Class here works on the means of expressing quantities of length, area, volume, capacity, and mass (or weight) in terms of standard units. For works on units used in the measurement of other quantities, including velocity, pressure, energy, temperature, see the particular field of application
	Cf. BS680.W4 Weights and measures in the Bible
	Cf. HF5711+ Tables of weights and measures (Business mathematics)
	Cf. QA465 Measurement (Mathematics)
	Cf. QB214 Time measuring instruments
	Cf. QC535+ Electric measurements
81	Periodicals, societies, congresses, serial publications
	For governmental standardizing bureaus, including serial publications issued by them see QC100.A3+
	Museums. Exhibitions
81.5.A1	General works
81.5.A2-Z	By region or country, A-Z
	Subarrange each country by Table Q5
82	Dictionaries and encyclopedias
	History
83	General works
84	Ancient
85	Medieval
86	Modern
87	Early works through 1800
88	General works, treatises, and advanced textbooks
	Including works with an alphabetical arrangement of countries
89.A-Z	By region or country, A-Z
	Subarrange each country by Table Q4
90	Elementary textbooks
90.5	Popular works

Weights and measures -- Continued
90.6 Juvenile works
Special systems
Metric system. International system (SI)
Cf. T50.5 Metric system in industry
90.8 Periodicals, societies, congresses, serial publications
91 General works, treatises, and textbooks
92.A-Z By region or country, A-Z
Subarrange each country by Table Q4
92.2 Popular works
92.5 Juvenile works
92.6 Addresses, essays, lectures
93 Study and teaching. Research
94 Conversion tables
International system see QC90.8+
96 Other systems (not A-Z)
97 Study and teaching. Research
99 Miscellany and curiosa
Including pyramid metrology
Standards (General). Governmental standardizing bureaus
100.A2 General works, treatises, and textbooks
100.A3-Z By region or country, A-Z
Measuring instruments (General)
100.5 General works
100.8 Catalogs
Measurement of special quantities
Including instruments used in measurement
Length
101 Standards
102 Measurement and instruments
102.5 Thickness
Including micrometers
103 Angles
Including goniometers
Cf. QA482 Plane geometry
Cf. TA603 Surveying
104 Volume
104.5 Area measurement
Mass and weight
105 Standards
Measurement
Cf. QC172+ Atomic mass
Cf. QC454.M3 Mass spectrometry
106 General works
107 Weighing instruments, balances, scales, etc.
Cf. TS410 Manufactures
Density and specific gravity

Weights and measures
Measurement of special quantities
Mass and weight
Density and specific gravity -- Continued
111 General works
114 Tables, etc.
Descriptive and experimental mechanics
For theoretical and analytical mechanics see QA801+
Cf. QC71.82+ Force and energy (General)
Cf. QC176+ Solid state physics
Cf. TA349+ Applied mechanics
120 Periodicals, societies, congresses, serial publications
121 Collected works (nonserial)
121.6 Dictionaries and encyclopedias
121.8 Nomenclature, terminology, notation, abbreviations
History
For general history of mechanics see QA802
122 General works
122.2.A-Z By region or country, A-Z
123 Early works through 1800
General works, treatises, and advanced textbooks
125 1801-1969
125.2 1970-
127 Elementary textbooks
127.3 Popular works
127.4 Juvenile works
127.6 Addresses, essays, lectures
Study and teaching. Research
128 General works
129 Problems, exercises, examinations
129.5 Laboratory manuals
131 Special aspects of the subject as a whole
Dynamics. Motion
Cf. QA843+ Analytic mechanics
133 General works, treatises, and textbooks
133.5 Juvenile works
135 Kinematics
136 Vibrations
Cf. QA865+ Analytic mechanics (Dynamics)
Cf. QA935+ Vibrations of elastic bodies
Cf. QC231 Sound
Cf. TA355 Engineering
137 Inertia
Including Mach's principle
Velocity. Speed
Cf. QC233 Velocity of sound
Cf. QC407 Velocity of light

Descriptive and experimental mechanics
Dynamics. Motion
Velocity. Speed -- Continued
137.5 General works, treatises, and textbooks
137.52 Juvenile works
Fluids. Fluid mechanics
Including liquids
Cf. QA901+ Analytic mechanics
Cf. TA357+ Applied fluid mechanics
138 Periodicals, societies, congresses, serial publications
139 Dictionaries and encyclopedias
140 Nomenclature, terminology, notation, abbreviations
141 History
142 Early works through 1500
General works, treatises, and textbooks
143 1501-1700
144 1701-1800
145 1801-1969
145.2 1970-
145.24 Juvenile works
145.26 Addresses, essays, lectures
145.28 Study and teaching
145.3 Handbooks, tables, formulas, etc.
145.4.A-Z Special properties of liquids, A-Z
145.4.A25 Acoustic properties
145.4.C6 Compressibility
145.4.D5 Diffusion
145.4.E45 Electric properties
145.4.E9 Expansion
145.4.M27 Magnetic properties
145.4.O6 Optical properties
145.4.P73 Pressure
145.4.T5 Thermal properties
145.4.V5 Viscosity
145.45.A-Z Special liquefied gases, A-Z
145.45.A75 Argon
145.45.F5 Fluorine
145.45.H4 Helium
145.45.H9 Hydrogen
145.48.A-Z Special liquids, A-Z
145.48.P6 Polywater
145.48.S9 Supercooled liquids
Hydrostatics. Floating bodies
Cf. QC183 Surface tension
Cf. TC165+ Technical hydraulics
Cf. TJ836+ Fluid power technology
145.5 Periodicals, societies, congresses, serial publications

Descriptive and experimental mechanics
Fluids. Fluid mechanics
Hydrostatics. Floating bodies -- Continued
145.7 Collected works (nonserial)
145.8 Dictionaries and encyclopedias
145.9 Nomenclature, terminology, notation, abbreviations
147 General works, treatises, and textbooks
147.5 Juvenile works
148 Addresses, essays, lectures
Study and teaching. Research
148.2 General works
148.24 Laboratory manuals
148.4 Instruments and apparatus
Including hydrometers, flowmeters
Fluid dynamics. Hydrodynamics
Cf. QA911+ Analytic mechanics
Cf. TC171+ Technical hydraulics
Cf. TJ266+ Turbine engineering
Cf. TP156.F6 Chemical engineering
150 Periodicals, societies, congresses, serial publications
151 General works, treatises, and textbooks
151.2 Juvenile works
151.5 Addresses, essays, lectures
151.7 Special aspects of the subject as a whole
152 Incompressible fluids
152.5 Compressible fluids
153 Nonhomogeneous fluids
154 Viscous fluids
Cf. QA929 Analytic mechanics
Cf. QC189.5.A1+ Rheology, Non-Newtonian fluids
155 Flows in porous media
155.5 Flows in viscous media
155.7 Flows in continuous media
Cf. QA808.2 Analytic mechanics
Quantum and relativistic hydrodynamics see QA912
Magnetohydrodynamics (Analytic mechanics) see QA920
Magnetohydrodynamics (Plasma physics) see QC718.5.M36
157 Waves
Cf. QA927 Analytic mechanics
Cf. QC718.5.W3 Plasma physics
158 Jets and cavities
159 Vortex flows
Cf. QA925 Analytic mechanics
Liquids see QC138+

Descriptive and experimental mechanics
Fluids. Fluid mechanics -- Continued
Gases. Pneumatics
Including air
Cf. QD531 Manipulation of gases, etc.
Cf. QD535 Liquefaction of gases
161 General works, treatises and textbooks
161.2 Juvenile works
161.5 Handbooks, tables, formulas, etc.
Special properties of gases
162 Adsorption and absorption
Including occlusion
163 Compressibility
163.5 Diffusion
164 Expansion
164.5 High temperatures
Occlusion see QC162
165 Pressure
Including manometers, etc.
165.3 Optical properties
165.5 Thermal properties
Vacuum
Including vacuum production, etc.
Cf. TJ940+ Vacuum technology
166 General works
166.5 Ultrahigh vacuum
167 Viscosity
Gas dynamics. Motion of gases
Including thermodynamic aspects
Cf. QA930 Analytic mechanics
Cf. QC717+ Ion flow dynamics
Cf. TJ1025+ Mechanical engineering
Cf. TL570+ Aerodynamics
167.5 Periodicals, societies, congresses, serial publications
168 General works, treatises, and textbooks
168.2 Addresses, essays, lectures
Study and teaching. Research
168.4 General works
168.6 Problems, exercises, etc.
168.7 Technique
168.8 Handbooks, tables, formulas, etc.
168.85.A-Z Special topics, A-Z
168.85.D46 Detonation waves
168.85.M53 Migration
168.85.R45 Relaxation
168.85.S45 Shock waves
168.86 Rarefied gas dynamics

Atomic physics. Constitution and properties of matter
Including molecular physics
Cf. QC770+ Nuclear physics
Cf. QD450+ Physical chemistry
Cf. TA401+ Materials of engineering and construction
170 Periodicals, societies, congresses, serial publications
General works, treatises, and textbooks
171 Through 1969
171.2 1970-
Constitution of matter and antimatter (General)
Cf. QC671 Aberration
Cf. QC793+ Elementary particle physics
172 Periodicals, societies, congresses, serial publications
172.2 Collected works (nonserial)
173 General works, treatises, and textbooks
173.16 Juvenile works
173.18 Addresses, essays, lectures
173.25 Study and teaching. Research
Properties of matter and antimatter (General)
Cf. QC182+ Special properties of matter and antimatter
173.28 Periodicals, societies, congresses, serial publications
173.3 General works, treatises, and textbooks
173.36 Juvenile works
173.38 Addresses, essays, lectures
173.39 Special aspects of the subject as a whole
173.397 Handbooks, tables, formulas, etc.
173.4.A-Z Special topics, A-Z
173.4.A82 Atom cooling
173.4.A85 Atomic beams
Atomic clusters see QC173.4.M48
173.4.A87 Atomic structure
Clusters, Atomic see QC173.4.M48
173.4.C63 Composite materials
(173.4.C65) Condensed matter
see QC173.45+
173.4.C74 Critical phenomena
173.4.E65 Equations of state
173.4.H95 Hyperfine structure
173.4.I53 Inhomogeneous materials
173.4.I57 Interfaces
173.4.L55 Liquid crystals
Cf. QD923 Crystallography
173.4.L56 Liquid metals
Cf. TA463 Engineering
173.4.M48 Microclusters
Including atomic clusters and molecular clusters
Cf. QC793.3.S8 Nuclear cluster theory

Atomic physics. Constitution and properties of matter
Properties of matter and antimatter (General)
Special topics, A-Z -- Continued

173.4.M5 Microphysics
173.4.M65 Molecular beams
Molecular clusters see QC173.4.M48
173.4.M67 Momentum distributions
173.4.M85 Multiple scattering
173.4.O73 Order-disorder models
173.4.P64 Polarizibility
173.4.P65 Polymers
Class here works on physical properties
For general works on chemical and physical properties see QD380+
173.4.P67 Porous materials
173.4.Q36 Quasicrystals
Cf. QD926 Crystallography
173.4.Q37 Quasimolecules
173.4.R44 Relaxation phenomena
173.4.S94 Surfaces
173.4.T48 Thomas-Fermi theory

Condensed matter physics

173.45 Periodicals, societies, congresses, serial publications
173.452 Directories
173.454 General works, treatises, and advanced textbooks
173.456 Study and teaching. Research
173.457.A-Z Special methods, A-Z
173.457.C64 Computer simulation
173.457.S7 Statistical methods
173.458.A-Z Special topics, A-Z
173.458.C78 Crystalline interfaces
173.458.D43 Defects
173.458.E43 Electric properties
173.458.E53 Energy dissipation
173.458.F72 Fractals
173.458.M33 Magnetic properties
173.458.M38 Mathematics
173.458.O66 Optical properties
173.458.R33 Radiation effects
173.458.S62 Soft condensed matter
173.458.S64 Spectra
173.458.S75 Structure
173.458.S87 Surfaces
173.458.T48 Thermal properties
173.458.U54 Universalities

Atomic physics. Constitution and properties of matter -- Continued
Relativity physics
Cf. QA808.5 Relativistic mechanics
Cf. QC175.3+ Kinetic theory of liquids
173.5 Periodicals, societies, congresses, serial publications
173.51 Collected works (nonserial)
173.52 History
173.55 General works, treatises, and textbooks
173.57 Popular works
173.575 Juvenile works
173.58 Addresses, essays, lectures
173.585 Special aspects of the subject as a whole
Including criticism of relativity
173.59.A-Z Special topics, A-Z
173.59.G44 Geometrodynamics
173.59.M3 Mathematical methods
173.59.S56 Simultaneity
173.59.S65 Space and time
173.59.T5 Time dilatation
173.59.T53 Time reversal
Special types of relativity theories
173.6 General
173.65 Special
Field theories. Unified field theories
Cf. QA808.2 Continuum mechanics
Cf. QC174.45+ Quantum field theory
Cf. QC178 Theories of gravitation
Cf. QC793.3.F5 Elementary particle physics
173.68 Periodicals, societies, congresses, serial publications
173.7 General works, treatises, and textbooks
173.72 Addresses, essays, lectures
173.75.A-Z Special topics, A-Z
173.75.T5 Thermodynamics
173.75.T85 Twistor theory
Quantum theory. Quantum mechanics
Cf. QB991.Q36 Cosmology
Cf. QC446.15+ Quantum optics
173.96 Periodicals, societies, congresses, serial publications
173.97 Collected works (nonserial)
173.975 Dictionaries and encyclopedias
173.98 History
174 Early works through 1926
Class here works on quantum theory prior to the Bohr atom
174.12 General works, treatises, and textbooks
Class here works on quantum theory after 1926
174.125 Addresses, essays, lectures

QC

Atomic physics. Constitution and properties of matter
Quantum theory. Quantum mechanics -- Continued
174.13 Special aspects of the subject as a whole
Study and teaching. Research
174.14 General works
174.15 Problems, exercises, examinations
174.17.A-Z Special topics, A-Z
174.17.A53 Angular momentum
174.17.A66 Approximation theory
174.17.B45 Bell's theorem
174.17.B6 Bound states
174.17.C45 Chaos
174.17.C6 Commutation relations
174.17.C63 Complementarity
Constant curvature, Spaces of see QC174.17.S63
174.17.C65 Correspondence principle
174.17.C67 Coulomb potential
Curvature, Spaces of constant see QC174.17.S63
174.17.D37 Data processing
174.17.D44 Density matrices
174.17.E58 Entanglement
174.17.F3 Factorization method
Few-body problem see QC174.17.P7
174.17.F45 Feynman integrals
174.17.F54 Finite element method
174.17.G46 Geometric quantization
174.17.G5 Gibbs' paradox
174.17.G56 Gleason measures
174.17.G68 Green's functions
174.17.G7 Group theory
Cf. QA174+ Algebra
174.17.H3 Hamiltonian operator
174.17.H4 Heisenberg principle
Cf. QC6.4.D46 Determinism
174.17.H55 Hilbert space
174.17.I58 Integral equations
174.17.I76 Irreversible processes
Cf. QC318.I7 Thermodynamics
Many-body problem see QC174.17.P7
174.17.M33 Markov processes
174.17.M35 Mathematical logic. Quantum logic
174.17.M4 Measure theory. Quantum measure theory
174.17.O63 Operator theory
174.17.P27 Path integrals
174.17.P3 Pauli exclusion principle
174.17.P45 Perturbation
174.17.P68 Probabilities

Atomic physics. Constitution and properties of matter
Quantum theory. Quantum mechanics
Special topics, A-Z -- Continued

174.17.P7 Problem of many bodies
Including few-body problem
Quantum computers see QA76.889
174.17.Q33 Quantum interference
Quantum logic see QC174.17.M35
174.17.Q35 Quantum maps
Quantum measure theory see QC174.17.M4
174.17.Q38 Quantum teleportation
174.17.Q385 Quantum trajectories
174.17.R32 Racah algebra
174.17.R37 Rate processes
174.17.R46 Renormalization theory
174.17.R65 Rotation groups
174.17.S3 Schrödinger operator
174.17.S32 Schwinger action principle
174.17.S36 Semigroups
174.17.S6 Sommerfeld polynomial method
174.17.S63 Spaces of constant curvature
174.17.S76 Stochastic processes
174.17.S77 Sum rules
Supergravity see QC174.17.S9
174.17.S78 Superposition
174.17.S9 Symmetry. Invariance
Including supergravity
Cf. QC793.3.S9 Elementary particle physics
Teleportation see QC174.17.Q38
174.17.T7 Transformations
174.17.V35 Variational principles
174.17.V4 Vector analysis
Wave mechanics
Cf. QC793.3.W3 Elementary particle physics
174.2.A1 Periodicals, societies, congresses, serial publications
174.2.A2 Collected works (nonserial)
174.2.A6-Z General works, treatises, and textbooks
174.22 Addresses, essays, lectures
174.23 Special aspects of the subject as a whole
174.24.A-Z Special types of wave mechanics, A-Z
174.24.G4 Geometrical
174.24.N6 Nonlinear
174.24.N64 Nonrelativistic
174.24.R4 Relativistic
174.26.A-Z Special topics, A-Z
Atomic and molecular orbitals see QD461
174.26.A8 Atomic transition probabilities

Atomic physics. Constitution and properties of matter
Quantum theory. Quantum mechanics
Wave mechanics
Special topics, A-Z -- Continued

174.26.B58 Bivectors
Spinor analysis see QA433
174.26.W28 Wave equations
Including solitons
174.26.W3 Wave functions

Matrix mechanics
Cf. QC793.3.M36 Elementary particle physics
174.3.A1 Periodicals, societies, congresses, serial publications
174.3.A6-Z General works, treatises, and textbooks
174.32 Handbooks, tables, formulas, etc.
174.35.A-Z Special theories, A-Z
174.35.R2 R-matrix theory
174.35.S2 S-matrix theory

Quantum statistics
Cf. QC793.3.S77 Statistical mechanics of elementary particles
174.4.A1 Periodicals, societies, congresses, serial publications
174.4.A2 Collected works (nonserial)
174.4.A6-Z General works, treatises, and textbooks
174.42 Addresses, essays, lectures
174.43 Special aspects of the subject as a whole

Quantum field theory
Cf. QC679+ Quantum electrodynamics
Cf. QC793.3.M36 Matrix theories of elementary particles
174.45.A1 Periodicals, societies, congresses, serial publications
174.45.A2 Collected works (nonserial)
174.45.A6-Z General works, treatises, and textbooks
174.46 Addresses, essays, lectures
174.52.A-Z Special topics, A-Z
174.52.A43 Algebra of currents
Cf. QC793.3.A4 Elementary particle physics
174.52.C66 Conformal invariants
174.52.D43 Degree of freedom
174.52.F8 Functional analysis
174.52.K56 Knot theory
174.52.L6 Lorentz transformations
174.52.O6 Operator theory
174.52.P37 Path integrals
174.52.S32 Scattering
174.52.S94 Symplectic manifolds
174.52.V33 Vacuum
174.52.Y36 Yang-Baxter equation

Atomic physics. Constitution and properties of matter
Quantum theory. Quantum mechanics
Quantum field theory
Special topics, A-Z -- Continued

174.52.Y37 Yang-Mills theory

Statistical physics
Including statistical mechanics and dynamics
Cf. QC311.5 Statistical thermodynamics
Cf. QC793.3.S77 Elementary particle physics

174.7 Periodicals, societies, congresses, serial publications
174.8 General works, treatises, and textbooks
174.82 Addresses, essays, lectures
174.84 Special aspects of the subject as a whole
Study and teaching. Research
174.842 General works
174.844 Problems, exercises, examinations
174.85.A-Z Special topics, A-Z
174.85.F47 Fermi liquid theory
174.85.H35 Hamiltonian systems
174.85.I8 Ising model
174.85.L38 Lattice theory
174.85.M43 Mean field theory
174.85.M64 Monte Carlo method
174.85.O6 Open systems
Cf. QC318.O63 Thermodynamics
174.85.P45 Percolation
174.85.P48 Phase space
Phase transformations see QC175.16.P5
174.85.P76 Probabilities
174.85.Q83 Quantum entropy
Cf. QC318.E57 Entropy (Thermodynamics)
174.85.R36 Random fields
174.85.R364 Random matrices
174.85.R37 Random walks
174.85.S34 Scaling
174.85.S46 Set theory
174.85.W85 Wulff construction
174.86.A-Z Special types of statistical mechanics, A-Z
174.86.C6 Classical
174.86.N65 Nonequilibrium
174.9 Kinetic theory of matter
Kinetic theory of gases
Cf. QC702.5 Ionized gases
175.A1 Periodicals, societies, congresses, serial publications
175.A6-Z General works, treatises, and textbooks
175.13 Special aspects of the subject as a whole
175.15 Study and teaching. Research

Atomic physics. Constitution and properties of matter
Statistical physics
Kinetic theory of gases -- Continued
175.16.A-Z Special topics, A-Z
175.16.B6 Boltzmann's distribution law
175.16.B65 Bose-Einstein gas
175.16.C6 Condensed gases
175.16.E6 Electron gas
Joule-Thomson effect see QC318.J6
175.16.M6 Molecules
175.16.P5 Phase transformations
175.16.R3 Rarefied gases
Transport theory
Cf. QC176.8.E9 Excitons
Cf. QC793.3.T7 Transport theory of elementary particles
Cf. QC809.E6 Energy budget (Geophysics)
175.2.A1 Periodicals, societies, congresses, serial publications
175.2.A6-Z General works, treatises, and textbooks
175.23 Addresses, essays, lectures
175.25.A-Z Special topics, A-Z
175.25.C6 Collision integrals
175.25.I6 Invariant imbedding
175.25.L5 Linear transport theory
175.25.R3 Radiative transfer
175.25.S4 Second sound
175.25.S8 Stochastic processes
Kinetic theory of liquids
175.3 General works, treatises, and textbooks
175.32 Addresses, essays, lectures
175.35 Special aspects of the subject as a whole
175.36.A-Z Special topics, A-Z
175.36.R4 Relativity
Superfluid physics
Cf. QC611.9+ Superconductivity
175.4.A1 Periodicals, societies, congresses, serial publications
175.4.A6-Z General works, treatises, and textbooks
175.45 Addresses, essays, lectures
175.47.A-Z Special topics, A-Z
175.47.B65 Bose-Einstein condensation
Solids. Solid state physics
Class here works on solids, including works that also deal in part with crystals.
For works that deal exclusively with crystals see QD901+
Cf. QD478 Solid state chemistry
Cf. TN689+ Physical metallurgy
176.A1 Periodicals, societies, congresses, serial publications

Atomic physics. Constitution and properties of matter
Solids. Solid state physics -- Continued

176.A3 Dictionaries and encyclopedias
176.A6-Z General works, treatises, and textbooks
176.2 Addresses, essays, lectures
176.3 Juvenile works
Study and teaching. Research
176.5 General works
176.515 Problems, exercises, examinations
176.52.A-Z By region or country, A-Z
176.8.A-Z Special topics, A-Z
176.8.A3 Acoustic properties
Cf. TA418.84 Engineering materials
176.8.A35 Adhesion
176.8.A44 Amorphous substances
176.8.A54 Anderson model
176.8.A6 Annealing
176.8.C45 Channeling
176.8.C6 Compressibility
176.8.D44 Defects
176.8.D5 Diffusion
Elastic properties see QC191
176.8.E35 Electric properties
176.8.E4 Electronic states
176.8.E9 Excitons
176.8.E94 Expansion
176.8.F4 Fermi surface
176.8.F74 Free electron theory of metals
Hole burning, Optical see QC176.8.O58
176.8.H66 Hopping conduction
176.8.L3 Lattice dynamics
Cf. QD921+ Crystal structure
176.8.M3 Magnetic properties
176.8.M46 Mesoscopic phenomena
176.8.M48 Metal-insulator transitions
176.8.M5 Micromechanics
176.8.N35 Nanostructures
Noncrystalline solids see QC176.8.A44
176.8.N65 Nonmetallic solids
176.8.O58 Optical hole burning
176.8.O6 Optical properties
176.8.P45 Phase transformations
176.8.P5 Phonons
176.8.P54 Plasma effects
176.8.P55 Plasmons
176.8.P6 Polaritons
176.8.P62 Polarons

Atomic physics. Constitution and properties of matter
Solids. Solid state physics
Special topics, A-Z -- Continued

176.8.Q35 Quantum wells
176.8.R3 Radiation effects
176.8.R35 Rare gas solids
176.8.S68 Spin glasses
176.8.S72 Sputtering
176.8.S8 Surface properties
Cf. QD506+ Surface chemistry
Cf. TA418.7+ Surface technology
176.8.T4 Thermal properties
Cf. QC295 Specific heat
Cf. TA418.52+ Engineering materials
176.8.T8 Tunneling
176.8.V34 Valence fluctuations
176.8.W3 Wave propagation

Thin films

176.82 Periodicals, societies, congresses, serial publications
176.825 Collected works (nonserial)
176.83 General works, treatises, and textbooks
176.835 Addresses, essays, lectures
176.84.A-Z Special topics, A-Z
176.84.D54 Diffusion
176.84.E5 Electric properties
176.84.M3 Magnetic properties
176.84.O7 Optical properties
176.84.R3 Radiation effects
176.84.S49 Size effects
176.84.S93 Surface properties
176.9.A-Z Special thin film substances and types, A-Z
176.9.M84 Multilayered
176.9.N64 Nonmetallic
176.9.O73 Organic
176.9.P64 Polycrystalline
176.9.R37 Rare earths
176.95.A-Z Special substances, A-Z
176.95.I25 Ice
Cf. QC926.3+ Snow
177 Theories of ether
178 Theories of gravitation
Including antigravity, quantum gravity
179 Gravitational waves. Gravitational radiation

Special properties of matter and antimatter

182 Absorption and adsorption
Cf. QC162 Adsorption and absorption of gases

Atomic physics. Constitution and properties of matter
Special properties of matter and antimatter -- Continued
183 Capillarity
Including surface tension, cohesion
Cf. QA274.75 Brownian motion processes
Cf. QD506+ Surface chemistry
184 Brownian motion
185 Diffusion. Transpiration
Cf. QA274.75 Diffusion processes
Cf. QC145.4.D5 Diffusion in liquids
Cf. QC163.5 Diffusion in gases
Cf. QC176.8.D5 Diffusion in solids
Osmosis (Cytology) see QH615
Osmosis (Physical chemistry) see QD543
Osmosis (Plant physiology) see QK871
Viscosity
Cf. QC145.4.V5 Viscosity of liquids
Cf. QC167 Viscosity of gases
189.A1 Periodicals, societies, congresses, serial publications
189.A2 Collected works (nonserial)
189.A6-Z General works, treatises, and textbooks
189.2 Handbooks, tables, formulas, etc.
Rheology
Including non-Newtonian liquids
Cf. QA931+ Plasticity (Analytic mechanics)
Cf. TA418.14+ Plastic properties of materials
Cf. TP156.R45 Chemical engineering
189.5.A1 Periodicals, societies, congresses, serial publications
189.5.A2 Collected works (nonserial)
189.5.A6-Z General works, treatises, and textbooks
189.8 Thixotropy
191 Elastic properties of solids
Cf. QA931+ Analytic mechanics
Cf. QD933 Crystallography
Cf. TA418+ Mechanical properties of materials
192 Thermal properties
193 Deformation
197 Friction, etc.
Cf. TA418.72 Friction properties of materials
Sound, light, and heat as a whole
220 General works
220.5 Acoustooptics

Class	Caption
	Acoustics. Sound
	Cf. ML3805 Music acoustics
	Cf. NA2800 Architectural acoustics
	Cf. QC176.8.A3 Acoustical properties of solids
	Cf. QP460+ Bioacoustics
	Cf. TA365+ Acoustics in engineering
	Cf. TA418.84 Acoustical properties of materials
	Cf. TH1725 Soundproof construction
	Cf. TK5981+ Electroacoustics
221	Periodicals, societies, congresses, serial publications
221.5	Dictionaries and encyclopedias
221.7	History
222	Early works through 1800
223	Mathematical theory
	General works, treatises, and advanced textbooks
225	1801-1969
225.15	1970-
225.2	Elementary textbooks
225.3	Popular works
225.5	Juvenile works
225.6	Addresses, essays, lectures
225.7	Special aspects of the subject as a whole
	Study and teaching. Research
226	General works
226.6	Experiments
227	Laboratory manuals
	Laboratories
228.A1	General works
228.A3-Z	By region or country, A-Z
	Subarrange each country by Table Q6
228.2	Technique
228.3	Instruments and apparatus
228.8	Handbooks, tables, formulas, etc.
229	Miscellany and curiosa
	Special topics
231	Kinematics of vibrations and wave motion
233	Propagation of sound
	Including velocity, reflection, transmission
	Vibrations
235	Gases in tubes, etc. Resonance
241	Strings, rods, membranes, plates, tuning forks
	Underwater acoustics
	Cf. TK5103.52 Acoustical telecommunication systems
242	Periodicals, societies, congresses, serial publications
242.2	General works, treatises, and textbooks
242.25	Addresses, essays, lectures

Acoustics. Sound
Special topics
Underwater acoustics -- Continued
242.4 Instruments and apparatus
Cf. TK5987 Hydrophone design and construction
242.5.A-Z Special topics, A-Z
242.5.O23 Ocean tomography
Sound waves
Cf. TD894 Noise measurement
242.8 Periodicals, societies, congresses, serial publications
243 General works, treatises, and textbooks
243.2 Juvenile works
243.3.A-Z Special topics, A-Z
243.3.A25 Acoustic streaming
243.3.A4 Amplitude
243.3.D3 Damping
243.3.D53 Diffraction
243.3.E5 Energy
243.3.P7 Pressure of sound
243.3.R3 Radiation pressure
243.3.R4 Reverberation. Reverberation time
Cf. NA2800 Architectural acoustics
243.3.S3 Scattering
Transmission see QC233
243.5 Infrasonics
244 Ultrasonics
Cf. QC480.2 Sonoluminescence
Cf. TA417.4 Ultrasonic testing
244.2 Nonlinear acoustics
244.5 Acoustic holography
246 Analysis of sounds. By phonograph, etc.
For acoustic phonetics see P221.5
Heat
For thermal properties of solids see QC176.8.T4
Cf. QC220+ Sound, light, and heat as a whole
251 Periodicals, societies, congresses, serial publications
251.4 Collected works (nonserial)
251.6 Dictionaries and encyclopedias
252 History and philosophy
252.2 Nomenclature, terminology, notation, abbreviations
253 Early works through 1800
General works, treatises, and advanced textbooks
254 1801-1969
254.2 1970-
255 Elementary textbooks
256 Juvenile works
257 Addresses, essays, lectures

Heat -- Continued
Study and teaching. Research
For programmed texts see QC254+
261 General works
261.5 Problems, exercises, examinations
263 Experiments
263.5 Laboratory manuals
265 Technique
266 Handbooks, tables, formulas, etc.
267 Miscellany and curiosa
Thermometers. Thermometry
Including temperature measurements and temperature measuring instruments
Cf. GC177 Oceanographic instruments
270 Periodicals, societies, congresses, serial publications
270.5 Collected works (nonserial)
270.7 Dictionaries and encyclopedias
271 General works, treatises, and textbooks
271.4 Juvenile works
271.5 Addresses, essays, lectures
271.6 Special aspects of the subject as a whole
271.8.A-Z Special aspects of instrumentation, A-Z
271.8.A95 Automatic control
271.8.C3 Calibration
271.8.T4 Testing
Special types of thermometers
272 Mercury and other liquids
273 Air and gases
274 Electrical. Resistance thermometers. Thermocouples
275.A-Z Other, A-Z
High temperatures
276 General works
277 Pyrometers and pyrometry
Low temperatures
Cf. QD536 Thermochemistry
Cf. TP480+ Low temperature engineering
277.9 Periodicals, societies, congresses, serial publications
278 General works, treatises, and textbooks
278.2 Juvenile works
278.4 Addresses, essays, lectures
278.6 Instruments and apparatus
High pressure
280 Periodicals, societies, congresses, serial collections
280.2 General works, treatises, and textbooks
280.4 Study and teaching. Research
280.6 Technique
280.8 Instruments and apparatus

Heat -- Continued

Relations between pressure, volume, and temperature

281 General works

281.5.A-Z Special topics, A-Z

281.5.C6 Compressibility

281.5.E9 Expansion

(282) Solids

see QC176+

(284) Liquids

see QC138+

(286) Gases

see QC161+

Calorimeters and calorimetry

Cf. QD510+ Thermochemistry

Cf. TP315+ Fuel (Chemical technology)

290 Periodicals, societies, congresses, serial publications

291 General works, treatises, and textbooks

292 Addresses, essays, lectures

293.A-Z Special types of calorimeters, A-Z

293.A3 Adiabatic

293.F5 Fluid

293.F8 Fuel

293.G3 Gas

293.M5 Microcalorimeter

293.R3 Radiation

293.V3 Vacuum

295 Specific heat of solids and liquids

297 Specific heat of gases and vapors

Change of state

301 General works, treatises, and textbooks

303 Fusion and solidification. Heat of fusion

304 Saturated vapors. Vapor pressure. Evaporation. Ebullition. Heat of vaporization

Cf. QC915.5+ Meteorology

Cf. QD533 Vapor densities

Cf. QD535 Liquefaction of gases

307 Continuity of state. Critical state. Critical point. Equations of state

309 Vaporization of solids. Sublimation

310 Heat of formation, solution, wetting, etc.

Cf. QD516 Thermochemistry

Thermodynamics

Cf. QC718.5.T5 Plasma physics

Cf. QD510+ Chemical thermodynamics

Cf. TJ255+ Heat engines. Engineering thermodynamics

Cf. TN689+ Metallurgical thermodynamics

310.15 Periodicals, societies, congresses, serial publications

Heat
Thermodynamics -- Continued
310.2 Collected works (nonserial)
310.3 Dictionaries and encyclopedias
310.5 Nomenclature, terminology, notation, abbreviations
311 General works, treatises, and advanced textbooks
311.15 Elementary textbooks
311.19 Addresses, essays, lectures
311.2 Special aspects of the subject as a whole
Study and teaching. Research
311.25 General works
311.28 Problems, exercises, examinations
311.29 Data processing
311.3 Handbooks, tables, formulas, etc.
Special types of thermodynamics
311.5 Statistical
311.7 Relativistic
312 Mechanical equivalent of heat
318.A-Z Other special topics, A-Z
318.E55 Enthalpy
318.E57 Entropy
Cf. QC174.85.Q83 Quantum entropy
Equilibrium thermodynamics see QC318.T47
Force and energy see QC71.82+
Gases see QC167.5+
318.I7 Irreversible processes
Including nonequilibrium thermodynamics
Cf. QC174.17.I76 Quantum theory
318.J6 Joule-Thomson effect
Low temperatures see QC277.9+
318.M3 Mass transfer
318.M35 Maxwell's demon
Nonequilibrium thermodynamics see QC318.I7
318.O63 Open systems
318.P6 Planck radiation law
318.T47 Thermodynamic equilibrium
318.T5 Thermodynamic potentials
319 Miscellany and curiosa
Heat transfer
319.8 Periodicals, societies, congresses, serial publications
319.9 Collected works (nonserial)
320 General works, treatises, and textbooks
320.14 Juvenile works
320.16 Addresses, essays, lectures
320.2 Special aspects of the subject as a whole
320.22.A-Z Special topics, A-Z
320.22.E4 Electromechanical analogies

Heat
Heat transfer
Special topics, A-Z -- Continued
320.22.E43 Electronic data processing
320.22.F5 Film boiling
Study and teaching. Research
320.3 General works
320.34 Problems, exercises, examinations
320.36 Experiments
320.38 Instruments and apparatus
320.4 Handbooks, tables, formulas, etc.
Conduction
320.8 Periodicals, societies, congresses, serial publications
321 General works, treatises, and textbooks
321.3 Juvenile works
321.5 Addresses, essays, lectures
321.6 Special aspects of the subject as a whole
321.7.A-Z Special topics, A-Z
321.7.E4 Electromechanical analogies
321.7.T55 Thermal diffusivity
323 Experiments
Convection
Cf. TH7435+ Heating of buildings
326 Periodicals, societies, congresses, serial publications
327 General works, treatises, and textbooks
327.4 Handbooks, manuals, etc.
328 Addresses, essays, lectures
330 Free convection
330.2 Bénard cells
Radiation and absorption. Laws of cooling
331 General works
Instruments
338 General works, treatises, and textbooks
338.5.A-Z Special, A-Z
338.5.B6 Bolometers
338.5.P95 Pyroelectric detectors
338.5.R3 Radiometers
338.5.R33 Radiomicrometers
Thermopiles see QC274
Optics. Light
Cf. QC220+ Sound, light, and heat as a whole
Cf. QC494+ Color
Cf. QP474+ Physiological optics
Cf. TA1501+ Applied optics. Lasers
350 Periodicals, societies, congresses, serial publications
351 Collected works (nonserial)
351.2 Dictionaries and encyclopedias

Optics. Light -- Continued

351.5	Nomenclature, terminology, notation, abbreviations
352	History
	Biography
352.4	Collective
352.5.A-Z	Individual, A-Z
353	Early works through 1800
	General works, treatises, and advanced textbooks
355	1801-1969
355.2	1970-2000
355.3	2001-
358	Elementary textbooks
358.5	Popular works
360	Juvenile works
361	Addresses, essays, lectures
362	Pictorial works and atlases
	Study and teaching. Research
363	General works
363.2	Outlines, syllabi
363.4	Problems, exercises, examinations
365	Experiments
366	Laboratory manuals
367	Optical measurements
368	Optical constants
369	Handbooks, tables, formulas, etc.
369.2	Miscellany and curiosa
370	Information theory in optics
	Optical instruments and apparatus (General) Cf. QC385+ Lens and mirror systems Cf. QC787.O6 Nuclear fission, atomic energy, and radioactivity instruments Cf. TS510+ Optical instrument manufacture
370.5	Periodicals, societies, congresses, serial publications
370.6	Collected works (nonserial)
370.7	Dictionaries and encyclopedias
371	General works, treatises, and textbooks
371.4	Juvenile works
371.5	Addresses, essays, lectures
372	Special aspects of the subject as a whole
372.2.A-Z	Special topics, A-Z
372.2.D4	Design
	Study and teaching. Research
372.22	General works
372.24	Laboratory manuals
372.6	Handbooks, tables, formulas, etc.
373.A-Z	Special instruments, A-Z
373.B3	Beam splitters

Optics. Light
Optical instruments and apparatus (General)
Special instruments, A-Z -- Continued

373.B55 Binoculars. Field glasses
373.C64 Collimators
Diffraction gratings see QC417
Field glasses see QC373.B55
Hand lenses see QC373.M33
373.H5 Heliostat
Interference microscopes see QH212.I5
373.K3 Kaleidoscopes
373.L5 Light filters
373.M33 Magnifying glasses. Hand lenss
Mass spectrometers see QC454.M3
Microscopes see QH211+
373.O59 Optical detectors
373.P7 Polariscope
Polarizing apparatus see QH217
373.Q2 Q-switching
Reflectometer see QC425.4
Refractometers see QC426.4
373.R4 Reticles
Scanning systems see TK7882.S3
373.S3 Schlieren apparatus
Including schlieren methods
373.S7 Spectrograph. Spectrometer
373.S8 Stereoscope
373.S85 Stroboscopes
Telemeter see TK399
Telescopes see QB88+
Materials for optical instruments, etc.
374 General works
374.5 Diamond
375 Glass
376 Quartz
378 Thin films
379 Miscellany and curiosa
Geometrical optics
Cf. QC974.5+ Meteorological optics
Cf. TR220 Photographic optics
380 Early works through 1800
381 General works, treatises, and advanced textbooks
381.2 Elementary textbooks
381.4 Popular works
381.6 Juvenile works
Study and teaching. Research
382 General works

Optics. Light
Geometrical optics
Study and teaching. Research -- Continued
382.2 Problems, exercises, examinations
382.6 Laboratory manuals
383 Mathematical theory
Lens and mirror systems
Cf. QB88+ Astronomical instruments
Cf. RE961 Ophthalmology
Cf. TC379 Lighthouse lenses
Cf. TP867 Mirrors and mirror frames
Cf. TR270+ Camera lenses
Cf. TS517.3+ Manufacture of optical surfaces
385 General works
385.2.A-Z Special topics, A-Z
385.2.D47 Design
Cf. QC372.2.D4 Optical instrument design
385.5 Experiments
387 Refractive indices
Cf. QC426.4 Refractometers
389 Transmission of radiation
391 Photometry. Microphotometry
Including densitometers
Cf. QB135 Astronomical photometry
Cf. TK4367 Electric light testing
Cf. TP754 Gas light testing
Physical optics
392 Periodicals, societies, congresses, serial publications
393 Collected works (nonserial)
393.2 Dictionaries and encyclopedias
394 Early works through 1800
General works, treatises, and advanced textbooks
395 1801-1969
395.2 1970-
396 Elementary textbooks
397 Addresses, essays, lectures
397.5.A-Z Special topics, A-Z
397.5.I53 Images
397.5.O77 Optical losses
Study and teaching. Research
398 General works
398.2 Problems, exercises, examinations
Theories of light
401 General works
402 Corpuscular theory
Cf. QC446.15+ Quantum optics

Optics. Light
Physical optics
Theories of light -- Continued
403 Wave theory
Cf. QC669+ Electromagnetic theory
406 Miscellaneous speculations
407 Velocity of light
Interference
Including Newton's rings, interferometer
Cf. QH212.I5 Interference microscopes
410.9 Periodicals, societies, congresses, serial publications
411 General works, treatises, and textbooks
411.4 Instruments and apparatus
Diffraction
414.8 Periodicals, societies, congresses, serial publications
414.9 Collected works (nonserial)
415 General works, treatises, and textbooks
416 Addresses, essays, lectures
417 Instruments and apparatus
Including diffraction gratings
Reflection
425 General works
425.2 Juvenile works
425.4 Instruments and apparatus
Including reflectometers
Refraction
425.9 Collected works (nonserial)
426 General works, treatises, and textbooks
426.2 Juvenile works
426.4 Instruments and apparatus
Including refractometers
426.6 Handbooks, tables, formulas, etc.
426.8.A-Z Special topics, A-Z
426.8.D68 Double refraction
426.8.N44 Negative refraction
Scattering (General)
427 Periodicals, societies, congresses, serial publications
427.4 General works, treatises, and textbooks
427.6 Handbooks, tables, formulas, etc.
427.8.A-Z Special topics, A-Z
427.8.C7 Critical opalescence
427.8.C73 Critical scattering
427.8.M5 Mie scattering
427.8.R3 Rayleigh scattering
427.8.S64 Speckle
Cf. TA1671+ Lasers and laser applications
Dispersion

Optics. Light
Physical optics
Dispersion -- Continued
431 General works
435 Anomalous dispersion
437 Incidence
Including grazing incidence
Polarization
Cf. QD481 Stereochemistry
Cf. TP382 Saccharimetry
440 Periodicals, societies, congresses, serial publications
441 General works, treatises, and textbooks
442 Addresses, essays, lectures
443 Production and measurement
445 Rings and brushes of crystals
Cf. QD941 Optical properties of crystals
446.A-Z Other special topics, A-Z
446.D5 Dichroism
Nonlinear optics. Quantum optics
For maser and laser physics see QC685+
446.15 Periodicals, societies, congresses, serial publications
446.2 General works, treatises, and textbooks
446.3.A-Z Special topics, A-Z
446.3.A54 Angular momentum
446.3.C45 Chaos
446.3.H37 Harmonics (Electric waves)
446.3.O65 Optical bistability
446.3.O67 Optical phase conjugation
446.3.O68 Optical pumping
446.3.S67 Squeezed light
Magnetooptics see QC675+
(447) Electronic optics
see QC793.5.E62+
Fiber optics
Cf. TA1800+ Applied fiber optics
447.9 Periodicals, societies, congresses, serial publications
448 General works, treatises, and textbooks
448.2 Addresses, essays, lectures
Holography
Cf. HD9707.5.H34+ Holography industry
Cf. QC244.5 Acoustic holography
Cf. TA1540+ Applied holography
449 General works
449.3 Electron holography
449.5 Optical tomography

Optics. Light -- Continued
Spectroscopy
Class here general works on the theory of spectroscopy and works intended primarily for physicists, including the spectroscopy of all electromagnetic radiations
Class here also compilations of spectra of elements, groups of elements, organic and inorganic compounds
For works on the application of spectroscopy in analytical chemistry and theoretical works intended primarily for chemists, see QD95-QD96; QD272.S6

450 Periodicals, societies, congresses, serial publications
450.15 Collected works (nonserial)
450.3 Dictionaries and encyclopedias
450.5 History
451 General works, treatises, and textbooks
451.2 Pictorial works and atlases
451.4 Addresses, essays, lectures
451.6 Special aspects of the subject as a whole
Study and teaching. Research
451.8 General works
451.82 Laboratory manuals
452 Data processing
452.5 Instruments and apparatus
453 Handbooks, tables, formulas, etc.
Including wavelength tables
454.A-Z Special types of spectra and spectroscopy, A-Z
454.A2 Absorption spectra
454.A25 Accelerator mass spectrometry
Alpha ray spectroscopy see QC793.5.A22+
454.A7 Arc spectra
454.A8 Atomic spectroscopy
Band spectra see QC454.M6
454.B39 Beam-foil spectroscopy
Beta spectroscopy see QC793.5.B42+
454.B74 Broadband dielectric spectroscopy
454.C634 Collision spectroscopy
454.E4 Electron spectroscopy
454.E46 Emission spectroscopy
454.F6 Flame spectroscopy
454.F7 Fourier transform spectroscopy
454.F85 Frequency spectra
Gamma spectroscopy see QC793.5.G32+
454.G3 Gas spectra
454.H33 Hadamard transform spectroscopy
Hadron spectroscopy see QC793.5.H32+
454.H618 High resolution spectroscopy
454.H9 Hyperfine spectra

Optics. Light
Spectroscopy
Special types of spectra and spectroscopy, A-Z -- Continued

	In-beam gamma ray spectroscopy see QC793.5.G32+
	Infrared spectrum see QC457
454.I48	Integral field spectroscopy
454.I5	Internal reflection spectroscopy
454.L3	Laser spectroscopy
454.L58	Level-crossing spectroscopy
454.L63	Light-beating spectroscopy
	Luminescence spectroscopy see QC476.6
	Magnetic resonance spectroscopy see QC762
454.M3	Mass spectroscopy
454.M32	Matrix isolation spectroscopy
454.M5	Microwave spectroscopy
454.M6	Molecular spectroscopy
	Mössbauer spectroscopy see QC491
	Neutron spectroscopy see QC793.5.N462+
	Nuclear magnetic resonance spectroscopy see QC762
454.N8	Nuclear spectroscopy Cf. QC793.5.A22+ Particle spectra
454.O66	Optical spectroscopy
454.O68	Optogalvanic spectroscopy
	Particle spectra see QC793.5.A22+
454.P46	Photodetachment threshold spectroscopy
454.P48	Photoelectron spectroscopy
	Plasma spectroscopy see QC718.5.S6
454.R3	Radiofrequency spectroscopy
454.R36	Raman spectroscopy
454.R4	Reflectance spectroscopy
454.R47	Resonance ionization spectroscopy
454.R5	Resonant ultrasound spectroscopy
	Rotational spectra see QD481
	Scintillation spectroscopy see QC491.5+
	Solar spectroscopy (Meteorology) see QC910.2+
	Solar spectroscopy (Optics) see QC455
454.S7	Spark spectroscopy
454.T47	Terahertz spectroscopy
	Time-of-flight mass spectroscopy see QC454.M3
454.T75	Tunneling spectroscopy
	Ultraviolet spectroscopy see QC459+
454.V5	Vibrational spectra
	X-ray spectroscopy see QC482.S6
454.Z44	ZEKE spectroscopy

Optics. Light
Spectroscopy -- Continued

455 Solar spectrum
Including wavelength measurements and maps
For works relating to the constitution and physical condition of the sun see QB551

457 Infrared spectrum
Cf. TA1570 Infrared technology

Ultraviolet spectrum
Cf. TA1501+ Applied optics. Lasers

459 General works

459.5 Far ultraviolet spectrum

Spectra of special substances

462.A-Z Special elements and groups of elements, A-Z (Table Q1 modified)

462.C65 Colloids
462.M47 Metal vapors
462.M49 Metals
462.R2 Rare earths
462.T85 Trace elements
462.T86 Transition metals

Organic compounds

462.5 General works, treatises, and textbooks
462.85 Handbooks, tables, formulas, etc.
463.A-Z Special organic compounds, A-Z
463.A4 Alcohols
463.A47 Alkaloids
463.A8 Amines
463.A84 Anthracene and derivatives
463.A86 Anthraquinones
463.B4 Benzene
463.B5 Biphenyl compounds
463.C3 Carbohydrates
463.C5 Chelates
463.C54 Chlorophyll
463.C57 Chroman
463.C78 Coordination compounds
463.E68 Essences and essential oils
463.E69 Esters
463.E7 Ethers and oxides
463.F55 Fluorocarbons
463.F6 Formaldehyde
463.F8 Furans
463.G84 Gums and resins
463.H4 Heterocyclic compounds
463.H9 Hydrocarbons
463.I44 Imidazole

Optics. Light
Spectroscopy
Spectra of special substances
Organic compounds
Special organic compounds, A-Z -- Continued

463.I5 Indole alkaloids
463.M38 Metal carbonyls
463.N35 Naphthoquinone
463.O7 Organometallic compounds
463.O72 Organophosphorus compounds
463.O73 Organosilicon compounds
463.P46 Plasticizers
463.P5 Polymers
463.P55 Polyurethanes
463.P6 Porphyrin
463.P7 Proteins
463.P92 Pyridines
463.Q5 Quinoline
463.Q54 Quinone
Resins see QC463.G84
463.S23 Saccharides
463.S72 Solvents
463.S8 Steroids
463.S9 Sulfur organic compounds
463.S94 Surface active agents
463.T4 Terpenes
464.A-Z Inorganic substances, A-Z
464.A43 Alkali metal halides
464.A44 Alkaline earth ferricyanides
464.A47 Ammonia
464.B67 Borates
464.C34 Calcium fluoride
464.C37 Carbon dioxide
464.C375 Carbon disulfide
464.F45 Ferroelectric crystals
464.F87 Fused salts
464.G55 Glass
464.H93 Hydrides
464.H934 Hydrochloric acid
464.H936 Hydrogen fluoride
464.M47 Mercury compounds
464.M48 Metallic oxides
464.M53 Mica
464.N57 Nitrates
464.N574 Nitric acid
464.N577 Nitrogen dioxide
464.N64 Nonmetallic minerals

Optics. Light
Spectroscopy
Spectra of special substances
Inorganic substances, A-Z -- Continued
464.P44 Phosphates
464.P46 Phosphorus compounds
464.P68 Potassium hydride
464.P685 Potassium phosphates
464.Q37 Quartz
464.S45 Selenium compounds
464.S54 Silicates
464.S546 Silver chloride
464.S63 Sodium halides
464.S635 Sodium hydride
464.S637 Sodium nitroferricyanide
464.S94 Sulfur dioxide
464.T44 Tellurium chlorides
464.T54 Thallium chloride
464.U73 Uranium compounds
464.W37 Water
464.Z57 Zirconium oxide
465 Instruments and apparatus
Including absorptionmeter
467 Structure of spectral lines. Effect of pressure. Stark effect, etc.
Cf. QC675.5.Z4 Zeeman phenomenon
Radiation physics (General)
Cf. QA935+ Wave propagation in elastic solids
Cf. QB531 Astronomy
Cf. QC191 Elastic properties of solids
Cf. QC331+ Thermal radiation
Cf. QC787.C6 Nuclear counters, etc.
Cf. QC793.5.A+ Radiation of special particles
Cf. QC910.2+ Solar radiation
Cf. QD601+ Radiation chemistry
Cf. QP82.2.R3 Physiological effect
474 Periodicals, societies, congresses, serial publications
474.5 Collected works (nonserial)
475 General works, treatises, and textbooks
475.25 Juvenile works
475.5 Study and teaching. Research
475.6 Special aspects of the subject as a whole
475.7 Technique
475.8 Instruments and apparatus
476.A-Z Special topics, A-Z
476.C6 Coherence
Duality, Wave-particle see QC476.W38

Radiation physics (General)
Special topics, A-Z -- Continued
476.S6 Sources of radiation
476.S86 Superradiance
476.W38 Wave-particle duality
Cf. QC401+ Theories of light
Luminescence
Cf. QC976.A3 Airglow
Cf. QD505.8 Chemiluminescence
476.4 Periodicals, societies, congresses, serial publications
476.45 Collected works (nonserial)
476.5 General works, treatises, and textbooks
476.6 Luminescence spectroscopy
Luminescent materials. Phosphors. Scintillators
Cf. QC787.S34 Scintillation counters
476.7 General works
476.75 Inorganic scintillators
476.77 Organic scintillators
Photoluminescence (General)
476.8 General works
Fluorescence
477 General works
477.2 Instruments and apparatus
Including fluorimeters
477.4 Sensitized fluorescence
Phosphorescence
Cf. QD79.P4 Phosphorimetry
Cf. QH641 Bioluminescence
Cf. TK454.4.P5 Phosphors (Electrical engineering)
Cf. TK7871.15.P4 Phosphors (Electronics)
477.8 Periodicals, societies, congresses, serial publications
477.9 Collected works (nonserial)
478 General works, treatises, and textbooks
479 Thermoluminescence
479.5 Cathodoluminescence
480 Electroluminescence
480.2 Sonoluminescence
X-rays. Roentgen rays
Cf. QB472+ X-ray astronomy
Cf. QC710+ Discharges through gases
Cf. QH212.X2 X-ray microscopes
Cf. RC78+ Medical radiography
Cf. RM845+ Radiotherapy
Cf. TR750 Radiography (Photography)
480.8 Periodicals, societies, congresses, serial publications
480.9 Dictionaries and encyclopedias
481 General works, treatises, and textbooks

Radiation physics (General)
X-rays. Roentgen rays -- Continued
481.5 Instruments and apparatus
Cf. RC78.5 Radiography
Cf. RM862.5 Radiotherapy
Cf. TR750 Applied photography
482.A-Z Special topics, A-Z
Crystallography see QD945
482.D5 Diffraction
482.G68 Grenz rays
482.P6 Polarization
482.S3 Scattering
482.S6 Spectroscopy
Study and teaching. Research
482.2 General works
482.3 Experiments
(483) Electric radiations (General)
see QC660.5+
484 Blackbody radiation
Bremsstrahlung
484.2 Periodicals, societies, congresses, serial publications
484.3 General works, treatises, and textbooks
484.5 Study and teaching. Research
484.6.A-Z Special topics, A-Z
484.6.I5 Inner Bremsstrahlung
Cosmic ray physics
Cf. QB463+ Nuclear astrophysics
Cf. QC770+ Nuclear physics
Cf. QC809.V3 Van Allen radiation belts
484.8 Periodicals, societies, congresses, serial publications
484.85 Collected works (nonserial)
484.9 History
485 General works, treatises, and textbooks
485.4 Popular works
485.42 Juvenile works
485.5 Addresses, essays, lectures
485.55 Special aspects of the subject as a whole
Observations. Data summaries
485.57 General works, treatises, and textbooks
485.575.A-Z By region or country, A-Z
485.6 Technique
485.7 Instruments and apparatus
Cf. QC785.5+ Nuclear instruments and apparatus
485.75 Handbooks, tables, formulas, etc.
485.8.A-Z Special topics, A-Z
485.8.B8 Bursts
Cosmic ray particles see QC793.3.C6

Radiation physics (General)
Cosmic ray physics
Special topics, A-Z -- Continued
485.8.F6 Forbush decreases
485.8.O7 Origin
485.8.S5 Showers
485.8.S8 Stars
485.8.V3 Variations, Diurnal, etc.
Including effects due to altitude, longitude, etc.
485.9.A-Z Special types, A-Z
485.9.A8 Atmospheric cosmic rays
485.9.G34 Galactic cosmic rays
485.9.P7 Primary cosmic rays
485.9.S4 Secondary cosmic rays
485.9.S6 Solar cosmic rays
485.9.U6 Underground cosmic rays
Other radiations
Alpha radiations see QC793.5.A22+
Beta rays see QC793.5.B42+
Cherenkov radiation
490.4 General works, treatises, and textbooks
Instruments and apparatus see QC787.C6
Gamma rays see QC793.5.G32+
Infrared rays. Infrared spectrometry see QC457
Radiation and spectra of isotopes see QC795.8.S6
491 Mössbauer effect. Mössbauer spectroscopy
Scintillation spectroscopy
491.5 Periodicals, societies, congresses, serial publications
492 General works, treatises, and textbooks
Instruments and apparatus see QC787.S34
Van Allen radiation see QC809.V3
Color
Cf. BF789.C7 Psychology
Cf. ML3840 Music and color
Cf. QD113 Colorimetry in analytic chemistry
Cf. QD473 Color in relation to atomic structure
Cf. QP483 Physiological effect
Cf. RM840 Phototherapy
Cf. TR510+ Color photography
Cf. TR977 Photomechanical color processes
494 Periodicals, societies, congresses, serial publications
494.15 Collected works (nonserial)
494.2 Dictionaries and encyclopedias
494.3 Nomenclature, terminology, notation, abbreviations
494.7 History
494.8 Early works through 1800
495 General works, treatises, and advanced textbooks

Radiation physics (General)
Color -- Continued
495.15 Elementary textbooks
495.2 Pictorial works and atlases
495.3 Popular works
495.5 Juvenile works
495.7 Addresses, essays, lectures
495.8 Special aspects of the subject as a whole
Study and teaching. Research
496 General works
496.15 Outlines, syllabi
496.3 Experiments
496.4 Laboratory manuals
496.6 Instruments and apparatus
Including colorimeters
496.8 Handbooks, manuals, etc.
496.9 Miscellany and curiosa
Electricity and magnetism
Cf. QC960.5+ Atmospheric electricity
Cf. TK1+ Electrical engineering
Electricity
Including works that deal collectively with electricity and magnetism
For electric properties of solids see QC176.8.E35
501 Periodicals, societies, congresses, serial publications
503 Collected works (nonserial)
505 Dictionaries and encyclopedias
506 Philosophy. Theory
506.5 Nomenclature, terminology, notation, abbreviations
507 History
Biography
514 Collective
515.A-Z Individual, A-Z
e.g.
515.A6 Ampère
515.O4 Ohm
Early works
516 Through 1700
517 1701-1850
General works, treatises, and advanced textbooks
1851-1969
518 Treatises
521 Descriptive and experimental works
522 1970-
523 Elementary textbooks
527 Popular works
527.2 Juvenile works

Electricity and magnetism

Electricity -- Continued

527.4 Addresses, essays, lectures

527.5 Special aspects of the subject as a whole

528.A-Z Special topics, A-Z

528.E4 Electromechanical analogies

Maxwell's equations see QC669+

528.V4 Vector theory

529 Handbooks, tables, formulas, etc.

Study and teaching. Research

For programmed texts see QC518+

530 General works

531 Outlines, syllabi

532 Problems, exercises, examinations

533 Experiments

534 Laboratory manuals

Electric measurements

Cf. TK275+ Electrical engineering

535 General works

536 Electric units

537 Standards

Laboratories

541.A1 General works

541.A3-Z By region or country, A-Z

Subarrange each country by Table Q6

Instruments and apparatus (General)

543 General works, treatises, and textbooks

544.A-Z Special instruments, A-Z

(544.A5) Ammeter

see QC645

(544.C3) Cathode ray tubes

see TK7871.73

Coils see QC645

544.C8 Current balance

Cyclotrons see QC787.C8

Decremeters see QC667

Electric meters see TK301+

544.E3 Electrodynamometer

544.E4 Electrometer

544.E45 Electophori

544.E5 Electrostatic lenses

544.G2 Galvanometer

(544.G3) Gas tubes

see TK7871.8+

544.P5 Phonic wheel

544.P8 Potentiometer

544.Q3 Quadruple lenses

Electricity and magnetism
Electricity
Instruments and apparatus (General)
Special instruments, A-Z -- Continued

(544.V3) Vacuum tubes
see TK7871.72+

561 Miscellany and curiosa

Electrostatics. Frictional electricity
Cf. QA825+ Attractions and potential
Cf. QC960.5+ Atmospheric electricity
Cf. TP156.E5 Electrostatic separation

570 Periodicals, societies, congresses, serial publications
571 General works, treatises, and textbooks
571.4 Juvenile works
571.5 Addresses, essays, lectures

Study and teaching. Research
572 General works
572.4 Experiments

573 Instruments and apparatus
Including frictional and induction machines

577 Electrocapillary phenomena
581.A-Z Other topics, A-Z
581.E4 Electric charge and distribution
581.I5 Induction
581.P6 Potential difference
581.V6 Volta effect

Dielectrics
Cf. TK3401+ Electric insulation

584 Periodicals, societies, congresses, serial publications
584.2 Collected works (nonserial)
585 General works, treatises, and textbooks
585.4 Addresses, essays, lectures
585.5 Study and teaching. Research
585.7.A-Z Special topics, A-Z
585.7.B7 Breakdown
585.7.C6 Constant
585.7.D5 Dielectrophoresis
585.7.E43 Electric discharge
585.7.H4 Heating
585.7.L6 Loss
585.7.M3 Magnetic properties
585.7.O6 Optical properties
585.7.R3 Radiation effects
585.7.R4 Relaxation
585.75.A-Z Specific dielectric substances, A-Z
585.75.S55 Silica
585.8.A-Z Special types of dielectrics, A-Z

Electricity and magnetism
Electricity
Electrostatics. Frictional electricity
Dielectrics
Special types of dielectrics, A-Z -- Continued
585.8.E4 Electrets
585.8.G38 Gaseous
585.8.L56 Liquid
589 Measurement of capacity
Cf. TK2805 Condensers (Dynamoelectric machinery)
Cf. TK7872.C65 Condensers (Electronics)
595 Pyroelectricity
Cf. QD939 Electric properties of crystals
Cf. TK7872.O7 Oscillators
595.5 Piezoelectricity
Cf. TK7872.P54 Piezoelectric devices
Ferroelectricity
Cf. QC715.17 Photoferroelectric effect
Cf. QD939 Electric properties of crystals
596 Periodicals, societies, congresses, serial publications
596.5 General works, treatises, and textbooks
596.9 Addresses, essays, lectures
Electric current (General)
Cf. QC641 Alternating currents
Cf. QD551+ Electrolysis
Cf. TK454+ Electric circuits and networks
601 General works
607 Ohm's law
(610) Conduction in gases and vapors
see QC710+
Electric conductivity
Cf. TK3301+ Electric conductors
610.3 Periodicals, societies, congresses, serial publications
610.4 General works, treatises, and textbooks
Electric resistance
Cf. QC761+ Magnetic induction
Cf. QC809.E15 Earth resistance
Cf. TK7872.R4 Electric resistors
610.6 General works
610.7 Magnetoresistance
Semiconductor physics
Class here general works on the physical properties of semiconductor materials
For works on semiconductor materials used in electronic engineering see TK7871.85+
Cf. QC176.8.E4 Solid-state electronics
610.9 Periodicals, societies, congresses, serial publications

Electricity and magnetism
Electricity
Electric current (General)
Electric conductivity
Semiconductor physics -- Continued

610.92	Collected works (nonserial)
610.94	Nomenclature, terminology, notation, abbreviations
610.96	History
611	General works, treatises, and textbooks
611.2	Addresses, essays, lectures
611.24	Special aspects of the subject as a whole
	Study and teaching. Research
611.26	General works
611.28	Problems, exercises, examinations
611.3	Laboratory manuals
611.4	Instruments and apparatus
611.45	Handbooks, tables, formulas, etc.
611.6.A-Z	Special topics, A-Z
611.6.A36	Acoustic properties
611.6.D4	Defects
611.6.D5	Diffusion
611.6.D6	Doping
611.6.E43	Electron-hold droplets
611.6.E45	Electron transport
	Energy-band theory see QC176.8.E4
611.6.G3	Galvanometric effects
611.6.H6	Holes
611.6.H67	Hot carriers
611.6.J85	Junctions
611.6.M64	Molecular beam epitaxy
611.6.O6	Optical effects
611.6.P52	Photoelectromagnetic effects
611.6.P55	Plasma effects
611.6.Q35	Quantum dots
611.6.Q36	Quantum optics
611.6.R3	Radiation effects
611.6.R43	Recombination
	Reliability see TK7871.85+
611.6.S9	Surface properties
611.6.T4	Thermal properties
611.8.A-Z	Specific semiconducting substances and types, A-Z
611.8.A44	Alloys
611.8.A5	Amorphous substances
611.8.C34	Cadmium arsenide
611.8.C45	Chalcopyrite
611.8.C6	Compensated semiconductors
611.8.C64	Compound semiconductors

Electricity and magnetism
Electricity
Electric current (General)
Electric conductivity
Semiconductor physics
Specific semiconducting substances and types, A-Z -- Continued

611.8.D66 Doped semiconductors
611.8.G3 Gallium arsenide
611.8.G4 Germanium
611.8.I52 Indium arsenide
611.8.L4 Lead chalcogenides
611.8.L5 Liquids
611.8.L68 Low-dimensional semiconductors
611.8.M25 Magnetic substances
611.8.M27 Many-valley semiconductors
611.8.M38 Mercury telluride
611.8.M4 Metal oxides
611.8.N33 Nanocrystals
611.8.N35 Narrow gap semiconductors
611.8.O68 Ore minerals
611.8.O7 Organic substances
611.8.P64 Polycrystalline semiconductors
611.8.R37 Rare earths
611.8.S44 Selenium
611.8.S45 Semimetals
611.8.S5 Silicon
611.8.S86 Superlattices
611.8.T44 Tellurium
611.8.W53 Wide gap semiconductors

Superconductivity physics
Cf. QC175.4+ Superfluid physics

611.9 Periodicals, societies, congresses, serial collections
611.917 History
611.92 General works, treatises, and textbooks
611.922 Juvenile works
611.924 Handbooks, tables, formulas, etc.

Superconducting materials. Superconductors
Cf. QC761.3 Superconducting magnets
Cf. TK7872.C77 Cryoelectronic devices
Cf. TK7872.S8 Engineering
Cf. TK7895.C7 Cryotrons

611.94 Periodicals, societies, congresses, serial collections
611.95 General works, treatises, and textbooks

Study and teaching. Research
611.96 General works
By region or country

Electricity and magnetism
Electricity
Electric current (General)
Electric conductivity
Superconductivity physics
Superconducting materials. Superconductors
Study and teaching. Research
By region or country -- Continued
United States
611.962 General works
611.964.A-Z By region or state, A-Z
611.966.A-Z Other regions or countries, A-Z
611.97.A-Z Special topics, A-Z
611.97.C54 Chemistry
611.97.E69 Equilibrium
Including nonequilibrium
611.97.F58 Fluctuations
611.97.M34 Magnetic properties
Nonequilibrium see QC611.97.E69
611.97.R33 Radiation effects
611.97.S64 Spectra
611.97.T46 Temperature effects
Including transition temperature
611.97.T54 Thermal properties
Transition temperature see QC611.97.T46
611.97.T86 Tunneling
611.98.A-Z Special superconducting materials or types of superconductors, A-Z
611.98.A44 Alloys
611.98.A48 Aluminum
611.98.A58 Anyon superconductivity
611.98.C47 Ceramic superconductors
611.98.C53 Chalcogenides
611.98.C63 Composites
611.98.C64 Copper
611.98.D33 d-band metals
611.98.D57 Dirty superconductors
611.98.H54 High temperature superconductors
611.98.M34 Magnetic
611.98.N54 Niobium
611.98.O74 Organic superconductors
611.98.R88 Ruthenium
611.98.T37 Ternary superconductors
611.98.T55 Thin film superconductors
611.98.T73 Transition metal oxides
611.98.T86 Type I superconductors
611.98.T87 Type II superconductors

Electricity and magnetism
Electricity
Electric current (General)
Electric conductivity
Superconductivity physics
Superconducting materials. Superconductors
Special superconducting materials or types of superconductors, A-Z -- Continued

611.98.V35 Vanadium
611.98.Z56 Zinc
612.A-Z Other special topics, A-Z
612.H3 Hall effect
Cf. TK7872.H3 Hall effect devices
612.P5 Photoconductivity
Cf. TK8330+ Photoconductive cells
612.P6 Potential barrier
612.S6 Skin effect
Superconductivity see QC611.9+
613 Electric resonance
Cf. QC762 Nuclear magnetism
Cf. QC794.6.R4 Nuclear interaction
615 Measurements of currents
Including ammeters, voltameters
618 Electromotive force
Including voltmeters
Thermoelectricity. Thomson effect. Peltier effect
Cf. TK2950+ Applied thermoelectricity
621 General works
623 Heating effects of currents
625 Electrokinetics

Electrodynamics
Cf. QA920 Magnetohydrodynamic theory
Cf. QC717+ Ion flow dynamics
Cf. QC718.5.M36 Magnetohydrodynamics (Plasma physics)
Cf. QC809.E55 Geophysics

630 Periodicals, societies, congresses, serial publications
630.15 Collected works (nonserial)
630.2 Dictionaries and encyclopedias
630.5 History
631 General works, treatises, and textbooks
631.2 Addresses, essays, lectures
631.3 Special aspects of the subject as a whole
Study and teaching. Research
631.7 General works
631.75 Problems, exercises, examinations
631.8 Laboratory manuals

Electricity and magnetism
Electricity
Electrodynamics -- Continued
638 Inductance. Induction
641 Alternating currents (Theory)
Cf. TK1141+ Alternating current engineering
Cf. TK2711+ Alternating current machinery
Electric corona
642.5 Periodicals, societies, congresses, serial publications
643 General works, treatises, and textbooks
643.5 Instruments and apparatus
643.7.A-Z Special topics, A-Z
643.7.D5 Discharge
643.7.P7 Pressure
645 Electric coils
Including induction coils
Cf. TK2391 Electric coils (Dynamoelectric machinery
Cf. TK2805 Condensers (Dyanmoelectric machinery)
Cf. TK7872.C56 Electronics
648 Vacuum polarization
Electric oscillations. Electric waves
Including electromagnetic waves
Cf. QB460+ Astrophysics
Cf. QC809.E55 Cosmic electrodynamics
660.5 Periodicals, societies, congresses, serial publications
661 General works, treatises, and textbooks
662 Addresses, essays, lectures
665.A-Z Special topics, A-Z
665.D3 Damping
665.D5 Diffraction
665.D54 Diffusion
665.E36 Electric displacement
665.E38 Electric fields
665.E4 Electromagnetic fields
665.E45 Electromechanical analogies
665.P5 Photoabsorption
665.P6 Polarization
665.Q3 Quadrupole moment
665.S3 Scattering
665.T7 Transmission
665.V4 Velocity
Study and teaching. Research
666 General works
666.5 Problems, exercises, examinations
667 Instruments and apparatus
Including decremeters

Electricity and magnetism
Electricity
Electric oscillations. Electric waves -- Continued
Electromagnetic theory
Including Maxwell's equations
669 Periodicals, societies, congresses, serial publications
670 General works, treatises, and textbooks
Study and teaching. Research
670.7 General works
670.75 Problems, exercises, examinations
671 Aberrations and moving media
Cf. QB163 Correction of astronomical observations
Electrooptics (General)
Cf. TA1750+ Applied electrooptics
673 General works
673.5.A-Z Special topics, A-Z
673.5.K4 Kerr effect
Magnetooptics (General)
675 General works
675.5.A-Z Special topics, A-Z
675.5.F3 Faraday effect
675.5.Z4 Zeeman effect
675.8 Microwave optics (General)
Radio waves (Theory)
Cf. QC972.6+ Radio meteorology
Cf. TK6540+ Radio engineering
676 Periodicals, societies, congresses, serial publications
676.4 General works, treatises, and textbooks
676.6 Addresses, essays, lectures
676.7.A-Z Special topics, A-Z
676.7.D5 Diffraction
676.7.S3 Scattering
676.7.S35 Scintillation
676.7.T7 Transmission
Microwaves (Theory)
Cf. QC718.5.M5 Plasma physics
Cf. TK7871.4 Masers
Cf. TK7876+ Electronics
677 Periodicals, societies, congresses, serial publications
678 General works, treatises, and textbooks
678.2 Addresses, essays, lectures
Study and teaching. Research
678.4 General works
678.6 Laboratory manuals
Quantum electrodynamics
Cf. QC793.3.E4 Elementary particle physics
679 Periodicals, societies, congresses, serial publications

Electricity and magnetism
Electricity
Quantum electrodynamics -- Continued
679.6 Collected works (nonserial)
680 General works, treatises, and textbooks
680.5 Addresses, essays, lectures
Quantum electronics
Including maser and laser physics
Cf. TA1671+ Lasers
Cf. TK7871.4 Masers
685 Periodicals, societies, congresses, serial publications
686 Collected works (nonserial)
687 Dictionaries and encyclopedias
687.2 History
688 General works, treatises, and textbooks
689 Addresses, essays, lectures
689.5.A-Z Special topics, A-Z
689.5.L35 Laser manipulation
689.5.L37 Laser pulses
689.55.A-Z Special types of lasers, A-Z
689.55.F75 Free electron lasers
689.55.P53 Plasma lasers
689.55.S45 Semiconductor lasers
700 Field emission
Electric discharge
701 General works, treatises, and textbooks
Ions. Ionization. Thermionic emission (General)
Cf. QC972.6+ Radio meteorology
Cf. QD561+ Electrochemistry
Cf. QD601+ Radiochemistry
701.7 Periodicals, societies, congresses, serial publications
702 General works, treatises, and textbooks
702.3 Instruments and apparatus
Cf. QC787.I6 Ionization chambers
702.5 Ionization of specific gases, liquids, etc.
702.7.A-Z Other special topics, A-Z
702.7.A9 Auger effect
702.7.B65 Bombardment
702.7.E38 Electron impact ionization
702.7.E4 Emission, Secondary ion
702.7.H42 Heavy ions
702.7.I55 Ion implantation
702.7.I57 Ion swarms
Magnetic ions see QC754.2.M333
702.7.M84 Multiply charged ions
702.7.N4 Negative ions. Anions

Electricity and magnetism
Electricity
Electric discharge
Ions. Ionization. Thermionic emission (General)
Other special topics, A-Z -- Continued
702.7.P48 Photoionization
Class here works on the physics of ionization produced by photons of light, X-rays or gamma rays.
For general works on chemical and physical aspects of photoionization see QD716.P48
702.7.P6 Positive ions
702.7.R4 Recombination of ions
702.7.S3 Scattering
Secondary ion emission see QC702.7.E4
702.7.T73 Trapped ions
Spark discharge (General)
Cf. QC454.A+ Spectra of special elements
Cf. QC966+ Lightning
703 General works
703.5 Breakdown of spark
703.7 Exploding wire phenomenon
705 Arc discharge
Cf. TK4311+ Arc lighting
Electric discharge through gases
Including cathode rays, canal rays
Cf. QC480.8+ X-rays
Cf. QC793.5.E62+ Electron emission
Cf. TK7871.7+ Electron tubes
710 Periodicals, societies, congresses, serial publications
711 General works, treatises, and textbooks
711.3 Addresses, essays, lectures
711.4 Special aspects of the subject as a whole
711.6.A-Z Electric discharge through specified gases, A-Z
711.6.A7 Argon
711.6.O9 Oxygen
711.8.A-Z Special topics, A-Z
711.8.A34 Afterglow
711.8.B7 Breakdown of spark
711.8.D5 Dissociation
711.8.G5 Glow discharge
711.8.P6 Polarization
711.8.R35 Radio frequency discharges

Electricity and magnetism
Electricity
Electric discharge -- Continued
Photoelectricity. Photoelectric cells
Including other effects of light, X-rays, etc., on discharge
Cf. QC391 Photometry
Cf. QC793.5.P42+ Photons
Cf. QC794.8.P4 Photonuclear interactions
Cf. QD701+ Photochemistry
Cf. TK8300+ Optoelectronic devices. Photoelectronic devices

715 General works
715.15 Photoemission
715.17 Photoferroelectric effect
715.2 Photoelectric properties of special substances
Including sensitivity
715.4 Photoelectric cells
Including photovoltaic effect

Ion flow dynamics
717 General works
717.5.A-Z Special topics, A-Z
717.5.I6 Ionic mobility

Plasma physics. Ionized gases
Cf. QA920 Magnetohydrodynamics
Cf. QC790.95+ Nuclear fusion
Cf. QC809.P5 Plasma (Cosmic physics)
Cf. TA2001+ Plasma engineering
Cf. TK2970 Magnetohydrodynamic generators
Cf. TL783.6 Plasma rockets

717.6 Periodicals, societies, congresses, serial publications
717.8 Collected works (nonserial)
718 General works, treatises, and textbooks
718.15 Addresses, essays, lectures
718.4 Special aspects of the subject as a whole
718.5.A-Z Special topics, A-Z
Accelerators see QC718.5.M36
Collisions with matter see QC718.5.P5
Collisions with particles see QC718.5.P55
Conductivity see QC718.5.T7
718.5.C65 Confinement
Controlled fusion see QC791.7+
718.5.C9 Cyclotron waves
718.5.D38 Dense plasma focus
718.5.D4 Density
718.5.D5 Diagnostics
Diffusion see QC718.5.T7
718.5.D7 Drift

Electricity and magnetism
Electricity
Plasma physics. Ionized gases
Special topics, A-Z -- Continued

718.5.D84 Dusty plasmas
718.5.D9 Dynamics
718.5.E37 Electric fields
718.5.E4 Electrodynamics
718.5.E45 Electromagnetics
Electron oscillations and resonances see QC718.5.W3
718.5.E48 Electrostatics
718.5.E66 Equilibrium
Including nonequilibrium
718.5.G95 Gyrotrons
Heat conduction see QC718.5.T7
718.5.H5 High temperature
718.5.H9 Hydrodynamics
Instabilities see QC718.5.S7
Ion waves see QC718.5.W3
Kinetics see QC718.5.T5
718.5.L3 Laser-produced plasmas
718.5.L6 Low temperature
718.5.M3 Magnetic fields
718.5.M36 Magnetohydrodynamics
Including plasma accelerators
Cf. QA920 Magnetohydrodynamic theory
718.5.M5 Microwaves
718.5.N4 Neutrality
Including nonneutrality
Nonequilibrium see QC718.5.E66
718.5.O6 Optical phenomena
Oscillations see QC718.5.W3
718.5.P45 Pinch effect
Plasma accelerators see QC718.5.M36
718.5.P5 Plasma reactions with matter
718.5.P55 Plasma reactions with particles
Plasma resonance see QC718.5.W3
718.5.P58 Plasmoids
718.5.Q17 Q-machines
718.5.R3 Radiation
718.5.S4 Sheaths
Cf. TL3028 Space vehicle communication systems
Shock waves see QC718.5.W3
718.5.S6 Spectroscopy
718.5.S7 Stability
Including instability
718.5.S78 Statistical behavior

Electricity and magnetism
Electricity
Plasma physics. Ionized gases
Special topics, A-Z -- Continued

718.5.S83 Strongly coupled plasmas
718.5.T5 Thermodynamics
718.5.T7 Transport
Including diffusion, conductivity, heat conductance, velocity
718.5.T8 Turbulence
Velocity see QC718.5.T7
718.5.W3 Waves

Study and teaching. Research
718.6 General works
718.612 Problems, exercises, examinations
718.613 Experiments

Laboratories
718.614 General works
718.615.A-Z Individual laboratories, A-Z
718.62 Technique
718.64 Instruments and apparatus
718.7 Handbooks, tables, formulas, etc.
718.8 Miscellany and curiosa
(721) Physics of electrons, protons, and other particles
see QC793+

Magnetism
Cf. QB462.8 Cosmic magnetic fields
Cf. QC176.8.M3 Solid-state physics
Cf. QC718.5.M36 Plasma physics
Cf. QC811+ Geomagnetism
Cf. QD591 Magnetochemistry

750 Periodicals, societies, congresses, serial publications
750.15 Collected works (nonserial)
750.3 Philosophy. Theory
750.4 History
751 Early works through 1800

General works, treatises, and textbooks
753 1801-1969
753.2 1970-
753.5 Popular works
753.7 Juvenile works
753.8 Recreations
Including amateur experiments
753.9 Addresses, essays, lectures
754 Special aspects of the subject as a whole
754.2.A-Z Special topics, A-Z
754.2.B35 Band theory

Electricity and magnetism
Magnetism
Special topics, A-Z -- Continued
754.2.E3 Electromechanical analogies
754.2.H9 Hysteresis
754.2.M3 Magnetic fields
Cf. QC809.M25 Cosmic magnetism
754.2.M32 Magnetic force
754.2.M33 Magnetic induction
754.2.M333 Magnetic ions
754.2.M336 Magnetic structure
754.2.M34 Magnetization
754.2.M35 Magnetostatics
754.2.M36 Magnetostriction
754.2.P4 Permeability
754.2.P45 Photomagnetic effect
754.2.P6 Potential
754.2.Q34 Quantum theory
754.2.S8 Susceptibility
Therapeutic use see RZ422
Study and teaching. Research
755 General works
755.2 Problems, exercises, examinations
755.3 Experiments
Cf. QC753.8 Amateur experiments
755.4 Laboratory manuals
Magnetic measurements
755.6 General works
755.65 Units and standards
Instruments and apparatus
755.67 General works, treatises, and textbooks
755.675.A-Z Special instruments, A-Z
755.675.H9 Hysteresigraph
755.7 Handbooks, tables, formulas, etc.
755.8 Miscellany and curiosa
Magnets
756.7 Periodicals, societies, congresses, serial publications
757 General works, treatises, and textbooks
757.5 Juvenile works
757.7 Addresses, essays, lectures
757.8 Bonded magnets
757.9 Permanent magnets
757.92 Wiggler magnets
Electromagnetism
Cf. QH656 Magnetic fields (Cytology)
759.6 Periodicals, societies, congresses, serial publications
759.8 History

Electricity and magnetism
Magnetism
Electromagnetism -- Continued
760 General works, treatises, and textbooks
760.2 Juvenile works
760.25 Addresses, essays, lectures
760.4.A-Z Special topics, A-Z
760.4.M33 Magnetic monopoles
760.4.M37 Mathematics
Study and teaching. Research
760.5 General works
760.52 Problems, exercises, examinations
760.54 Data processing
760.6 Handbooks, tables, formulas, etc.
Electromagnets
Cf. QC787.C3 Calutrons
Cf. TJ1366 Lifting magnets
Cf. TK454.4.E5 Electrical engineering
761 General works
761.2 Juvenile works
761.3 Superconducting magnets
Paleomagnetism see QE501.4.P35
761.4 Ferrimagnetism
Cf. QC766.F3 Ferrites
761.5 Ferromagnetism. Antiferromagnetism
761.8 Thermomagnetism
Nuclear magnetism
761.9 General works
762 Nuclear magnetic resonance
762.6.A-Z Other special topics, A-Z
762.6.A25 Acoustic nuclear magnetic resonance
762.6.E45 Electron nuclear double resonance
762.6.G53 Giant nuclear magnetic resonance
762.6.H94 Hyperfine interactions
762.6.M34 Magnetic resonance imaging
762.6.R44 Relaxation
762.6.S64 Spin-lattice relaxation
762.6.S65 Spin waves
762.6.T73 Translational motion
Paramagnetism
762.9 General works
763 Electron paramagnetic resonance
764 Diamagnetism
Magnetic materials
Cf. TK454.4.M3 Electrical engineering
764.5 Periodicals, societies, congresses, serial publications
764.52 Dictionaries and encyclopedias

Electricity and magnetism
Magnetism
Magnetic materials -- Continued
765 General works
766.A-Z Special magnetic materials, A-Z
Alloys, Magnetic see QC766.M34
766.A4 Amorphous substances
766.C6 Cobalt
766.F3 Ferrites
Fluids, Magnetic see QC766.M36
766.I7 Iron
766.M34 Magnetic alloys
766.M36 Magnetic fluids
766.M4 Metallic oxides
766.R3 Rare earths
766.T56 Thorium
Nuclear and particle physics. Atomic energy. Radioactivity
Cf. QC170+ Constitution of matter. Atomic physics
Cf. QD601+ Radiochemistry
Cf. TK9001+ Nuclear engineering
Cf. UG1282.A8 Atomic bombs
770 Periodicals, societies, congresses, serial publications
771 Collected works (nonserial)
772 Dictionaries and encyclopedias
Communication of information
772.2 General works
772.4 Information services
History
773.A1 Development and projects leading to production of first atomic bombs
773.A2-Z General works
773.3.A-Z By region or country, A-Z
Biography
774.A2 Collective
774.A3-Z Individual, A-Z
774.2 Directories
776 General works, treatises, and advanced textbooks
777 Elementary textbooks
778 Popular works
778.5 Juvenile works
780 Addresses, essays, lectures
782 Special aspects of the subject as a whole
782.5.A-Z Special topics, A-Z
782.5.P4 Photography
Cf. QC787.N78 Nuclear emulsions
783 Handbooks, tables, formulas, etc.
Data processing

Nuclear and particle physics. Atomic energy. Radioactivity
Data processing -- Continued
783.3 General works, treatises, and textbooks
783.4 Laboratory manuals
783.5 Pictorial works and atlases
Study and teaching
783.8 General works
783.85 Problems, exercises, examinations
784 Laboratory manuals
784.5 Atomic and nuclear measurements
Including atomic units
Instruments and apparatus
785.5 Periodicals, societies, congresses, serial publications
785.7 Collected works (nonserial)
786 General works, treatises, and textbooks
786.2 Addresses, essays, lectures
Nuclear reactors for research. Reactor physics
Cf. TK9202+ Nuclear reactor engineering
786.4 Periodicals, societies, congresses, serial publications
History
786.42 General works
786.43.A-Z By region or country, A-Z
786.45 Directories
786.5 General works, treatises, and textbooks
786.55 Addresses, essays, lectures
786.6.A-Z Special topics, A-Z
Accidents see TK9001+
786.6.C6 Computer programs
786.6.D4 Design and construction
Fuel elements see TK9360+
786.6.K5 Kinetics
786.6.P68 Power distribution
786.6.S73 Statistical methods
786.6.T4 Thermal neutrons
Cf. QC793.5.T42+ Elementary particle physics
Study and teaching. Research
786.7 General works
786.75 Experiments
786.8 Handbooks, tables, formulas, etc.
787.A-Z Other instruments, A-Z
787.B4 Betatrons
Bevatron see QC787.S9
787.B8 Bubble chambers
787.C3 Calutrons
787.C56 Cloud chambers
787.C58 Coincidence circuits
Cold cathode tubes see TK7871.84.C6

Nuclear and particle physics. Atomic energy. Radioactivity
Instruments and apparatus
Other instruments, A-Z

787.C59 Colliders
787.C6 Counters
Cf. TK9180 Nuclear engineering
787.C8 Cyclotrons
787.D35 Damping rings
787.D74 Drift chambers
787.E37 Electret ionization chambers
787.E39 Electron accelerators
787.E4 Electrostatic accelerators
787.E42 Electrostatic analyzers
787.F75 Fricke dosimeters
787.G32 Gamma ray detectors
787.G34 Gas calorimeters
787.G4 Geiger-Müller counters
787.H53 High-brightness accelerators
787.H54 High pressure ionization chambers
787.I6 Ionization chambers
787.K55 Klystrons
787.L5 Linear accelerators
787.L53 Linear colliders
787.M3 Magnetic analyzers
787.N78 Nuclear emulsions
787.N83 Nuclear track detectors
787.O6 Optical instruments
787.P3 Particle accelerators (General)
Cf. TK9340 Nuclear engineering
787.P34 Particle analyzers
Photoelectric multipliers see TK8314
787.P46 Photon detectors
787.P69 Proportional counters
787.P7 Proton accelerators
787.P73 Proton antiproton colliders
Including proton synchrotron colliders
787.P8 Pulse height analyzers
787.R43 Recirculating electron accelerators
787.S3 Scanning systems
787.S34 Scintillation counters
787.S4 Sector focused cyclotrons
787.S45 Self-quenching counters
787.S55 Spark chambers
787.S6 Spectrometer
787.S8 Storage rings
787.S83 Supercolliders
Including Superconducting Super Collider

Nuclear and particle physics. Atomic energy. Radioactivity
Instruments and apparatus
Other instruments, A-Z -- Continued

787.S85 Synchrocyclotrons
787.S9 Synchrotrons
787.T35 Targets
787.V3 Van de Graaff generators
787.V45 Vertex detectors

Research
Including laboratories and projects

788 General works
789.2.A3-Z By region or country, A-Z
Subarrange each country by Table Q6

Nuclear fission

789.7 Periodicals, societies, congresses, serial publications
790 General works, treatises, and textbooks
790.3 Addresses, essays, lectures
790.4.A-Z Special topics, A-Z
790.4.A6 Angular distribution
Delayed neutrons see QC793.5.D42+
790.4.E6 Energy loss
790.4.F5 Fission products (General)
Neutron transport theory see QC793.3.T7
790.4.P4 Photofission
790.4.P5 Pile theory
790.4.S9 Symmetrical fission
790.6 Instruments and apparatus
790.8.A-Z Fission of specific elements, A-Z (Table Q1)

Nuclear fusion
Cf. UG1282.A8 Hydrogen bomb

790.95 Periodicals, societies, congresses, serial publications
790.97 Collected works (nonserial)
791 General works, treatises, and textbooks
791.4 Popular works
791.5 Juvenile works
791.6 Addresses, essays, lectures

Controlled fusion

791.7 Periodicals, societies, congresses, serial publications
791.72 Collected works (nonserial)
791.725 Directories
791.73 General works, treatises, and textbooks
791.735 Popular works
791.74 Addresses, essays, lectures

Study and teaching. Research

791.745 General works

By region or country
United States

Nuclear and particle physics. Atomic energy. Radioactivity
Nuclear fusion
Controlled fusion
Study and teaching. Research
By region or country
United States -- Continued
791.75 General works
791.755.A-Z By region or state, A-Z
791.76.A-Z Other regions or countries, A-Z
791.77.A-Z Special devices, A-Z
791.77.S7 Stellarators
791.775.A-Z Special topics, A-Z
791.775.C64 Cold fusion
Inertial confinement fusion see QC791.775.P44
791.775.L37 Laser fusion
791.775.P44 Pellet fusion. Inertial confinement fusion
791.8.A-Z Other special topics, A-Z
Neutron transport theory see QC793.3.T7
Thermonuclear reactions see QC791.7+
Atomic energy
Cf. BR115.A83 Moral and religious aspects
Cf. HD9698+ Economic aspects
Cf. QC913.2.A8 Meteorological aspects
Cf. TK9001+ Atomic power
791.9 Periodicals, societies, congresses, serial publications
791.915 Collected works (nonserial)
791.92 Dictionaries and encyclopedias
Communication of information
791.93 General works
791.94 Information services
Nuclear regulatory commissions
791.948 General works
791.95.A-Z By region or country, A-Z
791.96 History
791.98 Directories
792 General works, treatises, and textbooks
792.4 Popular works
792.5 Juvenile works
792.6 Addresses, essays, lectures
792.7 Special aspects of the subject as a whole
Including peaceful uses of atomic energy
Study and teaching. Research
792.72.A-.Z8 General works
792.72.Z9 Catalogs of audiovisual materials
By region or country
United States
792.74 General works

Nuclear and particle physics. Atomic energy. Radioactivity
Atomic energy
Study and teaching. Research
By region or country
United States -- Continued
792.76.A-Z By region or state, A-Z
792.78.A-Z Other regions or countries, A-Z
Laboratories
792.79 General works
792.8.-Z By region or country, A-Z
Subarrange each country by Table Q6
Elementary particle physics
Cf. QC170+ Structure of matter and other theories
793 Periodicals, societies, congresses, serial publications
793.12 Collected works (nonserial)
793.13 Philosophy
793.15 Classification
793.16 History
793.2 General works, treatises, and advanced textbooks
793.24 Elementary textbooks
793.26 Popular works
793.27 Juvenile works
793.28 Addresses, essays, lectures
793.29 Special aspects of the subject as a whole
793.3.A-Z Special topics, A-Z
793.3.A4 Algebra of currents
Cf. QC174.52.A43 Quantum field theory
793.3.A5 Angular momentum
793.3.B4 Particle beams
793.3.B5 Binding energy. Nuclear forces
793.3.B6 Bootstrap theory
793.3.C53 Charm
793.3.C54 Chirality
793.3.C56 Collective excitations
793.3.C57 Color confinement
793.3.C58 Conservation laws
793.3.C6 Cosmic ray and ionospheric influences
793.3.C67 Coupling constants
793.3.D4 Decay. Lifetime
793.3.D43 Degree of freedom
793.3.D5 Diffraction
793.3.D55 Diffusion
793.3.D9 Dynamics
793.3.E4 Electrodynamics
793.3.E45 Electromagnetism
Electronic data processing see QC793.47.E4
793.3.E5 Energy ranges

Nuclear and particle physics. Atomic energy. Radioactivity
Elementary particle physics
Special topics, A-Z -- Continued
Energy spectra see QC793.5.A22+
Exciton theory see QC794.6.E9
793.3.E93 Exotic nuclei
793.3.F5 Field theories
Flavor see QC793.3.Q37
793.3.G38 Gauge fields
Including gauge theories
793.3.H44 Helicity
793.3.H5 High energy physics
Invariance see QC793.3.S9
Ionospheric influences see QC793.3.C6
Isospin see QC793.3.S6
793.3.K5 Kinematics
793.3.L53 Lie algebras
Lifetime see QC793.3.D4
Magnetic dipole moment see QC793.3.S6
793.3.M3 Magnetic fields
793.3.M36 Matrix theories
Molecules, Nuclear see QC793.3.N82
Momentum see QC793.3.S6
Nuclear cluster theory see QC793.3.S8
Nuclear emulsions see QC793.47.P4
Nuclear forces see QC793.3.B5
793.3.N8 Nuclear matter
Nuclear models see QC793.3.S8
793.3.N82 Nuclear molecules
Nuclear orientation see QC793.3.S6
793.3.N83 Nuclear shapes
Particle accelerators see QC787.P3
Particle beams see QC793.3.B4
Phase shift see QC794.6.S3
Photography. Nuclear emulsions see QC793.47.P4
Polarization see QC794.6.S3
Problem of many bodies see QC174.17.P7
793.3.Q35 Quantum chromodynamics
793.3.Q37 Quantum flavor dynamics
Quantum theory see QC174.45+
793.3.R4 Regge trajectories
Cf. QC174.17.G7 Group theory applied to quantum theory
Relaxation see QC762.6.R44
Renormalization theory see QC174.17.R46
Resonance. Resonance integral see QC794.6.R4
Scattering see QC794.6.S3

Nuclear and particle physics. Atomic energy. Radioactivity
Elementary particle physics
Special topics, A-Z -- Continued
Shapes, Nuclear see QC793.3.N83
793.3.S57 Space and time
Cf. QC173.59.S65 Relativity physics
Spectroscopy see QC454.N8
793.3.S6 Spin. Moments. Magnetic dipole moment. Nuclear orientation
793.3.S77 Statistical mechanics
793.3.S8 Structure
Including nuclear models and nuclear cluster theory
793.3.S9 Symmetry. Invariance
Cf. QC174.17.S9 Quantum theory
793.3.T67 Tracks
Transitions see QC454.N8
793.3.T7 Transport theory
793.3.V5 Violations
793.3.W3 Wave mechanics
793.3.W4 Weight diagrams
Study and teaching. Research
793.4 General works
793.412 Experiments
793.42 Problems, exercises, examinations
Technique
793.46 General works
793.47.A-Z Special, A-Z
793.47.E4 Electronic data processing
793.47.P4 Photography. Nuclear emulsions
793.47.S83 Statistical methods
Instruments and apparatus see QC785.5+
793.49 Miscellany and curiosa
793.5.A-Z Special nuclear and subnuclear particles, antiparticles, and families of particles, A-Z
793.5.A22-.A229 Alpha particles. Alpha rays (Table Q2)
793.5.A25-.A259 Anyons (Table Q2)
793.5.B32-.B329 Baryons (Table Q2)
793.5.B42-.B429 Beta particles. Beta rays (Table Q2)
793.5.B62-.B629 Bosons (Table Q2)
Including intermediate, W, and Z bosons
793.5.C64-.C649 Cold neutrons (Table Q2)
Including ultracold neutrons
793.5.D42-.D429 Delayed neutrons (Table Q2)
793.5.D442-.D4429 Delayed protons (Table Q2)
793.5.D482-.D4829 Deuterons (Table Q2)

Nuclear and particle physics. Atomic energy. Radioactivity
Elementary particle physics
Special nuclear and subnuclear particles, antiparticles, and families of particles, A-Z -- Continued

793.5.E62-.E629 Electrons (Table Q2)
Including synchrotron radiation
Cf. QC449.3 Electron holography
793.5.F32-.F329 Fast neutrons (Table Q2)
793.5.F42-.F429 Fermions (Table Q2)
793.5.G32-.G329 Gamma rays (Table Q2)
793.5.G552-.G5529 Gluons (Table Q2)
793.5.H32-.H329 Hadrons (Table Q2)
Cf. QC794.8.S8 Strong interactions
793.5.H34-.H349 Heavy leptons (Table Q2)
793.5.H42-.H429 Hyperons (Table Q2)
Including sigma particles and Y-particles
Intermediate bosons see QC793.5.B62+
Kaons see QC793.5.M42+
793.5.L42-.L429 Leptons (Table Q2)
Cf. QC793.5.H34+ Heavy leptons
Cf. QC794.8.W4 Weak interactions
793.5.M32-.M329 Magnons (Table Q2)
793.5.M42-.M429 Mesons (Table Q2)
Including kaons, muons, and pions
Muons see QC793.5.M42+
793.5.N42-.N429 Neutrinos (Table Q2)
793.5.N462-.N4629 Neutrons (Table Q2)
793.5.N82-.N829 Nucleons (Table Q2)
793.5.N862-.N8629 Nuclides (Table Q2)
Phonons see QC176.8.P5
793.5.P42-.P429 Photons (Table Q2)
Cf. QC176.8.P6 Polaritons
Cf. QC794.8.E4 Electromagnetic interactions
Pions see QC793.5.M42+
Polarons see QC176.8.P62
793.5.P58-.P589 Pomerons (Table Q2)
793.5.P62-.P629 Positrons (Table Q2)
793.5.P642-.P6429 Prompt neutrons (Table Q2)
793.5.P72-.P729 Protons (Table Q2)
793.5.Q252-.Q2529 Quarks (Table Q2)
793.5.Q32-.Q329 Quasi-particles (Table Q2)
Sigma particles see QC793.5.H42+
793.5.S62-.S629 Slow neutrons (Table Q2)
793.5.S72-.S729 Strange particles (Table Q2)
793.5.T32-.T329 Tachyons (Table Q2)
793.5.T37-.T379 Thermal electrons (Table Q2)
793.5.T42-.T429 Thermal neutrons (Table Q2)

Nuclear and particle physics. Atomic energy. Radioactivity
Elementary particle physics
Special nuclear and subnuclear particles, antiparticles, and families of particles, A-Z -- Continued
W bosons see QC793.5.B62+
Y-particles see QC793.5.H42+
Z bosons see QC793.5.B62+
Nuclear interactions
Cf. QC454.N8 Nuclear spectroscopy
793.9 Periodicals, societies, congresses, serial publications
793.95 Collected works (nonserial)
794 General works, treatises, and textbooks
794.5 Addresses, essays, lectures
794.6.A-Z Special topics, A-Z
794.6.A5 Angular distribution. Angular correlations
794.6.C58 Coherence
794.6.C6 Collisions
794.6.C7 Cross section of interactions
Decay see QC794.6.R3
794.6.E9 Excitation
Cf. QC795.8.E5 Energy levels
794.6.F4 Feynman diagrams
794.6.F65 Form factor
794.6.G7 Grand unified theories
794.6.I5 Internal conversion
794.6.I8 Isotone shift. Isotope shift
794.6.K5 Kinematics
794.6.M6 Moments
794.6.M85 Multiplicity
Polarization see QC794.6.S3
794.6.R25 Radiative capture
794.6.R3 Radioactivity. Decay
794.6.R4 Resonance. Resonance integral
794.6.S3 Scattering
Including elastic scattering, inelastic scattering, polarization, etc.
794.6.S75 Standard model
794.6.S8 Stopping power
794.6.S85 String models
Including superstring theories
Transitions see QC454.N8
794.8.A-Z Special types of interactions, A-Z
794.8.D57 Direct
794.8.E35 Effective
794.8.E4 Electromagnetic
Cf. QC793.5.P42+ Photons
794.8.E44 Electroweak

Nuclear and particle physics. Atomic energy. Radioactivity
Nuclear interactions
Special types of interactions, A-Z -- Continued

794.8.E93 Exclusive
794.8.G7 Gravitational
794.8.H4 Heavy ion induced
Including heavy ion collisions
794.8.H5 High energy
Cf. QC793.3.H5 High energy physics
Hyperfine see QC762.6.H94
794.8.I52 Inclusive
794.8.P4 Photonuclear
Cf. QC715+ Photoelectricity
794.8.S7 Spallation
794.8.S8 Strong
Cf. QC793.5.H32+ Hadrons
794.8.W4 Weak
Cf. QC793.5.L42+ Leptons

Radioactivity and radioactive substances
Including ionizing radiation
Cf. QC474+ Radiation physics
Cf. QC913+ Meteorological aspects
Cf. QD601+ Radiochemistry
Cf. QE501.4.N9 Nuclear geophysics
Cf. QH543.5+ Radiobiology

794.95 Periodicals, societies, congresses, serial publications
794.96 Collected works (nonserial)
794.97 Dictionaries and encyclopedias
794.98 History
795 General works, treatises, and textbooks
795.26 Popular works
795.27 Juvenile works
795.28 Addresses, essays, lectures
795.3 Special aspects of the subject as a whole
795.32.A-Z Special topics, A-Z
795.32.R3 Radiation dosimetry in physics
795.32.S3 Safety measures for physicists
Cf. RA1231.R2 Toxicology
Cf. TK9152+ Nuclear engineering

Study and teaching. Research
795.34 General works
795.36 Experiments
795.38 Laboratory manuals

Laboratories see QD604.8+

Technique
Cf. TK9151.4+ Radiation environment procedures
795.4 General works

Nuclear and particle physics. Atomic energy. Radioactivity
Radioactivity and radioactive substances
Technique -- Continued
795.42 Measurement of radioactivity and ionizing radiation
795.5 Instruments and apparatus (General)
For individual instruments see QC785.5+
795.52 Handbooks, tables, formulas, etc.
795.55.A-Z Special types of radioactivity, A-Z
795.55.I5 Induced radioactivity
Radioactive substances and radioisotopes
Cf. TK9400+ Nuclear engineering
795.6 Periodicals, societies, congresses, serial publications
795.64 Dictionaries and encyclopedias
795.7 General works, treatises, and textbooks
795.74 Juvenile works
Study and teaching. Research
795.76 General works
795.77 Experiments
795.78 Laboratory manuals
795.8.A-Z Special topics, A-Z
Prefer classification by specific substance in QC796
795.8.D4 Decay
795.8.E5 Energy levels
795.8.F5 Fission products
795.8.H3 Half-life
795.8.I5 Internal conversion
Isobars, Nuclear see QC795.8.N8
795.8.N8 Nuclear isomers. Nuclear isobars
795.8.R3 Radionuclides
795.8.S6 Spectra
For spectra of specific substances see QC462+
Standards see TK9400+
795.8.T45 Thermal properties
Transportation see HE199.5.R3+
796.A-Z Special radioactive substances and radioisotopes, A-Z (Table Q1)
796.2 Superheavy elements
Cf. QD172.S93 Inorganic chemistry
Applications
For applications in special fields, see the field, e.g. QH324.3, Tracers in biological research; RM858, Radioisotopes in therapeutics; TK9400-9401, Radioactive substances in industry
798.A1 General works, treatises, and textbooks
798.A2-Z Individual, A-Z
798.D3 Dating
798.T7 Tracers

	Geophysics. Cosmic physics
	Cf. GB5000+ Natural disasters
801	Periodicals, societies, congresses, serial publications
801.3	International Geophysical Committee. International Geophysical Year
801.4	International Years of the Quiet Sun
801.5	Collected works (nonserial)
801.9	Dictionaries and encyclopedias
	Observations
802.A1	General works, treatises, and textbooks
802.A2-Z	By name of issuing observatory, A-Z
	Prefer QC803
803.A-Z	By region or country, A-Z
804	History
	Biography
805.A2	Collective
805.A3-Z	Individual, A-Z
806	General works, treatises, and textbooks
806.4	Juvenile works
806.6	Addresses, essays, lectures
807	Special aspects of the subject as a whole
	Study and teaching. Research
807.5	General works
807.52	Problems, exercises, examinations
807.6.A-Z	By region or country, A-Z
	Observatories
808.A2	General works
808.A5-Z	By region or country, A-Z
	Under each country:
	.x — *General works*
	.x2A-.x2Z — *Individual observatories. By name, A-Z*
808.5	Technique. Instructions for observers
808.6	Data processing
808.7	Instruments and apparatus
808.8	Handbooks, tables, formulas, etc.
809.A-Z	Special topics, A-Z
809.A25	Acoustic phenomena
809.C6	Cosmic noise
	Earth radiation see QC809.T4
809.E15	Earth resistance
809.E2	Earth tides
809.E5	Elastic waves
809.E55	Electrodynamics
	Cf. QB460+ Astrophysics
809.E6	Energy budget. Heat budget
809.F5	Fluid dynamics

Geophysics. Cosmic physics
Special topics, A-Z -- Continued
Heat budget see QC809.E6
809.M25 Magnetic fields. Geomagnetic micropulsations
809.M3 Magnetohydrodynamics
809.M35 Magnetosphere. Magnetopause
809.M37 Mathematics
Nuclear astrophysics see QB463+
Nuclear geophysics see QE501.4.N9
809.P3 Paleogeophysics
809.P5 Plasmasphere. Space plasmas
809.R3 Radiation
Solar wind see QB529+
Space plasmas see QC809.P5
809.S67 Spectral theory
809.T38 Terrestrial heat flow
809.T4 Terrestrial radiation
809.V3 Van Allen radiation belts
Geomagnetism
Cf. QC750+ Magnetism
Cf. QE501.4.P35 Paleomagnetism
811 Periodicals, societies, congresses, serial publications
811.15 Collected works (nonserial)
813 History
814 Early works through 1800
General works, treatises, and textbooks
815 1801-1969
815.2 1970-
815.5 Juvenile works
815.7 Addresses, essays, lectures
816 Special aspects of the subject as a whole
Observatories
818.A2 General works
818.A5-Z By region or country, A-Z
Under each country:
.x *General works*
.x2A-.x2Z *Individual observatories. By name, A-Z*
819 Instruments and apparatus
Including magnetometer
820 Technique. Instruction for observers
820.6 Data processing
821 Handbooks, tables, formulas, etc.
822 Maps and mapping
Including construction, use, and interpretation of maps
Magnetic surveys
Geographic areas below are not subarranged by country

Geomagnetism
Magnetic surveys -- Continued
825 General works
825.1 North America
825.2 Mexico, Central America, and West Indies
825.3 South America
825.4 Europe
825.5 Asia
825.6 Africa
825.7 Australia
825.75 New Zealand
825.8 Arctic regions
825.9 Antarctica
826.A-Z Oceanic areas, A-Z
Geomagnetic field (Analysis and theory)
827 General works
828 Secular variation
Magnetic observations
830.A-Z General works. By name of issuing observatory, A-Z
831 Diurnal variations
833 Other periodic variations
835 Magnetic disturbances
Including magnetic storms
Geomagnetism and related aspects
836 Sunspot periods
837 Eclipses
839 Meteorological phenomena
841 Geological structure
843 Earthquakes
845 Earth currents
849 Deviation of the magnetic compass and other magnetic instruments. Magnetism of ships and aircraft
Cf. TL589.2.C6 Aeronautical instruments
Cf. VK577 Nautical instruments

Meteorology. Climatology
Including the earth's atmosphere and atmospheric physics
For works on the composite generalization of weather conditions of specific geographic areas during a specific period of time with reference to average conditions and their variability see QC980+
Cf. GB2801+ Hydrometeorology
Cf. N72.M48 Art and meteorology
Cf. QB603.A85 Planetary meteorology
Cf. S600+ Agricultural meteorology
Cf. SD390.5+ Forest meteorology
Cf. SH343.3 Fishery meteorology
Cf. TA197+ Engineering meteorology
Cf. TL556+ Aeronautical meteorology
Cf. UG467 Military meteorology

851 Periodicals, societies, congresses, serial publications
852 Collected works (nonserial)
854 Dictionaries and encyclopedias
854.15 Communication of meteorological information
For computer network resources see QC866.5.C67
For exchange of meteorological information see QC866.5.E93
854.2 Nomenclature, terminology, notation, abbreviations
History
855 General works
857.A-Z By region or country, A-Z
Biography
858.A2 Collective
858.A3-Z Individual, A-Z
859 Early works through 1800
General works, treatises, and advanced textbooks
861 1801-1969
861.2 1970-2000
861.3 2001-
863 Elementary textbooks
863.4 Popular works
Including works for hobbyists
863.5 Juvenile works
864 Handbooks, tables, formulas, etc.
Cf. QC871.4 Observers' manuals
Cf. QC873 Computation tables
865 Addresses, essays, lectures
866 Special aspects of the subject as a whole
866.5.A-Z Special topics, A-Z
866.5.C65 Communication systems
866.5.C67 Computer network resources
Including the Internet

Meteorology. Climatology
Special topics, A-Z -- Continued
866.5.E93 Exchange of meteorological information
866.5.G46 Geographic information systems
866.5.I5 International cooperation
Cf. QC875.2.A+ International projects, programs, etc.
866.5.P4 Photography (General)
Study and teaching. Research
869 General works
869.15 Outlines, syllabi
869.2 Programmed instruction
869.3 Problems, exercises, examinations
869.4.A-Z By region or country, A-Z
869.5 Meteorology as a profession. Vocational guidance
870 Miscellany and curiosa
Technique. Instructions for observers
871 Methods of observation
871.2 Observation forms, blanks, etc.
871.4 Observers' manuals
872 Telegraphic cipher codes for meteorological data
873 Computation tables (General)
Synoptic meteorology. Computation and analysis
874 General works
874.3 Data processing
874.5 Statistical methods
874.8 Laboratory manuals
Meteorological stations and observatories. Weather services
Including marine meteorological services
875.A2 General works
875.A5-Z By region or country, A-Z
Under each country:
.x *General works*
.x2A-.x2Z *Individual observatories. By name, A-Z*
875.2.A-Z Individual international projects, programs, etc. By name, A-Z
Meteorological instruments
For instruments of special fields, see the field, e.g., for Rain gauges see QC926
875.5 Periodicals, societies, congresses, serial publications
875.7 History
876 General works, treatises, and textbooks
876.5 Juvenile works
876.6 Addresses, essays, lectures
Museums. Exhibitions
876.7.A1 General works

Meteorology. Climatology
Meteorological instruments
Museums. Exhibitions -- Continued
876.7.A2-Z By region or country, A-Z
Subarrange each country by Table Q5
877 Weather signals, storm warnings, etc.
877.5 Weather broadcasting
Including radio and television weathercasting
878 Construction of weather maps, charts, etc.
Aeronomy. Upper atmosphere
878.5 Periodicals, societies, congresses, serial publications
878.6 Collected works (nonserial)
879 General works, treatises, and textbooks
879.15 Juvenile works
879.2 Addresses, essays, lectures
Study and teaching. Research
879.23 General works
879.232.A-Z By region or country, A-Z
879.25 Instruments and apparatus
Aeronautics in meteorology
Including sounding balloons, kites, etc.
Cf. TL556+ Meteorology in aeronautics
879.3 Periodicals, societies, congresses, serial publications
879.35 General works, treatises, and textbooks
879.36 Addresses, essays, lectures
Astronautics in meteorology
Including weather satellites, rockets, etc.
879.4 Periodicals, societies, congresses, serial publications
879.5 General works, treatises, and textbooks
879.53 Juvenile works
879.54 Addresses, essays, lectures
879.55.A-Z Special topics, A-Z
879.55.P4 Photography
Including automatic picture receiving and transmission, etc.
Stations, networks, and programs
879.56 General works
879.562.A2-Z By region or country, A-Z
Under each country:
.x *General works*
.x2A-.x2Z *Individual stations, networks, and programs. By name, A-Z*
879.57 Handbooks, tables, formulas, etc.
Observations. Data summaries
879.59.A1 General works, treatises, and textbooks
879.59.A3-Z By region or country, A-Z
Atmospheric chemistry

QC

Meteorology. Climatology
Atmospheric chemistry -- Continued
879.6 General works
Atmospheric ozone
Including ozone layer depletion
879.7 General works, treatises, and textbooks
879.712 Juvenile works
Observations. Data summaries
879.72 General
879.73.A-Z By region or country, A-Z
879.8 Atmospheric carbon dioxide
879.85 Atmospheric methane
879.9.A-Z Other chemical substances, A-Z
879.9.D55 Dimethyl sulfide
879.9.M47 Mercury
879.9.N57 Nitrogen compounds
879.9.O73 Organic compounds
879.9.P47 Peroxides
Radon see QC913.2.R3
Dynamic meteorology
Including mechanics and thermodynamics of the atmosphere (combined)
Cf. QC930.5+ Wind
880 General works
880.2 Addresses, essays, lectures
880.4.A-Z Special topics, A-Z
880.4.A3 Adiabatic processes
880.4.A5 Air masses
Cf. QC981.8.A5 Climatology
880.4.A8 Atmospheric circulation
880.4.B35 Baroclinicity
880.4.B55 Blocking
880.4.B65 Boundary layer
Clear air turbulence see QC880.4.T8
880.4.C64 Convection
880.4.C65 Coriolis force
880.4.C79 Cryosphere
880.4.D44 Diffusion
880.4.D5 Divergence. Convergence
Eddy flux see QC880.4.T8
880.4.E7 Equations of motion
880.4.F7 Fronts. Frontogenesis
880.4.L68 Low pressure systems
880.4.M52 Microbursts
880.4.P6 Power spectra
880.4.R6 Rossby waves
880.4.S56 Singularities

Meteorology. Climatology
Dynamic meteorology
Special topics, A-Z -- Continued

880.4.S65 Squalls. Squall lines
880.4.T5 Thermodynamics
880.4.T7 Transport phenomena
880.4.T8 Turbulence
Including clear air turbulence and eddy flux
880.4.V6 Vorticity
880.4.W3 Waves

Atmospheric shells (General)
Including composition of the atmosphere

881 General works
881.2.A-Z Specific shells, A-Z
881.2.C4 Chemosphere
881.2.D2 D region
881.2.E2 E region
881.2.E9 Exosphere
881.2.F2 F region
881.2.H43 Heliosphere
881.2.H48 Heterosphere
881.2.H6 Homosphere
881.2.I6 Ionosphere
Magnetosphere. Magnetopause see QC809.M35
881.2.M3 Mesosphere. Mesopause
881.2.M53 Middle atmosphere
881.2.N4 Neutrosphere
881.2.O9 Ozonosphere. Ozone layer
881.2.S8 Stratosphere. Stratopause
881.2.T4 Thermosphere
881.2.T7 Triptosphere. Triptopause
881.2.T75 Troposphere. Tropopause

Atmospheric pollutants
Cf. QC929.D9 Dust (Aqueous vapor)
Cf. TD881+ Air pollution

882 General works
Aerosols
882.4 Periodicals, societies, congresses, serial collections
882.42 General works, treatises, and textbooks
882.46 Technique
882.5 Dust
Cf. TD884.5 Air pollution
882.6 Smoke plumes
Cf. TD884 Air pollution

Cosmic relations. Influence on sun and moon, etc.
883 General works
883.2.A-Z Special topics, A-Z

Meteorology. Climatology
Cosmic relations. Influence on sun and moon, etc.
Special topics, A-Z -- Continued
883.2.A8 Atmospheric tides
883.2.C5 Climatic periodicity
883.2.S6 Solar activity. Solar climate
Mesometeorology
883.4 Periodicals, societies, congresses, serial publications
883.42 Collected works (nonserial)
883.5 General works, treatises, and textbooks
883.52 Addresses, essays, lectures
Observations. Data summaries
883.54 General works, treatises, and textbooks
883.56.A-Z By region or country, A-Z
Micrometeorology
883.7 Periodicals, societies, congresses, serial publications
883.72 Collected works (nonserial)
883.8 General works, treatises, and textbooks
883.82 Addresses, essays, lectures
Observations. Data summaries
883.84 General works, treatises, and textbooks
883.86.A-Z By region or country, A-Z
Paleoclimatology
Cf. QE697+ Geology
884 General works
884.2.A-Z Special topics, A-Z
884.2.C5 Climatic variations
884.2.D4 Dendroclimatology
Cf. QK477.2.A6 Annual rings
884.5.A-Z By region or country, A-Z
Atmospheric pressure
Cf. QC934 Relation to wind
885 General works, treatises, and textbooks
885.2 Charts, diagrams, maps, etc.
Observations. Data summaries
885.4 General works
885.6.A-Z By region or country, A-Z
Mercury barometers and barographs
886 General works
887 Tables for reductions
889 Distribution, isobars, etc.
891 Variations and oscillations
895 Barometric hypsometry
896 Aneroid barometers and barographs
Temperature and radiation

Meteorology. Climatology
Temperature and radiation -- Continued
Atmospheric temperature
Cf. QC934.2 Wind chill
Cf. TL557.A8 Aeronautical meteorology
Observations
Including distribution, isotherms
901.A1 General works, treatises, and textbooks
901.A3-Z By region or country, A-Z
902 Instruments and apparatus
Variations. Climatic changes
Including global temperature changes, etc.
902.8 Periodicals, societies, congresses, serial publications
Communication of information
902.9 General works
902.92 Information resources
902.93 Computer network resources
Including the Internet
Cf. QC981.8.G56 Global warming
903 General works, treatises, and textbooks
903.15 Juvenile works
903.2.A-Z By region or country, A-Z
905 Winter temperatures
906 Summer temperatures
(907) Temperature of the earth
see QE509
Temperature of the sea see GC160+
(909) Temperature of rivers, lakes, and springs
see GB651+
Solar radiation. Sunshine
910.2 Periodicals, societies, congresses, serial publications
910.5 Collected works (nonserial)
911 General works, treatises, and textbooks
911.2 Juvenile works
911.3 Addresses, essays, lectures
911.6 Handbooks, tables, formulas, etc.
Observations. Data summaries
911.8 General works, treatises, and textbooks
911.82.A-Z By region or country, A-Z
912 Instruments and apparatus
Including actinometers, pyrheliometers, sunshine recorders, etc.
912.2.A-Z Special topics, A-Z
912.2.S64 Solar constant
912.3 Atmospheric radiation
Including greenhouse effect
912.5 Albedo

Meteorology. Climatology
Temperature and radiation -- Continued

912.55 Global radiation
Atmospheric radioactivity
913 General works
913.2.A-Z Special topics, A-Z
913.2.A8 Atomic energy
Including radioactive fallout
Cf. TD887.R3 Radioactive pollution
913.2.R3 Radon
Aqueous vapor
Humidity. Hygrometry
915 General works
Evaporation and evapotranspiration
915.5 General works
Observations. Data summaries
915.6 General works
915.7.A-Z By region or country, A-Z
916 Instruments and apparatus
Including hydrometers, psychrometers, etc.
917 Handbooks, tables, formulas, etc.
920 Forms of water (General)
Clouds
Cf. TL557.C6 Aeronautical meteorology
920.7 Periodicals, societies, congresses, serial publications
920.8 Collected works (nonserial)
921 General works, treatises, and textbooks
921.3 Pictorial works and atlases
921.35 Juvenile works
921.37 Addresses, essays, lectures
Observations. Data summaries
921.375 General works, treatises, and textbooks
921.377.A-Z By region or country, A-Z
Cloud forms and classification. Formation
921.4 General works
921.43.A-Z Special forms, A-Z
921.43.C57 Cirrus
921.43.C8 Cumulus
921.43.N3 Nacreous (Mother-of-pearl)
Noctilucent see QC976.N6
921.43.S8 Stratus
Cloud physics
921.48 Periodicals, societies, congresses, serial publications
921.5 General works, treatises, and textbooks
921.55 Addresses, essays, lectures
921.6.A-Z Special topics, A-Z

Meteorology. Climatology
Aqueous vapor
Clouds
Cloud physics
Special topics, A-Z -- Continued
921.6.C6 Condensation nuclei
Including cloud droplets, ice crystals, etc.
921.6.C65 Convection
921.6.D95 Dynamics
921.6.E4 Electrification
921.6.T4 Thermodynamics of clouds
Observations of altitude, motion, etc.
922 General works, treatises, and textbooks
923 Instruments and apparatus
Including ceilometer
924.A-Z By region or country, A-Z
Rain and rainfall
Cf. BV283.F3 Prayers for rain
Cf. QE581 Erosion
Cf. S622+ Soil conservation
Cf. SD390.7.R34 Forest meteorology
Cf. TD418 Rainwater (Water supply)
924.5 Periodicals, societies, congresses, serial publications
924.6 Collected works (nonserial)
924.7 Juvenile works
925 General works, treatises, and textbooks
Observations. By region or country
North America, United States and Canada
925.1.A1 North America (General)
Canada
925.1.C2 General works
925.1.C3A-.C3Z By region, province, etc., A-Z
United States
925.1.U2-.U799 General works
925.1.U8A-.U8Z By region or state, A-Z
Mexico, Central America, and West Indies
925.2.A1 General works
925.2.A3-Z By country, island, or region, A-Z
Subarrange each country or island by Table Q4
South America
925.3.A1 General works
925.3.A3-Z By country, island, or region, A-Z
Subarrange each country or island by Table Q4
Europe
925.4.A1 General works
925.4.A3-Z By country, island, or region, A-Z
Subarrange each country or island by Table Q4

Meteorology. Climatology
Aqueous vapor
Rain and rainfall
Observations. By region or country -- Continued
Asia
925.5.A1 General works
925.5.A3-Z By country, island, or region, A-Z
Subarrange each country or island by Table Q4
Africa
925.6.A1 General works
925.6.A3-Z By country, island, or region, A-Z
Subarrange each country or island by Table Q4
Atlantic Ocean islands
925.65.A1 General works
925.65.A3-Z By country, island, or region, A-Z
Subarrange each country or island by Table Q4
Australia
925.7 General works
925.71.A-Z Local, A-Z
New Zealand
925.72 General works
925.73.A-Z Local, A-Z
Pacific Ocean islands
925.8.A1 General works
925.8.A3-Z By country, island, or region, A-Z
Subarrange each country or island by Table Q4
925.82 Tropics
925.9 Arctic regions
925.95 Antarctica
926 Instruments and apparatus
Including rain gauges
926.2 Data processing
926.24 Raindrops
Including raindrop size
Snow. Ice. Blizzards
Cf. GB641+ Frozen ground
Cf. GB2401+ Ice on the ground
Cf. GB2601+ Snow on the ground
926.3 Periodicals, societies, congresses, serial publications
926.32 General works, treatises, and advanced textbooks
926.36 Pictorial works
926.37 Juvenile works
By region or country
United States
926.43 General works
926.44.A-Z By region or state, A-Z
Subarrange each state by Table Q4

Meteorology. Climatology
Aqueous vapor
Snow. Ice. Blizzards
By region or country -- Continued
926.45.A-Z Other regions or countries, A-Z
Subarrange each country by Table Q4
Acid precipitation. Acid rain
Cf. TD195.4+ Environmental pollutants
926.5 Periodicals, societies, congresses, serial publications
926.52 General works, treatises, and advanced textbooks
By region or country
United States
926.55 General works
926.56.A-Z By region or state, A-Z
Subarrange each state by Table Q4
926.57.A-Z Other regions or countries, A-Z
Subarrange each country by Table Q4
Weather and cloud modification
Including weather control
Cf. QC921.48+ Cloud physics
926.6 Periodicals, societies, congresses, serial publications
928 General works, treatises, and textbooks
928.4 Juvenile works
928.6 Rainmaking. Cloud seeding
By region or country
United States
928.7 General works
928.72.A-Z By region or state, A-Z
928.74.A-Z Other regions or countries, A-Z
929.A-Z Other topics, A-Z
Including other forms of precipitation
929.A8 Avalanches
Blizzards see QC926.3+
929.D5 Dew formation
(929.D8) Droughts
see QC929.2+
929.D9 Dust influences
929.F7 Fog
Cf. TL557.F6 Aeronautical meteorology
929.F8 Forest influences
Frost see QC929.H6
929.G4 Glaze
929.H15 Hail
929.H6 Hoarfrost
Ice see QC926.3+
929.R17 Rain shadows
929.R2 Rain without clouds

Meteorology. Climatology
Aqueous vapor
Other topics, A-Z -- Continued
Rainmaking see QC928.6
929.S43 Sea salt aerosols
929.S5 Showers of miscellaneous matter
929.S6 Smoke influences
(929.S7) Snow. Ice. Blizzards
see QC926.3+
Droughts
929.2 Periodicals, societies, congresses, serial publications
929.24 General works, treatises, and advanced textbooks
929.25 Juvenile works
By region or country
United States
929.26 General works
929.27.A-Z By region or state, A-Z
Subarrange each state by Table Q4
929.28.A-Z Other regions or countries, A-Z
Subarrange each country by Table Q4
Wind
Cf. QC880+ Dynamic meteorology
Cf. TA654.5 Wind loads on structures
Cf. TL557.A5 Aeronautical meteorology
Cf. VK543+ Sailing
930.5 Periodicals, societies, congresses, serial publications
930.6 Collected works (nonserial)
930.7 Dictionaries and encyclopedias
931 General works, treatises, and textbooks
931.4 Juvenile works
931.6 Addresses, essays, lectures
931.8 Charts, diagrams, maps, etc.
932 Instruments and apparatus
Including anemometers
932.5 Handbooks, tables, formulas, etc.
933 Direction and velocity
934 Wind relation to atmospheric pressure
934.2 Wind in relation to atmospheric temperature. Wind chill
935 Upper currents. Jet stream
939.A-Z Constant, local, and periodic winds, A-Z
939.B67 Bora
939.F6 Föhn, Chinook, etc.
939.G73 Gregale
939.K37 Katabatic winds
939.L37 Land and sea breezes
939.M7 Monsoons

Meteorology. Climatology
Wind
Constant, local, and periodic winds, A-Z -- Continued
939.M8 Mountain and valley winds
Including Santa Ana
939.N8 Northers
Sea and land breezes see QC939.L37
939.T7 Trade winds
Observations
940.A1 General works, treatises, and textbooks
940.A2-Z By region or country, A-Z
e.g.
940.A8 North Atlantic Ocean
Storms. Cyclones
Cf. GC225+ Storm surges
Cf. QC926.3+ Snow. Ice. Blizzards
Cf. QC968+ Thunderstorms
Cf. TL557.S7 Aeronautical meteorology
940.6 Periodicals, societies, congresses, serial publications
941 General works, treatises, and textbooks
941.3 Juvenile works
941.8 Miscellany and curiosa
Theoretical aspects
Including dynamic meteorological aspects
942 General works
943 Application to navigation
943.5.A-Z By region or country, A-Z
Hurricanes and other cyclonic storms
944 General works, treatises, and textbooks
944.2 Juvenile works
By geographical location
945 Atlantic Ocean and West Indies
Including tropical cyclones, northeaster storms
947 India, Pakistan, and the Indian Ocean
948 China Seas and Pacific Ocean. Far East
Including typhoons
951 Instruments and apparatus
Including barocyclonometer
Tornadoes
955 General works
955.2 Juvenile works
955.5.A-Z By region or country, A-Z
957 Waterspouts
958 General works
959.A-Z By region or country, A-Z

Meteorology. Climatology -- Continued
Electrical phenomena in the atmosphere
Cf. QC801+ Geophysics. Cosmic physics
Cf. QC972.6+ Radio meteorology
960.5 Periodicals, societies, congresses, serial publications
961 General works, treatises, and textbooks
961.2 Addresses, essays, lectures
961.5 Technique. Instructions for observers
962 Instruments and apparatus
963 Observations of potential variation
Lightning (General)
Cf. GR640 Folklore
Cf. TH9057+ Protection of buildings from lightning
966 General works
966.5 Juvenile works
966.7.A-Z Special topics, A-Z
Arresters see TK3248
966.7.A84 Atmospheric ionization
966.7.B3 Ball lightning
966.7.D5 Discharge. Flash
Thunderstorms (General)
968 General works
968.2 Juvenile works
969 Miscellaneous electrical phenomena
Auroras
Cf. QB524+ Solar activity
Cf. QC835 Magnetic disturbance
Cf. QC976.A3 Airglow
970 Periodicals, societies, congresses, serial publications
971 General works, treatises, and textbooks
971.3 Pictorial works and atlases
971.4 Juvenile works
971.5 Addresses, essays, lectures
Observations
971.7.A1 General works, treatises, and textbooks
971.7.A2-Z By region or country, A-Z
972.A-Z Special topics, A-Z
972.L8 Luminescence
972.L85 Luminosity
972.P4 Photography
972.S6 Spectra
972.5.A-Z Special types of aurora, A-Z
972.5.A8 Australis
972.5.B6 Borealis
Northern lights see QC972.5.B6
Polaris see QC972.5.B6
972.5.R3 Radio auroras

Meteorology. Climatology -- Continued
Radio meteorology. Microwave meteorology
972.6 Periodicals, societies, congresses, serial publications
972.7 Collected works (nonserial)
973 General works, treatises, and textbooks
973.2 Addresses, essays, lectures
973.3 Instruments and apparatus
973.4.A-Z Special topics, A-Z
973.4.A85 Atmospherics
973.4.C4 Chorus. Dawn chorus
973.4.I6 Ionospheric radio waves
Including absorption, propagation, etc.
973.4.M33 Magnetospheric radio waves
Radio auroras see QC972.5.R3
973.4.R3 Radio noise
973.4.R35 Radio refractivity
Sferics see QC973.4.A85
973.4.T76 Tropospheric radio waves
Including absorption, propagation, etc.
973.4.V2 VLF emissions, propagation, etc.
973.4.W5 Whistlers
Radar meteorology
973.45 Periodicals, societies, congresses, serial publications
973.5 General works, treatises, and textbooks
973.6 Addresses, essays, lectures
Radar stations
973.62.A1 General works
973.62.A2-Z By region or country, A-Z
973.7 Instruments and apparatus
Including rawinsondes
973.8.A-Z Special topics, A-Z
973.8.E3 Echoes
973.8.R4 Refraction
973.8.W4 Weather radar networks
Meteorological optics
974.5 Periodicals, societies, congresses, serial publications
974.6 Collected works (nonserial)
General works, treatises, and textbooks
975 1801-1969
975.2 1970-
975.3 Juvenile literature
975.6 Addresses, essays, lectures
975.8 Handbooks, tables, formulas, etc.
Observations
975.9.A1 General works, treatises, and textbooks
975.9.A2-Z By region or country, A-Z
976.A-Z Special topics, A-Z

Meteorology. Climatology
Meteorological optics
Special topics, A-Z -- Continued
976.A3 Airglow
976.C6 Coloration of the sky
(976.C7) Counterglow
see QB761
Gegenschein see QB761
976.H15 Halos
976.L36 Laser beam propagation
976.M6 Mirages
976.N5 Night sky
976.N6 Noctilucent clouds
976.P7 Polarization
976.R15 Rain band spectrum
976.R2 Rainbow
976.R4 Atmospheric refraction
976.S3 Scattering
976.T6 Transmission of the atmosphere
976.T7 Transparency of the atmosphere
976.T8 Turbidity
976.T9 Twilight phenomena
976.U4 Ultraviolet rays
976.V5 Visibility
Cf. TL557.V5 Aeronautical meteorology
Climatology and weather
Class here works on the composite generalization of weather conditions of specific geographic areas during a specific period of time with reference to average conditions and their variability
Cf. BF353 Psychological aspects
Cf. GF71 Human ecology
Cf. NA2541 Architecture and climate
Cf. QC884+ Paleoclimatology
Cf. QH543+ Bioclimatology
Cf. RA791+ Medical climatology
Cf. S600+ Agricultural climatology
Cf. TA198 Industry and weather
Cf. TH7015 Heating and ventilation
Cf. TL556+ Aviation climatology
980 Periodicals, societies, congresses, serial publications
980.15 Collected works (nonserial)
Dictionaries and encyclopedias see QC854
980.4 Classification of climate
Including indexes
Biography see QC858.A2+
981 General works, treatises, and textbooks

Meteorology. Climatology
Climatology and weather -- Continued

981.2 Popular works
981.3 Juvenile works
981.4 Addresses, essays, lectures
981.45 Special aspects of the subject as a whole
981.5 Study and teaching. Research
981.6 Instruments and apparatus
Including frigorimeters
981.7.A-Z Special types of climatology, A-Z
981.7.C7 Cryptoclimatology
981.7.D94 Dynamic climatology
981.7.M3 Macroclimatology
981.7.M4 Mesoclimatology
981.7.M5 Microclimatology
Paleoclimatology see QC884+
981.7.S8 Synoptic climatology
981.7.T64 Topoclimatology
981.7.U7 Urban climatology
981.8.A-Z Special topics, A-Z
981.8.A5 Air masses in weather situations
Including cold and heat waves, etc.
(981.8.C5) Climatic changes
see QC902.8+
981.8.C53 Climatic extremes
Cold waves see QC981.8.A5
981.8.C65 Continentality
Droughts see QC929.2+
Forest influences see SD425
Glaciers and climate see QC981.8.I23
981.8.G56 Global warming
Heat waves see QC981.8.A5
981.8.I23 Ice sheets and climate. Glaciers and climate
981.8.S9 Sultriness
981.8.V65 Volcano effect on weather
981.8.Z6 Zones of climate
Geographic divisions
Including observations, weather reports, charts, etc., of special regions
International observations
982 General works
982.5.A-Z International areas not wholly within the divisions below. By name, A-Z
982.5.C64 Columbia River Watershed
982.5.D48 Developing countries
982.5.G7 Great Britain's colonies
982.5.G75 Great Lakes Region

Meteorology. Climatology
Climatology and weather
Geographic divisions
International observations
International areas not wholly within the divisions below. By name, A-Z -- Continued

982.5.N67 Northern Hemisphere
982.5.S68 Southern Hemisphere
982.8 North America (General)
United States
983 General works
984.A-Z By region or state, A-Z
Subarrange each state by Table Q4
Canada
985 General works
985.5.A-Z By region or province, A-Z
Subarrange each province by Table Q4
Mexico and Central America
986.A1 General works
986.A3-Z By country, island, or region, A-Z
Subarrange each country or island by Table Q4
West Indies
987.A1 General works
987.A3-Z By country, island, or region, A-Z
Subarrange each country or island by Table Q4
South America
988.A1 General works
988.A3-Z By country, island, or region, A-Z
Subarrange each country or island by Table Q4
Europe
989.A1 General works
989.A3-Z By country, island, or region, A-Z
Subarrange each country or island by Table Q4
Asia
990.A1 General works
990.A3-Z By country, island, or region, A-Z
Subarrange each country or island by Table Q4
Africa
991.A1 General works
991.A3-Z By country, island, or region, A-Z
Subarrange each country or island by Table Q4
Australia
992.A1 General works
992.A3-Z Local, A-Z
New Zealand
992.5.A1 General works
992.5.A3-Z Local, A-Z

Meteorology. Climatology
Climatology and weather
Geographic divisions -- Continued
993.A-Z Pacific and other oceanic islands. By island or group of islands, A-Z
993.5 Tropics (General). Tropical climatology and meteorology
993.6 Mountains (General). Mountain climatology and meteorology
993.7 Arid regions. Deserts (General). Arid zone climatology
Temperate zones. Temperate climate
For works on temperate climate in specific geographic regions, see QC982-QC994.9, Land; QC994.1-QC994.9, Oceans
993.75 General works
993.8 Mediterranean climate (General)
Class here works on Mediterranean climate regions in general. For works on Mediterranean climate in specific geographic regions, see QC983-QC993; QC994.3
Ocean areas. Maritime meteorology
Cf. GC190+ Ocean-atmosphere interaction
Cf. VK570 Ship routing
993.83 Periodicals, societies, congresses, serial publications
993.84 Observers' manuals. Handbooks, tables, formulas, etc.
Weather services see QC875.A2+
994 General works, treatises, and textbooks
By region
994.1 Atlantic Ocean (General)
994.2 Atlantic, North
994.3 Mediterranean Sea
994.4 Atlantic, South
994.5 Indian Ocean
994.55 Pacific Ocean (General)
994.6 Pacific, North
994.7 Pacific, South
Polar climatology and meteorology
994.75 General works
994.8 Arctic
994.9 Antarctic
Weather forecasting
Including analyses and forecasts
Cf. QC875.A2+ Weather services
Cf. QC877.5 Weather broadcasting
994.95 Periodicals, societies, congresses, serial publications
995 General works, treatises, and textbooks
995.3 Pictorial works and atlases
995.4 Popular works

Meteorology. Climatology
Climatology and weather
Weather forecasting -- Continued

995.43 Juvenile works
995.45 Addresses, essays, lectures
995.46 Study and teaching. Research
Technique (General)
Including graphical technique
995.48 General works
995.485 Observers' manuals
Types of weather forecasting
995.5 Hydrodynamic
996 Numerical
996.5 Statistical
997 Long-range
997.5 Short-range
997.75 Nowcasting
998 Weather lore
Cf. GR635+ Weather lore (as folklore)
999 Weather almanacs and miscellany

Chemistry
For applications of chemistry in special fields, see the field, e.g. RS402+ Medical and pharmaceutical chemistry; S583+ Agricultural chemistry
For chemical technology, including chemical engineering see TP1+

1 Periodicals, societies, congresses, serial publications
Museums
2.A1 General works
2.A2-Z By region or country, A-Z
Subarrange each country by Table Q5
3 Collected works (nonserial)
4 Encyclopedias
5 Dictionaries
6 Philosophy
7 Nomenclature, terminology, notation, abbreviations
Communication of chemical information
8 General works
8.3 Information services
8.5 Chemical literature
9 Abstracting and indexing
9.15 Language. Authorship
9.2 Translating. Translating services
9.3 Computer network resources
Including the Internet
History
11 General works
13 History of alchemy
14 Early works through 1800
15 1801-
18.A-Z By region or country, A-Z
20 Women in chemistry. Women chemists
For biography see QD21+
Biography of chemists
Cf. QD24.A2+ Alchemists
Cf. QD903.5+ Crystallographers
21 Collective
22.A-Z Individual, A-Z
e.g.
22.C8 Curie, Marie and Pierre
23 Directories
Alchemy
Cf. BR115.A57 Alchemy and Christianity
23.3 Periodicals, societies, congresses, serial publications
23.4 Collected works (nonserial)
23.5 Dictionaries and encyclopedias
History see QD13

	Alchemy -- Continued
	Biography
24.A2	Collective
24.A3-Z	Individual, A-Z
25	Early works through 1800
26	General works, treatises, and textbooks
26.5.A-Z	Special topics, A-Z
26.5.A4	Alkahest. Universal solvent
26.5.E4	Elixer of life
	Philosopher's stone see QD25
27	Early works through 1761
	General works, treatises, and advanced textbooks
28	1761-1860
31	1861-1969
31.2	1970-2000
31.3	2001-
	Elementary textbooks
33	To 2000
33.2	2001-
35	Juvenile works
37	Popular works
38	Recreations, home experiments, etc.
39	Addresses, essays, lectures
39.2	Special aspects of the subject as a whole
39.3.A-Z	Special topics, A-Z
39.3.C6	Computer programs
39.3.E4	Electromechanical analogies
39.3.E46	Electronic data processing. Cheminformatics Cf. RS418 Pharmaceutical chemistry
39.3.F33	Factor analysis
39.3.G73	Graph theory
39.3.M3	Mathematics
39.3.P45	Phlogiston
39.3.S55	Simulated annealing
39.3.S67	Spreadsheets
39.3.S7	Statistical methods
39.3.W37	Water
39.5	Chemistry as a profession. Vocational guidance
39.7	Social aspects
	Study and teaching. Research
40	General works
41	Outlines, syllabi
42	Problems, exercises, examinations For programmed textbooks see QD28+
43	Experiments Cf. QD38 Home experiments
45	Laboratory manuals

Study and teaching. Research -- Continued
By region or country
United States
47 General works
47.5.A-Z By region or state, A-Z
Subarrange each state by Table Q7
49.A-Z Other regions or countries, A-Z
Subarrange each country by Table Q7
Special teaching methods and aids
49.5 General works
49.6.A-Z Special methods, A-Z
49.6.P76 Process oriented guided inquiry learning
Laboratories
51 General works
51.5.A-Z By region or country, A-Z
Subarrange each country by Table Q6
Instruments and apparatus
53 General works
54.A-Z Special, A-Z
54.A3 Absorption apparatus
54.C4 Centrifuges
54.E8 Eudiometer
54.F85 Fume hoods
54.P5 Pipettes
54.S8 Sulfuric acid concentrator
54.T4 Thermostat
Techniques and operations
61 General works
63.A-Z Special, A-Z
Cf. QD258+ Operations in organic chemistry
63.D5 Dissolution
63.D6 Distillation
Electric furnace operations (Inorganic chemistry) see QD157
Electric furnace operations (Organic chemistry) see QD277
63.E83 Exchange reactions
63.E88 Extraction
63.F5 Filtration
63.G5 Glass manipulation
63.H87 Hydration
63.H9 Hydrogenation
63.I55 Ion exchange
63.L3 Laser techniques
63.M3 Masking
63.N5 Nitration
63.O9 Oxidation

Laboratories
Techniques and operations
Special, A-Z -- Continued
63.P4 Percolation
63.R4 Reduction
63.S4 Separation
63.V33 Vacuum techniques
63.5 Safety measures
64 Waste disposal
65 Handbooks, tables, formulas, etc.
Catalogs, pricelists, etc. see TP202
Analytical chemistry
For the analysis of special elements and their compounds see QD181.A+
For the analysis of organic compounds see QD271+
Cf. QE516.3 Analytical geochemistry
71 Periodicals, societies, congresses, serial publications
71.2 Collected works (nonserial)
71.5 Dictionaries and encyclopedias
71.8 Nomenclature, terminology, notation, abbreviations
History
72 General works
72.5.A-Z By region or country, A-Z
General works, treatises, and textbooks
75 Through 1970
75.2 1971-2000
75.22 2001-
75.25 Addresses, essays, lectures
75.3 Special aspects of the subject as a whole
75.4.A-Z Special topics, A-Z
75.4.A8 Automation
75.4.C34 Calibration
75.4.C45 Chemometrics
75.4.E4 Electronic data processing
Forensic chemistry see RA1057
75.4.K54 Kinetics
(75.4.M36) Mathematics
see QD75.4.C45
(75.4.M4) Measurement
see QD75.4.C45
Preparation of samples see QD75.4.S24
75.4.Q34 Quality control
Sample introduction see QD75.4.S24
75.4.S24 Sample preparation. Sample introduction
75.4.S25 Sampling
75.4.S73 Stable isotopes

Analytical chemistry
Special topics, A-Z -- Continued
(75.4.S8) Statistical methods
see QD75.4.C45
75.4.U48 Ultrasonic waves
Study and teaching. Research
75.7 General works
75.9 Problems, exercises, examinations
76 Laboratory manuals
77 Reagents, indicators, test papers, etc.
78 Handbooks, tables, formulas, etc.
79.A-Z Methods of analysis (Qualitative and quantitative), A-Z
Chemical microscopy see QH221
Chromatographic analysis
79.C4 General works
79.C45 Gas chromatography
79.C453 Ion exchange chromatography
79.C4537 Ligand exchange chromatography
79.C454 Liquid chromatography
79.C46 Paper chromatography
79.C52 Preparative layer chromatography
79.C75 Radiochromatography
79.C8 Thin layer chromatography
79.E4 Electron diffraction
79.E44 Electrophoresis
79.F4 Fluorimetry
79.I5 Instrumental analysis
79.M5 Microchemical analysis
Molecular emission cavity analysis see QD79.P4
79.O8 Oximetry
79.P4 Phosphorimetry. Molecular emission cavity analysis
79.P46 Photometry
Radiochemical analysis see QD605+
79.S4 Sedimentation analysis
Spectrum analysis see QD95+
79.T38 Thermal analysis
79.T4 Thermogravimetry
Qualitative analysis
81 General works, treatises, and advanced textbooks
83 Elementary textbooks
84 Laboratory manuals
85 Tables, outlines, etc.
87 Blowpipe analysis
Cf. QE367+ Determinative mineralogy

Analytical chemistry
Qualitative analysis -- Continued
Spectrum analysis (Qualitative and quantitative)
Class here works on the applications of spectroscopy in general analytical chemistry and theoretical works intended primarily for chemists.
For general works on the theory of spectroscopy and works intended primarily for physicists see QC450+
For compilations of spectra of elements, groups of elements, organic and inorganic compounds see QC462+
For works on the applications of spectroscopy in organic analytical chemistry see QD272.S6
Cf. CC79.S65 Spectrum analysis in archaeology

95 General works
95.5.A-Z Special topics, A-Z
95.5.D37 Data processing
95.5.S72 Statistical methods
96.A-Z Special methods and types of spectra, A-Z
96.A2 Absorption spectra
Including cavity-ringdown spectroscopy
96.A7 Arc spectra
96.A8 Atomic spectra
Cavity-ringdown spectroscopy see QD96.A2
96.D48 Deuteron magnetic resonance spectroscopy
96.E4 Electron paramagnetic resonance spectroscopy
96.E44 Electron spectroscopy
96.E46 Emission spectroscopy
96.F5 Flame spectroscopy
96.F56 Fluorescence spectroscopy
96.F68 Fourier transform spectroscopy
Cf. QD96.I5 Fourier transform infrared spectroscopy
Cf. QD96.N8 Fourier transform nuclear magnetic resonance spectroscopy
96.I47 Inductively coupled plasma spectrometry
Class here works on all types of spectrum analytical methods using inductively coupled plasmas
96.I5 Infrared spectroscopy
Including Fourier transform infrared spectroscopy
96.I54 Ion cyclotron resonance spectroscopy
Ion mobility spectroscopy see QD96.P62
96.L3 Laser spectroscopy
96.L85 Luminescence spectroscopy
96.M3 Mass spectroscopy
96.M33 Matrix isolation spectroscopy
96.M5 Microwave spectroscopy

Analytical chemistry
Qualitative analysis
Spectrum analysis (Qualitative and quantitative)
Special methods and types of spectra, A-Z -- Continued
96.M6 Mössbauer spectroscopy
96.M65 Molecular spectra
96.N8 Nuclear magnetic resonance spectroscopy
Including Fourier transform nuclear magnetic resonance spectroscopy
96.N84 Nuclear quadrupole resonance spectroscopy
96.O6 Optoacoustic spectroscopy
96.P5 Photoelectron spectroscopy
96.P54 Photothermal spectroscopy
96.P62 Plasma spectroscopy
Including ion mobility spectroscopy
Cf. QD96.I47 Inductively coupled plasma spectrometry
96.P7 Proton magnetic resonance spectroscopy
96.R3 Radiofrequency spectroscopy
96.R34 Raman spectroscopy
96.R4 Reflectance spectroscopy
96.R44 Relaxation spectroscopy
96.S43 Secondary ion mass spectroscopy
96.U4 Ultraviolet spectroscopy
96.V53 Vibrational spectra
96.X2 X-ray spectroscopy
98.A-Z Other special methods, A-Z
98.C4 Chromatography
98.E4 Electron microprobe
98.K5 Kinetic analysis
98.M5 Microchemical analysis
98.S6 Spot tests
Quantitative analysis
General works, treatises, and textbooks
101 Through 1970
101.2 1971-
111 Volumetric analysis
113 Colorimetric analysis
Electrochemical analysis
115 General works
116.A-Z Special methods, A-Z
116.C65 Conductometric analysis
116.I57 Impedance spectroscopy
116.P64 Polarography
116.P68 Potentiometry
116.V64 Voltammetry
117.A-Z Other special methods, A-Z

Analytical chemistry
Quantitative analysis
Other special methods, A-Z -- Continued

117.C5-.C52 Chromatography
117.C5 General works
117.C515 Gas chromatography
117.C517 Liquid chromatography
117.C52 Thin layer chromatography
117.E4 Electron diffraction
117.E42 Electron microprobe. Electron probe microanalysis
117.E45 Electrophoresis
117.F5 Fluorimetry
117.M5 Microchemical analysis. Microchemistry
117.P5 Photometry
117.R3 Radiometry. Radiation measurement
117.S64 Spectrophotometry
Spectrum analysis see QD95+
117.T4 Thermal analysis
121 Gas analysis
Including air analysis
Cf. TP754 Analysis, tests, etc. in the gas industry
Technical analysis
130 Periodicals, societies, congresses, serial publications
131 General works, treatises, and textbooks
Metals
132 General works
Assaying see TN550+
133 Iron and steel alloys
Alloys (General). Nonferrous alloys
135 General works
137.A-Z Special metal alloys, A-Z
For the analysis of metallic elements see QD181.A+
137.A6 Aluminum alloys
137.A8 Arsenic alloys
137.B3 Babbitt metal
137.C5 Chromium-iron-nickel alloys
137.C6 Copper alloys
137.F35 Ferrites (Magnetic materials)
137.F38 Ferroboron
137.F4 Ferrochromium
137.F44 Ferroniobium
137.F48 Ferrotungsten
137.G6 Gold alloys
Iron alloys (General) see QD133
137.M3 Magnesium alloys
137.N5 Nickel alloys

Analytical chemistry
Technical analysis
Metals
Alloys (General). Nonferrous alloys
Special metal alloys, A-Z -- Continued
137.S5 Silver alloys
Steel alloys see QD133
137.U73 Uranium alloys
137.Z5 Zinc alloys
139.A-Z Other special, A-Z
Air see QD121
Air pollution see TD890
Carbonated beverages see TP628+
Cement see TP882.3
Ceramics see TP810
139.C53 Cigarette smoke
Clay see TP811
Distilled beverages see TP609
139.E4 Electrolytes
Fats, oils, and waxes see TP671
Fermentation industries see TP511
Food see TX545
Gas see QD121
Gas industry see TP754
139.G5 Glass
Materials (General) see QD130+
Oils, fats, and waxes see TP671
Oils (Petroleum) see TP691
Plastics see TP1140
139.P6 Polymers
139.S44 Semiconductors
Sewage see TD735
139.S5 Silicon organic compounds
(139.T5) Textiles
see TS1449
139.T7 Trace elements
Water see QD142
Water supply see TD380+
Wine see TP548.5.A5
142 Water analysis
Cf. TD380+ Water supply
Inorganic chemistry
Cf. QD475 Physical inorganic chemistry
Cf. QE351+ Mineralogy
146 Periodicals, societies, congresses, serial publications
147 Collected works (nonserial)
148 Dictionaries and encyclopedias

Inorganic chemistry -- Continued
149 Nomenclature, terminology, notation, abbreviations
History
149.5 General works
149.7.A-Z By region or country, A-Z
150 Early works through 1800
General works, treatises, and advanced textbooks
151 1801-1969
151.2 1970-2000
151.3 2001-
151.5 Elementary textbooks
152 Addresses, essays, lectures
152.3 Special aspects of the subject as a whole
152.5.A-Z Special topics, A-Z
152.5.D46 Density functionals
152.5.M38 Mathematics
Reaction mechanisms see QD502.5
Study and teaching. Research
153 General works
153.5 Outlines, syllabi, etc
154 Problems, exercises, examinations
155 Laboratory manuals
155.5 Handbooks, tables, formulas, etc.
156 Inorganic synthesis
157 Electric furnace operations
Cf. QD277 Electric furnace operations (Organic)
Nonmetals
161 General works
162 Gases
163 Chemistry of the air
Cf. TD881+ Air pollution
165 Halogens: Bromine, chlorine, fluorine, iodine
167 Inorganic acids
Cf. QD477 General theory of acids and bases
169.A-Z Other, A-Z
169.C5 Chalcogenides
Heavy water see QD169.W3
169.W3 Water
Cf. GB855+ Natural water chemistry
Metals
Cf. TN600+ Metallurgy
171 General works, treatises, and textbooks
172.A-Z By group, A-Z
172.A3 Actinide elements
172.A4 Alkali metals
172.A42 Alkaline earth metals
172.I7 Iron group

Inorganic chemistry
Metals
By group, A-Z -- Continued
172.M4 Magnesium group
172.P8 Platinum group
172.P88 Precious metals
172.R2 Rare earth metals
172.S6 Spinel group
172.S93 Superheavy elements
Cf. QC796.2 Nuclear physics
172.T52 Titanium group
172.T6 Transition metals
172.T65 Transplutonium elements
172.T7 Transuranium elements
181.A-Z Special elements. By chemical symbol, A-Z (Table Q1)
Class here works on the origin, properties, preparation, reactions, isotopes, and analytical chemistry of individual elements and their inorganic compounds.
For the determination of atomic and molecular weights see QD464.A+
Salts
189 General works
191 Double salts
193 Complex salts
194 Oxysalts
196 Inorganic polymers and polymerization
197 Cyclic compounds
Organic chemistry
Cf. QD476 Physical organic chemistry
Cf. QD478 Solids. Solid state chemistry (Inorganic and organic)
241 Periodicals, societies, congresses, serial collections
(243) Yearbooks
see QD241
245 Collected works (nonserial)
246 Dictionaries and encyclopedias
History
248 General works
248.5.A-Z By region or country, A-Z
General works, treatises, and advanced textbooks
251 Through 1970
251.2 1971-2000
251.3 2001-
Elementary textbooks
253 To 2000
253.2 2001-

Organic chemistry -- Continued
Nomenclature, terminology, notation, abbreviations see QD291
254 Classification
255 Addresses, essays, lectures
255.4 Special aspects of the subject as a whole
255.5.A-Z Special topics, A-Z
255.5.E4 Electronic data processing
255.5.M35 Mathematics
255.5.R33 Radiation effects
Reaction mechanisms see QD502.5
Study and teaching. Research
256 General works
256.5 Outlines, syllabi
257 Problems, exercises, examinations
257.5 Experiments
257.7 Handbooks, tables, formulas, etc.
Operations in organic chemistry
258 General works
261 Laboratory manuals
262 Organic synthesis
Including general works on combinatorial chemistry
For works on pharmaceutical aspects of combinatorial chemistry see RS419
Organic analysis
Class here general works on the analysis of organic compounds
For the analysis of specific organic compounds or groups of compounds, see QD301
For works on the analysis of both organic and inorganic compounds see QD71+
271.A1 Periodicals, societies, congresses, serial publications
271.A2-Z General works, treatises, and textbooks
Reagents, indicators, test papers, etc.
271.3 General works
271.35.A-Z Special topics, A-Z
271.35.E54 Electrophiles. Superelectrophiles
271.4 Qualitative analysis
Prefer QD272 for special methods in qualitative analysis
271.7 Quantitative analysis
Prefer QD272 for special methods in quantitative analysis
272.A-Z Special methods of analysis (Qualitative and quantitative), A-Z
Chromatography
272.C4 General works
272.C44 Gas chromatography
272.C444 Gel permeation chromatography

Organic chemistry
Operations in organic chemistry
Organic analysis
Special methods of analysis (Qualitative and quantitative), A-Z
Chromatography -- Continued

272.C447 Liquid chromatography
272.C45 Thin layer chromatography
272.C6 Colorimetric analysis
272.E4 Electrochemical analysis
272.E43 Electrophoresis
272.E5 Enzymatic analysis
272.M5 Microchemical analysis
272.P5 Photometry
272.S57 Spectrophotometry
272.S6 Spectrum analysis
Works on the application of spectroscopy in general or inorganic analytical chemistry are classed in QD95
For compilations of spectra see QC462+
272.T45 Thermal analysis
272.V6 Volumetric analysis
273 Electrochemistry of organic compounds
Cf. QP517.B53 Bioelectrochemistry
275 Organic photochemistry
Cf. QP517.P45 Photobiochemistry
277 Electric furnace operations
281.A-Z Other special, A-Z
281.A2 Acylation
281.A5 Alkylation
281.A6 Amination
281.A63 Ammonolysis
281.B7 Bromination
281.C3 Catalysis
281.C5 Chlorination
281.C7 Condensation
Cyclization see QD281.R5
281.D4 Dehydrogenation
281.D47 Dialysis
281.D5 Distillation
281.E4 Elimination reactions
281.F5 Flotation
281.F55 Fluorination
281.F7 Fragmentation reactions
281.H3 Halogenation
281.H78 Hydroboration
281.H79 Hydroformylation
281.H8 Hydrogenation

QD

Organic chemistry
Operations in organic chemistry
Other special, A-Z -- Continued
281.H83 Hydrolysis
281.H84 Hydrosilylation
281.H85 Hydroxylation
281.I7 Isotopic exchange reactions
281.M48 Methylation
281.N5 Nitration
281.O9 Oxidation
281.O95 Ozonolysis. Ozonization
281.P46 Phosphorylation
281.P6 Polymerization. Telomerization
281.P9 Pyrolysis
281.Q5 Quinoidation
281.R35 Rearrangement reactions. Rearrangements
281.R4 Reduction
281.R5 Ring formation
Including ring breaking, enlargement, and closure, and ring-opening polymerization
281.S5 Silylation
281.S6 Solvolysis
281.S67 Substitution reactions
281.S7 Sulfonation
Telomerization see QD281.P6
291 Nomenclature, terminology, notation, abbreviations
Aliphatic compounds
300 Periodicals, societies, congresses, serial publications
301 General works, treatises, and textbooks
302 Special aspects of the subject as a whole
305.A-Z Special groups, A-Z
Including works on both aliphatic and aromatic aspects of functional groups
For works on special groups of aromatic compounds only see QD341.A+
305.A2 Acids and esters
305.A4 Alcohols
305.A6 Aldehydes and other carbonyl compounds
For ketones see QD305.K2
305.A7 Amides and hydrazides
Cf. QD315 Urea
Amino acids see QD431+
305.A8 Amino compounds
305.A9 Azo, hydrazo, and diazo compounds
305.C3 Carbanions and carbonium ions, free radicals, ylides
305.E7 Ethers and oxides

Organic chemistry
Aliphatic compounds
Special groups, A-Z -- Continued
305.F2 Fats and fatty oils
Cf. QP751+ Animal biochemistry
Cf. TP669+ Chemical technology
Free radicals see QD305.C3
Glycols see QD305.A4
305.H15 Halogen compounds
Hydrocarbons
305.H5 General works
305.H6 Alkanes (Paraffins)
305.H7 Alkenes (Olefins)
Cf. TP248.A554 Chemical technology
305.H8 Alkynes (Acetylene, etc.)
305.H9 Alicyclic compounds (Non-aromatic compounds with ring structure)
305.I6 Imides, imidoesters, etc.
305.K2 Ketones, ketenes, and oximes
305.N7 Nitriles and cyanogen derivatives
305.N8 Nitro and nitroso compounds
305.N84 Nitrogen derivatives (General)
305.P46 Phosphorus derivatives (General)
Radicals see QD305.C3
305.S54 Silicon compounds
305.S83 Sulfones
305.S84 Sulfur derivatives (General)
305.T45 Thio compounds
Ylides see QD305.C3
315 Urea and related compounds
Cf. QP801.U7 Animal biochemistry
Carbohydrates
Including sugars, starch, etc.
Cf. QP701+ Animal biochemistry
Cf. TP375+ Sugar manufacture
Cf. TP415+ Starch
320 Periodicals, societies, congresses, serial publications
321 General works, treatises, and textbooks
322.A-Z Special topics, A-Z
322.A52 Analysis
322.S95 Synthesis
323 Cellulose
Including hemicellulose
325 Glycosides
Including glucosides, mannosides, and galactosides
327 Tannins

Organic chemistry -- Continued
Aromatic compounds
Cf. QD390+ Condensed benzene rings
Cf. QD399+ Heterocyclic compounds
330 Periodicals, societies, congresses, serial publications
331 General works, treatises, and textbooks
335 Special aspects of the subject as a whole
341.A-Z Special groups, A-Z
341.A2 Acids and esters
341.A4 Alcohols
341.A6 Aldehydes and other carbonyl compounds
For ketones see QD341.K2
341.A7 Amides and hydrazides
Amino acids see QD431+
341.A8 Amino compounds
341.A83 Annulenes
341.A9 Azo, hydrazo, and diazo compounds
Benzene see QD341.H9
341.E7 Ethers and oxides
341.H8 Halogen compounds
341.H9 Hydrocarbons, benzene, etc.
341.I6 Imino compounds
341.K2 Ketones
341.N7 Nitriles and cyanogen derivatives
341.N8 Nitro and nitroso compounds
341.N83 Nitrogen derivatives (General)
341.P5 Phenols
341.P6 Pseudophenols
341.Q4 Quinones
341.S3 Sulfur derivatives (General)
341.S6 Sulfoxides and sulfones
341.S8 Sulfonium compounds
Antibiotics
Cf. QP801.A63 Animal biochemistry
Cf. RM265+ Therapeutics
375 General works, treatises, and textbooks
377.A-Z Special substances, A-Z
377.C4 Cephalosporin
377.C5 Chloromycetin
377.P4 Penicillin
377.P55 Pimaricin
377.S8 Streptomycin
377.S85 Streptothricin
377.T45 Tetracycline
377.V5 Viomycin

Organic chemistry -- Continued

Polymers. Macromolecules

Class here general works on chemical and physical properties of polymers

For works on physical properties see QC173.4.P65

Cf. QD139.P6 Technical analysis

Cf. QD196 Inorganic polymers

Cf. QD281.P6 Polymerization (Organic chemistry)

Cf. QD399+ Macrocyclic compounds

Cf. TP156.P6 Polymerization (Chemical engineering)

Cf. TP1080+ Polymer technology

380 Periodicals, societies, congresses, serial publications

380.3 Dictionaries and encyclopedias

380.6 Nomenclature, terminology, notation, abbreviations

380.7 Classification

381 General works, treatises, and textbooks

381.3 Juvenile works

381.7 Addresses, essays, lectures

381.8 Special aspects of the subject as a whole

381.9.A-Z Special topics, A-Z

381.9.A25 Acoustic properties

381.9.C64 Conformational analysis

381.9.D47 Deterioration

381.9.E38 Electric properties

381.9.E4 Electronic data processing

Fractionation see QD381.9.S44

381.9.M3 Mathematical models

381.9.M64 Molecular weights

381.9.O66 Optical properties

381.9.P45 Permeability

381.9.P56 Photochemistry

381.9.R3 Radiation effects

381.9.R43 Reduced gravity effects

381.9.R48 Rheology

Ring-opening polymerization see QD281.R5

381.9.S44 Separation. Fractionation

381.9.S65 Solubility and solutions

381.9.S87 Structure

381.9.S97 Surfaces and interfaces

381.9.T54 Thermal properties

382.A-Z Special types, A-Z

382.A47 Amphiphiles

382.B47 Biomimetic polymers

382.B5 Block copolymers

382.C66 Conducting polymers. Conjugated polymers

Conjugated polymers see QD382.C66

382.C67 Coordination polymers

Organic chemistry
Polymers. Macromolecules
Special types, A-Z -- Continued
Crosslinked polymers see QD382.P67
382.C78 Crystalline polymers
382.E48 Emulsion polymers
382.F55 Fluorescent polymers
382.G7 Graft copolymers
382.H4 Heat resistant polymers
382.H48 Heterochain polymers
382.I43 Imprinted polymers
382.I45 Ionomers
382.O43 Oligomers
Photochromic polymers see QD382.P45
382.P45 Photopolymers. Photochromic polymers
382.P64 Polyelectrolytes
Including polyampholytes
Polymer colloids see QD549.2.P64
Polymer liquid crystals see QD923
382.P67 Polymer networks. Crosslinked polymers
382.R43 Reactive polymers
382.S4 Semiconductors
382.T44 Telechelic polymers
382.W3 Water-soluble polymers
383.A-Z Special substances, A-Z
383.A27 Acrylic polymers
383.A55 Amine polymers
383.A95 Azo polymers
383.B67 Boron organic polymers
383.E66 Epoxy polymers
383.F48 Fluoropolymers
383.F84 Fullerene polymers
383.G57 Glutamic acid polymers
Methacrylate polymers see QD383.A27
383.S54 Silicon polymers
383.V56 Vinyl polymers
385 Laboratory manuals
388 Handbooks, tables, formulas, etc.
Condensed benzine rings
390 General works, treatises, and textbooks
390.3 Special aspects of the subject as a whole
391 Naphthalene and naphthalene derivatives
393 Anthracene and anthracene derivatives
395 Phenanthrene and phenanthrene derivatives
Heterocyclic and macrocyclic chemistry and compounds
399 Periodicals, societies, congresses, serial publications
400 General works, treatises, and textbooks

Organic chemistry
Heterocyclic and macrocyclic chemistry and compounds -- Continued
400.3 Special aspects of the subject as a whole
400.5.A-Z Special topics, A-Z
400.5.S95 Synthesis
401 Cyclic compounds containing N
403 Cyclic compounds containing S
405 Cyclic compounds containing O
406 Cyclic compounds containing P
Organometallic chemistry and compounds
Cf. QD882 Supramolecular organometallic chemistry
410 Periodicals, societies, congresses, serial publications
411 General works, treatises, and textbooks
411.5 Addresses, essays, lectures
411.7.A-Z Special topics, A-Z
411.7.A53 Analysis
411.7.B37 Barbier reactions
411.7.S94 Synthesis
411.7.T47 Thermal properties
411.8.A-Z Special groups of substances, A-Z
411.8.A47 Alkoxides
Including aryloxides
411.8.R37 Rare earth metals
411.8.T73 Transition metals
412.A-Z Special compounds. By chemical symbol of added element, A-Z (Table Q1)
412.5 Handbooks, tables, formulas, etc.
Biochemistry
Class here works on chemical aspects of biological materials
Cf. QD476.2 Physical biochemistry
Cf. QH345 General biochemistry of plants and animals
Cf. QK861+ Plant biochemistry
Cf. QP501+ Animal biochemistry
415.A1 Periodicals, societies, congresses, serial publications
415.A2 Collected works (nonserial)
415.A25 Dictionaries and encyclopedias
415.A3-Z General works, treatises, and textbooks
415.2 Addresses, essays, lectures
415.3 Problems, exercises, examinations
415.5 Laboratory manuals
415.7 Handbooks, tables, formulas, etc.
Antibiotics see QD375+
Terpenes, camphors, etc. Essential oils
Cf. TP958+ Essences (Chemical technology)
416.A1 Periodicals, societies, congresses, serial publications
416.A3-Z General works, treatises, and textbooks

QD

Organic chemistry
Biochemistry
Terpenes, camphors, etc. Essential oils -- Continued
416.2 Addresses, essays, lectures
416.3 Problems, exercises, examinations
416.5 Laboratory manuals
416.7 Handbooks, tables, formulas, etc.
Gums and resins
Cf. TP977+ Chemical technology
Cf. TP1101+ Plastic materials for synthetic gums and resins
419.A1 Periodicals, societies, congresses, serial publications
419.A3-Z General works, treatises, and textbooks
419.2 Addresses, essays, lectures
419.3 Problems, exercises, examinations
419.5 Laboratory manuals
419.7 Handbooks, tables, formulas, etc.
Alkaloids
Cf. QK898.A4 Plant constituent
Cf. RM666.A4 Therapeutics
Cf. RS431.A53 Pharmaceutical chemistry
421.A1 Periodicals, societies, congresses, serial publications
421.A3-Z General works, treatises, and textbooks
421.2 Addresses, essays, lectures
421.3 Problems, exercises, examinations
421.5 Laboratory manuals
421.7 Handbooks, tables, formulas, etc.
Steroids
Cf. QP752.S7 Animal biochemistry
Cf. RS163.S8 Materia medica
426.A1 Periodicals, societies, congresses, serial publications
426.A3-Z General works, treatises, and textbooks
426.2 Addresses, essays, lectures
426.3 Problems, exercises, examinations
426.5 Laboratory manuals
426.7 Handbooks, tables, formulas, etc.
Proteins, peptides, amino acids, etc.
Cf. QP551+ Animal biochemistry
Cf. TX553.P7 Special constituents of food
431.A1 Periodicals, societies, congresses, serial publications
431.A3-Z General works, treatises, and textbooks
431.2 Addresses, essays, lectures
431.25.A-Z Special topics, A-Z
431.25.A53 Analysis
431.25.D47 Derivatives
431.25.S85 Structure
431.25.S93 Synthesis

Organic chemistry
Biochemistry
Proteins, peptides, amino acids, etc. -- Continued
431.3 Problems, exercises, examinations
431.5 Laboratory manuals
431.7 Handbooks, tables, formulas, etc.
Nucleic acids
433.A1 Periodicals, societies, congresses, serial publications
433.A3-Z General works, treatises, and textbooks
433.5.A-Z Special topics, A-Z
433.5.S77 Structure
434 Ribonucleic acids
435 Deoxyribonucleic acids
436.A-Z Other related substances, A-Z
436.N85 Nucleotides
441 Colored compounds
Including phthaleins, eosin, animal and plant pigments
Cf. QK899 Botany
Cf. QP670+ Animal biochemistry
Cf. TP909.2+ Chemical technology
Physical and theoretical chemistry
Cf. QC170+ Constitution and properties of matter
450 Periodicals, societies, congresses, serial publications
450.2 Collected works (nonserial)
451 Dictionaries and encyclopedias
451.5 Nomenclature, terminology, notation, abbreviations
History
452 General works
452.5.A-Z By region or country, A-Z
General works, treatises, and textbooks
453 Through 1970
453.2 1971-2000
453.3 2001-
455 Addresses, essays, lectures
455.2 Special aspects of the subject as a whole
455.3.A-Z Special topics, A-Z
455.3.C64 Computer simulation
455.3.E4 Electronic data processing
455.3.F73 Fractals
455.3.G7 Graphic methods
455.3.G75 Group theory
455.3.L53 Lie algebras
455.3.M3 Mathematics
455.3.T65 Topology
Study and teaching. Research
455.5 General works
455.7 Outlines, syllabi

Physical and theoretical chemistry
Study and teaching. Research -- Continued
456 Problems, exercises, examinations
457 Laboratory manuals
457.2 Computer-assisted instruction
458 Handbooks, tables, formulas, etc.
461 Atomic and molecular theory and structure. Laws of chemical combination and chemical bonds. Molecular dimensions
Cf. QD469 Valence
461.5 Excited state chemistry
Quantum chemistry
462.A1 Periodicals, societies, congresses, serial publications
462.A3-Z General works, treatises, and textbooks
462.5 Addresses, essays, lectures
462.6.A-Z Special topics, A-Z
462.6.D38 Data processing
462.6.D45 Density functionals
462.6.D46 Density matrices
462.6.E53 Energy levels
462.6.M36 Many-body methods
462.6.M39 Mathematics
462.6.M66 Monte Carlo method
462.6.P68 Potential energy surfaces
462.6.R42 Relativistic effects
462.6.R44 Relaxation phenomena
462.6.S25 Scaling
462.6.S94 Symmetry groups
462.7 Problems, exercises, examinations
462.9 Handbooks, tables, formulas, etc.
Atomic and molecular weights
463 General works, treatises, and textbooks
464.A-Z Individual elements and their compounds. By chemical symbol of principal element, A-Z (Table Q1)
Chemical elements
Nature and properties
466 General works
466.5 Isotopes
For isotopes of individual elements see QD181.A+
Cf. QD601+ Radiochemistry
Cf. TK9400+ Radioisotopes in nuclear engineering
467 Classification. Periodic law
469 Valence
Cf. QC176.8.V34 Valence fluctuations
470 Allotropy
471 Chemical compounds - Structure and formulas
Including isomerism, mesomerism, tautomerism
Cf. QD481 Stereochemistry

Physical and theoretical chemistry -- Continued

473 Physical properties in relation to structure
Including odor, color, and optical properties
Cf. QD441 Colored organic compounds
Cf. QD931+ Physical properties of crystals

474 Complex compounds
Including clathrate and coordination compounds, chelates, and hydrates
Cf. QD410+ Organometallic compounds

475 Physical inorganic chemistry

476 Physical organic chemistry

476.2 Physical biochemistry

477 Acids and bases (General theory)

478 Solids. Solid state chemistry (Inorganic and organic)
Cf. QC176+ Solid state physics
Cf. QD506+ Surface chemistry
Cf. QD901+ Crystallography
Cf. TN689+ Physical metallurgy

480 Models of atoms, molecules, or chemical compounds

481 Stereochemistry. Molecular rotation
Cf. QP517.S83 Biochemistry

Conditions and laws of chemical reactions

501 General works

Chemical kinetics and mechanisms

502 General works

502.2 Nonlinear chemical kinetics. Oscillating chemical reactions

502.5 Reaction mechanisms
Including inorganic and organic mechanisms

503 Chemical equilibrium. Phase rule, etc.

504 Thermodynamics

505 Catalysis
Cf. QD569 Electrocatalysis
Cf. QD716.P45 Photocatalysis

505.5 Chemical affinity and reactivity

505.8 Chemiluminescence

Surface chemistry

506.A1 Periodicals, societies, congresses, serial publications

506.A3-Z General works, treatises, and textbooks

508 Addresses, essays, lectures

509.A-Z Special topics, A-Z

509.G37 Gas-solid interfaces

509.L54 Liquid-liquid interfaces

Liquid-solid interfaces see QD509.S65

509.M46 Metallic oxides

509.M65 Monomolecular films

509.S65 Solid-liquid interfaces

Physical and theoretical chemistry -- Continued
Thermochemistry
Cf. QC301+ Change of state (Physics)
Cf. QD79.T38 Thermal analysis (Analytical chemistry)
Cf. QD117.T4 Thermal analysis, Quantitative
Cf. QD157 Electric furnace operations (Inorganic chemistry)
Cf. QD277 Electric furnace operations (Organic chemistry)
510 Periodicals, societies, congresses, serial publications
511 General works, treatises, and textbooks
511.3 Addresses, essays, lectures
511.7 Problems, exercises, examinations
511.8 Handbooks, tables, formulas, etc.
515 Chemistry of high and low temperatures
516 Heat of formation, combustion, flame, explosion
Cf. TH9446.3+ Flammability of materials
Cf. TJ254.5+ Combustion engineering
517 Dissociation
518 Melting and boiling points
526 Fractional distillation
Cf. QD63.D6 Special operations in chemistry
Cf. QD281.D5 Operations in organic chemistry
Cf. TP156.D5 Chemical engineering processes
Cf. TP589+ Distilling industries
531 Manipulation of gases and vapors
Cf. TP242+ Chemical technology of gases
533 Vapor densities
535 Liquefaction of gases
Cf. TP243 Manufacture of liquefied gases
536 Research at low temperatures
Cf. TP480+ Low temperature engineering
538 Chemistry of high and low pressures
Theory of solution
Cf. QC182+ Special properties of matter
Cf. QD565 Electrolyte solutions
540 Periodicals, societies, congresses, serial publications
541 General works, treatises, and textbooks
543 Solubility, osmotic pressure, diffusion, etc.
Solvents
544 General works
544.3 Aqueous
544.5 Nonaqueous
Cf. TP247.5 Technology of organic solvents
545 Freezing points and vapor pressures
547 Flocculation, precipitation, adsorption, etc.

Physical and theoretical chemistry
Theory of solution -- Continued
548 Supersaturated solutions. Crystallization, etc.
Cf. QD921+ Crystal structure and growth
Colloids, sols, gels
Cf. QP525 Animal biochemistry
Cf. S593.3 Soil colloids
549 General works
549.2.A-Z Special topics, A-Z
549.2.C64 Colloidal crystals
549.2.C66 Complex fluids
549.2.P64 Polymer colloids
Electrochemistry. Electrolysis
Cf. QC610.3+ Electric conductivity, electromotive force
Cf. QD115+ Electrochemical analysis
Cf. QD272.E4 Electrochemical analysis of organic compounds
Cf. QD273 Electrochemistry of organic compounds
Cf. QD880 Electrochemistry of supramolecular compounds
Cf. QP517.B53 Bioelectrochemistry
Cf. TP250+ Industrial electrochemistry
551 Periodicals, societies, congresses, serial publications
552 Collected works (nonserial)
552.5 Dictionaries and encyclopedias
553 General works, treatises, and textbooks
554 Popular works
554.5 Juvenile works
555 Addresses, essays, lectures
555.5 Special aspects of the subject as a whole
555.6.A-Z Special topics, A-Z
555.6.E4 Electronic data processing
555.6.G74 Green's functions
555.6.I58 Interfaces
555.6.L37 Laser electrochemistry
555.6.M36 Mathematical models
555.6.N65 Nonaqueous solvents
555.6.S65 Spectrum analysis
555.8 Study and teaching. Research
556 Problems, exercises, examinations
557 Laboratory manuals
Electrochemical laboratories
558 General works
558.2.A-Z By region or country, A-Z
Subarrange each country by Table Q6
559 Instruments and apparatus
560 Handbooks, tables, formulas, etc.

Physical and theoretical chemistry
Electrochemistry. Electrolysis -- Continued
Ions and ionization
561 General works
562.A-Z Special topics, A-Z
562.A54 Anion separation
562.A75 Aqua ions
Dissociation see QD562.I65
562.E44 Electromotive force
562.E45 Electrophoresis
562.H93 Hydrogen-ion concentration
562.I63 Ion exchange. Ion exchange membranes
562.I65 Ionization. Dissociation
562.M54 Migration and velocity
Photodissociation see QD716.P48
Photoionization see QD716.P48
Velocity see QD562.M54
564 Electric double layer
565 Electrolytes, electrolyte solutions
Cf. TS672 Plating baths
568 Electrolytic cells
Cf. TK2901+ Electric power production from chemical action
569 Electrocatalysis
571 Electrode phenomena. Polarization, etc.
572.A-Z Special electrodes, A-Z
572.A65 Alkali metal
572.C37 Carbon
572.G53 Glass
572.H94 Hydrides
572.I66 Ion selective
572.I76 Iron
572.N53 Nickel
572.O85 Oxide
572.O88 Oxygen
572.S95 Sulfur
575.A-Z Special groups of substances, A-Z
575.C65 Complex compounds
575.G53 Glass
575.P67 Porous materials
576.A-Z Special substances. By chemical symbol of principal element, A-Z (Table Q1)
578 Photoelectrochemistry
581 Plasma chemistry
Cf. TP156.P5 Industrial plasma chemistry
591 Magnetochemistry
Cf. QD940 Magnetic properties of crystals

Physical and theoretical chemistry -- Continued
Radiochemistry. Nuclear chemistry
Cf. QC794.95+ Radioactivity, radioactive substances in nuclear physics
Cf. TK9350 Nuclear engineering
Cf. TP249 Industrial radiochemistry. Industrial radiation chemistry

601.A1 Periodicals, societies, congresses, serial publications
601.A2 Collected works (nonserial)
General works, treatises, and textbooks
601.A4-Z Through 1970
601.2 1971-2000
601.3 2001-
602 Addresses, essays, lectures
602.4 Special aspects of the subject as a whole
602.5.A-Z Special topics, A-Z
602.5.E4 Electronic data processing
603.A-Z Special substances. By chemical symbol of principal element, A-Z (Table Q1)
Study and teaching. Research
604 General works
604.3 Problems, exercises, examinations
604.5 Experiments
604.7 Laboratory manuals
Radiochemical laboratories. Hot laboratories
Cf. QC788+ Nuclear physics research laboratories and projects
604.8 General works
604.85.A-Z By region or country, A-Z
Subarrange each country by Table Q6
604.9 Handbooks, tables, formulas, etc.
Radiochemical analysis
605 General works
606 Radioactivation analysis. Nuclear activation analysis
607 Tracer techniques
For applications in special fields, see the field, e.g. QH324.3 Biology
608 Isotope dilution analysis
Radiation chemistry
Cf. QC474+ Radiation physics
Cf. TA418.6 Radiation effects and tests of materials
Cf. TP249 Industrial radiochemistry. Industrial radiation chemistry
625 Periodicals, societies, congresses, serial publications
626 Collected works (nonserial)
General works, treatises, and textbooks
635 Through 1970

Physical and theoretical chemistry
Radiation chemistry
General works, treatises, and textbooks -- Continued

636 1971-
641 Addresses, essays, lectures
642 Special aspects of the subject as a whole
643.A-Z Special topics, A-Z
643.C5 Chemical dosimetry
643.P84 Pulse radiolysis
Study and teaching. Research
646 General works
646.3 Problems, exercises, examinations
646.5 Experiments
646.7 Laboratory manuals
649 Handbooks, tables, formulas, etc.
651.A-Z Special substances. By name, A-Z
651.A36 Actinide elements
651.A4 Alcohol
651.A45 Ammonia
651.C37 Carbohydrates
651.H93 Hydrocarbons
651.M38 Mercapto compounds. Thiols
651.M4 Methanol
651.N5 Nitrous oxide
651.P6 Polymers
Thiols see QD651.M38
651.W3 Water
655 Particular types of radiation and chemical reaction, e.g. x-rays (not A-Z)

Photochemistry
Cf. QD275 Organic photochemistry
Cf. QD578 Photoelectrochemistry
Cf. QP517.P45 Photobiochemistry
Cf. TP249.5 Industrial photochemistry
Cf. TR200+ Photographic chemistry

701 Periodicals, societies, congresses, serial publications
General works, treatises, and textbooks
708 Through 1970
708.2 1971-
714 Addresses, essays, lectures
715 Special aspects of the subject as a whole
716.A-Z Special topics, A-Z
716.F54 Flash photolysis
716.L37 Laser photochemistry
Including femtochemistry
716.O95 Oxidation-reduction
716.P45 Photocatalysis

Physical and theoretical chemistry
Photochemistry
Special topics, A-Z -- Continued
716.P47 Photochromism
716.P48 Photodissociation. Photoionization
Class here general works on chemical and physical aspects of photoionization.
For works on the physics of ionization produced by photons of light, X-rays or gamma rays see QC702.7.P48
716.P5 Photopolymerization
Class here general works on photopolymerization
For works on inorganic polymerization see QD196
For works on organic polymerization see QD281.P6
719 Handbooks, tables, formulas, etc.
730.A-Z Special groups of substances, A-Z
730.C65 Coordination compounds
Polymers see QD381.9.P56
730.S35 Semiconductors
730.T73 Transition metal compounds
731.A-Z Special substances. By chemical symbol of principal element, A-Z (Table Q1)
801 Sonochemistry
Cf. TP156.A33 Industrial use of sounds and ultrasonics
850 Mechanical chemistry
Supramolecular chemistry
Cf. QD380+ Macromolecules
875 Periodicals, societies, congresses, serial publications
876 Dictionaries and encyclopedias
878 General works, treatises, and textbooks
880 Electrochemistry of supramolecular compounds
882 Supramolecular organometallic chemistry
Crystallography
Cf. QE372+ Descriptive mineralogy
901 Periodicals, societies, congresses, serial publications
901.2 Collected works (nonserial)
902 Dictionaries and encyclopedias
902.5 Nomenclature, terminology, notation, abbreviations
History
903 General works
903.3.A-Z By region or country, A-Z
Biography of crystallographers
903.5 Collective
903.6.A-Z Individual, A-Z
903.8 Directories
904 Early works through 1800
General works, treatises, and textbooks

Crystallography
General works, treatises, and textbooks -- Continued
905 1801-1969
905.2 1970-
906 Pictorial works and atlases
906.3 Juvenile works
906.5 Addresses, essays, lectures
906.6 Special aspects of the subject as a whole
906.7.A-Z Special topics, A-Z
906.7.E37 Electron microscopy
906.7.E4 Electronic data processing
906.7.N83 Nuclear magnetic resonance spectroscopy
Statistical methods see QD919
Study and teaching. Research
907 General works
907.3 Problems, exercises, examinations
907.5 Laboratory manuals
907.7 Instruments and apparatus
908 Handbooks, tables, formulas, etc.
Geometrical and mathematical crystallography
911 General works
912 Fundamental systems
Including tetragonal, orthorhombic, monoclinic systems
913 Diagrams
915 Goniometric measurements
919 Statistical methods
Crystal structure and growth
Including crystal lattices, defects, and dislocations
For lattice dynamics see QC176.8.L3
Cf. QD548 Crystallization in solutions
Cf. QD549.2.C64 Colloidal crystals
921 General works
923 Liquid crystals
Including polymer liquid crystals
Cf. QC173.4.L55 Physics
Cf. TP1180.P666 Chemical technology
924 Photonic crystals
925 Polycrystals
926 Quasicrystals
Cf. QC173.4.Q36 Physics
Physical properties of crystals
Cf. QC176+ Solids, solid state physics
931 General works
933 Mechanical properties
Including cohension, elasticity, plasticity, cleavage, hardness
937 Thermal properties

Crystallography
Physical properties of crystals -- Continued
939 Electric properties
Cf. QC595 Pyroelectricity
Cf. QC595.5 Piezoelectricity
940 Magnetic properties
941 Optical properties
Including isotropy, anisotropy, refractivity, reflectivity, crystal rotation
Cf. QC440+ Polarization
945 X-ray crystallography
947 Other physical properties (not A-Z)
951 Chemical crystallography
Including relationships between structure and bonding, isomorphism, polymorphism, pseudomorphism
999 Miscellany and curiosa

Geology
  For economic geology and mineral resources see TN1+
  Cf. QB603.G46 Planetary geology
  Cf. QH343.4 Geobiology
  Cf. TA703+ Engineering geology
  Cf. UG465+ Military geology

1 Periodicals, societies, congresses, serial publications
3 Collected works (nonserial)
4 Voyages and expeditions
5 Dictionaries and encyclopedias
6 Philosophy
7 Nomenclature, terminology, notation, abbreviations
History
11 General works
13.A-Z By region or country, A-Z
Biography
21 Collective
22.A-Z Individual, A-Z
e.g.
22.D25 Dana, James Dwight
22.L8 Lyell, Charles
22.S77 Steno, Nicolaus
23 Directories
25 Early works through 1800
General works, treatises, and advanced textbooks
26 1801-1969
26.2 1970-2000
26.3 2001-
Elementary textbooks
28 General
28.2 Physical geology
28.3 Historical geology
29 Juvenile works
31 Popular works
33 Special aspects of the subject as a whole
33.2.A-Z Special topics, A-Z
33.2.A3 Aerial photography in geology
33.2.A7 Artificial satellites in geology
33.2.B6 Borings
33.2.C48 Chaotic behavior in systems
33.2.C5 Charts, diagrams, etc.
Computer simulation see QE48.8
Data processing see QE48.8
33.2.F73 Fractals
33.2.M3 Mathematical geology
33.2.P47 Periodicity
33.2.P7 Practical geology

Special topics, A-Z -- Continued
33.2.R33 Radar in earth sciences
33.2.R4 Remote sensing
33.2.S6 Spectrum analysis in geology
33.2.S82 Statistical methods
33.2.S9 Subsurface geology
33.2.T45 Thermal analysis
33.2.T7 Translating services. Translating
33.2.W38 Wavelets
34 Geology as a profession. Vocational guidance
35 Addresses, essays, lectures
36 Geological maps
Class here works on making, interpretation, and use of geological maps
For the maps themselves see G3200+
Special fields
37 Agricultural geology
Engineering geology see TA703+
38 Environmental geology
38.5 Forensic geology
Military geology see UG465+
39 Submarine geology
For submarine geology of a particular body of water, see QE350.2+
Cf. GC83+ Submarine topography
Cf. QE511.7 Sea-floor spreading
39.5.A-Z Other, A-Z
Paleobiology see QE719.8
39.5.P25 Paleoceanography
Paleoclimatology see QC884+
Paleoecology see QE720+
Paleogeography see QE501.4.P3
39.5.P27 Paleohydrology
39.5.P3 Paleolimnology
Paleomagnetism see QE501.4.P35
Paleopedology see QE473
Paleoseismology see QE539.2.P34
39.5.U7 Urban geology
For urban geology of a particular place see QE65+
Study and teaching. Research
40 General works
41 Outlines, syllabi
42 Problems, exercises, examinations
43 Models, diagrams, etc.
44 Laboratory manuals
45 Fieldwork
By region or country

QE

Study and teaching. Research
By region or country -- Continued
United States
47.A1 General works
47.A2-Z By region or state, A-Z
Subarrange each state by Table Q7
48.A-Z Other regions or countries, A-Z
Subarrange each country by Table Q7
48.6 Awards
48.8 Data processing
Including computer simulation
Communication in geology
48.85 General works
48.86 Information services
48.87 Computer network resources
Including the Internet
Laboratories
49.A1 General works
49.A3-Z By region or country, A-Z
Subarrange each country by Table Q6
49.5 Instruments and apparatus
50 Collection and preservation
Museums. Exhibitions
51.A1 General works
51.A2-Z By region or country, A-Z
Subarrange each country by Table Q5
52 Handbooks, tables, formulas, etc.
53 Miscellany and curiosa
55 Dealers' catalogs of specimens
61 Surveys (History, organization, etc.)
Geographical divisions
65 Miscellaneous regions
e.g. British empire
70 Arctic regions. Greenland
America
70.5 General works
North America
71 General works
United States
72 Surveys (General)
73 Surveys, before 1861
74 Surveys, 1865-1879
United States Geological Survey
75 General publications of the USGS
76 Works about the USGS
77 General works
Special regions

Geographical divisions
America
North America
United States
Special regions -- Continued
78 Lake region and Saint Lawrence
78.3 North. Northeast. East. Appalachian Mountains
78.5 South. Southeast
78.7 Central. Mississippi Valley
79 Western states. Rocky Mountains
79.5 Southwest
By state
Class counties, physiographic regions, etc. in the local number
Alabama
81 General works
82.A-Z Local, A-Z
Alaska
83 General works
84.A-Z Local, A-Z
Arizona
85 General works
86.A-Z Local, A-Z
Arkansas
87 General works
88.A-Z Local, A-Z
California
89 General works
90.A-Z Local, A-Z
Colorado
91 General works
92.A-Z Local, A-Z
Connecticut
93 General works
94.A-Z Local, A-Z
Delaware
95 General works
96.A-Z Local, A-Z
97 District of Columbia
Florida
99 General works
100.A-Z Local, A-Z
Georgia
101 General works
102.A-Z Local, A-Z
Hawaii see QE349.H3
Idaho

Geographical divisions
America
North America
United States
By state
Idaho -- Continued

103	General works
104.A-Z	Local, A-Z
	Illinois
105	General works
106.A-Z	Local, A-Z
	Indiana
109	General works
110.A-Z	Local, A-Z
	Iowa
111	General works
112.A-Z	Local, A-Z
	Kansas
113	General works
114.A-Z	Local, A-Z
	Kentucky
115	General works
116.A-Z	Local, A-Z
	Louisiana
117	General works
118.A-Z	Local, A-Z
	Maine
119	General works
120.A-Z	Local, A-Z
	Maryland
121	General works
122.A-Z	Local, A-Z
	Massachusetts
123	General works
124.A-Z	Local, A-Z
	Michigan
125	General works
126.A-Z	Local, A-Z
	Minnesota
127	General works
128.A-Z	Local, A-Z
	Mississippi
129	General works
130.A-Z	Local, A-Z
	Missouri
131	General works
132.A-Z	Local, A-Z

Geographical divisions
America
North America
United States
By state -- Continued
Montana
133 General works
134.A-Z Local, A-Z
Nebraska
135 General works
136.A-Z Local, A-Z
Nevada
137 General works
138.A-Z Local, A-Z
New Hampshire
139 General works
140.A-Z Local, A-Z
New Jersey
141 General works
142.A-Z Local, A-Z
New Mexico
143 General works
144.A-Z Local, A-Z
New York
145 General works
146.A-Z Local, A-Z
North Carolina
147 General works
148.A-Z Local, A-Z
North Dakota
149 General works
150.A-Z Local, A-Z
Ohio
151 General works
152.A-Z Local, A-Z
Oklahoma
153 General works
154.A-Z Local, A-Z
Oregon
155 General works
156.A-Z Local, A-Z
Pennsylvania
157 General works
158.A-Z Local, A-Z
Rhode Island
159 General works
160.A-Z Local, A-Z

Geographical divisions
America
North America
United States
By state -- Continued
South Carolina
161 General works
162.A-Z Local, A-Z
South Dakota
163 General works
164.A-Z Local, A-Z
Tennessee
165 General works
166.A-Z Local, A-Z
Texas
167 General works
168.A-Z Local, A-Z
Utah
169 General works
170.A-Z Local, A-Z
Vermont
171 General works
172.A-Z Local, A-Z
Virginia
173 General works
174.A-Z Local, A-Z
Washington (State)
175 General works
176.A-Z Local, A-Z
West Virginia
177 General works
178.A-Z Local, A-Z
Wisconsin
179 General works
180.A-Z Local, A-Z
Wyoming
181 General works
182.A-Z Local, A-Z
Canada
185 General works
186 Alberta
187 British Columbia
188 Manitoba
189 New Brunswick
190 Nova Scotia
191 Ontario
192 Prince Edward Island

Geographical divisions
America
North America
Canada -- Continued
193 Québec (Province)
194 Saskatchewan
195 Yukon
196.A-Z Other northern territories, A-Z
(196.B3) Baffin Island
see QE196.N86
196.F7 Franklin
196.H8 Hudson Bay
(196.K4) Keewatin
see QE196.N86
Labrador see QE199
196.N7 Northwest Territories
Including Mackenzie
196.N86 Nunavut
Including Baffin Island, Keewatin
Ungava see QE193
199 Newfoundland and Labrador
Latin America
200 General works
Mexico
201 General works
203.A-Z Local, A-Z
Central America
210 General works
211 Belize
212 Costa Rica
213 Guatemala
214 Honduras
215 Nicaragua
216 Panama
217 El Salvador
West Indies. Caribbean Area
220 General works
221 Bahamas
222 Cuba
223 Haiti
224 Jamaica
225 Puerto Rico
226.A-Z Other islands, A-Z
229 Bermuda
South America
230 General works
231 Argentina

Geographical divisions
America
Latin America
South America -- Continued
233 Bolivia
235 Brazil
237 Chile
239 Colombia
241 Ecuador
Guianas
243 General works
243.2 Guyana (British Guiana)
243.3 Suriname (Dutch Guiana)
243.4 French Guiana
245 Paraguay
247 Peru
249 Uruguay
251 Venezuela
South Atlantic islands
256 General works
257 Falkland Islands
258.A-Z Other South Atlantic islands, A-Z
e.g.
258.S6 South Georgia Island
260 Europe
Great Britain
261 General works
England and Wales
262.A1 General works
262.A3-Z Local, A-Z
e.g.
262.A6 Anglesey
262.B75 Broads, The
262.D36 Dean, Forest of
262.E3 England
262.G5 Gloucestershire
262.L2 Lake District
262.M2 Man, Isle of
262.P8 Purbeck, Isle of
262.W2 Wales
262.W6 Wight, Isle of
264 Scotland
265 Ireland
266 Austria
266.2 Hungary
267 Czechoslovakia. Czech Republic
267.15 Slovakia

Geographical divisions
Europe -- Continued

267.2 Liechtenstein
268 France
269 Germany
271 Greece
272 Italy
272.5 Malta
273 Netherlands
274 Belgium
275 Luxembourg
276 Soviet Union. Russia (Federation)
Cf. QE315 Central Asia
276.3 Finland
276.5 Poland
Baltic States
276.7 General works
276.72 Estonia
276.74 Latvia
276.76 Lithuania
277 Scandinavia
278 Denmark
278.5 Faroe Islands
279 Iceland
281 Norway
282 Sweden
283 Spain
284 Portugal. Azores
285 Switzerland. Alps
Balkan States
287 General works
287.2 Albania
287.4 Bulgaria
287.6 Romania
287.8 Yugoslavia
288.A-Z Other regions or countries of Europe, A-Z
288.A33 Aegean Islands (Greece and Turkey)
288.B35 Baltic Sea Region
288.B38 Belarus
288.C276 Carpathian Mountains
288.C46 Central Europe
288.D56 Dinaric Alps
288.K75 Krkonoše (Czech Republic and Poland)
288.M629 Moldova
288.P36 Pannonia Region
288.P97 Pyrenees
288.S55 Silesia, Upper

Geographical divisions
Europe
Other regions or countries of Europe, A-Z -- Continued
288.U38 Ukraine
Asia
289 General works
290 Afghanistan
Arabian Peninsula
291.A1 General works
291.A3-Z By region or country, A-Z
291.A3 Aden
291.K9 Kuwait
291.M9 Muscat and Oman. Oman
Oman see QE291.M9
291.S28 Saudi Arabia
294 China
294.3 Taiwan
294.5 Mongolia
295 India
295.2 Burma. Myanmar
295.3 Sri Lanka
295.4 Pakistan
295.5 Bangladesh
296 Indochina
298 Thailand
299 Malay Peninsula. Straits Settlements
299.5 Malaysia
Indonesia. Dutch East Indies
301.A1 General works
301.A3-Z By region, island, etc., A-Z
e.g.
301.A5 Amboina
301.B7 Borneo
301.C4 Celebese
301.C45 Ceram
(301.D8) Dutch East Indies
see QE301.A1
301.J4 Java
301.K3 Kabaena Island
301.M7 Moluccas
301.S9 Sumatra
301.S94 Sunda Islands
301.T5 Timor
302 Philippines
304 Japan
305 Korea
Including South Korea

Geographical divisions
Asia -- Continued
305.2 North Korea
307 Iran
307.2 Iraq
315 Soviet Central Asia. Central Asia. Siberia
Cf. QE276 Russia (Federation)
316 Turkey
317 Armenia
318 Israel. Palestine
318.2 Jordan
318.3 Lebanon
318.4 Syria
319.A-Z Other regions or countries, A-Z
319.B46 Bengal Basin
319.C9 Cyprus
319.G35 Gangetic Plain
319.H5 Himalaya Mountains
319.N4 Near East. Middle East
319.O54 Oman Mountains (Oman and United Arab Emirates)
319.S67 Southeast Asia
319.5 Arab countries (General)
Africa
320 General works
321 Ethiopia
Former British possessions
325 South Africa
325.5 Central Africa (General)
326 East Africa (General)
327.A-Z Other, A-Z
327.B3 Basutoland. Lesotho.
327.B4 Bechuanaland. Botswana
Cameroon see QE339.C35
327.G6 Ghana. Gold Coast
327.K4 Kenya
Lesotho see QE327.B3
Malawi see QE327.N8
327.N5 Nigeria
327.N8 Nyasaland. Malawi
327.R55 Northern Rhodesia. Zambia
327.R6 Rhodesia, Southern. Zimbabwe
327.S2 Saint Helena
327.S5 Sierra Leone
327.S6 Sokotra (Yemen)
327.S77 Sudan
327.S8 Swaziland
327.T3 Tanzania. Tanganyika

Geographical divisions
Africa
Former British possessions
Other, A-Z -- Continued
327.U4 Uganda
West Cameroon see QE339.C35
Zambia see QE327.R55
327.Z3 Zanzibar
Zimbabwe see QE327.R6
328 Egypt
Former French possessions
329 Algeria
329.2 Tunisia
330 Madagascar
331.A-Z Other, A-Z
331.B45 Benin
Burkina Faso see QE331.U64
Cameroun see QE339.C35
Central African Republic see QE331.U2
331.C53 Chad
Côte d'Ivoire see QE331.I9
Dahomey see QE331.B45
331.D5 Djibouti
331.F65 French Equatorial Africa
French Somaliland see QE331.D5
331.F7 French West Africa
331.G3 Gabon
331.G8 Guinea
331.I9 Ivory Coast. Côte d'Ivoire
331.M27 Mali
331.M3 Mauritania
Morocco see QE339.M8
331.N5 Niger
331.U2 Ubangi-Shari. Central African Republic
331.U64 Upper Volta. Burkina Faso
332 Former German possessions
Cf. QE339.C35 Kamerun
334 Former Italian possessions. Libya
335 Congo (Democratic Republic). Zaire
335.5 Congo (Brazzaville)
Former Portuguese possessions
337 General works
337.3 Mozambique
337.5 Angola
337.6 Cape Verde
337.7 Guinea-Bissau
338 Spanish possessions

	Geographical divisions
	Africa -- Continued
339.A-Z	Other regions or countries, A-Z
339.B85	Burundi
339.C35	Cameroon
339.L5	Liberia
339.M8	Morocco
339.N34	Namibia
339.N66	Northeast Africa
339.N67	Northwest Africa
339.R85	Rwanda
339.S2	Sahara
339.S6	Somalia
339.S68	Southern Africa
339.S8	Sub-Saharan Africa
339.W46	West Africa
	Indian Ocean islands
339.5	General works
339.6.A-Z	By region, island, etc., A-Z
339.6.M35	Maldives
339.6.R48	Réunion
339.6.S48	Seychelles
	Australasia
339.8	General works
	Australia
340	General works
341	New South Wales
(342)	New Zealand see QE348.2
343	North Australia. Northern Territory
344	Queensland
345	South Australia
346	Tasmania
347	Victoria
348	Western Australia
348.2	New Zealand
348.4	Papua New Guinea
349.A-Z	Pacific islands, A-Z e.g.
349.F5	Fiji
349.H3	Hawaii
349.M35	Marshall Islands
349.N43	New Hebrides. Vanuatu
349.O4	Oceania
349.S64	Solomon Islands
349.T66	Tonga
350	Antarctica

QE

Geographical divisions -- Continued
Atlantic Ocean
350.2 General works
350.22.A-Z Local major divisions, A-Z
350.22.B34 Baltic Sea
350.22.B37 Barents Sea
350.22.B55 Black Sea
350.22.B65 Bothnian Sea
350.22.C37 Caribbean Sea
350.22.E52 English Channel
350.22.G53 Gibraltar, Straits of
350.22.G73 Greenland-Iceland Sea
350.22.L33 Labrador Sea
350.22.M32 Maine, Gulf of
350.22.M42 Mediterranean Sea
350.22.M48 Mexico, Gulf of
350.22.M5 Mid-Atlantic Bight
350.22.M52 Mid-Atlantic Ridge
350.22.N65 North Atlantic Ocean
350.22.N67 North Sea
350.22.N68 Norwegian Sea
350.22.R48 Reykjanes Ridge
350.22.S68 South Atlantic Ocean
Straits of Gibraltar see QE350.22.G53
Pacific Ocean
350.4 General works
350.42.A-Z Local major divisions, A-Z
350.42.A43 Alaska, Gulf of
350.42.B45 Bering Sea Region
350.42.C45 China Sea
350.42.E27 East China Sea
350.42.J34 Japan Sea
350.42.N65 North Pacific
350.42.O44 Okhotsk Sea
350.42.P45 Philippine Sea
350.42.S66 South China Sea
350.42.S68 South Pacific Ocean
350.42.T37 Tasman Sea
Indian Ocean
350.5 General works
350.52.A-Z Local major divisions, A-Z
350.52.A73 Arabian Sea
350.52.R43 Red Sea
Arctic Ocean
350.6 General works
350.62.A-Z Local major divisions, A-Z
350.62.C45 Chukchi Sea

	Mineralogy
	For crystallography see QD901+
	Cf. QB455.2 Astromineralogy
351	Periodicals, societies, congresses, serial publications
353	Collected works (nonserial)
355	Dictionaries and encyclopedias
357	Nomenclature, terminology, notation, abbreviations
	History
359.A1	General works
359.A2-Z	By region or country, A-Z
	Biography
361.A2	Collective
361.A3-Z	Individual, A-Z
	e.g.
361.C5	Clarke
	Dana, James Dwight see QE22.D25
361.H2	Haidinger
361.2	Directories
362	Early works through 1800
	General works, treatises, and textbooks
363	1801-1969
363.2	1970-
363.8	Pictorial works and atlases
364	Special aspects of the subject as a whole
364.2.A-Z	Special topics, A-Z
364.2.E4	Electronic data processing
364.2.F47	Fluid inclusions
364.2.F5	Fluorescent minerals
364.2.H4	Heavy minerals
364.2.H54	High pressure
364.2.M37	Metallogeny
364.2.M4	Metasomatism
364.2.P3	Paragenesis
364.2.R3	Radioactive minerals
	Rock-forming minerals see QE397
364.2.S7	Statistical methods
364.2.S87	Surfaces
364.2.T45	Thermodynamics
365	Popular works
365.2	Juvenile works
366	Study and teaching. Research
	Mineralogical laboratories
366.15	General works
366.16.A-Z	By region or country, A-Z
	Subarrange each country by Table Q6

Mineralogy -- Continued
366.2 Collection and preservation
For mineral collecting in specific geographic regions see QE373+
366.8 Handbooks, tables, formulas, etc.
Determinative mineralogy
For assaying see TN550+
Cf. QD87 Blowpipe analysis
General works, treatises, and textbooks
367 1801-1969
367.2 1970-
368.9 Special aspects of the subject as a whole
369.A-Z Special topics, A-Z
369.C6 Colloidal determinations
369.D5 Differential thermal analysis
369.F4 Fedorovskii method
369.I55 Immersion method
369.M5 Microscopic determinations
369.O6 Optical determinations
369.P49 Physical properties
369.S6 Specific gravity determinations
369.S65 Spectrum analysis
369.U4 Ultraviolet
369.X2 X-ray powder
371 Mineralogical chemistry
Descriptive mineralogy
General works, treatises, and textbooks
372 1801-1969
372.2 1970-
Geographical divisions
North America
373 General works
United States
375 General works
375.5.A-Z By region or state, A-Z
Canada
376 General works
376.5.A-Z By region, province, or territory, A-Z
Mexico
377 General works
377.5.A-Z By region or state, A-Z
Central America
377.7.A1 General works
377.7.A3-Z By region, country, or island, A-Z
Offshore islands generally class with adjacent mainland
West Indies. Caribbean Area
378.A1 General works

Mineralogy
Descriptive mineralogy
Geographical divisions
North America
West Indies. Caribbean Area -- Continued
378.A3-Z By region, country, or island, A-Z
Offshore islands generally class with adjacent mainland
South America
379.A1 General works
379.A3-Z By region, country, or island, A-Z
Offshore islands generally class with adjacent mainland
Europe
381.A1 General works
381.A3-Z By region, country, or island, A-Z
Offshore islands generally class with adjacent mainland
Asia
382.A1 General works
382.A3-Z By region, country, or island, A-Z
Offshore islands generally class with adjacent mainland
Africa
383.A1 General works
383.A3-Z By region, country, or island, A-Z
Offshore islands generally class with adjacent mainland
Australia
384 General works
384.2.A-Z By region, state, or territory, A-Z
New Zealand
384.5 General works
384.7.A-Z By region or statistical area, A-Z
Pacific islands
385.A1 General works
385.A3-Z By region, country, or island, A-Z
Offshore islands generally class with adjacent mainland
Arctic regions
385.5.A1 General works
385.5.A3-Z By region, country, or island, A-Z
Offshore islands generally class with adjacent mainland
Antarctica
385.6.A1 General works
385.6.A3-Z By region, country, or island, A-Z
Offshore islands generally class with adjacent mainland
Museums. Exhibitions
386.A1 General works
386.A2-Z By region or country, A-Z
Subarrange each country by Table Q5
387 Dealers' catalogs of specimens
388 Classification

	Mineralogy -- Continued
	Special groups of minerals
	Descriptive and determinative
389	General works
389.1	Native elements
389.2	Sulfides, selenides, tellurides, arsenides, antimonides
389.3	Sulfo salts (Sulfarsenites, sulfantimonites, sulfobismuthites)
389.4	Halides (Chlorides, bromides, iodides, fluorides)
389.5	Oxides
	Oxygen salts
389.6	General works
389.61	Carbonates
	Silicates, titanates
389.62	General works
389.625	Clay minerals
389.63	Niobates, tantalates
389.64	Phosphates, arsenates, vanadates, antimonates, nitrates
389.65	Borates, uranates
389.66	Sulfates, chromates, tellurates
389.67	Tungstates, molybdates
389.7	Salts of organic acids: oxalates, mellates, etc.
	Hydrocarbon compounds
389.8	General works
	Coal see TN805+
	Petroleum see TN870.5+
	Ore minerals (General)
390	General works
390.2.A-Z	Special ore minerals, A-Z
390.2.A58	Antimony ores
390.2.B46	Beryllium ores
390.2.B67	Boron ores
390.2.C58	Cobalt ores
390.2.C6	Copper ores
390.2.G65	Gold ores
390.2.I76	Iron ores
390.2.L43	Lead ores
390.2.L57	Lithium ores
390.2.M35	Manganese ores
390.2.M47	Mercury ores
390.2.N53	Nickel ores
390.2.P56	Platinum ores
390.2.R37	Rare earth ores
390.2.S55	Silver ores
390.2.T42	Tellurium ores
390.2.T45	Thorium ores
390.2.T48	Tin ores
390.2.T5	Titanium ores

Mineralogy
Special groups of minerals
Ore minerals (General)
Special ore minerals, A-Z -- Continued

390.2.T85	Tungsten ores
390.2.U7	Uranium ores
390.2.V36	Vanadium ores
390.2.Z54	Zinc ores
390.5	Hydrothermal deposits. Hydrothermal alteration
391.A-Z	Description of special minerals, A-Z
391.A18	Acmite
391.A2	Actinolite
	Agate see QE391.Q2
391.A4	Allanite
391.A45	Alunite
391.A48	Amazonite
391.A5	Amber
391.A53	Amphiboles
391.A55	Analcime
391.A57	Andesine
391.A572	Andorite
391.A573	Anhydrite
391.A6	Apatite
391.A8	Augite
391.B2	Babingtonite
391.B35	Barite
391.B5	Benitoite
391.B55	Bentonite
391.B6	Beryl
391.B64	Biotite
391.B7	Bøggildite
391.B73	Boehmite
391.B75	Botryogen
391.B78	Brannerite
391.B82	Brucite
391.C2	Calcite
391.C25	Cassiterite
391.C3	Celadonite
391.C32	Celestite
391.C35	Chalcocite
391.C38	Chalybite
391.C392	Chamosite
391.C396	Charoite
391.C4	Chert
391.C5	Chlorite
391.C6	Chondrodite
391.C65	Chromite

Mineralogy

Description of special minerals, A-Z -- Continued

391.C657	Chrysoberyl
391.C67	Chrysotile
391.C8	Colemanite
391.C84	Cookeite
391.C9	Corundum
391.C94	Cuprodescloizite
391.D3	Datolite
391.D6	Dolomite
391.D8	Durangite
391.E43	Electrum
391.E5	Endlichite
391.E6	Enstatite
391.E8	Epidote
391.E9	Evansite
391.F3	Feldspar
391.F4	Ferberite
391.F45	Ferrierite
	Flint see QE471.15.F47
391.F6	Fluorspar
391.G3	Galena
391.G37	Garnet
391.G5	Glauconite
391.G55	Gmelinite
391.G6	Gold
391.G8	Gunnbjarnite
391.G93	Gypsum
391.H34	Hedenbergite
391.H38	Helvite
391.H4	Hematite
391.H5	Hercynite
391.H55	Heulandite
391.H8	Hortonolite
391.H84	Huebnerite
	Iceland spar see QE391.C2
	Idocrase see QE391.V55
391.I4	Ilimaussite
391.I44	Ilmenite
391.I53	Indianite
391.I7	Iron
	Jade see QE394.J3
391.J25	Jarosite
	Jasper see QE391.Q2
391.K2	Kaolinite
391.L28	Lawsonite
391.L3	Lazurite

Mineralogy

Description of special minerals, A-Z -- Continued

391.L4	Leucite
	Leucoxene see QE396
391.L5	Liebigite
391.L8	Ludwigite
391.M2	Magnesite
391.M22	Magnetite
391.M25	Malachite
391.M3	Marcasite
391.M34	Meerschaum
391.M4	Melanosiderite
391.M45	Merumite
391.M6	Mica
391.M67	Moissanite
391.M7	Molybdenite
391.M75	Monazite
391.M8	Mordenite
391.M85	Muscovite
391.N27	Natrolite
391.N3	Naujakasite
	Nephrite see QE391.A2
391.O45	Olvine
	Opal see QE394.O7
	Palacheite see QE391.B75
391.P34	Palygorskite
391.P44	Pecoraite
391.P47	Perovskite
391.P48	Petalite
391.P5	Pickeringite
391.P55	Plagioclase
391.P56	Pollucite
391.P8	Pyrophyllite
391.P84	Pyroxene
391.P86	Pyroxmangite
391.P9	Pyrrhotite
391.Q2	Quartz
	Ramirite see QE391.C94
391.R5	Riebeckite
391.R7	Roscoelite
391.R88	Rutile
391.S25	Sapphirine
391.S28	Scapolite
391.S3	Scheelite
	Schungite see QE475.S39
	Sepiolite see QE391.M34
391.S47	Serpentine

Mineralogy
Description of special minerals, A-Z -- Continued

391.S49 Siderite
391.S5 Sillimanite
391.S6 Smectite
391.S65 Sphalerite
391.S67 Sphene
391.S68 Spinel
391.S7 Spodumene
391.S73 Stannite
391.S75 Staurolite
391.S77 Stenonite
391.S8 Stichtite
391.T2 Talc
391.T3 Tephroite
391.T4 Tetradymite
391.T6 Topaz
391.T7 Tourmaline
391.T8 Trona
391.T85 Tugtupite
391.U65 Uraninite
Uranothallite see QE391.L5
391.V35 Vanadinite
391.V5 Vermiculite
391.V55 Vesuvianite
391.V6 Villiaumite
391.V64 Vivianite
391.V68 Volkonskoite
391.W3 Wagnerite
391.W6 Wolframite
391.W66 Wollastonite
391.Z5 Zeolites
391.Z7 Zircon
391.Z8 Zoisite

Precious stones
Cf. NK7650+ Art industries
Cf. TN980+ Mining
Cf. TS747+ Jewelry manufacture

392 General works, treatises, and textbooks
392.2 Juvenile works
392.5.A-Z By region or country, A-Z
393 Diamonds
394.A-Z Other precious stones, A-Z
394.A4 Amethysts
394.E5 Emeralds
394.J3 Jade
394.J46 Jet

Mineralogy
Precious stones
Other precious stones, A-Z -- Continued
394.O7 Opals
394.R8 Rubies
394.S3 Sapphires
394.T8 Turquoise
396 Leucoxene
397 Rock-forming minerals
Meteorites see QB754.8+
399 Tektites
For fluorescent minerals see QE364.2.F5
399.2 Miscellany and curiosa
Petrology
Cf. TN950+ Building stones
420 Periodicals, societies, congresses, serial publications
421 Collected works (nonserial)
423 Dictionaries and encyclopedias
425 Nomenclature, terminology, notation, abbreviations
425.4 Classification
History
427.A1 General works
427.A2-Z By region or country, A-Z
430 Early works through 1800
General works, treatises, and textbooks
431 1801-1969
431.2 1970-
431.5 Special aspects of the subject as a whole
431.6.A-Z Special topics, A-Z
431.6.A25 Acoustic properties
431.6.E4 Electric properties
431.6.M3 Magnetic properties
431.6.M4 Mechanical properties
431.6.O7 Ores
431.6.P4 Petrogenesis
431.6.P5 Physical properties
431.6.P6 Porosity
431.6.T45 Thermal properties
431.6.W38 Water-rock interaction
432 Popular works
432.2 Juvenile works
432.5 Addresses, essays, lectures
Study and teaching. Research
432.7 General works
433 Laboratory manuals
433.5 Instruments and apparatus

Petrology -- Continued

433.6 Collection and preservation

For rock collecting in specific geographic regions see QE443+

433.7 Data processing

433.8 Handbooks, tables, formulas, etc.

434 Microscopic analysis of rocks. Thin sections

435 X-ray petrology

438 Chemical analysis of rocks

440 Petrofabric analysis

Including petrofabric diagrams

Museums. Exhibitions

442.A1 General works

442.A2-Z By region or country, A-Z

Subarrange each country by Table Q5

Geographical divisions

North America

443 General works

United States

444 General works

445.A-Z By region or state, A-Z

Canada

445.5 General works

446.A-Z By region or province, A-Z

Mexico

446.5 General works

446.6.A-Z By region or state, A-Z

Central America

447.A1 General works

447.A3-Z By region, country, or island, A-Z

Offshore islands generally class with adjacent mainland

West Indies. Caribbean Area

448.A1 General works

448.A3-Z By region, country, or island, A-Z

Offshore islands generally class with adjacent mainland

South America

449.A1 General works

449.A3-Z By region, country, or island, A-Z

Offshore islands generally class with adjacent mainland

Europe

451.A1 General works

451.A3-Z By region, country, or island, A-Z

Offshore islands generally class with adjacent mainland

Asia

452.A1 General works

452.A3-Z By region, country, or island, A-Z

Offshore islands generally class with adjacent mainland

Petrology
Geographical divisions -- Continued
Africa
453.A1 General works
453.A3-Z By region, country, or island, A-Z
Offshore islands generally class with adjacent mainland
Indian Ocean islands
453.2 General works
453.3.A-Z By region, country, or island, A-Z
Offshore islands generally class with adjacent mainland
Australia
453.5 General works
454.A-Z By region, state, or territory, A-Z
New Zealand
454.5 General works
454.6.A-Z By region or statistical area, A-Z
Pacific islands
455.A1 General works
455.A3-Z By region, country, or island, A-Z
Offshore islands generally class with adjacent mainland
Arctic regions
456.A1 General works
456.A3-Z By region, country, or island, A-Z
Offshore islands generally class with adjacent mainland
Antarctica
456.5.A1 General works
456.5.A3-Z By region, country, or island, A-Z
Offshore islands generally class with adjacent mainland
Igneous rocks, volcanic ash, tuff, etc.
461 General works
462.A-Z Special, A-Z
462.A35 Alaskite
462.A37 Albitite
462.A4 Alkalic igneous rocks
462.A5 Andesite
462.A55 Anorthosite
462.A63 Aplite
462.B3 Basalt
462.B65 Boninite
462.C36 Carbonatites
462.C5 Charnockite
462.D5 Diabase
462.D56 Diorite
462.F4 Fenite
462.G3 Gabbro
462.G7 Granite
462.G75 Granodiorite

	Petrology
	Igneous rocks, volcanic ash, tuff, etc.
	Special, A-Z -- Continued
462.G77	Greenstone
462.H67	Hornblendite
462.I35	Ignimbrite
462.K44	Keratophyre
462.K5	Kimberlite
462.K66	Komatiite
462.L35	Lamproite
462.L37	Latite
462.L48	Leucitite
462.M6	Monzonite
462.N4	Nepheline syenite
462.O28	Obsidian
462.O43	Olivinite
462.O6	Ophiolites
462.O73	Orangeite
462.P4	Pegmatites
462.P43	Pegmatoids
462.P45	Peridotite
462.P6	Porphyry
462.P7	Propylite
462.R4	Rhyolite
	Serpentinite see QE475.S47
462.S65	Spilites
462.S95	Syenite
462.T74	Trondhjemite
462.U4	Ultrabasic rocks
462.V64	Volcanite
	Sedimentary rocks. Sedimentology
	For sedimentation see QE571+
471	General works
471.15.A-Z	Special, A-Z
471.15.A68	Arenites
471.15.A7	Arkose
471.15.B32	Bauxite
471.15.B34	Beachrock
471.15.B4	Bentonite
471.15.B7	Breccia
471.15.C27	Calcretes
471.15.C3	Carbonate rocks
471.15.C4	Chert
471.15.C58	Concretions
471.15.C6	Conglomerate
471.15.D6	Dolomite
471.15.E8	Evaporites

	Petrology
	Sedimentary rocks. Sedimentology
	Special, A-Z -- Continued
471.15.F47	Flint
471.15.F5	Flysch
471.15.G4	Geodes
471.15.L5	Limestone
471.15.M44	Melanges
471.15.M83	Mudstone
471.15.O5	Oolite
	Phosphate rock see QE471.15.P48
471.15.P48	Phosphorite. Phosphate rock
471.15.S2	Salt
471.15.S25	Sandstone
471.15.S5	Shale
471.15.S54	Siltstone
471.15.T5	Tillite
471.15.T64	Tonsteins
471.15.T73	Travertine
471.15.T8	Turbidites
471.2	Sediments (Unconsolidated)
471.3	Clay
472	Sedimentary structures
473	Paleopedology
	Metamorphic rocks. Metamorphism
475.A2	General works, treatises, and textbooks
475.A3-Z	Special, A-Z
475.A4	Amphibolite
475.E25	Eclogite
475.G55	Gneiss
475.G7	Granulite
475.J27	Jadeite
475.J3	Jasperoid
475.L57	Listwanite
475.M3	Marble
475.M45	Metabasite
475.M5	Migmatite
475.M95	Mylonite
475.P47	Phyllite
475.Q3	Quartzite
475.S3	Schist
475.S39	Schungite
475.S47	Serpentinite
475.S6	Soapstone
475.T33	Tactite
475.T43	Tectonite
495	Laterite

Petrology -- Continued

496 Saprolites

499 Miscellany and curiosa

Dynamic and structural geology

Physical and tectonic

500 Periodicals, societies, congresses, serial publications

500.5 History

501 General works, treatises, and textbooks

Including physical history of the earth

501.2 Popular works

501.25 Juvenile works

501.3 Special aspects of the subject as a whole

501.4.A-Z Special topics, A-Z

Isotope geology see QE501.4.N9

501.4.M38 Mathematics

501.4.M6 Mohole project

501.4.N9 Nuclear geology. Isotope geology

501.4.P3 Paleogeography

501.4.P35 Paleomagnetism

Paleoweathering see QE570

501.4.P6 Polar wandering

501.4.R45 Remote sensing

501.4.U6 Upper mantle project

505 Addresses, essays, lectures

505.5 Study and teaching. Research

506 Geological cosmogony

507 Deluge, etc.

508 Geological time. Age of the earth

Including age determination, radioactive dating

Interior of the earth. Internal structure of the earth

509 General works

509.2 Core

509.3 Core-mantle boundary

509.4 Mantle

509.5 Temperature

511 Earth's crust. Isostasy

Including continental crust, cratons, and glacial isostasy

Cf. QB331 Gravity determinations

511.2 Island arcs

Plate tectonics

511.4 General works

511.42 Neotectonics

511.44 Morphotectonics

511.46 Subduction zones

511.48 Suture zones

511.5 Continental drift

Including Gondwana, Pangaea

Dynamic and structural geology -- Continued
511.7 Sea-floor spreading
512 Epeirogeny
513 Salt tectonics
Geochemistry
Cf. QH343.7+ Biogeochemistry
514 Periodicals, societies, congresses, serial publications
Biography
514.6 Collective
514.62.A-Z Individual, A-Z
515 General works, treatises, and textbooks
515.5.A-Z Special topics, A-Z
515.5.D37 Data processing
515.5.G43 Geochemical modeling
515.5.G45 Geochemical self-organization
515.5.K55 Kinetics
515.5.R45 Remote sensing
515.5.T46 Thermodynamics
516.A-Z Special elements and groups of elements, A-Z (Table Q1 modified)
516.A35 Alkali metals
516.C37 Carbon
Including geological carbon sequestration
516.H3 Halogens
516.M65 Metals
516.R15 Radioactive substances
516.R2 Rare earth metals
516.R23 Rare gases
516.T85 Trace elements
516.3 Analytical geochemistry
516.4 Environmental geochemistry
Nuclear geochemistry see QE501.4.N9
516.5 Organic geochemistry
Dynamic geology
517 Periodicals, societies, congresses, serial publications
517.5 General works, treatises, and textbooks
Volcanoes and earthquakes
521 General works, treatises, and textbooks
521.2 Popular works
521.3 Juvenile works
Volcanoes. Volcanism
Including supervolcanoes
521.5 Periodicals, societies, congresses, serial publications
522 General works, treatises, and textbooks
523.A-Z Individual volcanoes, A-Z
Including individually named groups
e.g.

	Dynamic and structural geology
	Volcanoes and earthquakes
	Volcanoes. Volcanism
	Individual, A-Z -- Continued
523.P8	Popocatepetl
	Western Hemisphere. America
	Including Hawaii
524	General works
524.2.A-Z	By region or country, A-Z
	For individual volcanoes see QE523.A+
	Eastern Hemisphere. Europe, Africa
526	General works
526.2.A-Z	By region or country, A-Z
	For individual volcanoes see QE523.A+
	Eastern Hemisphere. Asia, Australasia
527	General works
527.2.A-Z	By region or country, A-Z
	For individual volcanoes see QE523.A+
527.3	Pacific Area (General)
527.4	Antarctica
527.5	Prediction of volcanic activity
527.55	Remote sensing
527.56	Tephrochronology
527.6	Volcanic hazard analysis. Safety measures
	For hazard analysis or safety measures in specific geographic regions see QE523+
527.7	Volcanic plumes
527.73	Lava flows
527.75	Volcanic gases and vapors
528	Geysers, hot springs, etc.
529	Miscellany and curiosa
	Earthquakes. Seismology
	Cf. TC181 Earthquakes and hydraulic structures
	Cf. TC542.5 Earthquakes and dams
	Cf. TF539 Damage to railroads
	Cf. TH1095 Earthquakes and building
531	Periodicals, societies, congresses, serial publications
532.A-Z	Observations. By name of issuing observatory, A-Z
	Including serial collections issued by individual observatories
533	Early works through 1800
	General works, treatises, and textbooks
534	1801-1969
534.2	1970-2000
534.3	2001-
	Special
	Western Hemisphere. America

Dynamic and structural geology
Volcanoes and earthquakes
Earthquakes. Seismology
Special
Western Hemisphere. America -- Continued

535 General works
535.2.A-Z By region or country, A-Z
Eastern Hemisphere. Europe, Africa
536 General works
536.2.A-Z By region or country, A-Z
Eastern Hemisphere. Asia, Australasia
537 General works
537.2.A-Z By region or country, A-Z
537.5 Pacific Area (General)
538 Antarctica
538.5 Seismic waves. Elastic waves
538.8 Earthquake prediction
539 Special aspects of the subject as a whole
539.2.A-Z Special topics, A-Z
539.2.A4 Aftershocks
539.2.D36 Data processing
539.2.E42 Elastic rebound theory
Hazard analysis see QE539.2.S34
539.2.I46 Induced seismicity
539.2.I5 Intensity
539.2.M37 Mathematics
539.2.M5 Microseisms
539.2.P34 Paleoseismology
539.2.P4 Periodicity
539.2.R45 Remote sensing
539.2.S34 Safety measures. Hazard analysis
For safety measures or hazard analysis in specific geographic regions, see QE535+
539.2.S37 Seismic event location
539.2.S4 Seismic models
539.2.S43 Seismic traveltime inversion
539.2.S73 Statistical methods
Observatories. Seismic networks
540.A2 General works
540.A5-Z By region or country, A-Z
Under each country:

.x	*General works*
.x2A-.x2Z	*Individual observatories. By name, A-Z*

541 Instruments. Seismometry
Including tables, calculations, siesmograms, etc.

Dynamic and structural geology
Volcanoes and earthquakes
Earthquakes. Seismology -- Continued
(545) Volcanic gases and vapors
see QE527.75
Coral islands and reefs. Atolls
Cf. GB461+ Geomorphology
565 General works
565.5.A-Z By region or country, A-Z
For individual coral reefs and islands see QE566.A+
566.A-Z Individual, A-Z
e.g.
566.F35 Fangataufa Atoll
566.G7 Great Barrier Reef (Qld.)
566.M87 Mururoa Atoll
570 Weathering
Including paleoweathering
Sedimentation
Including erosion and deposition
For sedimentary rocks and sedimentology see QE471+
571 General works
573 Cryopedology
Glacial erosion
Cf. GB581+ Glacial landforms
Cf. QE697+ Pleistocene
575 Periodicals, societies, congresses, serial publications
576 General works, treatises, and textbooks
578 Moraines, eskers, kames
579 Drift. Loess
581 Aqueous erosion
Cf. S622+ Agriculture
587 Eversion
597 Aerial erosion
Earth movements. Mass movements
For descriptive works, disasters, etc., see DA+
598 Periodicals, societies, congresses, serial publications
598.2 General works, treatises, and textbooks
598.3 Juvenile works
598.5.A-Z By region or country, A-Z
Landslides. Rockslides
Including mudflows and mudslides
599.A1 Periodicals, societies, congresses, serial publications
599.A2 General works, treatises, and textbooks
599.A5-Z By region or country, A-Z
599.2 Landslide hazard analysis
For hazard analysis in specific geographic regions
see QE599.A5+

Dynamic and structural geology
Earth movements. Mass movements -- Continued
Subsidences
600 Periodicals, societies, congresses, serial publications
600.2 General works, treatises, and textbooks
600.3.A-Z By region or country, A-Z
Structural geology
601 General works, treatises, and textbooks
601.2 Special aspects of the subject as a whole
601.3.A-Z Special topics, A-Z
601.3.D37 Data processing
601.3.M38 Mathematics
601.3.S83 Stereographic projection
601.8 Problems, exercises, examinations
602 Stratification
604 Deformation
605 Joints and cleavages
Faults and folds
606 General works, treatises, and textbooks
606.5.A-Z By region or country, A-Z
Geosynclines
607 General works, treatises, and textbooks
607.5.A-Z By region or country, A-Z
(608) Metamorphism
see QE475
Veins, dikes, necks, bosses, laccoliths, and other intrusive bodies
Cf. TN263 Ore deposits
611 General works, treatises, and textbooks
611.5.A-Z By region or country, A-Z
Impact craters
612 General works, treatises, and textbooks
612.5.A-Z By region or country, A-Z
Cryptoexplosion structures
613 General works, treatises, and textbooks
613.5.A-Z By region or country, A-Z
Basins. Sedimentary basins
615 General works, treatises, and textbooks
615.5.A-Z By region or country, A-Z
Mountain building. Orogeny
621 General works
621.5.A-Z By region or country, A-Z
625 Effects of plants, animals, and man in geology
Cf. QR103 Geomicrobiology
Geographical divisions
North America
626 General works

Dynamic and structural geology

Geographical divisions

North America -- Continued

United States

627 General works

627.5.A-Z By region or state, A-Z

Canada

628 General works

628.5.A-Z By region, province, or territory, A-Z

Mexico

629 General works

629.5.A-Z By region or state, A-Z

Central America

630.A1 General works

630.A3-Z By region, country, or island, A-Z

Offshore islands generally class with adjacent mainland

West Indies. Caribbean Area

631.A1 General works

631.A3-Z By region, country, or island, A-Z

Offshore islands generally class with adjacent mainland

South America

632.A1 General works

632.A3-Z By region, country, or island, A-Z

Offshore islands generally class with adjacent mainland

Europe

633.A1 General works

633.A3-Z By region, country, or island, A-Z

Offshore islands generally class with adjacent mainland

Asia

634.A1 General works

634.A3-Z By region, country, or island, A-Z

Offshore islands generally class with adjacent mainland

Africa

635.A1 General works

635.A3-Z By region, country, or island, A-Z

Offshore islands generally class with adjacent mainland

Australia

636 General works

636.5.A-Z By region, state, or territory, A-Z

New Zealand

637 General works

637.5.A-Z By region or statistical area, A-Z

Pacific islands

638.A1 General works

638.A3-Z By region, country, or island, A-Z

Offshore islands generally class with adjacent mainland

Arctic regions

Dynamic and structural geology
  Geographical divisions
    Arctic regions -- Continued
639.A1 General works
639.A3-Z By region, country, or island, A-Z
  Offshore islands generally class with adjacent mainland
    Antarctica
639.5.A1 General works
639.5.A3-Z By region, country, or island, A-Z
  Offshore islands generally class with adjacent mainland

Stratigraphy
  Prefer stratigraphic to geographical classification
  For historical geology see QE28.3
640 Periodicals, societies, congresses, serial publications
645 Nomenclature, terminology, notation, abbreviations
  Class here general works as well as works on the nomenclature of particular regions, countries, etc.
651 General works, treatises, and textbooks
651.5 Cyclostratigraphy
652 Data processing
  Stratigraphic correlation
652.5 General works
652.55.A-Z By region or country, A-Z
  Precambrian
653 General works
653.3 Archaean
653.5 Proterozoic
  Paleozoic
654 General works
(655) Algonkian. Huronian. Precambrian in general
  see QE653
656 Cambrian
660 Ordovician
  Silurian
661 General works
(662) Lower (Ordovician)
  see QE660
(663) Upper (Silurian)
  see QE661
665 Devonian
  Carboniferous
671 General works
672 Mississippian
673 Pennsylvanian
  Cf. TN799.9+ Coal
673.5 Permo-Carboniferous
674 Permian

QE

Stratigraphy -- Continued
Mesozoic
675 General works
Triassic
676 General works
677 Lower
678 Middle
679 Upper
Jurassic
681 General works
682 Lower
683 Middle
684 Upper
Cretaceous
685 General works
686 Lower
687 Middle
688 Upper
689 Cretaceous-Tertiary boundary
Cenozoic
690 General works
Tertiary
691 General works
Paleogene
691.5 General works
692 Paleocene
692.2 Eocene
692.8 Eocene-Oligocene boundary
693 Oligocene
Neogene
693.5 General works
694 Miocene
695 Pliocene
695.5 Pliocene-Pleistocene boundary
Quaternary
696 General works
Pleistocene. Glacial epoch
697 General works
698 Cause of the glacial epoch
699 Holocene, Recent
Geological climate see QE698
Paleoclimatology see QC884+
Paleontology
701 Periodicals, societies, congresses, serial publications
702 Collected works (nonserial)
703 Dictionaries and encyclopedias
Communication of information

Paleontology
Communication of information -- Continued
704 General works
704.2 Information services
704.3 Computer network resources
Including the Internet
History
705.A1 General works
705.A2-Z By region or country, A-Z
Biography
707.A2 Collective
Including directories
707.A3-Z Individual, A-Z
e.g.
707.T4 Teilhard de Chardin, Pierre
707.Z8 Zittel, K.A.
Early works
709 Through 1790
710 1791-1830
General works, treatises, and textbooks
Including stratigraphic paleontology
711 1831-1969
711.2 1970-2000
711.3 2001-
713 Comprehensive systematic works
Including both zoological and botanical works
714 Pictorial works and atlases
714.2 Paleoart
Including paleontological illustration
714.3 Popular works
714.5 Juvenile works
714.7 Paleontology as a profession. Vocational guidance
715 Study and teaching
Museums. Exhibitions
Class catalogs of special subjects with the subject, e.g. British Museum catalog of fossil fishes in QE851
716.A1 General works
716.A2-Z By region or country, A-Z
Subarrange each country by Table Q5

Paleontology -- Continued

718 Collection and preservation

Class here general works on collection and preservation of fossils

For works on collection by stratigraphic division see QE724+

For works on collection by geographic division see QE743+

For works on collection and preservation of individual fossils see QE767

Micropaleontology

For fossil biomolecules see QP517.F66

719 General works

719.5 Prokaryotes. Bacteria

719.6 Protista

Cf. QE771+ Protozoa

Cf. QE955 Algae

719.8 Paleobiology

Cf. QE721.2.E85 Evolutionary paleobiology

Paleoecology

720 General works

720.2.A-Z By region or country, A-Z

720.5 Ichnology. Trace fossils

721 Special aspects of the subject as a whole

721.2.A-Z Special topics, A-Z

721.2.D37 Data processing

721.2.E85 Evolutionary paleobiology

721.2.E87 Evolutionary paleoecology

721.2.E97 Extinction

721.2.F6 Fossilization. Taphonomy

721.2.M63 Models and modelmaking

721.2.P24 Paleobiogeography

721.2.P26 Paleontological excavations

For geographical divisions see QE743+

721.2.P3 Paleotemperatures

721.2.S7 Statistical methods

Taphonomy see QE721.2.F6

721.2.V3 Variation

723 Addresses, essays, lectures

Stratigraphic divisions (General and zoological)

Corresponding classes for stratigraphic geology in QE653+

Precambrian

724 General works

724.5 Proterozoic

Paleozoic

725 General works

726 Cambrian

Paleontology
Stratigraphic divisions (General and zoological)
Paleozoic -- Continued
726.2 Ordovician
727 Silurian
728 Devonian
Carboniferous
729 General works
729.2 Mississippian
729.3 Pennsylvanian
730 Permian
Mesozoic
731 General works
732 Triassic
733 Jurassic
734 Cretaceous
734.5 Cretaceous-Tertiary boundary
Cenozoic
735 General works
Tertiary
736 General works
Paleogene
736.5 General works
736.8 Paleocene
737 Eocene
738 Oligocene
Neogene
738.5 General works
739 Miocene
740 Pliocene
Quaternary
741 General works
741.2 Pleistocene
741.3 Holocene, Recent
742 Amber fauna and flora
Geographical divisions (General and zoological)
Prefer the stratigraphic divisions above to geographical divisions
743 General works
743.5 Ocean bottom
744 Arctic regions
North America
745 General works
United States
746 General works
747.A-Z By region or state, A-Z
Canada

Paleontology
Geographical divisions (General and zoological)
North America
Canada -- Continued

748.A1 General works
748.A3-Z By region or province, A-Z
Offshore islands generally class with adjacent mainland

Mexico
749.A1 General works
749.A3-Z By region or state, A-Z
Offshore islands generally class with adjacent mainland

West Indies and Bermuda
750.A1 General works
750.A3-Z By region, country, or island, A-Z
Offshore islands generally class with adjacent mainland

Central America
751.A1 General works
751.A3-Z By region, country, or island, A-Z
Offshore islands generally class with adjacent mainland

South America
752.A1 General works
752.A3-Z By region, country, or island, A-Z
Offshore islands generally class with adjacent mainland

Europe
753 General works
754 Great Britain
755.A-Z Other regions or countries, A-Z

Asia
756.A1 General works
756.A3-Z By region, country, or island, A-Z
Offshore islands generally class with adjacent mainland

Africa
757.A1 General works
757.A3-Z By region, country, or island, A-Z
Offshore islands generally class with adjacent mainland

Australia
758.A1 General works
758.A3-Z By region, state, or territory, A-Z
Offshore islands generally class with adjacent mainland

758.5 New Zealand
759.A-Z Pacific islands, A-Z
Arctic regions see QE744
760 Antarctica

Paleozoology
760.8 Periodicals, societies, congresses, serial publications
761 General works, treatises, and textbooks
763 Popular works

Paleozoology -- Continued
765 Juvenile works
766 Marine animals
767 Plankton
For stratigraphic divisions see QE724+
For geographical divisions see QE743+
Invertebrates
770 General works, treatises, and textbooks
Protozoa
771 General works, treatises, and textbooks
772 Foraminifera
773 Radiolaria
774.A-Z Other Protozoa, A-Z
(774.D5) Dinoflagellates
see QE955
774.F5 Flagellata. Mastiogophora
774.P6 Polycystida
774.T5 Thecamoebae. Testacea
774.T55 Tintinnida
775 Porifera (Sponges)
Cnidaria
777 General works, treatises, and textbooks
778 Anthozoa (Corals)
779 Hydrozoa. Stromatoporoidea
For Graptolithina see QE840.5
780 Scyphozoa
Including Scyphomedusae and Conulata
780.5 Ctenophora
Echinodermata
781 General works, treatises, and textbooks
782 Crinozoa. Crinoidea
783.A-Z Other divisions, A-Z
783.A7 Asteroidea (True starfish)
783.B6 Blastoidea
783.C9 Cystoidea
783.D5 Diploporita
783.E2 Echinoidea
783.E3 Edrioasteroidea
783.H7 Holothurioidea
783.O6 Ophiuroidea
783.P3 Paracrinoidea
783.S8 Stelleroidea
783.S89 Stylophora
791 Worms and other vermiform invertebrates
Brachiopoda
796 General works, treatises, and textbooks
797.A-Z Systematic divisions, A-Z

Paleozoology
Invertebrates
Brachiopoda
Systematic divisions, A-Z -- Continued

797.A65 Articulata
797.A69 Athyrididae
797.A7 Atrypidae
797.C95 Cyrtinidae
797.D3 Delthyrididae
797.D5 Dielasmatidae
797.D6 Discinidae
797.I5 Inarticulata
797.K5 Kingenidae
797.L7 Lingulidae
797.O2 Obolidae
797.O7 Orthida
797.O75 Orthidae
797.P3 Paterinidae
797.P39 Pentamerida
797.P4 Pentameridae
797.P5 Playtstrophiinae
797.P9 Productidae
797.R5 Rhynchonellida
797.S4 Septirhynchiidae
797.S7 Spiriferidae
797.S8 Stringocephalidae
797.S89 Strophomenida
797.S9 Strophomenidae
797.T29 Terebratulida
(797.T3) Terebratulidae
see QE797.T29
797.T5 Thecidellinidae
797.T8 Trimerellidae
797.Z4 Zeilleriidae

Bryozoa. Polyzoa

798 General works, treatises, and textbooks
799.A-Z Systematic divisions, A-Z
799.C5 Cheilostomata
799.C7 Cryptostomata
799.C8 Ctenostomata
799.C9 Cyclostomata
799.E95 Expletocystida
799.G95 Gymnolaemata
799.M6 Monticuliporidae
799.S74 Stenolaemata
799.T7 Trepostomata

Mollusca

Paleozoology
Invertebrates
Mollusca -- Continued
801 General works, treatises, and textbooks
805 Monoplacophora. Amphineura. Aplacophora. Polyplacophora
Cephalopoda
806 General works, treatises, and textbooks
807.A-Z Systematic divisions, A-Z
807.A25 Actinoceratidae
807.A5 Ammonoidea
807.B4 Belemnitida
807.C65 Clymeniida
807.C7 Coleoidea
807.D5 Dibranchiata
Ecdyceras see QE807.H4
807.E4 Ellesmeroceratidae
807.E5 Endoceratoidea
807.G56 Goniatitidae
807.H4 Hebetoceratidae
807.L3 Lamellorthoceratidae
807.L7 Liparoceratidae
807.L98 Lytoceratidae
807.N4 Nautiloidea
807.O8 Orthoceratidae
807.P69 Placenticeratidae
807.S3 Salterellidae
807.S4 Sepiida
807.W8 Wutinoceratidae
Gastropoda
808 General works, treatises, and textbooks
809.A-Z Systematic divisions, A-Z
809.A18 Actaeonellidae
809.A2 Actaeonidae
809.A72 Archaeogastropoda
809.B8 Buccinidae
809.C4 Ceratopeidae
809.C48 Columbellidae
809.C52 Conidae
809.C9 Cypraeidae
809.E55 Eotomariidae
809.E64 Epitoniidae
809.E9 Euomphalidae
809.F3 Fasciolariidae
809.M25 Macluritidae
809.M4 Mesogastropoda
809.M8 Murchisoniata

Paleozoology
Invertebrates
Mollusca
Gastropoda
Systematic divisions, A-Z -- Continued

809.M85 Muricidae
809.N3 Nassariidae
809.N32 Naticidae
809.N45 Neritidae
809.O44 Olividae
809.O6 Opisthobranchia
809.P5 Platyceratidae
809.P7 Prosobranchia
809.P8 Pteropoda
809.P9 Pulmonata
809.P95 Pyramidellidae
809.T5 Thaididae
809.T88 Turridae
809.T9 Turritellidae
809.V2 Valencienniidae
809.V3 Vasidae
809.V7 Volutidae
809.Z9 Zonitidae

Bivalvia. Lamellibranchia. Pelecypoda

811 General works, treatises, and textbooks
812.A-Z Systematic divisions, A-Z
812.A8 Arcidae
(812.A84) Astartidae
see QE812.V45
812.B83 Buchiidae
812.C3 Cardiidae
812.C35 Carditidae
812.C5 Chondrodontidae
812.C6 Conocardiidae
Cypricardiacea see QE812.T34
812.D5 Diceratidae
812.D7 Dreissenidae
812.G7 Grammysiidae
812.G78 Gryphaeidae
812.H34 Halobiidae
812.H57 Hippuritidae
812.H573 Hippuritoida (Rudists)
812.I5 Inoceramidae
Leptonacea see QE812.V45
812.M2 Mactridae
812.M48 Megalodontacea
812.M6 Monotidae

Paleozoology
Invertebrates
Mollusca
Bivalvia. Lamellibranchia. Pelecypoda
Systematic divisions, A-Z -- Continued

812.M9 Myalinidae
812.M94 Mytilidae
812.N6 Noetiidae
812.N8 Nucloidae
812.O8 Ostreidae
812.O87 Ostreoida
812.P38 Pectinacea
812.P4 Pectinidae
812.P48 Pholadidae
812.P5 Pholadomyoida
812.P65 Praeheterodonta
812.P7 Pterinidae
812.R33 Radiolitidae
(812.R8) Rudista
see QE812.H573
812.S6 Solemyidae
812.S62 Solemyoida
812.T3 Tancrediidae
812.T34 Teleodesmacea
812.T37 Tellinidae
812.T4 Teredinidae
(812.T7) Trigoniidae
see QE812.T74
812.T74 Trigonioida
812.U6 Unionidae
812.V4 Veneridae
812.V45 Veneroida
813 Scaphopoda
814 Rostroconchia
Arthropoda
815 General works, treatises, and textbooks
Crustacea. Mandibulata
816 General works, treatises, and textbooks
817.A-Z Systematic divisions, A-Z
817.A6 Amphipoda
817.A7 Arthrostraca
817.B7 Branchiopoda
817.C5 Cirripedia
817.C6 Conchostraca
817.C7 Copepoda
817.D3 Decapoda
817.E5 Entomostraca

Paleozoology
Invertebrates
Arthropoda
Crustacea. Mandibulata
Systematic divisions, A-Z -- Continued

817.I8	Isopoda
817.L5	Leptostraca
817.M3	Malacostraca
817.O8	Ostracoda
	Phyllopoda see QE817.B7
817.S3	Schizopoda
817.S8	Stomatopoda
	Protarthropoda. Trilobitomorpha
821	General works, treatises, and textbooks
823.A-Z	Systematic divisions, A-Z
823.A35	Agnostida
823.C6	Corynexochida
823.M3	Marrellidae
823.P4	Pentastomida
823.P5	Phacopida
823.P53	Phillipsiidae
823.P75	Proetida
823.P76	Proetidae
823.P79	Ptychopariida
823.R4	Redlichiida
823.T2	Tardigrada
	Chelicerata. Merostomata. Arachnida
825	General works, treatises, and textbooks
826.A-Z	Systematic divisions, A-Z
826.A2	Acarina (Acari)
826.A6	Araneida (Araneae)
826.C5	Chernetidae (Pseudoscorpiones)
826.E8	Eurypterida
826.O63	Opiliones
826.P3	Pedipalpi
(826.P5)	Phalangida see QE826.O63
826.S4	Scorpionida
826.S6	Solifugae
826.X5	Xiphosurida
	Myriapoda
828	General works, treatises, and textbooks
829.A-Z	Systematic divisions, A-Z
829.C5	Chilopoda
829.D5	Diplopoda
	Hexapoda. Insects
831	General works, treatises, and textbooks

Paleozoology
Invertebrates
Arthropoda
Hexapoda. Insects -- Continued

832.A-Z	Systematic divisions, A-Z
832.A53	Anisoptera (Dragonflies)
832.A55	Anoplura
832.B55	Blattaria (Cockroaches)
832.C6	Coleoptera (Beetles)
832.C63	Collembola (Springtails)
832.D47	Dermaptera (Earwigs)
832.D6	Diptera (Flies, midges, mosquitoes)
832.E52	Embioptera
832.E65	Ephemeroptera (Mayflies)
832.H4	Hemiptera (True bugs)
832.H65	Homoptera
832.H9	Hymenoptera (Ants, bees, wasps)
832.I8	Isoptera (Termites)
832.L5	Lepidoptera (Butterflies and moths)
832.M34	Mallophaga (Biting lice)
832.M43	Mecoptera (Scorpionflies)
832.N5	Neuroptera
832.O36	Odonata
832.O7	Orthoptera
832.P45	Phasmatoptera (Stick insects)
832.P55	Plecoptera (Stoneflies)
832.P83	Psocoptera (Book lice)
832.S47	Siphonaptera (Fleas)
832.S87	Strepsiptera
832.T5	Thysanoptera (Thrips)
832.T8	Trichoptera (Caddisflies)
	Chordata
840.5	Cephalochordata. Tunicata. Hemichordata. Enteropneusta. Pterobranchia. Graptolithina
	Vertebrates
841	General works, treatises, and textbooks
842	Juvenile works
845	Fossil footprints
846	Fossil teeth
847	Amniotes
	Fishes
851	General works, treatises, and textbooks
851.2	Ichthyoliths
852.A-Z	Systematic divisions, A-Z
852.A25	Acipenseriformes
852.A33	Agnatha
852.A4	Amiiformes

Paleozoology
Chordata
Vertebrates
Fishes
Systematic divisions, A-Z -- Continued

852.A5 Anaspida
852.A53 Anguilliformes
852.A7 Arthrodira
852.B47 Beryciformes
852.C48 Chimaeriformes
852.C52 Chondrichthyes
852.C55 Clupeiformes
852.C58 Coelacanthiformes
852.C6 Coelolepida
852.C7 Crossopterygii
852.C95 Cypriniformes
852.D5 Dipnoi
852.D7 Drepanaspidae
852.E55 Edestidae
(852.E6) Elasmobranchii
see QE852.C52
852.E65 Elopiformes
852.G26 Gadiformes
Ganoidei see QE852.S4
852.G37 Gasterosteiformes
852.G65 Gonorhynchiformes
852.H4 Heterostraci
(852.H7) Holocephali
see QE852.C48
852.I35 Ichthyodectiformes
852.L35 Lamniformes
Cf. QL89.2.C37 Carcharocles megalodon
852.L45 Leptolepiformes
852.O45 Osteichthyes
852.O5 Osteostraci
852.P3 Palaeonisciformes
852.P4 Perciformes
852.P45 Pholidophoriformes
852.P5 Placodermi
Plagiostomi see QE852.C52
852.P8 Ptycholepiformes
852.P9 Pycnodontiformes
852.R35 Rajiformes
852.R4 Redfieldiiformes
852.S2 Salmoniformes
852.S4 Semionotiformes

Paleozoology
Chordata
Vertebrates
Fishes
Systematic divisions, A-Z -- Continued
(852.T2) Teleostei
see QE852.O45
852.T48 Tetraodontiformes
853 Fossil otoliths
Reptiles
861 General works, treatises, and textbooks
Dinosaurs
Class here works on dinosaurs in general
For works on specific orders of dinosaurs see QE862.A+
861.2 Periodicals, societies, congresses, serial publications
861.3 Dictionaries and congresses
861.35 Computer network resources
Including the Internet
861.4 General works
861.5 Juvenile works
861.6.A-Z Special topics, A-Z
861.6.B44 Behavior
861.6.E35 Eggs
861.6.E95 Extinction
861.6.F45 Flight
861.6.T72 Tracks
By region or country
United States
861.7 General works
861.8.A-Z By region or state, A-Z
Subarrange each state by Table Q4
861.9.A-Z Other regions or countries, A-Z
Subarrange each state by Table Q4
861.95 Miscellany and curiosa
862.A-Z Other systematic divisions, A-Z
862.C36 Captorhinidae
862.C5 Chelonia. Testudinata
862.C7 Cotylosauria
862.C8 Crocodylia
(862.D4) Dicynodontia
see QE862.T5
(862.D5) Dinosaurs
see QE861.2+
862.E9 Eunotosauridae
862.I2 Ichthyosauria
862.L2 Lacertilia

	Paleozoology
	Chordata
	Vertebrates
	Reptiles
	Systematic divisions, A-Z -- Continued
862.N7	Nothosauria
862.O6	Ophidia. Serpentes
862.O65	Ornithischia
	Ornithosauria see QE862.P7
862.P3	Pelycosauria
862.P35	Phytosauria
862.P37	Placodontia
862.P4	Plesiosauria
862.P7	Pterosauria
	Pythonomorpha see QE862.L2
862.R5	Rhynchocephalia
862.S3	Saurischia
862.S33	Sauropterygia
862.S65	Squamata
	Cf. QE862.L2 Lacertilia
	Cf. QE862.O6 Ophidia
(862.S8)	Synapsida
	see QE861
862.T4	Thalattosauria
862.T47	Thecodontia
862.T5	Therapsida
	Amphibians. Batrachia
867	General works, treatises, and textbooks
868.A-Z	Systematic divisions, A-Z
868.A46	Aistopoda
868.A48	Anthracosauria
868.A5	Anura
868.A6	Apoda
868.B7	Branchiosauridae
868.C2	Caudata
868.D5	Dissorophidae
	Ecaudata see QE868.A5
868.I25	Ichthyostegalia
868.L3	Labyrinthodontia
868.M53	Microsauria
868.P4	Pelobatidae
868.P5	Pipidae
868.R5	Rhachitomi
868.R53	Rhytidosteidae
	Stegocephala see QE868.L3
	Birds
871	General works, treatises, and textbooks

Paleozoology
Chordata
Vertebrates
Birds -- Continued

872.A-Z	Systematic divisions, A-Z
872.A15	Accipitres
872.A2	Aepyornithiformes
872.A3	Alcidae
872.A6	Anseriformes
872.A7	Apterygidae
872.A8	Archaeonithes (Sauriurae)
(872.A9)	Ardeiformes see QE872.C53
872.C3	Casuariiformes
872.C53	Ciconiiformes
	Coccyges see QE872.C9
872.C65	Coliiformes
872.C7	Columbidae
872.C75	Colymbidae (Gaviidae)
872.C77	Confuciusornithiformes
872.C8	Coraciiformes
872.C9	Cuculiformes
872.D5	Dinornithiformes
872.E52	Enantiornithiformes
872.G15	Galliformes (Galli)
872.G27	Gastornithiformes
	Gaviidae see QE872.C75
	Gressores see QE872.C53
872.G8	Gruiformes (Ralliformes)
872.O2	Odontognathae (Odontoholcae)
872.O6	Opisthocomidae
872.P2	Passeriformes
872.P4	Pelicaniformes
872.P5	Piciformes
872.P6	Podargidae
872.P65	Prophaethontiformes
872.P7	Psitaciformes
872.P8	Pteroclidae
	Ralliformes see QE872.G8
872.R37	Ratites
872.R4	Rheiformes
	Sauriruae see QE872.A8
872.S4	Sphenisciformes
872.S5	Steatornithes
	Steganpodes see QE872.P4
872.S8	Strigiformes
872.S9	Struthioniformes

Paleozoology
Chordata
Vertebrates
Birds
Systematic divisions, A-Z -- Continued
Teratornis see QE872.V9

872.T5 Threskiornithidae (Ibises and spoonbills)
872.T56 Tinamiformes
872.V9 Vulturidae
875 Fossil eggs

Mammals

881 General works, treatises, and textbooks
882.A-Z Systematic divisions, A-Z
882.C15 Carnivora
882.C5 Cetacea
882.C8 Chiroptera
882.C84 Cimolesta
882.C9 Creodonta
882.D4 Deltatheridia
882.D45 Desmostylia
882.D6 Docodonta
882.E2 Edentata. Xenarthra
882.E75 Erinaceomorpha
Cf. QE882.I5 Insectivora. Insectivores
882.E86 Eupantotheria
882.H47 Herbivora
882.I5 Insectivora. Insectivores
Cf. QE882.E75 Erinaceomorpha
Cf. QE882.S67 Soricomorpha
882.L3 Lagomorpha
882.M25 Macroscelidea

Marsupialia

882.M3 General works
882.M32 Dasyuromorphia
882.M33 Didelphimorphia
882.M34 Diprotodontia
882.M35 Microbiotheria
882.M36 Notoryctemorphia
882.M37 Paucituberculata
882.M38 Peramelemorphia
882.M39 Sparassodonta
882.M6 Monotremata
882.M8 Multituberculata
882.N6 Notoungulata
882.P3 Pantotheria
882.P45 Pholidota
882.P5 Pinnipedia

Paleozoology
Chordata
Vertebrates
Mammals
Systematic divisions, A-Z -- Continued

882.P7 Primates
Cf. GN282+ Human paleontology
882.P8 Proboscidea
882.R6 Rodentia
882.S32 Scandentia
882.S6 Sirenia
882.S67 Soricomorpha
Cf. QE882.I5 Insectivora. Insectivores
882.T34 Taeniodontia
(882.T49) Theria
see QE881
(882.T5) Tillodontia
see QE882.C84
882.T8 Tubulidentata
Ungulates
882.U2 General works
882.U3 Artiodactyla
882.U6 Perissodactyla
882.U8 Other
e.g. Dinocerata, Toxodontia
Xenarthra see QE882.E2
Fossils of doubtful affinity or origin
899 General works
899.2.A-Z Special groups, A-Z
899.2.A37 Acritarchs
899.2.C65 Conodonts
899.2.C67 Coprolites
899.2.D32 Dacryoconarida
899.2.T45 Tentaculitida
Paleobotany
901 Periodicals, societies, congresses, serial publications
903 Nomenclature, terminology, notation, abbreviations
History
904.A1 General works
904.A2-Z By region or country, A-Z
Biography
904.5 Collective
Including directories
904.52.A-Z Individual, A-Z
e.g.
904.52.S4 Seward, Sir Albert Charles, 1863-1941
905 General works, treatises, and textbooks

Paleobotany -- Continued

906 Juvenile works
907 Pictorial works and atlases
Museums. Exhibitions
908.A1 General works
908.A2-Z By region or country, A-Z
Subarrange each country by Table Q5
909 Study and teaching. Research
911 Addresses, essays, lectures
Stratigraphic divisions
Precambrian
914 General works
914.5 Proterozoic
Paleozoic
915 General works
916 Cambrian
916.5 Ordovician
917 Silurian
918 Devonian
Carboniferous
919 General works
919.3 Mississippian
919.5 Pennsylvanian
920 Permian
Mesozoic
921 General works
922 Triassic
923 Jurassic
924 Cretaceous
Cenozoic
925 General works
Tertiary
926 General works
Paleogene
926.5 General works
927 Paleocene
927.2 Eocene
928 Oligocene
Neogene
928.5 General works
929 Miocene
930 Pliocene
Quaternary
931 General works
931.2 Pleistocene
931.3 Holocene, Recent
932 Amber flora

Paleobotany -- Continued
Geographical divisions
Prefer the stratigraphic divisions

934 Arctic regions
North America
935 General works
United States
936 General works
937.A-Z By region or state, A-Z
Canada
938.A1 General works
938.A3-Z By region or province, A-Z
Mexico
939.A1 General works
939.A3-Z By region or state, A-Z
West Indies. Caribbean Area
940.A1 General works
940.A3-Z By region, country, or island, A-Z
Offshore islands generally class with adjacent mainland
Central America
941.A1 General works
941.A3-Z By region, country, or island, A-Z
Offshore islands generally class with adjacent mainland
South America
942.A1 General works
942.A3-Z By region, country, or island, A-Z
Offshore islands generally class with adjacent mainland
Europe
943 General works
944 Great Britain
945.A-Z Other regions or countries, A-Z
Asia
946.A1 General works
946.A3-Z By region, country, or island, A-Z
Offshore islands generally class with adjacent mainland
Africa
947.A1 General works
947.A3-Z By region, country, or island, A-Z
Offshore islands generally class with adjacent mainland
Australia
948.A1 General works
948.A3-Z By state or territory, A-Z
Offshore islands generally class with adjacent mainland
948.2 New Zealand
949.A-Z Pacific islands, A-Z
950 Antarctica
Systematic divisions

Paleobotany
Systematic divisions -- Continued
955 Algae
Including Characeae, Dasycladaceae, diatoms, dinoflagellates, nannofossils, and stromatolites
958 Fungi
959 Bryophyta (Liverworts and mosses)
Pteridophyta
960 General works
960.5 Psilophyta. Psilopsida
961 Pterophyta. Polypodiophyta (Ferns)
965 Sphenopsida. Equisetophyta
Hyeniales, Pseudoborniales, Calamitales, Equisetales, Sphenophyllales
971 Lycopsida
Protolepidodendrales, Lepidodendrales, Pleuromeiales, Isoetales, Lycopodiales, Selaginellales
Gymnosperms. Pinophyta
975 General works
Cycadophyta
976 General works
976.2 Cycadales
976.3 Cycadeoidales
976.4 Pteridospermales
Coniferophyta
977 General works
977.2 Coniferales
977.3 Ginkgoales
977.4 Gnetales
977.5 Taxales
978 Cordaitales
Angiospermophyta. Magnoliophyta
980 General works
981 Monocotyledons
983 Dicotyledons
989 Plants of unascertained position
990 Coal balls
991 Fossil woods. Fossil trees
992 Fossil leaves
Palynology
993 General works
993.2 Fossil pollen
996 Fossil spores
996.5 Fossil fruit and seeds

Natural history (General)
Periodicals, societies, congresses, serial publications
1 English
3 French
5 German
7 Other languages (not A-Z)
9 Collected works (nonserial)
9.5 International Biological Programme
11 Voyages and expeditions
Cf. Q115+ Scientific expeditions
Cf. QK5 Botanical expeditions
Cf. QL5 Zoological expeditions
13 Dictionaries and encyclopedias
Communication of information
13.2 General works
13.3 Information services
13.4 Computer network resources
Including the Internet
13.45 Natural history literature
14 Authorship
14.3 Philosophy
History
15 General works
21.A-Z By region or country, A-Z
Biography
26 Collective
31.A-Z Individual, A-Z
e.g.
31.A2 Agassiz
Audubon, John James see QL31.A9
31.D2 Darwin, Charles
31.H3 Haller
Linnaeus see QH44
31.M45 Mendel
31.W58 White, Gilbert
35 Directories
41 Pre-Linnaean works (through 1735)
Cf. QK41 Botany
Cf. QL41 Zoology
Works of Linnaeus (General)
43 General works
43.5 Minor works of Linnaeus
44 Works about Linnaeus
General works, treatises, and advanced textbooks
45 1736-1969
45.2 1970-
45.5 Popular works

46 Pictorial works and atlases
Cf. TR721+ Nature photography
46.5 Natural history illustration
47 Elementary textbooks
48 Juvenile works
49 Vocational guidance
Study and teaching. Research. Nature study
Cf. QH318.5 Biology fieldwork
50.5 Directories
51 General works
53 Outlines, syllabi. Nature study manuals
54 Problems, exercises, examinations
54.5 Activity programs
55 Experiments
57 Audiovisual aids
58 Nature trails
Cf. HV1664.N38 Natural history for people with visual disabilities
Technique
60 General works
60.2 Data processing
Collection and preservation
61 General works, treatises, and textbooks
63 Instruments and apparatus
68 Vivariums. Terrariums
Cf. SB417 Glass gardens. Wardian cases
Aquariums (Home and school) see SF456+
Aquariums (Public) see QL78+
Museums. Exhibitions
For research serial publications see QH1+
70.A1 General works
70.A2-Z By region or country, A-Z
Subarrange each country by Table Q5
72 Commercial lists, catalogs, etc.
Nature conservation. Landscape protection. Biodiversity conservation. Endangered species and ecosystems (General). Habitat conservation. Ecosystem management. Conservation biology
Including natural areas, nature reserves, wilderness areas, biosphere reserves, ecological reserves, environmentally sensitive areas
Cf. GF90+ Landscape assessment
Cf. GV191.67.W5 Recreational aspects of wilderness areas
Cf. QH91.8.B6 Marine biology
Cf. SK351+ Wildlife management areas
75.A1 Periodicals, societies, congresses, serial publications

Nature conservation. Landscape protection. Biodiversity conservation. Endangered species and ecosystems (General). Habitat conservation. Ecosystem management. Conservation biology -- Continued

75.A3-Z General works, treatises, and textbooks

By region or country

United States

76 General works

76.5.A-Z By region or state, A-Z

77.A-Z Other regions or countries, A-Z

77.3.A-Z Special topics, A-Z

77.3.C57 Citizen participation

77.3.C65 Communication of information

77.3.G46 Gender mainstreaming

77.3.T45 Teleology

78 Extinction (Biology)

Cf. QE721.2.E97 Paleontology

Cf. QL88+ Animal extinction

81 Addresses, essays, lectures. Nature books

Cf. GV191.2+ Outdoor life. Outdoor recreation

Cf. QH53 School manuals of nature study

Cf. QH58 Nature trails

Edible plants and animals. Wild food gathering

For cultivated plants and animals see S1+

Cf. QK98.5.A1+ Edible wild plants

Cf. QK617 Edible mushrooms

Cf. SH400+ Seafood gathering

Cf. SH401+ Fishing

Cf. SK1+ Hunting

82 General works

82.3.A-Z By region or country, A-Z

83 Classification. Nomenclature

Cf. QK91+ Plant classification

Cf. QL351+ Animal classification

83.5 Terminology, notation, abbreviations

Geographical distribution. Biogeography. Phylogeography

Cf. QH543.3 Dispersal of organisms by environmental factors

84 General works, treatises, and textbooks

Cold regions. Polar regions

Including Arctic regions

84.1 General works

84.2 Antarctica

84.3 Temperate regions

84.5 Tropics

Cf. QH86 Rain forests

Physiographic divisions

QH

Geographical distribution. Biogeography. Phylogeography
Physiographic divisions -- Continued
Land
For biology of a particular place see QH101+
84.8 Soils
85 Islands
86 Forests
Including rain forests, old growth forests, etc.
87 Mountains
87.2 Valleys
87.3 Wetlands
Including marshes, swamps, moors, bogs, etc.
(87.5) Moors
see QH87.3
87.7 Prairies. Grasslands
88 Deserts
88.5 Dunes
89 Caves
Water. Aquatic biology
For aquatic biology of a particular place see QH101+
Cf. GB855+ Natural water chemistry
90.A1 Periodicals, societies, congresses, serial publications
90.A4 Collected works (nonserial)
90.A5-Z General works, treatises, and textbooks
90.1 Addresses, essays, lectures
90.15 Popular works
90.16 Juvenile works
90.17 Pictorial works and atlases
90.2 Dictionaries and encyclopedias
90.25 History
For local history see QH101+
Biography
90.3.A2 Collective
90.3.A3-Z Individual, A-Z
90.35 Directories
90.45 Aquatic biology as a profession. Vocational guidance
Study and teaching. Research
90.5 General works
90.53 Outlines, syllabi
90.55 Laboratory manuals
90.56 Collection and preservation
Research methods and apparatus
90.57.A1 General works, treatises, and textbooks
90.57.A3-Z Special, A-Z
90.57.A77 Artificial substrates
90.57.B5 Biological assay. Biological assessment
90.57.D7 Dredging

Geographical distribution. Biogeography. Phylogeography
Physiographic divisions
Water. Aquatic biology -- Continued
Laboratories and stations
Cf. QH91.6+ Marine laboratories
Cf. QH96.6+ Freshwater laboratories
90.6 General works
90.65.A-Z By region or country, A-Z
Subarrange each country by Table Q6
Museums. Exhibitions
Serial publications see QH90.A1
90.7.A1 General works
90.7.A2-Z By region or country, A-Z
Subarrange each country by Table Q5
Aquatic parks and reserves
90.75.A1 General works, treatises, and textbooks
90.75.A3-Z By region or country, A-Z
90.8.A-Z Special topics, A-Z
90.8.B46 Benthos
Biodiversity see QH90.8.B56
90.8.B56 Biological diversity. Biodiversity. Biodiversity conservation
For aquatic biodiversity conservation of a particular region see QH76+
For aquatic biodiversity of a particular region see QH101+
Ecology see QH541.5.W3
90.8.I57 Introduced aquatic organisms
90.8.N44 Nekton
90.8.P5 Plankton (General)
Cf. QH91.8.P5 Marine plankton
Cf. QH96.8.P5 Freshwater plankton
Cf. QK933+ Phytoplankton
Cf. QL123 Zooplankton
90.8.T68 Toxicology
Marine biology
Cf. QH541.5.S3 Marine ecology
91.A1 Periodicals, societies, congresses, serial publications
91.A4 Collected works (nonserial)
91.A5-Z General works, treatises, and textbooks
91.1 Addresses, essays, lectures
91.15 Popular works
91.16 Juvenile works
91.17 Pictorial works and atlases
91.2 Dictionaries and encyclopedias
91.25 History
For local history see QH101+

QH

Geographical distribution. Biogeography. Phylogeography
Physiographic divisions
Water. Aquatic biology
Marine biology -- Continued
Biography
91.3.A2 Collective
91.3.A3-Z Individual, A-Z
91.35 Directories
91.45 Marine biology as a profession. Vocational guidance
Study and teaching. Research
91.5 General works
91.53 Outlines, syllabi
91.55 Laboratory manuals
91.56 Collection and preservation
Research methods and apparatus
91.57.A1 General works, treatises, and textbooks
91.57.A3-Z Special, A-Z
91.57.A4 Aeronautics
91.57.B5 Biological assay. Biological assessment
91.57.C68 Counting and measuring
91.57.D7 Dredging
91.57.E4 Electronic data processing
91.57.M38 Mathematical models
Measuring see QH91.57.C68
91.57.P4 Photosynthesis determination
91.57.P5 Plankton sampling
91.57.R47 Research ships
Laboratories and stations
91.6 General works
91.65.A-Z By region or country, A-Z
Subarrange each country by Table Q6
Museums. Exhibitions
Serial publications see QH90.A1
91.7.A1 General works
91.7.A2-Z By region or country, A-Z
Subarrange each country by Table Q5
Marine parks and reserves
91.75.A1 General works, treatises, and textbooks
91.75.A3-Z By region or country, A-Z
91.8.A-Z Special topics, A-Z
91.8.B4 Benthos
Biodiversity see QH91.8.B6
91.8.B5 Biological chemistry

Geographical distribution. Biogeography. Phylogeography
Physiographic divisions
Water. Aquatic biology
Marine biology
Special topics, A-Z -- Continued

91.8.B6 Biological diversity. Biodiversity. Biodiversity conservation
For marine biodiversity of a particular region see QH101+
For marine biodiversity conservation of a particular region see QH76+
For marine biodiversity and biodiversity conservation of a particular body of water see QH92+
Cf. QH91.8.S64 Species diversity

91.8.B63 Biological invasions

91.8.D44 Deep-sea biology
For deep-sea biology of a particular region see QH92+

91.8.E3 Echo scattering layers

Ecology see QH541.5.S3

91.8.E87 Eutrophication
For marine eutrophication of a particular region see QH92+

91.8.E94 Exotic marine organisms

91.8.M3 Marine borers. Marine fouling organisms

Marine eutrophication see QH91.8.E87

91.8.M34 Marine productivity

91.8.N37 Nekton

91.8.N4 Neuston

91.8.N46 Nitrogen cycle

91.8.O4 Oil pollution

91.8.P5 Plankton
Cf. QK934 Marine phytoplankton
Cf. QL123 Marine zooplankton

91.8.P7 Primary productivity

91.8.S64 Species diversity

By region
For marine biology of a particular region or country or off the coast of a particular region or country see QH101+

Atlantic Ocean

92 General works

North Atlantic Ocean

92.1 General works

Coast of North America

92.2 General works

QH

Geographical distribution. Biogeography. Phylogeography
Physiographic divisions
Water. Aquatic biology
Marine biology
By region
Atlantic Ocean
North Atlantic Ocean
Coast of North America -- Continued
92.3 Gulf of Mexico
92.4 Caribbean Sea
92.5.A-Z Other, A-Z
92.5.B33 Baffin Bay
92.5.G46 Georges Bank
92.5.M34 Maine, Gulf of
Coast of Europe
92.6 General works
92.7 Baltic Sea
92.8 North Sea
92.9.A-Z Other, A-Z
92.9.B57 Biscay Bay
92.9.E54 English Channel
Mediterranean Sea
93 General works
93.1 Adriatic Sea
93.2 Aegean Sea
93.3 Black Sea
93.4 Caspian Sea
93.5.A-Z Other, A-Z
South Atlantic Ocean
93.6 General works
Coast of Africa
93.7 General works
93.75 Gulf of Guinea
93.8 Coast of South America
93.9.A-Z Other, A-Z
Indian Ocean
94 General works
94.2 Arabian Sea
94.3 Red Sea
94.4 Persian Gulf
94.5 Bengal, Bay of
94.7.A-Z Other, A-Z
Pacific Ocean
95 General works
North Pacific Ocean
95.1 General works
Coast of Asia

Geographical distribution. Biogeography. Phylogeography
Physiographic divisions
Water. Aquatic biology
Marine biology
By region
Pacific Ocean
North Pacific Ocean
Coast of Asia -- Continued
95.2 General works
95.22 China Sea
95.23 Yellow Sea
95.24 Japan Sea
95.25 Sea of Okhotsk
95.26 Bering Sea
95.28.A-Z Other, A-Z
Coast of North America
95.3 General works
95.35 Gulf of Alaska
95.4 Coast of Mexico and Central America
95.45.A-Z Other, A-Z
South Pacific Ocean
95.5 General works
95.52 Coast of South America
95.53 Coral Sea
95.54 Tasman Sea
95.55.A-Z Other, A-Z
Arctic Ocean
Including polar oceans
95.56 General works
95.57.A-Z Arctic seas, A-Z
95.58 Antarctic Ocean
95.59 Tropical seas
95.6.A-Z Inland seas, A-Z
Cf. QH93+ Mediterranean Sea
Cf. QH93.4 Caspian Sea
95.7 Seashore biology
For works limited to a particular region or country see QH101+
95.8 Coral reefs
95.9 Brackish water. Saline water
Freshwater biology. Limnology
For works limited to specific geographic areas see QH101+
96.A1 Periodicals, societies, congresses, serial publications
96.A4 Collected works (nonserial)
96.A5-Z General works, treatises, and textbooks
96.1 Addresses, essays, lectures

Geographical distribution. Biogeography. Phylogeography
Physiographic divisions
Water. Aquatic biology
Freshwater biology. Limnology -- Continued

96.15 Popular works
96.16 Juvenile works
96.17 Pictorial works and atlases
96.2 Dictionaries and encyclopedias
96.25 History
For local history see QH101+
Biography
96.3.A2 Collective
96.3.A3-Z Individual, A-Z
96.35 Directories
96.45 Freshwater biology as a profession. Vocational guidance
Study and teaching. Research
96.5 General works
96.53 Outlines, syllabi
96.55 Laboratory manuals
96.56 Collection and preservation
Research methods and apparatus
96.57.A1 General works, treatises, and textbooks
96.57.A3-Z Special, A-Z
96.57.P75 Productivity measurement
96.57.R33 Radioactive tracers
96.57.S73 Statistical methods
Laboratories and stations
96.6 General works
96.65.A-Z By region or country, A-Z
Subarrange each country by Table Q6
Museums. Exhibitions
96.7.A1 General works
96.7.A2-Z By region or country, A-Z
Subarrange each country by Table Q5
Aquatic parks and reserves
96.75.A1 General works, treatises, and textbooks
96.75.A3-Z By region or country, A-Z
96.8.A-Z Special topics, A-Z
96.8.B4 Benthos
Biodiversity see QH96.8.B53
96.8.B5 Biological assay. Biological assessment

Geographical distribution. Biogeography. Phylogeography
Physiographic divisions
Water. Aquatic biology
Freshwater biology. Limnology
Special topics, A-Z -- Continued
96.8.B53 Biological diversity. Biodiversity. Biodiversity conservation
For freshwater biodiversity conservation of a particular region see QH76+
For freshwater biodiversity of a particular region see QH101+
Ecology see QH541.5.F7
96.8.E9 Eutrophication
96.8.I57 Introduced freshwater organisms
96.8.N48 Neuston
96.8.P43 Periphyton
96.8.P5 Plankton
Cf. QK935 Freshwater phytoplankton
Cf. QL143 Freshwater zooplankton
96.8.P7 Primary productivity
96.8.R34 Remote sensing
96.8.R35 Reservoir drawdown
Special freshwater environments
97 Streams
98 Lakes. Ponds
99 Springs
100 Snow and ice
Topographical divisions
America
101 General works
North America
102 General works
United States
104 General works
104.5.A-Z By region, A-Z
104.5.A6 Appalachian Mountains
104.5.A62 Appalachian Region, Southern
104.5.A74 Arkansas River
104.5.A84 Atlantic Coast
104.5.A85 Atlantic States
104.5.B42 Beartooth Mountains (Mont.and Wyo.)
104.5.B45 Bitterroot Range (Idaho and Mont.)
104.5.B47 Black Hills (S. D. and Wyo.)
104.5.B49 Blue Mountains (Or. and Wash.)
104.5.B5 Blue Ridge Mountains
104.5.C25 Caddo Lake and Region (La. and Tex.)
104.5.C3 Cascade Range

QH

Geographical distribution. Biogeography. Phylogeography
Topographical divisions
America
North America
United States
By region, A-Z -- Continued

104.5.C35 Champlain, Lake
104.5.C45 Chesapeake Bay
104.5.C48 Clinch River (Va. and Tenn.)
104.5.C58 Colorado Plateau
104.5.C6 Colorado River (Colo.-Mexico)
104.5.C64 Columbia Plateau. Columbia River
104.5.C74 Cross Timbers (Okla. and Tex.)
104.5.C85 Cumberland Mountains
104.5.D4 Death Valley (Calif. and Nev.). Death Valley National Park (Calif. and Nev.)
104.5.D44 Delaware River
104.5.D46 Delmarva Peninsula
104.5.D48 Detroit River (Mich. and Ont.)
Dismal Swamp see QH105.V8
104.5.E37 East
104.5.E73 Erie, Lake
Four Corners Region see QH104.5.S6
104.5.F76 Front Range (Colo. and Wyo.)
104.5.G68 Great Basin
104.5.G7 Great Lakes
104.5.G73 Great Plains
Great Smoky Mountains see QH105.N8
104.5.G84 Gulf Coast
104.5.H53 High Plains
104.5.H83 Hudson River
104.5.H86 Huron, Lake (Mich. and Ont.)
104.5.K55 Klamath Mountains (Or. and Calif.). Klamath River Watershed (Or. and Calif.)
104.5.L34 Lake States
104.5.M24 Maine, Gulf of
104.5.M39 Mexican-American Border Region
104.5.M44 Michigan, Lake
104.5.M45 Middle Atlantic States
104.5.M47 Middle West
104.5.M5 Mississippi River. Mississippi River Valley
104.5.M56 Missouri River
104.5.N36 Nanticoke River (Del. and Md.)
104.5.N4 New England
104.5.N45 New York Region
104.5.N54 Niobrara River (Wyo. and Neb.)
104.5.N58 Northeastern States

Geographical distribution. Biogeography. Phylogeography
Topographical divisions
America
North America
United States
By region, A-Z -- Continued
104.5.N6 Northwest, Pacific
104.5.N62 Northwestern States
104.5.O58 Ontario, Lake (N.Y. and Ont.)
104.5.O9 Ozark Mountains
104.5.P32 Pacific Coast
104.5.P54 Piedmont Region
104.5.P67 Potomac River
104.5.R33 Red River Valley (Minn. and N.D.- Man.)
104.5.R56 Rio Grande Region
104.5.R6 Rocky Mountains
104.5.S25 San Juan River
104.5.S255 San Luis Valley (Colo. and N.M.)
104.5.S27 Savannah River (Ga. and S. C.)
104.5.S54 Sierra Nevada
104.5.S545 Siskiyou Mountains (Calif. and Or.)
104.5.S55 Snake River
104.5.S58 Sonoran Desert
104.5.S59 Southern States
104.5.S6 Southwest. Four Corners Region
104.5.S85 Superior. Lake
104.5.T46 Tennessee River Valley
104.5.W29 Wasatch Range (Utah and Idaho)
104.5.W4 West (U.S.)
104.5.W47 White Mountains (Calif. and Nev.)
104.5.W48 White Mountains (N.H. and Me.)
104.5.Y44 Yellowstone River
105.A-.W By state, A-W
e.g.
Hawaii see QH198.H3
105.N8 North Carolina
Including Great Smoky Mountains
105.V8 Virginia
Including Dismal Swamp
Canada
106 General works
106.2.A-Z By region or province, A-Z
For regions that include both the United States and Canada see QH104.5.A+
Latin America
106.5 General works

Geographical distribution. Biogeography. Phylogeography
Topographical divisions
America
Latin America -- Continued
107 Mexico
For regions that include both the United States and Mexico see QH104.5.A+
Central America
108.A1 General works
108.A2-Z By region or country, A-Z
108.B43 Belize. British Honduras
British Honduras see QH108.B43
108.C6 Costa Rica
El Salvador see QH108.S3
108.G8 Guatemala
108.H6 Honduras
108.N5 Nicaragua
108.P3 Panama
108.S3 El Salvador
West Indies. Caribbean Area
109.A1 General works
109.A2-Z By island or group of islands, A-Z
109.A48 Antigue and Barbuda
109.A5 Antilles, Lesser
109.B3 Bahamas
109.B35 Barbados
Bermuda see QH110
109.B66 Bonaire
109.C38 Cayman Islands
109.C9 Cuba
109.C93 Curaçao
109.D65 Dominica
109.D66 Dominican Republic
109.F74 French West Indies
109.G74 Grenada
109.G8 Guadeloupe
109.H3 Haiti
Hispaniola see QH109.D66
Hispaniola see QH109.H3
109.J5 Jamaica
109.N48 Netherlands Antilles
Cf. QH109.B66 Bonaire
Cf. QH109.C93 Curaçao
Cf. QH109.S22 Saba
Cf. QH109.S55 Sint Eustatius
Cf. QH109.S56 Sint Maarten
109.P6 Puerto Rico

Geographical distribution. Biogeography. Phylogeography
Topographical divisions
America
Latin America
West Indies. Caribbean Area
By island or group of islands, A-Z -- Continued

109.S22 Saba
109.S24 Saint Kitts and Nevis
109.S25 Saint Lucia
109.S28 Saint Vincent and the Grenadines
109.S55 Sint Eustatius
109.S56 Sint Maarten
109.T8 Trinidad and Tobago
109.T82 Turks and Caicos Islands
109.V55 Virgin Islands
West Indies, French see QH109.F74
110 Bermuda
South America
111 General works
By region or country
112 Amazon River. Amazonia
113 Argentina
115 Bolivia
117 Brazil
119 Chile
121 Colombia
123 Ecuador
For Galapagos Islands see QH198.G3
Guianas
125 General works
125.2 French Guiana
125.4 Guyana (British Guiana)
125.6 Suriname (Dutch Guiana)
125.85 Orinoco River (Venezuela and Colombia)
127 Paraguay
128 Peru
128.5 Titicaca Lake (Peru and Bolivia)
129 Uruguay
130 Venezuela
Atlantic Ocean islands
132.A1 General works
132.A2-Z By island or group of islands, A-Z
132.A9 Azores
Bermuda see QH110
132.B68 Bouvet Island
132.C3 Canary Islands
132.C33 Cape Verde

Geographical distribution. Biogeography. Phylogeography
Topographical divisions
Atlantic Ocean islands
By island or group of islands, A-Z -- Continued
132.F34 Falkland Islands
132.F37 Faroe Islands
132.G73 Greenland
132.M28 Macaronesia
132.M3 Madeira Islands. Salvages Islands
Salvages Islands see QH132.M3
132.S644 South Georgia Island
132.S646 South Orkney Islands
West Indies see QH109.A1+
Europe
135 General works
By region or country
British Isles. Great Britain
137 General works
England
138.A1 General works
138.A3-Z Local, A-Z
e.g.
138.S4 Selborne
141 Scotland
143 Ireland
143.5 Northern Ireland
144 Wales
145 Austria
147 France
Including the Riviera
149 Germany
150 Mediterranean Region (General)
Including Islands of the Mediterranean
151 Greece
152 Italy
154 Malta
157 Belgium
158 Luxembourg
159 Netherlands
Russia. Soviet Union. Russia (Federation)
161 General works
Russia in Asia see QH191
161.5 Belarus
161.6 Moldova
161.7 Ukraine
162 Poland
164 Scandinavia (General)

Geographical distribution. Biogeography. Phylogeography
Topographical divisions
Europe
By region or country -- Continued

165 Denmark
Faroe Islands see QH132.F37
166 Iceland
168 Norway
169 Sweden
Spain
171 General works
171.2 Balearic Islands
Canary Islands see QH132.C3
173 Portugal
For Azores see QH132.A9
175 Switzerland
Including Alps (General)
177 Balkan Peninsula
Including Turkey in Europe
For Turkey in Asia see QH192
178.A-Z Other European regions or countries, A-Z
178.A47 Albania
178.A53 Andorra
178.A73 Ardennes
178.A85 Atlantic Coast
178.A95 Azov, Sea of (Ukraine and Russia)
178.B9 Bulgaria
178.C29 Caspian Sea
178.C36 Central Europe
178.C7 Crete
178.C73 Croatia
178.C8 Czechoslovakia. Czech Republic
178.D36 Danube River Valley
178.D54 Dnieper River Watershed
178.D6 Donets Basin (Ukraine and Russia)
178.E88 Estonia
178.F5 Finland
178.H8 Hungary
Islands of the Mediterranean see QH150
178.I87 Istria
178.J85 Jura Mountains
178.L28 Lapland
178.L34 Latvia
178.L45 Liechtenstein
178.L5 Lithuania
178.M23 Macedonia (Republic)
Mediterranean Region see QH150

Geographical distribution. Biogeography. Phylogeography
Topographical divisions
Europe
By region or country
Other European regions or countries, A-Z -- Continued

178.N67 North Sea Region
178.P53 Pieniny Range (Poland and Slovakia)
178.P97 Pyrenees
178.R55 Rhine River Valley
178.R57 Riga, Gulf of (Latvia and Estonia)
178.R8 Romania
178.S27 San Marino
178.S37 Serbia
178.S65 Slovakia
178.S66 Slovenia
178.T57 Tisza River Valley
178.Y8 Yugoslavia
178.5 Eurasia
Asia
179 General works
By region or country
181 China
183 India
183.5 Sri Lanka
Indochina
184 General works
184.2 Cambodia
184.4 Laos
184.6 Vietnam
185 Malaysia. Malay Peninsula
186 Indonesia
For Papua see QH186.5
186.5 New Guinea
Including Papua (Indonesia) and Papua New Guinea
187 Philippines
Japan
188 General works
188.3 Ryuku Islands
Including Okinawa Prefecture
189 Iran
190 Kuwait
191 Russia in Asia. Siberia. Russian Far East
Central Asia
191.3 General works
191.4 Kazakhstan
191.5 Kyrgyzstan
191.6 Tajikistan

Geographical distribution. Biogeography. Phylogeography
Topographical divisions
Asia
By region or country
Central Asia -- Continued
191.7 Turkmenistan
191.8 Uzbekistan
192 Turkey in Asia
192.5 Caucasus
Including Armenia, Azerbaijan, Georgia (Republic)
193.A-Z Other Asian regions or countries, A-Z
193.A34 Afghanistan
193.B35 Bangladesh
193.B48 Bhutan
193.B65 Borneo
193.B7 Brunei
193.B93 Burma. Myanmar
Caspian Sea see QH178.C29
193.C8 Cyprus
193.E18 East Asia
193.G35 Ganges River
193.G62 Gobi Desert
193.G64 Golan Heights
193.H5 Himalayan Mountains
193.I7 Iraq
193.I8 Israel. Palestine
193.J6 Jordan
193.K57 Kopet Dag (Turkmenistan and Iran)
193.K6 Korea
193.L42 Lebanon
193.M25 Macau
193.M28 Malacca, Strait of
193.M6 Mongolia
Myanmar see QH193.B93
193.N4 Nepal
193.O5 Oman
193.P28 Pakistan
Palestine see QH193.I8
193.P33 Pamir-Alai Mountains
193.P349 Persian Gulf
193.P35 Persian Gulf Region
193.P352 Persian Gulf States
193.Q2 Qatar
193.S28 Saudi Arabia
193.S46 Singapore
193.S59 South Asia
193.S6 Southeast Asia

Geographical distribution. Biogeography. Phylogeography
Topographical divisions
Asia
By region or country
Other Asian regions or countries, A-Z -- Continued

193.S9 Syria
193.T35 Taiwan
193.T46 Thailand
193.T48 Tien Shan
193.U5 United Arab Emirates
(193.V53) Vietnam
see QH184.6
193.Y4 Yemen

Africa
194 General works
195.A-Z By region or country, A-Z
Africa, Central see QH195.C37
195.A23 Africa, East
195.A233 Africa, Eastern
195.A24 Africa, French-speaking Equatorial
195.A25 Africa, French-speaking West
195.A3 Africa, North
Cf. QH150 Mediterranean Region
195.A312 Africa, Northeast
195.A323 Africa, Southern
Africa, Southwest see QH195.N29
Africa, Sub-Saharan see QH195.S87
Africa, West see QH195.W46
195.A4 Algeria
195.B6 Botswana
195.B92 Burkina Faso
195.C36 Cameroon
195.C37 Central Africa
195.C38 Central African Republic
195.C45 Chad
195.C46 Chad, Lake
195.C58 Congo (Brazzaville)
195.C6 Congo (Democratic Republic). Zaire
Côte d'Ivoire see QH195.I9
195.E4 Egypt
195.E76 Equatorial Guinea
195.E8 Ethiopia
195.G3 Gabon
195.G34 Gambia
195.G53 Ghana
195.G84 Guinea
195.G85 Guinea-Bissau

Geographical distribution. Biogeography. Phylogeography
Topographical divisions
Africa
By region or country, A-Z -- Continued

195.I9 Ivory Coast. Côte d'Ivoire
195.K3 Kalahari Desert
195.K4 Kenya
195.L47 Lesotho
195.L7 Liberia
195.M2 Madagascar
195.M47 Malawi
195.M475 Mali
195.M479 Mauritania
195.M4793 Mayumbe
195.M5 Morocco
195.M6 Mozambique
(195.N27) Namib Desert
see QH195.N29
195.N29 Namibia. Southwest Africa
195.N49 Niger River
195.N5 Nigeria
195.N55 Nile River. Nile River Watershed
195.O38 Okavango River
Rhodesia, Northern see QH195.Z3
Rhodesia, Southern see QH195.Z55
195.R53 Rift Valley
195.R9 Ruwenzori Mountains
195.R92 Rwanda
195.S3 Sahara
195.S33 Sahel
195.S34 Sao Tome and Principe
195.S36 Senegal
195.S53 Sierra Leone
195.S6 South Africa
195.S67 South Sudan
Southern Africa see QH195.A323
195.S72 Stanley Pool (Congo (Brazzaville) and Zaire)
195.S87 Sub-Sarahan Africa
195.S9 Sudan
195.S92 Sudan (Region)
195.T28 Tanganyika, Lake
195.T3 Tanzania
195.T53 Togo
195.U4 Uganda
United Arab Republic see QH195.E4
195.V5 Victoria, Lake
195.W46 West Africa

QH

Geographical distribution. Biogeography. Phylogeography
Topographical divisions
Africa
By region or country, A-Z -- Continued
195.Z3 Zambia
195.Z55 Zimbabwe
Indian Ocean islands
196.A1 General works
196.A2-Z By island or group of islands, A-Z
196.A4 Aldabra Islands
196.C53 Chagos Islands
196.C55 Christmas Island
196.C62 Cocos (Keeling) Islands
196.C64 Comoros
196.H43 Heard Island
196.K3 Kerguelen
Madagascar see QH195.M2
196.M35 Marion Island
196.M38 Mauritius
Including Rodrigues
196.M39 Mayotte
196.R4 Réunion
Rodrigues see QH196.M38
196.S2 Saint Paul
196.S4 Seychelles
Australasia
196.8 General works
Australia
197 General works
197.2.A-Z By state, territory, or region, A-Z
197.5 New Zealand
Pacific Area. Pacific islands
198.A1 General works
198.A2-Z By island or group of islands, A-Z
198.A44 American Samoa
198.B5 Bismarck Archipelago
198.C3 Campbell Island
198.C65 Cook Islands
198.E53 Enewetak Atoll
198.F3 Fanning Island
198.F55 Fiji
198.F74 French Polynesia
198.G3 Galapagos Islands
198.G8 Guam
198.H3 Hawaiian Islands
198.J64 Johnston Island
198.K57 Kiribati

Geographical distribution. Biogeography. Phylogeography
Topographical divisions
Australasia
Pacific Area. Pacific islands
By island or group of islands, A-Z -- Continued
198.M18 Mariana Islands
198.M2 Marquesas Islands
198.M34 Marshall Islands
198.M48 Micronesia
198.M5 Midway Islands
198.N4 New Caledonia
198.P4 Pelew Islands
Samoa see QH198.W5
198.S3 Samoan Islands
198.S5 Snares Islands (N.Z.)
198.S6 Solomon Islands
198.S67 Spratly Islands
198.T35 Tahiti
198.T66 Tonga
198.T88 Tuvalu
198.V35 Vanuatu
198.W5 Western Samoa. Samoa
(199) Arctic regions
see QH84.1
(199.5) Antarctica
see QH84.2
Tropical regions see QH84.5
Microscopy
201 Periodicals, societies, congresses, serial publications
202 Collected works (nonserial)
203 Dictionaries and encyclopedias
204 History
General works, treatises, and textbooks
Including handbooks
Cf. QH277 Popular works
205 Through 1969
205.2 1970-
206 Study and teaching. Research
207 Technique
Cf. QH231+ Preparation and mounting of objects
Microscopes
Cf. QC370.5+ Optical instruments
211 General works, treatises, and textbooks
Class application of microscopic techniques with the subject to which they are applied, e.g. QE434 Microscopic analysis of rocks

Microscopy
Microscopes -- Continued
212.A-Z Special microscopes, A-Z
Including the use and microscopy of special microscopes
212.A25 Acoustic microscopes
212.A76 Atom-probe field ion microscopes
212.A78 Atomic force microscopes
212.C6 Compound microscopes
Confocal microscopes see QH224
212.D5 Dissecting microscopes
212.E4 Electron microscopes
212.F5 Field ion microscopes
212.F55 Fluorescence microscopes
212.I5 Interference microscopes
212.M84 Multiphoton excitation microscopes
212.N43 Near-field microscopes
212.P5 Phase-contrast microscopes
212.P6 Polarizing microscopes
212.P7 Proton microscopes
212.S24 Scanning Auger electron microscopes
212.S28 Scanning electrochemical microscopes
212.S3 Scanning electron microscopes
Including low-voltage scanning electron microscopes
212.S32 Scanning force microscopes
212.S33 Scanning probe microscopes
212.S34 Scanning transmission electron microscopes
212.S35 Scanning tunneling microscopes
212.T7 Transmission electron microscopes
212.U48 Ultraviolet microscopes
212.X2 X-ray microscopes
213 Accessories and their use
215 Illuminating apparatus
217 Polarizing apparatus
Cf. QH212.P6 Polarizing microscopes
219 Catalogs of apparatus and supplies
221 Chemical microscopy
Cf. QD98.M5 Microchemical analysis
222 Video microscopy
224 Confocal microscopy
Including confocal fluorescence microscopy
225 Cryomicroscopy
Preparation of microscope specimens. Microtechnique
231 General works
233 Microtomy. Sectioning
234 Embedding
Including specific embedments
235 Fixation

Microscopy
Preparation of microscope specimens. Microtechnique -- Continued

236	Freeze etching
236.2	Freeze fracturing
237	Staining
239	Mounting
251	Photomicrography
255	Macrocinematography
	Microphotometry see QC391
261	Pictorial works and atlases
	Microscopic observations (General)
271	Through 1800
273	1801-1969
273.2	1970-
(274)	Microorganisms see QR
(275)	Aquatic microorganisms see QR105+
277	Popular works
278	Juvenile works
278.5	Recreations

Biology (General)
Cf. N72.B5 Biology and art
Cf. N72.B56
301 Periodicals, societies, congresses, serial publications
302 Collected works (nonserial)
302.5 Dictionaries and encyclopedias
Communication in biology
Cf. QH318 Biological illustration
303 General works, treatises, and textbooks
Information services
Including databases (General)
303.15 Directories
303.2 General works, treatises, and textbooks
303.4.A-Z By region or country, A-Z
Subarrange each country by Table Q5
303.5 Computer network resources
Including the Internet
303.6 Biological literature. Life sciences literature
304 Authorship
Including practical manuals and stylebooks
Cf. PE1475 Preparation of scientific papers in English
304.5 Terminology, notation, abbreviations
For nomenclature see QH83
History and conditions
Cf. QH361 History of evolution
305 General works
305.2.A-Z By region or country, A-Z
305.5 Women life scientists. Women biologists
306 Early works through 1860
General works and treatises
307 1861-1969
307.2 1970-
Textbooks
Advanced
308 Through 1969
308.2 1970-
Elementary
308.5 Through 1969
308.7 1970-
309 Popular works
309.2 Juvenile works
310 Handbooks, tables, formulas, etc.
311 Addresses, essays, lectures
313 Special aspects of the subject as a whole
313.5.A-Z Special topics, A-Z
313.5.F67 Forensic biology
314 Biology as a profession. Vocational guidance

Study and teaching. Research
315 General works
315.25 Teacher training
315.3 Audiovisual aids
315.5 Outlines, syllabi
316 Problems, exercises, examinations
316.4 Activity programs
316.5 Experiments
317 Laboratory manuals
318 Biological illustration
318.5 Fieldwork
Cf. QH58 Nature trails
By region or country
United States
319.A1 General works
319.A2-Z By region or state, A-Z
320.A-Z Other regions or countries, A-Z
Biological laboratories and stations
Class here descriptive works, administrative reports, etc.
For scientific contributions (serial) see QH301
Cf. QH90.6+ Aquatic biological laboratories
Cf. QH91.6+ Marine biological laboratories
Cf. QH96.6+ Freshwater biological laboratories
321 General works
By region or country
United States
321.5 General works
322.A-Z Individual laboratories and stations. By name, A-Z
323.A-Z Other regions or countries, A-Z
Subarrange each country by Table Q6
323.2 Safety measures
323.5 Biometry. Biomathematics. Mathematical models
Cf. QH507 Information theory in biology
Methods of research. Technique. Experimental biology
Cf. QH585+ Cytology
324 General works
324.15 Biological resource centers
Cf. QH442.4 Gene libraries
Data processing. Bioinformatics
324.2 General works
324.25 Artificial intelligence
Tracers
324.3 General works
324.35.A-Z Special elements. By chemical symbol, A-Z (Table Q1)
324.4 Germfree life
Instruments and apparatus (General)
324.42 General works

Methods of research. Technique
Instruments and apparatus (General) -- Continued

324.5 Catalogs of apparatus and supplies
324.8 Biological models
324.9.A-Z Other special, A-Z
324.9.A88 Autoclaving
324.9.A9 Autoradiography
324.9.B48 Biophotometry
324.9.B49 Biophysical labeling
324.9.B5 Biotelemetry
324.9.C3 Calorimetry
324.9.C4 Centrifugation
Centrifugation, Density gradient see QH324.9.D46
324.9.C7 Cryobiology. Freeze-drying
324.9.D46 Density gradient centrifugation
324.9.E36 Electron paramagnetic resonance
324.9.E38 Electron probe microanalysis
324.9.E4 Electrophoresis
324.9.E44 Ellipsometry
324.9.E5 Enzymatic analysis
(324.9.F38) Flow cytometry
see QH585.5.F56
324.9.F4 Fluorescence spectroscopy
Freeze-drying see QH324.9.C7
324.9.I5 Infrared spectroscopy
324.9.I8 Isolation perfusion
324.9.L37 Lasers
324.9.L5 Liquid chromatography
324.9.L53 Liquid scintillation counting
324.9.M28 Magnetic resonance
324.9.M3 Manometry
324.9.M5 Microprobe analysis
324.9.N48 Neutron scattering
324.9.N8 Nuclear magnetic resonance
324.9.R3 Radioactivation analysis
324.9.S4 Separation
324.9.S53 Spectrophotometry
324.9.S6 Spectroscopy
324.9.S62 Spin labels
324.9.S95 Synchrotron radiation
324.9.T45 Three-dimensional imaging
324.9.X2 X-ray microanalysis
325 Origin and beginnings of life
326 Exobiology
Cf. QB54 Extraterrestrial life

Space biology
Cf. QK760 Effect of space flight on plants
Cf. QP82.2.W4 Physiology of weightlessness
Cf. RC1150+ Human space physiology
Cf. TL943 Planetary quarantine
Cf. TL945 Space vehicle sterilization
327 General works
328 Space radiobiology
331 Philosophy of biology
332 Bioethics
Cf. R724+ Medical ethics
333 Social aspects of biology
341 Nature of life, vital force, etc.
343 Comparison of living and nonliving matter
343.4 Geobiology. Biosphere
Biogeochemistry
Cf. QR103 Geomicrobiology
343.7 General works
Biogeochemical cycles
Including cycles of individual elements, e.g. carbon cycle, nitrogen cycle, etc.
344 General works
344.3.A-Z By region or country, A-Z
345 General biochemistry of plants and animals
For works limited to chemical aspects of biological materials see QD415+
For the biochemistry of special substances see QP525+
Cf. QK861+ Plant biochemistry
Cf. QP501+ Animal biochemistry
Cf. QR148 Microbiological chemistry
347 Comparison of plants and animals
349 Miscellany and curiosa
351 Morphology
Cf. QK640+ Plant morphology
Cf. QL799+ Animal morphology
Population biology
Cf. HB848+ Demography
Cf. QH455 Population genetics
Cf. QK910 Vegetation dynamics
Cf. QL752 Animal populations
352 General works
352.5 Population viability analysis
353 Biological invasions. Introduced organisms
Cf. QH91.8.B63 Marine biological invasions

Evolution
For classification by organism, see in subclasses QK or QL
Cf. BL263 Religion and science
Cf. QE701+ Paleontology
359 Periodicals, societies, congresses, serial publications
360 Collected works (nonserial)
360.2 Dictionaries and encyclopedias
360.5 Philosophy
360.6 Nomenclature, terminology, notation, abbreviations
361 History
362 Study and teaching. Research
363 Early works through 1860
Works of Darwin
365.A1 Collected works. By date
365.A2-.Z8 Separate works, A-Z
The descent of man
365.D2 Editions. By date
365.D25 Selections. By editor
365.D3-.D79 Translations
Arrange alphabetically by language, then Cutter for translator
365.D8 Criticism and reviews
The expression of the emotions in man and animals
365.E2 Editions. By date
365.E25 Selections. By editor
365.E3-.E79 Translations
Arrange alphabetically by language, then Cutter for translator
365.E8 Criticism and reviews
365.O15-.O18 On the origin of species, previous essays
Essays written before or during the period of the creation of the main work
On the origin of species
365.O2 Editions. By date
365.O25 Selections. By editor
365.O3-.O79 Translations
Arrange alphabetically by language, then Cutter for translator, for example:
365.O5 German
365.O55 Hungarian
365.O68 Romanian
365.O7 Russian
365.O73 Spanish
365.O8 Criticism and reviews
The variation of animals and plants under domestication
365.V2 Editions. By date
365.V25 Selections. By editor

Evolution
Works of Darwin
Separate works, A-Z
The variation of animals and plants under domestication -- Continued
365.V3-.V79 Translations
Arrange alphabetically by language, then Cutter for translator
365.V8 Criticism and reviews
365.Z9 Selections from more than one work. By editor
General works, treatises, and textbooks
366 1861-1969
366.2 1970-
367 Popular works
367.1 Juvenile works
367.3 Critical works
Class here works that argue against the theory of evolution
Cf. BL263 Religion and science
367.5 Phylogenetic relationships
For the evolution of particular animals and groups of animals, see systematic sections, e.g. QL618.2 Evolution of fishes; QL708.5 Evolution of mammals
(368) Human evolution
see GN281+
(368.5) Plant evolution (General)
see QK980
369 Miscellany and curiosa
(371) Special aspects of the subject as a whole
see QH371.3.A+
371.3.A-Z Special aspects of the subject as a whole, A-Z
371.3.M37 Mathematical models
371.5 Macroevolution
372 Coevolution
372.5 Homoplasy
373 Convergence
375 Natural selection
376 Group selection
378 Symbiogenesis
380 Speciation
390 Mutation in evolution. Evolutionary genetics
395 Heterochrony
398 Punctuated equilibrium
Variation
401 General works
(405) Statistical methods
see QH323.5

Evolution
Variation -- Continued
(406) Plants
see QK983
408 Animals
408.5 Phenetics
409 Clines
411 Experimental study
Hybridization. Hybrid zones
421 General works
(423) Plants
see QK982
425 Animals
Class particular animals in QL or SF
Cf. SF105+ Animal breeding
Genetics
Class here general and experimental works in genetics
For studies made on the genetic constitution of an organism in order to elucidate its total function, see systematic divisions in QK, QL, or QR. For genetic studies for improvement of breed or variety, see the plant or animal in S
For endocrine genetics see QP187.5
For immunogenetics see QR184+
426 Periodicals, societies, congresses, serial publications
426.5 Collected works (nonserial)
427 Dictionaries and encyclopedias
History
428 General works
428.2.A-Z By region or country, A-Z
Biography
429 Collective
429.2.A-Z Individual, A-Z
e.g.
Mendel see QH31.M45
429.5 Directories
General works, treatises, and textbooks
430 General works
431 Human genetics (General)
Cf. HQ750+ Eugenics
Cf. RB155+ Medical genetics
432 Animal genetics (General)
Cf. QH408 Animal variation
Cf. SF105+ Animal breeding
(433) Plant genetics (General)
see QK981
434 Microbial genetics (General)
Cf. QR73 Variation

Genetics -- Continued

436 Pictorial works and atlases

437 Popular works

437.5 Juvenile works

438 Addresses, essays, lectures

438.4.A-Z Special aspects of the subject as a whole, A-Z

438.4.B55 Biochemical markers. Genetic markers

438.4.C45 Chemogenomics

Genetic markers see QH438.4.B55

438.4.M3 Mathematical models

438.4.M33 Mathematics

438.4.S73 Statistical methods

438.5 Heredity and environment. Nature and nurture

438.7 Social and moral aspects

439 Vocational guidance

Study and teaching. Research

440 General works

440.2 Outlines, syllabi

440.3 Problems, exercises, examinations

440.4 Experiments

440.5 Laboratory manuals

Laboratories

440.7 General works

440.8.A-Z By region or country, A-Z

Subarrange each country by Table Q6

441 Technique

441.2 Data processing

441.5 Cytogenetics

Cf. QH600+ Chromosomes

Cf. QP620+ Nucleic acids

Molecular genetics. Genetic engineering

Cf. QK981.5 Plant genetics

Cf. RB155+ Medical genetics

Cf. TP248.6 Genetic engineering applications

442 General works

442.2 Cloning

442.3 Gene targeting

442.4 Gene libraries

442.6 Transgenic organisms. Transgenic animals

Recombination mechanisms

443 General works

444 Segregation. Assortment

Crossing over

445 General works

Linkage and genetic mapping

445.2 General works

445.5 Sex linkage

Genetics
Recombination mechanisms
Crossing over -- Continued
445.7 Mosaicism
Genes. Alleles. Genome
Cf. QP98 Blood groups
447 General works
447.2 Dominance and recessiveness
447.5 Conversion
447.6 Polymorphisms
Lethal factors see QH463.5
447.8.A-Z Individual genes and genetic elements, A-Z
447.8.A28 Actin genes
447.8.B46 Beta-glucuronidase genes
447.8.H65 Homeobox genes
Ir genes see QR184.4
447.8.O43 Olfactory receptor genes
Oncogenes see RC268.42
447.8.R47 Reporter genes
447.8.S45 Selfish genetic elements
Recombination in microorganisms
448 General works
448.2 Conjugation
448.3 Transduction
448.4 Transformation
Genetic regulation. Gene expression
450 General works
450.2 Genetic code. Transcription
450.25 RNA editing
450.3 Gene amplification
450.5 Translation. Assembly
450.6 Post-translational modification of proteins
450.7 Epistasis
451 Cell fusion. Cell hybridization
452 Cytoplasmic inheritance
452.2 Microsatellites
Mobile genetic elements
Cf. QH462.I48 Insertion elements, DNA
452.3 General works
452.5 Episomes
452.6 Plasmids
Cf. QR76.6 Bacterial plasmids
452.7 Quantitative genetics
452.8 In situ hybridization
453 Developmental genetics

Genetics -- Continued
455 Population genetics
Cf. GN289+ Physical anthropology
Cf. HB848+ Population (Economic theory)
456 Ecological genetics
Endocrine genetics see QP187.5
Evolutionary genetics see QH390
Immunogenetics see QR184+
457 Behavior genetics
Cf. BF341+ Heredity of consciousness
Cf. BF699+ Genetic psychology
Mutations
Cf. QH390 Mutation in evolution
460 General works
461 Genetic mutation. Polyploidy. Aneuploidy
Chromosomal mutation
462.A1 General works, treatises, and textbooks
462.A2-Z By type, A-Z
462.B7 Breakage
462.D4 Deletion
462.D8 Duplication
462.G46 Gene fusion
462.I48 Insertion elements, DNA
462.I5 Inversion
462.N65 Nondisjunction
462.T7 Translocation
463 Gene mutation
463.2 Nonsense mutation
463.5 Lethal factors
464 Spontaneous mutation
Induced mutation. DNA damage
465.A1 General works, treatises, and textbooks
465.A2-Z By agent, A-Z
465.C3 Caffeine
465.C5 Chemicals (General)
465.C6 Colchicine
465.D55 DNA. Polynucleotides
465.N4 Neutrons
465.O44 Oil shale extracts
Polynucleotides see QH465.D55
465.R3 Radiation (General)
465.U4 Ultraviolet rays
465.X2 X-rays
465.5 Site-specific mutagenesis
467 Genetic repair mechanisms
468 Antimutagens

Genetics -- Continued
470.A-Z Experimental organisms, A-Z
Prefer classification by genetic aspect studied
470.A85 Aspergillus
470.C6 Corprinus
470.C64 Corn
470.D7 Drosophila
470.E8 Escherichia
Maize see QH470.C64
470.M52 Mice
470.N4 Neurospora
470.O35 Oenothera
470.S23 Saccharomyces cerevisiae
470.T6 Tobacco mosaic virus
470.T68 Tradescantia
470.T7 Trillium
Reproduction
Cf. QK825+ Plants
Cf. QP251+ Animals
471 General works, treatises, and textbooks
Asexual
Cf. QH442.2 Cloning (Genetic engineering)
475 General works, treatises, and textbooks
477 Fission
479 Budding
Sexual
481 General works, treatises, and textbooks
485 Fertilization
487 Parthenogenesis
489 Alternation of generations
491 Development. Morphogenesis
Including tissue remodeling
Cf. QK665 Plant embryology
Cf. QL951+ Animal embryology
499 Regeneration
Cf. QK840 Plant physiology
Cf. QP90.2 Animal physiology
Life
Cf. QK710+ Plants
Cf. QP1+ Animals
501 General works, treatises, and textbooks
Biochemistry see QH345
504 Biomagnetism
Cf. QP82.2.M3 Physiological effects of magnetic fields
Cf. QP345 Human magnetic fields
505 Biophysics

Life -- Continued
506 Molecular biology
Cf. QP187.3.M64 Molecular endocrinology
Homeostasis see QP90.4
507 Information theory in biology
508 Biological control sytems
509 Biological transport
Cf. QH615 Osmosis
509.5 Bioelectronics
510 Bioenergetics
510.5 Bioacoustics
511 Growth
512 Biomineralization
513 Biomechanics
Cf. QP303 Animal mechanics. Human mechanics
513.5 Fluid dynamics
514 Movement. Tropisms. Taxes
Including attachment mechanisms
515 Photobiology
Cf. QH641 Bioluminescence
Cf. QP517.P45 Photobiochemistry
516 Thermobiology
517 Electrophysiology
Cf. QP341 Animals
Cf. QP517.B53 Bioelectrochemistry
518 Respiration
518.5 Anaerobiosis
519 Nutrition
521 Metabolism
523 Dormancy
524 Cryptobiosis. Anhydrobiosis
527 Chronobiology. Periodicity. Biorhythms
Cf. QP84.6 Physiology
528 Degeneration
528.5 Longevity
Cf. QP85 Animals
529 Senescence. Aging
530 Death
Cf. QH671 Cell death
Cf. QP87 Animal death
530.5 Biodegradation
Cf. QP517.B5 Animals
Cf. QR135+ Microbial degradation
531 Miscellany and curiosa

Ecology
Class here works on general ecology and general animal ecology.
For works on ecology of individual animals and groups of animals, see the animal
For human ecology see GF1+
For ecology of a particular topographic area see QH101+
For plant ecology see QK900+
Cf. BL65.E36 Ecology and religion
Cf. HX550.E25 Communism and ecology
Cf. QH546 Ecological genetics

540 Periodicals, societies, congresses, serial publications
540.3 Collected works (nonserial)
540.4 Dictionaries and encyclopedias
540.5 Philosophy
540.6 Nomenclature, terminology, notation, abbreviations
540.7 Classification
History
540.8 General works
540.83.A-Z By region or country, A-Z
Biography see QH26+
541 General works, treatises, and textbooks
541.13 Popular works
541.14 Juvenile works
541.142 Handbooks, tables, formulas, etc.
541.145 Addresses, essays, lectures
541.15.A-Z Special aspects of the subject as a whole, A-Z
541.15.A9 Autoradiographic techniques
Biodiversity see QH541.15.B56
541.15.B54 Biological assay
541.15.B56 Biological diversity. Biodiversity
For local, see QH84.1+
For physiographic divisions see QH84.8+
Cf. QH75+ Biodiversity conservation
Cf. QH541.15.S64 Species diversity
Cf. QK46.5.D58 Plant diversity
541.15.B84 Buffer zones
541.15.C44 Chemical ecology
541.15.C55 Closed ecological systems
541.15.C67 Corridors
541.15.D6 Documentation
541.15.E19 Ecohydrology
541.15.E22 Ecological assessment (Biology)
541.15.E24 Ecological heterogeneity
541.15.E245 Ecological integrity
541.15.E248 Ecological zones
541.15.E25 Economic ecology

Ecology
Special aspects of the subject as a whole, A-Z -- Continued

541.15.E26 Ecophysiology
Cf. QP82+ Animal ecophysiology
541.15.E265 Ecosystem health
541.15.E267 Ecosystem services
541.15.E27 Ecotones
Including land-water ecotones
541.15.E45 Electronic data processing
541.15.F66 Food chains. Food webs
541.15.F73 Fragmented landscapes
541.15.G46 Geographic information systems
541.15.H34 Habitat suitability index models
Health, Ecosystem see QH541.15.E265
Heterogeneity, Ecological see QH541.15.E24
541.15.I5 Indicators (Biology)
Integrity, Ecological see QH541.15.E245
541.15.K48 Keystone species
541.15.L35 Landscape ecology
For local see QH101+
541.15.M23 Macroecology
541.15.M26 Mapping
541.15.M3 Mathematical models
Cf. QH541.15.H34 Habitat suitability index models
541.15.M34 Mathematics
541.15.M63 Molecular ecology
541.15.M64 Monitoring
541.15.N84 Null models
541.15.R34 Radioactive tracers
541.15.R4 Remote sensing
541.15.R45 Restoration ecology
For local see QH101+
For specific types of environments see QH541.5.A+
541.15.R57 Risk assessment
541.15.S5 Simulation methods
541.15.S62 Spatial ecology
541.15.S64 Species diversity
541.15.S68 Stable isotopes
541.15.S72 Statistical methods
541.15.S95 Surveys
Including general habitat surveys
541.15.T68 Toxicity testing
Zones, Ecological see QH541.15.E248

Communication in ecology
541.18 General works
541.183 Information services

QH

Ecology
Communication in ecology -- Continued
541.185 Computer network resources
Including the Internet
Study and teaching. Research
541.2 General works
541.215 Outlines, syllabi
Special teaching methods and aids
541.22 General works
541.23 Audiovisual aids
541.235.A-Z Other methods, A-Z
541.235.G34 Games
541.24 Experiments
541.25 Laboratory manuals
By region or country
United States
541.26 General works
541.262.A-Z By region or state, A-Z
541.264.A-Z Other regions or countries, A-Z
Ecological laboratories and stations
541.27 General works
541.273.A-Z By region or country, A-Z
541.28 Technique
541.29 Applied ecology
Cf. QH541.15.M64 Monitoring
Cf. QH541.15.R45 Restoration ecology
541.3 Biological productivity
Cf. QK909.5 Vegetation productivity
541.5.A-Z By type of environment, A-Z
For local see QH101+
Abyssal zone see QH541.5.D35
Antarctica see QH84.2
Aquatic see QH541.5.W3
Arctic regions see QH84.1
541.5.A74 Arid regions
541.5.B63 Bogs
Boreal forests see QH541.5.T3
Brackish waters see QH541.5.E8
Braided rivers see QH541.5.S7
541.5.C24 Canals
541.5.C3 Caves
Cerrados see QH541.5.P7
541.5.C5 Chaparral
541.5.C6 Cities. Urban ecology
541.5.C62 Cliffs
541.5.C63 Cloud forests
541.5.C65 Coasts

Ecology
By type of environment, A-Z -- Continued
541.5.C7 Coral reefs and islands. Reefs
541.5.C73 Coulees
541.5.C95 Cypress swamps
541.5.D35 Deep-sea zone. Abyssal zone
Including hydrothermal vents
541.5.D4 Deserts
541.5.E8 Estuaries. Brackish waters
541.5.F56 Fjords
Floodplains see QH541.5.V3
541.5.F6 Forests
Including forest canopy ecology and old growth forest ecology
Cf. QH541.5.C63 Cloud forests
Cf. QH541.5.P47 Permafrost forests
Cf. QH541.5.R27 Rain forests
Cf. QH541.5.T3 Taigas. Boreal forests
Cf. SD416+ Forest influences
Cf. SD418+ Deforestation
541.5.F7 Freshwater
541.5.G37 Gardens
Grasslands see QH541.5.P7
541.5.G76 Groundwater
541.5.H43 Heathlands
541.5.H65 Hot springs
Cf. QH541.5.D35 Hydrothermal vents
Cf. QR107 Microbial ecology
541.5.H67 Household ecology
Intertidal zones see QH541.5.S35
541.5.I8 Islands
541.5.J8 Jungle
541.5.K4 Kelp beds
541.5.L27 Lagoons
541.5.L3 Lakes
Cf. QH541.5.S22 Salt lakes
541.5.L53 Llanos
541.5.M27 Mangrove swamps
Marine ecology see QH541.5.S3
541.5.M3 Marshes. Wetlands
541.5.M4 Meadows
541.5.M44 Mediterranean-type
Cf. QH150 Mediterranean Region
541.5.M6 Moors
541.5.M65 Mountains
541.5.O24 Ocean bottom. Seabed
541.5.O25 Ocean currents
Oceans see QH541.5.S3

Ecology
By type of environment, A-Z -- Continued

541.5.P47 Permafrost forests
541.5.P6 Polar regions
541.5.P63 Ponds
541.5.P7 Prairies. Grasslands. Savannas. Cerrados. Steppes
Cf. QH541.5.S18 Sagebrush steppes
541.5.R27 Rain forests
541.5.R3 Rangelands
Reefs see QH541.5.C7
541.5.R4 Reservoirs
541.5.R52 Riparian areas
Rivers see QH541.5.S7
541.5.R62 Roads. Roadsides
541.5.S18 Sagebrush steppes
541.5.S22 Salt lakes
541.5.S24 Salt marshes. Tide marshes
541.5.S26 Sand dunes
Savannas see QH541.5.P7
541.5.S3 Sea. Marine ecology. Ocean ecology
Cf. QH541.5.D35 Deep-sea zone
Seabed see QH541.5.O24
541.5.S35 Seashore. Tidal pools
Including intertidal zones
541.5.S55 Shrublands
541.5.S57 Snow ecology
541.5.S6 Soil
541.5.S65 Springs
Cf. QH541.5.H65 Hot springs
Steppes see QH541.5.P7
541.5.S7 Streams. Rivers
Including braided rivers
Cf. QH541.5.C73 Coulees
541.5.S87 Sublittoral
541.5.S9 Swamps
Cf. QH541.5.C95 Cypress swamps
Cf. QH541.5.M27 Mangrove swamps
541.5.T3 Taigas. Boreal forests
Cf. QH541.5.P47 Permafrost forests
Tidal pools see QH541.5.S35
Tide marshes see QH541.5.S24
541.5.T7 Tropics
541.5.T8 Tundras
541.5.U55 Underground ecology
541.5.U64 Uplands
Cf. QH541.5.M65 Mountains
Urban ecology see QH541.5.C6

Ecology
By type of environment, A-Z -- Continued
541.5.V27 Vacant lots
541.5.V3 Valleys. Floodplains
Cf. QH541.5.C73 Coulees
541.5.W3 Water. Aquatic ecology
Water, Fresh see QH541.5.F7
Wetlands see QH541.5.M3
541.5.X45 Xeric ecology
(542) Paleoecology
see QE720
Geobiology see QH343.4
542.5 Biogeomorphology
Bioclimatology. Microclimatology
Cf. QH545.T4 Temperature as a factor in ecology
543 General works
543.2 Acclimatization
Cf. QK913 Plant acclimatization
543.3 Dispersal of organisms by environmental factors
Radioecology. Radiobiology
Cf. QH328 Space radiobiology
Cf. QH545.N8 Nuclear power plants, nuclear reactors
Cf. QH545.N83 Nuclear warfare
Cf. QH652+ Radiation effects on cells
543.5.A1 Periodicals. Congresses
543.5.A2 Collected works (nonserial)
543.5.A3-Z General works, treatises, and textbooks
Aquatic radioecology
543.58 General works
543.6 Marine radioecology
543.8 Brackish water radioecology. Estuarine radioecology
543.9 Freshwater radioecology
543.95 Ultraviolet radiation
544 Phenology
Influence of special factors in the environment
For works on the technical aspects (e.g., control, measurement, etc.) of pollution in general and of special kinds of pollution see TD172+
Cf. GF51 Human ecology
Cf. QH343.7+ Biogeochemistry
Cf. QK746+ Plants
Cf. QP82+ Animals
Cf. RA565+ Environmental health
545.A1 General works, treatises, and textbooks
545.A15-Z Special, A-Z
Acid precipitation see QH545.A17
545.A17 Acid rain. Acid precipitation. Acid deposition

	Ecology
	Influence of special factors in the environment
	Special, A-Z -- Continued
545.A2	Acids
545.A23	Actinide elements
545.A25	Agricultural chemicals
545.A3	Air pollution
545.A4	Aldrin
545.A42	All terrain bicycles. Mountain bikes Including all terrain cycling and mountain biking
545.A43	All terrain vehicles
545.A45	Ammonia
545.A77	Arsenic
	Atomic warfare see QH545.N83
545.B45	Benzene
545.B47	Beryllium
545.B55	Biological pest control agents
545.B57	Bird declines
545.B6	Boron
	Brines, Oil field see QH545.O47
545.C3	Cadmium
545.C34	Campfires
545.C35	Canals
545.C37	Carbon isotopes
545.C47	Chemical elements
545.C48	Chemical warfare. Chemical weapons
545.C5	Chloroform
545.C52	Cholecalciferol
545.C54	Chromium
545.C545	Cities and towns. Urban growth. Urban sprawl
545.C57	Coal-fired power plants
545.C59	Contaminated sediments
545.C6	Copper
545.C64	Coral fisheries
545.C78	Cruise ships
545.D35	Dams. Reservoirs
545.D4	Deicing chemicals
	Desalination plants see QH545.S33
545.D486	Diazinon
545.D5	Dichloromethane
545.D55	Dioxins Cf. QH545.T44 Tetrachlorodibenzodioxin
545.D57	Diquat
545.D7	Dredging
545.D713	Dredging (Fisheries)
545.D72	Dredging spoil
545.D74	Drilling muds

Ecology
Influence of special factors in the environment
Special, A-Z
545.D75 Drilling platforms
545.E35 El Niño Current
545.E38 Electric power plants
545.E4 Electromagnetic waves
545.E42 ELF electromagnetic fields
Energy development see QH545.E53
545.E53 Energy industries. Energy development
Erosion, Soil see QH545.S64
545.E98 Exterior lighting
545.F47 Fertilizers
545.F5 Fire. Fire ecology
545.F52 Fish culture
545.F53 Fisheries
545.F55 Flood control
Flood dams see QH545.D35
545.F67 Forest management
545.G37 Gas pipelines
545.G46 Geothermal power plants
545.G55 Glyphosate
Growth, Urban see QH545.C545
545.H34 Hang gliding
545.H42 Heavy metals
545.H47 Herbicides
545.H49 Hexazinone
545.H54 Hiking
545.H92 Hydrocarbons
Including polycyclic aromatic hydrocarbons
545.H93 Hydroelectric power plants
Insecticides see QH545.P4
545.L35 Lakeshore development
Land reclamation see QH545.R38
545.L4 Lead
545.L63 Logging
545.M3 Manganese
545.M34 Mariculture
Marine pollution see QH545.W3
545.M4 Mercury
545.M45 Metals
Metals, Heavy see QH545.H42
545.M52 Mineral industries
545.M6 Molybdenum
Mountain bikes see QH545.A42
Muds, Drilling see QH545.D74

Ecology
Influence of special factors in the environment
Special, A-Z -- Continued

545.M86 Munitions
Cf. QH545.C48 Chemical weapons
545.N3 Natural disasters
545.N47 Nickel
545.N5 Nitrogen
545.N65 Noise
545.N8 Nuclear power plants. Nuclear reactors
545.N83 Nuclear warfare
545.O32 Ocean acidification
Ocean fertilization see QH545.S43
545.O33 Ocean outfalls
Off-road vehicles see QH545.A43
545.O38 Offshore oil industry
Cf. QH545.D75 Drilling platforms
545.O47 Oil field brines
545.O5 Oil pollution
Cf. QH91.8.O4 Marine biology
545.O54 Oil sands extraction plants
545.O56 Oil shales
545.O57 Oil well drilling
545.O72 Organochlorine compounds
545.O74 Organometallic compounds
545.O76 Organophosphorus compounds
545.O87 Outdoor recreation
545.O94 Ozone
545.P37 Pentachlorophenol
545.P39 Persistent pollutants
545.P4 Pesticides
Including insecticides
545.P5 Phosphorus
Pipelines, Gas see QH545.G37
Pollution (General) see QH545.A1
Pollution, Air see QH545.A3
Pollution, Marine see QH545.W3
Pollution, Oil see QH545.O5
Pollution, Thermal see QH545.T48
Pollution, Water see QH545.W3
545.P6 Polychlorinated biphenyls
Polycyclic aromatic hydrocarbons see QH545.H92
Power plants, Coal-fired see QH545.C57
Power plants, Electric see QH545.E38
Power plants, Geothermal see QH545.G46
Power plants, Hydroelectric see QH545.H93
545.P73 Predator control

Ecology
Influence of special factors in the environment
Special, A-Z -- Continued
Radiation see QH543.5+
545.R38 Reclamation of land
545.R42 Recreation areas
545.R44 Reforestation
Reservoirs see QH545.D35
545.R58 River regulation
545.R62 Roads
545.S33 Saline water conversion plants. Desalination plants
545.S35 Saltwater encroachment
545.S37 Sand and gravel industry
545.S4 Scuba diving
545.S43 Seawater fertilization. Ocean fertilization
Sediments, Contaminated see QH545.C59
545.S45 Selenium
545.S49 Sewage
545.S493 Sewage sludge
545.S498 Shore protection
545.S5 Shotgun pellets
545.S55 Silver
545.S56 Skiing
Including snow grooming
Sludge, Sewage see QH545.S493
Snow grooming see QH545.S56
545.S6 Snowmobiles
545.S63 Soil amendments
545.S64 Soil erosion
Sprawl, Urban see QH545.C545
545.S8 Stream channelization
545.S84 Strip mining
545.S9 Sulfur
545.S92 Sulfur compounds
545.T37 Technetium
545.T4 Temperature
545.T44 Tetrachlorodibenzodioxin
545.T45 Textile industry
545.T48 Thermal pollution
545.T55 Tin compounds
545.T7 Trace elements
545.T74 Transuranium elements
545.T743 Trawls and trawling
545.T75 Triclopyr
545.T76 Tritium
545.T87 Turbidity
545.U7 Uranium mining

QH

Ecology
Influence of special facators in the environment
Special, A-Z
Urban growth see QH545.C545
Urban sprawl see QH545.C545
545.V3 Vanadium
Vehicles, All terrain see QH545.A43
545.W26 War
Cf. QH545.N83 Nuclear warfare
545.W28 Waste disposal
545.W3 Water pollution
Including marine pollution
Cf. QH90.8.T68 Aquatic toxicology
545.W33 Water resources development
Waterpower electric plants see QH545.H93
545.X44 Xenobiotics
545.Z56 Zinc
546 Adaptation
Including protective mechanisms, mimicry
Cf. QK912+ Plant adaptation
Cf. QH543.2 Acclimatization
546.3 Competition. Niche
547 Parasitism
Symbiosis
548 General works
548.3 Mutualism
549 Colonies
549.5 Animal-plant relationships
(555) Degeneration
see QH528
(558) Aging
see QH529
(559) Death
see QH530
Cytology
Class here general and experimental works in cytology.
For works on the cytology of particular animals written to elucidate the total organism, see the systematic divisions in QL
Cf. QH441.5 Cytogenetics
Cf. QK671 Plant cell anatomy
Cf. QK725 Plant cell physiology
573 Periodicals, societies, congresses, serial publications
574 Collected works (nonserial)
575 Dictionaries and encyclopedias
History
577 General works

	Cytology
	History -- Continued
578.A-Z	By region or country, A-Z
	General works, treatises, and textbooks
581	Through 1969
581.2	1970-
581.5	Addresses, essays, lectures
582	Pictorial works and atlases
582.4	Popular works
582.5	Juvenile works
	Study and teaching. Research
583	General works
583.15	Outlines, syllabi
583.2	Laboratory manuals
	Technique
	Cf. TP248.27.A53 Animal cell biotechnology
585	General works
	Cell culture
585.2	General works
585.3	Serum-free culture media
	Cell lines
585.4	General works
585.45	Continuous cell lines
585.457	Lymphoblastoid cell lines
585.5.A-Z	Special techniques, A-Z
585.5.C43	Cell fractionation
585.5.C44	Cell separation
585.5.C64	Colony-forming units assay
585.5.C98	Cytofluorometry
585.5.C984	Cytophotometry
585.5.D38	Data processing
585.5.E43	Electrodes, Ion selective
585.5.E46	Electrophoresis
585.5.E48	Electroporation
585.5.F56	Flow cytometry
585.5.I45	Immobilization of cells
585.5.L37	Lasers
585.5.M52	Micropipette techniques
585.5.M53	Microspectrophotometry
585.5.N82	Nuclear magnetic resonance spectroscopy
(585.5.S45)	Serum-free culture
	see QH585.3
585.5.S83	Subcellular fractionation
	Cell populations
587	General works
588.A-Z	Individual types of cells, A-Z
588.S83	Stem cells

Cytology -- Continued

591 Protoplasm. Cytoplasm

595 Nucleus

596 Nucleolus

597 Centrosome. Centriole

599 Chromatin

Chromosomes

Cf. QH462.A1+ Chromosomal mutation

600 General works

600.15 Artificial chromosomes

600.2 Centromere

600.3 Telomere

600.5 Sex chromosomes

600.6 Giant chromosomes. Lampbrush chromosomes

Cell membranes

601 General works

601.2 Nuclear membranes

602 Lipid membranes. Bilayer lipid membranes. Liposomes

603.A-Z Other special, A-Z

603.C4 Cell junctions

603.C43 Cell receptors

603.C63 Coated vesicles

603.C95 Cytoplasmic filaments

603.C96 Cytoskeleton

603.E6 Endoplasmic reticulum

603.E63 Endosomes

603.E93 Extracellular space

603.G6 Golgi apparatus

603.I49 Inclusion bodies

603.I54 Ion channels

603.L9 Lysosomes

603.M35 Microbodies

603.M4 Microsomes

603.M44 Microtubules

603.M5 Mitochondria

603.N83 Nuclear matrix

603.P47 Peroxisomes

603.R5 Ribosomes

603.S27 Sarcoplasmic reticulum

Control mechanisms. Cell regulation

Cf. QP187.3.C44 Endocrinology

604 General works

604.2 Cell interaction

Cf. QP517.C45 Cellular signal transduction

604.3 Cell compartmentation

604.5 Ion exchange

604.7 Cell growth. Cell proliferation

Cytology -- Continued
Cell division
605 General works
605.2 Mitosis
605.3 Meiosis
Cell differentiation
607 General works
Cf. QL963.5 Embryology
607.2.A-Z By type of cell, A-Z
607.2.C47 Chromatophores. Pigment cells
Pigment cells see QH607.2.C47
608 Aging of cells
Cf. QH671 Pathology and death
609 Cellular repair mechanisms
Physical and chemical properties
Cf. QH506 Molecular biology
611 General works
613 Histochemistry
615 Osmosis
621 Turgescence
622 Adsorption
623 Adhesion
Physiological properties
631 General works
633 Respiration
634 Ingestion. Pinocytosis, etc.
634.2 Exocytosis
634.5 Metabolism
635 Heat production. Energy
641 Light production. Bioluminescence
Cf. QP517.C54 Chemiluminescence
642 Optical properties
643 Radiation properties
645 Electric properties
645.5 Mechanical properties
646 Contraction
647 Motility. Irritability
Effect of physical and chemical agents on cells
Cf. QK746+ Plant physiology
Cf. QP82+ Animal physiology
650 General works
651 Light
Cf. QH515 Photobiology

Cytology
Effect of physical and chemical agents on cells -- Continued
Radiation
For the effect of radiation on specific organs, organisms, etc., see the specific organ, etc., e.g. QP356.5, Nervous system
Cf. QP82.2.R3 Radiation (Physiology)

652.A1 Periodicals, societies, congresses, serial publications
652.A2 Collected works (nonserial)
652.A3-Z General works, treatises, and textbooks
652.4 Ultraviolet radiation
(652.5) Radiogenetics
see QH465.R3
652.7 Acoustic radiation
653 Temperature
655 Electricity
656 Magnetic fields
657 Gravity
658 Pressure
659 Chemicals
671 Pathology and death
Cf. QH608 Aging of cells

Economic biology
Cf. S494.5.E25 Agriculture
Cf. SB107+ Economic botany
Cf. SF84+ Economic zoology

705 General works
705.5.A-Z By region or country, A-Z

	Botany
1	Periodicals, societies, congresses, serial publications
3	Collected works (nonserial)
5	Voyages and expeditions
7	Encyclopedias
9	Dictionaries
	Communication of information
9.2	General works
9.3	Information services
9.4	Computer network resources Including the Internet
10	Terminology, notation, abbreviations Cf. QK96 Nomenclature
11	Indexes of plants
13	Popular names
14.5	Botanical literature Including works on herbals
	History
15	General works
21.A-Z	By region or country, A-Z
	Biography
26	Collective
31.A-Z	Individual, A-Z e. g.
31.G8	Gray
31.T7	Torrey
35	Directories
	General works and treatises Cf. QK91 Works of Linnaeus (Botany only)
41	Early through 1753
45	1754-1969
45.2	1970-
46	Special aspects of the subject as a whole
46.5.A-Z	Special topics, A-Z
46.5.A47	Aerial photography
46.5.B66	Botanizers
	Botany for gardeners see QK50
46.5.D58	Diversity, Plant (General) Including centers of plant diversity For plant diversity conservation see QK86+ For local see QK102+
46.5.E4	Electronic data processing
46.5.F67	Forensic botany
46.5.H85	Human-plant relationships
46.5.M3	Mathematical models
46.5.S7	Statistical methods

Special topics, A-Z -- Continued
46.5.V44 Vegetation monitoring
For local see QK108+
47 Textbooks
48 Handbooks, tables, formulas, etc.
49 Juvenile works
50 Popular works
For plants of individual regions or countries see QK108+
50.5 Botany as a profession. Vocational guidance
Study and teaching. Research
51 General works
51.2.A-Z By region or country, A-Z
Each region or country subarranged by author
52 Outlines, syllabi
52.5 Problems, exercises, examinations
52.55 Activity programs
52.6 Experiments
53 Laboratory manuals
Cf. QK673 Anatomy and histology
Audiovisual aids
54 General works
55 Charts
57 Plant analysis blanks
61 Collection and preservation
61.4 Plant prints
62 Vegetation surveys
63 Vegetation mapping
Botanical gardens
Class here descriptions, catalogs, and administrative reports only.
Class other serial publications in QK1
Cf. QK479+ Arboretums
71 General works
73.A-Z By region or country, A-Z
Under each country:
.x *General works*
.x2A-.x2Z *Individual. By name, A-Z*
Herbariums
Class here descriptions, catalogs, and administrative reports only.
Class other serial publications in QK1
75 General works
76.A-Z By region or country, A-Z
77.A-Z Individual. By name, A-Z
Laboratories
Class here descriptions, catalogs, and administrative reports only.
Class other serial publications in QK1
78 General works

Laboratories -- Continued
78.5.A-Z By region or country, A-Z
Subarrange each country by Table Q6
Museums. Exhibitions
Class here descriptions, catalogs, and administrative reports only. Class other serial publications in QK1
79 General works
79.5.A-Z By region or country, A-Z
Subarrange each country by Table Q5
81 Addresses, essays, lectures
83 Plant lore
Cf. GR780+ Folklore
National plants. Official plants
Including state, provincial, etc. plants
84.8 General works
By region or country
85 United States
85.3.A-Z Other regions or countries, A-Z
85.5 Wild flowers
Prefer classification by area
Plant conservation. Rare plants. Endangered plants
Including plant diversity conservation and remnant vegetation conservation and management
86.A1 General works
86.A5-Z By region or country, A-Z
86.4 Plant reintroduction
86.5 Applied ethnobotany
Relict plants
86.7 General works
86.73.A-Z By region or country, A-Z
87 Miscellany and curiosa
89 Pressed plants with text. Bound herbaria
Classification
91 Works of Linnaeus (Botany only)
92 Linnaean system (Minor works)
Natural systems
Not to be used for systems developed after Darwin
93 General works, treatises, and textbooks
94 Minor works
Systematics and taxonomy. Philosophy and methodology
95 General works
95.4 Chemotaxonomy
For geographic treatment see QK108+
For systematic treatment see QK494.5.A+
95.6 Molecular aspects
96 Nomenclature
97 Comprehensive systematic works

QK

97.5 Identification
For geographic treatment see QK108+
98 Pictorial works and atlases (of plants)
Prefer classification by area
Atlases of botanical maps are classed in class G
Botanical illustration and artists
Cf. QK98 Pictorial works
History
98.15 General works
98.16.A-Z By region or country, A-Z
Biography
98.18 Collective
98.183.A-Z Individual, A-Z
Including collections of their illustrations
98.2 General works
98.24 Technique
98.3 Catalogs
98.4 Useful plants. Permaculture plants
98.4.A1 General works, treatises, and textbooks
98.4.A5-Z By region or country, A-Z
Economic botany see SB107+
Edible plants
Including edible wild plants
Cf. SB175+ Food crops
98.5.A1 General works, treatises, and textbooks
98.5.A5-Z By region or country, A-Z
Dye plants (General)
Cf. SB285+ Culture
98.7.A1 General works, treatises, and textbooks
98.7.A5-Z By region or country, A-Z
Medical botany (General)
Cf. RS164 Drugs of the vegetable kingdom
Cf. SB293 Culture
99.A1 General works, treatises, and textbooks
99.A5-Z By region or country, A-Z
Poisonous plants
Cf. SB617+ Poisonous plants as pests
100.A1 General works, treatises, and textbooks
100.A5-Z By region or country, A-Z
Geographical distribution. Phytogeography
101 General works, treatises, and textbooks
Aquatic flora (General)
For geographic treatment see QK108+
Cf. QK564+ Algae
102 General works
103 Marine flora (General)
105 Freshwater flora (General)

Geographical distribution. Phytogeography -- Continued
Topographical divisions
108 Special parts of the world
Including British Empire
America
109 General works
North America
110 General works
112 Illustrations of North American flora
United States
Including East (U.S.)
115 General works
By region
Northeast
117 General works
118 Popular handbooks
121 New England
121.5 Saint John River and Valley (Me. and N.B.)
Atlantic States. Atlantic Coast
122 General works
122.3 Appalachian Mountains
122.5 Middle Atlantic States
122.8 Chesapeake Bay
122.85 Potomac River
122.9 South Atlantic States
Southern States
124 General works
Southeast
Cf. QK122.9 South Atlantic States
125 General works
125.35 Blue Ridge Mountains
125.4 Great Smoky Mountains
125.8 Gulf States
128 Middle West
130 Great Lakes
West (U.S.)
133 General works
134 Ozark Mountains
135 Great Plains
139 Rocky Mountains Region
141 Great Basin
Southwest
142 General works
142.2 Chihuahuan Desert
142.3 Mojave Desert
142.4 Sonoran desert
Sierra Nevada

Geographical distribution. Phytogeography
Topographical divisions
America
North America
United States
By region
West (U.S.)
Sierra Nevada -- Continued
142.7 General works
142.75 Tahoe, Lake, Watershed (Calif. and Nev.)
143 Pacific coast
Northwest
144 General works
144.2 Columbia Basin
By state
145 Alabama
146 Alaska
147 Arizona
148 Arkansas
149 California
150 Colorado
151 Connecticut
152 Delaware
153 District of Columbia
154 Florida
155 Georgia
Hawaii see QK473.H4
156 Idaho
157 Illinois
159 Indiana
160 Iowa
161 Kansas
162 Kentucky
163 Louisiana
164 Maine
165 Maryland
166 Massachusetts
167 Michigan
168 Minnesota
169 Mississippi
170 Missouri
171 Montana
172 Nebraska
173 Nevada
174 New Hampshire
175 New Jersey
176 New Mexico

Geographical distribution. Phytogeography
Topographical divisions
America
North America
United States
By state -- Continued
177 New York
178 North Carolina
179 North Dakota
180 Ohio
181 Oklahoma
182 Oregon
183 Pennsylvania
184 Rhode Island
185 South Carolina
186 South Dakota
187 Tennessee
188 Texas
189 Utah
190 Vermont
191 Virginia
192 Washington
193 West Virginia
194 Wisconsin
195 Wyoming. Yellowstone Park
Canada
201 General works
203.A-Z By region or province, A-Z
For regions that include both the United States and Canada see QK115+
Latin America
205 General works
211 Mexico
Central America
215 General works
216 Belize
217 Costa Rica
218 Guatemala
219 Honduras
220 Nicaragua
221 Panama
222 El Salvador
West Indies. Caribbean area
225 General works
226 Bahamas
227 Cuba
Hispaniola

Geographical distribution. Phytogeography
Topographical divisions
America
Latin America
West Indies. Caribbean area
Hispaniola -- Continued

227.7	General works
227.8	Dominican Republic
228	Haiti
229	Jamaica
230	Puerto Rico
231.A-Z	Other, A-Z
231.A48	Antigua and Barbuda
231.A5	Antilles, Lesser
231.A78	Aruba
231.B3	Barbados
231.C35	Cayman Islands
231.C87	Curaçao
231.D59	Dominica
	Dominican Republic see QK227.8
231.F74	French West Indies
231.G73	Grenada
231.G8	Guadeloupe
231.M35	Martinique
231.N4	Netherlands Antilles
231.S3	Saint Bartholomew
231.S33	Saint Kitts and Nevis
231.S34	Saint Lucia
231.S35	Saint Martin
231.S38	Saint Vincent and the Grenadines
231.T75	Trinidad and Tobago
231.T87	Turks and Caicos Islands
231.V5	Virgin Islands
232	Bermuda
	South America
241	General works
261	Argentina
262	Bolivia
263	Brazil
264	Chile
265	Colombia
266	Ecuador
	Galapagos see QK473.G2
	Guiana
266.8	General works
267	Guyana (British Guiana)
268	Suriname (Dutch Guiana)

Geographical distribution. Phytogeography
Topographical divisions
America
Latin America
South America
Guiana -- Continued

269 French Guiana
270 Paraguay
271 Peru
272 Uruguay
273 Venezuela
274 Falkland Islands

Atlantic Ocean Islands

275.A1 General works
275.A3-Z By island or group of islands, A-Z
275.A9 Azores

Bermuda see QK232
Canary Islands see QK422

275.C4 Cape Verde

Falkland Islands see QK274

275.F37 Faroe Islands
275.M3 Madeira
275.S27 Saint Helena
275.S3 Salvages Islands
275.S68 South Orkney Islands
275.T74 Tristan da Cunha Island

Europe

281 General works

Zone and physiographic divisions

297 Alpine
303.A-Z Other, A-Z

By region or country
British Isles. Great Britain. England

306 General works
307 Ireland
307.5 Northern Ireland
308 Scotland
309 Wales
310 Austria
311 Hungary
313 France
313.5 Monaco
314 Germany

Including East and West Germany

(314.2) East Germany

see QK314

Geographical distribution. Phytogeography
Topographical divisions
Europe
By region or country -- Continued

314.5 Mediterranean Region
Including African coast
315 Greece
316 Italy
316.5 Malta
317 Benelux (Low Countries)
318 Belgium
319 Luxembourg
320 Netherlands (Holland)
321 Russia. Soviet Union. Russia (Federation)
Cf. QK372+ Former Soviet areas of Asia
Cf. QK375+ Russia (Federation) in Asia
321.5 Belarus
321.6 Moldova
321.7 Ukraine
322 Poland
323 Finland
324 Scandinavia (General)
Including Lapland
325 Denmark
325.5 Iceland
326 Norway
327 Sweden
Iberian Peninsula
328 General works
329 Spain
329.2 Gibraltar
330 Portugal
331 Switzerland
Balkan Peninsula
Including Turkey in Europe
332 General works
332.5 Bosnia and Hercegovina
333 Bulgaria
334 Croatia
334.5 Macedonia (Republic)
335 Romania
Serbia see QK336
335.5 Slovenia
336 Yugoslavia
Including Montenegro and Serbia
339.A-Z Other European regions, islands, or countries, A-Z
339.A5 Albania

Geographical distribution. Phytogeography
Topographical divisions
Europe
By region or country
Other European regions, islands, or countries, A-Z -- Continued
Alps see QK297
339.A54 Andorra
339.B34 Baltic States
339.C35 Carpathian Mountains
339.C45 Central Europe
339.C5 Channel Islands
339.C65 Constance, Lake of
339.C8 Czechoslovakia. Czech Republic
339.E37 Eastern Europe
339.E8 Estonia
339.J85 Jura Mountains (France and Switzerland)
339.L3 Latvia
339.L46 Liechtenstein
339.L5 Lithuania
Mediterranean Region see QK314.5
339.N67 Northern Europe
339.P95 Pyrenees (France and Spain)
339.S55 Slovakia
Yugoslavia see QK336
Asia
341 General works
352 Afghanistan
Arabian Peninsula
353 General works
353.2 Bahrain
353.3 Kuwait
353.4 Oman
353.5 Qatar
353.6 Saudi Arabia
353.7 United Arab Emirates
353.8 Yemen
354 Baluchistan
Cf. QK358.5 Baluchistan in Pakistan
China
355 General works
355.5 Hong Kong
355.6 Macau
356 Taiwan
357 Mongolia
South Asia. British Indian Empire
357.5 General works

Geographical distribution. Phytogeography
Topographical divisions
Asia
South Asia. British Indian Empire -- Continued

358 India
358.5 Pakistan
Including Baluchistan (Province)
358.7 Bangladesh
359 Sri Lanka
359.5 Nepal
359.6 Bhutan
Southeast Asia
For Malay Peninsula see QK365
360 General works
360.5 Burma. Myanmar
361 Cambodia. Laos. Vietnam. French Indonesia
364 Thailand
365 Malaysia
Including Malay Peninsula and Singapore
For Sabah and Sarawak see QK367
Malay Archipelago
365.5 General works
366 New Guinea
Including Papua (Indonesia) and Papua New Guinea
367 Indonesia
Including Borneo
For Papua see QK366
Brunei see QK367
368 Philippines
Japan
For Karafuto see QK375.2
369 General works
369.3 Ryukyu Islands
Including Okinawa-ken
370 Korea
371 Iran
Former Soviet areas of Asia
Cf. QK377 Caucasus
372 General works
Central Asia
374 General works
374.3 Kazakhstan
374.4 Kyrgyzstan
374.5 Tajikistan
374.6 Turkmenistan
374.7 Uzbekistan
Russia (Federation) in Asia. Siberia. Russian Far East

Geographical distribution. Phytogeography
Topographical divisions
Asia
Former Soviet areas of Asia
Russia (Federation) in Asia. Siberia. Russian Far East -- Continued

375 General works
375.2 Sakhalin
376 Asia Minor
Including Turkey in Asia
377 Caucasus
Including Armenia, Azerbaijan, Georgia (Republic)
377.3 Cyprus
377.5 Syria
377.7 Lebanon
378 Israel. Palestine
378.5 Jordan
379 Iraq
Bahrain see QK353.2
Kuwait see QK353.3
Oman see QK353.4
Qatar see QK353.5
Saudi Arabia see QK353.6
United Arab Emirates see QK353.7
Yemen see QK353.8
379.5.A-Z Other Asian regions or countries, A-Z
379.5.E38 East Asia
379.5.H55 Himalaya Mountains
379.5.M53 Middle East
379.5.P47 Persian Gulf
380 Arab countries
Africa
381 General works
By region or country
390 North Africa
391 Tropical Africa
Eastern Africa
Cf. QK401 East Africa
392 General works
392.4 Northeast Africa
393 West Africa
393.5 Central Africa
Cf. QK400 Former British Central Africa
394 Southern Africa
395 Ethiopia. Eritrea
Former British possessions
395.8 General works

Geographical distribution. Phytogeography
Topographical divisions
Africa
By region or country
Former British possessions -- Continued

396 South Africa
400 Central Africa (General)
401 East Africa (General)
402.A-Z Other special, A-Z
402.B6 Botswana
402.G3 Gambia
402.G5 Ghana
402.K4 Kenya
402.L48 Lesotho
402.M28 Malawi
Mauritius see QK429.M3
402.N34 Namibia
402.N5 Nigeria
402.R5 Rhodesia, Southern. Zimbabwe
402.S5 Sierra Leone
Somalia see QK415
402.S8 Swaziland
402.U2 Uganda
402.Z3 Zambia
Zimbabwe see QK402.R5
Mediterranean Region (General) see QK314.5
403 Egypt
404 Sudan
404.5 South Sudan
Former French possessions
405 Algeria
406 Tunisia
407 Madagascar
408 Senegal. Senegambia
409 Sahara
410.A-Z Other special, A-Z
410.B45 Benin
410.B85 Burkina Faso
Cameroon see QK412
410.C4 Central African Republic
410.C5 Chad
(410.D3) Dahomey
see QK410.B45
410.D55 Djibouti
410.G3 Gabon
410.G84 Guinea
410.I8 Ivory Coast. Côte d'Ivoire

Geographical distribution. Phytogeography
Topographical divisions
Africa
By region or country
Former French possessions
Other special, A-Z -- Continued
410.M38 Mauritania
Réunion see QK429.M27
410.T64 Togo
Former German possessions
411 Tanzania
411.5 Rwanda
412 Cameroon
413 Namibia. Southwest Africa
(414) Eritrea
see QK395
415 Somalia
416 Zaire. Congo (Democratic Republic)
416.4 Congo (Brazzaville)
417 Liberia
418 Morocco
419 Mozambique
420 Angola
420.5 Sao Tome and Principe
421 Guinea-Bissau
422 Canary Islands
423 Western Sahara
423.5 Equatorial Guinea
Including Fernando Po
424 Libya
Indian Ocean islands
428 General works
429.A-Z By island or group of islands, A-Z
429.A44 Aldabra Islands
429.C4 Christmas Island. Kiritimati
429.C6 Comoros
Madagascar see QK407
429.M24 Maldives
429.M27 Mascarene Islands
Including Réunion
429.M3 Mauritius
429.M34 Mayotte
429.P74 Prince Edward Islands
Réunion see QK429.M27
429.S4 Seychelles
429.S6 Sokotra
Australia

Geographical distribution. Phytogeography
Topographical divisions
Australia -- Continued
431 General works
445 New South Wales
Including Australian Capital Territory
Norfolk Island see QK473.N67
451 Northern Territory
453 Queensland
455 South Australia
457 Tasmania
459 Victoria
461 Western Australia
463 New Zealand and adjacent islands
Pacific islands. Oceania
471 General works
473.A-Z By island or group of islands, A-Z
Cf. QK463 New Zealand and adjacent islands
473.B6 Bonin Island
473.C48 Chuuk (Micronesia)
473.C55 Clipperton Island
473.E17 Easter Island
473.F5 Fiji Islands
473.F74 French Polynesia
473.G2 Galapagos Islands
473.G9 Guam
473.H4 Hawaiian Islands
473.J8 Juan Fernandez (Islands)
473.K55 Kiribati
473.K6 Kommander Islands
473.M3 Makatea
473.M34 Mariana Islands
473.M36 Marshall Islands
473.M5 Micronesia
473.M53 Midway Islands
473.N32 Nauru
473.N4 New Caledonia
New Guinea see QK366
Niihau see QK473.H4
473.N57 Niue (Island)
473.N67 Norfolk Island
Oceania see QK471+
Okinawa Islands see QK369.3
473.P3 Palmyra Island
473.P5 Pitcairn Island
473.P75 Polynesia
473.P78 Ponape Island

Geographical distribution. Phytogeography
Topographical divisions
Pacific islands. Oceania
By island or group of islands, A-Z -- Continued
473.R27 Raiatea
473.R3 Rarotonga
473.S3 Samoan Islands
473.S6 Society Islands (French Polynesia)
473.T3 Tahiti
473.T6 Tonga
473.T88 Tuvalu
473.V25 Vanuatu
473.W33 Wake Island
Polar regions
473.5 General works
Arctic regions
474 General works
474.2 Greenland
474.3 Svalbard
474.4 Antarctica
474.5 Tropics
Cf. QK391 Tropical Africa
Cf. QK936 Tropical plant ecology
Spermatophyta. Phanerogams
For general works, see general botany
Trees and shrubs
Cf. SD434+ Timber trees
474.8 Periodicals. Societies. Serials
474.83 Collected works (nonserial)
474.85 Congresses
474.87 Dictionaries and encyclopedias
475 General works, treatises, and textbooks
475.6 Pictorial works. Atlases
475.8 Juvenile works
476 Study and teaching. Research
477 Special aspects of the subject as a whole
For historic trees, see D
For folklore of trees see GR785
For national and state trees see QK84.8+
For remarkable trees see SD383+
477.2.A-Z Special topics, A-Z
477.2.A6 Annual rings
Cf. CC78.3 Archaeology
Cf. QC884.2.D4 Dendroclimatology
Flowering see QK830
Flowers see QK653+
477.2.I4 Identification

Spermatophyta. Phanerogams
Trees and shrubs
Special topics, A-Z -- Continued
Rings see QK477.2.A6
Roots see QK644
Arboretums. Fruticeta
479 General works
480.A-Z By region or country, A-Z
Under each country:
.x *General works*
.x2A-.x2Z *Local or individual. By name, A-Z*
(481-493.5) Local
see QK108+
Systematic divisions
Gymnosperms
Including orders and higher (not A-Z)
494 General works
494.5.A-Z By family, A-Z
Class species and genera by family
Abietaceae see QK494.5.P66
494.5.A7 Araucariaceae
494.5.C4 Cephalotaxaceae
Coniferae see QK494
Coniferales see QK494
494.5.C975 Cupressaceae
494.5.C995 Cycadaceae
494.5.E5 Ephedraceae
494.5.G48 Ginkgoaceae
494.5.G565 Gnetaceae
494.5.P58 Phyllocladaceae
494.5.P66 Pinaceae
494.5.P73 Podocarpaceae
494.5.S35 Sciadopityaceae (Japanese umbrella pine)
494.5.S8 Stangeriaceae
494.5.T25 Taxaceae
494.5.T3 Taxodiaceae
494.5.W4 Welwitschiaceae
494.5.Z35 Zamiaceae
Angiosperms
495.A1 General works, treatises, and textbooks
For geographical treatment see QK108+
For works limited to anatomy, morphology, and physiology see QK640+
495.A12 Dicotyledons
Including orders and higher (not A-Z)
495.A14 Monocotyledons
Including orders and higher (not A-Z)

Spermatophyta. Phanerogams
Systematic divisions
Angiosperms -- Continued

495.A15-Z By family, A-Z
Class species and genera by family

495.A1655 Acanthaceae
495.A17 Aceraceae (Maple)
495.A175 Achariaceae
495.A176 Achatocarpaceae
495.A177 Actinidiaceae
495.A178 Adoxaceae (Moschatel)
495.A185 Aextoxicaceae
495.A24 Agapanthaceae
495.A26 Agavaceae
495.A32 Aizoaceae (Ice plant)
495.A34 Akaniaceae
495.A36 Alangiaceae
495.A4 Alismataceae (Water plantain)
495.A42 Alliaceae (Onion; garlic; leek)
Aloaceae see QK495.A42
495.A48 Amaranthaceae (Amaranth)
495.A484 Amaryllidaceae (Amaryllis)
495.A485 Amborellaceae
495.A498 Anacardiaceae (Cashew)
495.A499 Ancistrocladaceae
495.A6 Annonaceae (Pawpaw)
495.A65 Aphyllanthaceae
Apiaceae see QK495.U48
495.A66 Apocynaceae (Dogbane)
495.A667 Aponogetonaceae
495.A67 Aquifoliaceae (Holly)
495.A685 Araceae (Arum)
495.A6853 Araliaceae (Ginseng)
Arecaceae see QK495.P17
495.A688 Aristolochiaceae (Dutchman's pipe)
495.A815 Asclepiadaceae (Milkweed)
495.A83 Asparagaceae (Asparagus)
495.A835 Asphodelaceae
Asteraceae see QK495.C74
495.A9 Austrobaileyaceae
495.B2 Balanopaceae
495.B23 Balanophoraceae
495.B25 Balsaminaceae (Touch-me-not)
495.B256 Basellaceae (Madeira vine)
495.B33 Bataceae
495.B4 Begoniaceae (Begonia)
495.B45 Berberidaceae (Barberry)

Spermatophyta. Phanerogams
Systematic divisions
Angiosperms
By family, A-Z -- Continued

495.B56 Betulaceae (Birch)
495.B62 Bignoniaceae (Catalpa)
495.B63 Bixaceae
495.B7 Bombacaceae
495.B73 Boraginaceae (Borage)
Brassicaceae see QK495.C9
495.B75 Bretschneideraceae
495.B76 Bromeliaceae (Bromelia)
495.B78 Brunelliaceae
495.B785 Bruniaceae
495.B786 Brunoniaceae (Blue-pincushion)
495.B7865 Buddlejaceae
495.B79 Burmanniaceae
495.B8 Burseraceae (Incense tree)
495.B83 Butomaceae (Flowering rush)
495.B85 Buxaceae (Box)
495.B9 Byblidaceae
495.C11 Cactaceae (Cactus)
495.C1153 Caesalpiniaceae
495.C1155 Callitrichaceae (Water starwort)
495.C15 Calycanthaceae (Spicebush)
495.C17 Calyceraceae
495.C18 Campanulaceae (Bellflower)
Candolleaceae see QK495.S87
495.C182 Canellaceae
495.C194 Cannabaceae
495.C196 Cannaceae (Canna)
Capparaceae see QK495.C198
495.C198 Capparidaceae (Spiderflower)
495.C199 Caprifoliaceae (Honeysuckle)
495.C1995 Cardiopteridaceae
495.C1997 Caricaceae (Papaya)
495.C2 Caryocaraceae
495.C24 Caryphyllaceae (Pink)
495.C27 Casuarinaceae (Beefwood)
495.C385 Celastraceae (Staff tree)
495.C39 Centrolepidaceae
495.C395 Cephalotaceae
495.C4 Ceratophyllaceae (Hornwort)
495.C43 Cercidiphyllaceae
495.C46 Chenopodiaceae (Goosefoot)
495.C47 Chloranthaceae
495.C48 Chrysobalanaceae

Spermatophyta. Phanerogams
Systematic divisions
Angiosperms
By family, A-Z -- Continued

495.C5 Cistaceae (Rockrose)
495.C55 Clethraceae
Clusiaceae see QK495.G87
495.C555 Cneoraceae
495.C6 Cochlospermaceae
495.C65 Columelliaceae
495.C7 Combretaceae (White mangrove)
495.C73 Commelinaceae (Spiderwort)
495.C74 Compositae (Sunflower)
495.C76 Connaraceae
495.C78 Convolvulaceae (Morning-glory)
495.C783 Coriariaceae
495.C785 Cornaceae (Dogwood)
495.C786 Corsiaceae
495.C787 Corynocarpaceae
495.C79 Crassulaceae (Stonecrop)
495.C797 Crossosomataceae
495.C9 Cruciferae (Mustard)
495.C93 Crypteroniaceae
495.C96 Cucurbitaceae (Gourd)
495.C965 Cunoniaceae (Lightwood)
495.C967 Cuscutaceae (Dodder)
495.C97 Cyanastraceae
495.C975 Cyclanthaceae (Panama-hat palm)
495.C979 Cymodoceaceae
495.C98 Cynomoriaceae
495.C997 Cyperaceae (Sedge)
495.C9973 Cyrillaceae (Leatherwood)
495.D325 Daphniphyllaceae
495.D33 Datiscaceae (Durango root)
495.D34 Davidiaceae
495.D35 Davidsoniaceae
495.D4 Degeneriaceae
495.D42 Desfontainiaceae
495.D43 Dialypetalanthaceae
495.D435 Diapensiaceae
495.D44 Dichapetalaceae
495.D45 Didiereaceae
495.D46 Didymelaceae
495.D47 Dilleniaceae
495.D48 Dioncophyllaceae
495.D54 Dioscoreaceae (Yam)
495.D545 Dipentodontaceae

Spermatophyta. Phanerogams
Systematic divisions
Angiosperms
By family, A-Z -- Continued

495.D56 Dipsacaceae (Teasel)
495.D564 Dipterocarpaceae
495.D76 Droseraceae (Sundew)
495.D9 Duckeodendraceae
495.D95 Dysphaniaceae
495.E25 Ebenaceae (Ebony)
495.E33 Elaeagnaceae
495.E35 Elaeocarpaceae
495.E37 Elatinaceae (Waterwort)
495.E44 Empetraceae (Crowberry)
495.E45 Epacridaceae
495.E64 Eremolepidaceae
495.E68 Ericaceae (Heath)
495.E685 Eriocaulaceae (Pipewort)
495.E695 Eriospermaceae
495.E82 Erythroxylaceae (Coca)
Escalloniaceae see QK495.S3
Eucalyptus see QK495.M9
495.E84 Eucommiaceae
495.E85 Eucryphiaceae
495.E9 Euphorbiaceae (Spurge)
495.E95 Eupomatiaceae
495.E96 Eupteleaceae
Euryalaceae see QK495.T4
Fabaceae see QK495.L52
495.F14 Fagaceae (Beech; Oak)
495.F55 Flacourtiaceae
495.F58 Flagellariaceae
495.F6 Fouquieriaceae (Ocotillo)
495.F67 Frankeniaceae (Alkali heath)
495.G26 Garryaceae (Silktassel bush)
495.G27 Geissolomataceae
495.G35 Gentianaceae (Gentian)
495.G37 Geosiridaceae
495.G38 Geraniaceae (Geranium)
495.G4 Gesneriaceae (African violet)
495.G56 Globulariaceae
495.G65 Gomortegaceae
495.G655 Goodeniaceae
495.G74 Gramineae (Grass)
495.G745 Griseliniaceae
495.G75 Grossulariaceae
495.G76 Grubbiaceae

Spermatophyta. Phanerogams
Systematic divisions
Angiosperms
By family, A-Z -- Continued

495.G83 Gunneraceae
495.G87 Guttiferae (St. Johnswort)
495.G877 Gyrostemonaceae
495.H15 Haemodoraceae (Bloodwort)
495.H2 Haloragaceae (Water milfoil)
Haloragidaceae see QK495.H2
495.H3 Hamamelidaceae (Witch hazel)
495.H35 Heliconiaceae
495.H38 Hemerocallidaceae (Daylily)
Henriqueziaceae see QK495.R85
495.H42 Hernandiaceae
495.H5 Himantandraceae
495.H65 Hippocastanaceae (Horse chestnut)
495.H66 Hippocrateaceae
495.H67 Hippuridaceae (Mare's tail)
495.H7 Hoplestigmataceae
Houmiriaceae see QK495.H8
495.H8 Humiriaceae
495.H83 Hyacinthaceae
495.H84 Hydnoraceae
(495.H85) Hydrocaryaceae
see QK495.T66
495.H86 Hydrocharitaceae (Elodea)
495.H88 Hydrophyllaceae (Waterleaf)
495.H885 Hydrostachyaceae
495.H9 Hypoxidaceae
495.I25 Icacinaceae
495.I4 Illiciaceae (Anise tree)
495.I75 Iridaceae (Iris)
495.J85 Juglandaceae (Walnut)
495.J855 Julianiaceae
495.J87 Juncaceae (Rush)
495.J875 Juncaginaceae (Arrow grass)
495.K7 Krameriaceae
Labiatae see QK495.L25
495.L152 Lacistemaceae
495.L153 Lactoridaceae
495.L25 Lamiaceae (Mint)
495.L32 Lardizabalaceae
495.L375 Lauraceae (Laurel)
495.L42 Lecythidaceae (Brazil nut)
495.L46 Leeaceae

Spermatophyta. Phanerogams
Systematic divisions
Angiosperms
By family, A-Z -- Continued

495.L52 Legumes
Cf. QK495.C1153 Caesalpiniaceae
Cf. QK495.M545 Mimosaceae
495.L524 Leitneriaceae (Corkwood)
495.L527 Lemnaceae (Duckweed)
495.L528 Lennoaceae
495.L53 Lentibulariaceae (Bladderwort)
495.L72 Liliaceae (Lily)
495.L73 Limnanthaceae (Meadowfoam)
495.L74 Linaceae (Flax)
495.L76 Lissocarpaceae
495.L78 Loasaceae (Evening star)
495.L785 Loganiaceae (Butterfly bush)
495.L87 Loranthaceae (Mistletoe)
495.L88 Lowiaceae
495.L9 Lythraceae (Crepe myrtle)
495.M24 Magnoliaceae (Magnolia)
495.M245 Malesherbiaceae
495.M26 Malpighiaceae
495.M27 Malvaceae (Mallow)
495.M28 Marantaceae (Arrowroot)
495.M285 Marograviaceae
495.M287 Martyniaceae (Devil's claw)
495.M3 Mayacaceae (Bogmoss)
495.M5 Medusagynaceae
495.M51 Medusandraceae
495.M5135 Melanthiaceae
495.M514 Melastomataceae (Meadow beauty)
495.M52 Meliaceae (Mahogany)
495.M524 Melianthaceae (Honey bush)
495.M537 Menispermaceae (Moonseed)
495.M5375 Menyanthaceae
495.M545 Mimosaceae
495.M55 Misodendraceae
495.M6 Molluginaceae
495.M67 Monimiaceae (Voldo)
495.M73 Moraceae (Mulberry)
495.M74 Moringaceae (Horseradish tree)
495.M78 Musaceae (Banana)
Musales see QK495.A14
495.M8 Myoporaceae
495.M83 Myricaceae (Wax myrtle)
495.M85 Myristicaceae (Nutmeg)

Spermatophyta. Phanerogams
Systematic divisions
Angiosperms
By family, A-Z -- Continued

495.M86 Myrothamnaceae
495.M87 Myrsinaceae
495.M9 Myrtaceae (Myrtle)
495.N3 Naiadaceae
495.N33 Nelumbonaceae
495.N35 Nepenthaceae
495.N37 Neuradaceae
495.N6 Nolanaceae
495.N9 Nyctaginaceae (Four-o'clock)
495.N97 Nymphaeaceae (Waterlily)
495.N975 Nyssaceae (Sour gum)
495.O3 Ochnaceae
495.O35 Olacaceae (Tallow-wood)
495.O44 Oleaceae (Olive)
495.O446 Oliniaceae
495.O46 Onagraceae (Evening-primrose)
495.O62 Opiliaceae
495.O64 Orchidaceae (Orchid)
495.O74 Orobanchaceae (Broomrape)
495.O98 Oxalidaceae (Wood sorrel)
495.P15 Paeoniaceae
495.P17 Palmae (Palm)
495.P175 Pandaceae
495.P18 Pandanaceae (Screw pine)
495.P22 Papaveraceae (Poppy)
Papaverales see QK495.A12
495.P28 Passifloraceae (Passionflower)
495.P42 Pedaliaceae (Benne)
495.P43 Penaeaceae
495.P44 Pentaphragmataceae
495.P445 Pentaphylacaceae
Peperomiaceae see QK495.P67
495.P446 Peridiscaceae
495.P45 Philydraceae
495.P453 Phyrmaceae (Lopseed)
495.P454 Phytolaccaceae (Poke)
495.P5 Picrodendraceae
495.P67 Piperaceae (Pepper)
495.P7 Pittosporaceae
495.P714 Plantaginaceae (Plantain)
495.P72 Platanaceae (Sycamore)
495.P725 Plumbaginaceae (Leadwort)
Poaceae see QK495.G74

QK

Spermatophyta. Phanerogams
Systematic divisions
Angiosperms
By family, A-Z -- Continued

495.P74 Podostemaceae (Riverweed)
495.P77 Polemoniaceae (Phlox)
495.P775 Polygalaceae (Milkwort)
495.P78 Polygonaceae (Buckwheat)
495.P783 Pontederiaceae (Pickerelweed)
495.P8 Portulacaceae
495.P83 Posidoniaceae
Potaliaceae see QK495.L785
495.P85 Potamogetonaceae (Pondweed)
495.P95 Primulaceae (Primrose)
495.P957 Proteaceae (Silk oak)
495.P9575 Ptaeroxylaceae
495.P958 Punicaceae (Pomegranate)
495.P997 Pyrolaceae
495.Q5 Quiinaceae
495.R15 Rafflesiaceae
Ranales see QK495.A12
495.R215 Ranunculaceae (Buttercup)
Ranunculales see QK495.A12
495.R3 Rapateaceae
495.R4 Resedaceae (Mignonette)
495.R42 Restionaceae
495.R45 Rhamnaceae (Coffeeberry)
495.R46 Rhizophoraceae (Mangrove)
Rhoeadales see QK495.A12
495.R465 Rhoipteleaceae
495.R468 Roridulaceae
495.R78 Rosaceae (Rose)
495.R85 Rubiaceae (Madder)
495.R956 Ruppiaceae
495.R98 Rutaceae (Citrus)
495.S15 Sabiaceae
495.S16 Salicaceae (Willow)
495.S165 Salvadoraceae (Toothbrush tree)
495.S18 Santalaceae (Sandalwood)
495.S19 Sapindaceae (Soapberry)
495.S2 Sapotaceae (Chicle)
495.S225 Sarcolaenaceae
495.S227 Sarcospermataceae
495.S23 Sargentodoxaceae
495.S24 Saraceniaceae (Pitcher plant)
495.S27 Saururaceae (Lizard's-tail)
495.S3 Saxifragaceae (Saxifrage)

Spermatophyta. Phanerogams
Systematic divisions
Angiosperms
By family, A-Z -- Continued

495.S35	Scheuchzeriaceae
495.S353	Schisandraceae (Bay-star vine)
	Scitamineae see QK495.A14
495.S43	Scrophulariaceae (Figwort; snapdragon)
495.S45	Scyphostegiaceae
495.S47	Scytopetalaceae
495.S59	Simaroubaceae (Tree of heaven)
495.S62	Siparunaceae
495.S65	Smilacaceae
495.S7	Solanaceae (Nightshade)
495.S74	Sonneratiaceae
495.S745	Sparganiaceae (Bar-reed)
495.S7455	Sphaerosepalaceae
495.S7456	Sphenocleaceae
495.S76	Stachyuraceae
495.S765	Stackhousiaceae
495.S77	Staphyleaceae (Bladdernut)
495.S78	Stemonaceae
495.S8	Sterculiaceae (Cacao)
495.S85	Strasburgeriaceae
495.S87	Stylidiaceae
495.S9	Styracaceae (Silverbell tree)
495.S95	Symplocaceae (Sweetleaf)
495.T3	Taccaceae
495.T35	Tamaricaceae (Tamarisk)
495.T355	Tetracentraceae
495.T4	Theaceae (Tea)
495.T45	Theligonaceae
495.T455	Themidaceae
495.T457	Theophrastaceae (Joewood)
495.T46	Thurniaceae
495.T48	Thymelaeaceae
495.T5	Tiliaceae (Linden)
495.T6	Tovariaceae
495.T66	Trapaceae (Water chestnut)
495.T7	Tremandraceae
495.T73	Trigoniaceae
495.T735	Trilliaceae
495.T74	Trimeniaceae
495.T745	Triuridaceae
495.T75	Trochodendraceae
495.T77	Tropaeolaceae (Nasturtium)
495.T8	Turneraceae

Spermatophyta. Phanerogams
Systematic divisions
Angiosperms
By family, A-Z -- Continued

495.T9 Typhaceae (Cattail)
495.U4 Ulmaceae (Elm)
495.U48 Umbelliferae (Parsley)
495.U7 Urticaceae (Nettle)
495.V3 Valerianaceae
495.V4 Velloziaceae
495.V48 Verbenaceae (Verbena)
495.V5 Violaceae (Violet)
495.V53 Viscaceae
495.V55 Vitaceae (Grape)
495.V6 Vochysiaceae
495.W5 Winteraceae
495.X3 Xanthorrhoeaceae
495.X9 Xyridaceae (Yelloweyed grass)
495.Z3 Zannichelliaceae
495.Z65 Zingiberaceae (Ginger)
495.Z7 Zosteraceae
495.Z9 Zygophyllaceae (Creosote-bush)

Cryptogams
Including Archegoniatae
For bacteria see QR1+

504 Periodicals, societies, congresses, serial publications
505 General works, treatises, and textbooks
505.5 Juvenile works
506 Anatomy, physiology, etc.
507 Classification. Systematic works

Local
509 North America
United States
510 General works
511.A-Z By region or state, A-Z
Canada
511.2 General works
511.3.A-Z By region or province, A-Z
Latin America
511.7 General works
Mexico
512 General works
512.2.A-Z By region or state, A-Z
512.4 Central America (Table Q3)
512.5 West Indies. Caribbean Area (Table Q3)
512.6 South America (Table Q3)
Europe

Cryptogams
Local
Europe -- Continued

512.7	General works
513	Great Britain
514.A-Z	Other European regions or countries, A-Z
515	Asia (Table Q3)
516	Africa (Table Q3)
517	Australia
517.5	New Zealand
518	Pacific islands (Table Q3)
519	Arctic regions
519.5	Antarctica
	Pteridophyta (Ferns, etc.)
520	Periodicals, societies, congresses, serial publications
521	Anatomy, physiology, etc.
522	General works, treatises, and textbooks
522.5	Juvenile works
523	Classification. Systematic works
523.3	Catalogs and collections
524.A-Z	Systematic divisions, A-Z
524.A25	Actiniopteridaceae
524.A29	Adiantaceae
(524.A65)	Aspidiaceae see QK524.D79
524.A7	Aspleniaceae
524.A76	Athyriaceae
524.A94	Azollaceae
524.C9	Cyatheaceae
524.D5	Dennstaedtiaceae
524.D55	Dicksoniaceae
524.D79	Dryopteridaceae
524.E6	Equisetaceae
524.H87	Huperziaceae
524.H9	Hymenophyllaceae
524.I8	Isoetaceae
524.L64	Lomariopsidaceae
524.L9	Lycopodiaceae
524.M3	Marattiaceae
524.M4	Marsileaceae
524.O7	Ophioglossaceae
524.O8	Osmundaceae
524.P3	Parkeriaceae
524.P7	Polypodiaceae
524.P77	Psilotaceae
	Pteridaceae see QK524.A29
524.S33	Salviniaceae

QK

Cryptogams
  Pteridophyta (Ferns, etc.)
    Systematic divisions, A-Z -- Continued
524.S35 Schizaeaceae
524.S46 Selaginellaceae
524.T54 Thelypteridaceae
    Geographical distribution
      For particular taxa see QK524.A+
524.35 General works
      Physiographic divisions (General)
524.37 Water
        Land see QK524.35
      Topographic divisions
        America
524.4 General works
          North America
524.5 General works
524.7 Great Lakes region
            United States
525 General works
525.5.A-Z By region or state, A-Z
            Canada
525.6 General works
525.7.A-Z By region or province, A-Z
          Latin America
525.8 General works
            Mexico
525.85 General works
525.9.A-Z By region or state, A-Z
526 Central America (Table Q3)
526.2 West Indies. Caribbean area (Table Q3)
526.4 South America (Table Q3)
        Europe
526.5 General works
527 Great Britain
528.A-Z Other European regions or countries, A-Z
529 Asia (Table Q3)
530 Africa (Table Q3)
531 Australia
531.5 New Zealand
532 Pacific islands (Table Q3)
  Bryophyta. Bryology
532.4 Periodicals. Societies. Serials
532.42 Congresses
532.5 Dictionaries and encyclopedias
    History
532.6 General works

	Cryptogams
	Bryophyta. Bryology
	History -- Continued
532.65.A-Z	By region or country, A-Z
	Biography
532.7	Collective
532.75.A-Z	Individual, A-Z
532.8	Directories
533	General works, treatises, and textbooks
533.3	Juvenile works
533.35	Addresses, essays, lectures
	Rare and endangered bryophytes
533.4	General works
533.5.A-Z	By region or country, A-Z
533.6	Anatomy, physiology, etc.
533.7	Classification. Systematic works
533.74	Catalogs and collections
	By region or country
	United States
533.8	General works
533.82.A-Z	By region or state, A-Z
533.84.A-Z	Other regions or countries, A-Z
	Musci (Mosses)
534	Periodicals, societies, congresses, serial publications
535	Anatomy, physiology, etc.
537	General works, treatises, and textbooks
537.5	Juvenile works
538	Classification. Systematic works
538.4	Catalogs and collections
539.A-Z	Systematic divisions, A-Z
539.A6	Amblystegiaceae
539.B68	Brachytheciaceae
539.B7	Bryaceae
539.B97	Buxbaumiaceae
539.D5	Dicranaceae
539.F5	Fissidentaceae
539.F6	Fontinalaceae
539.F98	Funariaceae
539.G7	Grimmiaceae
539.H68	Hookeriaceae
539.H95	Hypnobryales
539.H96	Hypopterygiaceae
539.M68	Mniaceae
539.O7	Orthotrichaceae
539.P7	Plagiotheciaceae
539.P78	Polytrichaceae
539.P8	Pottiaceae

	Cryptogams
	Bryophyta. Bryology
	Musci (Mosses)
	Systematic divisions, A-Z -- Continued
539.P93	Pterobryaceae
539.S46	Seligeriaceae
539.S75	Sphagnaceae
539.S76	Splachnaceae
539.S84	Stereophyllaceae
539.T58	Timmiaceae
	Local
	America
540.4	General works
	North America
540.5	General works
540.7	Great Lakes region
	United States
541	General works
541.5.A-Z	By region or state, A-Z
	Canada
541.6	General works
541.7.A-Z	By region or province, A-Z
541.8	Latin America
	Mexico
541.85	General works
541.9.A-Z	By region or state, A-Z
542	Central America (Table Q3)
542.2	West Indies. Caribbean area (Table Q3)
542.4	South America (Table Q3)
542.45	Atlantic islands (Table Q3)
	Europe
542.5	General works
543	Great Britain
544.A-Z	Other European regions or countries, A-Z
545	Asia (Table Q3)
546	Africa (Table Q3)
547	Australia
547.5	New Zealand
548	Pacific islands (Table Q3)
549	Arctic regions
549.5	Antarctica
	Hepaticae (Liverworts)
551	Anatomy, physiology, etc.
553	General works, treatises, and textbooks
554	Classification. Systematic works
555.A-Z	Systematic divisions, A-Z
555.A3	Adelanthaceae

Cryptogams
Bryophyta. Bryology
Hepaticae (Liverworts)
Systematic divisions, A-Z -- Continued

555.A5 Aneuraceae
(555.A6) Anthocerotaceae
see QK563.75+
555.B34 Balantiopsaceae
555.B7 Bryopteridaceae
555.D5 Dilaenaceae
555.F6 Fossombroniaceae
555.F9 Frullaniaceae
555.G44 Geocalycaceae
555.G7 Grimaldiaceae
555.H35 Haplomitriaceae
555.J9 Jungermanniaceae
555.L37 Lejeuneaceae
555.L4 Lepidoziaceae
555.L58 Lophocoleaceae
555.L6 Lophoziaceae
555.M2 Marchantiaceae
555.M4 Metzgeriaceae
555.P45 Plagiochilaceae
555.P6 Porellaceae
555.R5 Ricciaceae
555.S34 Scapaniaceae
555.T3 Targioniaceae

Local
America
555.4 General works
North America
555.5 General works
555.7 Great Lakes region
United States
556 General works
556.5.A-Z By region or state, A-Z
Canada
556.6 General works
556.7.A-Z By region or province, A-Z
Latin America
556.8 General works
Mexico
556.85 General works
556.9.A-Z By region or state, A-Z
557 Central America (Table Q3)
557.2 West Indies. Caribbean area (Table Q3)
557.4 South America (Table Q3)

Cryptogams
Bryophyta. Bryology
Hepaticae (Liverworts)
Local -- Continued
Atlantic Ocean islands
557.45 General works
557.47.A-Z By island or group of islands, A-Z
557.47.F34 Falkland Islands
Europe
557.5 General works
558 Great Britain
559.A-Z Other European regions or countries, A-Z
560 Asia (Table Q3)
561 Africa (Table Q3)
562 Australia
562.5 New Zealand
563 Pacific islands (Table Q3)
563.5 Arctic regions
563.7 Antarctica
563.725 Southern hemisphere
Hornworts
563.75 Periodicals, societies, congresses, serial publications
563.77 Anatomy, physiology, etc.
563.8 General works, treatises, and textbooks
563.84 Classification. Systematic works
563.85.A-Z By genus, A-Z
563.85.A57 Anthoceros
563.87.A-Z By region or country, A-Z
Algae. Algology
564 Periodicals. Societies. Serials
564.3 Congresses
564.5 Collected works (nonserial)
564.6 Dictionaries and encyclopedias
History
564.7 General works
564.73 By region or country, A-Z
Biography
564.75 Collective
564.77 Individual, A-Z
564.8 Directories
Anatomy, physiology, etc.
Including cytology, morphology
565 General works
565.2 Laboratory cultures and technique
565.5 Genetics
566 General works, treatises, and textbooks
566.3 Popular works

Cryptogams

Algae. Algology -- Continued

566.5 Juvenile works

567 Classification. Systematic works

567.5 Catalogs and collections

568.A-Z Special topics, A-Z

568.B55 Blooms

568.E26 Ecology

For systematic treatment see QK569.A+

For geographic treatment see QK570+

568.E85 Evolution

568.M52 Microalgae

For systematic treatment see QK569.A+

For geographic treatment see QK570+

568.T67 Toxic algae

Including toxic marine algae

569.A-Z Systematic divisions, A-Z

569.A27 Acrochaetiaceae

569.A43 Alariaceae

Audouinellaceae see QK569.A27

569.B15 Bacillariaceae

Bacillariophyceae. Bacillariophyta see QK569.D54

569.B2 Bangiaceae

569.B25 Batrachospermaceae

569.C37 Caulerpaceae

569.C39 Centrales

569.C4 Ceramiaceae

569.C44 Chaetangiaceae

569.C45 Chaetophoraceae

569.C455 Chaetophorales

569.C47 Characeae

569.C48 Characiaceae

569.C483 Charophyta

569.C484 Chattonellaceae

569.C486 Chlamydomonadaceae

569.C49 Chlorellaceae

569.C494 Chlorococcaceae

569.C496 Chloroccales

569.C6 Chlorophyta (Green algae)

569.C617 Chromophyta

569.C62 Chrysophyceae

569.C622 Chrysophytes

569.C624 Cladophoraceae

569.C63 Coccolithophoridaceae

569.C65 Codiaceae

569.C73 Coleochaetaceae

569.C8 Corallinaceae

Cryptogams
Algae. Algology
Systematic divisions, A-Z -- Continued

569.C86 Crossocarpaceae
569.C95 Cryptonemiaceae
569.C956 Cyanidiaceae
Cyanophyta see QR99.6+
569.C97 Cystoseiraceae
569.D3 Dasyaceae
569.D33 Dasycladaceae
569.D34 Dasycladales
569.D4 Delesseriaceae
569.D43 Desmerestiaceae
569.D46 Desmidiaceae
Desmidiales see QK569.D46
Desmidiales (Zygnematales) see QK569.Z82
569.D54 Diatoms (Bacillariophyceae. Bacillariophyta. Diatomophyceae)
569.D55 Dinamoebales
569.D56 Dinoflagellates
Dunaliellaceae see QK569.P65
569.E9 Euglenaceae
569.E93 Euglenids
569.F64 Florideae
569.F73 Fragilariaceae
569.F95 Fucaceae
569.G4 Gelidiaceae
569.G42 Gelidiales
569.G5 Gigartinaceae
569.G7 Gonidomataceae
569.G8 Gracilariaceae
569.H44 Hemidiscaceae
569.H46 Heteropediaceae
569.K3 Kallymeniaceae
569.L2 Laminariaceae
569.L34 Laminariales
569.L5 Lemaneaceae
569.L53 Lessoniaceae
569.L56 Lithodermataceae
569.M27 Mallomonadaceae
Melanophyceae see QK569.P5
569.M48 Mesotaeniaceae
569.M87 Myrionemataceae
Myxophyceae see QR99.6+
569.N37 Naviculaceae
569.N43 Nemaliales
569.N45 Nemastomataceae

Cryptogams
Algae. Algology
Systematic divisions, A-Z -- Continued

	Nostocaceae see QR99.7.N67
569.O37	Ochromonadaceae
569.O4	Oedogoniaceae. Oedogoniales
569.O6	Oocystaceae
	Oscillatoriaceae see QR99.7.O82
569.P25	Palmariaceae
569.P33	Peridiniales
569.P35	Peyssonneliaceae
569.P39	Pfiesteriaceae
569.P5	Phaeophyta
569.P54	Phyllophoraceae
569.P65	Polyblepharidaceae
569.P68	Porphyridiaceae
569.P9	Prasiolaceae
569.P93	Prochloraceae
(569.P94)	Protococcaceae see QK569.C486
569.P97	Protosiphonaceae
569.P974	Prymnesiophyceae
569.P98	Pseudoanemoniaceae
569.R26	Raphidophyceae
569.R37	Rhodomelaceae
569.R4	Rhodophyta. Rhodophyceae
569.R6	Rhodymeniaceae
569.S2	Sargassaceae
569.S32	Scenedesmaceae
	Schizophyceae see QR99.6+
569.S36	Scytosiphonaceae
569.S43	Selenastraceae
569.S53	Silicoflagellates
569.S56	Siphonocladaceae
569.S7	Sphacelariaceae
	Stigonemataceae see QR99.7.S85
569.T47	Thalassiosiraceae
569.T73	Trentepohliaceae
569.U46	Udoteaceae
569.U5	Ulotrichaceae
569.U55	Ulvaceae
569.U6	Ulvales
569.V3	Valoniaceae
569.V35	Vaucheriaceae
569.V9	Volvocaceae
569.V93	Volvocales
569.Z8	Zygnemataceae

Cryptogams
Algae. Algology
Systematic divisions, A-Z -- Continued
569.Z82 Zygnematales
Geographical distribution
For particular taxa see QK569.A+
570 General works
Physiographic divisions (General)
570.2 Marine
Cf. SH390+ Fisheries
570.25 Freshwater
Topographical divisions
America
570.4 General works
North America
570.5 General works
570.7 Great Lakes region
United States
571 General works
571.5.A-Z By region or state, A-Z
Canada
571.6 General works
571.7.A-Z By region or province, A-Z
Latin America
571.8 General works
Mexico
571.85 General works
571.9.A-Z By region or state, A-Z
572 Central America (Table Q3)
572.2 West Indies. Caribbean area (Table Q3)
572.4 South America (Table Q3)
Atlantic Ocean and islands
572.48 General works
572.5.A-Z By region, group of islands, or island, A-Z
Europe
572.9 General works
573 Great Britain
574.A-Z Other European regions or countries, A-Z
575 Asia (Table Q3)
576 Africa (Table Q3)
576.5 Indian Ocean
577 Australia
577.5 New Zealand
577.8 Pacific Ocean
578 Pacific Islands (Table Q3)
Polar regions
579 General works

Cryptogams
Algae. Algology
Geographical distribution
Topographical divisions
Polar regions -- Continued

580 Arctic regions
580.5 Antarctica

Lichens. Lichenology

580.7 Periodicals. Societies. Serials
580.74 Congresses
580.75 Collected works (nonserial)
580.77 Dictionaries and encyclopedias

Biography

580.85 Collective
580.86.A-Z Individual, A-Z
581 Anatomy, physiology, etc.
583 General works, treatises, and textbooks
584 Classification. Systematic works
584.2 Catalogs and collections
584.6.A-Z Special topics, A-Z
584.6.E64 Epiphytic lichens
585.A-Z Systematic divisions, A-Z
585.C28 Caliciales
585.C3 Caloplacaceae
585.C6 Cladoniaceae
585.C65 Collemataceae
585.G8 Graphidaceae
585.H48 Heppiaceae
585.L37 Lecanoraceae
585.L4 Lecidiaceae
585.L53 Lichinaceae
585.M44 Megalosporaceae
585.O63 Opegraphaceae
585.P17 Pannariaceae
585.P2 Parmeliaceae
585.P34 Peltigeraceae
585.P37 Pertusariaceae
585.P45 Physciaceae
585.R35 Ramalinaceae
585.R7 Roccellaceae
585.S64 Sphaerophoraceae
585.S78 Stereocaulaceae
585.S8 Stictaceae
585.T44 Teloschistaceae
585.T48 Thelenellaceae
585.T5 Thelotremataceae
585.T7 Trypetheliaceae

Cryptogams
Lichens. Lichenology
Systematic divisions, A-Z -- Continued
585.U5 Umbilicariaceae
585.V4 Verrucariaceae
Local
America
586.4 General works
North America
586.5 General works
586.7 Great Lakes region
United States
587 General works
587.5.A-Z By region or state, A-Z
Canada
587.6 General works
587.7.A-Z By region or province, A-Z
Latin America
587.8 General works
Mexico
587.85 General works
587.9.A-Z By region or state, A-Z
588 Central America (Table Q3)
588.2 West Indies. Caribbean area (Table Q3)
588.4 South America (Table Q3)
Atlantic Ocean and islands
588.47 General works
588.48.A-Z By region, group of islands or island, A-Z
Europe
588.5 General works
589 Great Britain
590.A-Z Other European regions or countries, A-Z
591 Asia (Table Q3)
592 Africa (Table Q3)
593 Australia
593.5 New Zealand
594 Pacific islands (Table Q3)
Arctic regions
597 General works
597.2 Greenland
597.3 Spitzbergen
597.5 Antarctica
597.7 Tropics
Fungi
Cf. QR111+ Soil fungi
Cf. QR245+ Pathogenic fungi
Cf. TA423.2+ Decay of wood

Cryptogams
Fungi -- Continued
600 Periodicals. Societies. Serials
600.2 Collected works (nonserial)
600.3 Congresses
600.35 Dictionaries and encyclopedias
Biography
600.44 Collective
600.45.A-Z Individual, A-Z
Study and teaching. Research
600.47 General works
600.473.A-Z By region or country, A-Z
600.476 Experiments
600.478 Laboratory manuals
600.48 Collection and preservation
Museums. Exhibitions
600.5 General works
600.53.A-Z By region or country, A-Z
Under each country:
.x General works
.x2A-.x2Z Individual. By name, A-Z
Catalogs and collections
600.7 General works
600.73.A-Z By region or country, A-Z
Under each country:
.x General works
.x2A-.x2Z Individual. By name, A-Z
601 Anatomy, physiology, etc.
Including cytology, morphology
602 Genetics, variation, etc.
603 General works, treatises, and textbooks
Classification. Systematic works
603.2 General works
603.3 Nomenclature
603.5 Juvenile works
604 Special aspects of the subject as a whole
604.2.A-Z Special topics, A-Z
604.2.A52 Anaerobic fungi
604.2.A56 Antagonistic fungi
Aquatic fungi see QK617.8+
604.2.C62 Colonies
604.2.C64 Communities
604.2.C66 Conservation
604.2.E26 Ecology
604.2.E27 Economic aspects
604.2.E28 Ecophysiology
Ectomycorrhizas see QK604.2.M92

Cryptogams
Fungi
Special topics, A-Z -- Continued
Edible fungi see QK617
604.2.E48 Endangered fungi
Endomycorrhizas see QK604.2.M92
604.2.E53 Endophytic fungi
604.2.E85 Evolution
604.2.H34 Hallucinogenic mushrooms
604.2.H95 Hypogeous fungi
604.2.I36 Identification
604.2.L53 Lichen-forming fungi
604.2.L54 Lichenicolous fungi
604.2.M64 Molecular biology
604.2.M89 Mycoparasitism
604.2.M92 Mycorrhizas. Mycorrhizal fungi
Including ectomycorrhizas and endomycorrhizas
Cf. SB106.M83 Plant culture
604.2.N45 Nematode-destroying fungi
Pathogenic fungi see QR245+
604.2.P45 Phytopathogenic fungi
Cf. SB733 Control of phytopathogenic fungi and fungal diseases of plants
604.2.P56 Pleomorphic fungi
Poisonous fungi see QK617
604.2.P64 Populations
604.2.P73 Predacious fungi
604.2.S25 Saprophytic fungi
Soil fungi see QR111+
604.2.S86 Straminipilous fungi
604.2.W65 Wood-decaying fungi
Cf. TA423.2+ Deterioration and preservation of wood
604.2.W66 Wood-staining fungi
Cf. TA423.4 Deterioration and preservation of wood
Yeast fungi see QK617.5
604.2.Z66 Zoosporic fungi
Local
America
604.4 General works
North America
604.5 General works
604.7 Great Lakes region
United States
605 General works
605.5.A-Z By region or state, A-Z
Canada
605.6 General works

Cryptogams
Fungi
Local
America
North America
Canada -- Continued
605.7.A-Z By region or state, A-Z
Latin America
605.8 General works
Mexico
605.85 General works
605.9.A-Z By region or state, A-Z
606 Central America (Table Q3)
606.2 West Indies. Caribbean area (Table Q3)
606.4 South America (Table Q3)
Europe
606.5 General works
607 Great Britain
608.A-Z Other European regions or countries, A-Z
609 Asia (Table Q3)
610 Africa (Table Q3)
611 Australia
611.5 New Zealand
612 Pacific islands (Table Q3)
615 Arctic regions
615.5 Antarctica
615.7 Tropics
617 Edible and poisonous fungi. Mushrooms (Popular works)
For geographic treatment see QK604.4+
For systematic treatment see QK621+
Cf. SB352.85+ Culture
617.5 Yeast fungi (General)
For geographic treatment see QK604.4+
For systematic treatment see QK621+
Cf. QR151+ Microorganisms of fermentation
Cf. TP433 Food processing and manufacture
Cf. TP580+ Brewing
Aquatic fungi (General)
For geographic treatment see QK604.4+
For systematic treatment see QK621+
617.8 General works
618 Marine fungi (General)
618.2 Freshwater fungi (General)
Systematic divisions
Phycomycetes
621.A1 General works, treatises, and textbooks
621.A2-Z Special, A-Z

	Cryptogams
	Fungi
	Systematic divisions
	Phycomycetes
	Special, A-Z -- Continued
621.A42	Albuginaceae
621.B37	Basidiobolus
621.B6	Blastocladiaceae
621.C48	Choanephoraceae
621.C5	Chytridiaceae
621.C63	Coelomomycetaceae
621.E3	Eccrinales
621.E47	Endogonaceae
621.E49	Entomophthoraceae
621.E5	Entophlyctaceae
621.L44	Leptomitales
	Molds see QK600+
621.M6	Monoblepharidaceae
621.M64	Mortierellaceae
621.M94	Mucoraceae
621.M96	Mucorales
621.O4	Olpidiaceae
	Oomycetes see QK621.A1
621.P45	Peronosporaceae
621.P47	Peronosporales
621.P9	Pythiaceae
621.R5	Rhipidiaceae
621.S24	Saprolegniaceae
621.S25	Saprolegniales
621.S9	Synchytriaceae
621.T45	Thraustochytriaceae
	Trichomycetes see QK621.A1
621.W6	Woroniaceae
	Ascomycetes
623.A1	General works, treatises, and textbooks
623.A2-Z	Special, A-Z
623.A8	Ascobolaceae
	Aspergillus see QK625.M7
623.C36	Capnodiaceae
623.C53	Chaetomiaceae
623.C55	Clavicipitaceae
623.C57	Clavicipitales
623.D47	Dermateaceae
623.D55	Diaporthales
	Discomycetes see QK623.A1
623.D72	Dothideaceae
623.D74	Dothideales

Cryptogams
Fungi
Systematic divisions
Ascomycetes
Special, A-Z -- Continued

623.E4 Elaphomycetaceae
623.E56 Endomycetaceae
623.E7 Erysiphaceae
623.E73 Erysiphales
(623.E85) Eurotiaceae
see QK623.T75
623.G55 Gnomoniaceae
623.G94 Gymnoascaceae
623.H35 Helotiaceae
623.H4 Helvellaceae
623.H76 Hyaloscyphaceae
623.H86 Hypocreaceae
623.H87 Hypomycetaceae
623.H88 Hysteriaceae
623.L3 Laboulbeniales
623.L39 Leotiaceae
623.L6 Lophiostomaceae
623.M38 Melanconidaceae
623.M39 Melanommatales
Meliolaceae see QK623.M4
623.M4 Meliolales. Meliolaceae
623.M5 Microthyriaceae
623.M63 Monascaceae
623.M65 Morchellaceae
623.M89 Mycocaliciales
623.M93 Mycosphaerellales. Mycosphaerellaceae
623.N43 Nectriaceae
623.O6 Ophiostomataceae
623.O75 Otideaceae
Patellariaceae see QK623.P5
Penicillium see QK625.M7
623.P5 Pezizaceae
623.P53 Pezizales
623.P6 Phacidiaceae
623.P63 Phyllachoraceae
623.P66 Pleosporaceae
623.P68 Pleosporales
623.P8 Pseudosphaeriaceae
Pyrenomycetes see QK623.A1
623.P93 Pyrenulaceae
623.P95 Pyronemataceae
623.R45 Rhytisamtaceae

Cryptogams
Fungi
Systematic divisions
Ascomycetes
Special, A-Z -- Continued

623.S23 Saccharomycetaceae
623.S26 Sarcoscyphaceae
623.S27 Sarcosomataceae
623.S3 Sclerotiniaceae
623.S6 Sordariaceae
623.S73 Sphaeriaceae
623.S76 Sphaeriales
623.T3 Taphrinaceae
623.T54 Thermoascaceae
623.T75 Trichocomaceae
623.T8 Tuberaceae
623.V35 Valsaceae
623.V46 Venturiaceae
623.X9 Xylariaceae
623.Z64 Zopfiaceae

Fungi imperfecti (Deuteromycetes)

625.A1 General works, treatises, and textbooks
625.A2-Z Special, A-Z
625.A48 Agonomycetaceae
625.C76 Cryptococcaceae
625.D4 Dematiaceae
Discellaceae see QK625.E9
625.E9 Excipulaceae
Hyphomycetes see QK625.A1
625.L4 Leptostromataceae
625.M4 Melanconiaceae
Melanconiales see QK625.M4
625.M7 Moniliaceae
625.M74 Moniliales
Mucedinaceae see QK625.M7
625.M9 Mycelia Sterilia
Nectrioidaceae see QK625.Z9
Phyllostictaceae see QK625.S5
Phyllostictales see QK625.S6
625.R4 Rhizoctonia
Sphaerioidaceae see QK625.S5
625.S5 Sphaeropsidaceae
625.S6 Sphaeropsidales
Stilbaceae see QK625.S7
625.S7 Stilbellaceae
625.T8 Tuberculariaceae
625.Z9 Zythiaceae

Cryptogams
Fungi
Systematic divisions -- Continued
Basidiomycota

626 General works, treatises, and textbooks

Teliomycetes

626.3 General works, treatises, and textbooks

626.5 Septobasidiales. Septobasidiaceae

Uredinales (Rust fungi)

627.A1 General works, treatises, and textbooks

627.A2-Z Special, A-Z

627.C65 Coleosporiaceae

627.C75 Cronartiaceae

627.M44 Melampsoraceae

627.P97 Pucciniaceae

Ustomycetes

627.3 General works, treatises, and textbooks

627.4 Cryptobasidiales. Cryptobasidiaceae

627.45 Cryptomycocolacales. Cryptomycocolacaceae

Exobasidiales

627.5 General works, treatises, and textbooks

627.53.A-Z Special, A-Z

627.53.E93 Exobasidiaceae

627.6 Graphiolales. Graphiolaceae

627.7 Platygloeales. Platygloeaceae

627.8 Sporidiales. Sporidiobolaceae

Ustilaginales (Smut fungi)

628.A1 General works, treatises, and textbooks

628.A2-Z Special, A-Z

628.T5 Tilletiaceae

628.U8 Ustilaginaceae

Basidiomycetes

628.5 General works, treatises, and textbooks

629.A-Z Special, A-Z

629.A4 Agaricaceae

629.A44 Agaricales

629.A53 Amanitaceae

(629.A58) Aphyllophorales
see QK628.5

629.A74 Athiliaceae

629.A8 Auriculales. Auriculariaceae

629.B58 Bolbitiaceae

629.B6 Boletaceae

629.B63 Boletales

629.C3 Cantharellaceae

629.C33 Cantharellales

629.C6 Clavariaceae

Cryptogams
Fungi
Systematic divisions
Basidiomycota
Basidiomycetes
Special, A-Z -- Continued

629.C783 Coriolaceae
629.C785 Corticiaceae
629.C787 Cortinariaceae
629.C83 Crepidotaceae
629.C95 Cyphellaceae
629.C97 Cystofilobasidiales. Cystofilobasidiaceae
629.D2 Dacrymycetaceae
629.E34 Echinodontiaceae
629.E56 Entolomataceae
(629.E9) Exobasidiaceae
see QK627.53.E93
629.F37 Favolaschiaceae
629.G18 Ganodermataceae
Gasteromycetes see QK626+
629.G4 Geastraceae
Geastrales see QK629.L92
629.G6 Gomphaceae
629.H8 Hydnaceae
629.H86 Hygrophoraceae
629.H89 Hymenochaetaceae
629.H9 Hymenogastraceae
Hymenomycetes see QK626+
629.L33 Lachnocladiaceae
629.L9 Lycoperdaceae
629.L92 Lycoperdales
629.M4 Melanogastraceae
629.N5 Nidulariales. Nidulariaceae
629.P55 Peniophoraceae
629.P6 Phallaceae
629.P63 Phallales
629.P64 Phanerochaetaceae
629.P67 Pluteaceae
629.P7 Polyporaceae
629.P74 Poriales
(629.R5) Rhodophyllaceae
see QK629.E56
629.R87 Russulaceae
629.S35 Sclerodermataceae
(629.S4) Septobasidiaceae
see QK626.5
629.S73 Stereaceae

Cryptogams
Fungi
Systematic divisions
Basidiomycota
Basidiomycetes
Special, A-Z -- Continued
629.S76 Strobilomycetaceae
629.S77 Strophariaceae
629.T4 Thelephoraceae
629.T67 Tremellaceae
629.T7 Tremellales
629.T73 Tricholomataceae
629.T8 Tulasnellaceae
(633) Myxobacterales
see QR82.M95
Myxomycetes (Slime molds)
635.A1 General works, treatises, and textbooks
635.A2-Z Special, A-Z
635.C4 Ceratiomyxaceae
635.D5 Dictyosteliaceae
635.D53 Dictyosteliales
635.P5 Physaraceae
635.P6 Plasmodiophoraceae
635.P65 Plasmodiophorales
635.S8 Stemonitaceae
(638) Eccrinales
see QK621.E3
Plant anatomy
Including plant morphology
Cf. QK665 Embryology
Cf. QK671 Histology
Cf. QK725 Cytology
640 Periodicals. Societies. Serials
640.2 Collected works (nonserial)
640.3 Congresses
640.4 Dictionaries and encyclopedias
641 General works, treatises, and textbooks
642 Pictorial works and atlases
642.5 Addresses, essays, lectures
(643) Individual plants and groups of plants
see QK495+
Vegetative organs
644 Root and modifications. Root tubercles
Bacteriology of root nodules see QR113
644.5 Haustoria
Shoot
Including buds, apexes, etc.

Plant anatomy
Vegetative organs
Shoot -- Continued
645 General works
Stem
Including bulbs, rhizomes, types of branching
646 General works
646.7 Tree trunks
647 Wood
648 Bark
649 Leaf and modifications. Stipules
650 Appendages
Including trichomas, thorns, spines, tendrils, scales, hairs, etc.
651 Thallus
Reproductive organs of spermatophytes
652 General works
Flower and inflorescence
653 General works
654 Receptacle
Perianth
655 General works
656 Calyx
657 Corolla
658 Androecium. Palynology
Including stamens, pollen, etc.
659 Gynoecium
Including pistils, ovary, etc.
Fruit and seed
660 General works
661 Seed
Cf. QK898.S43 Seed storage compounds
662 Reproductive organs of cryptogams
663 Alternation of generations
664 Teratology
665 Embryology
Including embryos, embryosacs, morphogenesis, spermatogenesis, etc.
(667) Phylogeny
see QK989
669 Nomenclature of color as applied to plant description
671 Histology
673 Technique
Including microscopy, microtechnique, photomicrography
(683-707) Individual parts
see QK644+
Plant physiology

Plant physiology -- Continued
710 Periodicals, societies, serial publications
710.2 Congresses
General works, treatises, and textbooks
711 Through 1969
711.2 1970-
711.5 Juvenile works
Study and teaching. Research
714 General works
714.3 Problems, exercises, examinations
714.4 Experiments
714.5 Laboratory manuals
Instruments and apparatus
715 General works
715.5 Phytotrons and growth chambers
717 Plant ecophysiology
Including plant resource allocation
For geographic treatment see QK108+
For systematic treatment see QK494+
For physiographic treatment see QK930+
Physical plant physiology
720 Physiology of the vegetative organs (General)
For individual organs and groups of organs see QK644+
725 Plant cells and tissues
728 Molecular biology
Growth. Development
Including pattern formation
Cf. QK665 Embryology
731 General works
740 Germination
745 Factors influencing growth
Chemical agents affecting plants
Cf. S631+ Fertilizers
Cf. SB742+ Deficiency diseases
Cf. SD408 Use of fertilizers
746 General works, treatises, and textbooks
Including nutritive matter, etc.
Pollutants
Cf. SB744.5+ Plant pathology
750 General works
751 Air pollutants
Cf. SB745 Plant pathology
753.A-Z Special chemicals, A-Z
753.A25 Acids
753.A4 Alkaloids
753.A45 Aluminum

Plant physiology
Physical plant physiology
Chemical agents affecting plants
Special chemicals, A-Z -- Continued

753.A78 Arsenic
Ascorbic acid see QK753.V58
753.A79 Atrazine
753.A8 Auxin
753.B4 Benzylaminopurine
753.B6 Borax
753.B7 Boron
753.C16 Cadmium
753.C2 Calcium
753.C3 Carbon dioxide
753.C58 Chelates
753.C6 Chlorides
753.C62 Chlorophenoxyacetic acid
753.C67 Cobalt
753.C7 Colchicine
753.C74 Copper
753.C743 Copper chlorides
753.D4 Detergents
753.D5 Dichlorophenoxyacetic acid
753.E7 Essences and essential oils
753.E8 Ethylene
753.F5 Fluorescein
753.F53 Fluorides
753.G45 Galactose
753.G47 Gases
753.G5 Gibberellins. Gibberellic acid
753.H4 Heavy metals
753.H45 Herbicides
Cf. SB744.25 Herbicide injuries
753.H93 Hydrogen-ion concentration
753.I5 Indolacetic acid
753.I54 Insecticides
753.I6 Iodine
753.I7 Iron
753.L37 Latex
753.M27 Magnesium
753.M3 Manganese
753.M47 Metals
753.M56 Minerals
753.M6 Molybdenum
753.N5 Nitrates
753.N54 Nitrogen
753.P37 Pentachlorophenol

Plant physiology
Physical plant physiology
Chemical agents affecting plants
Special chemicals, A-Z -- Continued

753.P4 Petroleum
753.P48 Phosphorus
753.P65 Poisons
753.P67 Polycyclic aromatic hydrocarbons
753.P7 Potassium
753.R33 Radioactive substances
Cf. SB746 Plant pathology
753.S3 Salt
753.S32 Salts
753.S5 Silicon
753.S57 Sodium fluoride
753.S6 Sodium sulfate
753.S65 Succinic acid
753.S7 Sugars
753.S8 Sulfates
753.S84 Sulfur
753.S85 Sulfur dioxide
753.T5 Thallium
753.T53 Thiamine
753.T55 Thioureas
753.T7 Trace elements
753.T75 Tritium
753.V58 Vitamin C
753.X45 Xenobiotics
753.Z5 Zinc

Physical agents affecting plants (General)
Cf. QK870+ Effect of floods, water levels, etc.

754 General works
754.4 Atmosphere
Climate
Cf. QK913 Acclimatization
Cf. QK914 Phenology
Cf. S600+ Crops and climate
Cf. SD390.5+ Forests and climate
754.5 General works
Local see QK108+
754.7.A-Z Special topics, A-Z
Drought tolerance see QK754.7.D75
754.7.D75 Droughts. Drought tolerance
Cf. SB791 Plant pathology
Frost see QK756
754.7.S55 Snow
Temperature see QK755+

Plant physiology

Physical plant physiology

Physical agents affecting plants (General)

Climate

Special topics, A-Z -- Continued

754.7.W55 Wind

Cf. SB793 Plant pathology

Temperature

755 General works

755.5 Heat

Including heat production in plants

756 Cold. Frost

Cf. SB781 Plant pathology

757 Radiation

Including light, X-rays, ultraviolet rays, etc.

758 Electricity

759 Mechanical forces

759.5 Volcanic eruptions

760 Space flight

761 Periodicity. Dormancy. Photoperiodism

Aging. Senescence

762.5 General works

763 Shedding of leaves, etc. Abscission

769 Miscellaneous special topics

Movements. Irritability in plants

771 General works

Movements affecting growth

773 Nutation. Torsion

Climbing plants, tendrils, etc.

776 Miscellaneous induced movements

Including geotropism, phototropism, heliotropism, etc.

791 Movements of variation (not affecting growth)

793 Mechanics

Reproduction

Cf. QK982 Hybridization

825 General works

826 Asexual reproduction

Sexual reproduction

827 General works

828 Fecundation. Fertilization. Sterility

830 Flowering

Cf. SB126.8 Plant culture

840 Reparative processes. Regeneration

Cf. SD406 Tree surgery, etc.

844 Luminescence. Light production

845 Electrophysiology of plants

Cf. QK758 Effect of electricity on plants

Plant physiology -- Continued
Botanical chemistry. Phytochemicals
Cf. QK981.3 Biochemical genetics
Cf. QR148 Microbiological chemistry
861 General works, treatises, and textbooks
Analysis and composition of plants
For chemistry of wood see TS932+
865 General works
(866) Chemical analysis of individual plants
see QK495+
Nutrition. Plant food. Assimilation of nitrogen, etc.
867 General works
Plant-water relationships
Including general works on the effects of water levels and floods on plants
Cf. SB785 Plant pathology
870 General works
871 Absorption of water. Osmosis, sap movements, wilting, translocation, etc.
873 Transpiration. Action of stomata, etc.
875 Gases in plants
876 Gases from plants
Metabolism
881 General works
882 Photosynthesis. Assimilation and utilization of carbon dioxide
887 Formation of new organic matter
891 Respiration
894 Anaerobiosis
896 Fermentation. Enzymes, diastase, etc.
897 Miscellaneous products
898.A-Z Special plant constituents, A-Z
898.A15 Abscisic acid
898.A156 Acetolactate synthase
898.A16 Acetylenes
898.A18 Adenosine triphosphatase
898.A2 Albumins
898.A3 Algin
898.A4 Alkaloids
Cf. QD421+ Chemistry
898.A43 Allelochemicals. Allelopathic agents
898.A5 Amino acids
898.A52 Aminoacyl-tRNA
898.A53 Amyloid
898.A55 Anthocyanins
898.A57 Antioxidants
898.A59 Antiviral proteins

Plant physiology
Botanical chemistry. Phytochemicals
Nutrition. Plant food. Assimilation of nitrogen, etc.
Special plant constituents, A-Z -- Continued

898.A67 Arabinoglactan
898.A7 Ascorbic acid
898.A74 Asparagine
898.A8 Auxin
898.B54 Bioactive compounds
898.B56 Biogenic amines
898.B85 Brassinosteroids
898.C2 Calcium
898.C3 Carbohydrates
898.C34 Carotenoids
898.C35 Carotin
898.C42 Cellulose
898.C44 Chlorides
898.C45 Chlorine
898.C5 Chlorophyll
898.C52 Chloroplast DNA
898.C6 Cobalt
898.C94 Cytokinins
898.D44 Deoxyribonucleic acid. DNA
898.D46 Depsides
898.D54 Dimethylpropiothetin
DNA see QK898.D44
898.E58 Enzymes
898.E75 Essences and essential oils
898.E8 Ethylene
898.F3 Fatty acids
898.F5 Flavonoids
898.F53 Flavonols
898.G45 Gibberellins
898.G475 Glucose
898.G48 Glutamate dehydrogenase
898.G485 Glutathione
898.G49 Gluten
898.G497 Glycoproteins
898.G5 Glycosides
898.H45 Hemicellulose
898.H67 Hormones
898.I53 Indole alkaloids
898.I55 Inositol
898.I7 Iron
898.I76 Isopentenoids
898.I78 Isoquinoline
898.I8 Isozymes

Plant physiology
Botanical chemistry. Phytochemicals
Nutrition. Plant food. Assimilation of nitrogen, etc.
Special plant constituents, A-Z -- Continued

898.L23 Laccase
898.L3 Latex
898.L42 Lectins
898.L5 Lignin
898.L54 Limonoids
898.L56 Lipids
898.L9 Lycopene
898.M25 Malate dehydrogenase
898.M28 Malonic acid
898.M3 Manganese
898.M8 Mucilage
898.N5 Nicotinic acid
898.N57 Nitrates
898.N58 Nitric oxide
898.N6 Nitrogen
898.N8 Nucleic acids
898.N83 Nucleotides
898.O4 Olive oil
898.O88 Oxalates
898.O9 Oxidases
898.O92 Oxygen
898.P2 Patellaric acid
898.P3 Patulin
898.P4 Pectin
898.P47 Peroxidase
898.P57 Phenols
898.P59 Phosphoproteins
898.P6 Phosphorus
898.P64 Phycobiliproteins
898.P65 Phytin
898.P66 Phytoalexins
898.P67 Phytochrome
898.P677 Phytoliths
898.P68 Phytomelanes
898.P7 Pigments
898.P73 Plastocyanin
898.P75 Plumieride
898.P756 Polyamines
898.P76 Polymers
898.P764 Polyphenols
898.P77 Polysaccharides
898.P79 Protein kinases
898.P8 Proteins

Plant physiology
Botanical chemistry. Phytochemicals
Nutrition. Plant food. Assimilation of nitrogen, etc.
Special plant constituents, A-Z -- Continued

898.P82 Proteolytic enzymes
898.P84 Protochlorophyllide
898.P97 Pyrrolizidines
898.S43 Seed storage compounds
For works limited to special compounds see the compound, e.g., Proteins see QK898.P8
898.S45 Selenium
898.S48 Sesquiterpene lactones
898.S49 Sesquiterpenes
898.S55 Shikimic acid
898.S64 Solanine
898.S67 Starch
898.S7 Steroids
898.S78 Sugar
898.S8 Sulfur
898.T2 Tannins
898.T4 Terpenes
898.U68 Uric acid
898.U7 Uronic acids
898.V5 Vitamins
899 Miscellaneous special topics

Plant ecology
Cf. QH540+ General ecology
900 Periodicals. Societies. Serials
900.2 Congresses
900.4 Dictionaries
History
900.7 General works
900.73.A-Z By region or country, A-Z
901 General works, treatises, and textbooks
(903) Ecological discussion of areas
see QK108+
(905) Plant ecophysiology
see QK717
909 Illustrations of floral ecology of regions
909.5 Vegetation productivity. Primary productivity
Cf. QK564+ Algae
Cf. QK882 Photosynthesis
Cf. QK933+ Phytoplankton
Cf. QK938.F6 Forest ecology
910 Vegetation dynamics
911 Vegetative interrelation. Plant communities. Phytosociology
Plant adaptation

Plant ecology
Plant adaptation -- Continued
912 General works
913 Acclimatization
Cf. QK754.5+ Vegetation and climate
914 Phenology
Nutritive adaptation
915 General works
916 Aquatics, ice plants, dew plants
917 Insectivorous plants. Carnivorous plants
918 Parasites, saprophytes, symbionts
Protective adaptations
921 General works
922 Epiphytes, xerophytes, salt-marsh and desert plants
Cf. QK938.D4 Desert flora
Cf. QK938.S27 Salt marsh flora
923 Spines, secretion, raphides
924 Myrmecophilism, acarophilism
924.5 Plant canopies
Reproductive interrelation
925 General works
926 Pollination
929 Dissemination
Physiographic regions (General)
For geographic treatment see QK108+
Water
930 General works
931 Marine
Cf. QK938.C6 Coasts
Freshwater
932 General works
932.7 Streams
Cf. QK105 Flora
Phytoplankton
933 General works
934 Marine
935 Freshwater
Land
General
see QK101+ and QK901+
936 Tropics
937 Mountains
938.A-Z Other special, A-Z
Bogs see QK938.M3
938.B8 Burned land
938.C3 Caves
Chalk see QK938.L5

Plant ecology
Physiographic regions (General)
Land
Other special, A-Z -- Continued

938.C55 Cloud forest plants
938.C6 Coasts
938.D4 Deserts
938.D9 Dunes
938.F6 Forests
Cf. QK938.C55 Cloud forest plants
Cf. QK938.M27 Mangrove forests and swamps
Cf. QK938.R34 Rain forests
Cf. QK938.T34 Taigas
Grasslands see QK938.P7
938.H4 Heathlands
938.H44 Hedges. Hegerows
938.I84 Islands
938.L5 Limestone, chalk, etc.
938.M27 Mangrove forests and swamps
938.M3 Marshes, bogs, swamps, etc.
Cf. QK938.M27 Mangrove forests and swamps
Cf. QK938.P42 Peat bogs
938.M4 Meadows, pastures
938.M45 Mediterranean-type plants
Cf. QK314.5 Mediterranean Region
938.M6 Moors
938.P3 Paramos
Pastures see QK938.M4; QK938.M45
938.P42 Peatlands. Peat bogs
938.P7 Prairies. Grasslands. Velds
938.R34 Rain forests
938.R6 Rocks
938.S27 Salt marshes. Tide marshes
Cf. QK922 Halophytes
Cf. QK938.M27 Margrove forests and swamps
938.S3 Sand barrens
938.S36 Seashore
938.S4 Semiarid regions
938.S45 Serpentines
938.S57 Shrublands
Swamps see QK938.M3
938.T34 Taigas
Tide marshes see QK938.S27
938.T8 Tundras
Velds see QK938.P7
938.V5 Vineyards

Plant ecology -- Continued
(940-977.5) Topographical divisions
see QK108+
Evolution of plants (General)
For works limited to specific divisions, classes, etc. see QK494+
For works limited to special crops see SB177.A+
980 General works
Genetics
981 General works
981.3 Biochemical genetics
981.35 Cytogenetics
981.4 Molecular genetics
981.45 Genome mapping
981.5 Genetic engineering
981.7 Germplasm resources
Cf. SB123.3+ Crop germplasm resources
982 Hybridization
983 Variation
985 Selection, natural and artificial
For works limited to plant-breeding see SB123+
987 Degeneration
989 Phylogeny

Zoology
For animal ecology see QH540+
For animal culture see SF1+
1 Periodicals, societies, congresses, serial publications
3 Collected works (nonserial)
5 Voyages and expeditions
7 Encyclopedias
9 Dictionaries
Communication of information
9.2 General works
9.3 Information services
9.4 Computer network resources
Including the Internet
Classification. Nomenclature see QL351+
10 Terminology, notation, abbreviations
Cf. QL353+ Nomenclature
History
15 General works
21.A-Z By region or country, A-Z
Biography
26 Collective
31.A-Z Individual, A-Z
e.g.
31.A9 Audubon
31.C9 Cuvier
35 Directories
General works and treatises
41 Early through 1759
45 1760-1969
45.2 1970-
46 Pictorial works and atlases
46.5 Zoological illustrating
Textbooks
Advanced
47 Through 1969
47.2 1970-
Elementary
48 Through 1969
48.2 1970-
49 Juvenile works
Cf. SF75.5 Domestic animals
50 Popular works
For stories and anecdotes see QL791+
50.5 Zoology as a profession. Vocational guidance
Study and teaching. Research
51 General works

Study and teaching. Research -- Continued
51.2.A-Z By region or country, A-Z
Each region or country subarranged by author
51.5 Problems, exercises, examinations
52 Outlines, syllabi
52.55 Activity programs
52.6 Experiments
53 Laboratory manuals
Cf. QL812+ Anatomy
Cf. QP44 Physiology
55 Laboratory animals
Class here general works only. Prefer systematic divisions for particular groups of animals
Cf. SF405.5+ Breeding and care
Cf. SF996.5 Diseases
57 Audiovisual aids
58 Other special
59 Wildlife attracting
Including gardening to attract wildlife
60 Wildlife watching
Including wildlife viewing sites
60.4 Radio tracking
60.5 Wildlife marking
Cf. QL645.6+ Amphibians and reptiles
Cf. QL677.5 Birds
60.7 Age determination
Collection and preservation
Class here general works only. For works on collecting particular animals or the fauna of particular places, see systematic or geographical subdivisions in QL
Cf. QL465 Insects
Cf. QL677.7 Birds
61 General works, treatises, and textbooks
Collecting techniques
62 General works
62.5 Immobilization
Cf. SF760.A55 Veterinary medicine
63 Taxidermy
Cf. QL618.6 Fish mounting
64 Models and modelmaking
67 Preservation techniques
Laboratories, institutes, university departments, etc.
Class here descriptions, catalogs, annual reports, etc.
For serial research publications see QL1
69.A1 General works
69.A3-Z By region or country, A-Z
Subarrange each country by Table Q6

Museums. Exhibitions
Class here descriptions, catalogs, annual reports, etc.
For serial research publications see QL1
71.A1 General works
71.A2-Z By region or country, A-Z
Subarrange each country by Table Q5
72 Commercial lists
Menageries
73.A1 General works
73.A2-Z By region or country, A-Z
Subarrange each country by Table Q5
Zoos. Zoological gardens
76 General works
76.5.A-Z By region or country, A-Z
Subarrange each country by Table Q5
77.5 Zoo animals
Cf. SF408+ Culture and care
Cf. SF995.84+ Veterinary medicine
Public aquariums
Cf. SF456+ Home aquariums
78 General and freshwater aquariums
78.5 Marine aquariums. Saltwater aquariums
79.A-Z By region or country, A-Z
Subarrange each country by Table Q5
81 Addresses, essays, lectures
Wildlife conservation. Rare animals. Endangered species.
Wildlife refuges. Wildlife habitat improvement
Including rare and endangered vertebrates
For conservation of particular animals and groups of animals, see QL366+
For habitat improvement of game animals see SK356.W54
Cf. HE5620.W54 Wildlife and traffic safety
Cf. QL676.5+ Bird refuges
Cf. SK351+ Wildlife management. Game protection
Cf. SK590+ Wild animal trade
81.5 Periodicals. Societies. Congresses
81.7 History (General)
For history of a particular place see QL84+
82 General works
83 Juvenile works
83.15 Study and teaching. Research
83.17 Wildlife monitoring
For local see QL101+
83.2 Wildlife rescue
Including wildlife relocation and replacement, rescue of injured or orphaned animals, etc.
Cf. SF996.45 Wildlife rehabilitation

Wildlife conservation. Rare animals. Endangered species.
Wildlife refuges. Wildlife habitat improvement -- Continued
83.4 Wildlife reintroduction
By region or country
North America
84 General works
United States
84.2 General works
84.22.A-Z By region or state, A-Z
Canada
84.24 General works
84.26.A-Z By region or province, A-Z
84.28 Mexico
Central America
84.285.A1 General works
84.285.A3-Z By region, country, or island, A-Z
West Indies
84.29.A1 General works
84.29.A3-Z By region, country, or island, A-Z
South America
84.3.A1 General works
84.3.A3-Z By region, country, or island, A-Z
Europe
84.4.A1 General works
84.4.A3-Z By region, country, or island, A-Z
Asia
84.5.A1 General works
84.5.A3-Z By region, country, or island, A-Z
Africa
84.6.A1 General works
84.6.A3-Z By region, country, or island, A-Z
Australia and Indo-Pacific islands
84.7.A1 Australia
84.7.A3-Z Other. By region, country, or island, A-Z
85 Animals and civilization. Human-animal relationships
86 Animal introduction. Introduced animals
For local see QL101+
Cf. QL606 Introduced vertebrates
Cf. SB990+ Pest introduction
Cf. SF87 Acclimatization of livestock
87 Animals in the ancient world
Bible zoology see BS663
87.5 Dead animals

Extinct animals
Including extinction
Cf. QL81.5+ Endangered animals
Cf. QL676.8 Extinct birds
Cf. QL707 Extinct mammals
88 General works
88.15.A-Z By region or country, A-Z
Cryptozoology
88.3 General works
88.5 Living fossils
Alleged animals
Cf. BF1484 Animal ghosts
Cf. GR705+ Animal folklore
Cf. GR825+ Mythical animals
Cf. GR910 Mermaids. Sea monsters
89 General works
89.2.A-Z By animal, A-Z
Abominable snowman see QL89.2.Y4
89.2.B43 Beast of Exmoor
89.2.C37 Carcharocles megalodon
Cf. QE852.L35 Paleozoology
89.2.C53 Champ (Monster)
89.2.C57 Chupacabras
89.2.D68 Dover demon
89.2.K73 Kraken
89.2.L6 Loch Ness monsters
89.2.M58 Mokele-mbembe
89.2.M6 Morag
89.2.M68 Mothman
89.2.O34 Ogopogo
89.2.R67 Ropen
89.2.S2 Sasquatch
89.2.S4 Sea serpents
89.2.S44 Serpents
89.2.Y4 Yeti
(95) Noxious animals
see SF84+
99 Medical zoology
Cf. RA639+ Transmission of disease
Dangerous animals. Poisonous animals
Cf. QL468.8 Insects
Cf. QL618.7 Fishes
Cf. QP631+ Toxins, venom, poisons
100 General works
100.5 Animal attacks
Geographical distribution
101 General works, treatises, and textbooks

Geographical distribution -- Continued
Polar regions
104 General works
105 Arctic regions
Including Greenland
Cf. QL126 Arctic Ocean
106 Antarctica
Cf. QL126.5 Antarctic Ocean
107 Temperate regions
109 Tropics
Physiographic divisions
Soil
Cf. QR111+ Soil microorganisms
110 General works
110.5 Compost
Land
111 Islands
Cf. QL125 Coral reefs
112 Forests
113 Mountains
Cf. QL254 Alps
113.77 Valleys. Floodplains
Wetlands
113.8 General works
114 Marshes. Tidemarshes
114.5 Swamps
115 Plains
Grasslands. Prairies
115.3 General works
115.5 Meadows. Fields
116 Deserts
117 Caves
118 Subterranean waters
Including groundwater
119 Gardens
Water
120 General works, treatises, and textbooks
120.5 Suspension feeders
Ocean
121 General works
122 Popular works
122.2 Juvenile works
123 Zooplankton
(124) Animal ecology of the ocean
see QH541.5.S3
125 Coral reefs
125.5 Deep-sea

Geographical distribution
Physiographic divisions
Water
Ocean -- Continued

125.6	Hydrothermal vents
126	Arctic Ocean
126.5	Antarctic Ocean
	Atlantic Ocean
127	General works
128	North Atlantic Ocean. North Sea, etc.
131	Baltic Sea
132	Black Sea. Sea of Azov
133	Mediterranean Sea
134	Gulf of Mexico
134.5	Caribbean Sea
135	South Atlantic Ocean
137	Indian Ocean. Red Sea
137.5	Indo-Pacific Region
138	Pacific Ocean
139	Brackish water. Estuaries
	Fresh water
141	General works
	Groundwater see QL118
142	Water surface. Surface films. Neuston
143	Zooplankton
145	Streams
146	Lakes
146.3	Ponds
147	Springs Including hot springs
148	Wells
149	Stagnant water
	Topographical divisions (Faunas)
	America
150	General works
	North America
151	General works
	United States
155	General works
157.A-Z	By region, A-Z
157.A84	Atlantic Coast
157.M52	Middle Atlantic States
157.M53	Middle West
157.N48	New England
157.N67	Northeastern States
157.P33	Pacific Coast
157.S68	Southern States

Geographical distribution
Topographical divisions (Faunas)
America
North America
United States
By region, A-Z -- Continued

157.S69 Southwestern States
Including Southwest, New

159 Alabama
161 Alaska
162 Arizona
163 Arkansas
164 California
165 Colorado
166 Connecticut
167 Delaware
168 District of Columbia
169 Florida
171 Georgia
Hawaii see QL345.H3
172 Idaho
173 Illinois
175 Indiana
176 Iowa
177 Kansas
178 Kentucky
179 Louisiana
181 Maine
182 Maryland
183 Massachusetts
184 Michigan
185 Minnesota
186 Mississippi
187 Missouri
188 Montana
189 Nebraska
191 Nevada
192 New Hampshire
193 New Jersey
194 New Mexico
195 New York
196 North Carolina
197 North Dakota
198 Ohio
199 Oklahoma
201 Oregon
202 Pennsylvania

Geographical distribution
Topographical divisions (Faunas)
America
North America
United States -- Continued
203 Rhode Island
204 South Carolina
205 South Dakota
206 Tennessee
207 Texas
208 Utah
209 Vermont
211 Virginia
212 Washington
213 West Virginia
214 Wisconsin
215 Wyoming
Including Yellowstone National Park
Canada
219 General works
221.A-Z By region or province, A-Z
Latin America
223 General works
225 Mexico
Central America
227 General works
228.A-Z By region or country, A-Z
West Indies. Caribbean Area
229.A2 General works
229.A4-Z By individual island or group of islands, A-Z
229.A58 Antilles, Lesser
229.B3 Bahamas
229.C39 Cayman Islands
229.C9 Cuba
229.D65 Dominica
229.H35 Haiti
229.H57 Hispaniola
229.I5 Inagua
229.L4 Leeward Islands
229.P6 Puerto Rico
229.T7 Trinidad
229.V57 Virgin Islands
234 Bermuda
South America
235 General works
By region or country
239 Argentina

Geographical distribution
Topographical divisions (Faunas)
America
Latin America
South America
By region or country -- Continued

241 Bolivia
242 Brazil
243 Chile
244 Colombia
245 Ecuador
For Galapagos Islands see QL345.G2
246 Guyana (British Guiana)
246.2 Suriname (Dutch Guiana)
246.4 French Guiana
247 Paraguay
247.4 Paraná River
248 Peru
249 Uruguay
251 Venezuela

Atlantic Ocean islands
252.A1 General works
252.A3-Z By individual island or group of islands, A-Z
Bermuda see QL234
252.C35 Cape Verde
252.F32 Faroe Islands

Europe
253 General works
254 Regions not limited to a single country (not A-Z)
Including Alps, Balkan Peninsula, Baltic States, etc.
British Isles. Great Britain
255 General works
256 England
257 Ireland
257.5 Northern Ireland
258 Wales
259 Scotland
261 Austria
262 Hungary
France
263 General works
264 Colonies and mandated territories
265 Germany
271 Greece
273 Italy
273.5 Malta
275 Netherlands

Geographical distribution
Topographical divisions (Faunas)
Europe -- Continued

277 Belgium
278 Luxembourg
281 Russia. Soviet Union. Russia (Federation)
Cf. QL331 Russia in Asia. Siberia. Russian Far East
Cf. QL332+ Central Asia
Cf. QL333.7 Caucasus
282 Belarus
282.5 Moldova
283 Ukraine
284 Poland
285 Finland
286 Scandinavia (General)
Denmark
287 General works
Faroe Islands see QL252.F32
288 Iceland
289 Norway
291 Sweden
293 Spain
294 Portugal
Including the Azores, Madeira, etc.
296 Switzerland
297 Turkey in Europe
For Balkan Peninsula (General) see QL254
For individual Balkan countries see QL298.A+
For Turkey in Asia see QL333.5
298.A-Z Other European countries, A-Z
298.B8 Bulgaria
298.C8 Czechoslovakia. Czech Republic
298.E86 Estonia
298.L3 Latvia
298.L58 Lithuania
298.R8 Romania
298.S65 Slovakia
298.Y8 Yugoslavia

Asia

300 General works
304 Afghanistan
305 Arabian Peninsula (General)
For individual countries see QL334.A+
(306) Baluchistan
307 China
307.2 Taiwan
308 East Indies

Geographical distribution
Topographical divisions (Faunas)
Asia
India -- Continued

309 India
Indochina. Malay Peninsula
312 General works
313 Vietnam
314 Cambodia
315 Laos
317 Thailand
318 Straits Settlements
Malay Archipelago
319 General works
319.5 Borneo. Kalimantan
320 Brunei
321 Indonesia
For Kalimantan see QL319.5
For Papua see QL322.5
322 Malaysia
322.5 New Guinea
Including Papua (Indonesia) and Papua New Guinea
323 Philippines
Japan
325 General works
325.3 Ryukyu Islands
Including Okinawa
327 Korea
329 Iran
331 Russia in Asia. Siberia. Russian Far East
Central Asia
332 General works
332.3 Kazakhstan
332.4 Kyrgyzstan
332.5 Tajikistan
332.6 Turkmenistan
332.7 Uzbekistan
333 Israel. Palestine
333.3 Syria
333.5 Turkey in Asia. Asia Minor
333.7 Caucasus
Including Armenia, Azerbaijan, Georgia (Republic)
334.A-Z Other regions or countries, A-Z
(334.A75) Asia, Western
see QL334.M53
334.B34 Bangladesh
334.B87 Burma. Myanmar

Geographical distribution
Topographical divisions (Faunas)
Asia
Other regions or countries, A-Z -- Continued

334.C4 Ceylon. Sri Lanka
334.M53 Middle East
334.M65 Mongolia
Myanmar see QL334.B87
334.N44 Nepal
334.O53 Oman
334.P4 Pakistan
334.S28 Saudi Arabia
334.S56 Singapore
Sri Lanka see QL334.C4
(334.T87) Turkmenistan
see QL332.6

Africa
336 General works
337.A-Z By region or country, A-Z
337.A44 Algeria
337.A5 Angola
337.B44 Benin
337.B68 Botswana. Bechuanaland
337.B8 British East Africa
337.B9 Burkina Faso. Upper Volta
337.B94 Burundi
337.C25 Cameroon
Cape Verde see QL252.C35
337.C43 Central Africa
337.C44 Central African Republic
337.C48 Chad
337.C57 Congo (Brazzaville)
337.C58 Congo (Democratic Republic). Zaire
Côte d'Ivoire see QL337.I8
337.D53 Djibouti
337.E25 East Africa
337.E3 Egypt
337.E75 Equatorial Guinea
337.E76 Eritrea
337.E8 Ethiopia
337.F7 French-speaking Equatorial Africa
337.F75 French-speaking West Africa
337.G32 Gabon
337.G34 Gambia
337.G56 Ghana
337.G77 Guinea
337.G8 Guinea-Bissau

Geographical distribution
Topographical divisions (Faunas)
Africa
By region or country, A-Z -- Continued

337.I8 Ivory Coast. Côte d'Ivoire
337.K3 Kalahari Desert
337.K4 Kenya
337.L46 Lesotho
337.L7 Liberia
337.L72 Libya
337.L83 Luangwa Valley
337.M2 Malagasy Republic. Madagascar
337.M28 Malawi
337.M33 Mali
337.M37 Mauritania
Mauritius see QL337.6.M36
337.M65 Morocco
337.M7 Mozambique
337.N27 Namibia
337.N47 Niger
337.N5 Nigeria
337.N55 Nimba, Mount, Region
Rhodesia, Northern see QL337.Z3
337.R4 Rhodesia, Southern. Zimbabwe
337.R95 Rwanda
337.S3 Sahara
337.S34 Sao Tome and Principe
337.S44 Senegal
337.S54 Sierra Leone
337.S6 Somalia
337.S65 South Africa
337.S656 South Sudan
337.S66 Southern Africa
Southwest Africa see QL337.N27
337.S78 Sub-Saharan Africa
337.S8 Sudan
337.S93 Swaziland
337.T27 Tanganyika, Lake
337.T3 Tanzania
337.T7 Togo
337.T84 Tunisia
337.U35 Uganda
337.W4 West Africa
337.W45 Western Sahara
337.Z3 Zambia
Zimbabwe see QL337.R4

Indian Ocean islands

Geographical distribution
Topographical divisions (Faunas)
Indian Ocean islands -- Continued
337.5 General works
337.6.A-Z By island or group of islands, A-Z
337.6.M34 Maldives
337.6.M36 Mauritius
Australia
338 General works
339.A-Z By state or territory, A-Z
340 New Zealand
Including adjacent islands
Pacific islands
345.A1 General works
345.A3-Z By individual island or group of islands, A-Z
345.C65 Cook Islands
345.F53 Fiji
345.G2 Galapagos Islands
345.G83 Guam
345.H3 Hawaii
345.M3 Marquesas Islands
345.M34 Marshall Islands
345.M53 Micronesia
345.N3 New Caledonia
New Guinea see QL322.5
345.P35 Palau
Ryukyu Islands see QL325.3
345.T3 Tahiti
345.T65 Tonga
Arctic regions, Antarctica see QL104+
Tropics see QL109
Classification. Systematics and taxonomy
351 Principles
352 Systems
Nomenclature
353 General works. Principles
354 Nomenclators and checklists
355 Popular names
Invertebrates
360 Dictionaries and encyclopedias
362 General works, treatises, and textbooks
362.4 Juvenile works
Rare and endangered species
362.45 General works
362.46.A-Z By region or country, A-Z
362.5 Classification
362.7 Catalogs and collections

Invertebrates -- Continued
362.75 Evolution
362.8 Methods, culture, etc.
362.85 Immunology
362.9 Genetics
363 Anatomy and morphology
363.5 Metamorphosis
363.8 Cytology
364 Physiology
364.15 Reproduction
364.18 Development
Including larvae
364.2 Behavior
364.3 Feeding and feeds
364.4 Ecology
364.5 Coloniality. Animal colonies
Class here works on groupings of physically interconnected animals having a common ancestry through asexual reproduction
365 Animalcules. Early works on infusoria
Geographical distribution
For geographical distribution of systematic divisions, see the division, e. g. QL366+, Protozoa
365.3 General works
Physiographic divisions
365.34 Soil
Aquatic
365.36 General works
365.363 Marine
365.365 Freshwater
Topographic divisions
365.4 North America (United States and Canada) (Table Q3)
Latin America
365.43 General works
365.44 Mexico, Central America, and West Indies (Table Q3)
365.45 South America (Table Q3)
365.46 Atlantic Ocean and islands (Table Q3)
365.47 Europe (Table Q3)
365.48 Asia (Table Q3)
365.5 Africa (Table Q3)
365.53 Indian Ocean and islands (Table Q3)
365.54 Australia
365.55 New Zealand
365.56 Pacific Ocean and islands. Oceania (Table Q3)
365.57 Arctic Ocean and regions
365.58 Antarctic Ocean and Antarctica
365.6 Tropics

Invertebrates -- Continued
Protozoa
Cf. QR251+ Pathogenic protozoa
366 General works, treatises, and textbooks
366.5 Classification
Geographical distribution
For geographical distribution of systematic divisions see QL368.A115+
367 General works
367.1 North America (United States and Canada) (Table Q3)
367.2 Mexico, Central America, and West Indies (Table Q3)
367.3 South America (Table Q3)
367.4 Europe (Table Q3)
367.5 Asia (Table Q3)
367.6 Africa (Table Q3)
367.7 Australia
367.75 New Zealand
367.8 Pacific islands (Table Q3)
367.9 Arctic regions
367.95 Antarctica
367.96 Tropics
Systematic divisions
368.A115 Plasmodroma
368.A12 Mastigophora (Phytomastigia; Zoomastigia). Flagellata
368.A14 Sarcodina (Rhizopoda; Actinopoda)
368.A16 Apicomplexa (Sporozoa)
368.A18 Cnidosporidia
368.A2 Ciliophora
368.A22 Ciliata (Holotricha; Spirotricha; Peritricha)
Suctoria see QL368.S9
368.A3-Z By order or higher taxa, A-Z
Class works on species, genera, and families by order
368.A32 Acantharia
368.A33 Acanthometrida
368.A335 Acanthophractida
368.A36 Aconchulinida
368.A38 Acrasida
368.A4 Actinomyxida
368.A44 Actinophryida
368.A5 Amoebida
368.A57 Apostomatida
368.A63 Arcellinida
368.A66 Archigregarinida
368.A8 Astomatida
368.A85 Athalamida
368.B5 Bicosoecida
368.B55 Blastocystida

Invertebrates
Protozoa
Systematic divisions
By order or higher taxa, A-Z -- Continued

368.C4	Centrohelida
368.C48	Chloromonadida
368.C5	Choanoflagellida
368.C54	Chonotrichida
368.C57	Chrysomonadida
368.C59	Coccidia
368.C6	Coccolithophorida
368.C8	Cryptomonadida
	Ctenostomatida see QL368.O4
368.D4	Desmothoracida
(368.D6)	Dinoflagellida see QK569.D56
368.D65	Diplomonadida
368.E2	Ebriida
368.E5	Entodiniomorphida
(368.E9)	Euglenida see QK569.E93
368.E92	Eugregarinida
368.E95	Eumycetosoida
368.F6	Foraminiferida
368.G8	Gregarinida
368.G85	Gromiida
368.G9	Gymnostomatida
368.H33	Haemosporida
368.H34	Haplosporida
368.H4	Helicosporida
368.H5	Heliozoida
368.H53	Heterochlorida. Xanthomonadida
368.H55	Heterotrichida
368.H87	Hymenostomatida
368.H9	Hypermastigida
368.H95	Hypotrichida
	Infusoria see QL366
368.K5	Kinetoplastida
368.L3	Labyrinthulida
368.L62	Lobosa
368.M5	Microsporida
368.M78	Mycetozoida
368.M8	Myxosporida
368.N4	Neogregarinida
368.O3	Oculosida
368.O4	Odontostomatida. Ctenostomatida
368.O5	Oligotrichida

Invertebrates
Protozoa
Systematic divisions
By order or higher taxa, A-Z -- Continued

368.O7 Opalinida
368.O9 Oxynomadida
368.P4 Peritirchida
Phytomonadida see QL368.V6
368.P52 Piroplasmida
368.P55 Plasmodiophorida
368.P62 Polymastigida
368.P65 Porulosida
368.P7 Proteomyxida
368.P74 Protococcida
Protomastigida see QL368.P76
368.P76 Protomonadida. Protomastigida
368.R2 Radiolarida
368.R43 Retortamonadida
368.R5 Rhizomastigida
Sarcosporida see QL368.T6
(368.S5) Silicoflagellida
see QK569.S53
368.S9 Suctorida
368.T4 Testacida
368.T5 Thigmotrichida
368.T55 Tintinnida
368.T6 Toxoplasmida. Sarcosporida
368.T7 Trichomonadida
368.T76 Trichostomatida
368.V6 Volvocida. Phytomonadida
Xanthomonadida see QL368.H53
368.X4 Xenophyophorida
368.Z66 Zooflagellates
369 Anatomy and morphology
369.2 Physiology
Porifera (Sponges)
370.7 Periodicals, societies, congresses, serial collections
371 General works, treatises, and textbooks
371.2 Pictorial works and atlases
371.4 Popular works
371.6 Juvenile works
Geographical distribution
For geographical distribution of systematic divisions
see QL373.A+
372 General works
372.1 North America (United States and Canada) (Table Q3)
372.2 Mexico, Central America, and West Indies (Table Q3)

Invertebrates
Porifera (Sponges)
Geographical distribution -- Continued

372.3 South America (Table Q3)
372.4 Europe (Table Q3)
372.5 Asia (Table Q3)
372.6 Africa (Table Q3)
372.7 Australia
372.75 New Zealand
372.8 Pacific islands (Table Q3)
372.9 Arctic regions
372.95 Antarctica
372.96 Tropics
373.A-Z Systematic divisions. By class, A-Z
Class here works on species, genera, families and orders
373.C2 Calcispongiae (Calcarea)
373.D4 Demospongiae
373.H6 Hyalospongea (Hexactinellida)
374 Anatomy and morphology
374.2 Physiology

Cnidaria

375 General works, treatises, and textbooks
375.2 Pictorial works and atlases
375.4 Popular works
375.6 Juvenile works

Geographical distribution
For geographical distribution of systematic divisions see QL377.A+

376 General works
376.1 North America (United States and Canada) (Table Q3)
376.2 Mexico, Central America, and West Indies (Table Q3)
376.3 South America (Table Q3)
376.4 Europe (Table Q3)
376.5 Asia (Table Q3)
376.6 Africa (Table Q3)
376.7 Australia
376.75 New Zealand
376.8 Pacific islands (Table Q3)
376.9 Arctic regions
376.95 Antarctica
376.96 Tropics
377.A-Z Systematic divisions. By class, A-Z
Anthozoa (Corals)
377.C5 General works
377.C6 Alcyonaria
377.C7 Zoantharia
Ctenophora see QL380+

Invertebrates
Cnidaria
Systematic divisions. By class, A-Z -- Continued
377.H9 Hydrozoa (Hydromedusae; hydroids)
377.S4 Scyphozoa (Scyphomedusae; jellyfish)
378 Anatomy and morphology
378.2 Physiology
379 Zoophyta (old sense)
Ctenophora
380 General works, treatises, and textbooks
Geographical distribution
For geographical distribution of systematic divisions see QL380.5.A+
380.3 General works
380.32 North America (United States and Canada) (Table Q3)
380.35 Mexico, Central America, and West Indies (Table Q3)
380.37 South America (Table Q3)
380.4 Europe (Table Q3)
380.42 Asia (Table Q3)
380.44 Africa (Table Q3)
380.46 Australasia and Indo-Pacific islands (Table Q3)
380.48 Polar regions
380.49 Tropics
380.5.A-Z Systematic divisions. By classes and orders
Class works on species, genera, and families by order
380.5.N8-.N83 Nuda
380.5.N8 General works
380.5.N83 Beroida
380.5.T4-.T47 Tentaculata
380.5.T4 General works
380.5.T42 Cestida
380.5.T429 Cydippida
380.5.T45 Lobata
380.5.T47 Platyctenea
380.7 Anatomy and morphology
380.8 Physiology
Echinodermata
381 General works, treatises, and textbooks
382 Classification
382.2 Catalogs and collections
Geographical distribution
For geographical distribution of systematic divisions see QL384.A+
383 General works
383.1 North America (United States and Canada) (Table Q3)
383.2 Mexico, Central America, and West Indies (Table Q3)
383.3 South America (Table Q3)

Invertebrates
Echinodermata
Geographical distribution -- Continued
383.35 Atlantic islands (Table Q3)
383.4 Europe (Table Q3)
383.5 Asia (Table Q3)
383.6 Africa (Table Q3)
383.7 Australia
383.75 New Zealand
383.8 Pacific islands (Table Q3)
383.9 Arctic regions
383.95 Antarctica
383.96 Tropics
384.A-Z Systematic divisions. By class, A-Z
Class works on species, genera, families, and orders by class
384.A8 Asteroidea (Starfishes)
384.C8 Crinoidea
384.E2 Echinoidea (Sea urchins)
384.H7 Holothurioidea (Sea cucumbers)
384.O6 Ophiuroidea (Brittle stars)
385 Anatomy and morphology
385.2 Physiology
Worms and other vermiform invertebrates
386.A1 Periodicals, societies, congresses, serial publications
386.A3-Z General works, treatises, and textbooks
Cf. QL392.A1+ Helminthology
386.6 Juvenile works
387 Classification
387.2 Catalogs and collections
Geographical distribution
For geographical distribution of systematic divisions see QL391.A+
388 General works, treatises, and textbooks
388.1 North America (United States and Canada) (Table Q3)
388.2 Mexico, Central America, and West Indies (Table Q3)
388.3 South America (Table Q3)
388.4 Europe (Table Q3)
388.5 Asia (Table Q3)
388.6 Africa (Table Q3)
388.7 Australia
388.75 New Zealand
388.8 Pacific islands (Table Q3)
388.9 Arctic regions
388.95 Antarctica
388.96 Tropics
391.A-Z Systematic divisions. By phylum, A-Z
391.A2 Acanthocephala (Spiny-headed worms)

Invertebrates
Worms and other vermiform invertebrates
Systematic divisions. By phylum, A-Z -- Continued

391.A6	Annelida (Segmented worms)
	Cestoda see QL391.P7
391.C6	Chaetognatha (Arrowworms)
391.E2	Echiura
391.G2	Gastrotricha
	Gephyrea (Gastrotricha) see QL391.E2
	Gephyrea (Sipuncula) see QL391.S5
391.G63	Gnathostomulida
	Hirudinea see QL391.A6
391.K5	Kinorhyncha (Echinodera)
391.L67	Loricifera
391.M4	Mesozoa
391.N4	Nematoda (Roundworms)
391.N5	Nematomorpha (Gordiacea; horsehair worms)
391.N6	Nemertina (Rhynchocoela; ribbonworms)
	Oligochaeta see QL391.A6
	Onycophora see QL448
	Pentastomida see QL447.3
391.P5	Phoronida
391.P7	Platyhelminthes (Flatworms)
(391.P85)	Pogonophora see QL391.A6
	Polychaeta see QL391.A6
391.P93	Priapulida
391.R8	Rotifera
391.S5	Sipuncula
	Trematoda see QL391.P7
	Turbellaria see QL391.P7
	Helminthology For geographic treatment see QL388+
392.A1	Periodicals, societies, congresses, serial publications
392.A3-Z	General works, treatises, and textbooks
393	Anatomy and morphology
394	Physiology
	Brachiopoda (Lamp shells)
395	General works, treatises, and textbooks
395.1	Classification
395.15	Catalogs and collectors
	Geographical distribution For geographical distribution of systematic divisions see QL395.8.A+
395.2	North America (United States and Canada) (Table Q3)
395.23	Mexico, Central America, and West Indies (Table Q3)
395.25	South America (Table Q3)

Invertebrates
Brachiopoda (Lamp shells)
Geographical distribution -- Continued
395.3 Europe (Table Q3)
395.4 Asia (Table Q3)
395.5 Africa (Table Q3)
395.6 Australia
395.63 New Zealand
395.67 Pacific islands (Table Q3)
395.7 Arctic regions
395.75 Antarctica
395.76 Tropics
395.8.A-Z Systematic divisions. By family, A-Z
Class here works on species, genera, and families
For works on higher taxa, see QL395+
395.8.C7 Craniidae
395.8.L7 Lingulidae
395.8.R5 Rhynchonellidae
395.8.T4 Terebratulidae
395.9 Anatomy and morphology
395.95 Physiology
Bryozoa (Ectoprocta; Polyzoa)
396 General works, treatises, and textbooks
396.5 Classification
396.7 Catalogs and collections
Geographical distribution
For geographical distribution of systematic divisions see QL398.A+
397 General works
397.1 North America (United States and Canada) (Table Q3)
397.2 Mexico, Central America, and West Indies (Table Q3)
397.3 South America (Table Q3)
397.4 Europe (Table Q3)
397.5 Asia (Table Q3)
397.6 Africa (Table Q3)
397.7 Australia
397.75 New Zealand
397.8 Pacific islands (Table Q3)
397.9 Arctic regions
397.95 Antarctica
397.96 Tropics
398.A-Z Systematic divisions. By order, A-Z
Class here works on species, genera, families, and orders
Class higher taxa in+
398.C5 Cheilostomata
398.C8 Ctenostomata
398.C9 Cyclostomata

Invertebrates
Bryozoa (Ectoprocta; Polyzoa)
Systematic divisions. By order, A-Z -- Continued
Ectoprocta see QL396+
Entoprocta see QL400+
398.L6 Lophopoda
399 Anatomy and morphology
399.2 Physiology
Entoprocta (Callyssozoa; Endoprocta)
400 General works, treatises, and textbooks
Geographical distribution
For geographical distribution of systematic divisions see QL400.5.A+
400.3 General works
400.32 North America (United States and Canada) (Table Q3)
400.35 Mexico, Central America, and West Indies (Table Q3)
400.37 South America (Table Q3)
400.4 Europe (Table Q3)
400.42 Asia (Table Q3)
400.44 Africa (Table Q3)
400.46 Australasia and the Indo-Pacific islands (Table Q3)
400.48 Polar regions
400.49 Tropics
400.5.A-Z Systematic divisions. By family, A-Z
Class here works on species, genera, and families
Class higher taxa in QL400+
400.5.L6 Loxosomatidae
400.5.P4 Pedicellinidae
400.5.U7 Urnatellidae
Mollusca
Cf. SH365+ Oyster culture and fisheries
401 Periodicals, societies, congresses, serial publications
402 Collected works (nonserial)
402.3 Dictionaries and encyclopedias
403 General works, treatises, and textbooks
404 Pictorial works and atlases
405 Popular works
405.2 Juvenile works
406 Classification
406.2 Catalogs and collections
406.5 Collection and preservation
406.55 Museums. Exhibitions
406.7 Evolution. Phylogeny. Speciation
Geographical distribution
For geographic distribution of systematic divisions see QL430.1+
Physiographic divisions

Invertebrates
Mollusca
Geographical distribution
Physiographic divisions -- Continued
Land
407 General works
407.5 Freshwater
Marine
For mollusks of particular coasts and islands see QL411+
408 General works
408.2 Atlantic Ocean
Cf. QL424.5 Atlantic islands
408.5 Pacific Ocean
Cf. QL428.5 Pacific islands
408.7 Indian Ocean
Topographical divisions
North America
411 General works
413 Canada
United States
414 General works
415.A-Z By region or state, A-Z
416 Atlantic Coast
417 Pacific Coast
(418) Pacific islands
see QL428.5
419 Gulf Coast
Latin America
420 General works
421 Mexico
422 Central America (Table Q3)
423 West Indies (Table Q3)
424 South America (Table Q3)
424.5 Atlantic islands (Table Q3)
425 Europe (Table Q3)
426 Asia (Table Q3)
427 Africa (Table Q3)
428 Australia
428.2 New Zealand
428.5 Pacific islands (Table Q3)
429 Arctic regions
429.5 Antarctica
429.6 Tropics
Systematic divisions
Aplacophora (Solenogasters)
430.12 General works and orders

Invertebrates
Mollusca
Systematic divisions
Aplacophora (Solenogasters) -- Continued

430.12.A-Z By family, A-Z
430.12.P76 Proneomeniidae
Polyplacophora (Chitons)
430.13 General works and orders
430.14.A-Z By family, A-Z
430.14.A26 Acanthochitonidae
430.14.C47 Chitonidae
430.14.I83 Ischnochitonidae
430.14.M64 Mopaliidae
430.15 Monoplacophora
Cephalopoda
430.2 General works and orders
430.3.A-Z By family, A-Z
430.3.A73 Architeuthidae
430.3.B3 Bathyteuthidae
430.3.C72 Cranchiidae
430.3.C9 Cycloteuthidae
430.3.E56 Enoploteuthidae
430.3.G66 Gonatidae
430.3.J68 Joubiniteuthidae
430.3.L8 Loliginidae
430.3.N4 Nautilidae
430.3.O2 Octopodidae (Octopuses)
430.3.O5 Ommastrephidae
430.3.O6 Onychoteuthidae
430.3.S47 Sepiidae
430.3.S49 Sepiolidae (Bobtail squids)
430.3.S65 Spirulidae
430.3.V35 Vampyroteuthidae
Gastropoda (Snails)
430.4 General works and orders
430.5.A-Z By family, A-Z
Abalones see QL430.5.H34
430.5.A18 Abyssochrysidae
430.5.A2 Achatinellidae
430.5.A22 Achatinidae
430.5.A23 Aciculidae
430.5.A24 Aclididae
430.5.A26 Acmaeidae
430.5.A28 Acroloxidae
430.5.A29 Actaeonidae
430.5.A45 Aeolidiidae
430.5.A5 Amastridae

Invertebrates
Mollusca
Systematic divisions
Gastropoda (Snails)
By family, A-Z -- Continued

	Amnicolidae see QL430.5.H9
430.5.A57	Ampullariidae
430.5.A63	Ancylidae
430.5.A66	Aplysiidae
430.5.A69	Architectonicidae
430.5.A7	Arionidae
430.5.A74	Arminidae
430.5.A8	Atlantidae
430.5.A85	Atyidae
	Auriculidae see QL430.5.E45
430.5.B37	Batillariidae
430.5.B58	Bithyniidae
430.5.B73	Bradybaenidae
430.5.B75	Buccinidae
430.5.B8	Bulimulidae
430.5.B84	Bulinidae
430.5.C18	Caecidae
430.5.C22	Calyptraeidae
430.5.C25	Camaenidae
430.5.C26	Cancellariidae
430.5.C3	Cassidae
430.5.C35	Cavolinidae
430.5.C38	Cerionidae
430.5.C4	Cerithiidae
430.5.C43	Cerithiopsidae
430.5.C49	Chilinidae
430.5.C53	Chondropomatidae
430.5.C56	Chromodorididae
430.5.C57	Clausiliidae
430.5.C6	Clionidae
430.5.C73	Columbellidae
430.5.C75	Conidae
	Cowries see QL430.5.C94
430.5.C82	Cyclophoridae
	Cyclostomidae see QL430.5.P63
	Cylindrellidae see QL430.5.U68
(430.5.C93)	Cymatiidae see QL430.5.R35
430.5.C94	Cypraeidae (Cowries)
430.5.D43	Diastomatidae
430.5.D55	Dolabriferidae
430.5.D6	Dorididae

Invertebrates
Mollusca
Systematic divisions
Gastropoda (Snails)
By family, A-Z -- Continued

430.5.E45	Ellobiidae
430.5.E48	Elysiidae
430.5.E5	Endodontidae
430.5.E55	Entoconchidae
430.5.E6	Epitoniidae
430.5.E9	Eulimidae
430.5.F2	Fasciolariidae
430.5.F53	Ficidae
430.5.F57	Fissurellidae
430.5.F58	Flabellinidae
430.5.G34	Gadiniidae
430.5.H34	Haliotidae (Abalones)
430.5.H37	Helicarionidae
430.5.H4	Helicidae
430.5.H45	Helicindae
430.5.H46	Helminthoglyptidae
	Hermaeidae see QL430.5.S75
430.5.H9	Hydrobiidae
430.5.J3	Janellidae
430.5.J36	Janthinidae
430.5.J8	Juliidae
430.5.L2	Lamellariidae
430.5.L33	Lepetidae
430.5.L4	Limacidae
	Limnaeidae see QL430.5.L85
430.5.L58	Littorinidae
430.5.L85	Lymnaeidae
430.5.M3	Marginellidae
	Melaniidae see QL430.5.T45
430.5.M44	Melanopsidae
430.5.M47	Melongenidae
430.5.M57	Mitridae
430.5.M9	Muricidae
430.5.N27	Nacellidae
430.5.N3	Nassariidae
430.5.N35	Naticidae
430.5.N5	Neritidae
430.5.O5	Olividae
430.5.O73	Oreohelicidae
430.5.O78	Orthalicidae
430.5.P15	Partulidae
430.5.P18	Patellidae

Invertebrates
Mollusca
Systematic divisions
Gastropoda (Snails)
By family, A-Z -- Continued

430.5.P2 Personidae
430.5.P23 Phasianellidae
430.5.P25 Philomycidae
430.5.P33 Phyllidiidae
430.5.P35 Phylliroidae
430.5.P37 Physidae
430.5.P46 Planaxidae
430.5.P48 Planorbidae
430.5.P49 Pleurobranchidae
430.5.P5 Pleuroceridae
430.5.P6 Polygyridae
430.5.P63 Pomatiasidae
430.5.P64 Pomatiopsidae
430.5.P68 Potamididae
Proserpinidae see QL430.5.H45
430.5.P9 Pupillidae
430.5.P92 Pupinidae
430.5.P95 Pyramidellidae
430.5.R35 Ranellidae
430.5.R45 Rhodopidae
430.5.R48 Rhytididae
430.5.R57 Rissoidae
Scalariidae see QL430.5.E6
430.5.S25 Scissurellidae
430.5.S56 Siphonariidae
430.5.S65 Spiraxidae
430.5.S74 Stiliferidae
430.5.S75 Stiligeridae
430.5.S78 Streptaxidae
430.5.S8 Strombidae
430.5.S83 Strophocheilidae
430.5.S87 Succineidae (Ambersnails)
430.5.T25 Terebridae
430.5.T3 Testacellidae
430.5.T35 Tethyidae
430.5.T45 Thiaridae
430.5.T63 Tonnidae
430.5.T65 Tornidae
430.5.T67 Tricoliidae
430.5.T7 Tritoniidae
430.5.T75 Trochidae
430.5.T78 Truncatellidae

QL

Invertebrates
Mollusca
Systematic divisions
Gastropoda (Snails)
By family, A-Z -- Continued

430.5.T85 Turbinellidae
430.5.T9 Turbinidae
430.5.T95 Turridae
430.5.T96 Turritellidae (Turretsnails, wormsnails)
430.5.U68 Urocoptidae
430.5.U7 Urocyclidae
Vaginulidae see QL430.5.V4
430.5.V34 Valloniidae
430.5.V36 Valvatidae
(430.5.V37) Vasidae
see QL430.5.T85
430.5.V4 Veronicellidae
430.5.V65 Vitronellidae
430.5.V7 Viviparidae
430.5.V75 Volutidae
430.5.V77 Volutomitridae
430.5.X46 Xenophoridae
430.5.Z6 Zonitidae

Bivalvia (Lamellibranchia; pelecypoda; clams)

430.6 General works and orders
430.7.A-Z By family, A-Z
430.7.A34 Amblemidae
430.7.A4 Anatinidae
430.7.A72 Arcidae
430.7.A74 Arcticidae
430.7.A8 Astartidae
430.7.C2 Cardiidae
430.7.C24 Carditidae
430.7.C53 Chamidae
430.7.C67 Corbiculidae
430.7.C69 Corbulidae
430.7.C8 Crassatellidae
Cyrenidae see QL430.7.C67
430.7.D55 Dimyidae
430.7.D65 Donacidae
430.7.D8 Dreisseniidae
430.7.G23 Gastrochaenidae
430.7.G55 Glossidae
430.7.G78 Gryphaeidae
430.7.H53 Hiatellidae
430.7.H87 Hyriidae
430.7.L35 Lametilidae

Invertebrates
Mollusca
Systematic divisions
Bivalvia (Lamellibranchia; pelecypoda; clams)
By family, A-Z -- Continued

430.7.L4 Ledidae
430.7.L5 Limidae
430.7.L8 Lucinidae
430.7.M3 Mactridae
430.7.M37 Margaritiferidae
430.7.M85 Mycetopodidae
430.7.M9 Myidae
430.7.M95 Mytilidae
430.7.N63 Noetiidae
430.7.N85 Nuculanidae
430.7.N9 Nuculidae
430.7.O9 Ostreidae (Oysters)
430.7.P3 Pectinidae
430.7.P48 Philobryidae
430.7.P5 Pholadidae
430.7.P56 Pinnidae
(430.7.P59) Pisidiidae
see QL430.7.S65
430.7.P7 Pristiglomidae
430.7.P75 Psammobiidae
430.7.P77 Pteriidae (Pearl oysters)
430.7.S43 Semelidae
430.7.S5 Siliculidae
430.7.S58 Solemyidae
430.7.S6 Solenidae (Razor clams)
430.7.S65 Sphaeriidae
430.7.S68 Spondylidae
430.7.T3 Tellinidae
430.7.T4 Teredinidae
430.7.T47 Thraciidae
430.7.T55 Tindariidae
430.7.T7 Tridacnidae
430.7.U6 Unionidae
430.7.V5 Veneridae
430.8 Scaphopoda (Tusk shells)
431 Anatomy and morphology
431.2 Physiology
431.3 Reproduction and spawning
431.4 Behavior
432 Miscellany and curiosa

Arthropoda

434.A1 Periodicals, societies, congresses, serial publications

Invertebrates
Arthropoda -- Continued

434.A3-Z General works, treatises, and textbooks
434.13 Pictorial works and atlases
434.14 Popular works
434.15 Juvenile works
434.2 Classification
434.3 Catalogs and collections
434.35 Evolution. Speciation
434.4 Study and teaching. Research
434.45 Poisonous arthropods. Dangerous arthropods

Geographical distribution

For geographical distribution of systematic divisions, see the division below

434.5 General works
434.52 North America (United States and Canada) (Table Q3)
434.53 Mexico, Central America, and West Indies (Table Q3)
434.54 South America (Table Q3)
434.55 Europe (Table Q3)
434.56 Asia (Table Q3)
434.57 Africa (Table Q3)
434.58 Australasia and Indo-Pacific islands (Table Q3)
434.59 Polar regions
434.6 Tropics
434.7 Anatomy and morphology
434.715 Cytology
434.72 Physiology
434.8 Behavior

Crustacea

435.A1 Periodicals, societies, congresses, serial publications
435.A3-Z General works, treatises, and textbooks
436 Pictorial works and atlases
437 Popular works
437.2 Juvenile works
438 Classification
438.2 Catalogs and collections
438.5 Evolution. Phylogeny

Geographical distribution

For geographical distribution of systematic divisions see QL444.A+

441 General works
441.1 North America (United States and Canada) (Table Q3)
441.2 Mexico, Central America, and West Indies (Table Q3)
441.3 South America (Table Q3)
441.4 Europe (Table Q3)
441.5 Asia (Table Q3)
441.6 Africa (Table Q3)

Invertebrates
Arthropoda
Crustacea
Geographical distribution -- Continued
441.7 Australia
441.75 New Zealand
441.8 Pacific islands (Table Q3)
441.9 Arctic regions
441.95 Antarctica
441.96 Tropics
444.A-Z Systematic divisions. By subclasses and orders, A-Z
Class here works on species, genera, and families by order
Branchiopoda
444.B8 General works
444.B815 Anostraca (Fairy shrimps)
444.B83 Cladocera (Water fleas)
444.B834 Conchostraca (Clam shrimps)
444.B86 Notostraca (Tadpole shrimps)
444.B9 Branchiura (Fish lice)
444.C4 Cephalocarida
Cirripedia
444.C5 General works
444.C52 Acrothoracica
444.C527 Ascothoracica
444.C57 Rhizocephala
444.C58 Thoracica (Barnacles)
Copepoda
444.C7 General works
444.C72 Calanoida
(444.C722) Caligoida
see QL444.C79
444.C73 Cyclopoida
444.C74 Harpacticoida
444.C75 Lernaepodoida
444.C756 Monstrilloida
444.C76 Notodelphyoida
444.C78 Poecilostomatoida
444.C79 Siphonostomatoida
Entomostraca see QL435+
Malacostraca
444.M3 General works
444.M315 Amphipoda (Sand hoppers; whale lice)
444.M317 Anaspidacea
444.M32 Bathynellacea
444.M328 Cumacea
444.M33 Decapoda (Shrimps; lobsters; crabs)
444.M338 Euphausiacea

Invertebrates
Arthropoda
Crustacea
Systematic divisions. By subclasses and orders, A-Z
Malacostraca -- Continued
444.M34 Isopoda (Pill bugs; wood lice)
444.M347 Leptostraca
444.M35 Mysidacea (Opossum shrimps)
444.M37 Spelaeogriphacea
444.M375 Stomatopoda
444.M378 Stygocaridacea
444.M38 Tanaidacea
444.M384 Thermosbaenacea
444.M9 Mystacocarida
Ostracoda (Seed shrimps)
444.O8 General works
444.O83 Halocyprida
444.O85 Myodocopida
444.O86 Podocopida
445 Anatomy and morphology
445.2 Physiology
447 Pycnogonida (Pantopoda)
447.3 Pentastomida (Linguatulida; tongue worms)
447.5 Tardigrada (Water bears)
447.7 Merostomata (Xiphosura)
448 Onychophora
Myriapoda
449 General works, treatises, and textbooks
Geographical distribution
For geographical distribution of systematic divisions see QL449.5+
449.3 General works
449.32 North America (United States and Canada) (Table Q3)
449.35 Mexico, Central America, and West Indies (Table Q3)
449.37 South America (Table Q3)
449.4 Europe (Table Q3)
449.42 Asia (Table Q3)
449.44 Africa (Table Q3)
449.46 Australasia and Indo-Pacific islands (Table Q3)
449.48 Polar regions
449.49 Tropics
Systematic divisions
Class here works on species, genera, and families by family; high taxa by class
Chilopoda (Centipedes)
449.5 General works and orders
449.55.A-Z By family, A-Z

Invertebrates
Arthropoda
Myriapoda
Systematic divisions
Chilopoda (Centipedes)
By family, A-Z -- Continued

449.55.C4 Cermatobiidae
449.55.C7 Craterostigmidae
449.55.C78 Cryptopidae
449.55.D5 Dignathodontidae
449.55.E8 Ethopolyidae
449.55.G4 Geophilidae
449.55.G66 Gonibregmatidae
449.55.G68 Gosibiidae
449.55.H4 Henicopidae
449.55.H5 Himantariidae
449.55.L5 Lithobiidae
449.55.M4 Mecistocephalidae
449.55.N4 Neogeophilidae
449.55.O7 Oryidae
449.55.S25 Schendylidae
449.55.S3 Scolopendridae
449.55.S37 Scutigeridae
449.55.S63 Sogonidae
449.55.S66 Soniphilidae
449.55.W3 Watobiidae

Diplopoda (Millipedes)

449.6 General works and orders
449.65.A-Z By family, A-Z
449.65.A6 Andrognathidae
449.65.A8 Atopetholidae
449.65.B4 Blaniulidae
449.65.C24 Callipodidae
449.65.C25 Cambalidae
449.65.C28 Caseyidae
449.65.C37 Chelodesmidae
449.65.C4 Chordeumidae
449.65.C5 Cleidogonidae
449.65.C6 Conotylidae
449.65.C72 Craspedosomidae
449.65.C79 Cryptodesmidae
449.65.E87 Eurymerodesmidae
449.65.E878 Euryuridae
449.65.G4 Gervaisiidae
449.65.G5 Glomeridae
449.65.G53 Glomeridesmidae
449.65.H37 Harpagophoridae

Invertebrates
Arthropoda
Myriapoda
Systematic divisions
Diplopoda (Millipedes)
By family, A-Z -- Continued

449.65.J8	Julidae
449.65.L4	Leioderidae
449.65.L9	Lysiopetalidae
449.65.N4	Nearctodesmidae
449.65.O6	Oniscodesmidae
449.65.O95	Oxydesmidae
449.65.P18	Pachybolidae
449.65.P22	Paeromopidae
449.65.P27	Paradoxsomatidae
449.65.P273	Paraiulidae
449.65.P42	Platydesmidae
449.65.P427	Platyrrhacidae
449.65.P64	Polydesmidae
449.65.P648	Polyxenidae
449.65.P649	Polyzoniidae
449.65.R4	Rhinocricidae
449.65.S56	Siphoniulidae
449.65.S565	Siphonophoridae
449.65.S64	Sphaeriodesmidae
449.65.S645	Sphaerotheridae
449.65.S65	Spirobolidae
449.65.S655	Spirostreptidae
	Strongylosomidae see QL449.65.P27
449.65.S88	Stylodesmidae
449.65.S95	Synxenidae
449.65.T56	Tingupidae
449.65.T75	Trichopolydesmidae
449.65.V34	Vanhoeffeniidae
449.65.X9	Xystodesmidae
	Pauropoda
449.7	General works
449.75.A-Z	By family, A-Z
449.75.B7	Brachypauropodidae
449.75.E8	Eurypauropodidae
449.75.P3	Pauropodidae
	Symphyla
449.8	General works
449.85.A-Z	By family, A-Z
449.85.G4	Geophilellidae
449.85.S25	Scolopendrellidae
449.85.S3	Scutigerellidae

Invertebrates
Arthropoda
Myriapoda -- Continued
449.9 Anatomy and morphology
449.92 Physiology
Arachnida (Scorpions; spiders; mites; etc.)
451 General works, treatises, and textbooks
452 Popular works
452.2 Juvenile works
452.8 Classification
453 Catalogs and collections
Geographical distribution
For geographical distribution of systematic divisions see QL458+
453.1 North America (United States and Canada) (Table Q3)
453.2 Mexico, Central America, and West Indies (Table Q3)
453.3 South America (Table Q3)
453.35 Atlantic islands (Table Q3)
453.4 Europe (Table Q3)
453.5 Asia (Table Q3)
453.6 Africa (Table Q3)
Australasia
453.68 General works
453.7 Australia
453.75 New Zealand
453.8 Pacific islands (Table Q3)
453.9 Arctic regions
453.95 Antarctica
453.96 Tropics
Systematic divisions
Acari (Acarina). Mites
458 General works
458.15.A-Z By order, A-Z
458.15.A33 Acariformes
Notostigmata see QL458.15.O65
458.15.O65 Opilioacariformes
458.15.P37 Parasitiformes
458.2.A-Z By family, A-Z
458.2.A3 Acaridae
458.2.A44 Alloptidae
458.2.A45 Ameronothridae
458.2.A5 Analgidae
458.2.A58 Anystidae
458.2.A74 Argasidae
458.2.A77 Arrenuridae
458.2.B4 Bdellidae
458.2.B7 Brachychthoniidae

Invertebrates
Arthropoda
Arachnida (Scorpions; spiders; mites; etc.)
Systematic divisions
Acari (Acarina). Mites
By family, A-Z -- Continued

458.2.C28 Caeculidae
458.2.C3 Carpoglyphidae
458.2.C37 Cercomegistidae
458.2.C39 Chaetodactylidae
458.2.C4 Cheyletidae
458.2.C8 Cunaxidae
458.2.C9 Cytoditidae
458.2.D45 Demodicidae
458.2.D47 Dermanyssidae
458.2.D475 Dermoglyphidae
458.2.D56 Diptilomiopidae
458.2.E45 Echimyopodidae
458.2.E6 Epidermoptidae
458.2.E73 Eremaeidae
458.2.E75 Eriophyidae
458.2.E78 Erythraeidae
458.2.E8 Eupodidae
458.2.E84 Eustathiidae
458.2.E9 Eylaidae
458.2.F3 Falculiferidae
458.2.G34 Galumnidae
Gamasidae see QL458.2.P3
458.2.G4 Glycyphagidae
458.2.H3 Halacaridae
458.2.H38 Hermanniidae
458.2.H4 Heterocheylidae
458.2.H9 Hydrachnidae
458.2.H98 Hydryphantidae
458.2.I9 Ixodidae
458.2.K5 Knemidokoptidae
458.2.L3 Labidocarpidae
458.2.L33 Laelapidae
458.2.L44 Leeuwenhoekiidae
458.2.L54 Limnocharidae
458.2.L58 Listrophoridae
458.2.L67 Lordalycidae
458.2.M3 Macronyssidae
458.2.M53 Microtrombidiidae
458.2.M9 Myobiidae
458.2.M93 Myocoptidae
458.2.N67 Nothridae

Invertebrates
Arthropoda
Arachnida (Scorpions; spiders; mites; etc.)
Systematic divisions
Acari (Acarina). Mites
By family, A-Z -- Continued

458.2.O74 Oribatidae
458.2.P3 Parasitidae
458.2.P35 Penthaleidae
458.2.P37 Phytoptidae
458.2.P4 Phytoseiidae
458.2.P44 Pionidae
458.2.P6 Podapolipodidae
458.2.P65 Pontarachnidae
458.2.P74 Proctophyllodidae
458.2.P8 Psoroptidae
458.2.P85 Pterolichidae
458.2.P87 Pterygosomatidae
458.2.P9 Pyemotidae
458.2.P95 Pyroglyphidae
458.2.R36 Raphignathidae
458.2.R45 Rhagidiidae
458.2.R47 Rhodacaridae
458.2.R66 Rosensteiniidae
458.2.S25 Sarcoptidae
458.2.S3 Scutacaridae
458.2.S7 Sperchonidae
458.2.S75 Spinturnicidae
458.2.S8 Stigmaeidae
458.2.S89 Syringobiidae
458.2.S9 Syringophilidae
458.2.T3 Tarsonemidae
458.2.T36 Tenuipalpidae
458.2.T4 Tetranychidae (Spider mites)
458.2.T5 Thyasidae
458.2.T7 Trachytidae
458.2.T75 Trombiculidae
458.2.T76 Trombidiidae
458.2.U5 Unionicolidae
458.2.U7 Uropodidae
458.2.V37 Varroidae
458.2.X65 Xolalgidae
458.2.Z4 Zerconidae

Amblypygi (Phrynichida)
458.3 General works
458.32.A-Z By family, A-Z
458.32.C4 Charonidae

Invertebrates
Arthropoda
Arachnida (Scorpions; spiders; mites; etc.)
Systematic divisions
Amblypygi (Phrynichida)
By family, A-Z -- Continued

458.32.P56 Phrynichidae
458.32.P57 Phrynidae
458.32.T3 Tarantulidae

Araneae (Araneida). Spiders

458.4 General works

Geographical distribution

458.41 North America (United States, Canada, and Greenland) (Table Q3)
458.412 Mexico, Central America, and West Indies (Table Q3)
458.413 South America (Table Q3)
458.4135 Atlantic islands (Table Q3)
458.414 Europe (Table Q3)
458.415 Asia (Table Q3)
458.416 Africa (Table Q3)
458.4165 Indian Ocean islands (Table Q3)

Australasia

458.417 General works
458.4173 Australia
458.4175 New Zealand
458.418 Pacific islands (Table Q3)

Polar regions

458.4185 General works
458.419 Arctic regions
458.4195 Antarctica
458.4197 Tropics
458.42.A-Z By family, A-Z
458.42.A2 Acanthoctenidae
458.42.A28 Actinopodidae
458.42.A3 Agelenidae
458.42.A4 Amaurobiidae

Amaurobioididae see QL458.42.A57

458.42.A45 Ammoxenidae
458.42.A48 Anapidae
458.42.A5 Antrodiaetidae
458.42.A57 Anyphaenidae
458.42.A7 Araneidae (Orb weavers)
458.42.A73 Archaeidae

Argiopidae see QL458.42.A7

Attidae see QL458.42.S24

458.42.A8 Atypidae

Invertebrates
Arthropoda
Arachnida (Scorpions; spiders; mites; etc.)
Systematic divisions
Araneae (Araneida). Spiders
By family, A-Z -- Continued

	Aviculariidae see QL458.42.T5
458.42.B3	Barychelidae
458.42.C3	Caponiidae
458.42.C4	Clubionidae
458.42.C67	Corinnidae
458.42.C8	Ctenidae
458.42.C83	Ctenizidae
458.42.C93	Cyatholipidae
	Deinopidae see QL458.42.D55
458.42.D44	Desidae
458.42.D5	Dictynidae
458.42.D53	Diguetidae
458.42.D55	Dinopidae. Deinopidae
458.42.D56	Dipluridae
458.42.D9	Dysderidae
458.42.E7	Eresidae
	Eusparassidae see QL458.42.H48
458.42.F5	Filistatidae
458.42.G5	Gnaphosidae
458.42.G7	Gradungulidae
458.42.H3	Hadrotarsidae
458.42.H33	Hahniidae
458.42.H47	Hersiliidae
458.42.H48	Heteropodidae
458.42.H6	Homalonychidae
458.42.H9	Hypochilidae
458.42.L3	Lamponidae
458.42.L4	Leptonetidae
458.42.L55	Linyphiidae
458.42.L555	Liocranidae
458.42.L56	Liphistiidae
458.42.L6	Loxoscelidae
458.42.L9	Lycosidae (Wolf spiders)
458.42.M4	Mecicobothriidae
458.42.M5	Microstigmatidae
458.42.M53	Migidae
458.42.M54	Mimetidae
458.42.M97	Mysmenidae
458.42.N37	Nemesiidae
458.42.N38	Nephilidae
458.42.N4	Nesticidae

Invertebrates
Arthropoda
Arachnida (Scorpions; spiders; mites; etc.)
Systematic divisions
Araneae (Araneida). Spiders
By family, A-Z -- Continued

458.42.O3	Ochyroceratidae
458.42.O4	Oecobiidae
458.42.O6	Oonopidae
458.42.O9	Oxyopidae
458.42.P34	Palpimanidae
458.42.P37	Paratropidae
458.42.P39	Philodromidae
458.42.P4	Pholcidae
458.42.P47	Pimoidae
458.42.P5	Pisauridae
458.42.P6	Platoridae
458.42.P64	Plectreuridae
458.42.P7	Prodidomidae
458.42.P8	Psechridae
458.42.P9	Pycnothelidae
458.42.S24	Salticidae (Jumping spiders)
458.42.S3	Scytodidae
458.42.S44	Selenopidae
458.42.S45	Senoculidae
458.42.S5	Sicariidaee
	Sparassidae see QL458.42.H48
458.42.S7	Stenochilida
458.42.S73	Stiphidiidae
458.42.S9	Symphytognathidae
458.42.T44	Telmidae
458.42.T45	Tengellidae
458.42.T46	Tetrabelmmidae
458.42.T48	Tetragnathidae
458.42.T5	Theraphosidae (Tarantulas)
458.42.T54	Theridiidae (Cobweb weavers)
458.42.T55	Theridiosomatidae
458.42.T56	Thomisidae
458.42.T6	Toxopidae
458.42.U4	Uloboridae
458.42.U7	Urocteidae
458.42.Z63	Zodariidae
458.42.Z67	Zoropsidae
	Opiliones (Opiliona; Phalangiida)
458.5	General works
458.52.A-Z	By family, A-Z
458.52.A8	Assamiidae

Invertebrates
Arthropoda
Arachnida (Scorpions; spiders; mites; etc.)
Systematic divisions
Opiliones (Opiliona; Phalangiida)
By family, A-Z -- Continued

458.52.C6 Cosmetidae
458.52.G6 Gonyleptidae
458.52.I7 Ischyropsalidae
458.52.L44 Leiobunidae
458.52.N4 Nemastomatidae
458.52.O5 Oncopodidae
458.52.P45 Phalangiidae
458.52.P46 Phalangodidae
458.52.S5 Sironidae
458.52.S9 Synthetonychidae
458.52.T75 Triaenonychidae
458.52.T76 Trogulidae

Palpigradi (Palpigradida)

458.55 General works
458.57.A-Z By family, A-Z
458.57.E9 Eukoeneniidae

Pseudoscorpiones (Book scorpions; Chelonethida; Pseudoscorpionida)

458.6 General works
458.62.A-Z By family, A-Z
458.62.C37 Chernetidae
458.62.C4 Chthoniidae
458.62.G3 Garypidae
458.62.H9 Hyidae
458.62.I3 Ideoroncidae
458.62.M4 Menthidae
458.62.N4 Neobisiidae
458.62.O4 Olpiidae
458.62.S9 Syarinidae
458.62.T7 Tridenchthoniidae

Ricinulei (Ricinuleida; Podogonata; Rhinogastra)

458.65 General works
458.67.A-Z By family, A-Z
458.67.R5 Ricinoididae

Schizomida

458.69 General works
458.692.A-Z By family, A-Z
458.692.H82 Hubbardiidae
458.692.P75 Protoschizomidae

Schizomidae see QL458.692.H82

Scorpiones (Scorpionida)

Invertebrates
Arthropoda
Arachnida (Scorpions; spiders; mites; etc.)
Systematic divisions
Scorpiones (Scorpionida) -- Continued

458.7 General works
458.72.A-Z By family, A-Z
458.72.B6 Bothriuridae
458.72.B8 Buthidae
458.72.C27 Caraboctonidae
458.72.C4 Chactidae
458.72.C45 Chaerilidae
458.72.D5 Diplocentridae
458.72.E88 Euscorpiidae
458.72.H45 Hemiscorpiidae
458.72.H48 Heteroscorpionidae
(458.72.I75) Ischnuridae
see QL458.72.H45
458.72.I95 Iuridae
458.72.M52 Microcharmidae
458.72.P75 Pseudochactidae
458.72.S3 Scorpionidae
458.72.S85 Superstitioniidae
458.72.T75 Troglotaoysicidae
(458.72.U75) Urodacidae
see QL458.72.S3
458.72.V4 Vaejovidae

Solpugida (Solifugae; Sun spiders; Wind scorpions)

458.8 General works
458.82.A-Z By family, A-Z
458.82.A4 Ammotrechidae
458.82.C4 Ceromidae
458.82.D3 Daesiidae
458.82.E7 Eremobatidae
458.82.G3 Galeodidae
458.82.H4 Hexisopodidae
458.82.K3 Karschiidae
458.82.M4 Melanoblossiidae
458.82.R4 Rhagodidae
458.82.S6 Solpugidae

Uropygi (Thelyphonida; Whip scorpions)

458.85 General works
458.87.A-Z By family, A-Z
(458.87.S3) Schizomidae
see QL458.692.H82
458.87.T4 Thelyphonidae
459 Anatomy and morphology

Invertebrates
Arthropoda
Arachnida (Scorpions; spiders; mites; etc.) -- Continued
459.2 Physiology
Insects
Cf. SB818+ Economic entomology
461 Periodicals, societies, congresses, serial publications
462 Collected works (nonserial)
462.3 Dictionaries and encyclopedias
462.4 Terminology, notation, abbreviations
462.5 History
463 General works, treatises, and textbooks
464 Field and laboratory manuals
465 Collection and preservation
466 Pictorial works and atlases
467 Popular works
467.2 Juvenile works
467.8 Rare and endangered species
467.9 Extinct insects
468 Classification. Nomenclature
468.2 Catalogs and collections
468.4 Entomology as a profession. Vocational guidance
468.5 Study and teaching. Research
468.7 Evolution. Phylogeny. Speciation
468.8 Poisonous insects. Dangerous insects
Geographical distribution
For geographical distribution of systematic divisions, see QL503+
469 General works
Physiographic divisions
Aquatic
472 General works
472.3 Marine
472.7 Urban
Topographic divisions
North America
473 General works
United States
474 General works
475.A-Z By region or state, A-Z
476 Canada
Latin America
476.5 General works
477 Mexico
478 Central America (Table Q3)
479 West Indies (Table Q3)
481 South America (Table Q3)

Invertebrates
Arthropoda
Insects
Geographical distribution
Topographic divisions -- Continued
Atlantic islands
481.4 General works
481.5 By individual island or group of islands, A-Z
482 Europe (Table Q3)
483 Asia (Table Q3)
485 Africa (Table Q3)
Indian Ocean islands
486 General works
486.3.A-Z By individual island or group of islands, A-Z
487 Australia
487.5 New Zealand
489 Pacific islands (Table Q3)
491 Arctic regions
491.5 Antarctica
491.6 Tropics
492.5 Immunology
493 Genetics
493.5 Molecular entomology
494 Anatomy and morphology
494.5 Metamorphosis
494.8 Cytology
Physiology
495 General works
495.5 Development
496 Behavior. Social life. Instinct
496.12 Parasitism
Including parasitic insects and parasitoids
496.15 Population dynamics
496.2 Migration
496.4 Ecology
496.5 Sound and sound production
496.7 Flight
497 Miscellany and curiosa
Apterygota
501 General works, treatises, and textbooks
Geographical distribution
For geographical distribution of systematic divisions see QL503+
502 General works
502.1 North America (United States and Canada) (Table Q3)
502.2 Mexico, Central America, and West Indies (Table Q3)

Invertebrates
Arthropoda
Insects
Apterygota
Geographical distribution -- Continued

502.3	South America (Table Q3)
502.4	Europe (Table Q3)
502.5	Asia (Table Q3)
502.6	Africa (Table Q3)
502.7	Australia
502.75	New Zealand
502.8	Pacific islands (Table Q3)
502.9	Arctic regions
502.95	Antarctica
502.96	Tropics
	Systematic divisions
	Collembola
503.A1	General works
503.A3-Z	By family, A-Z
503.A3	Actaletidae
503.D5	Dicyrtomidae
503.E5	Entomobryidae
503.H9	Hypogastruridae
503.I8	Isotomidae
503.N4	Neelidae
503.O5	Oncopoduridae
503.O56	Onychiuridae
503.P6	Poduridae
503.S6	Sminthuridae
503.T6	Tomoceridae
	Entotrophi (Diplura)
503.4.A1	General works
503.4.A3-Z	By family, A-Z
503.4.C3	Campodeidae
503.4.J3	Japygidae
503.4.P7	Projapygidae
	Protura
503.6.A1	General works
503.6.A3-Z	By family, A-Z
503.6.A3	Acerentomidae
503.6.E6	Eosentomidae
503.6.P7	Protentomidae
	Archaeognatha
503.7.A1	General works
503.7.A3-Z	By family, A-Z
503.7.M32	Machilidae
503.7.M44	Meinertellidae

QL

Invertebrates
Arthropoda
Insects
Apterygota
Systematic divisions -- Continued
Thysanura

503.8.A1 General works
503.8.A3-Z By family, A-Z
503.8.L4 Lepismatidae
(503.8.M3) Machilidae
see QL503.7.M32
(503.8.M4) Meinertellidae
see QL503.7.M44
503.8.N5 Nicoletiidae
504 Anatomy and morphology
504.2 Physiology

Ephemeroptera (Plectoptera; mayflies)

505 General works, treatises, and textbooks

Geographical distribution
For geographical distribution of systematic divisions see QL505.3.A+

505.1 General works
505.2 North America (United States and Canada) (Table Q3)
505.22 Mexico, Central America, and West Indies (Table Q3)
505.23 South America (Table Q3)
505.24 Europe (Table Q3)
505.25 Asia (Table Q3)
505.26 Africa (Table Q3)
505.27 Australasia and Indo-Pacific islands (Table Q3)
505.28 Polar regions
505.29 Tropics
505.3.A-Z Systematic divisions. By family, A-Z
Ametropodidae see QL505.3.S5
505.3.B33 Baetidae
505.3.B38 Baetiscidae
505.3.C3 Caenidae
505.3.E64 Ephemerellidae
505.3.E65 Ephemeridae
505.3.H4 Heptageniidae
505.3.L4 Leptophlebiidae
505.3.O4 Oligoneuridae
505.3.P3 Palingeniidae
505.3.P64 Polymitarcidae
505.3.P68 Potamanthidae
505.3.P76 Prosopistomatidae
505.3.S5 Siphlonuridae

Invertebrates
Arthropoda
Insects
Ephemeroptera (Plectoptera; mayflies) -- Continued

505.4 Anatomy and morphology
505.42 Physiology

Blattaria (Cockroaches)

505.5 General works

Geographical distribution

For geographical distribution of systematic divisions see QL505.7.A+

505.51 General works
505.6 North America (United States and Canada) (Table Q3)
505.62 Mexico, Central America, and West Indies (Table Q3)
505.63 South America (Table Q3)
505.64 Europe (Table Q3)
505.65 Asia (Table Q3)
505.66 Africa (Table Q3)
505.67 Australasia and Indo-Pacific islands (Table Q3)
505.68 Polar regions
505.69 Tropics
505.7.A-Z Systematic divisions. By family, A-Z
505.7.A73 Archiblattidae
505.7.A74 Areolariidae
505.7.A87 Attaphilidae
505.7.A88 Atticolidae
505.7.B4 Blaberidae
505.7.B48 Blattellidae
505.7.B485 Blattidae
505.7.C4 Chorisoneuridae
505.7.C6 Corydiidae
505.7.C7 Cryptocercidae
505.7.D5 Diplopteridae
505.7.E3 Ectobiidae
505.7.E7 Epilampridae
505.7.E9 Euthyrrhaphidae
505.7.H6 Homoeogamiidae
505.7.L3 Latindiidae
505.7.N62 Nocticolidae
505.7.N68 Nothoblattidae
505.7.N9 Nyctiboridae
505.7.O8 Ouloterygidae
505.7.O9 Oxyhaloidae
505.7.P33 Panchloridae
505.7.P34 Panesthiidae
505.7.P4 Perisphaeriidae

Invertebrates
Arthropoda
Insects
Blattaria (Cockroaches)
Systematic divisions. By family, A-Z -- Continued
505.7.P45 Phyllodromiidae
505.7.P6 Polyphagidae
505.8 Anatomy and morphology
505.82 Physiology
Mantodea (Mantids)
505.83 General works, treatises, and textbooks
Geographical distribution
For geographical distribution of systematic divisions see QL505.9.A+
505.84 General works
505.85 North America (United States and Canada) (Table Q3)
505.855 Mexico, Central America, and West Indies (Table Q3)
505.86 South America (Table Q3)
505.865 Europe (Table Q3)
505.87 Asia (Table Q3)
505.875 Africa (Table Q3)
505.88 Australasia and Indo-Pacific Islands (Table Q3)
505.885 Polar regions
505.89 Tropics
505.9.A-Z Systematic divisions. By family, A-Z
505.9.H94 Hymenopodidae
505.9.M35 Mantidae
505.95 Anatomy
505.96 Physiology
Orthoptera (Grasshoppers; locusts; etc.)
506 General works, treatises, and textbooks
Geographical distribution
For geographical distribution of systematic divisions see QL508.A+
507 General works
507.1 North America (United States and Canada) (Table Q3)
507.2 Mexico, Central America, and West Indies (Table Q3)
507.3 South America (Table Q3)
507.4 Europe (Table Q3)
507.5 Asia (Table Q3)
507.6 Africa (Table Q3)
507.7 Australia
507.75 New Zealand
507.8 Pacific islands (Table Q3)
507.9 Arctic regions

Invertebrates
Arthropoda
Insects
Orthoptera (Grasshoppers; locusts; etc.)
Geographical distribution -- Continued

507.95 Antarctica
507.96 Tropics
508.A-Z Systematic divisions. By family, A-Z
508.A2 Acrididae (Grasshoppers)
508.A56 Anostostomatidae
Bacillidae see QL509.7.P58
Bacteriidae see QL509.7.P53
Bacunculidae see QL509.7.P58
Blattidae see QL505.5+
508.C9 Cylindrachetidae
508.E5 Eneopteridae
508.G7 Gryllacrididae
508.G8 Gryllidae (Crickets)
(508.G86) Grylloblattidae
see QL509.3
508.G87 Gryllotalpidae (Mole crickets)
508.L45 Lentulidae
Locustidae see QL508.A2
(508.M4) Mantidae
see QL505.9.M35
508.M6 Mogoplistidae
508.M9 Myrmecophilidae
508.O4 Oecanthidae
508.P34 Pamphagidae
Phasmatidae see QL509.7.P53
508.P53 Phasmodidae
Phylliidae see QL509.7.P58
508.P6 Pneumoridae
508.P7 Proscopiidae
508.P97 Pyrgomorphidae
508.R45 Rhaphidophoridae
508.R65 Romaleidae (Lubber grasshoppers)
508.S7 Stenopelmatidae (Jerusalem crickets)
508.T38 Tetrigidae (Pigmy grasshoppers)
508.T4 Tettigoniidae (Katydids; Longhorn grasshoppers)
508.T45 Thericleidae
Timematidae see QL509.7.P58
508.T73 Tridactylidae (Pigmy mole crickets)
508.T74 Trigonidiidae
509 Anatomy and morphology
509.2 Physiology

Invertebrates
Arthropoda
Insects -- Continued
509.3 Grylloblattodea
Includes one family, Grylloblattidae
Phasmatoptera (Phasmida; Stick insects)
509.5 General works
Geographical distribution
For geographical distribution of systematic divisions see QL509.7.A+
509.55 General works
509.6 North America (United States and Canada) (Table Q3)
509.62 Mexico, Central America, and West Indies (Table Q3)
509.63 South America (Table Q3)
509.64 Europe (Table Q3)
509.65 Asia (Table Q3)
509.66 Africa (Table Q3)
509.67 Australasia and Indo-Pacific islands (Table Q3)
509.68 Polar regions
509.69 Tropics
509.7.A-Z Systematic divisions, A-Z
509.7.P53 Phasmatidae
509.7.P58 Phylliidae
Dermaptera (Earwigs)
510 General works, treatises, and textbooks
Geographical distribution
For geographical distribution of systematic divisions see QL510.3.A+
510.15 General works
510.2 North America (United States and Canada) (Table Q3)
510.22 Mexico, Central America, and West Indies (Table Q3)
510.23 South America (Table Q3)
510.24 Europe (Table Q3)
510.25 Asia (Table Q3)
510.26 Africa (Table Q3)
510.27 Australasia and Indo-Pacific islands (Table Q3)
510.28 Polar regions
510.29 Tropics
510.3.A-Z Systematic divisions. By family, A-Z
510.3.A4 Allostethidae
510.3.A5 Anataeliidae
510.3.A52 Ancistrogastridae
510.3.A54 Anechuridae
510.3.A6 Apachyidae
510.3.A7 Arixeniidae

Invertebrates
Arthropoda
Insects
Dermaptera (Earwigs)
Systematic divisions. By family, A-Z -- Continued

510.3.B7 Brachylabidae
510.3.C37 Carcinophoridae
510.3.C43 Chelidurldae
510.3.C48 Chelisochidae
510.3.D5 Diaperasticidae
510.3.D56 Diplatyidae
510.3.E3 Echinosomatidae
510.3.E8 Esphalmenidae
510.3.E9 Eudorniidae
510.3.F6 Forficulidae
510.3.H4 Hemimeridae
510.3.K3 Karschiellidae
510.3.L33 Labiduridae
510.3.L35 Labiidae
510.3.N46 Neolobophoridae
510.3.N48 Nesogastridae
510.3.O6 Opisthocosmiidae
510.3.P3 Parisolabidae
510.3.P4 Pericomidae
510.3.P5 Platylabiidae
510.3.P8 Psalididae
510.3.P94 Pygidicranidae
510.3.P97 Pyragridae
510.3.S6 Sparattidae
510.3.S66 Spongiphoridae
510.3.S8 Strongylopsalididae
510.3.V3 Vandicidae
510.4 Anatomy and morphology
510.42 Physiology

Neuroptera

511 General works, treatises, and textbooks

Geographical distribution

For geographical distribution of systematic divisions see QL513.A+

512 General works
512.1 North America (United States and Canada) (Table Q3)
512.2 Mexico, Central America, and West Indies (Table Q3)
512.3 South America (Table Q3)
512.4 Europe (Table Q3)
512.5 Asia (Table Q3)
512.6 Africa (Table Q3)

Invertebrates
Arthropoda
Insects
Neuroptera
Geographical distribution -- Continued

512.7 Australia
512.75 New Zealand
512.8 Pacific islands (Table Q3)
512.9 Arctic regions
512.95 Antarctica
512.96 Tropics
513.A-Z Systematic divisions. By family, A-Z
513.A6 Apochrysidae
513.A7 Ascalaphidae (Owlflies)
513.B4 Berothidae (Beaded lacewings)
513.C5 Chrysopidae (Lacewings)
513.C65 Coniopterygidae (Dusty-wings)
(513.C7) Corydalidae (Dobsonflies)
see QL514.7.C67
513.D5 Dilaridae (Pleasing lacewings)
Embiidae see QL539+
Ephemeroptera see QL505+
513.H5 Hemerobiidae (Brown lacewings)
513.I5 Inoceliidae
Isoptera see QL529+
513.I8 Ithonidae
513.M3 Mantispidae (Mantidflies)
513.M86 Myiodactylidae
513.M9 Myrmeleontidae (Antlions)
513.N4 Nemopteridae
513.N9 Nymphidae
Odonata see QL520+
513.O8 Osmylidae
Planipennia see QL511+
Plecoptera see QL530+
513.P6 Polystoechotidae (Giant lacewings)
Psocidae see QL515+
513.P8 Psychopsidae
(513.R3) Raphidiidae (Snakeflies)
see QL514.9.R35
(513.S6) Sialidae (Alderflies)
see QL514.7.S52
513.S65 Sisyridae (Spongillaflies)
513.S8 Stilbopterygidae
513.S9 Sympherobiidae
Termitidae see QL529+
513.T7 Trichomatidae

Invertebrates
Arthropoda
Insects
Neuroptera -- Continued
514 Anatomy and morphology
514.2 Physiology
Megaloptera
514.4 General works, treatises, and textbooks
Geographical distribution
For geographical distribution of systematic divisions see QL514.7.A+
514.5 General works
514.6 North America (United States and Canada) (Table Q3)
514.62 Mexico, Central America, and West Indies (Table Q3)
514.63 South America (Table Q3)
514.64 Europe (Table Q3)
514.65 Asia (Table Q3)
514.66 Africa (Table Q3)
514.67 Australasia and Indo-Pacific islands (Table Q3)
514.68 Polar regions
514.69 Tropics
514.7.A-Z Systematic divisions. By family, A-Z
514.7.C67 Corydalidae (Dobsonflies)
514.7.S52 Sialidae (Alderflies)
514.8 Anatomy and morphology
514.82 Physiology
Raphidioptera
514.86 General works, treatises, and textbooks
Geographical distribution
For geographical distribution of systematic divisions see QL514.9.A+
514.88 General works
514.8815 North America (United States and Canada) (Table Q3)
514.882 Mexico, Central America, and West Indies (Table Q3)
514.883 South America (Table Q3)
514.884 Europe (Table Q3)
514.885 Asia (Table Q3)
514.886 Africa (Table Q3)
514.887 Australasia and Indo-Pacific islands (Table Q3)
514.888 Polar regions
514.889 Tropics
514.9.A-Z Systematic divisions. By family, A-Z
514.9.R35 Raphidiidae (Snakeflies)
514.95 Anatomy and morphology
514.96 Physiology

Invertebrates
Arthropoda
Insects -- Continued
Psocoptera (Corrodentia)

515 General works
515.2.A-Z Systematic divisions, A-Z
515.2.P4 Peripsocidae
515.2.P73 Pseudocaecillidae
515.5 Zoraptera
Trichoptera (Caddisflies)
516 General works, treatises, and textbooks
Geographical distribution
For geographical distribution of systematic divisions see QL518.A+
517 General works
517.1 North America (United States and Canada) (Table Q3)
517.2 Mexico, Central America, and West Indies (Table Q3)
517.3 South America (Table Q3)
517.4 Europe (Table Q3)
517.5 Asia (Table Q3)
517.6 Africa (Table Q3)
517.7 Australia
517.75 New Zealand
517.8 Pacific islands (Table Q3)
517.9 Arctic regions
517.95 Antarctica
517.96 Tropics
518.A-Z Systematic divisions. By family, A-Z
518.A55 Anomalopsychidae
518.B4 Beraeidae
518.B7 Brachycentridae
518.C3 Calamoceratidae
518.G6 Goeridae
518.H4 Helicopsychidae
518.H94 Hydropsychidae
518.H95 Hydroptilidae
518.L48 Leptoceridae
518.L5 Limnephilidae
518.M6 Molannidae
518.O4 Odontoceridae
518.P45 Philopotamidae
518.P47 Phryganeidae
518.P6 Polycentropodidae
518.P8 Psychomyiidae
518.R4 Rhyacophilidae
518.S4 Sericostomatidae

Invertebrates
Arthropoda
Insects
Trichoptera (Caddisflies)
Systematic divisions. By family, A-Z -- Continued

518.X5 Xiphocentronidae
519 Anatomy and morphology
519.2 Physiology

Odonata (Dragonflies, etc.)

520 General works, treatises, and textbooks

Geographical distribution

For geographical distribution of systematic divisions see QL520.3.A+

520.15 General works
520.2 North America (United States and Canada) (Table Q3)
520.22 Mexico, Central America, and West Indies (Table Q3)
520.23 South America (Table Q3)
520.24 Europe (Table Q3)
520.25 Asia (Table Q3)
520.26 Africa (Table Q3)
520.27 Australasia and Indo-Pacific islands (Table Q3)
520.28 Polar regions
520.29 Tropics
520.3.A-Z Systematic divisions. By family, A-Z
520.3.A4 Aeshnidae (Darners)
520.3.A5 Agrionidae
520.3.A6 Amphipterygidae
520.3.C3 Calopterygidae
520.3.C4 Chlorocyphidae
520.3.C64 Coenagrionidae (Narrow-winged damselflies)
520.3.C67 Cordulegastridae (Biddies)
520.3.C68 Corduliidae (Green-eyed skimmers)
520.3.E6 Epallagidae
520.3.E65 Epiophlebiidae
520.3.G6 Gomphidae (Clubtails)
520.3.H44 Heliocharitidae
520.3.H45 Hemiphlebiidae
520.3.L45 Lestidae (Spread-winged damselflies)
520.3.L46 Lestoideidae
520.3.L6 Libellulidae (Skimmers)
520.3.M4 Megapodagrionidae
520.3.P4 Petaluridae (Graybacks)
520.3.P53 Platycnemididae
520.3.P58 Platystictidae
520.3.P6 Polythoridae
520.3.P7 Protoneuridae

Invertebrates
Arthropoda
Insects
Odonata (Dragonflies, etc.)
Systematic divisions. By family, A-Z -- Continued

520.3.P8 Pseudostigmatidae
520.3.S9 Synlestidae
520.4 Anatomy and morphology
520.42 Physiology

Hemiptera (Heteroptera; bugs)

521 General works, treatises, and textbooks

Geographical distribution

For geographical distribution of systematic divisions see QL523.A+

522 General works
522.1 North America (United States and Canada) (Table Q3)
522.2 Mexico, Central America, and West Indies (Table Q3)
522.3 South America (Table Q3)
522.4 Europe (Table Q3)
522.5 Asia (Table Q3)
522.6 Africa (Table Q3)
522.7 Australia
522.75 New Zealand
522.8 Pacific islands (Table Q3)
522.9 Arctic regions
522.95 Antarctica
522.96 Tropics
523.A-Z Systematic divisions. By family, A-Z
523.A14 Acanthosomatidae
523.A35 Aepophilidae
523.A4 Alydidae
523.A5 Anthocoridae (Flowerbugs)
523.A7 Aradidae (Flatbugs)
523.B4 Belostomatidae (Giant waterbugs)
523.B45 Berytidae

Capsidae see QL523.M5

523.C6 Cimicidae (Bedbugs, etc.)
523.C64 Colobothristidae
523.C67 Coreidae
523.C7 Corimelaenidae
523.C75 Corixidae (Water boatmen)
523.C9 Cydnidae (Burrower bugs)
523.D5 Dipsocoridae
523.D74 Drepanosiphidae
523.D9 Dysodiidae
523.E65 Enicocephalidae

Invertebrates
Arthropoda
Insects
Hemiptera (Heteroptera; bugs)
Systematic divisions. By family, A-Z -- Continued

523.G4 Gerridae (Water striders)
523.H4 Hebridae
523.H44 Helotrephidae
Henicocephalidae see QL523.E65
Heteroptera see QL521+
Homoptera see QL525+
523.H93 Hydrometridae
523.H96 Hyocephalidae
523.I83 Isodermidae
523.I85 Isometopidae
523.J6 Joppeicidae
523.L45 Leotichidae
523.L46 Leptopodidae
523.L9 Lygaeidae
523.M3 Macroveliidae
523.M4 Mesoveliidae
523.M47 Microphysidae
523.M5 Miridae (Plantbugs)
523.N3 Nabidae (Damsel bugs)
523.N4 Naucoridae (Creeping waterbugs)
523.N46 Neididae
523.N5 Nipidae (Water scorpions)
523.N53 Nerthridae
523.N6 Notonectidae (Back swimmers)
523.O3 Ochteridae
523.P5 Pentatomidae (Stinkbugs)
523.P53 Phymatidae (Ambushbugs)
523.P55 Piesmidae
523.P57 Plataspidae
523.P576 Ploiariidae
523.P62 Podopidae
523.P64 Polyctenidae
523.P9 Pyrrhocoridae
523.R4 Reduviidae (Assassin bugs)
523.R5 Rhopalidae
523.S25 Saldidae (Shorebugs)
523.S3 Schizopteridae
523.S4 Scutelleridae
523.T3 Tahitocoridae
523.T4 Termatophylidae
523.T43 Termitaphididae
523.T48 Thaumastotheriidae

Invertebrates
Arthropoda
Insects
Hemiptera (Heteroptera; bugs)
Systematic divisions. By family, A-Z -- Continued

523.T5 Tingidae (Lacebugs)
523.V45 Veliidae
523.V46 Velocipedidae
524 Anatomy and morphology
524.2 Physiology

Homoptera (Aphids; cicadas, etc.)

525 General works, treatises, and textbooks

Geographical distribution

For geographical distribution of systematic divisions see QL527.A+

526 General works
526.1 North America (United States and Canada) (Table Q3)
526.2 Mexico, Central America, and West Indies (Table Q3)
526.3 South America (Table Q3)
526.4 Europe (Table Q3)
526.5 Asia (Table Q3)
526.6 Africa (Table Q3)
526.7 Australia
526.75 New Zealand
526.8 Pacific islands (Table Q3)
526.9 Arctic regions
526.95 Antarctica
526.96 Tropics
527.A-Z Systematic divisions. By family, A-Z
527.A2 Acanaloniidae
527.A25 Achilidae
527.A259 Achilixiidae
527.A3 Adelgidae
527.A4 Aethialoniidae
527.A44 Agallidae

Aleurodidae see QL527.A5

527.A5 Aleyrodidae (Whiteflies)
527.A64 Aphididae (Aphids or plant lice)
527.A65 Apiomorphidae

Areopodidae see QL527.D44

527.A8 Asterolecaniidae (Pit scales)
527.B9 Bythoscopidae
527.C35 Callaphididae
527.C4 Cercopidae (Spittlebugs)
527.C43 Cerococcidae

Chermidae see QL527.P88

Invertebrates
Arthropoda
Insects
Homoptera (Aphids; cicadas, etc.)
Systematic divisions. By family, A-Z -- Continued

527.C49	Cicadellidae (Leafhoppers)
527.C5	Cicadidae (Cicadas)
527.C55	Cixiidae
527.C58	Clastopteridae
527.C6	Coccidae (Soft scales)
527.C62	Coelostomidiidae
527.C65	Conchaspididae
527.C9	Cylindrococcidae
527.D3	Dactylopiidae (Cochineal insects)
527.D44	Delphacidae
527.D47	Derbidae
527.D5	Diaspididae (Armored scales)
527.D53	Dictyopharidae
527.E73	Eriococcidae
527.E78	Eriosomatidae
527.E9	Euacanthidae
527.E97	Eurybrachidae
527.F4	Flatidae
527.F9	Fulgoridae
	Gyponidae see QL527.C49
527.I8	Issidae
	Jassidae see QL527.C49
527.K4	Kermesidae
527.K44	Kerridae (Lac scales)
527.K5	Kinnaridae
527.K6	Koebeliidae
	Lacciferidae see QL527.K44
(527.L4)	Lecaniidae see QL527.C6
527.L44	Ledridae
527.L6	Lophopidae
527.M3	Machaerotidae
527.M32	Macropsidae
527.M37	Margarodidae
527.M4	Meenoplidae
527.M45	Membracidae (Treehoppers)
	Monophlebidae see QL527.M37
527.N5	Nirvanidae
527.N6	Nogodinidae
527.O7	Ortheziidae (Ensign scales)
527.P3	Paropiidae
527.P44	Peloridiidae

QL

Invertebrates
Arthropoda
Insects
Homoptera (Aphids; cicadas, etc.)
Systematic divisions. By family, A-Z -- Continued

527.P45 Penthimiidae
527.P53 Phenacoleachiidae
527.P56 Phylloxeridae
527.P6 Pleidae
527.P83 Pseudococcidae (Mealybugs)
527.P88 Psyllidae (Jumping plant lice)
527.P93 Putoidae
527.P96 Pythamidae
527.R5 Ricaniidae
527.S5 Signoretiidae
527.S8 Stenocotidae
Tachardiidae see QL527.K44
Tettigellidae see QL527.C49
527.T43 Tettigometridae
527.T5 Thaumastoscopidae
527.T6 Tomaspididae
527.T7 Tropiduchidae
527.U4 Ulopidae
528 Anatomy and morphology
528.2 Physiology
Isoptera (Termites)
529 General works, treatises, and textbooks
Geographical distribution
For geographical distribution of systematic divisions see QL529.3.A+
529.15 General works
529.2 North America (United States and Canada) (Table Q3)
529.22 Mexico, Central America, and West Indies (Table Q3)
529.23 South America (Table Q3)
529.24 Europe (Table Q3)
529.25 Asia (Table Q3)
529.26 Africa (Table Q3)
529.27 Australasia and Indo-Pacific islands (Table Q3)
529.28 Polar regions
529.29 Tropics
529.3.A-Z Systematic divisions. By family, A-Z
529.3.H6 Hodotermitidae
529.3.K35 Kalotermitidae
529.3.M3 Mastotermitidae
529.3.R4 Rhinotermitidae
529.3.S47 Serritermitidae

Invertebrates
Arthropoda
Insects
Isoptera (Termites)
Systematic divisions. By family, A-Z -- Continued

529.3.T4 Termitidae
529.3.T5 Termopsidae
529.4 Anatomy and morphology
529.42 Physiology

Plecoptera (Stoneflies)

530 General works, treatises, and textbooks

Geographical distribution

For geographical distribution of systematic divisions see QL530.3.A+

530.15 General works
530.2 North America (United States and Canada) (Table Q3)
530.22 Mexico, Central America, and West Indies (Table Q3)
530.23 South America (Table Q3)
530.24 Europe (Table Q3)
530.25 Asia (Table Q3)
530.26 Africa (Table Q3)
530.27 Australasia and Indo-Pacific islands (Table Q3)
530.28 Polar regions
530.29 Tropics
530.3.A-Z Systematic divisions. By family, A-Z
530.3.A9 Austroperlidae
530.3.C3 Capniidae
530.3.C45 Chloroperlidae
530.3.E9 Eustheniidae
530.3.L47 Leptoperlidae
530.3.L49 Leuctridae (Rolled-wing stoneflies)
530.3.N4 Nemouridae
530.3.P44 Peltoperlidae
530.3.P47 Perlidae
530.3.P48 Perlodidae
530.3.P8 Pteronarcidae
530.3.T3 Taeniopterygidae
530.4 Anatomy and morphology
530.42 Physiology

Diptera (Flies)

531 General works, treatises, and textbooks
532 Pictorial works and atlases
533 Popular works
533.2 Juvenile works
534 Classification
534.2 Catalogs and collections

Invertebrates
Arthropoda
Insects
Diptera (Flies) -- Continued
Geographical distribution
For geographical distribution of systematic divisions see QL536+

535	General works
535.1	North America (United States and Canada) (Table Q3)
535.2	Mexico, Central America, and West Indies (Table Q3)
535.3	South America (Table Q3)
535.4	Europe (Table Q3)
535.5	Asia (Table Q3)
535.6	Africa (Table Q3)
535.7	Australia
535.75	New Zealand
535.8	Pacific islands (Table Q3)
535.9	Arctic regions
535.95	Antarctica
535.96	Tropics
	Systematic divisions. By family
536	Culicidae (Mosquitoes)
537.A-Z	Other families, A-Z
537.A3	Acroceridae
537.A4	Agromyzidae (Leafminerflies)
537.A45	Allactoneuridae
537.A5	Anthomyiidae
537.A53	Anthomyzidae
537.A6	Apioceridae
537.A85	Asilidae (Robberflies)
537.A88	Astiidae
537.A9	Aulacigastridae
537.B5	Bibionidae (Marchflies)
537.B56	Blepharoceridae
537.B64	Bolitophilidae
537.B65	Bombyliidae (Beeflies)
537.B7	Braulidae
537.C24	Calliphoridae (Blowflies)
537.C25	Canaceidae
537.C26	Canthyloscelidae
537.C27	Carnidae
537.C33	Cecidomyiidae (Gall midges)
537.C35	Celyphidae
537.C37	Ceratopogonidae (Biting midges)
537.C376	Ceroplatidae
537.C4	Chamaemyiidae

Invertebrates
Arthropoda
Insects
Diptera (Flies)
Systematic divisions. By family
Other families, A-Z -- Continued

537.C43 Chaoboridae (Phantom midges)
537.C455 Chiromyzidae
537.C456 Chironomidae (Tendipedidae; midges)
537.C46 Chloropidae
537.C49 Chyromyiidae
537.C5 Clusiidae
537.C56 Cnemospathidae
537.C634 Coelopidae
537.C636 Coenomyiidae
537.C65 Conopidae
537.C673 Cordyluridae
Corethridae see QL537.C43
537.C69 Corynoscelidae
537.C7 Cryptochaetidae
Culicidae see QL536
537.C8 Cuterebridae (Rabbit bots; rodent bots)
537.C9 Cylindrotomidae
537.D47 Deuterophlebiidae
537.D48 Dexiidae
537.D52 Diadocidiidae
537.D53 Diastatidae
537.D56 Diopsidae
537.D58 Ditomyiidae
537.D59 Dixidae
537.D6 Dolichopodidae (Long-legged flies)
537.D76 Drosophilidae (Vinegarflies)
537.D79 Dryomyzidae
537.E4 Empididae (Danceflies)
537.E7 Ephydridae
Euribiidae see QL537.T42
537.G3 Gasterophilidae (Horse bots)
537.G4 Glossinidae
Heleidae see QL537.C37
537.H44 Helomyzidae
537.H48 Hesperinidae
537.H54 Hilarimorphidae
537.H57 Hippoboscidae (Louseflies)
Hyperoscelididae see QL537.C26
Hypodermatidae see QL537.O4
537.I76 Ironomyiidae
537.K47 Keroplatidae

Invertebrates
Arthropoda
Insects
Diptera (Flies)
Systematic divisions. By family
Other families, A-Z -- Continued

537.L3 Lauxaniidae
537.L5 Limoniidae
537.L6 Lonchaeidae
537.L63 Lonchopteridae (Musidoridae)
537.L9 Lygistorrhinidae
537.M3 Macroceridae (Euphrosynidae)
537.M35 Manotidae
537.M4 Megamerinidae
Metopiidae see QL537.S25
537.M43 Micropezidae
537.M5 Milichiidae
537.M6 Mormotomyiidae
537.M8 Muscidae (Houseflies, etc.)
537.M9 Mycetobiidae
537.M92 Mycetophilidae (Fungivoridae)
537.M93 Mydaidae
537.M98 Mythicomyiidae
537.N44 Nemestrinidae
537.N46 Neottiophilidae
537.N47 Neriidae
537.N6 Nothybidae
537.N9 Nycteribiidae
537.N94 Nymphomyiidae
537.O3 Odiniidae
537.O4 Oestridae (Botflies; warbleflies)
537.O7 Opomyzidae
537.O8 Otitidae
537.P3 Pachyneuridae
537.P34 Pallopteridae
537.P35 Pantophthalmidae
537.P4 Periscelidae
537.P42 Petauristidae
537.P44 Phasiidae
537.P46 Phoridae (Humpbacked flies)
537.P49 Phytalmiidae
537.P56 Piophilidae (Skipperflies)
537.P57 Pipunculidae (Dorylaidae; bigheadedflies)
537.P63 Platypezidae (Clythiidae)
537.P65 Platystomatidae
537.P83 Psilidae (Rust flies)
537.P85 Psychodidae (Mothflies)

Invertebrates
Arthropoda
Insects
Diptera (Flies)
Systematic divisions. By family
Other families, A-Z -- Continued

537.P87 Pterocallidae
537.P89 Ptychopteridae (Liriopeidae)
537.P97 Pyrgotidae
537.R4 Rhagionidae (Snipeflies)
537.R457 Rhinophoridae
537.R458 Rhinoteridae
537.R46 Rhopalomeridae
537.R5 Richardiidae
537.S25 Sarcophagidae (Metopiidae; fleshflies)
537.S32 Scatopsidae
537.S34 Scenopinidae (Omphralidae)
537.S35 Sciadoceridae
537.S357 Sciaridae (Lycoriidae; fungus gnats)
537.S365 Sciomyzidae
537.S367 Sciophilidae
537.S4 Sepsidae
537.S54 Silvicolidae
537.S55 Simuliidae (Melusinidae; blackflies)
537.S6 Solvidae
537.S7 Sphaeroceridae
537.S84 Stratiomyidae (Soldier flies)
537.S86 Streblidae
537.S88 Synneuridae
537.S9 Syrphidae (Flowerflies; hoverflies)
537.T25 Tabanidae (Deerflies)
537.T28 Tachinidae (Larvaevoridae)
537.T3 Tachiniscidae
537.T35 Tanyderidae
537.T357 Tanypezidae
537.T42 Tephritidae
537.T447 Termitoxeniidae
537.T448 Tethinidae
537.T45 Thaumaleidae
537.T458 Thaumatoxenidae
537.T47 Therevidae
537.T49 Thyreophoridae
537.T6 Tipulidae (Craneflies)
537.T7 Trichoceridae (Winter craneflies)
537.T75 Trixoscelidae
Trypetidae see QL537.T42
Tylidae see QL537.M43

Invertebrates
Arthropoda
Insects
Diptera (Flies)
Systematic divisions. By family
Other families, A-Z -- Continued

537.U4 Ulidiidae
537.X9 Xylophagidae (Erinnidae)
538 Anatomy and morphology
538.2 Physiology

Embioptera (Embiodea; web spinners)

539 General works, treatises, and textbooks

Geographical distribution

For geographical distribution of systematic divisions see QL539.3.A+

539.15 General works
539.2 North America (United States and Canada) (Table Q3)
539.22 Mexico, Central America, and West Indies (Table Q3)
539.23 South America (Table Q3)
539.24 Europe (Table Q3)
539.25 Asia (Table Q3)
539.26 Africa (Table Q3)
539.27 Australasia and Indo-Pacific islands (Table Q3)
539.28 Polar regions
539.29 Tropics
539.3.A-Z Systematic divisions. By family, A-Z
539.3.A5 Anisembiidae
539.3.C4 Clothodidae
539.3.E4 Embiidae
539.3.N6 Notoligotomidae
539.3.O44 Oligembiidae
539.3.O46 Oligotomidae
539.3.T4 Teratembiidae
539.4 Anatomy and morphology
539.42 Physiology

Mallophaga (Chewing lice)

540 General works, treatises, and textbooks

Geographical distribution

For geographical distribution of systematic divisions see QL540.3.A+

540.15 General works
540.2 North America (United States and Canada) (Table Q3)
540.22 Mexico, Central America, and West Indies (Table Q3)
540.23 South America (Table Q3)
540.24 Europe (Table Q3)

Invertebrates
Arthropoda
Insects
Mallophaga (Chewing lice)
Geographical distribution -- Continued

540.25 Asia (Table Q3)
540.26 Africa (Table Q3)
540.27 Australasia and Indo-Pacific islands (Table Q3)
540.28 Polar regions
540.29 Tropics
540.3.A-Z Systematic divisions. By family, A-Z
540.3.B6 Boopiidae
540.3.D3 Dasyonygidae
540.3.G9 Gyropidae
540.3.H4 Heptapsogastridae
540.3.L3 Laemobothridae
540.3.M4 Menoponidae
540.3.N4 Nesiotinidae
540.3.P4 Philopteridae
540.3.R5 Ricinidae
540.3.T7 Trichodectidae
540.3.T72 Trichophilopteridae
540.3.T74 Trimenoponidae
540.4 Anatomy and morphology
540.42 Physiology

Lepidoptera (Butterflies; moths)

541 Periodicals, societies, congresses, serial publications
541.5 Dictionaries and encyclopedias
542 General works, treatises, and textbooks
543 Pictorial works and atlases
544 Popular works
544.2 Juvenile works
544.6 Butterfly attracting
Including butterfly gardens and gardening
545 Classification
545.2 Catalogs and collections

Geographical distribution
For geographical distribution of systematic divisions see QL561.A+

546 General works

North America

548 General works

United States

549 General works
551.A-Z By region or state, A-Z
552 Canada
553 Mexico, Central America, and West Indies (Table Q3)

Invertebrates
Arthropoda
Insects
Lepidoptera (Butterflies; moths)
Geographical distribution -- Continued

554	South America (Table Q3)
555	Europe (Table Q3)
556	Asia (Table Q3)
557	Africa (Table Q3)
557.5	Indian Ocean islands (Table Q3)
558	Australia
558.5	New Zealand
559	Pacific islands (Table Q3)
560	Arctic regions
560.5	Antarctica
560.6	Tropics
561.A-Z	Systematic divisions. By family, A-Z
561.A25	Acraeidae
561.A254	Acrolepiidae
561.A256	Acrolophidae
561.A3	Adelidae
	Aegeriidae see QL561.S47
561.A4	Agaristidae
561.A46	Agonoxenidae
561.A48	Alucitidae
561.A5	Amathusiidae
561.A57	Amphitheridae
	Amydriidae see QL561.T55
561.A65	Anomologidae
561.A67	Anthelidae
561.A7	Apoprogonidae
561.A8	Arctiidae (Tiger moths)
561.A84	Argyresthiidae
561.A865	Arrhenophandiae
561.A88	Ashinagidae
561.A93	Axiidae
561.B4	Blastobasidae
561.B6	Bombycidae (Silkworm moths)
561.B68	Brachodidae
561.B7	Brahmaeidae
561.C24	Callidulidae
561.C3	Carposinidae
561.C35	Castniidae
561.C4	Cecidosetidae
561.C42	Cercophanidae
561.C44	Charideidae
561.C46	Chlidanotidae

Invertebrates
Arthropoda
Insects
Lepidoptera (Butterflies; moths)
Systematic divisions. By family, A-Z -- Continued

561.C47 Choreutidae
561.C48 Chrysopolomidae
561.C5 Citheroniidae (Royal moths)
561.C57 Cochylidae
561.C58 Coleophoridae (Casebearer moths)
561.C59 Cosmopterigidae
561.C6 Cossidae (Carpenterworm moths)
Crambidae see QL561.P9
561.C8 Ctenuchidae
561.C9 Cyclotornidae
561.D25 Dalceridae (Milkweed butterflies)
561.D3 Danaidae (Milkweed butterflies)
561.D5 Dipotidae
561.D6 Douglasiidae
561.D7 Drepanidae
561.E4 Elachistidae
561.E5 Endromidae
561.E74 Epermeniidae
561.E75 Epicopeiidae
561.E754 Epimarptidae
561.E757 Epipaschiidae
561.E758 Epiplemidae
561.E759 Epipyropidae
561.E8 Eriocraniidae
561.E85 Ethmiidae
(561.E9) Eucleidae
see QL561.L54
561.E94 Eupterotidae
561.G3 Galleriidae (Wax moths)
561.G4 Gelechiidae
561.G6 Geometridae
561.G65 Glyphipterygidae
561.G7 Gracillariidae (Leafblotch miners)
561.H42 Heliconiidae
561.H44 Heliodinidae
561.H448 Heliozelidae (Shield bearers)
561.H47 Hepialidae
561.H5 Hesperiidae (Skippers)
561.H53 Heterogynidae
561.H9 Hyblaeidae
561.H97 Hyposmocomidae
561.I45 Immidae

Invertebrates
Arthropoda
Insects
Lepidoptera (Butterflies; moths)
Systematic divisions. By family, A-Z -- Continued

561.I5	Incurvariidae
561.L3	Lasiocampidae (Tent-caterpillar moths)
561.L37	Lecithoceridae
561.L4	Lemoniidae
561.L5	Libytheidae
561.L54	Limacodidae (Slug caterpillar moths)
	Lithosiidae see QL561.A8
561.L8	Lycaenidae
561.L9	Lymantriidae (Tussock moths)
561.L95	Lyonetiidae
561.M4	Megalopygidae (Flannel moths)
561.M42	Megathymidae (Skippers)
561.M44	Metachandidae
561.M44	Metachandidae
561.M48	Micropterygidae
561.M5	Mimallonidae
561.M55	Mnesarchaeidae
561.M6	Morphidae
561.N38	Neopseustidae
561.N4	Nepticulidae
561.N7	Noctuidae (Owlet moths; underwings)
561.N74	Nolidae
561.N8	Notodontidae
561.N87	Nyctemeridae
561.N9	Nymphalidae (Brushfooted butterflies)
561.O26	Ochsenheimeriidae
561.O43	Oecophoridae
	Oinophilidae see QL561.T55
561.O6	Olethreutidae
561.O7	Opostegidae
	Orenodidae see QL561.A48
561.O9	Oxychirotidae
561.O93	Oxytenididae
561.P17	Palaeosetidae
561.P18	Palaephatidae
561.P2	Papilionidae (Swallowtail butterflies)
	Phaloniidae see QL561.C57
	Phycitidae see QL561.P9
561.P48	Phyllocnistidae
561.P5	Pieridae
561.P55	Plutellidae (Diamondback moths)
561.P57	Prodoxidae (Yucca moths)

Invertebrates
Arthropoda
Insects
Lepidoptera (Butterflies; moths)
Systematic divisions. By family, A-Z -- Continued

561.P58 Prototheoridae
561.P6 Psychidae (Bagworm moths)
561.P8 Pterophoridae (Plume moths)
561.P85 Pterothysanidae
561.P9 Pyralidae
561.P96 Pyromorphidae
561.R3 Ratardidae
561.R53 Ridiaschinidae
561.R56 Riodinidae
561.S2 Saturniidae (Giant silkworm moths)
561.S3 Satyridae
561.S35 Scythridae
561.S44 Sematuridae
561.S47 Sesiidae (Clearwing moths)
Setomorphidae see QL561.T55
561.S7 Sphingidae (Sphinx moths)
561.S8 Stenomidae
561.S87 Strepsimanidae
561.T46 Thyatiridae
561.T48 Thyrididae
561.T55 Tineidae (Clothes moths)
561.T56 Tineodidae
561.T58 Tischeriidae
561.T8 Tortricidae (Leaf-roller moths)
561.U7 Uraniidae
561.X9 Xylorictidae
561.Y7 Yponomeutidae (Ermine moths)
561.Z9 Zygaenidae (Leaf-skeletonizer moths)
562 Anatomy and morphology
562.2 Physiology
562.4 Behavior. Social life. Instinct
562.6 Ecology
Hymenoptera (Ants; bees; wasps; etc.)
Cf. SF521+ Bee culture
563 General works, treatises, and textbooks
564 Pictorial works and atlases
565 Popular works
565.2 Juvenile works
566 Classification
566.2 Catalogs and collections

Invertebrates
Arthropoda
Insects
Hymenoptera (Ants; bees; wasps; etc.) -- Continued
Geographical distribution
For geographical distribution of systematic divisions see QL568.A+

567 General works
567.1 North America (United States and Canada) (Table Q3)
567.2 Mexico, Central America, and West Indies (Table Q3)
567.3 South America (Table Q3)
567.4 Europe (Table Q3)
567.5 Asia (Table Q3)
567.6 Africa (Table Q3)
567.7 Australia
567.75 New Zealand
567.8 Pacific islands (Table Q3)
567.9 Arctic regions
567.95 Antarctica
567.96 Tropics
568.A-Z Systematic divisions. By family, A-Z
568.A17 Acorduleceridae
568.A23 Agaontidae (Fig wasps)
568.A24 Agriotypidae
568.A3 Alienidae
568.A34 Alysiidae
568.A344 Alyssonidae
568.A36 Ampulicidae
568.A38 Anacharitidae
568.A4 Andrenidae
568.A48 Anthoboscidae
568.A53 Anthophoridae
568.A55 Aphelinidae
568.A57 Aphidiidae
568.A6 Apidae (Bumblebees; honeybees; stingless bees)
568.A7 Apterogynidae
568.A77 Argidae
568.A8 Aspiceridae
568.A9 Aulacidae
568.B36 Belytidae
Bembicidae see QL568.S7
568.B4 Bethylidae
568.B5 Blasticotomidae
568.B8 Braconidae
568.B83 Bradynobaenidae
568.C373 Cephidae (Stem sawflies)

Invertebrates
Arthropoda
Insects
Hymenoptera (Ants; bees; wasps; etc.)
Systematic divisions. By family, A-Z -- Continued

568.C375 Ceraphronidae
568.C377 Cerceridae
568.C4 Chalcididae
568.C44 Charipidae
568.C47 Chrysididae (Cuckoo wasps)
568.C5 Cimbicidae
568.C55 Cleonymidae
568.C56 Cleptidae
568.C6 Colletidae
568.C7 Crabronidae
568.C9 Cynipidae (Gall wasps)
568.D44 Diapriidae
568.D47 Dimorphidae
568.D5 Diprionidae (Conifer sawflies)
568.D7 Dryinidae
568.E4 Elasmidae
568.E5 Embolemidae
568.E6 Encyrtidae
568.E75 Eucharididae
568.E77 Eucoilidae
568.E8 Eulophidae
568.E84 Eumenidae
568.E845 Eupelmidae
568.E85 Eurytomidae
568.E9 Evaniidae (Ensign wasps)
568.F47 Fideliidae
568.F5 Figitidae
568.F7 Formicidae (Ants)
568.G3 Gasteruptionidae
568.G6 Gorytidae
568.H3 Halictidae (Sweat bees)
568.H4 Heloridae
568.I15 Ibaliidae
568.I2 Ichneumonidae
568.L3 Larridae
568.L47 Leptofoenidae
568.L49 Leucospididae
568.L56 Liopteridae
(568.M3) Masaridae
see QL568.V5
568.M4 Megachilidae (Leaf-cutting bees)
568.M44 Megalodontidae

Invertebrates
Arthropoda
Insects
Hymenoptera (Ants; bees; wasps; etc.)
Systematic divisions. By family, A-Z -- Continued

568.M45 Megalyridae
(568.M456) Meliponidae
see QL568.A6
568.M46 Melittidae
568.M466 Mellinidae
568.M48 Methocidae
568.M55 Miscogastridae
568.M56 Miscophidae
568.M6 Monomachidae
568.M8 Mutillidae (Velvet ants)
568.M94 Mymaridae (Fairyflies)
568.M944 Mymarommatidae
568.M97 Myrmosidae
568.N9 Nyssonidae
568.O25 Oberthuerellidae
568.O74 Ormyridae
568.O78 Orussidae (Parasitic wood wasps)
Oryssidae see QL568.O78
568.O8 Oxaeidae
568.O9 Oxybelidae
568.P3 Pamphiliidae (Web-spinning sawflies)
568.P43 Pelecinidae
Pemphredonidae see QL568.S7
568.P474 Pergidae
568.P475 Perilampidae
568.P5 Philanthidae
568.P55 Platygastridae
568.P58 Plumariidae
568.P6 Pompilidae (Spider wasps)
568.P9 Proctotrypidae
568.P94 Pteromalidae
568.P945 Pterostigmatidae
568.R4 Rhopalosomatidae
568.R6 Roproniidae
568.S2 Sapygidae
568.S3 Scelionidae
568.S34 Sclerogibbidae
568.S38 Scoliidae
568.S5 Sierolomorphidae
568.S57 Siricidae (Horntails)
568.S7 Sphecidae
568.S8 Stephanidae

Invertebrates
Arthropoda
Insects
Hymenoptera (Ants; bees; wasps; etc.)
Systematic divisions. By family, A-Z -- Continued

568.S85 Stizidae
568.S96 Syntexidae
568.T3 Tenthredinidae (Sawflies)
568.T34 Tetracampidae
568.T4 Thynnidae
568.T5 Tiphiidae
568.T6 Torymidae
568.T7 Trichogrammatidae
568.T74 Trigonalidae
568.T79 Trypoxylidae
568.V3 Vanhorniidae
568.V5 Vespidae (Hornets, etc.)
568.X5 Xiphydriidae (Wood wasps)
568.X7 Xyelidae
569 Anatomy and morphology
569.2 Physiology
569.4 Behavior. Social life. Instinct

Anoplura (Sucking lice)

570 General works, treatises, and textbooks

Geographical distribution

For geographical distribution of systematic divisions see QL570.3.A+

570.15 General works
570.2 North America (United States and Canada) (Table Q3)
570.22 Mexico, Central America, and West Indies (Table
570.23 South America (Table Q3)
570.24 Europe (Table Q3)
570.25 Asia (Table Q3)
570.26 Africa (Table Q3)
570.27 Australasia and Indo-Pacific islands (Table Q3)
570.28 Polar regions (Table Q3)
570.29 Tropics (Table Q3)
570.3.A-Z Systematic divisions. By family, A-Z
570.3.E3 Echinophthiriide
570.3.H34 Haematomyzidae
570.3.H37 Haematopinidae
570.3.H38 Haematopinoididae
570.3.H64 Hoplopleuridae
570.3.N4 Neolignathidae
570.3.P4 Pediculidae
570.3.P5 Phthiriidae

Invertebrates
Arthropoda
Insects -- Continued
Coleoptera (Beetles)

571 Periodicals, societies, congresses, serial publications
572 Collected works (nonserial)
573 General works, treatises, and textbooks
575 Pictorial works and atlases
576 Popular works
576.2 Juvenile works
577 Classification
577.2 Catalogs and collections
Geographical distribution
For geographical distribution of systematic divisions see QL596.A+
578 General works
580 America
North America
581 General works
United States
583 General works
584.A-Z By region or state, A-Z
585 Canada
Latin America
585.5 General works
586 Mexico
587 Central America (Table Q3)
588 West Indies (Table Q3)
589 South America (Table Q3)
591 Europe (Table Q3)
592 Asia (Table Q3)
593 Africa (Table Q3)
594 Australia
594.5 New Zealand
595 Pacific islands (Table Q3)
595.2 Arctic regions
595.4 Antarctica
595.6 Tropics
596.A-Z Systematic divisions. By family, A-Z
596.A23 Acanthoceridae
596.A27 Aculognathidae
596.A3 Aderidae
596.A37 Aegialiidae
596.A4 Aglycyderidae
596.A42 Alleculidae
596.A43 Alticidae
596.A45 Amphizoidae

Invertebrates
Arthropoda
Insects
Coleoptera (Beetles)
Systematic divisions. By family, A-Z -- Continued

596.A5	Anobiidae
596.A62	Anthicidae (Antlike flower beetles)
596.A63	Anthribidae (Fungus weevils)
596.A64	Aphodiidae
596.A8	Atractoceridae
596.A83	Attelabidae
596.B5	Bostrichidae (False powerpost beetles)
596.B54	Brachypteridae
596.B58	Brachyspectridae
596.B6	Brathinidae
596.B65	Brentidae
596.B7	Bruchidae (Seed beetles)
596.B8	Buprestidae (Metallic wood borers)
596.B97	Byrrhidae
596.B98	Byturidae (Fruitworm beetles)
596.C15	Cantharidae (Soldier beetles)
596.C2	Carabidae (Ground beetles)
	Cassididae see QL596.C5
596.C28	Catopochrotidae
596.C3	Cebrionidae
596.C37	Cephaloidae
596.C4	Cerambycidae (Longhorned beetles)
596.C415	Ceratocanthidae
596.C42	Cerophytidae
596.C43	Cetoniidae
596.C45	Chapuisiidae
596.C46	Chelonariidae
596.C48	Chlamisidae
596.C5	Chrysomelidae (Leaf beetles)
596.C56	Cincindelidae (Tiger beetles)
596.C6	Ciidae
596.C613	Cistelidae
596.C617	Clambidae
596.C618	Clavigeridae
596.C62	Cleridae (Checkered beetles)
596.C64	Clytridae
596.C65	Coccinellidae (Lady beetles)
596.C66	Colydiidae
596.C667	Corylophidae
596.C67	Corynetidae
596.C68	Cossyphodidae
596.C7	Crioceridae

Invertebrates
Arthropoda
Insects
Coleoptera (Beetles)
Systematic divisions. By family, A-Z -- Continued

596.C77 Cryptocephalidae
596.C78 Cryptophagidae
596.C8 Cucujidae (Flat-bark beetles)
596.C85 Cupidae
596.C9 Curculionidae (Snout beetles)
596.C93 Cyathoceridae
596.C933 Cybocephalidae
596.C94 Cyladidae
596.D37 Dascyllidae
596.D375 Dasytidae
596.D4 Dermestidae
596.D42 Derodontidae
596.D57 Diphyllidae
596.D58 Discolomidae
596.D6 Donaciidae
596.D67 Drilidae
596.D7 Dryopidae
596.D85 Dynastidae
596.D9 Dytiscidae (Predaceous diving beetles)
596.E3 Ectrephidae
596.E38 Elacatidae
596.E4 Elateridae (Click beetles)
596.E45 Elmidae
596.E5 Endomychidae
596.E7 Erotylidae
596.E76 Euchiridae
596.E77 Eucinetidae
596.E8 Eucnemidae
596.E84 Euglenidae
596.E85 Eumolpidae
596.E87 Eurystethidae
596.G3 Galerucidae
596.G47 Georyssidae
596.G48 Geotrupidae
596.G5 Glaphyridae
596.G6 Gnostidae
596.G8 Gyrinidae (Whirligig beetles)
596.H2 Haliplidae
596.H38 Helodidae
596.H4 Helotidae
596.H43 Hemipeplidae
596.H45 Heteroceridae

Invertebrates
Arthropoda
Insects
Coleoptera (Beetles)
Systematic divisions. By family, A-Z -- Continued

596.H48 Hispidae
596.H5 Histeridae (Hister beetles)
596.H78 Hybosoridae
596.H79 Hydraenidae
596.H8 Hydrophilidae (Water scavenger beetles)
596.H85 Hydroscaphidae
596.H9 Hygrobiidae
596.H95 Hypocephalidae
596.I7 Ipidae
596.J3 Jacobsoniidae
596.L23 Lagriidae
596.L25 Lamiidae
596.L27 Lamprosomatidae
596.L28 Lampyridae (Fireflies)
596.L29 Languriidae
596.L3 Lathridiidae
596.L35 Leiodidae (Round fungus beetles)
596.L4 Leptinidae
596.L43 Leptodiridae
596.L55 Limnichidae
596.L58 Limulodidae
596.L8 Lucanidae (Stag beetles)
596.L9 Lycidae (Netwinged beetles)
596.L92 Lyctidae (Powderpost beetles)
596.L94 Lyxmexylidae (Timber beetles)
596.M2 Malachiidae
596.M3 Megalopodidae
596.M34 Megascelidae
Melasidae see QL596.E8
596.M38 Meloidae (Blister beetles)
596.M4 Melolonthidae (Cockchafers)
596.M43 Melyridae
596.M47 Micromalthidae
596.M5 Micropeplidae
596.M53 Monoedidae
596.M55 Monommatidae
596.M57 Monotomidae
596.M6 Mordellidae (Tumbling flower beetles)
596.M8 Murmidiidae
596.M9 Mycetaeidae
596.M92 Mycetophagidae (Hairy fungus beetles)
596.N4 Nemonychidae

Invertebrates
Arthropoda
Insects
Coleoptera (Beetles)
Systematic divisions. By family, A-Z -- Continued

596.N54 Nilionidae
596.N57 Niponiidae
596.N58 Nitidulidae (Sap beetles)
596.N6 Nosodendridae
596.O25 Ochodaeidae
596.O4 Oedemeridae
596.O67 Orphnidae
596.O7 Orthoperidae
Ostomatidae see QL596.T8
596.P13 Pachypodidae
596.P17 Parandridae
596.P2 Passalidae
596.P25 Passandridae
596.P3 Pedilidae
596.P38 Petriidae
596.P4 Phaenocephalidae
596.P42 Phaenomeridae
596.P46 Phalacridae (Shining fungus beetles)
596.P47 Phenogodidae (Glowworms)
596.P5 Plastoceridae
596.P6 Platypodidae
596.P62 Platypsyllidae
596.P63 Pleocomidae
596.P7 Prionidae
596.P75 Proterhinidae
596.P8 Pselaphidae
596.P815 Psephenidae
596.P83 Ptiliidae
(596.P85) Ptinidae (Spider beetles)
see QL596.A5
596.P96 Pyrochroidae
596.P98 Phthidae
596.R4 Rhipiceridae
596.R485 Rhipiphoridae
596.R5 Rhizophagidae
596.R57 Rhysodidae
596.R8 Rutelidae
596.S23 Sagridae
596.S28 Scaphidiidae
596.S3 Scarabaeidae (Scarabs)
596.S35 Scolytidae (Bark beetles)
596.S353 Scolytoplatypodidae

Invertebrates
Arthropoda
Insects
Coleoptera (Beetles)
Systematic divisions. By family, A-Z -- Continued

596.S38 Scraptiidae
596.S4 Scydmaenidae
596.S45 Serropalpidae
596.S49 Silvanidae
596.S5 Silphidae (Carrion beetles)
596.S53 Sinodendridae
596.S6 Smicripidae
596.S65 Sphaeriidae
596.S66 Sphaeritidae
596.S68 Sphaerosomatidae
596.S7 Sphindidae
596.S75 Staphylinidae (Rove beetles)
596.S9 Synteliidae
596.T16 Telegeusidae
596.T2 Tenebrionidae (Darkling beetles)
596.T27 Tetratomidae
596.T35 Thorictidae
596.T4 Throscidae
596.T7 Trichiidae
Trichopterygidae see QL596.P83
596.T75 Trictenotomidae
596.T78 Trogidae
596.T8 Trogositidae
596.U75 Urodontidae
597 Anatomy and morphology
597.2 Physiology
Thysanoptera (Thrips)
598 General works, treatises, and textbooks
Geographical distribution
For geographical distribution of systematic divisions see QL598.3.A+
598.15 General works
598.2 North America (United States and Canada) (Table Q3)
598.22 Mexico, Central America, and West Indies (Table Q3)
598.23 South America (Table Q3)
598.24 Europe (Table Q3)
598.25 Asia (Table Q3)
598.26 Africa (Table Q3)
598.27 Australasia and Indo-Pacific islands (Table Q3)
598.28 Polar regions
598.29 Tropics

Invertebrates
Arthropoda
Insects
Thysanoptera (Thrips) -- Continued

598.3.A-Z Systematic divisions. By family, A-Z
598.3.A4 Aeolothripidae
598.3.C4 Ceratothripidae
598.3.C5 Chirothripoididae
598.3.E3 Ecacanthothripidae
598.3.E8 Eupatithripidae
598.3.F7 Franklinothripidae
598.3.H4 Heterothripidae
598.3.H9 Hystrichothripidae
598.3.I3 Idolothripidae
598.3.M44 Megathripidae
598.3.M45 Melanothripidae
598.3.M47 Merothripidae
598.3.M9 Mymarothripidae
598.3.O7 Orothripidae
598.3.P3 Panchaetothripidae
598.3.P45 Phlaeothripidae
598.3.P5 Phloeothripidae
598.3.P9 Pygothripidae
598.3.T4 Thripidae
598.3.U7 Urothripidae
598.4 Anatomy and morphology
598.42 Physiology

Mecoptera (Scorpionflies)

598.5 General works, treatises, and textbooks

Geographical distribution

For geographical distribution of systematic divisions see QL598.7.A+

598.52 General works
598.6 North America (United States and Canada) (Table Q3)
598.62 Mexico, Central America, and West Indies (Table Q3)
598.63 South America (Table Q3)
598.64 Europe (Table Q3)
598.65 Asia (Table Q3)
598.66 Africa (Table Q3)
598.67 Australasia and Indo-Pacific islands (Table Q3)
598.68 Polar regions
598.69 Tropics
598.7.A-Z Systematic divisions. By family, A-Z
598.7.B5 Bittacidae
598.7.B6 Boreidae
598.7.M4 Meropeidae

Invertebrates
Arthropoda
Insects
Mecoptera (Scorpionflies)
Systematic divisions. By family, A-Z -- Continued
598.7.N6 Notiothaumidae
598.7.P3 Panorpidae
598.8 Anatomy and morphology
598.82 Physiology
Strepsiptera (Twisted-winged parasites)
599 General works, treatises, and textbooks
Geographical distribution
For geographical distribution of systematic divisions see QL599.3.A+
599.15 General works
599.2 North America (United States and Canada) (Table Q3)
599.22 Mexico, Central America, and West Indies (Table Q3)
599.23 South America (Table Q3)
599.24 Europe (Table Q3)
599.25 Asia (Table Q3)
599.26 Africa (Table Q3)
599.27 Australasia and Indo-Pacific islands (Table Q3)
599.28 Polar regions
599.29 Tropics
599.3.A-Z Systematic divisions. By family, A-Z
599.3.C32 Callipharixenidae
599.3.E4 Elenchidae
599.3.H3 Halictophagidae
599.3.M45 Mengeidae
599.3.M46 Mengenillidae
599.3.M9 Myrmecolacidae
599.3.S85 Stichotrematidae
599.3.S89 Stylopidae
599.4 Anatomy and morphology
599.42 Physiology
Siphonaptera (Fleas)
599.5 General works, treatises, and textbooks
Geographical distribution
For geographical distribution of systematic divisions see QL599.7.A+
599.52 General works
599.6 North America (United States and Canada) (Table Q3)
599.62 Mexico, Central America, and West Indies (Table Q3)
599.63 South America (Table Q3)
599.64 Europe (Table Q3)

Invertebrates
Arthropoda
Insects
Siphonaptera (Fleas)
Geographical distribution -- Continued
599.65 Asia (Table Q3)
599.66 Africa (Table Q3)
599.67 Australasia and Indo-Pacific islands (Table Q3)
599.68 Polar regions
599.69 Tropics
599.7.A-Z Systematic divisions. By family, A-Z
599.7.C47 Ceratophyllidae
599.7.D6 Dolichopsyllidae
599.7.H4 Hectopsyllidae
599.7.H9 Hystrichopsyllidae
599.7.I3 Ischnopsyllidae
599.7.P8 Pulicidae
599.7.S8 Stephanocircidae
599.7.T8 Tungidae
599.8 Anatomy and morphology
599.82 Physiology
Chordates. Vertebrates
For behavior see QL750+
For anatomy see QL801+
For physiology see QP1+
605.A1 Periodicals, societies, congresses, serial publications
605.A2 Collected works (nonserial)
605.A3-Z General works, treatises, and textbooks
605.2 Popular works
605.3 Juvenile works
605.4 Dictionaries and encyclopedias
Rare and endangered species see QL81.5+
606 Introduced vertebrates
For local see QL606.5+
Geographical distribution
For geographical distribution of systematic divisions, see the division, e.g. QL619+, Fishes
606.5 General works
606.52 North America (United States and Canada) (Table Q3)
606.53 Mexico, Central America, and West Indies (Table Q3)
606.54 South America (Table Q3)
606.55 Europe (Table Q3)
606.56 Asia (Table Q3)
606.57 Africa (Table Q3)
606.58 Australasia and Indo-Pacific islands (Table Q3)
Arctic regions
606.59 General works

Chordates. Vertebrates
Geographical distribution
Arctic regions -- Continued
606.592 Bering Land Bridge Region. Beringia
606.594 Greenland
606.597 Antarctica
606.6 Tropics
607 Classification
607.2 Catalogs and collections
607.5 Evolution (General)
607.6 Population dynamics
607.9 Collection and preservation
Protochordata
610 General works
611 Cephalochordata
612 Hemichordata
613 Urochordata (Tunicata)
Fishes
Cf. SH1+ Fish culture, fisheries, angling
614 Periodicals, societies, congresses, serial publications
614.5 Collected works (nonserial)
614.7 Dictionaries and encyclopedias
Communication of information
614.73 General works
614.74 Information services
614.75 Computer network resources
Including the Internet
History of ichthyology
614.8 General works
614.83.A-Z By region or country, A-Z
Biography of ichthyologists see QL26+
614.9 Directories
615 General works, treatises, and textbooks
616 Pictorial works and atlases
617 Popular works
617.2 Juvenile works
Rare and endangered species
617.7 General works
617.73.A-Z By region or country, A-Z
618 Classification. Nomenclature
618.15 Catalogs and collections
618.2 Evolution. Speciation
618.3 Population dynamics
Study and teaching. Research
618.5 General works

Chordates. Vertebrates
Fishes
Study and teaching. Research -- Continued
618.55 Fish watching
For fish watching in individual regions or countries, see QL620+
618.6 Collection and preservation. Fish mounting
Cf. SH338+ Fisheries museums and exhibitions
618.65 Fish surveys
For fish surveys in individual regions or countries, see QL620+
618.7 Poisonous fishes. Dangerous fishes
Cf. QL638.93 Shark attacks
Geographical distribution
For geographical distribution of systematic divisions see QL637.9+
619 General works
Physiographic divisions
Marine fishes
For marine fishes of a particular coast see QL625+
620 General works
620.2 Circumpolar
Cf. QL637 Arctic Ocean
Cf. QL637.2 Antarctic Ocean
620.4 Circumtropical
620.45 Coral reefs
620.6 Intertidal fishes
Atlantic Ocean
Cf. QL632.5 Atlantic Ocean islands
621 General works
North Atlantic
621.2 General works
Eastern North Atlantic
Including the coast of Europe
621.3 General works
621.32 Greenland Sea
621.34 Norwegian Sea
621.35 Baltic Sea
Including the Gulf of Bothnia
621.36 Kattegat. Skagerrak
621.37 North Sea
621.38 English Channel
621.39 Irish Sea
621.395 Biscay, Bay of
Mediterranean Sea
621.4 General works
621.42 Adriatic Sea

Chordates. Vertebrates
Fishes
Geographical distribution
Physiographic divisions
Marine fishes
Atlantic Ocean
North Atlantic
Eastern North Atlantic
Mediterranean Sea -- Continued
621.44 Aegean Sea
621.46 Black Sea
Western North Atlantic
Including the coast of North America
621.5 General works
621.52 Baffin Bay
621.53 Davis Strait
621.54 Newfoundland Banks
621.56 Gulf of Mexico
621.58 Caribbean Sea
Central Atlantic. Tropical Atlantic
621.6 General works
621.62 Eastern Central Atlantic
621.65 Western Central Atlantic
South Atlantic
621.7 General works
Eastern South Atlantic
Including the coast of Africa
621.72 General works
621.75 Gulf of Guinea
621.77 Western South Atlantic
Including the coast of South America
Indian Ocean
Cf. QL636.7 Indian Ocean islands
622 General works
North Indian Ocean
622.2 General works
Arabian Sea
622.3 General works
622.32 Persian Gulf
622.34 Red Sea
622.36 Gulf of Aden
Bay of Bengal
622.4 General works
622.45 Andaman Sea
South Indian Ocean
622.5 General works
622.55 Mozambique Channel

Chordates. Vertebrates
Fishes
Geographical distribution
Physiographic divisions
Marine fishes -- Continued
Pacific Ocean
Cf. QL636.5 Pacific islands
623 General works
North Pacific
623.2 General works
623.3 Bering Sea
Eastern North Pacific
Including the coast of North America
623.4 General works
623.45 Gulf of Alaska
Western North Pacific
Including the coast of Asia
623.5 General works
623.52 Okhotsk Sea
623.53 Japan Sea
623.54 Yellow Sea
China Sea
623.548 General works
623.55 East China Sea
623.56 South China Sea
623.58 Philippine Sea
623.59 Tonkin, Gulf of
623.6 Central Pacific. Tropical Pacific
South Pacific
623.7 General works
623.8 Eastern South Pacific
Including the coast of South America
Western South Pacific
Including Australasia
623.9 General works
623.92 Java Sea
623.94 Coral Sea
623.96 Tasman Sea
623.98 Indo-Pacific region
Arctic Ocean see QL637
Antarctic Ocean see QL637.2
624 Freshwater fishes
Class here general works only
For fishes of a particular area see QL625+
Topographic divisions
North America
625 General works

Chordates. Vertebrates
Fishes
Geographical distribution
Topographic divisions
North America -- Continued
625.5 Great Lakes
Canada
626 General works
626.5.A-Z By region or province, A-Z
United States
627 General works
628.A-Z By region or state, A-Z
Cf. QL636.5 Hawaii
Latin America
628.5 General works
629 Mexico
630 Central America (Table Q3)
631 West Indies (Table Q3)
632 South America (Table Q3)
632.5 Atlantic Ocean islands (Table Q3)
633 Europe (Table Q3)
634 Asia (Table Q3)
635 Africa (Table Q3)
Australia
636 General works
636.15.A-Z By state, territory, or region, A-Z
636.2 New Zealand
636.5 Pacific islands (Table Q3)
636.7 Indian Ocean islands (Table Q3)
637 Arctic regions
Including the Arctic Ocean
637.2 Antarctica
Including the Antarctic Ocean
637.5 Tropics
Systematic divisions
637.9.A-Z Osteichthys (Bony fishes). By order, A-Z
Class species, genera, and families in QL638
Class single-family orders with family in QL638
For general works and works on higher groups of bony fishes, except dipnoid and ganoid fishes see QL615
For general works on dipnoid and ganoid fishes see QL638.3
637.9.A3 Acipenseriformes
Amiiformes see QL638.A37
637.9.A5 Anguilliformes (Eels)
637.9.A8 Atheriniformes

Chordates. Vertebrates
Fishes
Systematic divisions
Osteichthys (Bony fishes). By order, A-Z -- Continued

637.9.A93 Aulopiformes
Batrachoidiformes see QL638.B3
637.9.B36 Beloniformes
637.9.B4 Beryciformes
Ceratodontiformes see QL638.C356
637.9.C35 Cetomimiformes
Channiformes see QL638.C486
637.9.C38 Characiformes
637.9.C4 Clupeiformes
Coelacanthiformes see QL638.L26
Ctenothrissiformes see QL638.M13
637.9.C9 Cypriniformes
637.9.C95 Cyprinodontiformes
637.9.D3 Dactylopteriformes
637.9.D5 Dipteriformes
637.9.E4 Elopiformes
637.9.G3 Gadiformes
637.9.G37 Gasterosteiformes
Gobiesociformes see QL638.G6
637.9.G6 Gonorynchiformes
637.9.G94 Gymnotiformes
637.9.L3 Lampridiformes
Lepisosteiformes see QL638.L4
637.9.L6 Lophiiformes
637.9.M6 Mormyriformes
637.9.M93 Myctophiformes
637.9.N6 Notacanthiformes
637.9.O63 Ophidiiformes
637.9.O76 Osmeriformes
637.9.O8 Osteoglossiformes
Pegasiformes see QL638.P32
637.9.P46 Perciformes
637.9.P47 Percopsiformes
637.9.P5 Pleuronectiformes
Polypteriformes see QL638.P76
637.9.S3 Salmoniformes
637.9.S35 Scorpaeniformes
637.9.S5 Siluriformes
637.9.S9 Synbranchiformes
637.9.T4 Tetraodontiformes
637.9.Z4 Zeiformes
638.A-Z Osteichthyes (Bony fishes). By family, A-Z
Class here works on species, genera, and families

Chordates. Vertebrates
Fishes
Systematic divisions
Osteichthys (Bony fishes). By family, A-Z -- Continued

638.A15	Acanthoclinidae
638.A2	Acanthuridae (Surgeonfishes)
638.A25	Acipenseridae (Sturgeons)
638.A27	Acropomatidae
638.A29	Adrianichthyidae
638.A3	Ageneiosidae
638.A316	Agonidae (Poachers)
638.A32	Akysidae
	Alabetidae see QL638.G6
638.A335	Albulidae (Bonefishes)
638.A34	Alepisauridae (Lancetfishes)
638.A35	Alepocephalidae
638.A36	Amarsipidae
638.A364	Amblycipitidae
638.A366	Amblyopsidae (Cavefishes)
638.A37	Amiidae (Bowfins)
638.A4	Ammodytidae (Sand lances)
638.A44	Amphiliidae
638.A47	Amphipnoidae
638.A5	Anabantidae
638.A53	Anablepidae
638.A54	Anarhichadidae (Wolffishes)
638.A55	Anguillidae (Freshwater eels)
	Anisochromidae see QL638.P84
638.A556	Anomalopidae
638.A56	Anoplogasteridae
638.A567	Anoplopomatidae (Sablefishes)
638.A568	Anostomidae
638.A57	Anotopteridae (Daggertooths)
638.A577	Antennariidae (Frogfishes)
638.A6	Aoteidae
638.A63	Aphredoderidae (Pirate perches)
638.A64	Aploactinidae
638.A642	Aplocheilidae
638.A643	Aplochitonidae
638.A65	Aplodactylidae
638.A7	Apogonidae (Cardinalfishes)
638.A73	Apteronotidae
	Arapaimidae see QL638.O88
638.A75	Argentinidae
638.A755	Ariidae (Sea catfishes)
638.A77	Arripidae
638.A78	Aspredinidae

Chordates. Vertebrates
Fishes
Systematic divisions
Osteichthys (Bony fishes). By family, A-Z -- Continued

638.A785 Astroblepidae
638.A788 Astronesthidae
638.A79 Ateleopodidae
638.A8 Atherinidae (Silversides)
638.A83 Auchenipteridae
638.A84 Aulopodidae
638.A844 Aulorhynchidae
638.A848 Aulostomidae (Trumpetfishes)
638.B13 Bagridae
638.B15 Balistidae (Triggerfishes; filefishes)
638.B153 Balitoridae (Hillstream loaches)
638.B155 Banjosidae
638.B17 Barbourisiidae
638.B18 Bathyclupeidae
638.B2 Bathydraconidae
638.B23 Bathylaconidae
638.B25 Bathylagidae (Deepsea smelts)
638.B26 Bathymasteridae (Ronquils)
638.B27 Bathypteroidae
638.B3 Batrachoididae (Toadfishes)
638.B34 Belonidae (Needlefishes)
638.B347 Belontiidae
638.B4 Berycidae
638.B6 Blenniidae (Combtooth blennies)
638.B65 Bothidae (Lefteye flounders)
638.B67 Bovichthyidae
638.B7 Bracionichthyidae (Handfishes)
638.B8 Bramidae (Pomfrets)
638.B83 Branchiostegidae (Tilefishes)
638.B85 Bregmacerotidae (Codlets)
638.C12 Caesionidae
638.C14 Callichthyidae
638.C15 Callionymidae (Dragonets)
638.C2 Caproidae (Boarfishes)
638.C23 Caracanthidae
638.C25 Carangidae (Jacks; pompanos)
638.C26 Carapidae (Pearlfishes)
638.C265 Caristiidae
638.C27 Catostomidae (Suckers)
638.C28 Caulophrynidae
638.C3 Centrarchidae (Sunfishes)
638.C32 Centriscidae (Snipefishes)
638.C326 Centrolophidae

Chordates. Vertebrates
Fishes
Systematic divisions
Osteichthys (Bony fishes). By family, A-Z -- Continued

638.C33 Centrophrynidae
638.C34 Centropomidae (Snooks)
638.C347 Cepolidae
638.C35 Ceratiidae (Seadevils)
638.C356 Ceratodontidae
638.C36 Cetomimidae
638.C37 Cetopsidae
638.C385 Chacidae
638.C4 Chaenopsidae
638.C48 Chaetodontidae (Butterflyfishes)
638.C483 Champsodontidae
638.C484 Chanidae
638.C485 Channicthyidae
638.C486 Channidae
638.C5 Characidae (Characins; tetras)
638.C53 Chaudhuriidae
638.C534 Chauliodontidae (Viperfishes)
638.C5344 Chaunacidae
638.C536 Cheilodactylidae
638.C5365 Cheimarrhichthyidae
638.C54 Chiasmodontidae
638.C544 Chilodontidae
638.C547 Chironemidae
638.C549 Chlorophthalmidae (Greeneyes)
638.C55 Cichlidae (Cichlids)
638.C577 Cirrhitidae (Hawkfishes)
638.C578 Citharidae
638.C5785 Citharinidae
638.C6 Clariidae (Airbreathing catfishes)
638.C63 Clinidae (Clinids; blennies)
638.C64 Clupeidae (Herrings)
638.C647 Cobitidae (Loaches)
(638.C65) Coelacanthidae
see QL638.L26
638.C6535 Colocongridae
638.C654 Comephoridae
638.C655 Congiopodidae
638.C66 Congridae (Conger eels)
638.C666 Congrogadidae
638.C7 Coracinidae
Coregonidae see QL638.S2
638.C795 Coryphaenidae (Dolphinfishes)
Coryphaenoididae see QL638.M2

QL

Chordates. Vertebrates
Fishes
Systematic divisions
Osteichthys (Bony fishes). By family, A-Z -- Continued

638.C8 Cottidae (Sculpins)
638.C816 Cottocomephoridae
638.C818 Cottunculidae
638.C83 Cranoglanididae
638.C84 Creediidae
638.C88 Ctenoluciidae
638.C89 Curimatidae
638.C9 Cyclopteridae (Lumpsuckers; snailfishes)
638.C914 Cyemidae
638.C92 Cynodontidae
638.C93 Cynoglossidae (Tonguefishes)
638.C94 Cyprinidae (Minnows; carps)
638.C96 Cyprinodontidae (Killifishes)
638.D3 Dactylopteridae (Flying gurnards)
638.D35 Dactyloscopidae (Sand stargazers)
638.D4 Denticipitidae
638.D47 Derichthyidae
638.D5 Diceratiidae
638.D56 Diodontidae (Porcupinefishes)
638.D57 Diplomystidae
638.D577 Diretmidae
638.D58 Distichodontidae
638.D6 Doradidae
Dummumieriidae see QL638.C64
638.D93 Dysommidae (Arrowtooth eels)
638.D95 Dysomminidae
638.E2 Echeneidae (Remoras)
638.E34 Electrophoridae (Electric eel)
638.E4 Elopidae (Ladyfishes, etc.)
638.E5 Embiotocidae (Surfperches)
638.E53 Emmelichthyidae (Bonnetmouths)
638.E55 Engraulidae (Anchovies)
638.E556 Enoplosidae
638.E6 Ephippidae (Spadefishes)
638.E62 Epigonidae (Deepwater cardinalfishes)
638.E65 Erythrinidae
638.E7 Esocidae (Pikes)
638.E8 Eurypharyngidae
638.E83 Eutaeniophoridae
638.E87 Evermannellidae
638.E9 Exocoetidae (Flying fishes)
Fierasferidae see QL638.C26
638.F5 Fistulariidae (Cornetfishes)

Chordates. Vertebrates
Fishes
Systematic divisions
Osteichthys (Bony fishes). By family, A-Z -- Continued

638.F6 Formionidae
638.F86 Fundulidae
638.G2 Gadidae (Codfishes)
638.G23 Gadopsidae
638.G25 Galaxiidae
638.G266 Gasteropelecidae
638.G27 Gasterosteidae (Sticklebacks)
638.G4 Gempylidae (Snake mackerels)
638.G43 Gerridae (Mojarras)
638.G45 Gibberichthyidae
638.G455 Gigantactinidae
638.G5 Giganturidae
638.G55 Glaucosomitidae (Pearl perches)
638.G6 Gobiesocidae (Clingfishes)
638.G7 Gobiidae (Gobies)
638.G73 Gobioididae
638.G75 Gonorynchidae
638.G8 Gonostomatidae (Lightfishes)
638.G82 Goodeidae
638.G843 Grammicolepididae
638.G844 Grammidae
638.G848 Grammistidae (Soapfishes)
638.G85 Gregoryinidae
638.G87 Gymnarchidae
Gymnodontidae see QL638.T32
638.G9 Gymnotidae
638.G95 Gyrinocheilidae
638.H23 Haemulidae (Grunts)
638.H25 Halosauridae
638.H28 Harpagiferidae
638.H3 Harpodontidae
638.H444 Helogeneidae
638.H448 Helostomatidae
638.H45 Hemiodontidae
638.H46 Hemiramphidae (Halfbeaks)
638.H47 Hepsetidae
638.H484 Heterenchelyidae
638.H486 Heteropneustidae
638.H49 Hexagrammidae (Greenlings)
638.H54 Himantolophidae (Footballfishes)
638.H56 Hiodontidae (Mooneyes)
638.H64 Holocentridae (Squirrelfishes)

Chordates. Vertebrates
Fishes
Systematic divisions
Osteichthys (Bony fishes). By family, A-Z -- Continued

(638.H66) Homalopteridae
see QL638.B153

638.H67 Hoplichthyidae
638.H68 Horaichthyidae
638.H93 Hypophthalmidae
638.H935 Hypoptychidae
638.I13 Icelidae
638.I15 Ichthyboridae
638.I23 Icosteidae (Ragfishes)
638.I3 Ictaluridae (Freshwater catfishes)
638.I35 Idiacanthidae
638.I4 Indostomidae
638.I6 Ipnopidae
638.I86 Isonidae
638.I88 Istiophoridae (Billfishes)
638.J4 Jenynsiidae
638.K3 Kasidoridae
638.K5 Kneriidae
638.K6 Korsogasteridae
638.K7 Kraemeriidae
638.K8 Kuhliidae
638.K87 Kurtidae
638.K9 Kyphosidae (Sea chubs)
638.L115 Labracoglossidae
638.L12 Labridae (Wrasses)
638.L2 Lacteriidae
638.L24 Lampridae (Opahs)
638.L26 Latimeriidae
638.L28 Latridae
638.L3 Lebiasinidae
638.L35 Leiognathidae
638.L37 Lepidosirenidae
638.L4 Lepisosteidae (Gars)
638.L47 Leptoscopidae
638.L48 Lethrinidae
638.L5 Limnichthyidae
638.L55 Linophrynidae
Liparidae see QL638.C9
638.L57 Lipogenidae
638.L6 Lobotidae (Tripletails)
638.L75 Lophiidae (Goosefishes)
638.L77 Lophotidae (Crestfishes)
638.L785 Loricariidae (Armored catfishes)

Chordates. Vertebrates
Fishes
Systematic divisions
Osteichthys (Bony fishes). By family, A-Z -- Continued

638.L8 Luciocephalidae
638.L9 Lutjanidae (Snappers)
638.L95 Luvaridae (Louvars)
638.M13 Macristiidae
638.M16 Macrocephenchelyidae
638.M165 Macrorhamphosidae
638.M2 Macrouridae (Grenadiers)
638.M22 Macrurocyttidae
638.M24 Malacosteidae
638.M246 Malapteruridae
638.M28 Mastacembelidae
638.M33 Megalopidae (Tarpon)
638.M34 Melamphaeidae
638.M35 Melanocetidae
Melanostomiatidae see QL638.M3573
638.M3573 Melanostomiidae
638.M358 Melanotaeniidae
638.M37 Menidae
638.M4 Merlucciidae
638.M5 Microdesmidae (Wormfishes)
Microstomidae see QL638.B25
638.M57 Mirapinnidae
638.M6 Mochokidae
638.M64 Molidae (Molas)
638.M645 Monacanthidae
638.M65 Monocentridae
638.M653 Monodactylidae
638.M654 Monognathidae
638.M67 Moridae
638.M675 Moringuidae (Spaghetti eels)
638.M676 Mormyridae
638.M678 Moronidae
638.M8 Mugilidae (Mullets)
(638.M84) Mugiloididae
see QL638.P613
638.M85 Mullidae (Goatfishes)
638.M87 Muraenesocidae (Pike congers)
638.M875 Muraenidae (Morays)
638.M876 Muraenolepididae
638.M9 Myctophidae (Lanternfishes)
638.M97 Myrocongridae
638.N25 Nandidae
638.N3 Neenchelyidae

Chordates. Vertebrates
Fishes
Systematic divisions
Osteichthys (Bony fishes). By family, A-Z -- Continued

638.N33 Nematistiidae
638.N34 Nemichthyidae (Snipe eels)
638.N347 Nemipteridae
638.N36 Neoceratiidae
638.N38 Neoscopelidae
638.N387 Neostethidae
638.N4 Nessorhamphidae
638.N46 Nettastomatidae
638.N5 Nomeidae
638.N57 Normanichthyidae
638.N58 Notacanthidae (Spiny eels)
638.N586 Notograptidae
638.N5867 Notopteridae
638.N5873 Notosudidae
638.N6 Nototheniidae
Novumbridae see QL638.U5
638.O2 Odacidae
638.O23 Odontobutidae
638.O3 Ogcocephalidae (Batfishes)
638.O4 Olyridae
638.O45 Omosudidae
638.O5 Oneirodidae
638.O633 Ophichthidae (Snake eels)
638.O634 Ophiclinidae
638.O637 Ophidiidae (Cusk eels)
638.O65 Opisthognathidae (Jawfishes)
638.O657 Opisthoproctidae (Spookfishes)
638.O67 Oplegnathidae
638.O7 Oreosomatidae
638.O78 Oryziatidae
638.O84 Osmeridae (Smelts)
638.O87 Osphronemidae
638.O88 Osteoglossidae
638.O887 Ostraciontidae
638.O9 Owstoniidae
Oxudercidae see QL638.G7
638.P254 Pangasiidae
638.P258 Pantodontidae
638.P3 Paralepididae
638.P313 Paralichthyidae (Sand flounders)
638.P315 Parazenidae
638.P316 Parodontidae
638.P318 Pataecidae

Chordates. Vertebrates
Fishes
Systematic divisions
Osteichthys (Bony fishes). By family, A-Z -- Continued

638.P32 Pegasidae
638.P34 Pempheridae (Sweepers)
638.P35 Pentacerotidae (Armorheads)
638.P357 Penatpodidae
638.P358 Percichthyidae
638.P4 Percidae (Perches; darters)
638.P464 Percophididae (Flatheads)
638.P468 Percopsidae (Trout-perches)
638.P47 Peronedysidae
638.P5 Phallostethidae
638.P55 Pholidichthyidae
638.P56 Pholididae (Gunnels)
638.P57 Phractolaemidae
638.P58 Phycidae
638.P6 Pimelodidae
638.P613 Pinguipedidae (Sandperches)
638.P62 Platycephalidae
638.P63 Platytroctidae
638.P64 Plecoglossidae
638.P648 Plesiopidae
638.P7 Pleuronectidae (Righteye flounders)
638.P72 Plotosidae
638.P73 Poeciliidae (Livebearers)
638.P747 Polymixiidae (Beardfishes)
638.P75 Polynemidae (Threadfins)
638.P755 Polyodontidae (Paddlefishes)
638.P76 Polypteridae
638.P768 Pomacanthidae (Marine angelfishes)
638.P77 Pomacentridae (Damselfishes)
(638.P772) Pomadasyidae (Grunts)
see QL638.H23
638.P778 Pomatomidae (Bluefishes)
638.P785 Priacanthidae (Bigeyes)
638.P786 Prochilodontidae
638.P788 Profundulidae (Middle American killifishes)
638.P8 Psettodidae
638.P84 Pseudochromidae
638.P844 Pseudogrammidae
Pseudoplesiopidae see QL638.P84
638.P855 Psilorhynchidae
638.P88 Psychrolutidae
638.P9 Ptilichthyidae (Quillfishes)
Pygidiidae see QL638.T76

Chordates. Vertebrates
Fishes
Systematic divisions
Osteichthys (Bony fishes). By family, A-Z -- Continued

638.P97	Pyramodontidae
638.R3	Rachycentridae (Cobias)
638.R4	Regalecidae (Oarfishes)
638.R48	Retropinnidae
638.R5	Rhamphichthyidae
638.R55	Rhinoprenidae
638.R59	Rhyacichthyidae
638.R65	Rondeletiidae
638.R68	Rosauridae
638.S15	Saccopharyngidae
638.S18	Salangidae
638.S2	Salmonidae (Salmon; trout; whitefishes)
638.S3	Scaridae (Parrotfishes)
638.S32	Scatophagidae (Scats)
638.S334	Schilbeidae
638.S335	Schindleriidae
638.S34	Sciaenidae (Drums)
638.S347	Scomberesocidae (Sauries)
638.S35	Scombridae (Tuna; mackerel)
638.S374	Scopelarchidae (Pearleyes)
	Scopelosauridae see QL638.N5873
638.S38	Scophthalmidae
638.S42	Scorpaenidae (Scorpionfishes)
638.S45	Scytalinidae (Graveldivers)
(638.S47)	Searsidae (Tubeshoulders) see QL638.P63
638.S48	Serranidae (Sea basses)
(638.S483)	Serrasalmidae see QL638.C5
638.S485	Serrivomeridae
638.S5	Siganidae
638.S54	Sillaginidae
638.S6	Siluridae (Old World catfishes)
638.S64	Simenchelyidae
638.S68	Sisoridae
638.S7	Soleidae (Soles)
638.S73	Solenostomidae
638.S74	Sparidae (Porgies)
638.S77	Sphyraenidae (Barracudas)
638.S785	Stephanoberycidae
638.S8	Sternoptychidae
638.S83	Sternopygidae (Glass knifefishes)
638.S84	Stichaeidae (Pricklebacks)

Chordates. Vertebrates
Fishes
Systematic divisions
Osteichthys (Bony fishes). By family, A-Z -- Continued

638.S86 Stomiatidae
638.S87 Stromateidae (Butterfishes)
638.S88 Stylephoridae (Tube-eyes)
Synancejidae see QL638.S42
638.S892 Synaphobranchidae
638.S893 Synbranchidae
638.S9 Syngnathidae (Pipefishes; seahorses)
638.S96 Synodontidae (Lizardfishes)
638.T27 Teraponidae
Tetragonopteridae see QL638.C5
638.T3 Tetragonuridae
638.T32 Tetraodontidae (Puffers)
Theraponidae see QL638.T27
Thunnidae see QL638.S35
638.T55 Todaridae
638.T6 Toxotidae
638.T68 Trachichthyidae
638.T685 Trachinidae
638.T69 Trachipteridae (Ribbonfishes)
638.T695 Triacanthidae (Spikefishes)
638.T7 Trichiuridae (Cutlassfishes)
638.T73 Trichodontidae (Sandfishes)
638.T76 Trichomycteridae
638.T78 Trichonotidae
638.T8 Triglidae (Searobins)
638.T85 Triodontidae
638.T87 Tripterygiidae
638.T95 Trypauchenidae
638.U5 Umbridae (Mudminnows)
638.U7 Uranoscopidae (Stargazers)
638.V4 Veliferidae
638.X4 Xenocephalidae
638.X45 Xenocongridae (False morays)
638.X5 Xiphiidae (Swordfishes)
638.Z28 Zanclidae (Moorish idol)
638.Z3 Zaniolepididae
638.Z36 Zaproridae (Prowfishes)
638.Z4 Zeidae (Dories)
638.Z6 Zoarcidae (Eelpouts)

Agnatha (Jawless fishes)
638.12 General works
Myxini
Myxiniformes (Hagfishes)

Chordates. Vertebrates
Fishes
Systematic divisions
Agnatha (Jawless fishes)
Myxini
Myxiniformes (Hagfishes) -- Continued

638.14 General works
638.15.A-Z By family, A-Z
(638.15.B35) Bdellostomatidae
see QL638.15.M9
638.15.M9 Myxinidae
(638.15.P37) Paramyxinidae
see QL638.15.M9

Cephalaspidomorophi
638.18 General works
Petromyzontiformes (Lampreys)
638.2 General works
638.25.A-Z By family, A-Z
638.25.G45 Geotriidae
638.25.P48 Petromyzontidae

638.3 Dipnoid fishes
Class here general works only
For specific fishes see QL637.9+

638.5 Ganoid fishes
Class here general works only
For specific fishes see QL637.9+

Chondrichthyes (Cartilaginous fishes)
638.6 General works
Chimaeriformes
638.7 General works
638.75.A-Z By family, A-Z
638.75.C4 Chimaeridae (Chimaeras)
Pristiformes (Sawfishes)
638.77 General works
638.78.A-Z By family, A-Z
638.78.P75 Pristidae
Rajiformes (Rays)
638.8 General works
638.85.A-Z By family, A-Z
638.85.A5 Anacanthobatidae
638.85.A7 Arhynchobatidae
638.85.D3 Dasyatidae (Stingrays)
638.85.G9 Gymnuridae
638.85.H48 Hexatrygonidae (Sixgill stingrays)
638.85.M6 Mobulidae (Manta rays)
638.85.M9 Myliobatidae (Eagle rays)
638.85.P6 Potamotrygonidae (Freshwater stingrays)

Chordates. Vertebrates
Fishes
Systematic divisions
Chondrichthyes (Cartilaginous fishes)
Rajiformes (Rays)
By family, A-Z -- Continued
(638.85.P7) Pristidae (Sawfishes)
see QL638.78.P75
638.85.R3 Rajidae (Skates)
638.85.R4 Rhinobatidae (Guitarfishes)
Rhinopteridae see QL638.85.M9
638.85.R48 Rhynchobatidae
(638.85.T6) Torpedinidae
see QL638.875.T6
Urolophidae see QL638.85.D3
Torpediniformes (Electric rays)
638.87 General works
638.875.A-Z By family, A-Z
638.875.T6 Torpedinidae (Torpedo electric rays)
Sharks
638.9 General works
638.93 Shark attacks. Shark repellents
Systematic divisions
638.94.A-Z By order, A-Z
Class species, genera, and families in QL638.95
Class single-family orders with the family in QL638.95
638.94.C37 Carcharhiniformes (Ground sharks)
Heterodontiformes see QL638.95.H4
638.94.H49 Hexanchiformes
638.94.L36 Lamniformes
638.94.O74 Orectolobiformes (Carpet sharks)
Pristiophoriformes see QL638.95.P7
638.94.S75 Squaliformes
Squatiniformes see QL638.95.S88
638.95.A-Z By family, A-Z
638.95.A4 Alopiidae (Thresher sharks)
638.95.C3 Carcharhinidae (Requiem sharks)
Carchariidae see QL638.95.O3
638.95.C37 Cetorhinidae (Basking shark)
638.95.C4 Chlamydoselachidae (Frill shark)
638.95.D3 Dalatiidae (Kitefin sharks; sleeper sharks)
Echniorhinidae see QL638.95.S84
638.95.G55 Ginglymostomatidae (Nurse sharks)
638.95.H4 Heterodontidae (Bullhead sharks)
638.95.H48 Hexanchidae (Cow sharks)
Isuridae see QL638.95.L3

Chordates. Vertebrates
Fishes
Systematic divisions
Chondrichthyes (Cartilaginous fishes)
Sharks
Systematic divisions
By family, A-Z -- Continued

638.95.L3 Lamnidae (Mackerel sharks)
638.95.M44 Megachasmidae (Megamouth shark)
638.95.M58 Mitsukurinidae (Goblin shark)
638.95.O3 Odontaspididae (Sand tigers)
638.95.O7 Orectolobidae (Wobbegongs)
638.95.P7 Pristiophoridae (Saw sharks)
638.95.P8 Pseudotriakidae (False cat shark)
638.95.R4 Rhincodontidae (Whale shark)
638.95.S3 Scapanorhynichidae
638.95.S38 Scyliorinidae (Cat sharks)
Somniosidae see QL638.95.D3
638.95.S7 Sphyrnidae (Hammerhead sharks)
638.95.S84 Squalidae (Dogfish sharks)
638.95.S88 Squatinidae (Angel sharks)
638.95.S92 Stegostomatidae (Zebra shark)
638.95.T75 Triakidae (Houndsharks)
638.97 Immunology
638.99 Genetics
639 Anatomy and morphology
639.1 Physiology
Including electrophysiology and electric fishes
For effects of pollution, disease, etc. see SH171+
639.15 Age determination. Age/growth calculations. Length/weight relationships
For particular groups or species see QL637.9+
639.16 Racial analysis
639.2 Reproduction and spawning
Cf. SH155.6 Artificial spawning
Cf. SH155.7 Induced spawning
639.25 Development. Eggs and larvae
639.3 Behavior
639.4 Locomotion
639.5 Migration. Diadromy
Cf. SH156.8 Fish tagging
639.6 Vertical distribution
Including diel vertical migration
639.8 Ecology
Parasites see SH175
Reptiles and amphibians
640 Periodicals, societies, congresses, serial publications

Chordates. Vertebrates
Reptiles and amphibians -- Continued
640.5 Collected works (nonserial)
640.7 Dictionaries and encyclopedias
641 General works, treatises, and textbooks
643 Pictorial works and atlases
644 Popular works
644.2 Juvenile works
Rare and endangered species
644.7 General works
644.73.A-Z By region or country, A-Z
Extinct reptiles and/or amphibians
644.8 General works
644.83.A-Z By region or country, A-Z
645 Classification. Nomenclature
645.2 Catalogs and collections
Evolution
645.3 General works
645.4 Speciation
645.5 Variation
Study and teaching. Research
Including census taking, banding, marking, tagging, etc., and general works on amphibian and reptile watching and viewing sites
645.6 General works
645.63.A-Z By region or country, A-Z
645.65 Collection and preservation
645.7 Dangerous reptiles
Geographical distribution
Class here works on the reptiles and/or amphibians of a specific region
For geographical distribution of systematic divisions see QL666.A+
648 General works
North America
651 General works
United States
652 General works
653.A-Z By region or state, A-Z
Canada
654 General works
654.2.A-Z By region, province, or territory, A-Z
Latin America
654.5 General works
655 Mexico
Including Yucatán Peninsula
656 Central America (Table Q3)

QL

Chordates. Vertebrates
Reptiles and amphibians
Geographical distribution
Latin America -- Continued

656.5 West Indies (Table Q3)
657 South America (Table Q3)
658 Europe (Table Q3)
661 Asia (Table Q3)
662 Africa (Table Q3)
663 Australia
663.5 New Zealand
664 Pacific islands (Table Q3)
664.2 Arctic regions
664.4 Antarctica
664.6 Tropics

Systematic divisions
Reptiles

665 General works, treatises, and textbooks

Juvenile works see QL644.2
Physiographic divisions
Aquatic reptiles. Water reptiles

665.3 General works
665.5 Marine reptiles. Sea reptiles

Geographical distribution see QL648+

666.A-Z By order and family, A-Z

Amphisbaenia see QL666.L192+
Chelonia (Testudinata; turtles)

666.C5 General works
666.C52 Carettochelyidae (Pitted-shell turtles)
666.C535 Chelidae
666.C536 Cheloniidae
666.C539 Chelydridae
666.C54 Dermatemydidae
666.C546 Dermochelyidae (Leatherback turtle)
666.C547 Emydidae (Box turtles)
666.C55 Kinosternide
666.C57 Pelomedusidae
666.C584 Testudinidae (Tortoises)
666.C587 Trionychidae (Softshell turtles)

Crocodylia (Crocodilians)

666.C9 General works
666.C925 Crocodylidae (Alligators; crocodiles; caimans; gavial)
(666.C94) Gavialidae
see QL666.C925

Squamata

666.L19 General works

Chordates. Vertebrates
Reptiles and amphibians
Systematic divisions
Reptiles
Systematic divisions by family, A-Z
Squamata
Amphisbaenia

666.L192	General works
666.L193	Amphisbaenidae
666.L194	Bipedidae
	Lacertilia (Sauria; lizards)
666.L2	General works
(666.L21-.L2196)	Geographical distribution see QL648+
666.L223	Agamidae
	Amphisbaenidae see QL666.L192+
666.L225	Anelytropsidae
666.L2254	Anguidae (Glass lizards)
666.L2256	Anniellidae
666.L23	Chamaeleontidae (Chameleons)
666.L234	Cordylidae (Girdle-tailed lizards)
666.L236	Corytophanidae
666.L237	Crotaphytidae
666.L238	Dibamidae
666.L24	Eublepharidae
666.L243	Feylinidae
666.L245	Gekkonidae (Geckos)
666.L247	Helodermatidae (Gila monsters)
666.L248	Hoplocercidae
666.L25	Iguanidae
666.L255	Lacertidae
666.L2556	Lanthanotidae
666.L265	Opluridae
666.L267	Phrynosomatidae
666.L268	Polychrotidae
666.L27	Pygopodidae
666.L28	Scincidae (Skinks)
	Sphaerodactylidae see QL666.L245
666.L285	Teiidae
666.L287	Tropiduridae
666.L29	Varanidae (Monitor lizards)
666.L293	Xantusiidae
666.L295	Xenosauridae
	Serpentes (Ophidia; snakes)
666.O6	General works
666.O62	Acrochordidae (Wart snakes; file snakes)
666.O625	Aniliidae (False coral snakes; coral pipe snakes)

Chordates. Vertebrates
Reptiles and amphibians
Systematic divisions
Reptiles
By order and family, A-Z
Squamata
Serpentes (Ophidia; snakes)

666.O626 Anomalepididae (Primitive blind snakes; dawn blind snakes)
666.O6265 Anomochilidae (Dwarf pipe snakes)
666.O627 Atractaspididae (Mole vipers)
666.O63 Boidae (Boas)
666.O633 Bolyeriidae (Round Island boas)
666.O636 Colubridae
Crotalidae see QL666.O69
666.O638 Cylindrophiidae (Asian pipe snakes)
666.O64 Elapidae (Cobras; coral snakes; sea snakes)
(666.O645) Hydrophiidae
see QL666.O64
666.O65 Leptotyphlopidae (Slender blind snakes)
666.O66 Loxocemidae (Mexican burrowing pythons)
666.O67 Pythonidae
666.O68 Tropidophiidae (Dwarf boas)
666.O685 Typhlopidae (Blind snakes)
666.O688 Uropeltidae (Shield-tailed snakes)
666.O69 Viperidae (Vipers and pit vipers)
666.O694 Xenopeltidae (Sunbeam snakes)
Rhynchocephalia
666.R4 General works
666.R48 Sphenodontidae (Tuatara)
Squamata see QL666.L19+
Amphibians
667 General works, treatises, and textbooks
Juvenile works see QL644.2
Geographical distribution see QL648+
668.A-Z By order and family, A-Z
Gymnophiona (Apoda; caecilians)
668.A6 General works
668.A63 Caeciliidae
668.A65 Ichthyophiidae
668.A67 Rhinatrematidae
668.A68 Scolecomorphidae
668.A69 Uraeotyphlidae
Caudata (Urodela; salamanders; newts)
668.C2 General works
668.C23 Ambystomatidae (Mole salamanders)
668.C237 Amphiumidae

Chordates. Vertebrates
Reptiles and amphibians
Systematic divisions
Amphibians
By order and family, A-Z
Caudata (Urodela; salamanders; newts) -- Continued

668.C24 Cryptobranchidae (Giant salamanders)
668.C243 Dicamptodontidae
668.C25 Hynobiidae
668.C274 Plethodontidae (Lungless salamanders)
668.C277 Proteidae
668.C278 Rhyacotritonidae
668.C28 Salamandridae (Newts)
668.C285 Sirenidae

Ecaudata (Anura; Salientia; frogs; toads)

668.E2 General works
668.E214 Alytidae
668.E217 Ascaphidae (Tailed frogs)
(668.E22) Atelopodidae
see QL668.E227
668.E224 Bombinatoridae
668.E225 Brevicipitidae
668.E227 Bufonidae (Toads)
668.E23 Centrolenidae (Glass frogs)
668.E233 Dendrobatidae
668.E234 Dicroglossidae
(668.E235) Discoglossidae
see QL668.E214
668.E24 Hylidae (Tree frogs)
668.E244 Hyperoliidae
668.E255 Leiopelmatidae
668.E257 Leptodactylidae (Robber frogs)
668.E259 Mantellidae
668.E26 Microhylidae (Narrow-mouthed toads)
668.E2615 Myobatrachidae
668.E262 Pelobatidae (Eurasian spadefoot toads)
668.E2626 Pelodryadidae
668.E263 Pelodytidae
668.E264 Phrynomeridae
668.E265 Pipidae
668.E268 Pseudidae
668.E27 Ranidae (Frogs)
668.E274 Rhacophoridae
668.E275 Rhinophrynidae
668.E33 Scaphiopodidae (North American spadefoot toads)
668.5 Genetics
669 Anatomy and morphology

Chordates. Vertebrates
Reptiles and amphibians
Systematic divisions -- Continued
669.2 Physiology
669.25 Age determination. Life spans. Longevity
669.3 Reproduction
669.5 Behavior
669.8 Ecology
Birds
671 Periodicals, societies, congresses, serial publications
672 Collected works (nonserial)
672.2 Dictionaries and encyclopedias
Communication of ornithological information
672.5 Ornithological literature
672.6 Language. Authorship
History
672.7 General works
672.73.A-Z By region or country, A-Z
673 General works, treatises, and textbooks
674 Pictorial works and atlases
674.4 Ornithological illustration
675 Birds' eggs and nests
676 Popular works
676.2 Juvenile works
Bird protection. Bird refuges. Important bird areas. Bird attracting
Including birdhouses, bird feeders, birdcall whistles, and gardening to attract birds
Cf. SK351+ Wildlife management. Game protection
676.5 General works
By region or country
United States
676.55 General works
676.56.A-Z By region or state, A-Z
676.57.A-Z Other regions or countries, A-Z
676.7 Rare and endangered species
For local see QL676.55+
676.8 Extinct birds
677 Classification. Nomenclature
677.2 Catalogs and collections
677.3 Evolution
677.4 Population dynamics
For mortality see QL698.25
677.5 Study and teaching. Research
Including census taking, bird banding, and general works on bird watching and birding sites
677.7 Collection and preservation

Chordates. Vertebrates
Birds -- Continued
677.75 Dangerous birds
677.78 Birds of prey. Raptors
Cf. QL696.F3+ Falconiformes
Cf. QL696.S8+ Strigiformes
677.79.A-Z Other types of birds, A-Z
677.79.C38 Cavity-nesting birds
677.79.E85 Exotic birds
677.79.F55 Flightless birds
677.79.F67 Forest birds
Game birds
see SF508+ Animal culture; SK311+ Hunting
677.79.G73 Grassland birds
677.79.I58 Introduced birds
677.79.N63 Nocturnal birds
Ornamental birds see SF512+
677.79.P37 Parasitic birds
677.79.P57 Piscivorous birds
Talking birds see SF462.8
Water birds see QL678.5+
677.8 Aviaries. Bird exhibitions
Geographical distribution
For geographical distribution of systematic divisions see QL696.A+
678 General works
Physiographic divisions
For birds of a particular region or country or off the coast of a particular region or country see QL680+
Aquatic birds. Water birds
Including shore birds
For waterfowl see SF510.W3 Animal culture; SK331+ Hunting
678.5 General works
Marine birds. Sea birds
678.52 General works
By region
678.55 Atlantic Ocean
678.6 Indian Ocean
678.65 Pacific Ocean
Topographical divisions
679 Zone divisions
e.g. Palaearctic region
America
680 General works
North America and United States
681 General works

Chordates. Vertebrates
Birds
Geographical distribution
Topographical divisions
America
North America and United States -- Continued
United States
682 General works
683.A-Z By region, A-Z
684.A-.W By state, A-W
Canada
685 General works
685.5.A-Z By region or province, A-Z
Latin America
685.7 General works
686 Mexico
687 Central America (Table Q3)
688 West Indies (Table Q3)
689 South America (Table Q3)
690 Europe (Table Q3)
691 Asia (Table Q3)
691.5 Arab countries (General)
692 Africa (Table Q3)
Australasia
692.8 General works
Australia
693 General works
693.3.A-Z By state, territory, or region, A-Z
693.5 New Zealand
694 Pacific islands (Table Q3)
694.5 Atlantic islands (Table Q3)
694.7 Indian Ocean islands (Table Q3)
695 Arctic regions
695.2 Antarctica
695.5 Tropics
696.A-Z Systematic divisions. By order and family, A-Z
Accipitriformes see QL696.F3+
Alciformes see QL696.C4+
Anseriformes
696.A5 General works
696.A52 Anatidae (Ducks; geese; swans)
696.A53 Anhimidae (Screamers)
Apodiformes
696.A55 General works
696.A552 Apodidae (Swifts)
696.A554 Hemiprocnidae (Crested swifts)
696.A558 Trochilidae (Hummingbirds)

Chordates. Vertebrates
Birds
Systematic divisions. By order and family, A-Z -- Continued
Apterygiformes
696.A6 General works
696.A63 Apterygidae (Kiwis)
Ardeiformes see QL696.C5+
Caprimulgiformes
696.C2 General works
696.C22 Aegothelidae (Owlet frogmouths)
696.C23 Caprimulgidae (Goatsuckers)
696.C25 Nyctibiidae (Potoos)
696.C26 Podargidae (Frogmouths)
696.C28 Steatornithidae (Oilbirds)
Casuariiformes
696.C3 General works
696.C33 Casuariidae (Cassowaries)
696.C34 Dromiceidae (Emus)
Charadriiformes
696.C4 General works
696.C42 Alcidae (Auks; auklets; murres)
696.C428 Burhinidae (Thick-knees)
696.C43 Charadriidae (Plovers; turnstones; surfbirds)
696.C435 Chionididae (Sheathbills)
696.C44 Dromadidae (Crabplovers)
696.C448 Glareolidae (Pratincoles; coursers)
696.C452 Haematopodidae (Oystercatchers)
696.C457 Jacanidae (Jacanas)
696.C46 Laridae (Gulls; terns; skuas; jaegers)
696.C465 Pedionomidae
(696.C47) Phalaropodidae (Phalaropes)
see QL696.C48
696.C473 Recurvirostridae (Avocets; stilts)
696.C477 Rostratulidae (Painted snipes)
696.C479 Rynchopidae (Skimmers)
696.C48 Scolopacidae (Snipes; woodcocks; sandpipers; phalaropes)
(696.C488) Stercorariidae
see QL696.C46
696.C49 Thinocoridae (Seedsnipes)
Ciconiiformes
696.C5 General works
696.C52 Ardeidae (Herons; bitterns)
696.C525 Balaenicipitidae (Shoebill)
696.C53 Cathartidae (New World vultures)
696.C535 Ciconiidae (Storks; jabirus)
696.C536 Cochleariidae (Boatbilled herons)

Chordates. Vertebrates
Birds
Systematic divisions. By order and family, A-Z
Ciconiiformes -- Continued
696.C56 Phoenicopteridae (Flamingos)
696.C58 Scopidae (Hammerheads)
696.C585 Threskiornithidae (Ibises; spoonbills)
Coccyges see QL696.C8+
Coliiformes
696.C59 General works
696.C593 Coliidae (Colies)
Columbiformes
696.C6 General works
696.C63 Columbidae (Pigeons; doves)
696.C66 Pteroclidae (Sandgrouses)
696.C67 Raphidae (Dodos; solitaires)
Coraciiformes
696.C7 General works
696.C72 Alcedinidae (Kingfishers)
696.C725 Brachypteraciidae (Groundrollers)
696.C729 Bucerotidae (Hornbills)
696.C73 Coraciidae (Rollers)
696.C74 Leptosomatidae (Cuckoo rollers)
696.C754 Meropidae (Bee-eaters)
696.C756 Momotidae (Motmots)
(696.C77) Phoeniculidae (Wood hoopoes)
see QL696.U66
696.C78 Todidae (Todies)
(696.C79) Upupidae (Hoopoes)
see QL696.U68
Cuculiformes
696.C8 General works
696.C83 Cuculidae (Cuckoos; roadrunners; anis)
696.C85 Musophagidae (Plaintain-eaters; touracos)
Cypseliformes see QL696.A55+
Falconiformes
696.F3 General works
696.F32 Accipitridae (Hawks; Old World vultures; harriers)
Including vultures (General)
(696.F33) Cathartidae (New World vultures)
see QL696.C53
696.F34 Falconidae (Falcons; caracaras)
696.F36 Pandionidae (Ospreys)
696.F38 Sagittariidae (Secretarybirds)
Galliformes
696.G2 General works
696.G23 Cracidae (Curassows; guans; chachalacas)

Chordates. Vertebrates
Birds
Systematic divisions. By order and family, A-Z
Galliformes -- Continued
696.G25 Megapodiidae (Megapodes)
(696.G254) Meleagrididae (Turkeys)
see QL696.G27
696.G258 Numididae (Guineafowl)
696.G259 Odontophoridae (New World quails)
696.G26 Opisthocomidae (Hoatzins)
696.G27 Phasianidae (Pheasants, Old World quails, grouse, partridges, peafowls, turkeys)
(696.G285) Tetraonidae (Grouse)
see QL696.G27
Gaviiformes
696.G3 General works
696.G33 Gaviidae (Loons)
Gruiformes
696.G8 General works
696.G82 Aramidae (Limpkins)
696.G827 Cariamidae (Seriemas)
696.G83 Eurypgidae (Sunbitterns)
696.G84 Gruidae (Cranes)
696.G845 Heliornithidae (Sungrebes)
696.G85 Mesitornithidae (Roatelos)
696.G86 Otididae (Bustards)
Pedionomidae see QL696.C465
696.G874 Psophiidae (Trumpeters)
696.G876 Rallidae (Rails; coots)
696.G878 Rhynochetidae (Kagus)
696.G89 Turnicidae (Bustardquails)
Halcyones see QL696.C72
Lariformes see QL696.C46
Limicolae see QL696.C4+
Meropidae see QL696.C754
Musophagiformes see QL696.C85
Passeriformes
696.P2 General works
696.P212 Acanthisittidae (New Zealand wrens)
696.P213 Acanthizidae (Australasian warblers)
696.P2135 Aegithalidae (Long-tailed tits; bushtits)
Aegithinidae see QL696.P2344
696.P214 Alaudidae (Larks)
696.P216 Artamidae (Woodswallows; currawongs; Australian butcherbirds)
696.P218 Atrichornithidae (Scrubbirds)
696.P22 Bombycillidae (Waxwings)

Chordates. Vertebrates
Birds
Systematic divisions. By order and family, A-Z
Passeriformes -- Continued

696.P224 Callaeidae (Wattled crows; huias; saddlebacks)
696.P225 Campephagidae (Cuckoo shrikes)
696.P228 Catamblyrhynchidae (Plushcapped finches)
696.P23 Certhiidae (Creepers)
696.P234 Chamaeidae (Wrentits)
696.P2344 Chloropseidae (Leafbirds)
696.P235 Cinclidae (Dippers)
696.P2354 Climacteridae (Australasian treecreepers)
696.P236 Coerebidae (Honeycreepers)
696.P2365 Conopophagidae (Antpipits)
696.P2367 Corvidae (Crows; magpies; jays)
696.P2368 Cotingidae (Cotingas)
(696.P237) Cracticidae
see QL696.P216
696.P239 Cyclarhidae (Peppershrikes)
696.P24 Dendrocolaptidae (Woodhewers)
696.P242 Dicaeidae (Flowerpeckers)
696.P2427 Dicruridae (Drongos)
696.P243 Drepanididae (Hawaiian honeycreepers)
696.P2435 Dulidae (Palmchats)
696.P2438 Emberizidae (Buntings; American sparrows; wood warblers)
696.P2439 Eopsaltriidae (Australian robins)
696.P244 Estrildidae (Waxbills)
696.P245 Eurylaimidae (Broadbills)
696.P2455 Formicariidae (Ant thrushes)
696.P246 Fringillidae (Finches)
696.P2464 Furnariidae (Ovenbirds)
696.P2468 Grallinidae (Magpie larks)
696.P247 Hirundinidae (Swallows)
696.P2474 Hyposittidae (Caralbilled nuthatches)
696.P2475 Icteridae (Blackbirds; troupials)
Irenidae see QL696.P2585
696.P248 Laniidae (Shrikes)
696.P2485 Maluridae (Australian wrens)
696.P249 Meliphagidae (Honeyeaters)
696.P2495 Menuridae (Lyrebirds)
696.P25 Mimidae (Thrashers; mockingbirds)
696.P252 Motacillidae (Wagtails; pipits)
696.P255 Muscicapidae (Old World flycatchers)
696.P257 Nectariniidae (Sunbirds)
696.P2585 Oriolidae (Old World flycatchers)
696.P259 Oxyruncidae (Sharpbills)

Chordates. Vertebrates
Birds
Systematic divisions. By order and family, A-Z
Passeriformes -- Continued

696.P2595 Pachycephalidae
696.P26 Paradisaeidae (Birds of paradise)
696.P2612 Paradoxornithidae (Parrotbills; suthoras)
696.P2615 Paridae (Titmice; chickadees)
(696.P2618) Parulidae
see QL696.P2438
696.P262 Passeridae
696.P2625 Philepittidae (Asities; false sunbirds)
696.P2629 Phytotomidae (Plantcutters)
696.P263 Pipridae (Manakins)
696.P2634 Pittidae (Pittas)
696.P264 Ploceidae (Weaverbirds)
696.P265 Prionopidae (Weaverbirds)
696.P266 Prunellidae (Accentors)
696.P267 Ptilogonatidae (Silky flycatchers)
696.P2675 Ptilonorhynchidae (Bowerbirds)
696.P268 Pycnonotidae (Bulbuls)
696.P27 Regulidae (Kinglets)
696.P272 Remizidae
696.P273 Rhinocryptidae (Tapaculos)
696.P275 Sittidae (Nuthatches)
696.P278 Sturnidae (Starlings)
696.P279 Sylviidae (Old World warblers)
696.P28 Tersinidae (Swallow tanagers)
696.P282 Thraupidae (Tanagers)
696.P285 Timaliidae (Babblers)
696.P287 Troglodytidae (Wrens)
696.P288 Turdidae (Thrushes)
696.P289 Tyrannidae (Tyrant flycatchers)
696.P29 Vangidae (Vangas)
696.P294 Vireolaniidae (Shrike vireos)
696.P2945 Vireonidae (Vireos)
696.P296 Zeledoniidae (Wrenthrushes)
696.P298 Zosteropidae (White-eyes)

Pelecaniformes
696.P4 General works
696.P42 Anhingidae (Snake-birds)
696.P45 Fregatidae (Frigate birds)
696.P47 Pelecanidae (Pelicans)
696.P474 Phaethontidae (Tropicbirds)
696.P4745 Phalacrocoracidae (Cormorants)
696.P48 Sulidae (Boobies; gannets)

Phoenicopteriformes see QL696.C56

Chordates. Vertebrates
Birds
Systematic divisions. By order and family, A-Z -- Continued
Piciformes
696.P5 General works
696.P52 Bucconidae (Puffbirds)
696.P53 Capitonidae (Barbets)
696.P54 Galbulidae (Jacamars)
696.P55 Indicatoridae (Honeyguides)
696.P56 Picidae (Woodpeckers)
696.P57 Ramphastidae (Toucans)
Podicipediformes
696.P58 General works
696.P586 Podicipedidae (Grebes)
Procellariformes
696.P6 General works
696.P63 Diomedeidae (Albatrosses)
696.P64 Hydrobatidae (Storm petrels)
696.P66 Pelecanoididae (Diving petrels)
696.P665 Procellariidae (Shearwaters; fulmars)
696.P7 Psittaciformes (Parrots)
Puffinidae see QL696.P665
Pygopodes see QL696.P586
Pygopodes (Gaviidae) see QL696.G33
Rhamphastidae see QL696.P57
Rheiformes
696.R37 General works
696.R4 Rheidae (Rheas)
Scansores
see QL671+
Sphenisciformes
696.S47 General works
696.S473 Spheniscidae (Penguins)
Steganopodes see QL696.P4+
Strigiformes
696.S8 General works
696.S83 Strigidae (Owls)
696.S85 Tytonidae (Barn owls)
Struthioniformes
696.S87 General works
696.S9 Struthionidae (Ostriches)
Tinamiformes
696.T37 General works
696.T4 Tinamidae (Tinamous)
Trochili see QL696.A558
Trogoniformes
696.T67 General works

Chordates. Vertebrates
Birds
Systematic divisions. By order and family, A-Z
Trogoniformes -- Continued
696.T7 Trogonidae (Trogons)
Upupiformes
696.U6 General works
696.U66 Phoeniculidae (Wood hoopoes)
696.U68 Upupidae (Hoopoes)
696.5 Genetics
Anatomy and morphology
697 General works
697.4 Feathers. Plumage
698 Physiology
698.2 Reproduction
698.25 Mortality
698.26 Effect of roads
698.3 Behavior
Including social life and instinct
Eggs and nests see QL675
Bird banding see QL677.5
698.4 Food
698.5 Song. Vocalization
698.7 Flight
698.8 Navigation
698.85 Orientation
698.9 Migration
698.95 Ecology
699 Miscellany and curiosa
For birds of the Bible see BS664
Mammals
700 Periodicals, societies, congresses, serial publications
701 Collected works (nonserial)
701.2 Dictionaries and encyclopedias
Communication of information
701.5 General works
701.6 Information services
701.8 Computer network resources
Including the Internet
702 Mammalogical literature
703 General works, treatises, and textbooks
704 Compends
705 Pictorial works and atlases
706 Popular works
For popular works on domestic animals see SF41
706.2 Juvenile works
706.4 Study and teaching. Research

QL

Chordates. Vertebrates
Mammals -- Continued
706.5.A-Z Special topics, A-Z
706.5.D38 Data processing
Rare and endangered species
706.8 General works
706.83.A-Z By region or country, A-Z
707 Extinct mammals
708 Classification. Nomenclature
708.2 Catalogs and collections
708.4 Collection and preservation
708.5 Evolution. Speciation
708.6 Population dynamics
Geographical distribution
For geographical distribution of systematic divisions see QL737.A+
708.7 General works
Physiographic divisions
Aquatic
713 General works
Marine
713.2 General works
By region
For marine mammals of a particular region or country or off the coast of a particular region or country see QL715+
Atlantic Ocean
713.25 General works
713.28 North Atlantic Ocean
713.35 Pacific Ocean
Topographical divisions
North America
715 General works
United States
717 General works
719.A-Z By region or state, A-Z
Canada
721 General works
721.5.A-Z By region or province, A-Z
Latin America
721.8 General works
722 Mexico
723 Central America (Table Q3)
724 West Indies (Table Q3)
725 South America (Table Q3)
Europe
726 General works

Chordates. Vertebrates
Mammals
Geographical distribution
Topographical divisions
Europe -- Continued

727 Great Britain
728.A-Z Other regions or countries, A-Z
729 Asia (Table Q3)
731 Africa (Table Q3)
732 Indian Ocean islands (Table Q3)
Australasia
732.8 General works
Australia
733 General works
733.5.A-Z By state, territory, or region, A-Z
734 New Zealand
735 Pacific islands (Table Q3)
736 Arctic regions. Greenland
736.2 Antarctica
736.5 Tropics
737.A-Z Systematic divisions. By order and family, A-Z
Afrosoricida. Tenrecomorpha
737.A35 General works
737.A352 Chrysochloridae (Golden moles)
737.A357 Tenrecidae (Tenrecs)
Carnivora
737.C2 General works
737.C214 Ailuridae (Red panda)
737.C22 Canidae (Dogs)
For domestic dogs see SF421+
737.C23 Felidae (Cats)
For domestic cats see SF441+
737.C235 Herpestidae (Mongooses)
737.C24 Hyaenidae (Hyenas)
737.C248 Mephitidae (Skunks)
737.C25 Mustelidae (Weasels; badgers; otters)
737.C26 Procyonidae (Raccoons)
737.C27 Ursidae (Bears; giant panda)
737.C28 Viverridae (Civets, etc.)
Cetacea
737.C4 General works
Mysticeti (Baleen whales)
737.C42 General works
737.C423 Balaenidae (Right whales)
737.C424 Balaenopteridae (Rorquals)
737.C425 Eschrichtiidae (Gray whales)
737.C427 Neobalaenidae

Chordates. Vertebrates
Mammals
Systematic divisions. By order and family, A-Z
Cetacea -- Continued
Odontoceti (Toothed whales)
737.C43 General works
737.C432 Delphinidae (Dolphins)
Iniidae see QL737.C436
Lipotidae see QL737.C436
737.C433 Monodontidae (Narwhal; white whale)
737.C434 Phocoenidae (Porpoises)
737.C435 Physeteridae (Sperm whales)
737.C436 Platanistidae (River dolphins)
Pontoporiidae see QL737.C436
Stenidae see QL737.C432
737.C438 Ziphiidae (Beaked whales)
Chiroptera
737.C5 General works
737.C52 Desmodontidae (Vampires)
737.C525 Emballonuridae (Sac-winged bats)
737.C53 Furipteridae (Smoky bats)
737.C533 Hipposideridae (Old World leaf-nosed bats)
737.C535 Megadermatidae (False vampires)
737.C54 Molossidae (Free-tailed bats)
737.C543 Mormoopidae
737.C545 Mystacinidae (New Zealand short-tailed bats)
737.C55 Myzopodidae (Old World sucker-footed bats)
737.C555 Natalidae (Funnel-eared bats)
737.C56 Noctilionidae (Fisherman bats)
737.C565 Nycteridae (Slit-faced bats)
737.C57 Phyllostomidae (American leaf-nosed bats)
737.C575 Pteropodidae (Old World fruit bats)
737.C58 Rhinolophidae (Horseshoe bats)
737.C585 Rhinopomatidae (Mouse-tailed bats)
737.C59 Thyropteridae (Disk-winged bats)
737.C595 Vespertilionidae
Dermoptera
737.D35 General works
737.D4 Cynocephalidae (Flying lemurs)
Edentata. Xenarthra
737.E2 General works
737.E22 Bradypodidae (Three-toed tree sloths)
737.E23 Dasypodidae (Armadillos)
737.E238 Megalonychidae (Two-toed tree sloths)
737.E24 Myrmecophagidae (Anteaters)
Erinaceomorpha
737.E75 General works

Chordates. Vertebrates
Mammals
Systematic divisions. By order and family, A-Z
Erinaceomorpha -- Continued
737.E753 Erinaceidae (Hedgehogs)
Hyracoidea
737.H85 General works
737.H9 Procaviidae (Hyraxes)
Insectivora. Insectivores
737.I5 General works
(737.I52) Chrysochloridae
see QL737.A352
(737.I53) Erinaceidae
see QL737.E753
(737.I54) Macroscelididae (Elephant shrews)
see QL737.M242
(737.I545) Potamogalidae
QL737.S73
(737.I55) Solenodontidae
see QL737.S74
(737.I56) Soricidae
see QL737. S75
(737.I57) Talpidae
see QL737.S76
(737.I58) Tenrecidae
see QL737.A357
Lagomorpha
737.L3 General works
737.L32 Leporidae (Rabbits; hares)
737.L33 Ochotonidae (Pikas)
Macroscelidea
737.M24 General works
737.M242 Macroscelididae (Elephant shrews)
Marsupialia. Marsupials
737.M3 General works
Dasyuromorphia
737.M325 General works
737.M33 Dasyuridae (Marsupial mice, Marsupial cats)
737.M335 Myrmecobiidae (Numbat)
737.M336 Thylacinidae (Thylacine)
Didelphimorphia
737.M337 General works
737.M34 Didelphidae (American opossums)
Diprotodontia
737.M345 General works
737.M346 Acrobatidae
737.M347 Burramyidae (Pygmy possums)

Chordates. Vertebrates
Mammals
Systematic divisions. By order and family, A-Z
Marsupialia
Diprotodontia -- Continued

737.M348 Hypsiprymnodontidae (Rat-kangaroos)
Cf. QL737.M386 Potoroidae
737.M35 Macropodidae (Kangaroos, wallabies)
737.M373 Petauridae
737.M38 Phalangeridae (Phalangers)
737.M384 Phascolarctidae (Koalas)
737.M386 Potoroidae (Bettongs, potoroos, rat-kangaroos)
Cf. QL737.M348 Hypsiprymnodontidae
737.M387 Pseudocheiridae
737.M3875 Tarsipedidae
737.M39 Vombatidae (Wombats)

Microbiotheria
737.M43 General works
737.M435 Microbiotheriidae

Notoryctemorphia
737.M44 General works
737.M445 Notoryctidae (Marsupial moles)

Paucituberculata
737.M46 General works
737.M463 Caenolestidae (Rat opossums)

Peramelemorphia (Bandicoots)
737.M47 General works
737.M475 Peramelidae
(737.M476) Peroryctidae
see QL737.M475
737.M478 Thylacomyidae (Bilbies)

Monotremata
737.M7 General works
737.M72 Ornithorhynchidae (Platypus)
737.M73 Tachyglossidae (Echidnas)

Pholidota
737.P4 General works
737.P5 Manidae (Pangolins)

Pinnipedia
737.P6 General works
737.P62 Odobenidae (Walrus)
737.P63 Otariidae (Eared seals)
737.P64 Phocidae (Seals)

Primates
737.P9 General works
737.P915 Atelidae (Howler monkeys; muriquis; spider monkeys, woolly monkeys)

Chordates. Vertebrates
Mammals
Systematic divisions. By order and family, A-Z
Primates -- Continued

(737.P917) Callimiconidae
see QL737.P925

(737.P92) Callitrichidae
see QL737.P925

737.P925 Cebidae (Marmosets; tamarins; squirrel monkeys, capuchin monkeys)

737.P93 Cercopithecidae (Old World monkeys)

737.P933 Cheirogaleidae

737.P935 Daubentoniidae (Aye-ayes)

737.P937 Galagonidae (Galagos)

(737.P94) Hominidae
see GN51+

737.P945 Indridae

737.P95 Lemuridae (Large lemurs)

737.P955 Lorisidae (Lorises; pottos)

737.P957 Nyctipithecidae (Night monkeys)

737.P959 Pitheciidae (Sakis; titis; uakaris)

737.P96 Pongidae (Apes)

737.P965 Tarsiidae (Tarsiers)

(737.P968) Tupaiidae (Tree shrews)
see QL737.S254

Proboscidea

737.P97 General works

737.P98 Elephantidae (Elephants)

Rodentia

737.R6 General works

737.R62 Abrocomidae

737.R623 Agoutidae (Pacas)

737.R624 Anomaluridae (Scaly-tailed squirrels)

737.R626 Aplodontidae (Mountain beavers)

737.R628 Bathyergidae (African mole rats)

737.R63 Capromyidae (Hutias)

737.R632 Castoridae (Beavers)

737.R634 Caviidae (Cavies)

737.R636 Chinchillidae (Chinchillas)

(737.R638) Cricetidae (New World rats and mice)
see QL737.R666

737.R64 Ctenodactylidae (Gundis)

737.R642 Ctenomyidae (Tucu-tucos)

737.R644 Dasyproctidae (Agoutis; acouchis)

737.R646 Dinomyidae (Pacaranas)

737.R648 Dipodidae (Jerboas; birch mice; jumping mice)

737.R65 Echimyidae (Spiny rats)

Chordates. Vertebrates
 Mammals
  Systematic divisions. By order and family, A-Z
   Rodentia -- Continued
737.R652 Erethizontidae (New World porcupines)
737.R654 Geomyidae (Pocket gophers)
737.R656 Gliridae (Dormice)
737.R66 Heteromyidae (Pocket mice; kangaroo rats)
737.R662 Hydrochaeridae (Capybara)
737.R664 Hystricidae (Old World porcupine)
737.R666 Muridae (Mice; rats; voles; lemmings; gerbils; hamsters)
737.R668 Myocastoridae (Coypu; nutria)
737.R67 Octodontidae
737.R672 Pedetidae (Springhares)
737.R674 Petromuridae
(737.R676) Platacanthomyidae
 see QL737.R666
(737.R678) Rhizomyidae
 see QL737.R666
737.R68 Sciuridae (Squirrels)
737.R682 Seleviniidae (Desert dormice)
737.R684 Spalacidae
 see QL737.R666
737.R686 Thryonomyidae (Cane rats)
(737.R688) Zapodidae
 see QL737.R648
   Scandentia
737.S25 General works
737.S254 Tupaiidae (Tree shrews)
   Sirenia
737.S6 General works
737.S62 Dugongidae (Dugongs)
737.S63 Trichechidae (Manatees)
   Soricomorpha
737.S7 General works
737.S73 Potamogalidae (Water shrews)
737.S74 Solenodontidae (Solenodons)
737.S75 Soricidae (Shrews)
737.S76 Talpidae (Moles)
   Tubulidentata
737.T75 General works
737.T8 Orycteropodidae (Aardvarks)
   Ungulata
737.U4 General works
    Artiodactyla (Even-toed ungulates)
737.U5 General works

Chordates. Vertebrates
Mammals
Systematic divisions. By order and family, A-Z
Ungulata
Artiodactyla (Even-toed ungulates) -- Continued
737.U52 Antilocapridae (Pronghorn)
737.U53 Bovidae
For domestic cattle, sheep, and goats see SF1+
737.U54 Camelidae (Camels)
737.U55 Cervidae (Deer)
737.U56 Giraffidae
737.U57 Hippopotamidae (Hippopotami)
737.U575 Moschidae (Musk deer)
737.U58 Suidae (Old World pigs)
For domestic swine see SF391+
737.U59 Tayassuidae (Peccaries)
737.U595 Tragulidae (Chevrotains)
Perissodactyla (Odd-toed ungulates)
737.U6 General works
737.U62 Equidae (Horses)
For domestic horses see SF277+
737.U63 Rhinocerotidae (Rhinoceroses)
737.U64 Tapiridae (Tapirs)
Xenarthra see QL737.E2+
738 Miscellany and curiosa
738.5 Genetics
739 Anatomy and morphology
For anatomy of domestic animals see SF761+
Cf. QL801+ Comparative anatomy
739.15 Cytology
Physiology
For physiology of domestic animals see SF768+
Cf. QP1+ Animal physiology
739.2 General works
739.23 Reproduction
739.25 Age determination
Behavior
739.3 General works
739.5 Migration
739.8 Ecology

Animal behavior
Class here general works on animal behavior and general works on particular types of animal behavior
For works on the behavior of special groups or individual animals, see QL360+
For comparative psychology and behavior of animals and humans see BF660+
For works on the behavior of special groups of domestic animals or individual domestic animals see SF756.7

750 Periodicals, societies, congresses, serial publications
750.3 Dictionaries and encyclopedias
750.5 History
751 General works, treatises, and textbooks
Cf. QH540+ General and animal ecology
Cf. SF1+ Animal culture
751.5 Juvenile works
751.6 Addresses, essays, lectures
751.65.A-Z Special aspects of the subject as a whole, A-Z
751.65.D37 Data processing
751.65.M3 Mathematical models
751.65.M32 Mathematics
751.65.S55 Simulation methods
751.65.S73 Statistical methods
751.7 Laboratory manuals
Special topics
Behavioral endocrinology. Endocrine aspects of animal behavior see QP356.45
752 Animal populations
For population studies of a particular group of animals, see systematic sections
Cf. QL607.6 Vertebrate population dynamics
Cf. QL618.3 Fish population dynamics
Cf. QL677.4 Bird population dynamics
Periodicity. Seasonal habits
753 General works
754 Migration
Cf. QL496.2 Migration of insects
Cf. QL639.5 Migration of fishes
Cf. QL698.9 Migration of birds
Cf. QL739.3 Migration of mammals
755 Hibernation
Sleep behavior
755.3 General works
755.5 Nocturnal animals
Habitations
756 General works
756.15 Burrowing. Burrowing animals

Animal behavior
Special topics -- Continued
756.2 Territoriality
Food
756.5 General works
756.55 Bloodsucking animals
756.56 Browsing
756.57 Cannibalism
756.6 Health behavior. Medicinal use
756.7 Drug use
756.8 Symbiosis
757 Parasitology
Cf. QL392.A1+ Helminthology
Cf. QL496.12 Parasitic insects and parasitoids
Cf. RC119+ Parasitic diseases of man
Cf. SF810.A3+ Parasitic diseases of animals
758 Predation. Predatory animals
Cf. SF810.5+ Predator control
758.5 Aggression. Agonistic behavior
Cf. QL100.5 Animal attacks
758.7 Reconciliation
759 Defense mechanisms
760 Grooming behavior
761 Sexual behavior
761.5 Familial behavior. Kin recognition
762 Parental behavior
762.5 Infanticide
Developmental behavior
763 General works
763.2 Critical periods. Imprinting
763.5 Play behavior
765 Sound production. Vocalization
Cf. QL496.5 Insect sounds
767 Color
768 Animal tracks and signs
Including droppings
Cf. SK282 Tracking
775 Social relations. Animal societies
Cf. QL364.5 Coloniality
775.5 Altruistic behavior
776 Communication
780 Eliminative behavior
781 Instinct
781.3 Motivation
782 Navigation
Cf. QL698.8 Navigation by birds
782.5 Orientation

Animal behavior
Special topics -- Continued
783 Swarming
Psychology. Intelligence. Learning
785 General works
785.2 Memory
Cf. QP406 Physiology
785.24 Number concept
785.25 Consciousness
785.27 Emotions
785.3 Extrasensory perception
(785.5) Special animals
see QL362+ or SF (Domestic animals)
Stories and anecdotes
For circus animals see GV1829+
For animals in television see PN1992.8.A58
For animals in motion pictures see PN1995.9.A5
For domesticated animals see SF1+
For wild animals as pets see SF459.A+
791 General works
793 Famous animals
795.A-Z Special. By common name of animal, A-Z
795.A35 African wild dog
795.A4 Alligators
795.A6 Antelopes
795.A8 Asses, Wild
795.B2 Badgers
795.B3 Bats
795.B4 Bears
795.B5 Beavers
795.B53 Bees
795.B57 Birds
Cf. SF460+ Cage birds
795.B6 Bison
Black eagle see QL795.B57
795.B8 Buffaloes
795.B85 Butterflies
Canada goose see QL795.B57
795.C2 Cats, Wild
Cf. SF445.5 Stories about domestic cats
795.C3 Cattle, Wild
Cf. SF197.4 Stories about domestic cattle
795.C5 Chamois
795.C54 Cheetahs
795.C57 Chimpanzees
795.C6 Coyotes
795.C65 Crabs

Animal behavior
Stories and anecdotes
Special. By common name of animal, A-Z -- Continued

795.C67 Crocodiles
795.D3 Deer
795.D5 Dingoes
795.D6 Dogs
Cf. SF426.2 Stories about domestic dogs
795.D7 Dolphins
Ducks, Wild see QL795.B57
795.E4 Elephants
795.E94 European wildcat
795.F65 Fireflies
795.F7 Fishes
795.F8 Foxes
795.F85 Frogs
795.G3 Gazelles
795.G5 Gibbons
795.G55 Giraffe
795.G7 Gorillas
795.H3 Hamsters
795.H35 Hares
795.H4 Hedgehogs
795.H6 Hippopotami
795.H65 Hornets
795.H7 Horses, Wild
Cf. SF301 Stories about domestic horses
795.J27 Jackals
795.J3 Jaguars
795.K3 Kangaroos
795.K62 Koalas
795.L5 Leopards
795.L7 Lions
795.L9 Lynxes
795.M3 Marmots
795.M37 Mice
795.M5 Minks
795.M57 Moles
795.M6 Mongooses
795.M7 Monkeys
795.M8 Moose
Mules see SF362
795.M85 Musk-oxen
795.M87 Muskrats
795.O7 Orangutans
795.O8 Otters
795.P18 Pandas

Animal behavior
Stories and anecdotes
Special. By common name of animal, A-Z -- Continued

795.P2 Panthers
795.P28 Peccaries
Ponies, Wild see QL795.H7
795.P6 Porcupines
795.P85 Pumas
Rabbits, Wild see QL795.H35
795.R15 Raccoons
795.R2 Rats
795.R4 Reindeer
795.R45 Rhinoceroses
795.R5 Ring-tailed phalangers
795.S3 Salamanders
Sea otters see QL795.O8
795.S43 Seals
795.S46 Sharks
795.S47 Shrews
795.S55 Skunks
795.S6 Sloths
795.S65 Snakes
795.S7 Squirrels
795.S9 Swine
795.T47 Thylacine
795.T5 Tigers
795.T8 Turtles
795.W4 Weasels
795.W5 Whales
795.W6 Wild boars
Wild dog, African see QL795.A35
795.W8 Wolves
795.W83 Wombats
795.Z42 Zebras

Morphology

Class here general works on animal form, structure, body size, etc.

For particular animals, see QL363+

799 General works, treatises, and textbooks
799.3 Juvenile works
799.5 Study and teaching. Research

Anatomy

Here are classified general works on comparative anatomy and special works on the anatomy of individual organs.

For works on the general anatomy or the anatomy of specific organs of special groups of animals, see the preceding systematic divisions or SF Domestic animals

For invertebrate anatomy see QL363

For human anatomy see QM1+

801 Periodicals, societies, congresses, serial publications
803 Collected works (nonserial)
803.3 Dictionaries
803.5 Nomenclature, terminology, notation, abbreviations
804 Early works through 1800
805 General works, treatises, and textbooks
806 Pictorial works and atlases
806.5 Juvenile works
807 Comparative histology
For special tissues see QM559+
808 Addresses, essays, lectures
Study and teaching. Research
810 General works
810.5 Problems, exercises, examinations
811 Outlines, syllabi
Laboratory manuals
812 General works
812.5 Dissection
813.A-Z By laboratory animal, A-Z
For specific organs or parts of the body, see QL821+
813.C38 Cats
813.D64 Dogs
Dogfish shark see QL813.F57
813.F57 Fishes
813.F75 Frogs
813.G63 Goats
813.G73 Grasshoppers
813.H35 Hamsters
813.M55 Mice
813.M56 Minks
Perch see QL813.F57
813.P54 Pigs. Swine
813.R3 Rabbits
813.R37 Rats
Sharks see QL813.F57
813.S69 Squids
Museums. Exhibitions
814.A1 General works

	Anatomy
	Museums. Exhibitions -- Continued
814.A2-Z	By region or country, A-Z
	Subarrange each country by Table Q5
	Skeleton. Osteology
	For histology see QM569
821	General works
822	Skull
823	Catalogs of specimens
825	Articulations
827	Ligaments
831	Muscles
	For histology see QM571
	Vascular system
835	Blood vessels
838	Heart
841	Lymphatics
	Respiratory organs
845	General works
846	Branchiae (Gills)
847	Tracheae in Arthropoda
848	Lungs
849	Pleura
851	Diaphragm
852	Respiratory passages
853	Larynx
854	Trachea. Bronchi
855	Air sacs, swimming bladders, etc.
	Digestive organs
856	General works
857	Mouth
858	Teeth
861	Pharynx. Esophagus. Tonsils
862	Stomach
863	Intestines
863.5	Peritrophic membranes
864	Peritoneum. Mesentery and omentum
	Glands
865	Salivary glands
866	Pancreas
867	Liver
868	Ductless glands
	Including spleen, thyroid, thymus, suprarenal, pineal, pituitary, carotid, etc.
	Urogenital system
871	General works
	Excretory organs

Anatomy
Urogenital system
Excretory organs -- Continued

872 General works
872.5 Nephridia
872.7 Wolffian body
873 Kidneys
873.5 Ducts
874 Bladder
875 Urethra

Reproductive organs. Copulatory organs

876 General works
878 Male
881 Female

Nervous system

For histology see QM575

921 Periodicals, societies, congresses, serial publications
923 Collected works (nonserial)
925 General works, treatises, and textbooks
927 Laboratory manuals. Neurological technique
931 Neural elements: Cells, fibers, supporting structures, etc.

Central nervous system. Brain

933 General works, treatises, and textbooks

Special types

935 Invertebrate
937 Vertebrate
938.A-Z Special structures, A-Z
938.A35 Afferent pathways
938.B73 Brain stem
938.C46 Cerebral cortex
938.C47 Cerebral ventricles
938.D44 Dentate nucleus
938.D53 Diencephalon
938.D65 Dorsal ventricular ridge
938.H56 Hippocampus
938.H94 Hypothalamus
938.L55 Limbic system
938.M4 Mechanoreceptors
938.M43 Medial geniculate body
938.N45 Neocortex
938.N48 Neural crest
938.O44 Olivary nucleus
938.P7 Prosencephalon
938.R53 Rhinencephalon
938.S6 Spinal cord
938.T45 Thalamus
939 Peripheral nervous system. Sympathetic nervous system

Anatomy -- Continued
940 Animal weapons for defense and offense
Integument. Skin
941 General works
942 Hair. Fur. Bristles. Whiskers. Scales. Nails. Hoofs. Horns
943 Skin glands. Odoriferous glands
944 Mammae
Sense organs
945 General works
945.5 Antennae
946 Tongue
947 Nose
948 Ear
949 Eye
Topographical and regional anatomy
950.1 General works, treatises, and textbooks
950.2 External form of the body
Trunk
950.3 General works
950.39 Buttocks
950.4 Neck
950.5 Head
950.6 Tail
Limbs
950.7 General works
950.75 Flippers
950.8 Wings
950.9 Segmental anatomy
950.95 Body cavities
Embryology
For special organs see QL821+
For human embryology see QM601+
951 Periodicals, societies, congresses, serial publications
952 Nomenclature, terminology, notation, abbreviations
953 History
Biography
954 Collective
954.2.A-Z Individual, A-Z
955 General works, treatises, and textbooks
Including general works on vertebrates or invertebrates
956 Pictorial works and atlases
956.5 Juvenile works
957 Laboratory manuals
Individual orders, genera, species, etc.
958 Invertebrate
959 Vertebrate
Special topics

Embryology
Special topics -- Continued
961 Experimental embryology
962 Behavioral embryology
963 Chemical embryology
963.5 Cell differentiation
Cf. QH607+ Cytology
Germ cells
964 General works
965 Oogenesis and ovum
966 Spermatogenesis and spermatozoa
For fertilization see QP273
Development of the embryo
Including twins, multiple birth, etc.
971 General works
971.2 Organizer
973 Allantois. Placenta
975 Amnion. Amniotic fluid
977 Chorion
979 Myogenesis
979.5 Chondrogenesis
981 Metamorphosis
991 Teratology

QL

Human anatomy
Class here only works that deal with human anatomy
For physical anthropology see GN49+
For comparative anatomy see QL801+
For works that include both human physiology and anatomy see QP1+

1 Periodicals, societies, congresses, serial publications
5 Collected works (nonserial)
7 Dictionaries and encyclopedias
Nomenclature, terminology, notation, abbreviations see QM81
11 History
Biography
16.A2 Collective
16.A3-Z Individual, A-Z
e.g.
16.L4 Leonardo da Vinci
16.V5 Vesalius
17 Directories
21 Early works through 1800
General works, treatises, and textbooks
23 1801-1969
23.2 1970-
24 Comparative anatomy of humans
Cf. GN281+ Human evolution. Man's place in nature
24.5 Anatomy of the child
Cf. RJ131+ Growth and development of children
25 Pictorial works and atlases
26 Popular works
27 Juvenile works
28 Special aspects of the subject as a whole
Study and teaching. Research
30 General works
31 Outlines, syllabi
32 Problems, exercises, examinations
33 Charts, manikins, etc.
By region or country
United States
33.1 General works
33.2.A-Z By region or state, A-Z
Subarrange each state by Table Q7
33.3.A-Z Other regions or countries, A-Z
Subarrange each country by Table Q7
Dissection
33.4 History
33.5 General works, treatises, and textbooks
34 Manuals of practical anatomy. Laboratory manuals
35 Outline guides

Dissection -- Continued
39 Laboratory technique
Laboratories
41 General works
43.A-Z By region or country, A-Z
Subarrange each country by Table Q6
Museums. Exhibitions
51.A1 General works
51.A2-Z By region or country, A-Z
Subarrange each country by Table Q5
71 Addresses, essays, lectures
81 Nomenclature, terminology, notation, abbreviations
100 Musculoskeletal system
Skeleton. Osteology
Cf. RA1059 Forensic osteology
101 General works
105 Skull
Cf. GN71+ Craniology
111 Vertebral column
113 Ribs and sternum
115 Hipbone and pelvis
117 Bones of the extremities
Articulations. Joints
131 General works
141 Ligaments
142 Articular cartilage
Muscles
151 General works
155 Of the head and neck
161 Of the trunk
165 Of the limbs
170 Tendons
Vascular system
For works on the blood vessels of a particular organ or system, see the organ or system
178 General works
181 Heart. Pericardium
191 Arteries and veins
197 Lymphatics
Organs of respiration and voice
251 General works
255 Larynx
Cf. QP306 Larynx physiology
257 Trachea. Bronchi
261 Lungs. Pleura
265 Diaphragm
Organs of digestion

Organs of digestion -- Continued
301 General works
306 Mouth
311 Teeth
325 Salivary glands
331 Pharynx. Esophagus. Tonsils
341 Stomach
345 Intestines
351 Liver
352 Gallbladder
353 Pancreas
367 Peritoneum. Mesentery and omentum
Glands
Cf. QM325 Salivary glands
Cf. QM351 Liver
Cf. QM353 Pancreas
368 General works, treatises, and textbooks
371 Ductless glands
Including spleen, thyroid, thymus, suprarenal, pineal, pituitary, carotid
Urinary and reproductive organs
401 General works
404 Kidneys
408 Ureters
411 Bladder
413 Urethra
416 Generative organs, Male
421 Generative organs, Female
431 Perineum
Nervous system
For works on the innervation of a particular organ or system, see the organ or system
451 General works
455 Brain
465 Spinal cord
469 Meninges
471 Peripheral nervous system. Sympathetic nervous system. Cranial nerves, etc.
Integument
481 General works
484 External skin
485 Bursae mucosae
488 Hair. Nails
491 Skin glands
495 Mammae
Sense organs
501 General works

Sense organs -- Continued
503 Tongue
505 Nose
507 Ear
511 Eye
Regional anatomy
Including surgical and topographical anatomy
531 General works, treatises, and textbooks
Special regions
535 Head and neck. Jaws
Trunk
540 General works
541 Thorax
543 Abdomen
Limbs
548 Upper. Arm and hand
549 Lower. Leg and foot
Human and comparative histology
Including microscopic anatomy and ultrastructure
For general comparative histology see QL807
550 Periodicals, societies, congresses, serial publications
550.2 Dictionaries and encyclopedias
Biography
550.5 Collective
550.6.A-Z Individual, A-Z
551 General works, treatises, and textbooks
Study and teaching. Research
552 General works
553 Outlines, syllabi
554 Problems, exercises, examinations
555 Laboratory manuals
Laboratory technique
556 General works
556.5.A-Z Special methods, A-Z
Embedding, Plastic see QM556.5.P53
556.5.F5 Fixation
556.5.L9 Lyophilization
556.5.P53 Plastic embedding
557 Pictorial works and atlases
Special tissues
559 Pigment
561 Epithelium
Cf. QP88.4 Physiology
562 Endothelium
Cf. QP88.45 Physiology
563 Connective tissues
565 Adipose tissues

Human and comparative histology
Special tissues -- Continued
567 Cartilaginous tissues
569 Bony tissues
Including bone marrow
569.5 Hematopoietic system
570 Blood vessels
570.5 Heart
570.7 Lymphathics
571 Muscular tissues
575 Nerve tissues
575.5 Blood-brain barrier
576 Endocrine glands
Generative organs
577 General works
577.4 Male
577.8 Female
Human embryology
601 General works, treatises, and textbooks
602 Pictorial works and atlases
603 Popular works
608 Research. Experimentation
611 Special topics (not A-Z)
Teratology
Cf. GT6730 Manners and customs
690 Early works through 1800
691 1801-
695.A-Z By region, system, or organ of the body, A-Z
Class clinical aspects in R
695.B36 Basicranium
695.B7 Brain
695.C37 Cardiovascular system
695.E95 Extremities
695.F32 Face
695.G45 Generative organs
695.N45 Nervous system
695.P76 Prosencephalon
695.U74 Urinary organs
695.V55 Viscera

Physiology
For the physiology of special animals or groups of animals see the systematic divisions QL364+
Cf. GN221+ Physiological anthropology
1 Periodicals, societies, congresses, serial publications
6 Collected works (nonserial)
11 Dictionaries and encyclopedias
13 Nomenclature, terminology, notation, abbreviations
21 History
Biography
25 Collective
26.A-Z Individual, A-Z
e.g.
26.H3 Harvey
26.P35 Pavlov
29 Early works through 1800
General works, treatises, and textbooks
31 1801-1969
31.2 1970-
33 Comparative physiology
33.5 Special aspects of the subject as a whole
33.6.A-Z Special topics, A-Z
33.6.C48 Chaotic processes
33.6.D38 Data processing
33.6.M36 Mathematical models
Human physiology
Including general works on human biology
General works, treatises, and advanced textbooks
34 Through 1969
34.5 1970-
35 Handbooks, manuals, etc.
36 School textbooks of physiology and hygiene
37 Juvenile works
38 Popular works
Study and teaching. Research
Cf. RA440+ Hygiene
39 General works
40 Problems, exercises, examinations
41 Outlines, syllabi
Experimental physiology
42 Elementary works
Including laboratory manuals
43 Advanced works
44 Laboratory manuals
Data processing see QP33.6.D38
45 Vivisection
Cf. HV4905+ Anti-vivisection

Study and teaching. Research -- Continued
47.A-Z By region or country, A-Z
Laboratories
51 General works
53.A-Z By region or country, A-Z
Subarrange each country by Table Q6
54 Technique
55 Instruments and apparatus
71 Addresses, essays, lectures
77 Miscellany and curiosa
Phenomena of animal life (General)
81 General works
81.5 Sex differences
81.6 Sexual orientation. Homosexuality
Influence of the environment (General). Animal ecophysiology. Physiological adaptation
Cf. GF1+ Human ecology
82 General works
82.2.A-Z Special topics, A-Z
82.2.A2 Acceleration
82.2.A3 Air pollution
82.2.A36 Allostasis
82.2.A4 Altitude
Anoxemia see QP177
Biomagnetism see QP82.2.M3
82.2.C5 Climate. Weather
Cf. QP82.2.H8 Humidity
Cf. QP82.2.T4 Temperature
82.2.C6 Cold
82.2.E4 Electrolytes
82.2.E43 Electromagnetic waves
82.2.G35 Gamma waves
82.2.G7 Gravity
82.2.H4 Heat
82.2.H44 Heavy metals
82.2.H45 Heavy particles
82.2.H8 Humidity
Immersion in water see QP82.2.W35
82.2.I45 Infrasonic waves
82.2.I5 Ionized air
82.2.I53 Ionizing radiation
82.2.L3 Lasers
82.2.L5 Light
82.2.M3 Magnetism
82.2.M5 Microwaves
82.2.M54 Millimeter waves
82.2.N6 Noise

Phenomena of animal life (General)
Influence of the environment (General). Animal ecophysiology. Physiological adaptation
Special topics, A-Z -- Continued

82.2.N64 Nonionizing radiation
82.2.P4 Pesticides
82.2.P6 Pollution
82.2.P7 Pressure
82.2.R3 Radiation
Radiation, Ionizing see QP82.2.I53
Radiation, Nonionizing see QP82.2.N64
Radiation, Ultraviolet see QP82.2.U4
82.2.R33 Radio waves
82.2.S8 Stress (Physiology)
82.2.T4 Temperature
Cf. QP82.2.C6 Cold
Cf. QP82.2.H4 Heat
Cf. QP135 Thermoregulation
Traffic and wildlife see HE5620.W54
82.2.U37 Ultrasonic waves
82.2.U4 Ultraviolet rays
82.2.U45 Underwater physiology
Cf. RC1015 Human underwater physiology
82.2.V5 Vibration
82.2.W35 Water immersion
82.2.W36 Water pollution
Weather see QP82.2.C5
82.2.W4 Weightlessness
Cf. RC1151.W44 Human space physiology

Developmental physiology
Cf. QL971+ Animal fetal development
Cf. RG600+ Human fetal development
Cf. RJ131+ Children
Cf. RJ140+ Adolescents
Cf. RJ252 Infants

83.8 General works, treatises, and textbooks
84 Growth
84.4 Puberty
84.6 Chronobiology. Periodicity. Biorhythms
For special applications, see the field, e.g. T55.3.B56 Industrial safety
85 Longevity. Prolongation of life
86 Aging. Senescence
Cf. QH608 Cell aging
Cf. RC580.P7 Progeria
Cf. RC952+ Geriatrics

Developmental physiology -- Continued
87 Death
Cf. QH671 Cell death
Physiology of the tissues (General)
Including physical and chemical properties
88 General works
88.15 Adipose tissues. Brown adipose tissue
Cf. QM565 Histology
88.2 Bone
88.23 Connective tissues
88.3 Hair. Fur. Wool
88.4 Epithelium
Cf. QM561 Histology
88.45 Endothelium
Cf. QP88.45 Histology
Muscle see QP321+
Nerve see QP361+
88.5 Skin
Cf. QP220+ Skin secretions
Cf. QP369+ Skin nerves
Cf. QP372.9 Galvanic skin response
Cf. QP450+ Cutaneous senses
88.6 Teeth
Cf. QP149 Mastication
89 Transplantation
Cf. RD120.6+ Surgery
90 Rejuvenation
90.2 Regeneration
90.4 Homeostasis
90.5 Body fluids
For lymph see QP115
For secretions see QP190+
For cerebrospinal fluid see QP375
90.6 Osmoregulation
90.7 Acid-base equilibrium
Blood
91 General works
92 Formation. Hematopoiesis. Bone marrow
Composition and chemistry
93 General works
Coagulation
Including fibrin, fibrinogen, thrombin, prothrombin, thromboplastin
93.5 General works
93.7.A-Z Special factors, A-Z
93.7.A58 Antithrombins
93.7.P76 Protein C

Blood
Composition and chemistry
Coagulation
Special factors, A-Z -- Continued
93.7.T45 Thrombomodulin
93.7.V65 Von Willebrand factor
Corpuscles and platelets
94 General works
Leucocytes. White blood cells
Cf. QR185.8.L48 Immunology
95 General works
95.2 Basophils
95.3 Eosinophils
Cf. QR185.8.E58 Immunology
95.4 Granulocytes
Cf. QR185.8.G73 Immunology
95.5 Lymphocytes
Cf. QR185.8.L9 Immunology
95.7 Monocytes
95.8 Neutrophils
Cf. QR185.8.N47 Immunology
Erythrocytes. Red blood cells
96 General works
96.5 Hemoglobin
Cf. QP99.3.G55 Glycosylated hemoglobin
Cf. RC641.7.H35 Hemoglobinopathy
96.7 Reticulocytes
Platelets
Cf. QR185.8.P58 Immunology
97 General works
97.5 Megakaryocytes
98 Blood groups
99 Plasma and serum
99.3.A-Z Special constituents, A-Z
99.3.A4 Albumins
99.3.A45 Alpha macroglobulins
Antithrombins see QP93.7.A58
99.3.A65 Apolipoproteins
Including individual apolipoproteins
99.3.B5 Blood sugar
99.3.C3 Carbon dioxide
Fibrin and fibrinogen see QP93.5+
99.3.G3 Gases
Cf. RB45.2 Examination of blood gases
99.3.G55 Glycosylated hemoglobin
99.3.H3 Haptoglobin
99.3.H35 Hematin

	Blood
	Special constituents, A-Z -- Continued
99.3.H37	Hematoblasts
99.3.H4	Hemocyanin
99.3.H45	Hemoerythrin
	Hemoglobin see QP96.5
99.3.H53	High density lipoproteins
99.3.L5	Lipids
99.3.L52	Lipoproteins
99.3.L68	Low density lipoproteins
99.3.O6	Oocytin
99.3.O9	Oxygen
99.3.P5	Pigments
	Platelet activating factor see QP752.P62
99.3.P7	Proteins
	Prothrombin see QP93.5+
	Thrombin and thromboplastin see QP93.5+
99.3.T72	Trace elements
99.5.A-Z	Other special, A-Z
99.5.A3	Agglutination
99.5.E5	Electrophoresis
99.5.H4	Hemolysis
99.5.S4	Sedimentation
	Cardiovascular system. Circulation
101	General works, treatises, and textbooks
101.2	Periodicals, societies, congresses, serial publications
101.3	Collected works (nonserial)
101.4	History of discovery and ideas on circulation. Harvey
(102)	General works see QP101
103	Juvenile works
104	Study and teaching. Research
	Hemodynamics Including pressure, velocity, flow, viscosity, etc.
105	General works
105.15	Rheology
105.2	Measurement of pressure
105.4	Measurement of flow
	Systemic system
106	General works
106.2	Arterial. Aorta
106.4	Venous
106.6	Microcirculation. Capillaries
	Special systems
107	Pulmonary system
108	Coronary system
108.5.A-Z	Other, A-Z

Cardiovascular system. Circulation
Special systems
Other, A-Z -- Continued
108.5.C4 Cerebral circulation
108.5.P45 Peripheral circulation
109 Vasomoter control. Baroreflexes
110.A-Z Other special topics, A-Z
110.A37 Adrenergic receptors
110.A7 Artificial circulation
110.B5 Blood volume
110.C64 Collateral circulation
110.G45 Gene expression
110.R3 Radiation effects
110.V34 Vascular endothelium
110.V37 Vascular muscle
110.V38 Vascular resistance
Heart
(111) General works
see QP111.4
111.2 Periodicals, societies, congresses, serial publications
111.3 Collected works (nonserial)
111.4 General works, treatises, and textbooks
111.5 Pictorial works and atlases
111.6 Juvenile works
Study and teaching. Research
112 General works
Research techniques
112.4 General works
112.5.A-Z Special, A-Z
112.5.A55 Animal models
112.5.C3 Cardiography
112.5.E4 Electrocardiography
112.5.E46 Electrophysiology
112.5.M33 Magnetocardiography
112.5.N83 Nuclear magnetic resonance
112.5.R6 Radiography
113 Cardiac dynamics
Including beat, rate, output, acceleration, rhythm
113.2 Myocardium
For specific myocardial characteristics see QP114.A+
113.4 Nervous control
113.6 Cardiovascular sound
114.A-Z Other special topics, A-Z
114.A32 Adaptation
114.A35 Aging
114.A57 Aortic valve
114.A75 Arrest, Cardiac

Heart
Other special topics, A-Z -- Continued
Cardiac arrest see QP114.A75
Cardiac membranes see QP114.M46
114.C37 Cardiogenic reflexes
114.C44 Cells
114.C5 Chemical effects
Cold see QP114.H94
114.C65 Conduction system
114.D5 Diastole
114.D54 Dilatation
114.E53 Endocardium
114.E9 Exercise effects
Heart cells see QP114.C44
Heart membranes see QP114.M46
114.H6 Hormone control
114.H94 Hypothermia. Cold
114.I8 Isolation. Survival
114.L94 Lymphatics
114.M43 Mechanical properties
114.M46 Membranes
114.M48 Metabolism
114.M65 Molecular biology
114.R3 Radiation effects
114.R43 Receptors
Reflexes, Cardiogenic see QP114.C37
114.R45 Regeneration
115 Lymph and lymphatic system
Cf. QP114.L94 Heart lymphatics
Respiration. Respiratory organs
Cf. QP177 Oxygen and metabolism
Cf. RA782 Breathing and exercises
121.A1 Periodicals, societies, congresses, serial publications
121.A4-Z General works, treatises, and textbooks
123 Regulation of respiration
123.5 Cough
124 Pulmonary gas exchange
125 Trachea
135 Thermoregulation. Animal heat. Body temperature
Cf. QP82.2.T4 Ambient temperature
136 Appetite
Hunger and thirst
Cf. RC620+ Deficiency diseases
137 General works
Hunger
138 General works
138.5 Starvation

Hunger and thirst -- Continued
139 Thirst
Nutrition
Cf. RA784 Personal hygiene
Cf. RG559 Pregnancy
Cf. RM214+ Diet therapy
Cf. SF94.5+ Animal culture. Feeding and feeds
Cf. TX551+ Home economics
141.A1 Periodicals, societies, congresses, serial publications
141.A2-Z General works, treatises, and textbooks
Study and teaching. Research
143 General works
Research techniques
143.4 General works
143.5.A-Z Special, A-Z
143.5.A58 Anthropometric assessment
143.5.M37 Mathematical models
143.5.R33 Radioactive tracers
143.5.S73 Stable isotope tracers
143.7 Nutrient interactions
144.A-Z Other special topics, A-Z
144.A77 Avocado
144.B48 Beverages
144.C46 Chocolate. Cocoa
144.C58 Citrus fruit
Cocoa see QP144.C46
144.C63 Coconut
Dairy products see QP144.M54
144.E44 Eggs
144.F52 Fiber
144.F56 Fish. Seafood. Marine products
144.F78 Fruit
144.F85 Functional foods
144.G45 Genetics
144.G73 Grain
Marine products see QP144.F56
144.M43 Meat
144.M54 Milk. Dairy products
144.O44 Oilseeds. Vegetable oils
Including individual oilseeds and vegetable oils
144.R53 Rice
Seafood see QP144.F56
Vegetable oils see QP144.O44
144.V44 Vegetables
Physiology of the digestive tract. Digestion
145 General works
Special organs

Nutrition
Physiology of the digestive tract. Digestion
Special organs -- Continued
Mouth. Pharynx. Esophagus
Cf. QP88.6 Teeth
Cf. QP188.S2 Salivary glands
146 General works
147 Ingestion. Eating
148 Deglutition
149 Mastication
150 Drinking
151 Stomach
Cf. QP193 Gastric juice
156 Intestines
157 Peritoneum. Mesentery and omentum
159 Feces
165 Absorption
Metabolism
Cf. QH634.5 Cell metabolism
171 General works
176 Energy metabolism
177 Relation of oxygen to metabolism
Including oxidation, anoxemia, etc.
180 Gastrointestinal motility
185 Liver. Gallbladder
Cf. QP197 Bile
185.3 Bile ducts
Glands
186 General works
Endocrinology. Endocrine glands
Cf. QP252+ Reproductive endocrinology
Cf. QP356.4 Neuroendocrinology
Cf. QP356.45 Behavioral endocrinology
Cf. RC648+ Endocrine diseases
187.A1 Periodicals, societies, congresses, serial publications
187.A4-Z General works, treatises, and textbooks
187.3.A-Z Special topics, A-Z
187.3.A28 Adaptation
187.3.A34 Aging
187.3.C44 Cellular control mechanisms
187.3.D38 Data processing
187.3.E93 Exercise
187.3.M36 Mathematical models
187.3.M64 Molecular endocrinology
187.3.S42 Second messengers
187.5 Endocrine genetics
187.6 Developmental endocrinology

Glands
Endocrinology. Endocrine glands -- Continued
Individual endocrine glands see QP188.A+
Exocrine glands
187.7.A1 Periodicals, societies, congresses, serial publications
187.7.A4-Z General works, treatises, and textbooks
188.A-Z Special glands, A-Z
188.A28 Adrenal cortex
188.A3 Adrenal glands
188.A33 Adrenal medulla
188.A6 Aortic paraganglia
188.C35 Chromaffin cells
188.H88 Hypothalamic-pituitary-adrenal axis
188.H9 Hypothalamo-hypophyseal system
Cf. QP188.P58 Pituitary gland
Cf. QP356.4 Neuroendocrinology
Cf. QP383.7+ Hypothalamus
Islands of Langerhans see QP188.P26
188.M3 Mammary glands
Cf. QP246 Milk
188.P26 Pancreas. Islands of Langerhans
Cf. QP195 Pancreatic juice
188.P3 Parathyroid gland
188.P55 Pineal body
188.P58 Pituitary gland
Cf. QP188.H9 Hypothalamo-hypophyseal system
188.S2 Salivary glands
Cf. QP191 Saliva
188.S26 Salt glands
188.S43 Sebaceous glands
Cf. QP222 Sebum
188.S7 Spleen
188.S9 Sweat glands
Cf. QP221 Sweat
188.T4 Tear glands. Lacrimal organs
Cf. QP231 Tears
188.T5 Thymus gland
188.T54 Thyroid gland
Secretions
190 General works, treatises, and textbooks
Digestive organs and glands secretions
190.7 General works, treatises, and textbooks
191 Saliva
193 Gastric juice
Cf. QP552.G35 Gastric intrinsic factor
195 Pancreatic juice

Secretions
Digestive organs and glands secretions -- Continued
197 Bile
Cf. QP671.B5 Bile pigments
Cf. QP752.B54 Bile acids
211 Urinary organs secretions. Urine
215 Mucous membrane secretions. Mucus
Skin secretions
220 General works, treatises, and textbooks
221 Sweat
222 Sebum
231 Lacrimal organ secretions. Tears
Other
235 Venom
246 Milk
246.5 Synovial fluid
Urinary and reproductive organs
247 General works
Urinary organs
Cf. QP211 Urine
248 General works
249 Kidneys
250 Ureters
250.5 Bladder
250.8 Urethra
Reproduction. Physiology of sex
Cf. HQ31+ Sex instruction
Cf. QP81.6 Sexual orientation. Homosexuality
Cf. RA788 Sexual health
251 General works, treatises, and textbooks
251.5 Juvenile works
Reproductive endocrinology
Cf. RG159+ Endocrine gynecology
Cf. RG558.5 Obstetrical endocrinology
Cf. RG616 Fetus
252 General works
252.5 Reproductive immunology
Cf. RG557 Obstetrics
Male sex physiology
253 General works, treatises, and textbooks
255 Testes and semen
Cf. QL966 Spermatogenesis
257 Accessory male organs
Female sex physiology
259 General works, treatises, and textbooks
261 Ovary and ovulation
Cf. QL965 Oogenesis

Urinary and reproductive organs
Reproduction. Physiology of sex
Female sex physiology -- Continued
262 Uterus
263 Menstruation
Cf. RJ140+ Physiology of adolescents
265 Accessory female organs
267 Hermaphroditism
273 Fertilization. Fecundation
For fertility see QP251
275 Ovum implantation
277 Physiology of the embryo
Cf. QL951+ Embryology (Zoology)
Cf. QM601+ Human embryology
Cf. RG610+ Human fetus
278 Sex differentiation
278.5 Sex determination
Cf. QH600.5 Sex chromosomes
Cf. RG566 Determination of sex during pregnancy
279 Sex preselection
280 Viviparity. Ovoviviparity
281 Gestation
Cf. RG499.2+ Obstetrics
285 Parturition
Cf. RG651+ Labor
Musculoskeletal system. Movements
Including physiology of exercise
Cf. GN231+ Physical anthropology
Cf. QP114.E9 Exercise effects on heart
Cf. QP187.3.E93 Endocrinology
Cf. RC1235+ Physiology of sports
301 General works, treatises, and textbooks
303 Mechanics. Kinesiology
306 Voice and speech. Larynx
Cf. BF463.S64 Speech perception
Cf. MT821 Voice culture
Cf. QM255 Larynx anatomy
Cf. RC280.T5 Laryngeal tumors
Cf. RC423+ Speech disorders
Cf. RF510+ Laryngeal diseases
Cf. TK7895.S65 Speech recognition systems
309 Work physiology
310.A-Z Other special movements, A-Z
310.C5 Ciliary motion
310.C55 Climbing
310.D35 Dancing
Deglutition see QP148

Musculoskeletal system. Movements
Other special movements, A-Z -- Continued

310.F5 Flight
310.G34 Galloping
Cf. SF289 Horses
(310.H36) Hand movements
see QP334
(310.H43) Head movements
see QP325
Ingestion see QP147
310.I7 Irritability
310.J86 Jumping
Mastication see QP149
310.P5 Phototropism
310.R45 Rhythmic movements
310.R85 Running
310.S45 Skipping
(310.S65) Spinal movements
see QP330
310.S77 Stretching
310.S95 Swimming
310.T9 Typewriting
310.W3 Walking
310.W7 Writing
310.3 Posture
310.5 Hypokinesia. Inactivity
311 Miscellany and curiosa
Muscle
Cf. QP113.2 Myocardium
321 General works
321.5 Smooth muscle
Cf. QP110.V37 Vascular muscle
322 Sphincters
323 Joints
By region
Head and neck
325 General works
327 Face
330 Spine
Upper extremities
333 General works
334 Hand
Lower extremities
335 General works
336 Foot

341 Electrophysiology
Cf. QL639.1 Fishes
Cf. QP372.9 Galvanic skin response
Cf. QP447.5 Electroreceptors
345 Magnetic field generation
Neurophysiology and neuropsychology
351 Periodicals, societies, congresses, serial publications
352 Collected works (nonserial)
352.5 Dictionaries and encyclopedias
353 History
Biography
353.3 Collective
353.4.A-Z Individual, A-Z
354 Early works through 1800
General works, treatises, and textbooks
355 1801-1969
355.2 1970-
356 Special aspects of the subject as a whole
356.15 Comparative neurobiology
356.2 Molecular neurobiology
356.22 Neurogenetics
356.25 Developmental neurophysiology
356.3 Neurochemistry. Brain chemistry
356.4 Neuroendocrinology
Cf. QP188.H9 Hypothalamo-hypophyseal system
356.45 Psychoneuroendocrinology. Behavioral endocrinology
356.47 Neuroimmunology
356.5 Radiation effects on the nervous system
357 Laboratory manuals
Cf. BF79 Psychology laboratory manuals
357.5 Data processing
359 Miscellany and curiosa
Neuropsychology. Physiological psychology. Psychophysiology
Cf. BF1+ Psychology
360 General works
360.5 Cognitive neuroscience
360.6 Neuroanthropology
360.7 Neuroergonomics
Nervous system
361 General works, treatises, and textbooks
361.5 Juvenile works
363 Miscellaneous general functions
Including excitation, impulse propagation, etc.
363.2 Neuroglia
363.3 Neural circuitry. Neural networks
363.5 Neurogenesis. Developmental neurobiology

Neurophysiology and neuropsychology
Nervous system -- Continued
364 Synapses
364.5 Neural transmission
364.7 Neurotransmitters. Neurotransmitter receptors
365 Inhibition (General)
365.2 Sensitization
Peripheral nervous system
365.5 General works
Cerebrospinal nerves
366 Cranial nerves
367 Spinal nerves
Autonomic nervous system
368 General works
368.5 Sympathetic nervous system
368.7 Parasympathetic nervous system
368.8 Autonomic ganglia. Paraganglia
Somatic nervous system. Muscle and skin nerves
369 General works
369.5 Neuromuscular transmission. Myoneural junction
Central nervous system
370 General works
370.5 Pyramidal tract. Extrapyramidal tracts
371 Spinal cord
Reflexes
Cf. QP416 Conditioned response
372 General works
372.5 Stretch reflex
372.6 Startle reflex
372.8 Visceral reflex
372.9 Galvanic skin response
(374) Other special topics (not A-Z)
375 Cerebrospinal fluid
375.5 Blood-brain barrier. Choroid plexus
Brain
Cf. QP108.5.C4 Cerebral circulation
Cf. QP356.3 Neurochemistry
376 General works
376.5 Electroencephalography
376.6 Imaging
Brain stem
376.8 General works
377 Medulla oblongata
377.5 Pons Varolii
Midbrain. Mesencephalon
378 General works
378.3 Substantia nigra

Neurophysiology and neuropsychology
Nervous system
Central nervous system
Brain
Brain stem
Midbrain. Mesencephalon -- Continued
378.4 Periaqueductal gray matter
379 Cerebellum
Cerebrum. Cerebral hemispheres
381 General works
382.A-Z Special lobes, A-Z
382.F7 Frontal
382.O22 Occipital
382.P3 Parietal
382.T4 Temporal
382.2 Corpus callosum
Cortex
383 General works
383.12 Neocortex
383.15 Sensorimotor cortex
383.17 Prefrontal cortex
383.2 Limbic system
383.25 Hippocampus
Basal ganglia
383.3 General works
383.5 Thalamus. Optic thalamus
383.6 Claustrum
Hypothalamus
Cf. QP188.H9 Hypothalamo-hypophyseal system
383.7 General works
383.8 Suprachiasmatic nucleus
383.9 Corpus striatum
384.3 Encephalic photoreceptors
Localization of functions
385 General works
385.5 Cerebral dominance
388 Brain stimulation techniques
Time relations of central processes, reaction time, etc. see BF317
Association of ideas see BF365+
395 Higher nervous activity
396 Information processing
398 Intellect
Cf. BF431+ Psychology

Neurophysiology and neuropsychology
Nervous system
Central nervous system
Brain -- Continued
399 Language. Speech
Cf. BF455+ Psychology
Cf. QP306 Speech
401 Emotions. Pleasure and pain
Cf. BF511 Psychology
402 Personality
405 Attention and volition
406 Memory
Cf. BD181.7 Philosophy
Cf. BF370+ Psychology
408 Learning
Cf. BF318 Psychology
Cf. LB1060+ Education
409 Motivation
Cf. BF501+ Psychology
411 Consciousness, subconsciousness, and unconsciousness
416 Conditioned response
421 Fatigue
Cf. BF482 Psychology
Cf. QP321+ Muscle
Sleep. Hypnotic conditions, etc.
425 General works
426 Dreaming
Cf. BF1074+ Parapsychology
427 Napping
430 Other special topics (not A-Z)
Senses. Sensation. Sense organs
Cf. BF231+ Psychology
Cf. QP137+ Hunger and thirst
431 General works, treatises, and textbooks
434 Juvenile works
435 General special
Perceptual process
441 General works
442 Intersensory effects. Multisensory processing
Multisensory processing see QP442
443 Space
Including orientation
Cf. QP471+ Equilibrium
Cf. QP491+ Visual space perception
445 Time
Sensory receptors

Neurophysiology and neuropsychology
Senses. Sensation. Sense organs
Sensory receptors -- Continued
447 General works
Chemoreceptors see QP455+
447.5 Electroreceptors
447.7 Magnetoreceptors
Nociceptors see QP451.4
447.8 Photoreceptors
For encephalic photoreceptors see QP384.3
Proprioceptors see QP454
Thermoreceptors see QP451.6
Special senses
Somesthesia
448 General works
Cutaneous senses
450 General works
451 Touch
451.2 Pressure
451.4 Pain
Including nociceptors
451.6 Temperature
Including thermoreceptors
454 Proprioception. Sense of movement. Muscular sense
Chemical senses. Chemoreceptors
455 General works
456 Taste
458 Smell
Hearing. Physiological acoustics
Cf. ML3820+ Physiology of music
Cf. QC221+ Sound (Physics)
460 Periodicals, societies, congresses, serial publications
461 General works, treatises, and textbooks
462 Popular works
462.2 Juvenile works
463 Limits of hearing
(464) Speech perception
see BF463.S64
465 Pitch and tone perception and discrimination
467 Rhythm. Melody
469 Localization of sound
469.3 Bone conduction
Equilibrium. Labyrinths of the ear
471 General works
471.2 Cochlea
Vision. Physiological optics
Cf. RE1+ Ophthalmology

Neurophysiology and neuropsychology
Senses. Sensation. Sense organs
Special senses
Vision. Physiological optics -- Continued
474 Periodicals, societies, congresses, serial publications
475 General works, treatises, and textbooks
475.5 Popular works
475.7 Juvenile works
Eyeball
476 General works
476.3 Intraocular pressure
477 Accommodation. Refraction
477.5 Movement
477.8 Cornea
478 Lens
479 Retina
Light perception and discrimination
481 General works
482 Night vision
482.5 After-images
483 Color vision
Binocular vision
487 General works
487.5 Binocular rivalry
Visual space perception
491 General works
492 Form, solidity, size
493 Movement
494 Peripheral vision
495 Optical illusions
Animal biochemistry
For works limited to chemical aspects of biological materials see QD415+
Cf. QH345 General biochemistry and plants and animals
Cf. QR148 Microbiological chemistry
Cf. RB112.5 Clinical biochemistry
Cf. RS400+ Pharmaceutical chemistry
501 Periodicals, societies, congresses, serial publications
509 Collected works (nonserial)
History
511 General works
511.5.A-Z By region or country, A-Z
Biography
511.7 Collective
511.8.A-Z Individual, A-Z
512 Dictionaries and encyclopedias
513 Early works through 1800

Animal biochemistry -- Continued
General works, treatises, and textbooks
514 1801-1969
514.2 1970-
517.A-Z Special topics, A-Z
517.A55 Allosteric regulation
517.B42 Binding sites
517.B44 Bioactive compounds
517.B48 Biochemical templates
517.B49 Bioconjugates
517.B5 Biodegradation
517.B53 Bioelectrochemistry
517.B54 Bioenergetics
Bioluminescence see QH641
517.B56 Biomimetics
517.B57 Biosynthesis
Biothermodynamics see QP517.T48
517.B58 Biotransformation
517.C45 Cellular signal transduction
Including second messengers
517.C49 Charge transfer in biology
517.C54 Chemiluminescence
517.C57 Chirality
Computer simulation see QP517.M3
517.C66 Cooperative binding
517.C78 Cryobiochemistry
517.D57 Dissociation
517.F66 Fossil biomolecules
517.H53 High pressure biochemistry
517.H93 Hydrogen bonding
517.L54 Ligand binding
517.M3 Mathematical models. Computer simulation
517.M65 Molecular dynamics
517.M66 Molecular orbitals
517.M67 Molecular recognition
517.P45 Photobiochemistry
517.P49 Physical biochemistry
517.P76 Protein binding
517.Q34 Quantum biochemistry
517.R4 Reaction rates
517.R48 Rheology
Second messengers see QP517.C45
Signal transduction, Cellular see QP517.C45
517.S83 Stereochemistry
517.S85 Structure-activity relationships
Cf. RM301.42 Pharmacology
517.S87 Surface chemistry

Animal biochemistry
Special topics, A-Z -- Continued
Templates, Biochemical see QP517.B48
517.T48 Thermodynamics
517.5 Biological chemistry as a profession. Vocational guidance
Study and teaching. Research
518 General works
518.3 Outlines, syllabi
518.5 Problems, exercises, examinations
519 Laboratory manuals
Technique. Analytical biochemistry
519.7 General works
519.9.A-Z Special methods, A-Z
519.9.A35 Affinity chromatography
519.9.A36 Affinity electrophoresis
519.9.A37 Affinity labeling
519.9.A94 Autoradiography
519.9.B55 Bioluminescence assay
519.9.B84 Buffer solutions
519.9.C34 Calorimetry
519.9.C36 Capillary electrophoresis
519.9.C37 Capillary liquid chromatography
519.9.C44 Centrifugation
Centrifugation, Density gradient see QP519.9.D45
519.9.C47 Chromatography
Chromatography, Affinity see QP519.9.A35
Chromatography, Countercurrent see QP519.9.C68
Chromatography, Gas see QP519.9.G37
Chromatography, Gel permeation see QP519.9.G44
Chromatography, High performance liquid see QP519.9.H53
Chromatography, Ion exchange see QP519.9.I54
Chromatography, Liquid see QP519.9.L55
Chromatography, Thin layer see QP519.9.T55
519.9.C57 Circular dichroism
519.9.C68 Countercurrent chromatography
519.9.D45 Density gradient centrifugation
519.9.E42 Electrochemical analysis
519.9.E43 Electrodes, Ion selective
519.9.E433 Electron paramagnetic resonance spectroscopy
519.9.E4333 Electron probe microanalysis
519.9.E434 Electrophoresis
519.9.E46 Enzymatic analysis
519.9.E48 Enzyme-linked immunosorbent assay
519.9.F52 Flash photolysis
519.9.F55 Flow injection analysis
519.9.F56 Fluorescence spectroscopy. Fluorescent probes

Animal biochemistry
Technique. Analytical biochemistry
Special methods, A-Z -- Continued

519.9.F58	Fluorimetry
519.9.G37	Gas chromatography
519.9.G42	Gel electrophoresis
519.9.G44	Gel permeation chromatography
519.9.H53	High performance liquid chromatography
519.9.I42	Immunoassay
519.9.I43	Immunoblotting
	Immunoblotting, Western see QP519.9.W47
	Immunoelectrophoresis see QR187.I47
519.9.I44	Immunoenzyme technique
519.9.I48	Infrared spectroscopy
519.9.I54	Ion exchange chromatography
519.9.I8	Isoelectric focusing
519.9.I84	Isotachophoresis
519.9.I87	Isotopes
519.9.L37	Laser spectroscopy
519.9.L55	Liquid chromatography
	Liquid chromatography, High performance see QP519.9.H53
519.9.L82	Luminescence immunoassay
519.9.L84	Luminescence spectroscopy
519.9.M3	Mass spectrometry
519.9.M64	Molecular probes
519.9.N8	Nuclear activation analysis
519.9.N83	Nuclear magnetic resonance spectroscopy
519.9.P48	Photoaffinity labeling
	Photolysis, Flash see QP519.9.F52
519.9.P68	Positron emission tomography
519.9.P84	Pulsed-field gel electrophoresis
	Radioactivation analysis see QP519.9.N8
519.9.R28	Radioactive tracers
519.9.R3	Radioimmunoassay
519.9.R34	Radioligand assay
519.9.R36	Raman spectroscopy
519.9.S45	Separation (Technology)
519.9.S58	Spectrophotometry
519.9.S6	Spectroscopy
	Spectroscopy, Electron paramagnetic resonance see QP519.9.E433
	Spectroscopy, Fluorescence see QP519.9.F56
	Spectroscopy, Laser see QP519.9.L37
	Spectroscopy, Nuclear magnetic resonance see QP519.9.N83
	Spectroscopy, Raman see QP519.9.R36

Animal biochemistry
Technique. Analytical biochemistry
Special methods, A-Z -- Continued
Spectroscopy, X-ray see QP519.9.X73
519.9.S85 Supercritical fluid extraction. Supercritical fluid chromatography
519.9.T55 Thin layer chromatography
519.9.T59 Time-resolved spectroscopy
519.9.T84 Two-dimensional electrophoresis
519.9.U47 Ultracentrifugation
519.9.U48 Ultratrace analysis
519.9.W47 Western immunoblotting
519.9.X72 X-ray crystallography
519.9.X73 X-ray spectroscopy
520 Handbooks, tables, formulas, etc.
521 Miscellany and curiosa
Special substances
525 Colloids
527 Radicals
Xenobiotics
529 General works
529.5 Plant compounds
Inorganic substances
531 General works, treatises, and textbooks
532 Metals
533 Minerals
534 Trace elements
Cf. TX553.T7 Food value
535.A-Z Elements and their inorganic compounds. By chemical symbol of principal element, A-Z (Table Q1)
Organic substances
550 General works, treatises, and textbooks
Proteins, amino acids, etc.
551 General works, treatises, and textbooks
551.5 Protein-protein interactions
552.A-Z Special proteins (other than amino acids, enzymes, or hormones), A-Z
552.A27 Actin
552.A32 Actomyosin
552.A43 Albumins
552.A436 Allosteric proteins
552.A439 Alpha fetoproteins
552.A45 Amyloid
552.A56 Antifreeze proteins
Antigens and antibodies see QR186.5+
Apolipoproteins see QP99.3.A65
552.A65 Aquaporins

Animal biochemistry
Special substances
Organic substances
Proteins, amino acids, etc.
Special proteins (other than amino acids, enzymes, or hormones), A-Z -- Continued

552.A87 ATP-binding cassette transporters
552.A94 Avidin
552.B65 Bone morphogenetic proteins
552.C17 C-reactive protein
552.C22 Calcitonin gene-related peptide
552.C24 Calcium-binding proteins
552.C28 Calmodulin
552.C29 Calreticulin
552.C3 Carnosine
552.C34 Carrier proteins
552.C35 Casein
552.C38 Cbl proteins
552.C42 Cell adhesion molecules
552.C45 Cerebrospinal fluid proteins
552.C48 Chromogranins
552.C56 Clusterin
552.C6 Collagen
552.C62 Collectins
552.C63 Connexins
552.C64 Copper proteins
552.C94 Cytochromes
552.C96 Cytoskeletal proteins
552.D95 Dystrophin
552.E4 Elastin
552.E53 Endorphins
552.E54 Endothelins
552.E55 Enkephalins
552.E59 Epidermal growth factor
552.E95 Extracellular matrix proteins
552.F37 Fatty acid-binding proteins
552.F47 Ferritin
Fetoproteins, Alpha see QP552.A439
Fibrinogen see QP93.5+
552.F5 Fibroblast growth factors
552.F53 Fibronectins
552.F54 Flavoproteins
552.G16 G proteins
552.G25 Galanin
552.G3 Gamma globulins
552.G35 Gastric intrinsic factor
552.G4 Gelatin

Animal biochemistry
Special substances
Organic substances
Proteins, amino acids, etc.
Special proteins (other than amino acids, enzymes, or hormones), A-Z -- Continued

552.G5 Globin
552.G55 Globulins
552.G58 Glutathione
552.G59 Glycoproteins. Glycopeptides
552.G7 Gramicidins
552.G73 Green fluorescent protein
552.G76 Growth factors
552.H3 Haptoglobins
552.H43 Heat shock proteins
Hemoglobin see QP96.5
552.H46 Hemoproteins
552.H48 Hepatocyte growth factor
552.H5 Histones
552.H9 Hypoglycin
Immunoglobulins see QR186.7+
552.I54 Insulin-like growth factor-binding proteins
552.I55 Integrins
552.I56 Interphotoreceptor retinoid-binding protein
Intrinsic factor see QP552.G35
552.I67 Iron proteins
552.I7 Iron-sulfur proteins
552.K4 Keratin
552.K46 Kinesin
552.K5 Kinins
552.L3 Lactalbumin
552.L345 Lactoferrins
552.L35 Lactoglobulin
552.L42 Lectins
552.L48 Lipocortins
552.L5 Lipoproteins
552.M44 Membrane proteins
552.M46 Metalloproteins
552.M47 Metallothionein
552.M54 Milk proteins
552.M64 Molecular chaperones
552.M8 Mucins
552.M85 Muscle proteins
552.M88 Myelin proteins. Myelin basic protein
552.M9 Myohemoglobin
552.M93 Myosin
552.N36 Nerve growth factor

Animal biochemistry
Special substances
Organic substances
Proteins, amino acids, etc.
Special proteins (other than amino acids, enzymes, or hormones), A-Z -- Continued

552.N37 Nerve proteins
552.N38 Neuropeptide Y
552.N39 Neuropeptides
552.N4 Neurophysins
552.N43 Neuropilins
552.N46 NF-kappa B (DNA-binding protein)
552.N62 Nonhistone chromosomal proteins
552.N67 Notch proteins
552.N82 Nucleopeptides
Nucleoproteins see QP625.N87
552.O65 Opioid peptides
552.O77 Osteopontin
552.O94 Ovomucoid
552.P25 p53 protein
552.P4 Peptides
552.P45 Peptones
552.P5 Phosphoproteins
Plasma proteins see QP99.3.P7
552.P56 Platelet-derived growth factor
552.P6 Polypeptides
552.P65 Pregnancy proteins
552.P7 Protamines
Protectins see QP552.L42
552.P73 Proteoglycans
Prothrombin see QP93.5+
552.Q55 Quinoproteins
Receptor-specific proteins see QP552.L42
552.S32 Semaphorins
552.S35 Seminal proteins
552.S37 Septins
552.S4 Sericin
Serum albumin see QP99.3.A4
552.S65 Somatomedin
552.S74 Steroid-binding proteins
552.S9 Substance P
Sulfur-iron proteins see QP552.I7
552.T33 Tachykinins
552.T37 Tenascin
552.T43 Thaumatins
552.T45 Thioredoxin
Thrombin see QP93.5+

Animal biochemistry
Special substances
Organic substances
Proteins, amino acids, etc.
Special proteins (other than amino acids, enzymes, or hormones), A-Z -- Continued

552.T47 Thrombospondins
552.T5 Thyroglobulin
552.T55 Thyroprotein
552.T68 Transcription factors
552.T7 Transferrin
552.T72 Transforming growth factors
552.T77 TRP channels
552.T82 Tubulins
552.T83 Tuftsin
552.U24 Ubiquitin
552.U86 Uteroglobin
552.V58 Vitamin K-dependent proteins
552.W58 Wnt proteins
552.Z55 Zinc proteins

Amino acids

561 General works, treatises, and textbooks
562.A-Z Constituents of proteins, A-Z
562.A7 Arginine
562.A8 Aspartic acid
562.B73 Branched chain amino acids
562.C9 Cystine
562.D53 Diamino amino acids
562.G5 Glutamic acid
562.G55 Glutamine
562.G58 Glycine
Glycocoll see QP562.G58
562.H5 Histidine
562.L4 Leucine
562.L8 Lysine
562.M4 Methionine
562.P5 Phenylalanine
562.P7 Proline
562.T5 Threonine
562.T7 Tryptophan
562.T9 Tyrosine
562.V3 Valine
563.A-Z Other, A-Z
563.A3 Adenosylmethionine
563.A38 Agmatine
563.A48 Aminobutyric acid
563.A5 Aminocapric acid

Animal biochemistry
Special substances
Organic substances
Proteins, amino acids, etc.
Amino acids
Other, A-Z -- Continued

563.C5 Citrulline
563.D5 Dihydroxyphenylalanine
DOPA see QP563.D5
563.D66 Dopamine
563.G32 GABA
Gamma-aminobutyric acid see QP563.G32
563.K33 Kainic acid
563.K9 Kynurenine
563.O7 Ornithine
563.T5 Thyroxine

Hormones
571 General works, treatises, and textbooks
571.5 Hormone inhibition
571.7 Hormone receptors
572.A-Z Special, A-Z
ACTH see QP572.A35
572.A27 Adrenaline
572.A3 Adrenocortical hormones
572.A35 Adrenocorticotrophic hormone
572.A4 Aldosterone
572.A48 Amylin
572.A5 Androgens
572.A52 Androstenedione
572.A54 Angiotensins
Including individual angiotensins
572.A82 Atrial natriuretic peptides
572.C3 Calcitonin
572.C33 Calcium regulating hormones
572.C36 Catechol estrogens
572.C47 Chalones
572.C5 Cholecystokinin
572.C53 Chorionic gonadotropins
572.C6 Corticosterone
572.C62 Corticotropin releasing hormone
572.C65 Cortisone
572.E25 Ecdysone
572.E27 Ecdysteroids
572.E8 Estradiol
572.E85 Estrogen
Cf. QP572.P48 Phytoestrogens
Estrogens, Catechol see QP572.C36

Animal biochemistry
Special substances
Organic substances
Proteins, amino acids, etc.
Hormones
Special, A-Z -- Continued

572.F6 Follicle-stimulating hormone
572.G3 Gastrin
572.G35 Gastrointestinal hormones
572.G45 Ghrelin
572.G5 Glucagon
572.G52 Glucagon-like peptide 1
572.G54 Glucocorticoids
572.G58 Glycoprotein hormones
572.G6 Gonadotropin
Growth hormone see QP572.S6
572.G75 Growth hormone releasing factor
572.H85 Hydroxyprogesterone
572.H9 Hypothalamic hormones
572.I47 Inhibin
572.I5 Insulin
Intermedin see QP572.M75
Lactogenic hormones see QP572.P74
572.L48 Leptin
572.L5 Lipocaic
572.L56 Lipotropin
572.L84 Luteinizing hormone
572.L85 Luteinizing hormone releasing hormone
572.M44 Melatonin
572.M66 Motilin
572.M75 MSH
572.N47 Neurotensin
Noradrenalin see QP572.N6
572.N6 Norepinephrine
572.O74 Orexins
572.O9 Oxytocin
572.P3 Parathyroid hormone
572.P33 Parathyroid hormone-related protein
572.P4 Peptide hormones
572.P47 Pheromones
572.P48 Phytoestrogens
572.P5 Pituitary hormone releasing factors
572.P52 Pituitary hormones
572.P57 Placental hormones
572.P67 Pregnenolone
572.P7 Progesterone
572.P74 Prolactin

Animal biochemistry
Special substances
Organic substances
Proteins, amino acids, etc.
Hormones
Special, A-Z -- Continued

572.P75 Prosecretin
572.P77 Protein hormones
572.R46 Relaxin
572.S34 Secretin
572.S4 Sex hormones
572.S59 Somatostatin
572.S6 Somatotropin
572.S7 Steroid hormones
572.T4 Testosterone
572.T46 Thymic hormones
572.T5 Thyroid hormones
Including thyroxine, thyronines, triiodothyronine
572.T55 Thyrotropin
572.T56 Thyrotropin releasing factor
572.V28 Vasoactive intestinal peptides
572.V3 Vasopressin

Enzymes
Cf. QK896 Plant enzymes
601 General works, treatises, and textbooks
601.2 Isoenzymes
601.3 Enzyme kinetics
Enzyme regulation
For works on regulation of individual enzymes or enzyme classes, see QP601.7+
601.4 General works
601.45 Enzyme activation
For works on activation of individual enzymes or enzyme classes, see QP601.7+
601.5 Enzyme inhibition
For works on inhibition of individual enzymes or enzyme classes, see QP601.7+
601.6 Extracellular enzymes
Metalloenzymes
601.7 General works
601.75.A-Z Special, A-Z
601.75.M35 Manganese enzymes
601.75.M64 Molybdenum enzymes
601.75.Z54 Zinc enzymes
601.8 Thiamin pyrophosphate-dependent enzymes
Oxidoreductases
602 General works, treatises, and textbooks

Animal biochemistry
Special substances
Organic substances
Proteins, amino acids, etc.
Enzymes
Oxidoreductases -- Continued

603.A-Z	Special, A-Z
603.A34	Alcohol dehydrogenase
603.A35	Aldehyde dehydrogenase
603.A37	Alpha-keto acid dehydrogenase
603.A4	Amino acid oxidases
	Amino oxidase see QP603.M6
603.A8	Ascorbate oxidase
603.C3	Catalase
	Catechol oxidase see QP603.D5
603.C45	Cholesterol hydroxylase
	Cytochrome c reductase see QP603.R4
603.C85	Cytochrome oxidase
603.C9	Cytochrome peroxidase
603.D4	Dehydrogenases
603.D5	Diphenol oxidase
603.F47	Ferredoxin-NADP reductase
603.G55	Glucose dehydrogenase
603.G57	Glucosephosphate dehydrogenase
603.H45	Heme oxygenase
603.H55	Histaminase
603.H88	Hydrogenase
603.H9	Hydroxylases
603.H92	Hydroxymethylglutaryl coenzyme A reductases
603.I54	IMP dehydrogenase
603.L33	Lactate dehydrogenase
603.L56	Lipoxygenases
603.M48	Methylenetetrahydrofolate reductase
603.M6	Monamine oxidase
603.M65	Monooxygenases
603.N58	Nitrogenase
603.O8	Oxidases
603.O85	Oxygenases
603.P4	Peroxidase
603.P43	Phenol oxidase
603.P74	Proline hydroxylase
603.P76	Prostaglandin synthase
603.P8	Pyruvate oxidase
603.R4	Reduced nicotinamide adenine dinucleotide dehydrogenase
603.R52	Ribonucleoside diphosphate reductase
603.S9	Succinate dehydrogenase

Animal biochemistry
Special substances
Organic substances
Proteins, amino acids, etc.
Enzymes
Oxidoreductases
Special, A-Z -- Continued

603.S94 Superoxide dismutase
603.T78 Tryptophan oxygenase
Tyraminase see QP603.M6
Tyrosinase see QP603.P43
603.U7 Urate oxidase
Uricase see QP603.U7

Transferases
605 General works, treatises, and textbooks
606.A-Z Special, A-Z
606.A33 Acetyltransferases
606.A43 Aminotransferases
606.A8 Aspartate aminotransferase
606.C45 Choline acetylase
606.C73 Creatine kinase
606.D46 Deoxyribonucleate nucleotidyltransferases. DNA polymerases
606.F7 Fructokinase
606.G5 Glucan phosphorylase
606.G57 Glucokinase
606.G573 Glucuronosyltransferase
606.G58 Glutamic-aspartic transaminase
606.G59 Glutathione transferase
606.G592 Glycogen phosphorylase
606.G6 Glycosyltransferases
Kinase, Protein see QP606.P76
606.M48 Methyltransferases
606.P53 Phosphofructokinase
606.P55 Phosphotransferases
606.P76 Protein kinases
606.P78 Protein-tyrosine kinase
606.R48 Reverse transcriptase
606.R53 Ribonucleate nucleotidyltransferases. RNA polymerases
606.S85 Sulfotransferases
606.T44 Telomerase
Transaminases see QP606.A43
606.T73 Transglutaminases
606.T75 Transketolase
606.U7 Uridine diphosphoglucuronosyltransferase

Hydrolases

Animal biochemistry
Special substances
Organic substances
Proteins, amino acids, etc.
Enzymes
Hydrolases -- Continued

608 General works, treatises, and textbooks
609.A-Z Special, A-Z
609.A25 Acetylcholinesterase
609.A3 Adenosine triphosphatase
609.A38 Alanine aminopeptidase
609.A4 Alkaline phosphatase
609.A43 Allantoinase
609.A438 Amidases
609.A44 Aminopeptidases
609.A45 Amylase
609.A53 Angiotensin converting enzyme
609.A7 Arginase
609.A77 Arylsulphatases
609.A86 Aspartic proteinases
609.A88 Astacins
609.B46 Beta lactamases
609.C26 Calpain
609.C3 Carboxypeptidase
609.C35 Cathepsin
609.C37 Cellulase
609.C38 Cellulose 1,4-beta-cellobiosidase
609.C39 Chitinase
609.C4 Cholinesterase
Chymosin see QP609.R4
609.C45 Chymotrypsin
609.C6 Coagulase
609.C64 Collagenase
Converting enzyme, Angiotensin see QP609.A53
609.C92 Cyclic nucleotide phosphodiesterases
609.C93 Cyclin-dependent kinases
609.C94 Cysteine proteinases
609.D4 Deoxyribonucleases
609.D48 Dextranase
Diastase see QP609.A45
609.D52 Digestive enzymes
609.D54 Dipeptidases
DNA restriction enzymes see QP609.R44
609.E38 Elastases
609.E4 Emulsin
609.E44 Endonucleases
609.E7 Erepsin

Animal biochemistry
Special substances
Organic substances
Proteins, amino acids, etc.
Enzymes
Hydrolases
Special, A-Z -- Continued

609.E8 Esterases
609.F7 Fructofuranosidase
Fructose diphosphatase see QP609.H5
609.G3 Galactosidase
609.G38 Glucose-6-phosphatase
609.G4 Glucosidases
609.G44 Glycoasparaginase
609.G45 Glycosidases
609.G83 Guanosine triphosphatase
609.H5 Hexosediphosphatase
609.H8 Hyaluronidase
Invertase see QP609.F7
609.K3 Kallikrein
Lactamases, Beta see QP609.B46
Lactase see QP609.G3
609.L43 Lecithinase
609.L5 Lipase
609.L55 Lipolytic enzymes
609.L9 Lysozyme
609.N48 Neutral proteinases
609.N78 Nucleases
609.N8 Nucleosidases
609.P3 Papain
609.P35 Paraoxonase
Pectinase see QP609.P6
609.P4 Pepsin
609.P45 Peptidases (Exopeptidases)
609.P5 Phosphatases
609.P52 Phosphatidate phosphatase
609.P53 Phosphodiesterase
609.P55 Phospholipase
609.P553 Phospholipase A2
609.P555 Phospholipase C
609.P56 Phosphoprotein phosphatases
609.P6 Polygalacturonase
Proteases see QP609.P78
609.P75 Proteinases (Endopeptidases)
609.P78 Proteolytic enzymes
609.P85 Pullulanase
609.R38 Renin

Animal biochemistry
Special substances
Organic substances
Proteins, amino acids, etc.
Enzymes
Hydrolases
Special, A-Z -- Continued

609.R4 Rennin
609.R44 Restriction enzymes, DNA
609.R49 Rho GTPases
609.R53 Ribonucleases
609.S47 Serine proteinases
609.S63 Sodium-potassium ATPase
609.S93 Subtilisins
609.S95 Sulfatases
Thrombin see QP93.5+
609.T7 Trypsin
Trypsinogen see QP609.T7
609.U7 Urease

Lyases
612 General works, treatises, and textbooks
613.A-Z Special, A-Z
613.A33 Adenylate cyclase
613.A4 Aldolases
613.A75 Aromatic amino acid decarboxylase
Carbonate dehydratase see QP613.C37
613.C37 Carbonic anhydrase
Carboxylase see QP613.P9
613.E56 Enolase
613.G8 Guanylate cyclase
613.O75 Ornithine decarboxylase
613.P54 Phenylalanine ammonia lyase
Phosphopyruvate hydratase see QP613.E56
613.P9 Pyruvate decarboxylase

Isomerases
615 General works, treatises, and textbooks
616.A-Z Special, A-Z
616.D54 DNA helicases
616.D56 DNA topoisomerases
616.P46 Peptidyloprolyl isomerase
616.P76 Protein disulfide isomerase

Ligases
618 General works, treatises, and textbooks
619.A-Z Special, A-Z
619.A45 Aminoacyl-tRNA synthetases
619.D53 DNA ligases
619.G58 Glutamine synthetase

Animal biochemistry
Special substances
Organic substances
Proteins, amino acids, etc.
Enzymes
Ligases
Special, A-Z -- Continued

619.L9 Lysyl ribonucleic acid synthetase
619.P87 Pyruvate carboxylase

Nucleic acids

620 General works, treatises, and textbooks

Ribonucleic acids

623 General works, treatises, and textbooks
623.5.A-Z Special, A-Z
623.5.A58 Antisense RNA
623.5.C36 Catalytic RNA
623.5.M47 Messenger RNA
623.5.S63 Small interfering RNA
623.5.T73 Transfer RNA

RNA-ligand interactions

623.7 General works
623.8.A-Z Special ligands, A-Z
623.8.P75 Proteins

Deoxyribonucleic acids

624 General works, treatises, and textbooks
624.5.A-Z Special topics, A-Z
624.5.A57 Antisense DNA
624.5.C57 Circular DNA
624.5.D72 DNA fingerprinting
624.5.D726 DNA microarrays
624.5.D73 DNA probes
624.5.M46 Methylation
624.5.M58 Mitochondrial DNA
624.5.R33 Radiation effects
624.5.R48 Replication
624.5.S26 Satellite DNA
624.5.S73 Stability
624.5.S78 Structure

DNA-ligand interactions

624.74 General works, treatises, and textbooks
624.75.A-Z Special ligands, A-Z
624.75.D77 Drugs
624.75.P74 Proteins
625.A-Z Other related substances, A-Z
625.A25 Adenine nucleotides
625.A27 Adenosine
625.A29 Adenosine diphosphate ribose

Animal biochemistry
Special substances
Organic substances
Nucleic acids
Other related substances, A-Z -- Continued

625.A3 Adenosine triphosphate
625.A35 Adenylic acid
625.B76 Bromodeoxyuridine
625.D56 Binucleoside polyphosphates
625.I54 Inosine
625.N34 NAD (Coenzyme)
625.N8 Nuclein
625.N86 Nucleohistones
625.N87 Nucleoproteins
625.N88 Nucleosides
625.N89 Nucleotides
625.O45 Oligoadenylates
625.O47 Oligonucleotides
625.P74 Pseudouridine
625.P87 Purine nucleotides
625.P96 Pyridine nucleotides
625.Q33 Quadruplex nucleic acids
625.T75 Triple-helix-forming oligonucleotides

Toxins and antitoxins
Cf. QR180+ Immunology
Cf. RM278 Immunotherapy

631 General works, treatises, and textbooks
632.A-Z Special, A-Z
632.B3 Bacterial toxins
632.B64 Bombesin
632.B66 Botulinum toxin
632.C87 Cyanobacterial toxins
632.C9 Cytochalasins
632.D54 Digitoxin
632.E4 Endotoxins
632.I57 Insect venoms
632.M37 Marine toxins. Marine venoms
632.M52 Microbial toxins
632.M9 Mycotoxins
632.P47 Pertussis toxin
632.R43 Recombinant toxins
632.S27 Saxitoxin
632.S65 Snake toxins. Snake venoms
632.T46 Tetrodotoxin
632.T75 Trichothecenes
632.V46 Venom
Cf. QP632.I57 Insect venoms

Animal biochemistry
Special substances
Organic substances -- Continued
Pigments

670 General works, treatises, and textbooks
671.A-Z Special, A-Z
671.B5 Bile pigments
671.B55 Bilirubin
671.C3 Carotenes. Carotin
671.C35 Carotenoids. Carotinoids
671.C45 Chlorophyll
671.C78 Cytochrome b
671.C8 Cytochrome c
671.C83 Cytochrome P-450
671.C85 Cytochromes
671.F5 Flavins
671.F52 Flavonoids
671.H4 Hematoporphyrin
671.H45 Heme
671.I5 Iodopsin
671.L52 Lipofuscins
671.M44 Melanin
671.P6 Porphyrins
671.V5 Visual pigments
671.X3 Xanthopterin

Carbohydrates

701 General works, treatises, and textbooks
702.A-Z Special, A-Z
702.A3 Agar
702.A35 Aglucones
702.A4 Amino sugars
702.A48 Amyloses
702.C5 Chitin
702.C55 Chondroitin sulfates
702.C8 Cyclitols
702.D38 Deoxy sugars
702.D4 Deoxyribose
702.F58 Fluorocarbohydrates
702.F68 Fructans
702.F7 Fructose
702.F73 Fructose-2,6-bisphosphate
702.G3 Galactose
702.G48 Glucans
702.G5 Glucides
702.G55 Glucosamine
702.G56 Glucose
702.G57 Glucuronic acid

Animal biochemistry
Special substances
Organic substances
Carbohydrates
Special, A-Z -- Continued

702.G572 Glucuronides
702.G577 Glycoconjugates
702.G58 Glycogen
702.G59 Glycosides
702.H4 Heparin
702.H45 Hexosamines
702.H8 Hyaluronic acid
702.I45 Imino sugars
Inosítol see QP772.I5
702.I5 Inulin
702.L3 Lactose
702.M8 Mucopolysaccharides
702.O44 Oligosaccharides
702.P4 Pectins
702.P45 Pentoses
702.P47 Peptidoglycans
702.P6 Polysaccharides
702.S28 Saponins
702.S6 Sorbitol
702.S75 Starch
702.S8 Sucrose
702.S85 Sugars
702.X87 Xylans
702.X89 Xylitol
702.X9 Xylose

Lipids

Cf. TP676 Chemical technology of animal fats and oils
Cf. TX553.L5 Lipids as a food constituent

751 General works, treatises, and textbooks
752.A-Z Special, A-Z
752.A25 Acetic acid
752.A5 Androstane
752.A7 Arachidonic acid
752.B54 Bile acids
Bile pigments see QP671.B5
752.C37 Ceramides
752.C4 Cerebrosides
Cholesterin see QP752.C5
752.C5 Cholesterol
752.C53 Cholesterol oxides
752.C55 Cholic acid

Animal biochemistry
Special substances
Organic substances
Lipids
Special, A-Z -- Continued

752.C6 Corticosteroids
752.C7 Croton oil
752.D54 Diglycerides
752.D63 Docosahexaenoc acid
752.E53 Eicosanoids
752.E84 Essential fatty acids
752.F3 Fats
752.F35 Fatty acids
752.F57 Fish oils
752.G3 Gangliosides
752.G5 Glycerides
Glycerin see QP752.G55
752.G55 Glycerol
752.G56 Glycolipids
752.G58 Glycosphingolipids
752.I8 Isobutyric acid
Isopentenoids see QP752.T47
Isoprenoid compounds see QP752.T47
752.L4 Lecithin
752.L5 Linoleic acids
752.L515 Linolenic acids
752.L52 Lipoxins
752.L8 Lysolecithin
752.L83 Lysophospholipids acid
752.M45 Membrane lipids
752.M9 Myelin
752.O42 Olive oil
752.O44 Omega-3 fatty acids
752.O45 Omega-6 fatty acids
752.O89 Oxysterols
752.P35 Palm oil
Phosphatides see QP752.P53
752.P52 Phosphoinositides
752.P53 Phospholipids
752.P62 Platelet activating factor
752.P65 Polyketides
752.P69 Prostacyclin
Prostaglandins see QP801.P68
752.P7 Protagon
752.P84 Pulmonary surfactant
752.S37 Saturated fatty acids
752.S6 Sphingolipids

Animal biochemistry
Special substances
Organic substances
Lipids
Special, A-Z -- Continued
Steroid hormones see QP572.S7
752.S7 Steroids
752.S75 Sterols
752.T47 Terpenes. Isopentenoids. Isoprenoid compounds
752.T63 Trans fatty acids
752.T7 Tributyrin
752.T74 Triglycerides
752.W3 Waxes
Vitamins
771 General works, treatises, and textbooks
772.A-Z Special, A-Z
Adermine see QP772.P9
772.A4 Aminobenzoic acids
Aneurine see QP772.T5
Antihemorrhage vitamin see QP772.V55
Antipernicious anemia vitamin see QP772.C9
Antirickets vitamin see QP772.V53
Antiscurvy vitamin see QP772.A8
Antisterility vitamin see QP772.T6
Antixerophthalmia vitamin see QP772.V5
772.A8 Ascorbic acid. Vitamin C
772.B5 Bioflavonoids. Vitamin P
772.B55 Biotin. Vitamin H
772.C3 Carnitine. Vitamin BT
772.C5 Choline
772.C9 Cyanocobalamine. Vitamin B12
772.E74 Ergocalciferol. Vitamin D2
772.F37 Fat-soluble vitamins
Folacin see QP772.F6
772.F6 Folic acid. Vitamin M
772.I5 Inositol
Lipoic acid see QP772.T54
Niacin see QP772.N55
Niacin amide see QP772.N5
772.N5 Nicotinamide. Vitamin PP
772.N55 Nicotinic acid. Niacin
Nicotinic acid amide see QP772.N5
772.P3 Pangamic acid. Vitamin B15
772.P35 Pantothenic acid. Vitamin B5
Pellagra preventive factor see QP772.N5
Pteroylglutamic acid see QP772.F6
772.P9 Pyridoxine. Vitamin B6

Animal biochemistry
Special substances
Organic substances
Vitamins
Special, A-Z -- Continued
Retinol see QP772.V5
772.R5 Riboflavin. Vitamin B2
772.T5 Thiamine. Vitamin B1
772.T54 Thioctic acid
772.T6 Tocopherol. Vitamin E
772.V5 Vitamin A
772.V52 Vitamin B complex
Vitamin B1 see QP772.T5
Vitamin B2 see QP772.R5
Vitamin B5 see QP772.P35
Vitamin B6 see QP772.P9
Vitamin B12 see QP772.C9
Vitamin B15 see QP772.P3
Vitamin BT see QP772.C3
Vitamin C see QP772.A8
772.V53 Vitamin D
Vitamin D2 see QP772.E74
Vitamin E see QP772.T6
Vitamin G see QP772.R5
Vitamin H see QP772.B55
772.V55 Vitamin K
772.V56 Vitamin K2
Vitamin M see QP772.F6
Vitamin P see QP772.B5
Vitamin PP see QP772.N5
801.A-Z Miscellaneous organic substances, A-Z
801.A25 Acetone
801.A26 Acids
801.A3 Alcohol
801.A33 Aldehydes
801.A34 Alkaloids
801.A35 Allantoin
801.A48 Amines
801.A63 Antibiotics
801.A65 Antimetabolites
801.A66 Antioxidants
801.A67 Antivitamins
801.A75 Aromatic compounds
801.A84 Aspartame
801.B5 Benzene
801.B52 Benzimidazoles
801.B53 Benzodiazepines

Animal biochemistry
Special substances
Organic substances
Miscellaneous organic substances, A-Z -- Continued

801.B55	Betaines
801.B66	Biogenic amines
801.B69	Biopolymers
801.C24	Caffeine
801.C27	Cannabis
801.C3	Carbolic acid
801.C3115	Carbolines
801.C312	Carboxylic acids
801.C33	Catecholamines
801.C4	Cerebrin
801.C48	Chlorophenols
801.C63	Citrates
801.C65	Citric acid
	Coca see QP801.C68
801.C68	Cocaine
801.C69	Colchicine
801.C7	Colicins
801.C75	Complex compounds
801.C8	Creatine. Creatinine
801.C83	Crown ethers
801.C86	Cyclic adenylic acid
	Cynurenic acid see QP801.K8
801.E28	Ecstasy (Drug)
801.F45	Flavor components
801.F5	Fluorine organic compounds
801.F67	Formaldehyde
801.F87	Furylbenzimidazole
801.G47	Germanium organic compounds
801.G57	Glutaric acid
801.G63	Glycolic acid
(801.G74)	Growth factors see QP552.G76
801.G8	Guanidine
801.G83	Guanidines
801.H34	Halogen organic compounds
801.H45	Hippuric acid
801.H5	Histamine
801.H78	Hydrazines
801.H9	Hydrocarbons
801.I4	Indican (metabolic product)
801.I43	Indocyanine green
801.I45	Indole
	Inositol see QP772.I5

Animal biochemistry
Special substances
Organic substances
Miscellaneous organic substances, A-Z -- Continued

801.I48 Insecticides
Interleukins see QR185.8.I56
801.I55 Ionophores
(801.I76) Isoprenoid compounds
see QP752.T47
801.K4 Ketones
801.K8 Kynurenic acid
801.L3 Lactic acid
Leucomaines see QP801.P7
801.L47 Leukotrienes
801.L53 Lignans
801.L97 Lysergic acid diethylamide
Macromolecules see QP801.P64
Marijuana see QP801.C27
801.M37 Mercapto compounds. Thiols
801.M39 Metformin
801.M42 Methoxyhydroxphenylglycol
801.M425 Methylxanthines
801.M43 Metiamide
801.M45 Mevalonic acid
Milk, Human see QP246
801.N44 Neopterin
801.N48 Nicotine
801.N55 Nitrogen organic compounds
Organo ...
For compounds with names beginning "Organo..." the Cutter number is determined by the element or substance following this prefix
801.O74 Orotic acid
801.O8 Oxalic acid
801.P28 Pantethine
801.P36 Penicillin
801.P374 Pentoxifylline
801.P38 Pesticides
801.P39 Phenethylamines
801.P4 Phenols
801.P56 Phosphonic acids
801.P63 Phosphorus organic compounds
801.P634 Phytic acid
801.P636 Phytochemicals
801.P638 Polyamines
801.P639 Polycyclic aromatic hydrocarbons
801.P64 Polymers. Macromolecules

Animal biochemistry
Special substances
Organic substances
Miscellaneous organic substances, A-Z -- Continued

801.P643 Polyurethanes
801.P654 PQQ
801.P68 Prostaglandins
801.P686 Psoralens
801.P69 Pteridines
801.P7 Ptomaines. Leucomaines
801.P8 Purines
801.P85 Pyrimidines
801.P855 Pyrrolizidines
801.P86 Pyruvic acid
801.Q5 Quinones
801.R4 Reductones
801.R47 Retinoids
801.S4 Serotonin
801.S44 Shikimic acid
801.S47 Sialic acid
801.S79 Succinic acid
801.S85 Sulfonic acids
801.T3 Taurine
Tetrahydrocannabinol see QP801.C27
801.T4 Thiocyanates
Thiols see QP801.M37
801.T57 Tobacco
801.T6 Tolylenediamine
801.U24 Ubiquinones
801.U7 Urea
Vitamins see QP771+
801.X45 Xenobiotics

(901-981) Experimental pharmacology

The Library of Congress has not classed new material on experimental pharmacology in these numbers since approximately 1981.

For works on the physiological effects of chemical substances on the animal body see QP501+

For works on experimental toxicology see RA1199+

For works on experimental pharmacology in general see RM301.25+

(911-981) Individual chemical substances

see QP525+ for the physiological effects of individual chemical substances on the animal body

For works on the physiological effects of drugs on the human body see RM300+

Microbiology
1 Periodicals, societies, congresses, serial publications
6 Collected works (nonserial)
9 Dictionaries and encyclopedias
11 Terminology, notation, abbreviations
12 Classification. Nomenclature
Cf. QR81 Bacteria
Cf. QR394 Viruses
13 Evolution
History
21 General works
22.A-Z By region or country, A-Z
Biography
30 Collective
31.A-Z Individual, A-Z
e.g.
31.F5 Fleming, Alexander
31.K6 Koch, Robert
Pasteur, Louis see Q143.P2
General works, treatises, and textbooks
41 Through 1969
41.2 1970-
By discipline
46 Medical microbiology
Cf. QR67+ Diagnostic technique
Cf. QR171.A1+ Microorganisms in the animal body
Cf. RC109+ Infections and parasitic diseases
46.5 Pharmaceutical microbiology
47 Dental microbiology
Cf. RK325 Oral sepsis
48 Sanitary microbiology
Cf. QR105+ Aquatic microbiology
Cf. TD1+ Sanitary engineering
Veterinary microbiology see SF780.2
51 Agricultural microbiology
Cf. QR111+ Soil microbiology
Cf. QR121 Dairy microbiology
Cf. QR351 Microorganisms of plant diseases
Geomicrobiology see QR103
Industrial microbiology
Cf. QR115+ Food microbiology
Cf. QR135+ Microbial degradation
Cf. QR151+ Microorganisms of fermentation
Cf. TP248.27.M53 Microbial biotechnology
53 General works, treatises, and textbooks
53.5.A-Z By industry or products, etc., A-Z
53.5.A44 Alloys

By discipline
Industrial microbiology
By industry or products, etc., A-Z -- Continued
53.5.C73 Coal
53.5.C76 Cosmetics
53.5.P48 Petroleum
53.5.R34 Railroads
Including railroad tracks, railroad ties, railroad beds, etc.
54 Pictorial works and atlases
56 Popular works
57 Juvenile works
58 Addresses, essays, lectures
60 Special aspects of the subject as a whole
Study and teaching. Research
61 General works
61.5 Problems, exercises, examinations
61.7 Experiments
62 Outlines, syllabi
63 Laboratory manuals
Laboratories
Cf. R108 Medical laboratories
64.A1 General works
64.A3-Z By region or country, A-Z
Subarrange each country by Table Q6
64.5 Culture collections
64.7 Safety measures
64.8 Quality control
Technique
65 General works
Culture technique
66 General works
66.3 Culture media
66.4 Continuous culture
Diagnostic technique
67 General works
67.2 Diagnostic bacteriology
Microscope technique
Cf. QH201+ Microscopy
68 General works
68.5.A-Z Special, A-Z
68.5.E45 Electron microscopy
69.A-Z Special topics, A-Z
69.A56 Anti-infective agent testing
69.A57 Antibiotic testing
Antiinfective agent testing see QR69.A56
69.A88 Automation
69.B53 Bioluminescence assay

	Technique
	Special topics, A-Z -- Continued
69.C3	Cataphoresis
69.C79	Cryopreservation
69.D35	Data processing
69.D48	Disintegration
69.D54	DNA probes
69.E43	Electric impedance measurement
69.E58	Enzyme-linked immunosorbent assay
69.F56	Flow cytometry
69.F7	Freeze-drying. Drying
69.G27	Gas chromatography
69.H54	High performance liquid chromatography
69.M33	Mass spectrometry
69.M48	Microbiological assay
69.M5	Micrurgy
69.N83	Nuclear magnetic resonance spectroscopy
69.P6	Population counts
69.S7	Staining
69.S75	Sterilization
69.V53	Viability counts
71	Laboratory equipment
72	Statistical methods
72.5	Handbooks, manuals, etc.
	Microbial genetics see QH434
73	Diversity and variation Cf. QR392 Virus variation
73.4	Development
73.5	Differentiation
73.6	Aggregation
73.7	Cell cycle
73.8	Microbial populations
74	Molecular microbiology
74.5	Protista Cf. QK564+ Algae Cf. QK600+ Fungi Cf. QK635.A1+ Slime molds Cf. QL366+ Protozoa
	Bacteria
74.8	General works
	Morphology. Ultrastructure
75	General works
75.3	Size
75.5	Shape
76	Protoplasm
76.3	Protoplasts
76.5	Nuclear materials

Bacteria
Morphology. Ultrastructure -- Continued

76.6 Plasmids
76.7 Pigments
77 Cell membranes
Cell walls
77.3 General works
77.35 Cell surfaces
77.5 Capsules. Slime layers
78 Flagella
78.5 Pili
79 Spores
79.5 Colonies
80 Terminology, notation, abbreviations
81 Classification. Nomenclature
81.5 Catalogs and collections
81.7 Evolution
82.A-Z Systematic divisions. By family or higher taxa, A-Z
Class individual genera under the family.
For unassigned genera and species see QR82.Z9
For bacteria of specific diseases see QR201.A+
82.A3 Achromatiaceae
82.A35 Actinomycetaceae
82.A355 Actinoplanaceae
82.A39 Aegyptianella
Aerobacter cloacae see QR82.E6
82.A43 Aeromonadaceae
82.A69 Archaebacteria
82.A9 Azotobacteraceae
82.B3 Bacillaceae
82.B35 Bacteroidaceae
82.B4 Beggiatoaceae
82.B95 Brucellaceae
82.C35 Chlamydiaceae
82.C4 Chlorobiaceae
82.C45 Chromatiaceae
82.C6 Corynebacteriaceae
82.C88 Cystobacteraceae
82.C9 Cytophagaceae
82.D37 Deinococcaceae
82.D4 Dermatophilaceae
82.E6 Enterobacteriaceae
82.F7 Frankiaceae
82.L3 Lactobacillaceae
82.L4 Leucotrichaceae
82.M38 Methylobacteriaceae
82.M4 Methylomonadaceae

Systematic divisions. By family or higher taxa, A-Z -- Continued
82.M45 Microbacteriaceae
82.M5 Micrococcaceae
82.M55 Micromonosporaceae
82.M8 Mycobacteriaceae
82.M95 Myxococcaceae
82.N4 Neisseriaceae
82.N5 Nitrobacteraceae
82.N6 Nocardiaceae
82.P25 Pasteurellaceae
82.P44 Pelonemataceae
82.P45 Peloplocaceae
82.P47 Peptococcaceae
82.P6 Polyangiaceae
82.P7 Propionibacteriaceae
82.P78 Pseudomonadaceae
82.R45 Rhizobiaceae
82.R46 Rhodospirillaceae
82.R47 Rhodospirillales
82.S5 Simonsiellaceae
82.S6 Spirillaceae
82.S7 Spirochaetaceae
82.S78 Streptococcaceae
82.S8 Streptomycetaceae
82.T7 Treponemataceae
82.V4 Veillonellaceae
82.V53 Vibrionaceae
82.Z9 Genera and species as yet unassigned (not A-Z)
Physiology
84 General works
Growth
Cf. QR66+ Culture technique
84.5 General works
84.7 Psychrophilic bacteria
84.8 Thermophilic bacteria
86 Nutrition
86.5 Reproduction
Metabolism
88 General works
88.2 Autotrophy
88.3 Biosynthesis
88.4 Methylotrophy
88.5 Photosynthesis
Cf. QK882 Plant physiology
88.7 Chemoautotrophy
Respiration
89 General works

Bacteria
Physiology
Metabolism
Respiration -- Continued

89.5	Anaerobic
89.7	Nitrogen fixation Cf. TP245.N8 Chemical engineering
90	Enzymes
92.A-Z	Other substances, A-Z
92.A3	Acetic acid
92.A49	Alkanes
92.A6	Amino acids
92.B3	Bacteriocins
92.B7	Branched chain amino acids
92.C27	Calcium
92.C3	Carbohydrates
92.C33	Carbon dioxide
92.C55	Chlorinated aromatic compounds
92.C57	Citric acid
92.C74	Creatine
92.D45	Deoxyribonucleic acid. DNA
	DNA see QR92.D45
92.F3	Fatty acids
92.F87	Furans
92.G35	Galactose
92.G5	Glucose
92.H6	Hormones
92.H8	Hydrogen
92.I4	Immunoglobulin-binding proteins
92.I7	Iron
92.L5	Lipids
92.M45	Metals
92.M46	Methane
92.M47	Methyl groups
92.M5	Minerals
92.N5	Nicotinic acid
92.N6	Nitrogen
92.N8	Nucleic acids
92.N82	Nucleotides
	Oxygen see QR89+
92.P37	Peptides
92.P39	Peptidoglycans
92.P4	Phenols
92.P45	Phosphates
92.P58	Poly-beta-hydroxyalkanoates
92.P59	Polymers
92.P6	Polysaccharides

Bacteria
Physiology
Metabolism
Other substances, A-Z -- Continued

92.P7 Propionic acid
Protein A, Staphylococcal see QR92.S68
92.P75 Proteins
92.P87 Purines
92.S3 Salts
92.S53 Siderophores
92.S68 Staphylococcal protein A
92.S7 Steroids
92.S79 Sugars
92.S8 Sulfur
92.V5 Vitamins
92.X35 Xanthan gum
93 Anhydrobiosis
94 Heat production
95 Light production
96 Motility. Irritability
96.5 Interaction. Communication
96.8 Adhesion
Environmental factors
97.A1 General works
97.A2-Z By factor, A-Z
97.A3 Acidity. Alkalinity. Hydrogen-ion concentration
Alkalinity see QR97.A3
97.A57 Anti-infective agents
97.A58 Antibiotics
97.B32 Bactericides
97.C3 Carbon dioxide
97.C5 Chemicals
97.E5 Electrolytes
97.H4 Heat
Hydrogen-ion concentration see QR97.A3
97.L5 Light
97.M34 Magnetism
(97.M6) Moisture
see QR97.W37
97.O8 Oxygen
97.P47 Pesticides
97.P7 Pressure
97.R3 Radiation
97.S3 Salinity
97.T4 Temperature
Cf. QR84.7 Psychrophilic bacteria
Cf. QR84.8 Thermophilic bacteria

Bacteria
Physiology
Environmental factors
By factor, A-Z -- Continued
97.W37 Water. Moisture
97.X46 Xenobiotics
Antibiosis
Cf. QP801.A63 Biochemistry of antibiotics
Cf. QR69.A57 Testing
Cf. QR175 Virulence
Cf. RM265+ Antibiotic therapy
Cf. RM666.A+ Pharmacology of individual antibiotic drugs
Cf. RS431.A6 Pharmaceutical chemistry of antibiotics
99 General works
99.5 Resistance
Cyanobacteria
99.6 Periodicals. Serials
99.62 Congresses
99.63 General works, treatises, and textbooks
99.64 Pictorial works and atlases
99.65 Popular works
99.66 Juvenile works
99.67 Classification. Nomenclature
99.69.A-Z Special topics, A-Z
99.69.B55 Blooms
Cyanobacterial blooms see QR99.69.B55
99.7.A-Z Systematic divisions. By family, A-Z
99.7.E57 Entophysalidaceae
99.7.N67 Nostocaceae
99.7.O82 Oscillatoriaceae
99.7.S39 Scytonemataceae
99.7.S85 Stigonemataceae
99.8.A-Z By region or country, A-Z
Microbial ecology. Geographical distribution
100 General works, treatises, and textbooks
100.8.A-Z By type of relationship, A-Z
100.8.B55 Biofilms
100.8.C65 Competition
100.8.D46 Denitrification
Including denitrifying bacteria
100.8.M37 Mats
100.8.S9 Symbiosis
By type of environment
100.9 Extreme environments (General)
101 Air and dust
103 Geomicrobiology. Microbial effect on geological processes

Microbial ecology
By type of environment -- Continued
Water. Aquatic microbiology
105 General works
105.5 Freshwater
Cf. TD384 Water supply analysis
Seawater. Marine microbiology
106 General works
106.5 Hydrothermal vents
107 Hot springs. Calderas
Soil
Including soil fungi
Cf. QK604.2.M92 Mycorrhizal fungi
111 General works
113 Root nodules
Cf. S652 Soil inoculation
Foods
Cf. TP371.2+ Preservation in food processing
Cf. TX599+ Food preservation in the home
115 General works
116 Eggs
117 Meat
118 Fish. Shellfish
119 Breads. Cereals
121 Dairy products
Cf. SF253 Milk analysis
122 Fruit. Vegetables (General)
123 Canned foods
129.A-Z Other food products, A-Z
129.B44 Beer
129.C6 Corn oil
129.F7 Fruit juice
129.S8 Sugar
129.T65 Tomatoes
130 Space microbiology
131.A-Z Other environments, A-Z
131.G58 Glaciers
Pathogenic fungi see QR245+
Microbial degradation
135 General works
135.5.A-Z Special substances, A-Z
135.5.C65 Compost
135.5.M37 Metals

148 Microbiological chemistry
Cf. QK861+ Plant biochemistry
Cf. QP501+ Animal biochemistry
Cf. QR88.3 Bacterial biosynthesis
Cf. QR467 Biochemistry of viruses
Microorganisms of fermentation. Yeasts, etc.
Including diseases of wine and beer
Cf. TP371.44 Preserving food by fermentation
Cf. TP568+ Brewing
151 General works
(155) Yeasts and yeastlike fungi in the body
see QR171
160 Microorganisms of cellulose and other plant products
Microorganisms in the animal body
Cf. QR201.A+ Pathogenic microorganisms
Cf. QR245+ Pathogenic fungi
Cf. QR301+ Pathogenic fungi
Cf. RM666.P835 Probiotics
171.A1 General works, treatises, and textbooks
171.A2-Z By organ or system, etc., A-Z
171.A43 Alimentary canal
171.B5 Blood
171.E9 Eye
171.F4 Feces. Manure
171.F45 Female generative organs
171.G29 Gastrointestinal system
171.G4 Generative organs
Generative organs, Female see QR171.F45
171.G47 Germplasm
171.I6 Intestines
171.L8 Lungs
Manure see QR171.F4
Mouth see QR47
171.N3 Nasopharyngeal system
171.R85 Rumen
171.S5 Skin
171.S8 Stomach
Teeth see QR47
171.U7 Urinary system
175 Virulence. Pathogenic action in general
Cf. QP631+ Toxins (Animal biochemistry)
177 Drug resistance

Immunology
Cf. QL362.85 Invertebrates
Cf. QL638.97 Fishes
Cf. QP252.5 Reproductive immunology
Cf. QP356.47 Neuroimmunology
Cf. RA638 Public health
Cf. RC581+ Immunologic diseases
Cf. RG557 Obstetrics
Cf. RM270+ Immunotherapy
Cf. RM370+ Immunopharmacology
Cf. SF757.2+ Veterinary immunology

180 Periodicals, societies, serial publications
180.2 Collected works (nonserial)
180.3 Congresses
180.4 Dictionaries and encyclopedias
Biography
180.7 Collective
180.72.A-Z Individual, A-Z
181 General works, treatises, and textbooks
181.5 Addresses, essays, lectures
181.7 Popular works
181.8 Juvenile works
182 Special aspects of the subject as a whole
182.2.A-Z Special topics, A-Z
182.2.A54 Animal models
Including specific animal models
182.2.C65 Computer simulation
182.2.E94 Evolution
182.2.I46 Immunoinformatics
182.2.M36 Mathematical models
182.2.N86 Nutritional aspects
Space flight see RC1151.I45
182.2.S7 Statistical methods
Study and teaching. Research
182.5 General works
182.55 Outlines, syllabi
182.6 Problems, exercises, examinations
Laboratory methods
For specific tests see QR187.A2+
183 General works
183.2 Tracers
183.5 Immunotechnology
183.6 Immunochemistry
Cf. QR187.I45 Immunocytochemistry
183.8 Immunotaxonomy
Immunogenetics
184 General works

QR

Immunology

Immunogenetics -- Continued

184.2 Human immunogenetics

Histocompatibility. H-2 locus

184.3 General works

184.315 Major histocompatibility complex

184.32 HLA antigens

Minor histocompatibility antigens

184.34 General works

184.35 H-Y antigen

184.4 Ir genes. Ia antigens

184.5 Developmental immunology

184.6 Phylogeny of the immune system

Types of immunity

185.2 Natural

Acquired

185.3 General works

185.33 Maternally acquired immunity

185.35 Immunologic memory

185.4 Humoral

185.5 Cellular

185.6 Molecular aspects. Molecular immunology

Immune structures

185.7 General works

185.8.A-Z By type, A-Z

Antibody-drug conjugates see RS201.A56

185.8.A58 Antibody-toxin conjugates

185.8.A59 Antigen presenting cells

185.8.B15 B cells

185.8.B54 Biological response modifiers

185.8.C45 Chemokines

185.8.C6 Complement

Cf. QR187.C6 Complement fixation

185.8.C95 Cytokines

185.8.D45 Dendritic cells

185.8.E58 Eosinophils

Cf. QP95.3 Physiology

185.8.F33 Fc receptors

185.8.G4 Germinal centers

185.8.G73 Granulocytes

Cf. QP95.4 Physiology

185.8.H93 Hybridomas

Cf. QH451 Cell fusion

185.8.I45 Immune complexes

185.8.I56 Interleukins

Including interleukin-1, interleukin-2, etc.

185.8.K54 Killer cells

Immunology
Immune structures
By type, A-Z -- Continued
185.8.L35 Langerhans cells
185.8.L48 Leucocytes
Cf. QP95+ Physiology
185.8.L49 Leukolysins
185.8.L9 Lymphocytes
185.8.L93 Lymphokines
185.8.M28 Macrophage migration inhibitory factor
185.8.M3 Macrophages
185.8.M35 Mast cells
185.8.M36 Mathematical models
185.8.N47 Neutrophils
185.8.O7 Opsonin
Cf. QR187.P4 Phagocytosis
185.8.P45 Phagocytes
Cf. QR187.P4 Phagocytosis
185.8.P58 Platelets
Cf. QP97+ Physiology
185.8.S65 Spleen
185.8.S96 Suppressor cells
185.8.T2 T cells
185.8.T24 Th cells
Thrombocytes see QR185.8.P58
185.8.T48 Thymus
185.8.T67 Transfer factor
Cf. RM282.T7 Therapeutic use
185.8.T7 Trophoblast
185.8.T84 Tumor necrosis factor
185.9.A-Z By organ or system, etc., A-Z
185.9.G37 Gastrointestinal system
185.9.L58 Liver
185.9.M83 Mucous membrane
185.95 Immune recognition
Immune response
Class here works on the mechanism of immune response in humans or laboratory animals
For works on the immunology of specific animals or groups of animals, other than laboratory animals, see the systematic divisions in QL. For works on the immune response to particular diseases or parasites, see the disease or parasite in R or SF
186 General works
186.3 Idiotypic networks
Antigens
186.5 General works

Immunology
Antigens -- Continued

186.6.A-Z By type, A-Z
186.6.B33 Bacterial antigens
Blood group antigens see QP98
186.6.C37 Carbohydrates
186.6.C42 CD antigens
Including CD23 antigen, CD26 antigen, etc.
186.6.C44 Cell surface antigens
186.6.F85 Fungal antigens
186.6.G73 Granulocyte antigens
H-Y antigen see QR184.35
186.6.H3 Haptens
186.6.H42 Heat shock proteins
Histocompatibility antigens see QR184.3+
HLA antigens see QR184.32
186.6.L94 Lysozyme
186.6.P38 Parasite antigens
186.6.P76 Proteins
186.6.S64 Spermatozoa
186.6.S94 Superantigens
186.6.S95 Synthetic antigens
186.6.T48 Thy-1 antigen
186.6.T57 Tissue-specific antigens
186.6.T6 Toxins
186.6.T65 Toxoids
Tumor antigens see QR188.6
186.6.V57 Viral antigens

Antibodies. Immunoglobulins
186.7 General works
186.8.A-Z By type, A-Z
186.8.A2 IgA. Immunoglobulin A
186.8.D2 IgD. Immunoglobulin D
186.8.E2 IgE. Immunoglobulin E
186.8.G2 IgG. Immunoglobulin G
186.8.M2 IgM. Immunoglobulin M
Autoantibodies
186.82 General works
186.83.A-Z By type, A-Z
186.83.P48 Phospholipid antibodies
186.83.R48 Rheumatoid factor
186.85 Monoclonal antibodies
Cf. RM282.M65 Therapeutic use
186.87 Recombinant antibodies
186.9 Specificity

Antigen-antibody reactions
Class tests with type of reaction

Immunology
Antigen-antibody reactions -- Continued
187.A1 General works, treatises, and textbooks
187.A2-Z By type, A-Z
187.A3 Agglutination
187.A8 Autolysis
187.B3 Bacteriolysis
187.C48 Chemiluminescence immunoassay
187.C6 Complement fixation
187.C65 Conglutination
187.D3 Danysz phenomenon
187.F58 Fluorescent antigen technique
187.H38 Hemagglutination tests
187.H4 Hemolysis
187.H45 Hemolytic plaque technique
187.H57 Histocompatibility testing
187.I44 Immunoadsorption
187.I45 Immunocytochemistry
187.I46 Immunodiffusion
187.I47 Immunoelectrophoresis
187.I48 Immunofluorescence
187.I482 Immunogold labeling
187.I486 Immunophenotyping
187.L47 Leucocyte adherence inhibition test
187.P4 Phagocytosis
187.P7 Precipitation
187.S4 Sedimentation
187.3 Adjuvants
187.4 Chemotaxis
187.5 Interferons
188 Hypersensitivity. Allergy
Cf. RC583+ Diseases
188.3 Autoimmunity
For autoantibodies see QR186.82+
Cf. RC600 Autoimmune diseases
188.35 Immunodeficiency
Cf. RC606+ Medicine
Cf. RJ387.D42 Pediatrics
188.4 Tolerance
Immunosuppression
188.45 General works
188.46 Virus-induced immunosuppression
188.5 Radiation immunology
188.6 Tumor immunology
Cf. RC268.3 Immunological aspects

QR

	Immunology -- Continued
188.8	Transplantation immunology
	Cf. QP89 Physiology of the tissues
	Cf. RD120.6+ Surgery
	Vaccines
	Cf. RA638 Vaccination in public health
	Cf. RM281 Vaccinotherapy
189	General works, treatises, and textbooks
189.2	Synthetic vaccines
189.5.A-Z	By disease or type, A-Z
189.5.A33	AIDS (Disease)
189.5.A56	Anti-idiotypic
189.5.B33	Bacterial diseases
	BGC vaccine see QR189.5.T72
189.5.C45	Chickenpox
189.5.D53	DNA vaccines
189.5.E5	Encephalitis
189.5.E53	Enterobacterial vaccines
189.5.H46	Hepatitis
189.5.H48	Herpesvirus disease
189.5.I5	Influenza
189.5.M34	Malaria
189.5.M4	Measles
189.5.N48	Newcastle disease
189.5.P36	Papillomavirus
189.5.P46	Pertussis
189.5.P54	Pleuropneumonia
189.5.P58	Pneumococcal infections
189.5.P6	Poliomyelitis
189.5.P76	Protozoan diseases
189.5.R3	Rabies
189.5.R8	Rubella
189.5.S48	Sexually transmitted diseases
189.5.S6	Smallpox
	Tuberculosis
189.5.T7	General works
189.5.T72	BCG vaccine
189.5.T9	Typhoid
189.5.V5	Virus diseases
201.A-Z	Pathogenic microorganisms. By disease, A-Z
201.A16	Acinetobacter infections
201.A2	Actinomycosis
201.A27	Adenovirus diseases
201.A3	Adiaspiromycosis
201.A35	African swine fever
201.A37	AIDS (Disease). HIV infections
201.A55	Amebiasis

Pathogenic microorganisms. By disease, A-Z -- Continued

201.A57 Anaerobic infections
201.A6 Anthrax
201.A72 Arbovirus infections
201.A74 Arenavirus diseases
201.A85 Aspergillosis
201.B318 Babesiosis
201.B32 Bacteremia
201.B34 Bacterial diseases
201.B37 Bartonella infections
201.B55 Blastomycosis
201.B66 Borna disease
Borreliosis see QR201.R45
201.B7 Botulism
201.B74 Bovine spongiform encephalopathy
201.B8 Brucellosis. Undulant fever
201.C25 Campylobacter infections
(201.C26) Campylobacter pylori infections
see QR201.H44
Cancer see QR201.T84
201.C27 Candidiasis
201.C29 Chagas' disease
201.C47 Chlamydia infections
201.C5 Cholera
201.C54 Clostridium diseases
201.C58 Coccidioidomycosis
201.C59 Coccidiosis
201.C6 Conjunctivitis
201.C65 Coxsackievirus infections
201.C9 Cystitis
201.C94 Cytomegalovirus infections
201.D4 Diarrhea
Diarrhea, Viral see QR201.V53
201.D5 Diphtheria
201.D6 Diphtheroid organisms
201.D9 Dysentery. Bacillary dysentery
201.E16 Ebola virus disease
201.E2 Edema, Malignant
201.E45 Erlichiosis
201.E6 Endocarditis, Bacterial
201.E64 Enterococcal infections
201.E75 Epstein-Barr virus diseases
201.E82 Escherichia coli infections
201.F6 Food poisoning
Cf. QR201.B7 Botulism
201.F62 Foodborne diseases
201.F63 Foot-and-mouth disease

QR

	Pathogenic microorganisms. By disease, A-Z -- Continued
201.G45	Giardiasis
201.G5	Glanders
201.G7	Gonorrhea
201.G76	Gram-positive bacterial infections
201.H22	Haemophilus infections
201.H24	Hantavirus infections
201.H44	Helicobacter pylori infections
201.H46	Hepatitis, Viral
201.H48	Herpesvirus infections
	HIV infections see QR201.A37
201.H7	Hog cholera
201.H86	HTLV infections
201.I6	Influenza
	Jaundice see QR201.L6
201.L44	Legionnaires' disease
201.L5	Leprosy
201.L6	Leptospirosis. Jaundice
201.L64	Leukemia
201.L7	Listeriosis
201.L88	Lyme disease
201.L9	Lymphocytic choriomeningitis
201.M3	Malaria
	Malignant edema see QR201.E2
201.M4	Mastitis
201.M43	Measles
201.M6	Meningitis
201.M73	Microsporidiosis
201.M96	Mycobacterial diseases
201.M97	Mycoplasma diseases
201.M98	Mycotoxicoses
201.N4	Necrosis
201.N45	Neisseria infections
201.N5	Newcastle disease
201.O6	Oidiomycosis
201.O8	Osteomyelitis
201.P26	Papillomavirus diseases
201.P27	Parasitic diseases
201.P28	Paratuberculosis
201.P3	Paratyphoid fever
201.P33	Parvovirus infections
201.P4	Peritonitis
201.P45	Picornavirus infections
201.P5	Plague
201.P7	Pneumococcal pneumonia
201.P73	Poliomyelitis
201.P732	Polyomavirus infections

Pathogenic microorganisms. By disease, A-Z -- Continued

201.P733 Porphyromonas gingivalis infections
201.P737 Prion diseases
201.P74 Pseudomonas aeruginosa infections
201.P75 Pseudotuberculosis
201.P8 Psittacosis
201.Q2 Q fever
201.R3 Rabies
201.R45 Relapsing fever. Borreliosis
201.R47 Retrovirus infections
201.R5 Rheumatic fever
201.R53 Rheumatism
201.R59 Rickettsial diseases
Rocky Mountain spotted fever see QR201.S65
201.R67 Rotavirus infections
201.S25 Salmonella infections
201.S27 Sarcocystosis
201.S28 SARS (Disease)
201.S3 Scarlatina
201.S35 Schistosomiasis
201.S47 Serratia diseases
201.S55 Shigellosis
201.S6 Smallpox
201.S65 Spotted fever, Rocky Mountain
201.S68 Staphylococcal infections
201.S7 Streptococcus infections
201.S9 Syphilis
201.T3 Tetanus
201.T5 Torulosis
201.T53 Toxoplasmosis
201.T54 Trachoma
201.T55 Trichomoniasis
201.T6 Tuberculosis
201.T8 Tularemia
201.T84 Tumors. Cancer
201.T9 Typhoid fever
201.T95 Typhus fever
Undulant fever see QR201.B8
201.V53 Viral diarrhea
Viral hepatitis see QR201.H46
201.V55 Virus diseases
201.W6 Whooping cough
201.Y4 Yellow fever
201.Y45 Yersinia infections

Medical mycology. Pathogenic fungi
Class here general works only
For particular fungi see QK621+
Cf. QK604.2.P45 Phytopathogenic fungi
Cf. RC117.A+ Mycotic diseases
Cf. SB733 Fungus diseases of plants
Cf. SF780.7 Veterinary mycology
245 General works
248 Diagnostic mycology
Medical parasitology
Class here general works only
For particular protozoa see QL368.A115+
For pathogenic microorganisms see QR201.A+
Cf. QR201.P27 Parasitic diseases
Cf. RC118+ Spirochetal and protozoan diseases
Cf. SF781+ Veterinary medicine
251 General works
255 Diagnostic parasitology
Microorganisms of animals
Cf. QR171.A1+ Microorganisms in the animal body
Cf. SF951+ Diseases of special classes of animals
301 General works
Vertebrates
For domestic animals see SF780.2
302 General works
Humans see QR46
303 Mammals
311 Birds
314 Amphibians
315 Reptiles
321 Fishes
Cf. SF458.5 Aquarium fish diseases
Cf. SH171+ Diseases and pests of fish
Invertebrates
325 General works
327 Insects
330 Poikilotherms
Microorganisms of microorganisms
340 General works
Bacteriophages
342 General works
342.2.A-Z Individual phages or groups of phages, A-Z
342.2.F37 fd
342.2.I43 IKe
342.2.M82 Mu
342.2.T14 T4
343 Fungal viruses

351 Microorganisms of plants
Cf. SB621+ Microbial diseases of plants
Mycoplasmas
352 General works
352.5.A-Z Systematic divisions. By family, A-Z
352.5.A3 Acholeplasmataceae
352.5.M9 Mycoplasmataceae
Rickettsias
353 General works
353.5.A-Z Systematic divisions. By family, A-Z
353.5.A5 Anaplasmataceae
353.5.B3 Bartonellaceae
(353.5.C4) Chlamydiaceae
see QR82.C35
353.5.R5 Rickettsiaceae
Virology
Cf. QR201.V55 Virus diseases
Cf. SF780.4 Veterinary virology
Cf. TD427.V55 Viral pollution of water
355 Periodicals, societies, congresses, serial publications
357 Collected works (nonserial)
358 Dictionaries and encyclopedias
History
359 General works
359.5.A-Z By region or country, A-Z
Biography
359.7 Collective
359.72.A-Z Individual, A-Z
360 General works, treatises, and textbooks
363 Pictorial works and atlases
364 Popular works
365 Juvenile works
368 Addresses, essays, lectures
370 Special aspects of the subject as a whole
372.A-Z Special topics, A-Z
Bacteriophages see QR342+
372.M32 Macromolecules
372.O58 Oncogenic DNA viruses
372.O6 Oncogenic viruses
Cf. QR201.T84 Tumors
Study and teaching. Research
375 General works
376 Laboratory manuals
Laboratories
380.A1 General works
380.A3-Z By region or country, A-Z
Subarrange each country by Table Q6

Virology
Laboratories -- Continued
383 Culture collections
Technique
385 General works
385.5 Isolation
386 Culture technique
387 Diagnostic technique
387.5 Electron microscopy. Ultrastructural studies
388 Counting and measuring
Statistical methods see QR72
389 Molecular virology
392 Variation
Cf. QH434 Microbial genetics
393 Terminology, notation, abbreviations
394 Classification. Nomenclature
Systematic divisions
For classification for viruses of specific diseases see QR201.A+
394.5 DNA viruses
Cf. QR372.O58 Oncogenic DNA viruses
395 RNA viruses
396 Adenoviruses
398 Arboviruses
398.5 Baculoviruses
398.6 Bromoviridae
398.7 Bunyaviruses
398.8 Caliciviruses
399 Coronaviruses
Herpesviruses
400 General works
400.2.A-Z Special, A-Z
400.2.E68 Epstein-Barr virus
400.2.H47 Herpes simplex virus
400.2.V37 Varicella-zoster virus
401 Iridoviruses
401.5 Luteoviridae. Luteoviruses
402 Mosaic viruses
403 Nidoviruses
For coronaviruses see QR399
404 Orthomyxoviruses. Myxoviruses
Paramyxoviruses
404.15 General works
404.2.A-Z Special, A-Z
404.2.N55 Nipah virus
404.2.S45 Sendai virus
Orthopoxviruses

Virology
  Systematic divisions
    Orthopoxviruses -- Continued
405 General works
405.2.A-Z Special, A-Z
405.2.B83 Buffalopox virus
    Papillomaviruses. Polyomaviruses
406 General works
406.2.A-Z Special, A-Z
406.2.S56 Simian virus 40. SV40
      SV40 see QR406.2.S56
    Parvoviruses. Picodnaviruses
408 General works
408.2.A-Z Special, A-Z
408.2.C35 Canine parvovirus
    Picornaviruses
410 General works
410.2.A-Z Special, A-Z
410.2.E55 Enteroviruses
410.2.R45 Rhinoviruses
    Polyomaviruses see QR406+
411 Potyviridae. Potyviruses
412 Poxviruses
414 Reoviruses
    Retroviruses
414.5 General works
414.6.A-Z Special, A-Z
414.6.F6 Foamy viruses
414.6.H58 HIV
415 Rhabdoviruses
415.5 Togaviruses
416.A-Z Other groups of viruses, A-Z
416.C35 California group viruses
416.R8 Rubella viruses
  Viruses of particular hosts see QR301+
  Viruses of particular diseases see QR201.A+
  Viruses of particular body organs or systems see QR171.A1+
  Virus structure
450 General works
451 Size
452 Shape
453 Capsid
454 Envelope
456 DNA
458 RNA
460 Protein

Virology
Virus structure -- Continued

462	Enzymes
465	Virus function
467	Biochemistry
469	Adsorption
470	Replication
472	Transformation
474	Lysogeny
	Effect of environment
478.A1	General works, treatises, and textbooks
478.A2-Z	By agent, A-Z
478.R3	Radiation
478.T4	Temperature
480	Virus-virus interaction
482	Virus-host interaction
484	Virus-vector interaction
500	Viroids
502	Prions

.A2	Ac Actinium
.A3	Ag Silver (Argentum)
	Alabamine see Q1 .A8
.A4	Al Aluminum
.A5	Am Americium
	Antimony see Q1 .S3
	Argentum see Q1 .A3
.A6	Ar Argon
.A7	As Arsenic
.A8	At Astatine (Alabamine)
.A9	Au Gold (Aurum)
.B1	B Boron
.B2	Ba Barium
.B4	Be Beryllium (Glucinum)
.B5	Bi Bismuth
.B55	Bk Berkelium
.B7	Br Bromine
.C1	C Carbon
.C2	Ca Calcium
.C3	Cd Cadmium
	Cassiopeium see Q1 .L8
	Celtium see Q1 .H5
.C4	Ce Cerium
.C45	Cf Californium
.C5	Cl Chlorine
.C55	Cm Curium
.C6	Co Cobalt
.C7	Cr Chromium
.C8	Cs Cesium
	Columbium see Q1 .N3
.C9	Cu Copper (Cuprum)
	Didymium see Q1 .N4
.D8	Dy Dysprosium
.E6	Er Erbium
.E7	Es Einsteinium
.E8	Eu Europium
.F1	F Fluorine
.F4	Fe Iron (Ferrum)
.F5	Fm Fermium
	Ferrum see Q1 .F4
.F7	Fr Francium
.G2	Ga Gallium
.G4	Gd Gadolinium
.G5	Ge Germanium
	Glucinum see Q1 .B4
	Gold see Q1 .A9
.H1	H Hydrogen

.H4	He Helium
.H5	Hf Hafnium (Celtium)
.H6	Hg Mercury (Hydrargyrum)
.H7	Ho Holmium
	Hydrargyrum see Q1 .H6
.I1	I Iodine
	Illinium see Q1 .P5
.I5	In Indium
.I7	Ir Iridium
	Iron see Q1 .F4
.K1	K Potassium (Kalium)
.K6	Kr Krypton
.L2	La Lanthanum
	Lead see Q1 .P3
.L5	Li Lithium
.L8	Lu Lutetium (Cassiopeium)
.L9	Lw Lawrencium
.M3	Md Mendelevium
.M4	Mg Magnesium
.M6	Mn Manganese
	Mercury see Q1 .H6
.M7	Mo Molybdenum
	Natrium see Q1 .N2
.N1	N Nitrogen
.N2	Na Sodium (Natrium)
.N3	Nb Niobium (Columbium)
.N4	Nd Neodymium (Didymium)
.N5	Ne Neon
.N6	Ni Nickel
	Niton see Q1 .R6
.N65	No Nobelium
.N7	Np Neptunium
.O1	O Oxygen
.O7	Os Osmium
.P1	P Phosphorus
.P2	Pa Protactinium
.P3	Pb Lead (Plumbum)
.P4	Pd Palladium
	Plumbum see Q1 .P3
.P5	Pm Promethium (Illinium)
.P6	Po Polonium
	Potassium see Q1 .K1
.P7	Pr Praseodymium
.P8	Pt Platinum
.P9	Pu Plutonium
.R1	Ra Radium
.R3	Rb Rubidium

.R4	Re Rhenium
.R45	Rf Rutherfordium
.R5	Rh Rhodium
.R6	Rn Radon (Niton)
.R9	Ru Ruthenium
.S1	S Sulfur
.S3	Sb Antimony (Stibium)
.S4	Sc Scandium
.S5	Se Selenium
.S55	Sg Seaborgium
.S6	Si Silicon
	Silver see Q1 .A3
.S65	Sm Samarium
.S7	Sn Tin (Stannum)
	Sodium see Q1 .N2
	Stannum see Q1 .S7
	Stibium see Q1 .S3
.S8	Sr Strontium
.T2	Ta Tantalum
.T3	Tb Terbium
.T35	Tc Technetium
.T4	Te Tellurium
.T5	Th Thorium
	Tin see Q1 .S7
.T6	Ti Titanium
.T7	Tl Thallium
.T8	Tm Thulium
	Tungsten see Q1 .W1
.U7	U Uranium
.V2	V Vanadium
.W1	W Tungsten (Wolfram)
.X4	Xe Xenon
.Y1	Y Yttrium
.Y3	Yb Ytterbium
.Z6	Zn Zinc
.Z7	Zr Zirconium

.x	General works
.x2	Particle source
.x3	Effect of particles
.x4	Moments. Resonance. Spin. Symmetry
.x5	Capture. Decay. Lifetime
.x6	Charge. Density. Mass
.x7	Energy spectra. Radiation
.x8	Particle interactions. Scattering
(.x9)	Instrumentation see QC785.5+

.A1	General works
.A3-.Z	By region, country, or island, A-Z Offshore islands generally class with adjacent mainland

TABLES

.x	General works
.x2A-.x2Z	Local, A-Z

.x	General works
.x2A-.x2Z	Special. By city, A-Z

TABLE OF SUBARRANGEMENT FOR LABORATORIES, STATIONS, OR PROJECTS (CUTTER NO.)

Q6

.x	General works
.x2A-.x2Z	Individual laboratories, stations, or projects. By name, A-Z

.x	General works
.x2A-.x2Z	Local, A-Z
.x3A-.x3Z	Special schools or universities. By name, A-Z

A

A stars: QB843.A12
Aardvarks
  Zoology: QL737.T8
Abalones: QL430.5.H34
Abbreviations
  Analytical chemistry: QD71.8
  Biology: QH304.5
  Natural history: QH83.5
Abdomen
  Regional anatomy: QM543
Abduction (Logic)
  Philosophy of science: Q175.32.A24
Abelian functions: QA345
Abelian groups: QA180
Aberration
  Electromagnetic theory: QC671
  Spherical astronomy: QB163
Abominable snowman: QL89.2.Y4
Abrocomidae: QL737.R62
Abscisic acid
  Plant constituent: QK898.A15
Abscission
  Plant physiology: QK763
Absolute, The
  Physics: QC6.4.A27
Absorption
  Atomic physics: QC182
  Gas mechanics: QC162
  Heat transfer: QC331+
  Nutrition: QP165
Absorption apparatus
  Chemical laboratories: QD54.A3
Absorption of water
  Phytochemistry: QK871
Absorption spectra
  Analytical chemistry: QD96.A2
  Physics: QC454.A2
Absorptionmeter: QC465
Abstract algebra: QA162
Abstract automata
  Algebra: QA267+
Abstract data types
  Computer science: QA76.9.A23
Abstract harmonic analysis: QA403+
Abstract machines
  Algebra: QA267+
Abstracting and indexing
  Chemistry: QD9
Abyssal zone
  Ecology: QH541.5.D35
Abyssochrysidae: QL430.5.A18
Acanaloniidae: QL527.A2
Acanthaceae: QK495.A1655
Acantharia: QL368.A32
Acanthisittidae: QL696.P212
Acanthizidae: QL696.P213
Acanthocephala: QL391.A2
Acanthoceridae: QL596.A23
Acanthochitonidae: QL430.14.A26
Acanthoclinidae: QL638.A15
Acanthoctenidae: QL458.42.A2
Acanthometrida: QL368.A33
Acanthophractida: QL368.A335
Acanthosomatidae: QL523.A14
Acanthuridae: QL638.A2
Acari
  Paleozoology: QE826.A2
  Zoology: QL458+
Acaridae: QL458.2.A3
Acariformes: QL458.15.A33
Acarina
  Paleozoology: QE826.A2
  Zoology: QL458+
Acarophilism: QK924
Acceleration
  Physiological effect: QP82.2.A2
Accelerator mass spectrometry
  Physics: QC454.A25
Accentors: QL696.P266
Access control
  Computer science: QA76.9.A25
Accessory female organs: QP265
Accessory male organs: QP257
Accipitres
  Paleozoology: QE872.A15
Accipitridae: QL696.F32
Accipitriformes: QL696.F3+
Acclimatization
  Ecology: QH543.2
  Plant ecology: QK913

Accommodation, Eye
  Physiology: QP477
Accretion (Astrophysics): QB466.A25
Aceraceae: QK495.A17
Acerentomidae: QL503.6.A3
Acetic acid
  Animal biochemistry: QP752.A25
  Microbial metabolism: QR92.A3
Acetolactate synthase
  Plant constituent: QK898.A156
Acetone
  Animal biochemistry: QP801.A25
Acetylcholinesterase
  Animal biochemistry: QP609.A25
Acetylene
  Aliphatic compounds: QD305.H8
Acetylenes
  Plant constituent: QK898.A16
Acetyltransferases
  Animal biochemistry: QP606.A33
Achariaceae: QK495.A175
Achatinellidae: QL430.5.A2
Achatinidae: QL430.5.A22
Achatocarpaceae: QK495.A176
Achilidae: QL527.A25
Achilixiidae: QL527.A259
Acholeplasmataceae
  Microbiology: QR352.5.A3
Achondrites: QB758.5.A47
Achromatiaceae: QR82.A3
Aciculidae: QL430.5.A23
Acid-base equilibrium
  Physiology: QP90.7
Acid deposition
  Effect on plants and animals:
    QH545.A17
Acid precipitation
  Effect on plants and animals:
    QH545.A17
  Meteorology: QC926.5+
Acid rain
  Effect on plants and animals:
    QH545.A17
  Meteorology: QC926.5+
Acidity
  Bacterial physiology: QR97.A3
Acids
  Aliphatic compounds: QD305.A2
  Animal biochemistry: QP801.A26
  Aromatic compounds: QD341.A2
  Effect on plants: QK753.A25
  Effect on plants and animals:
    QH545.A2
  Theoretical chemistry: QD477
Acinetobacter infections
  Microbiology: QR201.A16
Acipenseridae: QL638.A25
Acipenseriformes: QL637.9.A3
  Paleozoology: QE852.A25
Aclididae: QL430.5.A24
Acmaeidae: QL430.5.A26
Acmite
  Mineralogy: QE391.A18
Aconchulinida: QL368.A36
Acordulecerídae: QL568.A17
Acouchis: QL737.R644
Acoustic holography: QC244.5
Acoustic microscopes: QH212.A25
Acoustic nuclear magnetic resonance:
  QC762.6.A25
Acoustic phenomena
  Geophysics: QC809.A25
Acoustic properties
  Liquids: QC145.4.A25
  Petrology: QE431.6.A25
  Polymers: QD381.9.A25
  Semiconductors: QC611.6.A36
  Solid state physics: QC176.8.A3
Acoustic radiation
  Effect on cells: QH652.7
Acoustic streaming: QC243.3.A25
Acoustics
  Physics: QC221+
Acoustics, Nonlinear: QC244.2
Acoustics, Underwater: QC242+
Acoustooptics: QC220.5
Acquired immunity: QR185.3+
Acraeidae: QL561.A25
Acrasida: QL368.A38
Acrididae: QL508.A2
Acritarchs
  Paleozoology: QE899.2.A37
Acrobatidae: QL737.M346

Adipose tissues
  Physiology: QP88.15
Adjuvants
  Immunology: QR187.3
Adobe Acrobat
  File conversion software: QA76.9.F48
Adoxaceae: QK495.A178
Adrenal cortex
  Physiology: QP188.A28
Adrenal glands
  Physiology: QP188.A3
Adrenal medulla
  Physiology: QP188.A33
Adrenaline
  Animal biochemistry: QP572.A27
Adrenergic receptors
  Cardiovascular system: QP110.A37
Adrenocortical hormones
  Animal biochemistry: QP572.A3
Adrenocorticotrophic hormone
  Animal biochemistry: QP572.A35
Adrianichthyidae: QL638.A29
Adsorption
  Atomic physics: QC182
  Cytology: QH622
  Gas mechanics: QC162
  Physical chemistry: QD547
  Virology: QR469
Aegeriidae: QL561.S47
Aegialiidae: QL596.A37
Aegithalidae: QL696.P2135
Aegithinidae: QL696.P2344
Aegothelidae: QL696.C22
Aegyptianella: QR82.A39
Aeolidiidae: QL430.5.A45
Aeolothripidae: QL598.3.A4
Aepophilidae: QL523.A35
Aepyornithiformes
  Paleozoology: QE872.A2
Aerial erosion
  Geology: QE597
Aerial photography in botany:
  QK46.5.A47
Aerial photography in geology:
  QE33.2.A3
Aerodynamics
  Fluid dynamics: QA930
Aerolites
  Astronomy: QB758+
Aeromonadaceae: QR82.A43
Aeronautical almanacs
  Ephimerides: QB8.A+
Aeronautics in astronomy: QB135.5
Aeronautics in marine biology:
  QH91.57.A4
Aeronautics in meteorology: QC879.3+
Aeronomy: QC878.5+
Aerosols
  Atmospheric pollutants: QC882.4+
Aeshnidae: QL520.3.A4
Aesthetics
  Philosophy of science: Q175.32.A47
Aethialoniidae: QL527.A4
Aextoxicaceae: QK495.A185
Afferent pathways
  Anatomy: QL938.A35
Affine geometry: QA477
Affinity, Chemical
  Physical chemistry: QD505.5
Affinity chromatography: QP519.9.A35
Affinity electrophoresis: QP519.9.A36
Affinity labeling: QP519.9.A37
African mole rats: QL737.R628
African swine fever
  Microbiology: QR201.A35
African violet
  Botany: QK495.G4
African wild dog
  Anecdotes: QL795.A35
Afrosoricida: QL737.A35+
After-images
  Physiology: QP482.5
Afterglow
  Electric discharge: QC711.8.A34
Aftershocks
  Seismology: QE539.2.A4
Agallidae: QL527.A44
Agamidae: QL666.L223
Agaontidae: QL568.A23
Agapanthaceae: QK495.A24
Agar
  Animal biochemistry: QP702.A3
Agaricaceae: QK629.A4
Agaricales: QK629.A44

Agaristidae: QL561.A4
Agassiz
  Natural history: QH31.A2
Agates
  Mineralogy: QE391.Q2
Agavaceae: QK495.A26
Age determination
  Fishes: QL639.15
  Mammals: QL739.25
  Reptiles and amphibians: QL669.25
  Zoology: QL60.7
Age/growth calculations
  Fishes: QL639.15
Age of solar system: QB503
Age of the earth: QE508
Agelenidae: QL458.42.A3
Ageneiosidae: QL638.A3
Agglutination
  Antigen-antibody reactions:
    QR187.A3
  Blood physiology: QP99.5.A3
Aggregation
  Microbiology: QR73.6
Aggression
  Animals: QL758.5
Aging
  Biology: QH529
  Cells: QH608
  Developmental physiology: QP86
  Endocrine glands: QP187.3.A34
  Heart: QP114.A35
  Plant physiology: QK762.5+
Aglucones
  Animal biochemistry: QP702.A35
Aglycyderidae: QL596.A4
Agmatine
  Animal biochemistry: QP563.A38
Agnatha
  Paleozoology: QE852.A33
  Zoology: QL638.12+
Agnostida
  Paleozoology: QE823.A35
Agonidae: QL638.A316
Agonistic behavior
  Animals: QL758.5
Agonomycetaceae: QK625.A48
Agonoxenidae: QL561.A46
Agoutidae: QL737.R623
Agoutis: QL737.R644
Agricultural chemicals
  Effect on plants and animals:
    QH545.A25
Agricultural geology: QE37
Agricultural microbiology: QR51
Agrionidae: QL520.3.A5
Agriotypidae: QL568.A24
Agromyzidae: QL537.A4
AIDS (Disease)
  Microbiology: QR201.A37
  Vaccines: QR189.5.A33
AIDS vaccines: QR189.5.A33
Ailuridae: QL737.C214
Air
  Chemistry: QD163
  Fluid mechanics: QC161+
  Microbiology: QR101
Air almanacs
  Ephimerides: QB8.A+
Air analysis
  Analytical chemistry: QD121
Air masses
  Climatology: QC981.8.A5
  Meteorology: QC880.4.A5
Air pollution
  Effect on plants: QK751
  Effect on plants and animals:
    QH545.A3
  Physiological effect: QP82.2.A3
Air sacs
  Anatomy: QL855
Air thermometers: QC273
Airbreathing catfishes: QL638.C6
Airglow: QC976.A3
Aistopoda
  Paleozoology: QE868.A46
Aizoaceae: QK495.A32
Akaniaceae: QK495.A34
Akysidae: QL638.A32
Alabetidae: QL638.G6
Alangiaceae: QK495.A36
Alanine aminopeptidase
  Animal biochemistry: QP609.A38
Alariaceae: QK569.A43
Alaskite: QE462.A35

Alaudidae: QL696.P214
Albamine
  Chemical element: Q1 .A8
Albatrosses
  Zoology: QL696.P63
Albedo: QC912.5
Albitite: QE462.A37
Albuginaceae: QK621.A42
Albulidae: QL638.A335
Albumins
  Animal biochemistry: QP552.A43
  Blood constituents: QP99.3.A4
  Plant constituent: QK898.A2
Alcedinidae: QL696.C72
Alchemy: QD23.3+
  History: QD13
Alcidae: QL696.C42
  Paleozoology: QE872.A3
Alciformes: QL696.C4+
Alcohol
  Animal biochemistry: QP801.A3
  Radiation chemistry: QD651.A4
Alcohol dehydrogenase
  Animal biochemistry: QP603.A34
Alcohols
  Aliphatic compounds: QD305.A4
  Aromatic compounds: QD341.A4
  Spectra: QC463.A4
Alcyonaria: QL377.C6
Aldehyde dehydrogenase
  Animal biochemistry: QP603.A35
Aldehydes
  Aliphatic compounds: QD305.A6
  Animal biochemistry: QP801.A33
  Aromatic compounds: QD341.A6
Alderflies
  Zoology: QL514.7.S52
Aldolases
  Animal biochemistry: QP613.A4
Aldosterone
  Animal biochemistry: QP572.A4
Aldrin
  Effect on plants and animals: QH545.A4
Alephcephalidae: QL638.A35
Alepisauridae: QL638.A34
Aleyrodidae: QL527.A5
Algae: QK564+
  Paleontolology: QE955
Algebra: QA150+
Algebra of currents
  Atomic physics: QC174.52.A43
  Elementary particle physics: QC793.3.A4
Algebraic fields: QA247+
Algebraic functions: QA341
Algebraic geometry: QA564+
  Mathematical physics: QC20.7.A37
Algebraic logic: QA10+
Algebraic logic (Mathematical physics): QC20.7.A4
Algebraic numbers: QA247+
Algebraic topology: QA612+
Algin
  Plant constituent: QK898.A3
ALGOL (Computer program language)
  Computer science: QA76.73.A24
Algol systems: QB833+
Algology: QK564+
Algorithms: QA9.58
  Computer science: QA76.9.A43
Alicyclic compounds: QD305.H9
Alienidae: QL568.A3
Alimentary canal
  Microbiology: QR171.A43
Aliphatic compounds: QD300+
Alismataceae: QK495.A4
Alkahest: QD26.5.A4
Alkali heath
  Botany: QK495.F67
Alkali metal electrodes: QD572.A65
Alkali metal halides
  Spectra: QC464.A43
Alkali metals
  Geochemistry: QE516.A35
  Inorganic chemistry: QD172.A4
Alkalic igneous rocks: QE462.A4
Alkaline earth ferricyanides
  Spectra: QC464.A44
Alkaline earth metals
  Inorganic chemistry: QD172.A42
Alkaline phosphatase
  Animal biochemistry: QP609.A4

Aluminum
Chemical element: Q1 .A4
Effect on plants: QK753.A45
Superconductors: QC611.98.A48
Aluminum alloys
Analytical chemistry: QD137.A6
Alunite
Mineralogy: QE391.A45
Alydidae: QL523.A4
Alysiidae: QL568.A34
Alyssonidae: QL568.A344
Alytidae: QL668.E214
Amanitaceae: QK629.A53
Amaranth
Botany: QK495.A48
Amaranthaceae: QK495.A48
Amarsipidae: QL638.A36
Amaryllidaceae: QK495.A484
Amaryllis
Botany: QK495.A484
Amastridae: QL430.5.A5
Amathusiidae: QL561.A5
Amaurobiidae: QL458.42.A4
Amaurobioididae: QL458.42.A57
Amazonite
Mineralogy: QE391.A48
Amber
Mineralogy: QE391.A5
Amber fauna
Paleontology: QE742
Amber flora
Paleobotany: QE932
Paleontology: QE742
Ambersnails: QL430.5.S87
Ambient intelligence
Computer science: QA76.9.A48
Amblemidae: QL430.7.A34
Amblycipitidae: QL638.A364
Amblyopsidae: QL638.A366
Amblypygi: QL458.3+
Amblystegiaceae: QK539.A6
Amborellaceae: QK495.A485
Ambushbugs: QL523.P53
Ambystomatidae: QL668.C23
Amebiasis
Microbiology: QR201.A55
America Online: QA76.57.A43
American leaf-nosed bats: QL737.C57
American opossums: QL737.M34
American sparrows
Zoology: QL696.P2438
Americium
Chemical element: Q1 .A5
Ameronothridae: QL458.2.A45
Amethysts
Mineralogy: QE394.A4
Ametropodidae: QL505.3.S5
Amidases
Animal biochemistry: QP609.A438
Amides
Aliphatic compounds: QD305.A7
Aromatic compounds: QD341.A7
Amiidae: QL638.A37
Amiiformes
Paleozoology: QE852.A4
Amination
Organic chemistry: QD281.A6
Amine polymers
Organic chemistry: QD383.A55
Amines
Animal biochemistry: QP801.A48
Amino acid oxidases
Animal biochemistry: QP603.A4
Amino acids
Animal biochemistry: QP561+
Biochemistry: QD431+
Microbial metabolism: QR92.A6
Plant constituent: QK898.A5
Amino compounds
Aliphatic compounds: QD305.A8
Aromatic compounds: QD341.A8
Amino oxidase
Animal biochemistry: QP603.M6
Amino sugars
Animal biochemistry: QP702.A4
Aminoacyl-tRNA
Plant constituent: QK898.A52
Aminoacyl-tRNA synthetases
Animal biochemistry: QP619.A45
Aminobenzoic acids
Animal biochemistry: QP772.A4
Aminobutyric acid
Animal biochemistry: QP563.A48

Aminocapric acid
  Animal biochemistry: QP563.A5
Aminopeptidases
  Animal biochemistry: QP609.A44
Aminotransferases
  Animal biochemistry: QP606.A43
Amintes
  Spectra: QC463.A8
Ammeters
  Physics: QC615
Ammodytidae: QL638.A4
Ammonia
  Effect on plants and animals: QH545.A45
  Radiation chemistry: QD651.A45
  Spectra: QC464.A47
Ammonoidea
  Paleozoology: QE807.A5
Ammonolysis
  Organic chemistry: QD281.A63
Ammotrechidae: QL458.82.A4
Ammoxenidae: QL458.42.A45
Amnicolidae: QL430.5.H9
Amnion
  Embryology: QL975
Amniotes: QE847
Amniotic fluid
  Embryology: QL975
Amoebida: QL368.A5
Amorphous substances
  Magnetic materials: QC766.A4
  Semiconductor physics: QC611.8.A5
  Solid state physics: QC176.8.A44
Amphibian watching: QL645.6+
Amphibians
  Paleozoology: QE867+
  Zoology: QL667+
Amphibians and reptiles
  Zoology: QL640+
Amphiboles: QE391.A53
Amphibolite: QE475.A4
Amphiliidae: QL638.A44
Amphineura
  Paleozoology: QE805
Amphiphiles
  Organic chemistry: QD382.A47
Amphipnoidae: QL638.A47
Amphipoda: QL444.M315
  Paleozoology: QE817.A6
Amphipterygidae: QL520.3.A6
Amphisbaeni: QL666.L192+
Amphisbaenidae: QL666.L193
Amphitheridae: QL561.A57
Amphiumidae: QL668.C237
Amphizoidae: QL596.A45
Amplitude
  Sound waves: QC243.3.A4
Ampulicidae: QL568.A36
Ampullariidae: QL430.5.A57
Amydriidae: QL561.T55
Amylase
  Animal biochemistry: QP609.A45
Amylin
  Animal biochemistry: QP572.A48
Amyloid
  Animal biochemistry: QP552.A45
  Plant constituent: QK898.A53
Amyloses
  Animal biochemistry: QP702.A48
Anabantidae: QL638.A5
Anablepidae: QL638.A53
Anacanthobatidae: QL638.85.A5
Anacardiaceae: QK495.A498
Anacharitidae: QL568.A38
Anaerobic bacteria
  Microbiology: QR89.5
Anaerobic fungi: QK604.2.A52
Anaerobic infections
  Microbiology: QR201.A57
Anaerobiosis
  Biology: QH518.5
  Phytochemistry: QK894
Analcime
  Mineralogy: QE391.A55
Analgidae: QL458.2.A5
Analog computers: QA76.4
Analysis
  Biochemistry: QD431.25.A53
  Mathematical physics: QC20.7.A5
  Mathematics: QA299.6+
  Organic chemistry
    Carbohydrates: QD322.A52
  Organometallic chemistry: QD411.7.A53

Anthrax
  Microbiology: QR201.A6
Anthribidae: QL596.A63
Anthropometric assessment
  Nutrition research: QP143.5.A58
Anti-idiotypic vaccines: QR189.5.A56
Anti-infective agents
  Bacterial physiology: QR97.A57
  Testing: QR69.A56
Antibiosis: QR99+
Antibiosis resistance: QR99.5
Antibiotic testing
  Microbiology: QR69.A57
Antibiotics
  Animal biochemistry: QP801.A63
  Bacterial physiology: QR97.A58
  Organic chemistry: QD375+
Antibodies
  Immunology: QR186.7+
Antibody-toxin conjugates:
  QR185.8.A58
Antiferromagnetism
  Physics: QC761.5
Antifreeze proteins
  Animal biochemistry: QP552.A56
Antigen-antibody reactions
  Microbiology: QR187.A1+
Antigen presenting cells: QR185.8.A59
Antigens
  Immunology: QR186.5+
Antigravity: QC178
Antihemorrhage vitamin
  Animal biochemistry: QP772.V55
Antilocapridae: QL737.U52
Antimatter, Constitution of: QC172+
Antimatter, Properties of: QC173.28+
Antimetabolites
  Animal biochemistry: QP801.A65
Antimonates
  Mineralogy: QE389.64
Antimonides
  Mineralogy: QE389.2
Antimony
  Chemical element: Q1 .S3
Antimony ores
  Mineralogy: QE390.2.A58
Antimutagens: QH468
Antioxidants
  Animal biochemistry: QP801.A66
  Plant constituent: QK898.A57
Antipernicious anemia vitamin
  Animal biochemistry: QP772.C9
Antirickets vitamin
  Animal biochemistry: QP772.V53
Antiscurvy vitamin
  Animal biochemistry: QP772.A8
Antisense DNA
  Animal biochemistry: QP624.5.A57
Antisense RNA
  Animal biochemistry: QP623.5.A58
Antisterility vitamin
  Animal biochemistry: QP772.T6
Antithrombins: QP93.7.A58
Antitoxins
  Animal biochemistry: QP631+
Antiviral proteins
  Plant constituent: QK898.A59
Antivitamins
  Animal biochemistry: QP801.A67
Antixerophthalmia vitamin
  Animal biochemistry: QP772.V5
Antlike flower beetles: QL596.A62
Antlions: QL513.M9
Antpipits: QL696.P2365
Antrodiaetidae: QL458.42.A5
Ants
  Paleozoology: QE832.H9
  Zoology: QL568.F7
Anura: QL668.E2+
  Paleozoology: QE868.A5
Anyon superconductivity:
  QC611.98.A58
Anyons
  Elementary particle physics:
    QC793.5.A25+
Anyphaenidae: QL458.42.A57
Anystidae: QL458.2.A58
Aorta
  Physiology: QP106.2
Aortic paraganglia
  Physiology: QP188.A6
Aortic valve
  Physiology: QP114.A57
Aoteidae: QL638.A6

Apachyidae: QL510.3.A6
Apatite
  Mineralogy: QE391.A6
Aperiodic tilings
  Discrete geometry: QA640.72
Apes
  Zoology: QL737.P96
Apexes
  Plant anatomy: QK645+
Aphelinidae: QL568.A55
Aphididae: QL527.A64
Aphidiidae: QL568.A57
Aphids
  Zoology: QL525+
Aphodiidae: QL596.A64
Aphredoderidae: QL638.A63
Aphyllanthaceae: QK495.A65
Apicomplexa: QL368.A16
Apidae: QL568.A6
Apioceridae: QL537.A6
Apiomorphidae: QL527.A65
APL (Computer program language): QA76.73.A27
Aplacophora: QL430.1+
  Paleozoology: QE805
Aplite: QE462.A63
Aploactinidae: QL638.A64
Aplocheilidae: QL638.A642
Aplochitonidae: QL638.A643
Aplodactylidae: QL638.A65
Aplodontidae: QL737.R626
Aplysiidae: QL430.5.A66
Apochrysidae: QL513.A6
Apocynaceae: QK495.A66
Apoda: QL668.A6+
  Paleozoology: QE868.A6
Apodidae: QL696.A552
Apodiformes: QL696.A55+
Apogonidae: QL638.A7
Apolipoproteins
  Blood constituents: QP99.3.A65
Aponogetonaceae: QK495.A667
Apoprogonidae: QL561.A7
Apostomatida: QL368.A57
Appetite
  Physiology: QP136
Application program interfaces
  Computer science: QA76.76.A63
Application software
  Computer software: QA76.76.A65
Applied ethnobotany: QK86.5
Approximation theory
  Algebra: QA221+
  Quantum mechanics: QC174.17.A66
Apterogynidae: QL568.A7
Apteronotidae: QL638.A73
Apterygidae: QL696.A63
  Paleozoology: QE872.A7
Apterygiformes: QL696.A6+
Apterygota
  Zoology: QL501+
Aqua ions
  Electrochemistry: QD562.A75
Aquaporins
  Animal biochemistry: QP552.A65
Aquariums, Freshwater: QL78
Aquariums, Public: QL78+
Aquatic biology
  Biogeography: QH90+
Aquatic biology as a profession: QH90.45
Aquatic birds
  Zoology: QL678.5+
Aquatic ecology: QH541.5.W3
Aquatic flora
  Botany: QK102+
Aquatic fungi
  Botany: QK617.8+
Aquatic insects
  Zoology: QL472+
Aquatic microbiology: QR105+
Aquatic parks
  Freshwater biology: QH96.75.A1+
Aquatic plants
  Botany: QK930+
Aquatic radioecology: QH543.58+
Aquatic reptiles: QL665.3+
Aquatics
  Plant ecology: QK916
Aqueous erosion
  Geology: QE581
Aqueous solvents
  Physical chemistry: QD544.3

Aqueous vapor
  Meteorology: QC915+
Aquifoliaceae: QK495.A67
Arabinoglactan
  Plant constituent: QK898.A67
Araceae: QK495.A685
Arachidonic acid
  Animal biochemistry: QP752.A7
Arachnida
  Paleozoology: QE825+
Aradidae: QL523.A7
Arakelov theory
  Algebra: QA242.6
Araliaceae: QK495.A6853
Aramidae: QL696.G82
Araneae: QL458.4+
  Paleozoology: QE826.A6
Araneida: QL458.4+
  Paleozoology: QE826.A6
Araneidae: QL458.42.A7
Arapaimidae: QL638.O88
Araucariaceae: QK494.5.A7
Arboretums
  Botany: QK479+
Arbovirus infections
  Microbiology: QR201.A72
Arboviruses
  Virology: QR398
Arc discharge
  Electric discharge: QC705
Arc measures
  Geodesy: QB291
Arc spectra
  Analytical chemistry: QD96.A7
  Physics: QC454.A7
Arcellinida: QL368.A63
Archaean
  Stratigraphy: QE653.3
Archaebacteria: QR82.A69
Archaeidae: QL458.42.A73
Archaeogastropoda
  Paleozoology: QE809.A72
Archaeognatha: QL503.7.A1+
Archaeonithes
  Paleozoology: QE872.A8
Archiblattidae: QL505.7.A73
Archigregarinida: QL368.A66
Architectonicidae: QL430.5.A69
Architecture, Computer: QA76.9.A73
Architeuthidae: QL430.3.A73
Arcidae: QL430.7.A72
  Paleozoology: QE812.A8
Arctic Ocean
  Zoology: QL126
Arctic regions
  Biogeography: QH84.1+
Arcticidae: QL430.7.A74
Arctiidae: QL561.A8
Ardeidae: QL696.C52
Ardeiformes: QL696.C5+
Area
  Measurement: QC104.5
Areas and volumes
  Surfaces
    Infinitesimal geometry: QA636
Arenavirus diseases
  Microbiology: QR201.A74
Arenites: QE471.15.A68
Areolariidae: QL505.7.A74
Areopodidae: QL527.D44
Argasidae: QL458.2.A74
Argentinidae: QL638.A75
Argentum
  Chemical element: Q1 .A3
Argidae: QL568.A77
Arginase
  Animal biochemistry: QP609.A7
Arginine
  Animal biochemistry: QP562.A7
Argiopidae: QL458.42.A7
Argon
  Chemical element: Q1 .A6
  Electric discharge: QC711.6.A7
  Fluid mechanics: QC145.45.A75
Argyresthiidae: QL561.A84
Arhynchobatidae: QL638.85.A7
Arid regions
  Climatology: QC993.7
  Ecology: QH541.5.A74
Arid regions ecology: QH541.5.A74
Ariidae: QL638.A755
Arionidae: QL430.5.A7
Aristolochiaceae: QK495.A688
Arithmetic: QA101+

Ascorbic acid
  Animal biochemistry: QP772.A8
  Effect on plants: QK753.V58
  Plant constituent: QK898.A7
Ascothoracica: QL444.C527
Asexual reproduction
  Biology (General): QH475+
  Plant physiology: QK826
Ashinagidae: QL561.A88
Asian philosophy
  Physics: QC6.4.A85
Asian pipe snakes: QL666.O638
Asilidae: QL537.A85
Asities: QL696.P2625
Asparagaceae: QK495.A83
Asparagine
  Plant constituent: QK898.A74
Asparagus: QK495.A83
Aspartame
  Animal biochemistry: QP801.A84
Aspartate aminotransferase
  Animal biochemistry: QP606.A8
Aspartic acid
  Animal biochemistry: QP562.A8
Aspartic proteinases
  Animal biochemistry: QP609.A86
Aspergillosis
  Microbiology: QR201.A85
Aspergillus
  Experimental genetics: QH470.A85
Asphodelaceae: QK495.A835
Aspiceridae: QL568.A8
Aspidiaceae: QK524.A65
Aspleniaceae: QK524.A7
Aspredinidae: QL638.A78
Assamiidae: QL458.52.A8
Assassin bugs: QL523.R4
Assemblers
  Computer software: QA76.76.A87
Assembly
  Genetics: QH450.5
Asses, Wild
  Anecdotes: QL795.A8
Assignment problems
  Mathematical optimization: QA402.6
Assimilation of nitrogen
  Phytochemistry: QK867+
Associative rings and algebras:
  QA251.5
Assortment
  Genetics: QH444
Astacins
  Animal biochemistry: QP609.A88
Astartidae: QL430.7.A8
  Paleozoology: QE812.V45
Astatine
  Chemical element: Q1 .A8
Asteroidea: QL384.A8
  Paleozoology: QE783.A7
Asteroids: QB651+
  Perturbations: QB377+
Asterolecaniidae: QL527.A8
Astiidae: QL537.A88
Astomatida: QL368.A8
Astroblepidae: QL638.A785
Astrogeology
  Astronomy: QB454+
Astrolabe, Prismatic: QB328.P7
Astrolabes: QB85
Astrology
  Medieval astronomy: QB25+
Astrometry: QB807
Astromineralogy
  Astronomy: QB455.2
Astronautics in astronomy: QB136
Astronautics in meteorology: QC879.4+
Astronautics in science: Q180.7
Astronesthidae: QL638.A788
Astronomical geography: QB630+
Astronomical globes: QB66
Astronomical instrument makers:
  QB84.7+
Astronomical instruments, Portable:
  QB105
Astronomical observatories: QB81+
Astronomical photographic equipment:
  QB121.5
Astronomical photography: QB121+
Astronomical photometry: QB135
Astronomical refraction: QB155+
Astronomical spectroscopy: QB465
Astronomy: QB1+
Astronomy as a profession: QB51.5
Astronomy, Descriptive: QB494.2+

Atomic orbitals
  Physical chemistry: QD461
Atomic physics: QC170+
Atomic spectra
  Analytical chemistry: QD96.A8
Atomic spectroscopy
  Physics: QC454.A8
Atomic structure
  Atomic physics: QC173.4.A87
  Physical chemistry: QD461
Atomic theory
  Physical chemistry: QD461
Atomic transition probabilities:
  QC174.26.A8
Atomic units: QC784.5
Atomic warfare
  Effect on plants and animals:
    QH545.N83
Atomic weights
  Physical chemistry: QD463+
Atopetholidae: QL449.65.A8
ATP-binding cassette transporters:
  QP552.A87
Atractaspididae: QL666.O627
Atractoceridae: QL596.A8
Atrazine
  Effect on plants: QK753.A79
Atrial natriuretic peptides
  Animal biochemistry: QP572.A82
Atrichornithidae: QL696.P218
Atrypidae
  Paleozoology: QE797.A7
Attachment mechanisms
  Biology: QH514
Attaphilidae: QL505.7.A87
Attelabidae: QL596.A83
Attention
  Neurophysiology: QP405
Atticolidae: QL505.7.A88
Attidae: QL458.42.S24
Attractions and potential
  Analytic mechanics: QA825+
Attractors
  Topology: QA614.813
Atyidae: QL430.5.A85
Atypidae: QL458.42.A8
Auchenipteridae: QL638.A83
Audiovisual aids
  Botany: QK54+
  Mathematics: QA18+
  Science teaching: Q190+
Auditing
  Data processing activities:
    QA76.9.A93
Audouinellaceae: QK569.A27
Audubon, John James: QL31.A9
Auger effect
  Electric discharge: QC702.7.A9
Augite
  Mineralogy: QE391.A8
Auklets: QL696.C42
Auks: QL696.C42
Aulacidae: QL568.A9
Aulacigastridae: QL537.A9
Aulopiformes: QL637.9.A93
Aulopodidae: QL638.A84
Aulorhynchidae: QL638.A844
Aulostomidae: QL638.A848
Auriculales: QK629.A8
Auriculariaceae: QK629.A8
Auriculidae: QL430.5.E45
Aurora australis: QC972.5.A8
Aurora borealis: QC972.5.B6
Aurora polaris: QC972.5.B6
Auroral photography: QC972.P4
Auroras: QC970+
Aurum
  Chemical element: Q1 .A9
Ausdehnungslehre: QA205
Australasian treecreepers:
  QL696.P2354
Australasian warblers: QL696.P213
Australian butcherbirds: QL696.P216
Australian robins: QL696.P2439
Australian wrens: QL696.P2485
Austrobaileyaceae: QK495.A9
Austroperlidae: QL530.3.A9
Authorship
  Biology: QH304
  Chemistry: QD9.15
  Zoology: QL672.6
Autoclaving
  Biological research: QH324.9.A88

Autoimmunity
Immunology: QR188.3
Autolysis
Antigen-antibody reactions: QR187.A8
Automata, Conscious: Q325+
Automatic differentiations
Computer software: QA76.76.A98
Automatic hypothesis formation
Computer science: QA76.9.A955
Automatic theorem proving
Computer science: QA76.9.A96
Automation
Analytical chemistry: QD75.4.A8
Microbiology: QR69.A88
Automorphic functions
Analysis: QA353.A9
Autonomic computing: QA76.9.A97
Autonomic ganglia
Neurophysiology: QP368.8
Autonomic nervous system
Neurophysiology: QP368+
Autoradiographic techniques
Ecology: QH541.15.A9
Autoradiography
Analytical biochemistry: QP519.9.A94
Biological research: QH324.9.A9
Autotrophic bacteria: QR88.2
Autumn
Astronomy: QB637.7
Auxin
Effect on plants: QK753.A8
Plant constituent: QK898.A8
Avalanches
Meteorology: QC929.A8
Aviaries: QL677.8
Aviculariidae: QL458.42.T5
Avidin
Animal biochemistry: QP552.A94
Avocado
Nutrition: QP144.A77
Avocets
Zoology: QL696.C473
Awards
Geology: QE48.6
Mathematics: QA20.3
Axiidae: QL561.A93
Axioms
Plane geometry: QA481
Aye-ayes: QL737.P935
Azimuth: QB207
Azo compounds
Aliphatic compounds: QD305.A9
Aromatic compounds: QD341.A9
Azo polymers
Organic chemistry: QD383.A95
Azollaceae: QK524.A94
Azotobacteraceae: QR82.A9

B

B cells: QR185.8.B15
B method
Computer science: QA76.9.B22
B stars: QB843.B12
Babbitt metal
Analytical chemistry: QD137.B3
Babblers: QL696.P285
Babesiosis
Microbiology: QR201.B318
Babingtonite
Mineralogy: QE391.B2
Bacillaceae: QR82.B3
Bacillariaceae: QK569.B15
Bacillariophyceae: QK569.D54
Bacillariophyta: QK569.D54
Bacillary dysentery
Microbiology: QR201.D9
Back propagation
Cybernetics: Q325.78
Back swimmers
Zoology: QL523.N6
Background radiation, Cosmic: QB991.C64
Backup processing
Computer science: QA76.9.B32
Bacteremia
Microbiology: QR201.B32
Bacteria
Microbiology: QR74.8+
Micropaleontology: QE719.5
Bacteria, Autotrophic: QR88.2
Bacteria, Chemoautotrophic: QR88.7
Bacterial adhesion: QR96.8

Barometric hypsometry
  Meteorology: QC895
Baroreflexes
  Physiology: QP109
Barracudas
  Zoology: QL638.S77
Bartonella infections
  Microbiology: QR201.B37
Bartonellaceae
  Microbiology: QR353.5.B3
Barychelidae: QL458.42.B3
Baryons
  Elementary particle physics:
    QC793.5.B32+
Basal ganglia
  Neurophysiology: QP383.3+
Basalt: QE462.B3
Base measuring
  Geodetic surveying: QB303
Basellaceae: QK495.B256
Bases
  Theoretical chemistry: QD477
BASIC (Computer program language):
  QA76.73.B3
Basicranium
  Human embryology: QM695.B36
Basidiobolus: QK621.B37
Basidiomycetes: QK628.5+
Basidiomycota: QK626+
Basins: QE615+
Basins, Multiring: QB456
Basking shark: QL638.95.C37
Basophils
  Physiology: QP95.2
Bataceae: QK495.B33
Batch processing
  Computer science: QA76.9.B38
Batfishes: QL638.O3
Bathyclupeidae: QL638.B18
Bathydraconidae: QL638.B2
Bathyergidae: QL737.R628
Bathylaconidae: QL638.B23
Bathylagidae: QL638.B25
Bathymasteridae: QL638.B26
Bathynellacea: QL444.M32
Bathypteroidae: QL638.B27
Bathyteuthidae: QL430.3.B3
Batillariidae: QL430.5.B37
Batrachia
  Paleozoology: QE867+
Batrachoididae: QL638.B3
Batrachospermaceae: QK569.B25
Bats
  Anecdotes: QL795.B3
Bauxite
  Petrology: QE471.15.B32
Bay-star vine
  Botany: QK495.S353
Bayesian statistical decision theory
  Mathematical physics: QC20.7.B38
Bayesian statistics: QA279.5
Bdellidae: QL458.2.B4
Be stars: QB843.B25
Beachrock: QE471.15.B34
Beaded lacewings: QL513.B4
Beaked whales
  Zoology: QL737.C438
Beam-foil spectroscopy
  Physics: QC454.B39
Beam splitters
  Optical instruments: QC373.B3
Beardfishes: QL638.P747
Bears
  Anecdotes: QL795.B4
  Zoology: QL737.C27
Beast of Exmoor: QL89.2.B43
Beavers
  Anecdotes: QL795.B5
  Zoology: QL737.R632
Bedbugs
  Zoology: QL523.C6
Bee-eaters: QL696.C754
Beech
  Botany: QK495.F14
Beeflies: QL537.B65
Beefwood
  Botany: QK495.C27
Beer
  Microbiology: QR129.B44
Bees
  Anecdotes and stories: QL795.B53
  Paleozoology: QE832.H9
  Zoology: QL563+

Beta rays
  Elementary particle physics:
    QC793.5.B42+
Betaines
  Animal biochemistry: QP801.B55
Betatrons: QC787.B4
Bethe-ansatz technique
  Mathematical physics: QC20.7.B47
Bethylidae: QL568.B4
Bettongs: QL737.M386
Betulaceae: QK495.B56
Bevatrons: QC787.S9
Beverages
  Nutrition: QP144.B48
BGC vaccine: QR189.5.T72
Bibionidae: QL537.B5
Bicosoecida: QL368.B5
Bicycles, All terrain
  Effect on plants and animals:
    QH545.A42
Biddies: QL520.3.C67
Biela comet: QB723.B5
Bifurcation theory
  Differential equations: QA380
  Mathematical physics: QC20.7.B54
Big bang theory (Cosmology):
  QB991.B54
Bigeyes: QL638.P785
Bigheadedflies: QL537.P57
Bignoniaceae: QK495.B62
Bikes, Mountain
  Effect on plants and animals:
    QH545.A42
Biking, Mountain
  Effect on plants and animals:
    QH545.A42
Bilayer lipid membranes
  Cytology: QH602
Bile
  Physiology: QP197
Bile acids
  Animal biochemistry: QP752.B54
Bile ducts
  Physiology: QP185.3
Bile pigments
  Animal biochemistry: QP671.B5
Bilinear forms
  Number theory: QA243
Bilirubin
  Animal biochemistry: QP671.B55
Billfishes: QL638.I88
Binaries, X-ray: QB830
Binary system: QA141.4
Binary systems of stars: QB821+
Binding, Cooperative
  Animal biochemistry: QP517.C66
Binding energy
  Elementary particle physics:
    QC793.3.B5
Binding, Ligand
  Animal biochemistry: QP517.L54
Binding, Protein
  Animal biochemistry: QP517.P76
Binding sites
  Animal biochemistry: QP517.B42
Binocular rivalry
  Physiology: QP487.5
Binocular vision
  Physiology: QP487+
Binoculars
  Optical instruments: QC373.B55
Binomial coefficients: QA161.B48
Binomial theorem: QA161.B5
Binucleoside polyphosphates
  Animal biochemistry: QP625.D56
Bioacoustics
  Biology: QH510.5
Bioactive compounds
  Animal biochemistry: QP517.B44
  Plant constituent: QK898.B54
Biochemical genetics
  Plants: QK981.3
Biochemical markers
  Genetics: QH438.4.B55
Biochemical templates
  Animal biochemistry: QP517.B48
Biochemistry
  Organic chemistry: QD415+
  Viruses: QR467
Biochemistry, Animal: QP501+
Biochemistry, High pressure
  Animal biochemistry: QP517.H53

Biomagnetism
  Biology: QH504
  Physiological effect: QP82.2.M3
Biomathematics: QH323.5
Biomechanics
  Biology: QH513
Biometry: QH323.5
Biomimetic polymers
  Organic chemistry: QD382.B47
Biomimetics
  Animal biochemistry: QP517.B56
Biomineralization
  Biology: QH512
Biomolecules, Fossil
  Animal biochemistry: QP517.F66
Bionics: Q317+
Biophotometry
  Biological research: QH324.9.B48
Biophysical labeling
  Biological research: QH324.9.B49
Biophysics
  Biology: QH505
Biopolymers
  Animal biochemistry: QP801.B69
Biorhythms
  Biology: QH527
  Developmental physiology: QP84.6
Biosphere
  Biology: QH343.4
Biosphere reserves: QH75+
Biosynthesis
  Animal biochemistry: QP517.B57
  Bacterial physiology: QR88.3
Biotelemetry
  Biological research: QH324.9.B5
Biothermodynamics
  Animal biochemistry: QP517.T48
Biotin
  Animal biochemistry: QP772.B55
Biotite
  Mineralogy: QE391.B64
Biotransformation
  Animal biochemistry: QP517.B58
Bipartite graphs
  Algebra: QA166.14
Bipedidae: QL666.L194
Biphenyl compounds
  Spectra: QC463.B5
Biquadratic equations: QA215
Birch
  Botany: QK495.B56
Birch mice: QL737.R648
Bird areas: QL676.5+
Bird attracting: QL676.5+
Bird banding: QL677.5
Bird declines
  Effect on plants and animals:
    QH545.B57
Bird exhibitions: QL677.8
Bird feeders: QL676.5+
Bird food: QL698.4
Bird protection
  Zoology: QL676.5+
Bird refuges: QL676.5+
Bird watching: QL677.5
Birdcall whistles: QL676.5+
Birdfood: QL698.4
Birdhouses: QL676.5+
Birding sites: QL677.5
Birds
  Anecdotes and stories: QL795.B57
  Paleozoology: QE871+
  Zoology: QL671+
Birds' eggs: QL675
Birds' nests: QL675
Birds of paradise: QL696.P26
Birds of prey
  Zoology: QL677.78
Birth, Multiple
  Embryology: QL971+
Bismuth
  Chemical element: Q1 .B5
Bison
  Anecdotes and stories: QL795.B6
Bithyniidae: QL430.5.B58
Biting lice
  Paleozoology: QE832.M34
Biting midges: QL537.C37
Bittacidae: QL598.7.B5
Bitterns
  Zoology: QL696.C52
Bivalvia
  Paleozoology: QE811+

Bose algebras (Mathematical physics):
  QC20.7.B58
Bose-Einstein condensation:
  QC175.47.B65
Bose-Einstein gas: QC175.16.B65
Bosons
  Elementary particle physics:
    QC793.5.B62+
Bosses
  Geology: QE611+
Bostrichidae: QL596.B5
Botanical chemistry: QK861+
Botanical gardens
  Botany: QK71+
Botanical illustration: QK98.15+
Botanizers: QK46.5.B66
Botany: QK1+
Botany as a profession: QK50.5
Botflies: QL537.O4
Bothidae: QL638.B65
Bothriuridae: QL458.72.B6
Botryogen
  Mineralogy: QE391.B75
Botulinum toxin
  Animal biochemistry: QP632.B66
Botulism
  Microbiology: QR201.B7
Bound herbaria
  Botany: QK89
Bound states (Quantum mechanics):
  QC174.17.B6
Boundary layer
  Meteorology: QC880.4.B65
Boundary value problems
  Differential equations: QA379
  Mathematical physics: QC20.7.B6
Bovichthyidae: QL638.B67
Bovidae: QL737.U53
Bovine spongiform encephalopathy
  Microbiology: QR201.B74
Bowerbirds: QL696.P2675
Bowfins: QL638.A37
Box
  Botany: QK495.B85
Bøggildite
  Mineralogy: QE391.B7
Brachionichthyidae: QL638.B7
Brachiopoda
  Paleozoology: QE796+
  Zoology: QL395+
Brachodidae: QL561.B68
Brachycentridae: QL518.B7
Brachychthoniidae: QL458.2.B7
Brachyladidae: QL510.3.B7
Brachypauropodidae: QL449.75.B7
Brachypteraciidae: QL696.C725
Brachypteridae: QL596.B54
Brachyspectridae: QL596.B58
Brachytheciaceae: QK539.B68
Brackish water
  Aquatic biology: QH95.9
  Zoology: QL139
Brackish water radioecology: QH543.9
  Ecology: QH543.8
Brackish waters
  Ecology: QH541.5.E8
Braconidae: QL568.B8
Bradybaenidae: QL430.5.B73
Bradynobaenidae: QL568.B83
Brahmaeidae: QL561.B7
Braid theory
  Topology: QA612.23
Braided rivers
  Ecology: QH541.5.S7
Brain
  Anatomy: QL933+
  Human anatomy: QM455
  Human embryology: QM695.B7
  Invertebrates: QL935
  Neurophysiology: QP376+
  Vertebrates: QL937
Brain chemistry: QP356.3
Brain drain: Q150+
Brain stem
  Anatomy: QL938.B73
  Neurophysiology: QP376.8+
Brain stimulation techniques
  Neurophysiology: QP388
Bramidae: QL638.B8
Branched chain amino acids
  Animal biochemistry: QP562.B73
  Microbial metabolism: QR92.B7
Branchiae
  Anatomy: QL846

C

Capsidae: QL523.M5
Capsules
  Microbiology: QR77.5
Captorhinidae
  Paleozoology: QE862.C36
Capture of the moon by the earth:
  QB392.C3
Capuchin monkeys: QL737.P925
Capybara: QL737.R662
Carabidae: QL596.C2
Caraboctonidae: QL458.72.C27
Caracanthidae: QL638.C23
Caracaras (Birds): QL696.F34
Carangidae: QL638.C25
Carapidae: QL638.C26
Carbanions
  Aliphatic compounds: QD305.C3
Carbohydrates
  Animal biochemistry: QP701+
  Immunology: QR186.6.C37
  Microbial metabolism: QR92.C3
  Organic chemistry: QD320+
  Plant constituent: QK898.C3
  Radiation chemistry: QD651.C37
  Spectra: QC463.C3
Carbolic acid
  Animal biochemistry: QP801.C3
Carbolines
  Animal biochemistry: QP801.C3115
Carbon
  Chemical element: Q1 .C1
  Geochemistry: QE516.C37
Carbon cycle: QH344+
Carbon dioxide
  Bacterial physiology: QR97.C3
  Blood constituents: QP99.3.C3
  Effect on plants: QK753.C3
  Microbial metabolism: QR92.C33
  Photosysthesis: QK882
  Spectra: QC464.C37
Carbon disulfide
  Spectra: QC464.C375
Carbon electrodes: QD572.C37
Carbon isotopes
  Effect on plants and animals:
    QH545.C37
Carbon sequestration, Geological
  Geochemistry: QE516.C37
Carbonate dehydratase
  Animal biochemistry: QP613.C37
Carbonate rocks: QE471.15.C3
Carbonates
  Mineralogy: QE389.61
Carbonatites: QE462.C36
Carbonic anhydrase
  Animal biochemistry: QP613.C37
Carboniferous
  Paleobotany: QE915, QE919+
  Paleontology: QE729+
  Stratigraphy: QE671+
Carbonium ions
  Aliphatic compounds: QD305.C3
Carbonyl compounds
  Aliphatic compounds: QD305.A6
  Aromatic compounds: QD341.A6
Carboxylase
  Animal biochemistry: QP613.P9
Carboxylic acids
  Animal biochemistry: QP801.C312
Carboxypeptidase
  Animal biochemistry: QP609.C3
Carcharhinidae: QL638.95.C3
Carcharhiniformes: QL638.94.C37
Carchariidae: QL638.95.O3
Carcharocles megalodon
  Cryptozoology: QL89.2.C37
Carcinophoridae: QL510.3.C37
Cardiac arrest
  Physiology: QP114.A75
Cardiac dynamics
  Physiology: QP113
Cardiidae: QL430.7.C2
  Paleozoology: QE812.C3
Cardinalfishes: QL638.A7
Cardiogenic reflexes
  Physiology: QP114.C37
Cardiography: QP112.5.C3
Cardiopteridaceae: QK495.C1995
Cardiovascular sound
  Physiology: QP113.6
Cardiovascular system
  Human embryology: QM695.C37
  Physiology: QP101+

Cell interaction
Cytology: QH604.2
Microbiology: QR96.5
Cell junctions
Cytology: QH603.C4
Cell lines
Cytology: QH585.4+
Cell membranes
Cytology: QH601+
Microbiology: QR77
Cell metabolism: QH634.5
Cell pathology: QH671
Cell populations
Cytology: QH587+
Cell proliferation
Cytology: QH604.7
Cell receptors
Cytology: QH603.C43
Cell regulation
Cytology: QH604+
Cell respiration: QH633
Cell separation
Cytology: QH585.5.C44
Cell surface antigens
Immunology: QR186.6.C44
Cell walls
Bacteria: QR77.3+
Cells, Cardiac
Physiology: QP114.C44
Cells, Chromaffin
Physiology: QP188.C35
Cells, Electrolytic
Electrochemistry: QD568
Cells, Nerve
Anatomy: QL931
Cellular automata
Algebra: QA267.5.C45
Cellular control mechanisms
Endocrine glands: QP187.3.C44
Cellular immunity: QR185.5
Cellular osmosis
Cytology: QH615
Cellular repair mechanisms
Cytology: QH609
Cellular signal transduction
Animal biochemistry: QP517.C45
Cellulase
Animal biochemistry: QP609.C37
Cellulose
Organic chemistry: QD323
Plant constituent: QK898.C42
Cellulose 1,4-beta-cellobiosidase
Animal biochemistry: QP609.C38
Cellulose microorganisms: QR160
Celtium
Chemical element: Q1 .H5
Celyphidae: QL537.C35
Cenozoic
Paleobotany: QE925+
Paleontology: QE735+
Stratigraphy: QE690+
Census
Birds: QL677.5
Census taking
Reptiles and amphibians: QL645.6+
Center of mass
Analytic mechanics: QA839
Centers of plant diversity: QK46.5.D58
Centipedes: QL449.5+
Central nervous system
Anatomy: QL933+
Neurophysiology: QP370+
Central projection: QA511+
Centrales: QK569.C39
Centrarchidae: QL638.C3
Centrifugation
Animal biochemistry: QP519.9.C44
Biological research: QH324.9.C4
Centrifuges
Chemical laboratories: QD54.C4
Centriole
Cytology: QH597
Centriscidae: QL638.C32
Centrohelida: QL368.C4
Centrolenidae: QL668.E23
Centrolepidaceae: QK495.C39
Centrolophidae: QL638.C326
Centromere
Cytology: QH600.2
Centrophrynidae: QL638.C33
Centropomidae: QL638.C34
Centrosome
Cytology: QH597

Circulation of blood
  Physiology: QP101+
Circumstellar matter: QB792
Cirrhitidae: QL638.C577
Cirripedia: QL444.C5+
  Paleozoology: QE817.C5
Cirrus clouds: QC921.43.C57
Cistaceae: QK495.C5
Cistelidae: QL596.C613
Citharidae: QL638.C578
Citharinidae: QL638.C5785
Citheroniidae: QL561.C5
Cities
  Ecology: QH541.5.C6
Cities and towns
  Effect on plants and animals: QH545.C545
Citizen participation
  Nature conservation: QH77.3.C57
Citrates
  Animal biochemistry: QP801.C63
Citric acid
  Animal biochemistry: QP801.C65
  Microbial metabolism: QR92.C57
Citrulline
  Animal biochemistry: QP563.C5
Citrus
  Botany: QK495.R98
Citrus fruit
  Nutrition: QP144.C58
Civets
  Zoology: QL737.C28
Civilization and computers: QA76.9.C66
Cixiidae: QL527.C55
Cladocera: QL444.B83
Cladoniaceae: QK585.C6
Cladophoraceae: QK569.C624
Clam shrimps: QL444.B834
Clambidae: QL596.C617
Clams: QL430.6+
Clariidae: QL638.C6
Classical logical systems
  Mathematical logic: QA9.25+
Classical statistical mechanics: QC174.86.C6
Classification
  Chemical elements: QD467
  Climate: QC980.4
  Fungi: QK603.2+
  Invertebrates: QL362.5
  Mollusca: QL406
  Natural history: QH83
  Sciences: Q177
  Scientific research: Q180.55.C55
  Zoology: QL351+
Classification of curves and surfaces: QA603
Clastopteridae: QL527.C58
Clathrate compounds
  Physical chemistry: QD474
Clausiliidae: QL430.5.C57
Claustrum
  Neurophysiology: QP383.6
Clavariaceae: QK629.C6
Clavicipitaceae: QK623.C55
Clavicipitales: QK623.C57
Clavigeridae: QL596.C618
Clay
  Petrology: QE471.3
Clear air turbulence
  Meteorology: QC880.4.T8
Clearwing moths: QL561.S47
Cleavage
  Crystallography: QD933
  Geology: QE605
Cleidogonidae: QL449.65.C5
Cleonymidae: QL568.C55
Cleptidae: QL568.C56
Cleridae: QL596.C62
Clethraceae: QK495.C55
Click beetles: QL596.E4
Client/server computing
  Computer science: QA76.9.C55
Clifford algebras: QA199
  Mathematical physics: QC20.7.C55
Cliffs
  Ecology: QH541.5.C62
Climacteridae: QL696.P2354
Climate
  Effect on plants: QK754.5+
  Mars (Planet): QB643.C55
  Physiological effect: QP82.2.C5

Cobalt
  Effect on plants: QK753.C67
  Magnetic materials: QC766.C6
  Plant constituent: QK898.C6
Cobalt ores
  Mineralogy: QE390.2.C58
Cobias: QL638.R3
Cobitidae: QL638.C647
COBOL (Computer program language): QA76.73.C25
Cobordism
  Differential topology: QA613.66
Cobras: QL666.O64
Cobweb weavers: QL458.42.T54
Coca
  Animal biochemistry: QP801.C68
  Botany: QK495.E82
Cocaine
  Animal biochemistry: QP801.C68
Coccidae: QL527.C6
Coccidia: QL368.C59
Coccidioidomycosis
  Microbiology: QR201.C58
Coccidiosis
  Microbiology: QR201.C59
Coccinellidae: QL596.C65
Coccolithophorida: QL368.C6
Coccolithophoridaceae: QK569.C63
Coccyges: QL696.C8+
  Paleozoology: QE872.C9
Cochineal insects
  Zoology: QL527.D3
Cochlea
  Neurophysiology: QP471.2
Cochleariidae: QL696.C536
Cochlospermaceae: QK495.C6
Cochylidae: QL561.C57
Cockchafers: QL596.M4
Cockroaches
  Paleozoology: QE832.B55
  Zoology: QL505.5+
Cocoa
  Nutrition: QP144.C46
Coconut
  Nutrition: QP144.C63
Codes, Telegraphic
  Meteorology: QC872
Codfishes: QL638.G2
Codiaceae: QK569.C65
Coding theory
  Machine theory
    Algebra: QA268
Codlets: QL638.B85
Coelacanthiformes
  Paleozoology: QE852.C58
Coelolepida
  Paleozoology: QE852.C6
Coelomomycetaceae: QK621.C63
Coelopidae: QL537.C634
Coelostats
  Astronomical instruments: QB97
Coelostomidiidae: QL527.C62
Coenagrionidae: QL520.3.C64
Coenomyiidae: QL537.C636
Coerebidae: QL696.P236
Coevolution
  Biology: QH372
Coffeeberry
  Botany: QK495.R45
Cognitive neuroscience: QP360.5
Coherence
  Nuclear interactions: QC794.6.C58
  Radiation physics: QC476.C6
Coherent state (Physics): QC6.4.C56
Cohesion
  Crystallography: QD933
Cohesion of matter and antimatter: QC183
Cohomology theory
  Mathematical physics: QC20.7.H65
  Topology: QA612.3+
Coincidence circuits: QC787.C58
Coincidences
  Topology: QA612.24
Colchicine
  Animal biochemistry: QP801.C69
  Effect on plants: QK753.C7
  Genetic effects: QH465.C6
Cold
  Effect on plants: QK756
  Heart physiology: QP114.H94
  Physiological effect: QP82.2.C6
Cold fusion: QC791.775.C64

Colorimetric analysis
  Organic chemistry: QD272.C6
Colubridae: QL666.O636
Columbellidae: QL430.5.C73
  Paleozoology: QE809.C48
Columbidae: QL696.C63
  Paleozoology: QE872.C7
Columbiformes: QL696.C6+
Columbium
  Chemical element: Q1 .N3
Columelliaceae: QK495.C65
Colydiidae: QL596.C66
Colymbidae
  Paleozoology: QE872.C75
Comas Sola comet: QB723.C6
Combinations
  Algebra: QA165
Combinatorial analysis
  Algebra: QA164+
Combinatorial analysis (Mathematical physics): QC20.7.C58
Combinatorial chemistry
  Organic synthesis: QD262
Combinatorial geometry: QA167+
Combinatorial group theory
  Algebra: QA182.5
Combinatorial probabilities
  Mathematics: QA273.45
Combinatorial topology: QA612+
Combinatorics
  Algebra: QA164+
Combinatory logic
  Mathematical logic: QA9.5
Combretaceae: QK495.C7
Combtooth blennies: QL638.B6
Comephoridae: QL638.C654
Comets: QB717+
Commelinaceae: QK495.C73
Commonsense reasoning
  Artificial intelligence: Q338.85
Communication
  Animals: QL776
  Microbiology: QR96.5
Communication in astronomy: QB14.2+
Communication in biology: QH303+
Communication in geology: QE48.85+
Communication in physics: QC5.3+
Communication in science: Q223+
Communication in space sciences: QB497.2
Communication of information
  Botany: QK9.2+
  Climatic change: QC902.9+
  Fishes: QL614.73+
  Mammals: QL701.5+
  Natural history: QH13.2+
  Nature conservation: QH77.3.C65
  Paleontology: QE704+
  Zoology: QL9.2+
Communication of meteorological information: QC854.15
Communication of ornithological information: QL672.5+
Communication of planetological information: QB600.3+
Communities
  Fungi: QK604.2.C64
Commutation relations (Quantum mechanics): QC174.17.C6
Commutative rings and algebras: QA251.3
Compact objects
  Astrophysics: QB466.C65
Compact spaces
  Topology: QA611.23
Compactifications
  Topology: QA611.23
Comparative anatomy: QL801+
Comparative histology: QL807
  Human anatomy: QM550+
Comparative human anatomy: QM24
Comparative neurobiology: QP356.15
Comparative physiology: QP33
Compatibility of software: QA76.76.C64
Compensated semiconductors: QC611.8.C6
Competition
  Ecology: QH546.3
  Microbial ecology: QR100.8.C65
Competitions
  Mathematics: QA20.3
Compilers
  Computer software: QA76.76.C65

Computer network resources
  Fishes: QL614.75
  Geology: QE48.87
  Mammals: QL701.8
  Mathematics: QA41.6
    Study and teaching: QA11.5
  Meteorology: QC866.5.C67
  Natural history: QH13.4
  Paleontology: QE704.3
  Physics: QC5.4
  Planets: QB600.34
  Science communication: Q224.5
  Science research: Q179.97
  Science study and teaching: Q182.7
  Zoology: QL9.4
Computer organization: QA76.9.C643
Computer programs
  Chemistry: QD39.3.C6
Computer science: QA75.5+
Computer science as a profession: QA76.25
Computer security: QA76.9.A25
Computer simulation: QA76.9.C65
  Animal biochemistry: QP517.M3
  Immunology: QR182.2.C65
  Physical chemistry: QD455.3.C64
Computer software: QA76.75+
Computer software, Free: QA76.76.F75
Computer system failures: QA76.9.F34
Computer systems: QA75.5+
Computer viruses: QA76.76.C68
Computers
  Social aspects: QA76.9.C66
Computers and children: QA76.9.C659
Computers and civilization: QA76.9.C66
Computers and family: QA76.9.F35
Computers and older people: QA76.9.O43
Computers and women: QA76.9.W65
Concave functions
  Analysis: QA353.C64
Conceptual structures
  Information theory: Q387.2
Conchaspididae: QL527.C65
Conchostraca: QL444.B834
  Paleozoology: QE817.C6
Concretions: QE471.15.C58
Condensation
  Organic chemistry: QD281.C7
Condensation nuclei
  Cloud physics: QC921.6.C6
Condensed benzene rings
  Organic chemistry: QD390+
Condensed gases
  Statistical physics: QC175.16.C6
Condensed matter physics: QC173.45+
Conditioned response
  Neurophysiology: QP416
Conducting polymers
  Organic chemistry: QD382.C66
Conduction
  Physics: QC320.8+
Conduction system
  Heart physiology: QP114.C65
Conductivity
  Plasma physics: QC718.5.T7
Conductometric analysis
  Electrochemical analysis: QD116.C65
Confidence intervals
  Mathematical statistics: QA276.74
Configuration management
  Computer software: QA76.76.C69
Configurations
  Algebra: QA166.25+
Confinement of plasma: QC718.5.C65
Confocal fluorescence microscopy: QH224
Confocal microscopy: QH224
Conformal geometry: QA609
Conformal representation
  Differential geometry: QA646
  Mathematics: QA360
Conformal variants
  Atomic physics: QC174.52.C66
Conformational analysis
  Polymers: QD381.9.C64
Confuciusornithiformes
  Paleozoology: QE872.C77
Conger eels: QL638.C66
Congiopodidae: QL638.C655
Conglomerate
  Petrology: QE471.15.C6

Conglutination
Antigen-antibody reactions: QR187.C65
Congridae: QL638.C66
Congrogadidae: QL638.C666
Congruences
Algebraic geometry: QA608
Conic sections
Analytic geometry: QA552
Conics
Analytic geometry: QA559
Plane geometry: QA485
Conidae: QL430.5.C75
Paleozoology: QE809.C52
Conifer sawflies: QL568.D5
Coniferales
Paleobotany: QE977.2
Coniferophyta
Paleobotany: QE977+
Coniopterygidae: QL513.C65
Conjugated polymers %b Organic chemistry: QD382.C66
Conjugation
Genetics: QH448.2
Conjunctivitis
Microbiology: QR201.C6
Connaraceae: QK495.C76
Connective tissues
Human histology: QM563
Physiology: QP88.23
Connectivity of graphs: QA166.243
Connexes
Algebraic geometry: QA608
Connexins
Animal biochemistry: QP552.C63
Conocardiidae
Paleozoology: QE812.C6
Conodonts
Paleozoology: QE899.2.C65
Conopidae: QL537.C65
Conopophagidae: QL696.P2365
Conotylidae: QL449.65.C6
Conscious automata: Q325+
Consciousness
Animals: QL785.25
Neurophysiology: QP411
Physics: QC6.4.C57
Conservation
Fungi: QK604.2.C66
Conservation biology: QH75+
Conservation laws
Elementary particle physics: QC793.3.C58
Conservation of energy: QC73.8.C6
Constant of gravitation
Geodesy: QB341
Constants
Dielectrics: QC585.7.C6
Optics: QC368
Constants, Cosmological: QB991.C658
Constellation figures: QB802
Constellations of the zodiac
Astronomy: QB803
Constitution of antimatter: QC172+
Constitution of matter: QC172+
Atomic physics: QC170+
Constrained motion
Particle dynamics: QA853
Constraint databases: QA76.9.C67
Constraint programming
Digital computers: QA76.612
Constraints
Artificial intelligence: Q340
Physics: QC6.4.C58
Constructive mathematics: QA9.56+
Constructive realism
Philosophy of science: Q175.32.C66
Contact geometry: QA665
Contaminated sediments
Effect on plants and animals: QH545.C59
Continental crust
Geology: QE511
Continental drift
Geology: QE511.5
Continentality
Meteorology: QC981.8.C65
Continuity
Physics: QC6.4.C6
Continuity of state
Physics: QC307
Continuous cell lines
Cytology: QH585.45

Cracidae: QL696.G23
Cracillariidae: QL561.G7
Crambidae: QL561.P9
Cranchiidae: QL430.3.C72
Craneflies: QL537.T6
Cranes (Birds): QL696.G84
Cranial nerves
  Human anatomy: QM471
  Neurophysiology: QP366
Craniidae: QL395.8.C7
Cranoglanididae: QL638.C83
Craspedosomidae: QL449.65.C72
Crassatellidae: QL430.7.C8
Crassulaceae: QK495.C79
Cratering of planets: QB603.C7
Craterostigmidae: QL449.55.C7
Craters, Impact
  Geology: QE612+
Craters, Meteorite: QB754.8+
Cratons
  Geology: QE511
Creatine
  Animal biochemistry: QP801.C8
  Microbial metabolism: QR92.C74
Creatine kinase
  Animal biochemistry: QP606.C73
Creatinine
  Animal biochemistry: QP801.C8
Creative ability in science: Q172.5.C74
Creediidae: QL638.C84
Creepers (Birds): QL696.P23
Creeping waterbugs: QL523.N4
Cremona transformations: QA602
Creodonta
  Paleozoology: QE882.C9
Creosote-bush
  Botany: QK495.Z9
Crepe myrtle
  Botany: QK495.L9
Crepidotaceae: QK629.C83
Crested swifts: QL696.A554
Crestfishes: QL638.L77
Cretaceous
  Paleobotany: QE924
  Paleontology: QE734
  Stratigraphy: QE685+
Cretaceous-Tertiary boundary:
  QE734.5
  Stratigraphy: QE689
Crickets
  Zoology: QL508.G8
Crinoidea: QL384.C8
  Paleozoology: QE782
Crinozoa
  Paleozoology: QE782
Crioceridae: QL596.C7
Critical opalescence: QC427.8.C7
Critical periods
  Animal behavior: QL763.2
Critical phenomena
  Atomic physics: QC173.4.C74
Critical point
  Physics: QC307
Critical point theory
  Topology: QA614.7
Critical scattering: QC427.8.C73
Critical state
  Physics: QC307
Crocodiles
  Anecdotes and stories: QL795.C67
  Zoology: QL666.C925
Crocodilians: QL666.C9+
Crocodylia: QL666.C9+
  Paleozoology: QE862.C8
Crocydylidae: QL666.C925
Cronartiaceae: QK627.C75
Cross section of interactions
  Nuclear interactions: QC794.6.C7
Crossing over
  Genetics: QH445+
Crosslinked polymers
  Organic chemistry: QD382.P67
Crossocarpaceae: QK569.C86
Crossopterygii
  Paleozoology: QE852.C7
Crossosomataceae: QK495.C797
Crotalidae: QL666.O69
Crotaphytidae: QL666.L237
Croton oil
  Animal biochemistry: QP752.C7
Crowberry
  Botany: QK495.E44

D

Darwin, Charles
  Biography: QH31.D2
  Works: QH365.A1+
Dascyllidae: QL596.D37
Dasyaceae: QK569.D3
Dasyatidae: QL638.85.D3
Dasycladaceae: QK569.D33
  Paleontology: QE955
Dasycladales: QK569.D34
Dasyonygidae: QL540.3.D3
Dasypodidae: QL737.E23
Dasyproctidae: QL737.R644
Dasytidae: QL596.D375
Dasyuridae: QL737.M33
Dasyuromorphia: QL737.M325+
  Paleozoology: QE882.M32
Data compression
  Computer science: QA76.9.D33
Data entry
  Computer science: QA76.9.D337
Data marts
  Computer science: QA76.9.D34
Data mining
  Computer science: QA76.9.D343
Data preparation
  Computer science: QA76.9.D345
Data processing: QA75.5+
  Analytic geometry: QA551.5
  Analytical chemistry: QD75.4.E4
  Animal behavior: QL751.65.D37
  Artificial intelligence: Q336
  Astronomy: QB51.3.E43
  Astrophysics: QB462.2
  Biological research: QH324.2+
  Calculus: QA303.5.D37
  Chemistry: QD39.3.E46
  Crystallography: QD906.7.E4
  Cytology: QH585.5.D38
  Differential equations: QA371.5.D37
  Electrochemistry: QD555.6.E4
  Electromagnetism: QC760.54
  Endocrine glands: QP187.3.D38
  Galaxies: QB857.5.D37
  Genetics: QH441.2
  Geochemistry: QE515.5.D37
  Geodesy: QB297
  Geology: QE48.8
Data processing
  Geometry: QA448.D38
  Gravity observations: QB336
  Group theory: QA174.7.D36
  Heat transfer: QC320.22.E43
  Linear algebra: QA185.D37
  Mammals: QL706.5.D38
  Marine biology: QH91.57.E4
  Mathematical statistics: QA276.4+
  Microbiology: QR69.D35
  Mineralogy: QE364.2.E4
  Multilinear algebra: QA185.D37
  Natural history (General): QH60.2
  Neurophysiology: QP357.5
  Nuclear chemistry: QD602.5.E4
  Organic chemistry: QD255.5.E4
  Paleontology: QE721.2.D37
  Physical chemistry: QD455.3.E4
  Physiology: QP33.6.D38
  Planets: QB602.95
  Polymers: QD381.9.E4
  Quantum chemistry: QD462.6.D38
  Rain and rainfall: QC926.2
  Science: Q183.9
  Seismology: QE539.2.D36
  Spectroscopy: QC452
  Stratigraphy: QE652
  Structural geography: QE601.3.D37
  Thermodynamics: QC311.29
Data recovery
  Computer science: QA76.9.D348
Data structures
  Computer science: QA76.9.D35
Data summaries
  Atmospheric pressure: QC885.4+
Data warehousing
  Computer science: QA76.9.D37
Database design: QA76.9.D26
Database management: QA76.9.D3
Database security: QA76.9.D314
Databases: QA76.9.D32
  Biology: QH303.15+
Dating
  Radioactive substances: QC798.D3
Datiscaceae: QK495.D33
Datolite
  Mineralogy: QE391.D3

Daubentoniidae: QL737.P935
Davidiaceae: QK495.D34
Davidsoniaceae: QK495.D35
Dawn chorus
  Radio meteorology: QC973.4.C4
Daylily: QK495.H38
Dead animals
  Zoology: QL87.5
Death
  Biology: QH530
  Cells: QH671
  Developmental physiology: QP87
Debugging in computer science:
  QA76.9.D43
Decapoda: QL444.M33
  Paleozoology: QE817.D3
Decay
  Elementary particle physics:
    QC793.3.D4
  Nuclear interactions: QC794.6.R3
  Radioactive substances: QC795.8.D4
Decidability
  Mathematical logic: QA9.65
Decimal system: QA141.35
Decision theory
  Mathematical statistics: QA279.4+
Declarative programming
  Digital computers: QA76.615
Decompilers: QA76.76.D57
Decomposition method
  Mathematical physics: QC20.7.D4
  System analysis: QA402.2
Decremeters: QC667
Deductive systems
  Mathematical logic: QA9.65+
Deep-sea biology
  Marine biology: QH91.8.D44
Deep-sea zone
  Ecology: QH541.5.D35
Deep-sea zoology: QL125.5
Deepsea smelts: QL638.B25
Deepwater cardinalfishes: QL638.E62
Deer
  Anecdotes and stories: QL795.D3
  Zoology: QL737.U55
Deerflies: QL537.T25
Default reasoning
  Artificial intelligence: Q339
Defects
  Condensed matter physics:
    QC173.458.D43
  Semiconductor physics: QC611.6.D4
  Solid state physics: QC176.8.D44
Defects in crystals: QD921+
Defense mechanisms
  Animals: QL759
Deformable bodies, Mechanics of
  Analytic mechanics: QA901+
Deformation
  Geology: QE604
Deformation of matter and antimatter:
  QC193
Deformation of surfaces
  Differential geometry: QA648
Deformations of structures
  Topology: QA614.97
Degenerate differential equations:
  QA377.5
Degeneration
  Biology: QH528
  Plants: QK987
Degeneriaceae: QK495.D4
Deglutition
  Physiology: QP148
Degree of freedom
  Atomic physics: QC174.52.D43
  Elementary particle physics:
    QC793.3.D43
Dehydrogenases
  Animal biochemistry: QP603.D4
Dehydrogenation
  Organic chemistry: QD281.D4
Deicing chemicals
  Effect on plants and animals:
    QH545.D4
Deinococcaceae: QR82.D37
Deinopidae: QL458.42.D55
Delavan comet: QB723.D45
Delayed neutrons
  Elementary particle physics:
    QC793.5.D42+

Delayed protons
  Elementary particle physics:
    QC793.5.D442+
Delesseriaceae: QK569.D4
Deletion
  Chromosomal mutation: QH462.D4
Delphacidae: QL527.D44
DELPHI (Videotex system):
  QA76.57.D44
Delphinidae: QL737.C432
Delsalination plants
  Effect on plants and animals:
    QH545.S33
Delta Scuti stars: QB843.D44
Deltatheridia
  Paleozoology: QE882.D4
Delthyrididae
  Paleozoology: QE797.D3
Deluge
  Geology: QE507
Dematiaceae: QK625.D4
Demodicidae: QL458.2.D45
Demospongiae: QL373.D4
Dendritic cells: QR185.8.D45
Dendrobatidae: QL668.E233
Dendroclimatology
  Paleoclimatology: QC884.2.D4
Dendrocolaptidae: QL696.P24
Denitrification
  Microbial ecology: QR100.8.D46
Denitrifying bacteria
  Microbial ecology: QR100.8.D46
Denning comet: QB723.D5
Dennstaedtiaceae: QK524.D5
Dense plasma focus
  Plasma physics: QC718.5.D38
Densitometers: QC391
Density
  Measurement: QC111+
  Plasma physics: QC718.5.D4
Density functionals
  Inorganic chemistry: QD152.5.D46
  Mathematical physics: QC20.7.D43
  Quantum chemistry: QD462.6.D45
Density gradient centrifugation
  Analytical biochemistry: QP519.9.D45
  Biological research: QH324.9.D46
Density matrices
  Quantum chemistry: QD462.6.D46
  Quantum mechanics: QC174.17.D44
Dental microbiology: QR47
Dentata nucleus
  Anatomy: QL938.D44
Denticipitidae: QL638.D4
Deoxy sugars
  Animal biochemistry: QP702.D38
Deoxyribonucleases
  Animal biochemistry: QP609.D4
Deoxyribonucleate
  nucleotidyltransferases
  Animal biochemistry: QP606.D46
Deoxyribonucleic acid
  Microbial metabolism: QR92.D45
  Plant constituent: QK898.D44
Deoxyribonucleic acids
  Animal biochemistry: QP624+
  Organic chemistry: QD435
Deoxyribose
  Animal biochemistry: QP702.D4
Deposition
  Geology: QE571+
Depsides
  Plant constituent: QK898.D46
Derbidae: QL527.D47
Derichthyidae: QL638.D47
Derivatives
  Proteins, peptides, amino acids, etc.:
    QD431.25.D47
Dermanyssidae: QL458.2.D47
Dermaptera
  Paleozoology: QE832.D47
  Zoology: QL510+
Dermateaceae: QK623.D47
Dermatemydidae: QL666.C54
Dermatophilaceae: QR82.D4
Dermestidae: QL596.D4
Dermochelyidae: QL666.C546
Dermoglyphidae: QL458.2.D475
Dermoptera: QL737.D35+
Derodontidae: QL596.D42
Description logics
  Information theory: Q387.3
Descriptive astronomy: QB494.2+
Descriptive geometry: QA501+

Descriptive mechanics
Physics: QC120+
Descriptive mineralogy: QE372+
Desert climatology: QC993.7
Desert dormice: QL737.R682
Desert ecology: QH541.5.D4
Desert meteorology: QC993.7
Desert plants
Plant ecology: QK922
Deserts
Biogeography: QH88
Ecology: QH541.5.D4
Plant ecology: QK938.D4
Zoology: QL116
Desfontainiaceae: QK495.D42
Desidae: QL458.42.D44
Design
Algebra: QA166.25+
Desmerestiaceae: QK569.D43
Desmidiaceae: QK569.D46
Desmidiales: QK569.Z82
Desmodontidae: QL737.C52
Desmostylia
Paleozoology: QE882.D45
Desmothoracida: QL368.D4
Detergents
Effect on plants: QK753.D4
Deterioration
Polymers: QD381.9.D47
Determinants
Mathematical physics: QC20.7.D45
Matrices: QA191
Determination of the ecliptic
Spherical astronomy: QB171
Determination, Sex
Physiology: QP278.5
Determinative mineralogy: QE367+
Determinism (Physics): QC6.4.D46
Detonation waves (Gas dynamics): QC168.85.D46
Deuteron magnetic resonance spectroscopy
Analytical chemistry: QD96.D48
Deuterons
Elementary particle physics: QC793.5.D482+
Deuterophlebiidae: QL537.D47
Development
Biology: QH491
Computer software: QA76.76.D47
Fishes: QL639.25
Insects: QL495.5
Invertebrates: QL364.18
Microbiology: QR73.4
Plant physiology: QK731+
Developmental behavior
Animals: QL763+
Developmental endocrinology: QP187.6
Developmental genetics: QH453
Developmental immunology: QR184.5
Developmental neurobiology
Physiology: QP363.5
Developmental neurophysiology: QP356.25
Developmental physiology: QP83.8+
Deviation of the magnetic compass: QC849
Device drivers
Computer software: QA76.76.D49
Devil's claw
Botany: QK495.M287
Devonian
Paleobotany: QE918
Paleontology: QE728
Stratigraphy: QE665
Dew formation
Meteorology: QC929.D5
Dew plants
Plant ecology: QK916
Dexiidae: QL537.D48
Dextranase
Animal biochemistry: QP609.D48
Diabase: QE462.D5
Diadocidiidae: QL537.D52
Diadromy
Fishes: QL639.5
Diagnostic bacteriology: QR67.2
Diagnostic mycology
Microbiology: QR248
Diagnostic parasitology
Microbiology: QR255
Diagnostic technique
Microbiology: QR67+
Virology: QR387

Diagnostics
  Plasma physics: QC718.5.D5
Diagrams
  Mathematics teaching aid: QA19.C45
Dialectical materialism
  Philosophy of science: Q175.32.D52
Dialectical materialism (Physics):
  QC6.4.D5
Dialogue
  Philosophy of science: Q175.32.D53
Dialypetalanthaceae: QK495.D43
Dialysis
  Organic chemistry: QD281.D47
Diamagnetism
  Physics: QC764
Diameter of the sun: QB523
Diameters, Stellar: QB818
Diamino amino acids: QP562.D53
Diamondback moths: QL561.P55
Diamonds
  Mineralogy: QE393
Diamonds in optical instruments:
  QC374.5
Diapensiaceae: QK495.D435
Diaperasticidae: QL510.3.D5
Diaphragm
  Anatomy: QL851
  Human anatomy: QM265
Diaporthales: QK623.D55
Diapriidae: QL568.D44
Diarrhea
  Microbiology: QR201.D4
Diarrhea, Viral
  Microbiology: QR201.V53
Diaspididae: QL527.D5
Diastase
  Animal biochemistry: QP609.A45
  Phytochemistry: QK896
Diastatidae: QL537.D53
Diastole
  Heart physiology: QP114.D5
Diastomatidae: QL430.5.D43
Diatomophyceae: QK569.D54
Diatoms: QK569.D54
  Paleontology: QE955
Diazinon
  Effect on plants and animals:
    QH545.D486
Diazo compounds
  Aliphatic compounds: QD305.A9
  Aromatic compounds: QD341.A9
Dibamidae: QL666.L238
Dibranchiata
  Paleozoology: QE807.D5
Dicaeidae: QL696.P242
Dicamptodontidae: QL668.C243
Diceratidae
  Paleozoology: QE812.D5
Diceratiidae: QL638.D5
Dichapetalaceae: QK495.D44
Dichloromethane
  Effect on plants and animals:
    QH545.D5
Dichlorophenoxyacetic acid
  Effect on plants: QK753.D5
Dichroism: QC446.D5
Dicksoniaceae: QK524.D55
Dicotyledons: QK495.A12
  Paleobotany: QE983
Dicranaceae: QK539.D5
Dicroglossidae: QL668.E234
Dicruridae: QL696.P2427
Dictynidae: QL458.42.D5
Dictyopharidae: QL527.D53
Dictyosteliaceae: QK635.D5
Dictyosteliales: QK635.D53
Dicyrtomidae: QL503.D5
Didelphidae: QL737.M34
Didelphimorphia: QL737.M337+
  Paleozoology: QE882.M33
Didiereaceae: QK495.D45
Didymelaceae: QK495.D46
Didymium
  Chemical element: Q1 .N4
Diel vertical migration
  Fishes: QL639.6
Dielasmatidae
  Paleozoology: QE797.D5
Dielectric heating: QC585.7.H4
Dielectric loss: QC585.7.L6
Dielectrics: QC584+
Dielectrophoresis: QC585.7.D5

Dignathodontidae: QL449.55.D5
Diguetidae: QL458.42.D53
Dihydroxyphenylalanine
  Animal biochemistry: QP563.D5
Dikes
  Geology: QE611+
Dilaenaceae: QK555.D5
Dilaridae: QL513.D5
Dilatation
  Heart physiology: QP114.D54
Dilatation of time (Relativity physics): QC173.59.T5
Dilleniaceae: QK495.D47
Dimensional analysis
  Mathematical physics: QC20.7.D55
Dimethyl sulfide
  Meteorology: QC879.9.D55
Dimethylpropiothetin
  Plant constituent: QK898.D54
Dimorphidae: QL568.D47
Dimyidae: QL430.7.D55
Dinamoebales: QK569.D55
Dingoes
  Anecdotes and stories: QL795.D5
Dinocerata
  Paleozoology: QE882.U8
Dinoflagellates: QK569.D56
  Paleontology: QE955
Dinomyidae: QL737.R646
Dinopidae: QL458.42.D55
Dinornithiformes
  Paleozoology: QE872.D5
Dinosaur tracks: QE861.6.T72
Dinosaurs
  Paleozoology: QE861.2+
Diodontidae: QL638.D56
Diomedeidae: QL696.P63
Dioncophyllaceae: QK495.D48
Diophantine analysis
  Number theory: QA242
Diopsidae: QL537.D56
Dioptidae: QL561.D5
Diorite: QE462.D56
Dioscoreaceae: QK495.D54
Dioxins
  Effect on plants and animals: QH545.D55
Dipentodontaceae: QK495.D545
Dipeptidases
  Animal biochemistry: QP609.D54
Diphenol oxidase
  Animal biochemistry: QP603.D5
Diphtheria
  Microbiology: QR201.D5
Diphtheroid organisms
  Microbiology: QR201.D6
Diphyllidae: QL596.D57
Diplatyidae: QL510.3.D56
Diplocentridae: QL458.72.D5
Diplomonadida: QL368.D65
Diplomystidae: QL638.D57
Diplopoda: QL449.6+
  Paleozoology: QE829.D5
Diploporita
  Paleozoology: QE783.D5
Diplopteridae: QL505.7.D5
Diplura: QL503.4.A1+
Dipluridae: QL458.42.D56
Dipnoi
  Paleozoology: QE852.D5
Dipnoid fishes: QL638.3
Dipodidae: QL737.R648
Dippers: QL696.P235
Diprionidae: QL568.D5
Diprotodontia: QL737.M345+
  Paleozoology: QE882.M34
Dipsacaceae: QK495.D56
Dipsocoridae: QL523.D5
Diptera
  Paleozoology: QE832.D6
  Zoology: QL531+
Dipteriformes: QL637.9.D5
Dipterocarpaceae: QK495.D564
Diptilomiopidae
  Zoology: QL458.2.D56
Diquat
  Effect on plants and animals: QH545.D57
Direcmidae: QL638.D577
Direct interactions
  Nuclear physics: QC794.8.D57
Directed graphs
  Algebra: QA166.15
Dirichlet problem: QA425

DNA-ligand interactions: QP624.74+
DNA ligases
  Animal biochemistry: QP619.D53
DNA microarrays
  Animal biochemistry: QP624.5.D726
DNA polymerases
  Animal biochemistry: QP606.D46
DNA probes
  Animal biochemistry: QP624.5.D73
  Microbiology: QR69.D54
DNA restriction enzymes
  Animal biochemistry: QP609.R44
DNA topoisomerases
  Animal biochemistry: QP616.D56
DNA vaccines: QR189.5.D53
DNA viruses
  Virology: QR394.5
Dobsonflies
  Zoology: QL514.7.C67
Docodonta
  Paleozoology: QE882.D6
Docosahexaenoc acid
  Animal biochemistry: QP752.D63
Documentation
  Computer science: QA76.9.D6
  Ecology: QH541.15.D6
Documentation of software:
  QA76.76.D63
Dodder
  Botany: QK495.C967
Dodos
  Zoology: QL696.C67
Dogbane
  Botany: QK495.A66
Dogfish shark
  Laboratory manuals: QL813.F57
Dogfish sharks: QL638.95.S84
Dogs
  Anecdotes and stories: QL795.D6
  Laboratory manuals: QL813.D64
  Zoology: QL737.C22
Dogwood
  Botany: QK495.C785
Dolabriferidae: QL430.5.D55
Dolichopodidae: QL537.D6
Dolichopsyllidae: QL599.7.D6
Dolomite: QE471.15.D6
Dolomite
  Mineralogy: QE391.D6
Dolphinfishes: QL638.C795
Dolphins
  Anecdotes and stories: QL795.D7
  Zoology: QL737.C432
Dominance
  Genetics: QH447.2
Donacidae: QL430.7.D65
Donaciidae: QL596.D6
DOPA
  Animal biochemistry: QP563.D5
Dopamine
  Animal biochemistry: QP563.D66
Doped semiconductors: QC611.8.D66
Doping
  Semiconductor physics: QC611.6.D6
Doradidae: QL638.D6
Dorididae: QL430.5.D6
Dories
  Zoology: QL638.Z4
Dormancy
  Biology: QH523
  Effect on plants: QK761
Dormice: QL737.R656
Dorsal ventricular ridge
  Anatomy: QL938.D65
Dorylaidae: QL537.P57
DOS
  Computer software
    Operating systems: QA76.774.D67
Dothideaceae: QK623.D72
Dothideales: QK623.D74
Double layer, Electric
  Electrochemistry: QD564
Double layers
  Astrophysics: QB462.72
Double refraction
  Optics: QC426.8.D68
Double salts
  Inorganic chemistry: QD191
Double star systems theory
  Celestial mechanics: QB421
Double stars: QB821+
Douglasiidae: QL561.D6
Dover demon: QL89.2.D68

Doves
  Zoology: QL696.C63
Dragonets: QL638.C15
Dragonflies
  Paleozoology: QE832.A53
  Zoology: QL520+
Drawings of the moon
  Descriptive astronomy: QB595
Drawings of the planets
  Descriptive astronomy: QB605
Dreaming
  Physiology: QP426
Dredging
  Aquatic biology: QH90.57.D7
  Effect on plants and animals:
    QH545.D7
  Marine biology: QH91.57.D7
Dredging (Fisheries)
  Effect on plants and animals:
    QH545.D713
Dredging spoil
  Effect on plants and animals:
    QH545.D72
Dreissenidae
  Paleozoology: QE812.D7
Dreisseniidae: QL430.7.D8
Drepanaspidae
  Paleozoology: QE852.D7
Drepanidae: QL561.D7
Drepanididae: QL696.P243
Drepanosiphidae: QL523.D74
Drift
  Geology: QE579
  Plasma physics: QC718.5.D7
Drift chambers
  Nuclear physics: QC787.D74
Drilidae: QL596.D67
Drilling muds
  Effect on plants and animals:
    QH545.D74
Drilling platforms
  Effect on plants and animals:
    QH545.D75
Drinking
  Physiology: QP150
Driving clocks
  Astronomical instruments: QB97
DRL (Computer program language):
  QA76.73.D25
Dromadidae: QL696.C44
Dromiceidae: QL696.C34
Drongos: QL696.P2427
Droppings, Animal: QL768
Droseraceae: QK495.D76
Drosophila
  Experimental genetics: QH470.D7
Drosophilidae: QL537.D76
Drought tolerance
  Plant physiology: QK754.7.D75
Droughts
  Effect on plants: QK754.7.D75
  Meteorology: QC929.2+
Drug resistance
  Microbiology: QR177
Drug use
  Animals: QL756.7
Drugs
  DNA-ligand interactions:
    QP624.75.D77
Drums (Fishes)
  Zoology: QL638.S34
Drying
  Microbiology: QR69.F7
Dryinidae: QL568.D7
Dryomyzidae: QL537.D79
Dryopidae: QL596.D7
Dryopteridaceae: QK524.D79
Dualism (Physics): QC6.4.D8
Duckeodendraceae: QK495.D9
Ducks
  Zoology: QL696.A52
Ducks, Wild
  Anecdotes and stories: QL795.B57
Duckweed
  Botany: QK495.L527
Ductless glands
  Anatomy: QL868
  Human anatomy: QM371
Ducts, Bile
  Physiology: QP185.3
Ducts, Excretory
  Anatomy: QL873.5
Dueteromycetes: QK625.A1+
Dugongidae: QL737.S62

Dugongs
  Zoology: QL737.S62
Dulidae: QL696.P2435
Dunaliellaceae: QK569.P65
Dunes
  Biogeography: QH88.5
  Botany: QK938.D9
Duodecimal system: QA141.5.A1+
Duplication
  Chromosomal mutation: QH462.D8
Duplication of the cube
  Elementary geometry: QA469
Durangite
  Mineralogy: QE391.D8
Durango root: QK495.D33
Dussumieriidae
  Zoology: QL638.C64
Dust
  Atmospheric pollutants: QC882.5
  Microbiology: QR101
Dust influences
  Meteorology: QC929.D9
Dust storms
  Mars (Planet): QB643.D87
Dusty plasmas
  Plasma physics: QC718.5.D84
Dusty-wings: QL513.C65
Dutchman's pipe
  Botany: QK495.A688
Dwaft galaxies: QB858
Dwarf boas: QL666.O68
Dwarf novae: QB843.D85
Dwarf pipe snakes: QL666.O6265
Dwarf planets: QB698+
Dwarf stars: QB843.D9
Dye plants
  Botany: QK98.7.A1+
Dynamic climatology: QC981.7.D94
Dynamic geology: QE517+
Dynamic meteorology: QC880+
Dynamics
  Analytic mechanics: QA843+
  Cloud physics: QC921.6.D95
  Elementary particle physics: QC793.3.D9
  Physics: QC133+
  Plasma physics: QC718.5.D9
Dynamics, Molecular
  Animal biochemistry: QP517.M65
Dynamics of a particle
  Analytic mechanics: QA851+
Dynamics, Stellar: QB810+
Dynastidae: QL596.D85
Dysderidae: QL458.42.D9
Dysentery
  Microbiology: QR201.D9
Dysodiidae: QL523.D9
Dysommidae: QL638.D93
Dysomminidae: QL638.D95
Dysphaniaceae: QK495.D95
Dysprosium
  Chemical element: Q1 .D8
Dystiscidae: QL596.D9
Dystrophin
  Animal biochemistry: QP552.D95

E

E region
  Meteorology: QC881.2.E2
Eagle rays: QL638.85.M9
Ear
  Anatomy: QL948
  Human anatomy: QM507
Ear labyrinths
  Physiology: QP471+
Eared seals
  Zoology: QL737.P63
Early stars: QB843.E2
Earth
  Age: QE508
  Crust: QE511
  Internal structure: QE509+
  Mean density: QB341
  Physical history: QE501
Earth as a planet: QB630+
Earth capture of the moon: QB392.C3
Earth currents
  Geomagnetism: QC845
Earth interior: QE509+
Earth, Mathematical theory of the figure of the: QB283
Earth movements
  Geology: QE598+

Electronics in astronomy: QB127+
Electrons
  Elementary particle physics:
    QC793.5.E62+
Electrooptics: QC673+
Electrophiles
  Organic analysis: QD271.35.E54
Electrophoresis
  Analytical chemistry: QD79.E44
  Animal biochemistry: QP519.9.E434
  Biological research: QH324.9.E4
  Blood physiology: QP99.5.E5
  Cytology: QH585.5.E46
  Electrochemistry: QD562.E45
  Organic chemistry: QD272.E43
  Quantitative analysis: QD117.E45
Electrophoresis, Capillary
  Animal biochemistry: QP519.9.C36
Electrophoridae: QL638.E34
Electrophysiology: QP112.5.E46
  Biology: QH517
  Fishes: QL639.1
  Physiology: QP341
  Plant physiology: QK845
Electroporation
  Cytology: QH585.5.E48
Electroreceptors
  Physiology: QP447.5
Electrostatic accelerators
  Nuclear physics: QC787.E4
Electrostatic analyzers
  Nuclear physics: QC787.E42
Electrostatic lenses: QC544.E5
Electrostatics
  Physics: QC570+
  Plasma physics: QC718.5.E48
Electroweak interactions
  Nuclear physics: QC794.8.E44
Electrum
  Mineralogy: QE391.E43
Elementary geometry: QA451+
Elementary mathematics: QA101+
Elementary particle physics: QC793+
Elements, Chemical
  Inorganic chemistry: QD181.A+
  Physical chemistry: QD466+
Elements, Individual
  Cycles: QH344+
Elenchidae: QL599.3.E4
Elephant shrews: QL737.M242
Elephantidae: QL737.P98
Elephants
  Anecdotes and stories: QL795.E4
  Zoology: QL737.P98
ELF electromagnetic fields
  Effect on plants and animals:
    QH545.E42
Elimination
  Matrices: QA192
Elimination reactions
  Organic chemistry: QD281.E4
Eliminative behavior
  Animals: QL780
Elixer of life
  Alchemy: QD26.5.E4
Ellesmeroceratidae
  Paleozoology: QE807.E4
Ellipsoids
  Statics: QA827
Ellipsometry
  Biological research: QH324.9.E44
Elliptic curves: QA567.2.E44
Elliptic functions
  Analysis: QA343
Elliptic integrals
  Analysis: QA343
Elliptical galaxies: QB858.4
Ellobiidae: QL430.5.E45
Elm
  Botany: QK495.U4
Elmidae: QL596.E45
Elodea
  Botany: QK495.H86
Elopidae: QL638.E4
Elopiformes: QL637.9.E4
  Paleozoology: QE852.E65
Elysiidae: QL430.5.E48
Emballonuridae: QL737.C525
Embedding of microscope specimens:
  QH234
Embedding theorems
  Mathematical physics: QC20.7.E48
Emberizidae: QL696.P2438

Epiphytes
  Plant ecology: QK922
Epiphytic lichens: QK584.6.E64
Epiplemidae: QL561.E758
Epipyropidae: QL561.E759
Episomes: QH452.5
Epistasis
  Genetics: QH450.7
Epitaxy, Molecular beam:
  QC611.6.M64
Epithelium
  Human histology: QM561
  Physiology: QP88.4
Epitoniidae: QL430.5.E6
  Paleozoology: QE809.E64
Epoxy polymers
  Organic chemistry: QD383.E66
Epstein-Barr virus
  Virology: QR400.2.E68
Epstein-Barr virus diseases
  Microbiology: QR201.E75
Equation of time
  Astronomy: QB217
Equations of motion
  Meteorology: QC880.4.E7
Equations of state
  Astrophysics: QB466.E65
  Atomic physics: QC173.4.E65
  Physics: QC307
Equations, Theory of
  Algebra: QA211+
Equatorial mountings
  Astronomical instruments: QB97
Equidae: QL737.U62
Equilibrium
  Physiology: QP471+
  Plasma physics: QC718.5.E66
  Statics: QA831
  Superconductors: QC611.97.E69
Equilibrium, Punctuated
  Biology: QH398
Equipment and supplies
  Astronomical photography: QB121.5
Equipollence
  Analytic geometry: QA556.5
Equisetaceae: QK524.E6
Equisetales
  Paleobotany: QE965
Equisetophyta
  Paleobotany: QE965
Erbium
  Chemical element: Q1 .E6
Eremaeidae: QL458.2.E73
Eremobatidae: QL458.82.E7
Eremolepidaceae: QK495.E64
Erepsin
  Animal biochemistry: QP609.E7
Eresidae: QL458.42.E7
Erethizontidae: QL737.R652
Ergocalciferol
  Animal biochemistry: QP772.E74
Ergodic theory: QA611.5
  Integral calculus: QA313
Ericaceae: QK495.E68
Erinaceidae: QL737.E753
Erinaceomorpha: QL737.E75+
  Paleozoology: QE882.E75
Erinnidae: QL537.X9
Eriocaulaceae: QK495.E685
Eriococcidae: QL527.E73
Eriocraniidae: QL561.E8
Eriophyidae: QL458.2.E75
Eriosomatidae: QL527.E78
Eriospermaceae
  Botany: QK495.E695
Ermine moths: QL561.Y7
Erosion
  Geology: QE571+
Erosion, Aerial
  Geology: QE597
Erosion, Aqueous
  Geology: QE581
Erosion, Glacial
  Geology: QE575+
Erosion, Soil
  Effect on plants and animals:
    QH545.S64
Erotylidae: QL596.E7
Error messages
  Computer science: QA76.9.E77
Errors of adjustment
  Astronomy: QB154
Errors, Scientific: Q172.5.E77

eWorld (Online service): QA76.57.E88
Excavations, Paleontological:
  QE721.2.P26
Exchange of meteorological information:
  QC866.5.E93
Exchange reactions
  Chemistry: QD63.E83
Excipulaceae: QK625.E9
Excitation
  Nervous system: QP363
  Nuclear interactions: QC794.6.E9
Excited state chemistry: QD461.5
Exclusive interactions
  Nuclear and particle physics:
    QC794.8.E93
Excretory organs
  Anatomy: QL872+
Exercise
  Endocrine glands: QP187.3.E93
  Physiology: QP301+
Exercise effects
  Heart physiology: QP114.E9
Exhibitions
  Botany: QK79+
  Fungi: QK600.5+
Exobasidiaceae: QK627.53.E93
Exobasidiales: QK627.5+
Exocoetidae: QL638.E9
Exocrine glands
  Physiology: QP187.7.A1+
Exocytosis
  Cells: QH634.2
Exopeptidases
  Animal biochemistry: QP609.P45
Exosphere
  Meteorology: QC881.2.E9
Exotic birds
  Zoology: QL677.79.E85
Exotic marine organisms
  Marine biology: QH91.8.E94
Exotic nuclei
  Elementary particle physics:
    QC793.3.E93
Expanding universe (Cosmology):
  QB991.E94
Expansion
  Gases: QC164
Expansion
  Liquids: QC145.4.E9
  Pressure, volume and temperature
    relations: QC281.5.E9
  Solid state physics: QC176.8.E94
Expansions
  Topology: QA611.29
Expeditions
  Geology: QE4
  Natural history: QH11
Expeditions and voyages, Scientific:
  Q115+
Experimental biology: QH324+
Experimental design
  Mathematical statistics: QA279+
Experimental embryology: QL961
Experimental mechanics
  Physics: QC120+
Experimental physiology: QP42+
Experiments
  Biology: QH316.5
  Botany: QK52.6
  Organic chemistry: QD257.5
  Space science research: QB500.264
Expert systems
  Computer software: QA76.76.E95
Explanation
  Philosophy of science: Q175.32.E97
Expletocystida
  Paleozoology: QE799.E95
Exploding wire phenomenon
  Electric discharge: QC703.7
Exploration
  Moon: QB582.5
Explosion
  Thermochemistry: QD516
Exponential functions
  Analysis: QA342
Exponential sums
  Number theory
    Algebra: QA246.7+
Exponents
  Algebra: QA161.E95
Exterior algebra: QA205
Exterior lighting
  Effect on plants and animals:
    QH545.E98

External skin
  Human anatomy: QM484
Extinct amphibians: QL644.8+
Extinct animals
  Zoology: QL88+
Extinct birds: QL676.8
Extinct insects: QL467.9
Extinct mammals: QL707
Extinct reptiles: QL644.8+
Extinction
  Dinosaurs: QE861.6.E95
  Paleontology: QE721.2.E97
  Zoology: QL88+
Extinction (Biology): QH78
Extra-meridian instruments: QB103
Extracellular enzymes
  Animal biochemistry: QP601.6
Extracellular matrix proteins
  Animal biochemistry: QP552.E95
Extracellular space
  Cytology: QH603.E93
Extraction
  Chemistry: QD63.E88
Extragalactic distances: QB857.5.E97
Extrapolation
  Mathematics: QA281
Extrapyramidal tracts
  Neurophysiology: QP370.5
Extrasensory perception
  Animals: QL785.3
Extrasolar planets: QB820
Extraterrestrial life
  Astronomy: QB54
Extraterrestrial seismology: QB455.5
Extreme environments
  Microbiology: QR100.9
Extremities
  Human embryology: QM695.E95
Extremities, Bones of
  Human anatomy: QM117
Eye
  Anatomy: QL949
  Human anatomy: QM511
  Microbiology: QR171.E9
Eye movement
  Neurophysiology: QP477.5
Eyeball
  Neurophysiology: QP476+
Eyepieces
  Astronomical instruments: QB111
Eylaidae: QL458.2.E9

F

F region
  Meteorology: QC881.2.F2
Face
  Human embryology: QM695.F32
Face muscles
  Physiology: QP327
Factor analysis
  Chemistry: QD39.3.F33
  Mathematical statistics: QA278.5
Factor tables: QA51
Factorization
  Number theory: QA242
Factorization method
  Quantum mechanics: QC174.17.F3
Factors
  Algebra: QA161.F3
Faculae: QB526.F3
Fagaceae: QK495.F14
Failures of computer systems:
  QA76.9.F34
Failures of software: QA76.76.F34
Fairy shrimps: QL444.B815
Fairyflies: QL568.M94
Falconidae: QL696.F34
Falconiformes: QL696.F3+
Falcons
  Zoology: QL696.F34
Falculiferidae: QL458.2.F3
False cat shark: QL638.95.P8
False coral snakes: QL666.O625
False morays: QL638.X45
False powerpost beetles: QL596.B5
False sunbirds: QL696.P2625
False vampires: QL737.C535
Familial behavior
  Animals: QL761.5
Family and computers: QA76.9.F35
Famous animals: QL793

Fangataufa Atoll
  Geology: QE566.F35
Far ultraviolet spectrum
  Optics: QC459.5
Faraday effect: QC675.5.F3
Fasciolariidae: QL430.5.F2
  Paleozoology: QE809.F3
Fast neutrons
  Elementary particle physics:
    QC793.5.F32+
Fat-soluble vitamins
  Animal biochemistry: QP772.F37
Fatigue
  Neurophysiology: QP421
Fats
  Aliphatic compounds: QD305.F2
  Animal biochemistry: QP752.F3
Fatty acid-binding proteins
  Animal biochemistry: QP552.F37
Fatty acids
  Animal biochemistry: QP752.F35
  Microbial metabolism: QR92.F3
  Plant constituent: QK898.F3
Fatty oils
  Aliphatic compounds: QD305.F2
Fault-tolerant computing: QA76.9.F38
Faults
  Geology: QE606+
Favolaschiaceae: QK629.F37
Faye comet: QB723.F2
Fc receptors: QR185.8.F33
fd bacteriophage: QR342.2.F37
Feathers
  Birds: QL697.4
Feces
  Microbiology: QR171.F4
  Physiology: QP159
Fecundation
  Physiology: QP273
  Plant physiology: QK828
Fedorovskii method
  Determinative mineralogy: QE369.F4
Feeding and feeds
  Invertebrates: QL364.3
Feldspar
  Mineralogy: QE391.F3
Felidae: QL737.C23
Female generative organs
  Human anatomy: QM421
  Microbiology: QR171.F45
Female organs, Accessory: QP265
Female reproductive organs
  Anatomy: QL881
Female sex physiology: QP259+
Femtochemistry: QD716.L37
Fenite: QE462.F4
Ferberite
  Mineralogy: QE391.F4
Fermat's theorem: QA244
Fermentation
  Phytochemistry: QK896
Fermi liquid theory (Statistical physics):
  QC174.85.F47
Fermi surface
  Solid state physics: QC176.8.F4
Fermions
  Elementary particle physics:
    QC793.5.F42+
Fermium
  Chemical element: Q1 .F5
Fermo meteorite: QB756.F47
Ferns
  Botany: QK520+
  Paleobotany: QE961
Ferredoxin-NADP reductase
  Animal biochemistry: QP603.F47
Ferrierite
  Mineralogy: QE391.F45
Ferrimagnetism: QC761.4
Ferrites
  Analytical chemistry: QD137.F35
  Magnetism: QC766.F3
Ferritin
  Animal biochemistry: QP552.F47
Ferroboron
  Analytical chemistry: QD137.F38
Ferrochromium
  Analytical chemistry: QD137.F4
Ferroelectric crystals
  Spectra: QC464.F45
Ferroelectricity
  Physics: QC596+
Ferromagnetism
  Physics: QC761.5

Ferroniobium
  Analytical chemistry: QD137.F44
Ferrotungsten
  Analytical chemistry: QD137.F48
Ferrum
  Chemical element: Q1 .F4
Fertilization
  Physiology: QP273
  Plant physiology: QK828
  Sexual reproduction: QH485
Fertilizers
  Effect on plants and animals: QH545.F47
Fetal development, Animal: QL971+
Few-body problem
  Theoretical astronomy: QB362.F47
Feylinidae: QL666.L243
Feynman diagrams
  Nuclear interactions: QC794.6.F4
Feynman integrals: QC174.17.F45
Fiber
  Nutrition: QP144.F52
Fiber bundles
  Topology: QA612.6+
Fiber optics: QC447.9+
Fiber spaces
  Topology: QA612.6+
Fiberings
  Topology: QA612.6+
Fibers, Nerve
  Anatomy: QL931
Fibrin: QP93.5+
Fibrinogen: QP93.5+
Fibroblast growth factors
  Animal biochemistry: QP552.F5
Fibronectins
  Animal biochemistry: QP552.F53
Ficidae
  Zoology: QL430.5.F53
Fideliidae: QL568.F47
Field emission
  Electricity: QC700
Field glasses
  Optical instruments: QC373.B55
Field ion microscopes: QH212.F5
Field theories
  Atomic physics: QC173.68+
Field theories
  Elementary particle physics: QC793.3.F5
Fields
  Zoology: QL115.5
Fieldwork
  Biology: QH318.5
Fierasferidae: QL638.C26
Fifth generation computers: QA76.85
Fig wasps: QL568.A23
Figitidae: QL568.F5
Figure of the earth
  Astronomy: QB283
Figures of equilibrium of rotating masses of fluid
  Celestial mechanics: QB410
Figures of planets: QB603.F5
Figwort
  Botany: QK495.S43
File conversion
  Computer science: QA76.9.F48
File organization
  Computer science: QA76.9.F5
File processing
  Computer science: QA76.9.F53
File snakes: QL666.O62
Filefishes: QL638.B15
Filistatidae: QL458.42.F5
Film boiling
  Heat transfer: QC320.22.F5
Films in science teaching: Q192
Filtration
  Chemistry: QD63.F5
Finches
  Zoology: QL696.P246
Finding the time
  Astronomy: QB213
Finite element method
  Mathematical physics: QC20.7.F56
  Quantum mechanics: QC174.17.F54
Finite fields
  Algebra: QA247.3+
Finite geometries: QA167.2
Finite groups
  Algebra: QA177

Fluorescent polymers
  Organic chemistry: QD382.F55
Fluorescent probes
  Analytical biochemistry: QP519.9.F56
Fluorides
  Effect on plants: QK753.F53
  Mineralogy: QE389.4
Fluorimeters: QC477.2
Fluorimetry
  Analytical chemistry: QD79.F4
  Animal biochemistry: QP519.9.F58
  Quantitative analysis: QD117.F5
Fluorination
  Organic chemistry: QD281.F55
Fluorine
  Chemical element: Q1 .F1
  Fluid mechanics: QC145.45.F5
Fluorine organic compounds
  Animal biochemistry: QP801.F5
Fluorocarbohydrates
  Animal biochemistry: QP702.F58
Fluorocarbons
  Spectra: QC463.F55
Fluoropolymers
  Organic chemistry: QD383.F48
Fluorspar
  Mineralogy: QE391.F6
Flying fishes
  Zoology: QL638.E9
Flying gurnards: QL638.D3
Flying lemurs: QL737.D4
Flysch: QE471.15.F5
Foamy viruses: QR414.6.F6
Fog
  Meteorology: QC929.F7
Föhn
  Meteorology: QC939.F6
Folacin
  Animal biochemistry: QP772.F6
Folds (Geology): QE606+
Foliations
  Differential topology: QA613.62
Folic acid
  Animal biochemistry: QP772.F6
Follicle-stimulating hormone
  Animal biochemistry: QP572.F6
Fontinalaceae: QK539.F6
Food
  Animals: QL756.5+
  Birds: QL698.4
  Microbiology: QR115+
Food chains
  Ecology: QH541.15.F66
Food microbiology: QR115+
Food poisoning
  Microbiology: QR201.F6
Food webs
  Ecology: QH541.15.F66
Foodborne diseases
  Microbiology: QR201.F62
Foot
  Regional anatomy: QM549
Foot-and-mouth disease
  Microbiology: QR201.F63
Foot muscles
  Physiology: QP336
Footballfishes: QL638.H54
Footprints, Fossil: QE845
Foraminifera
  Paleozoology: QE772
Foraminiferida: QL368.F6
Forbush decreases
  Cosmic ray physics: QC485.8.F6
Force and energy (Physics): QC71.82+
Forces and couples in three dimensions
  Statics: QA831
Forensic biology: QH313.5.F67
Forensic botany: QK46.5.F67
Forensic geology: QE38.5
Forest birds
  Zoology: QL677.79.F67
Forest canopy ecology: QH541.5.F6
Forest ecology: QH541.5.F6
Forest influences
  Meteorology: QC929.F8
Forest management
  Effect on plants and animals:
    QH545.F67
Forests
  Biogeography: QH86
  Botany: QK938.F6
  Ecology: QH541.5.F6
  Zoology: QL112
Forficulidae: QL510.3.F6

Fruticeta: QK479+
Fucaceae: QK569.F95
Fuchsian functions
  Analysis: QA353.A9
Fuchsian groups: QA335
Fuel calorimeters: QC293.F8
Fulgoridae: QL527.F9
Fullerene polymers
  Organic chemistry: QD383.F84
Fulmars: QL696.P665
Fume hoods
  Chemical laboratories: QD54.F85
Funariaceae: QK539.F98
Function spaces
  Functional analysis: QA323
Functional analysis: QA319+
  Atomic physics: QC174.52.F8
  Mathematical physics: QC20.7.F84
Functional equations
  Analysis: QA431
Functional foods
  Nutrition: QP144.F85
Functional integration
  Mathematical physics: QC20.7.F85
Functional programming
  Digital computers: QA76.62
Functional programming languages
  Digital computers: QA76.62
Functionality, Window
  Computer software: QA76.76.W56
Functions, Special
  Mathematical physics: QC20.7.F87
Functions, Theory of
  Analysis: QA331+
Functions, Zeta
  Mathematical physics: QC20.7.Z47
Functors
  Homological algebra: QA169
Fundulidae: QL638.F86
Fungal antigens
  Immunology: QR186.6.F85
Fungal communities: QK604.2.C64
Fungal viruses
  Microbiology: QR343
Fungi
  Botany: QK600+
  Paleobotany: QE958
Fungi imperfecti: QK625.A1+
Fungivoridae: QL537.M92
Fungus gnats: QL537.S357
Fungus weevils: QL596.A63
Funnel-eared bats: QL737.C555
Fur
  Anatomy: QL942
  Physiology: QP88.3
Furans
  Microbial metabolism: QR92.F87
  Spectra: QC463.F8
Furipteridae: QL737.C53
Furnariidae: QL696.P2464
Furylbenzimidazole
  Animal biochemistry: QP801.F87
Fused salts
  Spectra: QC464.F87
Fusion
  Physics: QC303
Fuzzy automata
  Algebra: QA267.5.F89
Fuzzy decision making
  Mathematical statistics: QA279.6
Fuzzy graphs
  Algebra: QA166.175
Fuzzy logic
  Mathematics: QA9.64
Fuzzy measure theory
  Integral calculus: QA312.5
Fuzzy sets
  Algebra: QA248.5
Fuzzy statistics
  Mathematical statistics: QA276.5
Fuzzy topology: QA611.2

G

G proteins
  Animal biochemistry: QP552.G16
GABA
  Animal biochemistry: QP563.G32
Gabbro: QE462.G3
Gadidae: QL638.G2
Gadiformes: QL637.9.G3
  Paleozoology: QE852.G26
Gadiniidae: QL430.5.G34

Gadolinium
  Chemical element: Q1 .G4
Gadopsidae: QL638.G23
Galactic bulges: QB857.5.B84
Galactic center of the Milky Way: QB857.72
Galactic clusters: QB858.7+
Galactic cosmic rays: QC485.9.G34
Galactic nuclei, Active: QB858.3+
Galactose
  Animal biochemistry: QP702.G3
  Effect on plants: QK753.G45
  Microbial metabolism: QR92.G35
Galactosidase
  Animal biochemistry: QP609.G3
Galactosides
  Organic chemistry: QD325
Galagonidae: QL737.P937
Galagos: QL737.P937
Galanin
  Animal biochemistry: QP552.G25
Galaxies: QB856+
Galaxiidae: QL638.G25
Galbulidae: QL696.P54
Galena
  Mineralogy: QE391.G3
Galeodidae: QL458.82.G3
Galerucidae: QL596.G3
Galileo
  Biography as an astronomer: QB36.G2
Gall midges: QL537.C33
Gall wasps: QL568.C9
Gallbladder
  Human anatomy: QM352
  Physiology: QP185
Galleriidae: QL561.G3
Galli
  Paleozoology: QE872.G15
Galliformes: QL696.G2+
  Paleozoology: QE872.G15
Gallium
  Chemical element: Q1 .G2
Gallium arsenide
  Semiconductor physics: QC611.8.G3
Galloping
  Physiology: QP310.G34
Galumnidae: QL458.2.G34
Galvanic skin response
  Neurophysiology: QP372.9
Galvanometer: QC544.G2
Galvanometric effects
  Semiconductor physics: QC611.6.G3
Game theory
  Algebra: QA269+
Games
  Mathematics teaching aid: QA20.G35
    Elementary geometry: QA462.2.G34
Games of chance
  Algebra: QA271
Games of strategy
  Algebra: QA270
Gamma-aminobutyric acid
  Animal biochemistry: QP563.G32
Gamma functions
  Analysis: QA353.G3
Gamma globulins
  Animal biochemistry: QP552.G3
Gamma ray astronomy: QB471.A1+
Gamma ray detectors
  Nuclear physics: QC787.G32
Gamma rays
  Elementary particle physics: QC793.5.G32+
Gamma waves
  Physiological effect: QP82.2.G35
Gangliosides
  Animal biochemistry: QP752.G3
Gannets
  Zoology: QL696.P48
Ganodermataceae: QK629.G18
Ganoid fishes: QL638.5
Ganoidei
  Paleozoology: QE852.S4
Garbage collection
  Computer science: QA76.9.G37
Garden ecology: QH541.5.G37
Gardening to attract birds: QL676.5+
Gardens
  Ecology: QH541.5.G37
  Zoology: QL119
Garlic: QK495.A42

Glass blowing and working
Chemical laboratories: QD63.G5
Glass electrodes: QD572.G53
Glass frogs: QL668.E23
Glass in optical instruments: QC375
Glass knifefishes: QL638.S83
Glass lizards: QL666.L2254
Glauconite
Mineralogy: QE391.G5
Glaucosomitidae: QL638.G55
Glaze
Meteorology: QC929.G4
Gleason measures (Quantum mechanics): QC174.17.G56
Gliridae: QL737.R656
Global analysis
Mathematical physics: QC20.7.G55
Topology: QA614+
Global differential geometry: QA670+
Global radiation
Meteorology: QC912.55
Global Riemannian geometry: QA671
Global temperature changes: QC902.8+
Global warming
Meteorology: QC981.8.G56
Globes, Astronomical: QB66
Globin
Animal biochemistry: QP552.G5
Globular clusters: QB853.5
Globulariaceae: QK495.G56
Globulins
Animal biochemistry: QP552.G55
Glomeridae: QL449.65.G5
Glomeridesmidae: QL449.65.G53
Glossidae: QL430.7.G55
Glossinidae: QL537.G4
Glow discharge
Electric discharge through gases: QC711.8.G5
Glowworms: QL596.P47
Glucagon
Animal biochemistry: QP572.G5
Glucagon-like peptide 1
Animal biochemistry: QP572.G52
Glucan phosphorylase
Animal biochemistry: QP606.G5
Glucans
Animal biochemistry: QP702.G48
Glucides
Animal biochemistry: QP702.G5
Glucinum
Chemical element: Q1 .B4
Glucocorticoids
Animal biochemistry: QP572.G54
Glucokinase
Animal biochemistry: QP606.G57
Glucosamine
Animal biochemistry: QP702.G55
Glucose
Animal biochemistry: QP702.G56
Microbial metabolism: QR92.G5
Plant constituent: QK898.G475
Glucose-6-phosphatase
Animal biochemistry: QP609.G38
Glucose dehydrogenase
Animal biochemistry: QP603.G55
Glucosephosphate dehydrogenase
Animal biochemistry: QP603.G57
Glucosidases
Animal biochemistry: QP609.G4
Glucosides
Organic chemistry: QD325
Glucuronic acid
Animal biochemistry: QP702.G57
Glucuronides
Animal biochemistry: QP702.G572
Glucuronosyltransferase
Animal biochemistry: QP606.G573
Gluons
Elementary particle physics: QC793.5.G552+
Glutamate dehydrogenase
Plant constituent: QK898.G48
Glutamic acid
Animal biochemistry: QP562.G5
Glutamic acid polymers
Organic chemistry: QD383.G57
Glutamic-aspartic transaminase
Animal biochemistry: QP606.G58
Glutamine
Animal biochemistry: QP562.G55
Glutamine synthetase
Animal biochemistry: QP619.G58

Glutaric acid
Animal biochemistry: QP801.G57
Glutathione
Animal biochemistry: QP552.G58
Plant constituent: QK898.G485
Glutathione transferase
Animal biochemistry: QP606.G59
Gluten
Plant constituent: QK898.G49
Glycerides
Animal biochemistry: QP752.G5
Glycerol
Animal biochemistry: QP752.G55
Glycine
Animal biochemistry: QP562.G58
Glycoasparaginase
Animal biochemistry: QP609.G44
Glycocoll
Animal biochemistry: QP562.G58
Glycoconjugates
Animal biochemistry: QP702.G577
Glycogen
Animal biochemistry: QP702.G58
Glycogen phosphorylase
Animal biochemistry: QP606.G592
Glycolic acid
Animal biochemistry: QP801.G63
Glycolipids
Animal biochemistry: QP752.G56
Glycopeptides
Animal biochemistry: QP552.G59
Glycoprotein hormones
Animal biochemistry: QP572.G58
Glycoproteins
Animal biochemistry: QP552.G59
Plant constituent: QK898.G497
Glycosidases
Animal biochemistry: QP609.G45
Glycosides
Animal biochemistry: QP702.G59
Organic chemistry: QD325
Plant constituent: QK898.G5
Glycosphingolipids
Animal biochemistry: QP752.G58
Glycosylated hemoglobin
Blood constituents: QP99.3.G55
Glycosyltransferases
Animal biochemistry: QP606.G6
Glycyphagidae: QL458.2.G4
Glyphipterygidae: QL561.G65
Glyphosate
Effect on plants and animals: QH545.G55
Gmelinite
Mineralogy: QE391.G55
Gnaphosidae: QL458.42.G5
Gnathostomulida: QL391.G63
Gneiss: QE475.G55
Gnetaceae: QK494.5.G565
Gnetales
Paleobotany: QE977.4
GNN
Data processing system: QA76.57.G48
Gnomoniaceae: QK623.G55
Gnostidae: QL596.G6
Goatfishes: QL638.M85
Goats
Laboratory manuals: QL813.G63
Goatsuckers: QL696.C23
Gobies: QL638.G7
Gobiesocidae: QL638.G6
Gobiidae: QL638.G7
Gobioididae: QL638.G73
Goblin shark: QL638.95.M58
Gödel numbers: QA9.65
Gödel's theorem: QA9.65
Goeridae: QL518.G6
Gold
Chemical element: Q1 .A9
Mineralogy: QE391.G6
Gold alloys
Analytical chemistry: QD137.G6
Gold ores
Mineralogy: QE390.2.G65
Golden moles: QL737.A352
Golgi apparatus
Cytology: QH603.G6
Gomortegaceae: QK495.G65
Gomphaceae: QK629.G6
Gomphidae: QL520.3.G6
Gonadotropin
Animal biochemistry: QP572.G6

H

Hadamard transform spectroscopy
  Physics: QC454.H33
Hadrons
  Elementary particle physics:
    QC793.5.H32+
Hadrotarsidae: QL458.42.H3
Haematomyzidae: QL570.3.H34
Haematopinidae: QL570.3.H37
Haematopinoididae: QL570.3.H38
Haematopodidae: QL696.C452
Haemodoraceae: QK495.H15
Haemophilus infections
  Microbiology: QR201.H22
Haemosporida: QL368.H33
Haemulidae: QL638.H23
Hafnium
  Chemical element: Q1 .H5
Hagfishes: QL638.14+
Hahniidae: QL458.42.H33
Hail
  Meteorology: QC929.H15
Hair
  Anatomy: QL942
  Human anatomy: QM488
  Physiology: QP88.3
Hairs
  Shoots: QK650
Hairy fungus beetles: QL596.M92
Halacaridae: QL458.2.H3
Hale-Bopp comet: QB723.H17
Half-life
  Radioactive substances: QC795.8.H3
Halfbeaks: QL638.H46
Halictidae: QL568.H3
Halictophagidae: QL599.3.H3
Halides
  Mineralogy: QE389.4
Haliotidae: QL430.5.H34
Haliplidae: QL596.H2
Hall effect: QC612.H3
Halley's comet: QB723.H2
Hallucinogenic mushrooms:
  QK604.2.H34
Halobiidae
  Paleozoology: QE812.H34
Halocyprida: QL444.O83
Halogen compounds
  Aliphatic compounds: QD305.H15
  Aromatic compounds: QD341.H8
Halogen organic compounds
  Animal biochemistry: QP801.H34
Halogenation
  Organic chemistry: QD281.H3
Halogens
  Geochemistry: QE516.H3
  Inorganic chemistry: QD165
Haloragaceae: QK495.H2
Halos
  Galaxies: QB857.5.H34
  Meteorological optics: QC976.H15
Halosauridae: QL638.H25
Hamamelidaceae: QK495.H3
Hamiltonian graph theory
  Algebra: QA166.18
Hamiltonian operator
  Quantum mechanics: QC174.17.H3
Hamiltonian systems
  Mathematical physics: QC20.7.H35
  Statistical physics: QC174.85.H35
  Topology: QA614.83
Hamilton's equations
  Analytic mechanics: QA871
Hammerhead sharks: QL638.95.S7
Hammerheads: QL696.C58
Hamsters: QL737.R666
  Anecdotes and stories: QL795.H3
  Laboratory manuals: QL813.H35
Hand
  Regional anatomy: QM548
Hand lenses
  Optical instruments: QC373.M33
Hand muscles
  Physiology: QP334
Handfishes: QL638.B7
Handlebodies
  Differential topology: QA613.658
Hang gliding
  Effect on plants and animals:
    QH545.H34
Hantavirus infections
  Microbiology: QR201.H24
Haplomitriaceae: QK555.H35
Haplosporida: QL368.H34

Haptens
  Immunology: QR186.6.H3
Haptoglobin
  Blood constituents: QP99.3.H3
Haptoglobins
  Animal biochemistry: QP552.H3
Hard disk management: QA76.9.H35
Hardness
  Crystallography: QD933
Hares
  Anecdotes and stories: QL795.H35
  Zoology: QL737.L32
Harmonic analysis: QA403+
Harmonic functions
  Potential theory: QA405
Harmonic maps: QA614.73
Harmonic motion
  Analytic mechanics: QA867
Harmonics (Electric waves)
  Physical optics: QC446.3.H37
Harpacticoida: QL444.C74
Harpagiferidae: QL638.H28
Harpagophoridae: QL449.65.H37
Harpodontidae: QL638.H3
Harriers (Birds): QL696.F32
Harvey
  Discovery of blood circulation:
    QP101.4
Hashing
  Computer science: QA76.9.H36
Haustoria
  Plant anatomy: QK644.5
Hawaiian honeycreepers: QL696.P243
Hawkfishes: QL638.C577
Hawks
  Zoology: QL696.F32
Hazard analysis
  Seismology: QE539.2.S34
  Volcanoes: QE527.6
Head
  Anatomy: QL950.5
  Regional anatomy: QM535
Head muscles
  Human anatomy: QM155
Health behavior
  Animals: QL756.6
Health, Ecosystem: QH541.15.E265
Hearing
  Physiology: QP460+
Hearing limits
  Physiology: QP463
Heart
  Anatomy: QL838
  Human histology: QM570.5
  Physiology: QP111+
Heart beat
  Physiology: QP113
Heart cells
  Physiology: QP114.C44
Heart membranes
  Physiology: QP114.M46
Heart vascular system
  Human anatomy: QM181
Heat
  Bacterial physiology: QR97.H4
  Effect on plants: QK755.5
  Physics: QC251+
  Physiological effect: QP82.2.H4
Heat, Animal
  Physiology: QP135
Heat budget
  Geophysics: QC809.E6
Heat conductance
  Plasma physics: QC718.5.T7
Heat of combustion: QD516
Heat of formation: QD516
  Physics: QC310
Heat of fusion
  Physics: QC303
Heat of solution
  Physics: QC310
Heat of vaporization
  Physics: QC304
Heat of wetting
  Physics: QC310
Heat production
  Cells: QH635
  Microbiology: QR94
Heat production in plants (Botany):
  QK755.5
Heat resistant polymers
  Organic chemistry: QD382.H4
Heat shock proteins
  Animal biochemistry: QP552.H43

Hematite
  Mineralogy: QE391.H4
Hematoblasts
  Blood constituents: QP99.3.H37
Hematopoiesis
  Physiology: QP92
Hematopoietic system
  Human histology: QM569.5
Hematoporphyrin
  Animal biochemistry: QP671.H4
Heme
  Animal biochemistry: QP671.H45
Heme oxygenase
  Animal biochemistry: QP603.H45
Hemerobiidae: QL513.H5
Hemerocallidaceae: QK495.H38
Hemicellulose
  Organic chemistry: QD323
  Plant constituent: QK898.H45
Hemichordata: QL612
  Paleozoology: QE840.5
Hemidiscaceae: QK569.H44
Hemimeridae: QL510.3.H4
Hemiodontidae: QL638.H45
Hemipeplidae: QL596.H43
Hemiphlebiidae: QL520.3.H45
Hemiprocnidae: QL696.A554
Hemiptera
  Paleozoology: QE832.H4
  Zoology: QL521+
Hemiramphidae: QL638.H46
Hemiscorpiidae: QL458.72.H45
Hemocyanin
  Blood constituents: QP99.3.H4
Hemodynamics
  Physiology: QP105+
Hemoerythrin
  Blood constituents: QP99.3.H45
Hemoglobin
  Blood constituents: QP96.5
Hemolysis
  Antigen-antibody reactions: QR187.H4
  Blood physiology: QP99.5.H4
Hemolytic plaque technique
  Antigen-antibody reactions: QR187.H45
Hemoproteins
  Animal biochemistry: QP552.H46
Henicocephalidae: QL523.E65
Henicopidae: QL449.55.H4
Heparin
  Animal biochemistry: QP702.H4
Hepaticae: QK551+
Hepatitis vaccines: QR189.5.H46
Hepatitis, Viral
  Microbiology: QR201.H46
Hepatocyte growth factor
  Animal biochemistry: QP552.H48
Hepialidae: QL561.H47
Heppiaceae: QK585.H48
Hepsetidae: QL638.H47
Heptageniidae: QL505.3.H4
Heptapsogastridae: QL540.3.H4
Herbicides
  Effect on plants: QK753.H45
  Effect on plants and animals: QH545.H47
Herbig-Haro objects
  Astronomy: QB855.55
Herbivora
  Paleozoology: QE882.H47
Hercynite
  Mineralogy: QE391.H5
Heredity and environment
  Genetics: QH438.5
Heresy in science: Q172.5.H47
Hermaeidae: QL430.5.S75
Hermanniidae: QL458.2.H38
Hermaphroditism
  Physiology: QP267
Hernandiaceae: QK495.H42
Herons
  Zoology: QL696.C52
Herpes simplex virus
  Virology: QR400.2.H47
Herpestidae: QL737.C235
Herpesvirus infections
  Microbiology: QR201.H48
Herpesvirus vaccines: QR189.5.H48
Herpesviruses
  Virology: QR400+
Herrings
  Zoology: QL638.C64

Hersiliidae: QL458.42.H47
Hesperiidae: QL561.H5
Hesperinidae: QL537.H48
Heterenchelyidae: QL638.H484
Heteroceridae: QL596.H45
Heterochain polymers
  Organic chemistry: QD382.H48
Heterocheylidae: QL458.2.H4
Heterochlorida: QL368.H53
Heterochrony
  Biology: QH395
Heterocyclic chemistry
  Organic chemistry: QD399+
Heterocyclic compounds
  Organic chemistry: QD399+
  Spectra: QC463.H4
Heterodontidae: QL638.95.H4
Heterogeneous computing: QA76.88
Heterogynidae: QL561.H53
Heteromyidae: QL737.R66
Heteropediaceae: QK569.H46
Heteropneustidae: QL638.H486
Heteropodidae: QL458.42.H48
Heteroptera
  Zoology: QL521+
Heteroscorpionidae: QL458.72.H48
Heterosphere
  Meteorology: QC881.2.H48
Heterostraci
  Paleozoology: QE852.H4
Heterothripidae: QL598.3.H4
Heterotrichida: QL368.H55
Heulandite
  Mineralogy: QE391.H55
Hexactinellida: QL373.H6
Hexagrammidae: QL638.H49
Hexahedrites
  Astronomy: QB757.5.H49
Hexanchidae: QL638.95.H48
Hexanchiformes: QL638.94.H49
Hexapoda
  Paleozoology: QE831+
Hexatrygonidae: QL638.85.H48
Hexazinone
  Effect on plants and animals: QH545.H49
Hexisopodidae: QL458.82.H4
Hexosamines
  Animal biochemistry: QP702.H45
Hexosediphosphatase
  Animal biochemistry: QP609.H5
Hiatellidae: QL430.7.H53
Hibernation
  Animal behavior: QL755
Hierarchies
  Recursion theory
    Mathematical logic: QA9.62
Hieroglyphics
  Mathematics teaching: QA20.H54
High-brightness accelerators
  Nuclear physics: QC787.H53
High density lipoproteins
  Blood constituents: QP99.3.H53
High energy interactions
  Nuclear physics: QC794.8.H5
High energy physics
  Elementary particle physics: QC793.3.H5
High performance computing: QA76.88
High performance liquid chromatography
  Animal biochemistry: QP519.9.H53
  Microbiology: QR69.H54
High pressure
  Mineralogy: QE364.2.H54
  Physics: QC280+
High pressure biochemistry
  Animal biochemistry: QP517.H53
High pressure chemistry: QD538
High pressure ionization chambers
  Nuclear physics: QC787.H54
High resolution spectroscopy
  Physics: QC454.H618
High temperature
  Plasma physics: QC718.5.H5
High temperature chemistry: QD515
High temperature superconductors: QC611.98.H54
High temperatures
  Physics: QC276+
High temperatures of gases: QC164.5
Higher albegraic curves: QA565+
Higher algebra: QA155
Higher algebraic surfaces: QA571+

Hydroxymethylglutaryl coenzyme A reductases
Animal biochemistry: QP603.H92
Hydroxyprogesterone
Animal biochemistry: QP572.H85
Hydrozoa: QL377.H9
Paleozoology: QE779
Hydryphantidae: QL458.2.H98
Hyenas
Zoology: QL737.C24
Hyeniales
Paleobotany: QE965
Hygrobiidae: QL596.H9
Hygrometry
Meteorology: QC915+
Hygrophoraceae: QK629.H86
Hyidae: QL458.62.H9
Hylidae: QL668.E24
Hymenochaetaceae: QK629.H89
Hymenogastraceae: QK629.H9
Hymenomycetes: QK626+
Hymenophyllaceae: QK524.H9
Hymenopodidae: QL505.9.H94
Hymenoptera
Paleozoology: QE832.H9
Zoology: QL563+
Hymenostomatida: QL368.H87
Hynobiidae: QL668.C25
Hyocephalidae: QL523.H96
Hyperbolic tables: QA55+
Hyperelliptic functions: QA345
Hyperfine interactions
Nuclear magnetism: QC762.6.H94
Hyperfine spectra
Physics: QC454.H9
Hyperfine structure
Atomic physics: QC173.4.H95
Hypergeometric functions
Analysis: QA353.H9
Hypergraphs
Algebra: QA166.23
Hypermastigida: QL368.H9
Hypermedia
Computer software: QA76.76.I59
Hyperoliidae: QL668.E244
Hyperons
Elementary particle physics: QC793.5.H42+
Hyperoscelididae: QL537.C26
Hypersensitivity
Immunology: QR188
Hyperspace
Geometry: QA691+
Hypertext document markup languages: QA76.76.H94
Hypertext systems
Computer software: QA76.76.H94
Hyphomycetes: QK625.A1
Hypnobryales: QK539.H95
Hypnotic conditions
Physiology: QP425+
Hypocephalidae: QL596.H95
Hypochilidae: QL458.42.H9
Hypocreaceae: QK623.H86
Hypodermatidae: QL537.O4
Hypogastruridae: QL503.H9
Hypoglycin
Animal biochemistry: QP552.H9
Hypogoeus fungi: QK604.2.H95
Hypokinesia
Physiology: QP310.5
Hypomycetaceae: QK623.H87
Hypophthalmidae: QL638.H93
Hypopterygiaceae: QK539.H96
Hypoptychidae: QL638.H935
Hyposittidae: QL696.P2474
Hyposmocomidae: QL561.H97
Hypothalamic hormones
Animal biochemistry: QP572.H9
Hypothalamic-pituitary-adrenal axis: QP188.H88
Hypothalamo-hypophyseal system
Physiology: QP188.H9
Hypothalamus
Anatomy: QL938.H94
Neurophysiology: QP383.7+
Hypothermia
Heart physiology: QP114.H94
Hypotheses, Testing of
Mathematical statistics: QA277+
Hypotrichida: QL368.H95
Hypoxidaceae: QK495.H9

Imidoesters
  Aliphatic compounds: QD305.I6
Imino compounds
  Aromatic compounds: QD341.I6
Imino sugars
  Animal biochemistry: QP702.I45
Immersion in water
  Physiological effect: QP82.2.W35
Immersion method
  Determinative mineralogy: QE369.I55
Immidae: QL561.I45
Immobilization
  Cells: QH585.5.I45
  Zoology collecting technique: QL62.5
Immune complexes: QR185.8.I45
Immune recognition
  Immunology: QR185.95
Immune response
  Immunology: QR186+
Immune structures
  Immunology: QR185.7+
Immune system
  Phylogeny: QR184.6
Immunity
  Molecular aspects: QR185.6
Immunity, Acquired: QR185.3+
Immunity, Cellular: QR185.5
Immunity, Humoral: QR185.4
Immunity, Maternally acquired: QR185.33
Immunity, Natural: QR185.2
Immunoadsorption: QR187.I44
Immunoassay
  Animal biochemistry: QP519.9.I42
Immunoblotting
  Animal biochemistry: QP519.9.I43
Immunochemistry: QR183.6
Immunocomputers: QA76.875
Immunocytochemistry
  Immunology: QR187.I45
Immunodeficiency
  Immunology: QR188.35
Immunodiffusion: QR187.I46
Immunoelectrophoresis
  Microbiology: QR187.I47
Immunoenzyme technique
  Animal biochemistry: QP519.9.I44
Immunofluorescence: QR187.I48
Immunogenetics
  Immunology: QR184+
Immunoglobulin A: QR186.8.A2
Immunoglobulin-binding proteins
  Microbial metabolism: QR92.I4
Immunoglobulin D: QR186.8.D2
Immunoglobulin E: QR186.8.E2
Immunoglobulin G: QR186.8.G2
Immunoglobulin M: QR186.8.M2
Immunoglobulins
  Immunology: QR186.7+
Immunogold labeling: QR187.I482
Immunoinformatics: QR182.2.I46
Immunologic adjuvants: QR187.3
Immunologic memory: QR185.35
Immunology
  Fishes: QL638.97
  Insects: QL492.5
  Invertebrates: QL362.85
  Microbiology: QR180+
Immunology, Developmental: QR184.5
Immunology, Reproductive
  Physiology: QP252.5
Immunophenotyping: QR187.I486
Immunosuppression
  Immunology: QR188.45+
Immunotaxonomy: QR183.8
Immunotechnology: QR183.5
IMP dehydrogenase
  Animal biochemistry: QP603.I54
Impact
  Elasticity: QA937
Impact craters
  Geology: QE612+
Impedance spectroscopy
  Electrochemical analysis: QD116.I57
Imprinted polymers: QD382.I43
Imprinting
  Animals: QL763.2
Impulse propagation
  Nervous system: QP363
In situ hybridization: QH452.8
Inactivity
  Physiology: QP310.5
Inarticulata
  Paleozoology: QE797.I5

Incense tree
  Botany: QK495.B8
Incidence
  Optics: QC437
Inclusion bodies
  Cytology: QH603.I49
Inclusive interactions
  Nuclear physics: QC794.8.I52
Incompressible fluids
  Fluid dynamics: QC152
Incurvariidae: QL561.I5
Indefinite inner product spaces
  Functional analysis: QA322.5
Index theorems
  Topology: QA614.92
Indexes of plants: QK11
Indianite: QE391.I53
Indican
  Animal biochemistry: QP801.I4
Indicatoridae: QL696.P55
Indicators
  Analytical chemistry: QD77
  Ecology: QH541.15.I5
  Organic chemistry: QD271.3+
Indium
  Chemical element: Q1 .I5
Indium arsenide
  Semiconductor physics: QC611.8.I52
Individual device drivers
  Computer software: QA76.76.D49
Individualized instruction
  Mathematics: QA20.I53
Indocyanine green
  Animal biochemistry: QP801.I43
Indolacetic acid
  Effect on plants: QK753.I5
Indole
  Animal biochemistry: QP801.I45
Indole alkaloids
  Plant constituent: QK898.I53
  Spectra: QC463.I5
Indostomidae: QL638.I4
Indridae: QL737.P945
Induced mutation
  Genetics: QH465.A1+
Induced radioactivity
  Physics: QC795.55.I5
Induced seismicity: QE539.2.I46
Inductance
  Electrodynamics: QC638
Induction
  Electrodynamics: QC638
  Electrostatics: QC581.I5
Induction coils
  Electrodynamics: QC645
Induction machines: QC573
Inductively coupled plasma
  spectrometry: QD96.I47
Industrial microbiology: QR53+
Inelastic scattering
  Nuclear interactions: QC794.6.S3
Inequalities of the moon's motion:
  QB392.I5
Inertia
  Descriptive mechanics: QC137
Inertial confinement fusion:
  QC791.775.P44
Infanticide
  Animals: QL762.5
Inference
  Philosophy of science: Q175.32.I54
Inferior planets: QB606+
Infinitary languages
  Mathematical logic: QA9.37
Infinite groups
  Algebra: QA178
Infinite products
  Mathematical series: QA295
Infinitesimal geometry: QA615+
Infinitesimal transformations: QA385+
Inflationary universe: QB991.I54
Inflorescence
  Spermatophytes: QK653+
Influenza
  Microbiology: QR201.I6
Influenza vaccines: QR189.5.I5
Information centers
  Science: Q223.2+
Information processing
  Neurophysiology: QP396
Information resources
  Climatic change: QC902.92
Information services
  Biology: QH303.15+

Information services
  Botany: QK9.3
  Chemistry: QD8.3
  Computer science information:
    QA76.162
  Ecology: QH541.183
  Fishes: QL614.74
  Geology: QE48.86
  Mathematics: QA41.5
  Natural history: QH13.3
  Paleontology: QE704.2
  Physics: QC5.35
  Planets: QB600.32
  Science: Q223.2+
  Zoology: QL9.3
Information theory
  Biology: QH507
  Cybernetics: Q350+
  Mathematics: QA10.4
  Optics: QC370
Information visualization
  Computer science: QA76.9.I52
Infrared astronomy: QB470.A1+
Infrared radition
  Planets: QB603.I52
Infrared spectroscopy
  Analytical chemistry: QD96.I5
  Animal biochemistry: QP519.9.I48
  Biological research: QH324.9.I5
Infrared spectrum
  Physics: QC457
Infrasonic waves
  Physiological effect: QP82.2.I45
Infrasonics (Physics): QC243.5
Infusoria
  Invertebrates: QL365
Ingestion
  Cells: QH634
  Physiology: QP147
Inhibin
  Animal biochemistry: QP572.I47
Inhibition
  Neurophysiology: QP365
Inhomogeneous materials
  Atomic physics: QC173.4.I53
Iniidae: QL737.C436
Initial value problems
  Differential equations: QA378
Injured wildlife, Rescue of
  Zoology: QL83.2
Inner Bremsstrahlung: QC484.6.I5
Inner product spaces
  Functional analysis: QA322.4
Inoceliidae: QL513.I5
Inoceramidae
  Paleozoology: QE812.I5
Inorganic acids
  Inorganic chemistry: QD167
Inorganic chemistry: QD146+
Inorganic chemistry, Physical: QD475
Inorganic polymers: QD196
Inorganic reaction mechanisms:
  QD502.5
Inorganic scintillators
  Radiation physics: QC476.75
Inorganic substances
  Animal biochemistry: QP531+
  Spectra: QC464.A+
Inorganic synthesis: QD156
Inosine
  Animal biochemistry: QP625.I54
Inositol
  Animal biochemistry: QP772.I5
  Plant constituent: QK898.I55
Input design
  Computer science: QA76.9.I55
Insect venoms
  Animal biochemistry: QP632.I57
Insecticides
  Animal biochemistry: QP801.I48
  Effect on plants: QK753.I54
Insectivora: QL737.I5+
  Paleozoology: QE882.I5
Insectivores: QL737.I5+
  Paleozoology: QE882.I5
Insectivorous plants
  Plant ecology: QK917
Insects
  Paleozoology: QE831+
  Zoology: QL461+
Insertion elements, DNA: QH462.I48
Instability
  Plasma physics: QC718.5.S7

Internet
  Astronomy: QB14.3
  Biology: QH303.5
  Botany: QK9.4
  Chemistry: QD9.3
  Climatic change: QC902.93
  Dinosaurs: QE861.35
  Ecology: QH541.185
  Fishes: QL614.75
  Geology: QE48.87
  Mammals: QL701.8
  Mathematics: QA41.6
    Study and teaching: QA11.5
  Meteorology: QC866.5.C67
  Natural history: QH13.4
  Paleontology: QE704.3
  Physics: QC5.4
  Planets: QB600.34
  Science communication: Q224.5
  Science research: Q179.97
  Science study and teaching: Q182.7
  Zoology: QL9.4
Internet programming
  Digital computers: QA76.625
Interphotoreceptor retinoid-binding protein
  Animal biochemistry: QP552.I56
Interplanetary dust: QB603.I55
Interplanetary medium: QB603.I55
Interpolation
  Mathematics: QA281
Intersection graph theory
  Algebra: QA166.185
Intersection homology theory: QA612.32
Intersensory effects
  Physiology: QP442
Interstellar hydrogen: QB791.5
Interstellar magnetic fields: QB791.7
Interstellar matter: QB790+
Intertidal fishes
  Zoology: QL620.6
Intertidal zones
  Ecology: QH541.5.S35
Interval analysis
  Numerical analysis: QA297.75
Intestines
  Anatomy: QL863
  Human anatomy: QM345
  Microbiology: QR171.I6
  Physiology: QP156
Intramercurial planets: QB607
Intranet programming
  Digital computers: QA76.625
Intraocular pressure
  Neurophysiology: QP476.3
Intrinsic factor
  Animal biochemistry: QP552.G35
Introduced animals
  Zoology: QL86
Introduced aquatic organisms
  Aquatic biology: QH90.8.I57
Introduced birds
  Zoology: QL677.79.I58
Introduced freshwater organisms
  Freshwater biology: QH96.8.I57
Introduced organisms
  Biology: QH353
Introduced vertebrates
  Zoology: QL606
Intrusive bodies
  Geology: QE611+
Intuitionistic mathematics
  Mathematical logic: QA9.47
Inulin
  Animal biochemistry: QP702.I5
Invariance
  Elementary particle physics: QC793.3.S9
  Quantum mechanics: QC174.17.S9
Invariant embedding
  Statistical physics: QC175.25.I6
Invariants
  Vector and tensor algebra: QA201
Inverse problems
  Differential equations: QA378.5
Inversion
  Chromosomal mutation: QH462.I5
Inversions
  Modern geometry: QA473+
Invertase
  Animal biochemistry: QP609.F7
Invertebrate embryology: QL958

Invertebrates
  Nervous system: QL935
  Paleozoology: QE770+
  Zoology: QL360+
Iodides
  Mineralogy: QE389.4
Iodine
  Chemical element: Q1 .I1
  Effect on plants: QK753.I6
Iodopsin
  Animal biochemistry: QP671.I5
Ion channels
  Cytology: QH603.I54
Ion cyclotron resonance spectroscopy
  Analytical chemistry: QD96.I54
Ion exchange
  Chemistry: QD63.I55
  Cytology: QH604.5
  Electrochemistry: QD562.I63
Ion exchange chromatography
  Analytical chemistry: QD79.C453
  Animal biochemistry: QP519.9.I54
Ion exchange membranes
  Electrochemistry: QD562.I63
Ion flow dynamics
  Electricity: QC717+
Ion-hydrogen concentration
  Electrochemistry: QD562.H93
Ion implantation
  Electric discharge: QC702.7.I55
Ion mobility spectroscopy: QD96.P62
Ion selective electrodes
  Animal biochemistry: QP519.9.E43
  Cytology: QH585.5.E43
  Electrochemistry: QD572.I66
Ion swarms
  Electric discharge: QC702.7.I57
Ion waves
  Plasma physics: QC718.5.W3
Ionic mobility
  Electricity: QC717.5.I6
Ionization
  Electrochemistry: QD562.I65
  General: QD561+
  Physics: QC701.7+
Ionization chambers: QC787.I6
Ionized air
  Physiological effect: QP82.2.I5
Ionized gases
  Physics: QC717.6+
Ionizing radiation
  Nuclear physics: QC794.95+
  Physiological effect: QP82.2.I53
Ionomers
  Organic chemistry: QD382.I45
Ionophores
  Animal biochemistry: QP801.I55
Ionosphere
  Meteorology: QC881.2.I6
  Planets: QB603.I57
Ionospheric influences
  Elementary particle physics:
    QC793.3.C6
Ionospheric radio wave absorption:
  QC973.4.I6
Ionospheric radio waves
  Radio meteorology: QC973.4.I6
Ions
  Electrochemistry: QD561+
  Physics: QC701.7+
iOS
  Computer software
    Operating systems: QA76.774.I67
iPad: QA76.8.I63
iPhone: QA76.8.I64
Ipidae: QL596.I7
Ipnopidae: QL638.I6
Ir genes: QR184.4
Irenidae: QL696.P2585
Iridaceae: QK495.I75
Iridium
  Chemical element: Q1 .I7
Iridoviruses
  Virology: QR401
Iris
  Botany: QK495.I75
Iron
  Chemical element: Q1 .F4
  Effect on plants: QK753.I7
  Magnetic materials: QC766.I7
  Microbial metabolism: QR92.I7
  Mineralogy: QE391.I7
  Plant constituent: QK898.I7

K

Kinematics of fluids: QA913
Kinematics of vibrations: QC231
Kinesin
  Animal biochemistry: QP552.K46
Kinesiology
  Physiology: QP303
Kinetic analysis
  Analytical chemistry: QD98.K5
Kinetic theory of gases: QC175+
Kinetic theory of liquids: QC175.3+
Kinetics
  Analytical chemistry: QD75.4.K54
  Geochemistry: QE515.5.K55
  Plasma physics: QC718.5.T5
Kinetoplastida: QL368.K5
Kingenidae
  Paleozoology: QE797.K5
Kingfishers: QL696.C72
Kinglets: QL696.P27
Kinins
  Animal biochemistry: QP552.K5
Kinnaridae: QL527.K5
Kinorhyncha: QL391.K5
Kinosternide: QL666.C55
Kitefin sharks: QL638.95.D3
Kites
  Meteorology: QC879.3+
Kiwis
  Zoology: QL696.A63
KK-theory
  Topology: QA612.33
Klamath Mountains (Or. and Calif.): QH104.5.K55
Kloosterman sums: QA246.8.K58
Klystrons
  Nuclear physics: QC787.K55
Knemidokoptidae: QL458.2.K5
Kneriidae: QL638.K5
Knot polynomials
  Mathematical physics: QC20.7.K56
Knot theory
  Atomic physics: QC174.52.K56
  Topology: QA612.2+
Knowledge representation
  Information theory: Q387+
Knowledge, Theory of
  Philosophy of science: Q175.32.K45
Koalas
  Anecdotes and stories: QL795.K62
  Zoology: QL737.M384
Koebeliidae: QL527.K6
Kolmogorov complexity
  Machine theory: QA267.7
Komatiite: QE462.K66
Korsogasteridae: QL638.K6
Kraemeriidae: QL638.K7
Kraken: QL89.2.K73
Krameriaceae: QK495.K7
Krypton
  Chemical element: Q1 .K6
Kuhliidae: QL638.K8
Kuiper Belt: QB695
Kurinelli meteorite: QB756.K87
Kurtidae: QL638.K87
Kynurenic acid
  Animal biochemistry: QP801.K8
Kynurenine
  Animal biochemistry: QP563.K9
Kyphosidae: QL638.K9

L

Labidocarpidae: QL458.2.L3
Labiduridae: QL510.3.L33
Labiidae: QL510.3.L35
Laboratories
  Botany: QK78+
  Chemistry: QD51+
  Computer science: QA76.35+
  Electrochemistry: QD558+
  Limnology: QH96.6+
  Marine biology: QH91.6+
  Nuclear chemistry: QD604.8+
  Physiology: QP51+
  Science teaching: Q183.A1+
  Virology: QR380+
Laboratories, Computation
  Mathematics: QA74
Laboratories, Science: Q180.56+
Laboratory equipment
  Microbiology: QR71
Laboratory manuals
  Animal behavior: QL751.7
  Ecology: QH541.25

Laboratory manuals
  Experimental physiology: QP42
Laboubelniales: QK623.L3
Labracoglossidae: QL638.L115
Labridae: QL638.L12
Labyrinthodontia
  Paleozoology: QE868.L3
Labyrinths of the ear
  Physiology: QP471+
Labyrinthulida: QL368.L3
Lac scales
  Zoology: QL527.K44
Laccase
  Plant constituent: QK898.L23
Lacciferidae: QL527.K44
Laccoliths
  Geology: QE611+
Lacebugs: QL523.T5
Lacertidae: QL666.L255
Lacertilia: QL666.L2+
  Paleozoology: QE862.L2
Lacewings: QL513.C5
Lachnocladiaceae: QK629.L33
Lacistemaceae: QK495.L152
Lacrimal organs
  Physiology: QP188.T4, QP231
Lactalbumin
  Animal biochemistry: QP552.L3
Lactamases, Beta
  Animal biochemistry: QP609.B46
Lactariidae: QL638.L2
Lactase
  Animal biochemistry: QP609.G3
Lactate dehydrogenase
  Animal biochemistry: QP603.L33
Lactic acid
  Animal biochemistry: QP801.L3
Lactobacillaceae: QR82.L3
Lactoferrins
  Animal biochemistry: QP552.L345
Lactogenic hormones
  Animal biochemistry: QP572.P74
Lactoglobulin
  Animal biochemistry: QP552.L35
Lactoridaceae: QK495.L153
Lactose
  Animal biochemistry: QP702.L3
Lady beetles: QL596.C65
Ladyfishes: QL638.E4
Laelapidae: QL458.2.L33
Laemobothridae: QL540.3.L3
Lagomorpha: QL737.L3+
  Paleozoology: QE882.L3
Lagoon ecology: QH541.5.L27
Lagoons
  Ecology: QH541.5.L27
Lagrange's equations
  Analytic mechanics: QA871
Lagriidae: QL596.L23
Lake ecology: QH541.5.L3
Lakes
  Ecology: QH541.5.L3
  Freshwater biology: QH98
  Zoology: QL146
Lakeshore development
  Effect on plants and animals:
    QH545.L35
Lambda calculus: QA9.5
Lamé functions (Ellipsoidal harmonics):
  QA409
Lamellariidae: QL430.5.L2
Lamellibranchia
  Paleozoology: QE811+
  Zoology: QL430.6+
Lamellorthoceratidae
  Paleozoology: QE807.L3
Lametilidae: QL430.7.L35
Lamiaceae: QK495.L25
Lamiidae: QL596.L25
Laminariaceae: QK569.L2
Laminariales: QK569.L34
Lamnidae: QL638.95.L3
Lamniformes: QL638.94.L36
  Paleozoology: QE852.L35
Lamp shells
  Zoology: QL395+
Lampbrush chromosomes: QH600.6
Lamponidae: QL458.42.L3
Lampreys: QL638.2+
Lampridae: QL638.L24
Lampridiformes: QL637.9.L3
Lamproite: QE462.L35
Lamprosomatidae: QL596.L27
Lampryidae: QL596.L28

INDEX

Lytoceratidae
  Paleozoology: QE807.L98

M

M stars: QB843.M16
M87 (Galaxy)
  Radio astronomy: QB479.55.M18
Mac OS
  Computer software
    Operating systems: QA76.774.M33
Machaerotidae: QL527.M3
Machilidae: QL503.7.M32
Machine learning: Q325.5+
Machine theory
  Algebra: QA267+
Machines, Mathematical: QA71+
Mach's principle: QC137
Macintosh OS
  Computer software
    Operating systems: QA76.774.M33
Mackerel
  Zoology: QL638.S35
Mackerel sharks: QL638.95.L3
Macluritidae
  Paleozoology: QE809.M25
Macristiidae: QL638.M13
Macrocephenchelyidae: QL638.M16
Macroceridae: QL537.M3
Macrocinematography
  Microscopy: QH255
Macroclimatology: QC981.7.M3
Macrocyclic compounds
  Organic chemistry: QD399+
Macroecology
  Ecology: QH541.15.M23
Macroevolution
  Biology: QH371.5
Macroglobulins, Alpha
  Blood constituents: QP99.3.A45
Macromolecules
  Animal biochemistry: QP801.P64
  Organic chemistry: QD380+
  Virology: QR372.M32
Macronyssidae: QL458.2.M3
Macrophage migration inhibitory factor
  Immunology: QR185.8.M28
Macrophages
  Immunology: QR185.8.M3
Macropsidae: QL527.M32
Macrorhamphosidae: QL638.M165
Macroscelidea: QL737.M24+
  Paleozoology: QE882.M25
Macroscelidide: QL737.M242
Macrouridae: QL638.M2
Macroveliidae: QL523.M3
Macrurocyttidae: QL638.M22
Mactridae: QL430.7.M3
  Paleozoology: QE812.M2
Madder
  Botany: QK495.R85
Madeira vine
  Botany: QK495.B256
Magellanic Clouds: QB858.5.M33
Magic cubes
  Algebra: QA165
Magic labelings
  Algebra: QA166.197
Magic squares
  Algebra: QA165
Magic tricks
  Mathematics teaching aid: QA20.M33
Magnesite
  Mineralogy: QE391.M2
Magnesium
  Chemical element: Q1 .M4
  Effect on plants: QK753.M27
Magnesium alloys
  Analytical chemistry: QD137.M3
Magnesium group
  Inorganic chemistry: QD172.M4
Magnetic alloys
  Magnetic materials: QC766.M34
Magnetic analyzers
  Nuclear physics: QC787.M3
Magnetic compass deviation: QC849
Magnetic dipole moment
  Elementary particle physics:
    QC793.3.S6
Magnetic disturbances
  Geomagnetism: QC835
Magnetic field generation
  Physiology: QP345
Magnetic fields: QB817.5

Marking
  Reptiles and amphibians: QL645.6+
Markov chains
  Stochastic processes: QA274.7+
Markov processes
  Quantum mechanics: QC174.17.M33
  Stochastic processes: QA274.7+
Marmosets: QL737.P925
Marmots
  Anecdotes and stories: QL795.M3
Marograviaceae: QK495.M285
Marrellidae
  Paleozoology: QE823.M3
Mars (Planet): QB641+
  Perturbations: QB376
  Satellites: QB403
  Solar parallax: QB516
Marsh ecology: QH541.5.M3
Marshes
  Biogeography: QH87.3
  Botany: QK938.M3
  Ecology: QH541.5.M3
  Zoology: QL114
Marsileaceae: QK524.M4
Marsupial cats: QL737.M33
Marsupial mice: QL737.M33
Marsupial moles: QL737.M445
Marsupialia: QL737.M3+
  Paleozoology: QE882.M3+
Marsupials: QL737.M3+
Martingales
  Stochastic processes: QA274.5
Martyniaceae: QK495.M287
Maser physics: QC685+
Masking
  Chemistry: QD63.M3
Mass
  Planets: QB603.M3
  Sun: QB523
Mass and weight measurements:
  QC105+
Mass loss
  Astrophysics: QB466.M37
Mass movements
  Geology: QE598+
Mass spectrometry
  Animal biochemistry: QP519.9.M3
Mass spectrometry
  Microbiology: QR69.M33
Mass spectroscopy
  Analytical chemistry: QD96.M3
Mass transfer
  Thermodynamics: QC318.M3
Masses, Stellar: QB814
Mast cells
  Immunology: QR185.8.M35
Mastacembelidae: QL638.M28
Mastication
  Physiology: QP149
Mastigophora: QL368.A12
Mastiogophora
  Paleozoology: QE774.F5
Mastitis
  Microbiology: QR201.M4
Mastotermitidae: QL529.3.M3
Maternally acquired immunity:
  QR185.33
Mathematical crystallography
  Chemistry: QD911+
Mathematical geology: QE33.2.M3
Mathematical literature: QA41.7
Mathematical logic: QA8.9+
  Quantum mechanics: QC174.17.M35
Mathematical models
  Animal behavior: QL751.65.M3
  Animal biochemistry: QP517.M3
  Biology: QH323.5
  Botany: QK46.5.M3
  Ecology: QH541.15.M3
  Electrochemistry: QD555.6.M36
  Endocrine glands: QP187.3.M36
  Evolution: QH371.3.M37
  Genetics: QH438.4.M3
  Immune structures: QR185.8.M36
  Immunology: QR182.2.M36
  Marine biology: QH91.57.M38
  Nutrition research: QP143.5.M37
  Philosophy of science: Q175.32.M38
  Physiology: QP33.6.M36
  Polymers: QD381.9.M3
  Scientific research: Q180.55.M38

Mathematical optimization
  Analytical methods used in the solution of physical problems: QA402.5+
  Mathematical physics: QC20.7.M27
Mathematical physics: QC19.2+
  Mathematical theory: QA401+
Mathematical statistics: QA276+
Mathematical theory of sound: QC223
Mathematics: QA1+
  Analytical chemistry: QD75.4.C45
  Animal behavior: QL751.65.M32
  Astrophysics: QB462.3
  Chemistry: QD39.3.M3
  Condensed matter physics: QC173.458.M38
  Ecology: QH541.15.M34
  Electromagnetism: QC760.4.M37
  Genetics: QH438.4.M33
  Geophysics: QC809.M37
  Inorganic chemistry: QD152.5.M38
  Organic chemistry: QD255.5.M35
  Physical chemistry: QD455.3.M3
  Quantum chemistry: QD462.6.M39
  Seismology: QE539.2.M37
  Structural geography: QE601.3.M38
  Structural geology: QE501.4.M38
Mathematics as a profession: QA10.5
Mathematics, Computer: QA76.9.M35
Mathematics, Reverse: QA9.25+
Mathematics, Use of electronic computers in: QA76.95
Matrices
  Algebra: QA184+
  Linear and multilinear algebra: QA188+, QA188
Matrices, Random
  Algebra: QA196.5
Matrix isolation spectroscopy
  Analytical chemistry: QD96.M33
  Physics: QC454.M32
Matrix logic
  Mathematical logic: QA9.9
Matrix mechanics
  Quantum mechanics: QC174.3+
Matrix theories
  Elementary particle physics: QC793.3.M36
Matrix theory
  Mathematical physics: QC20.7.M3
Matroids
  Algebra: QA166.6
Mats
  Microbial ecology: QR100.8.M37
Matter, Constitution of: QC172+
Matter, Properties of: QC173.28+
Maxima and minima
  Analytic geometry: QA563
Maxwell's demon
  Thermodynamics: QC318.M35
Maxwell's equations: QC669+
Mayacaceae: QK495.M3
Mayflies
  Paleozoology: QE832.E65
  Zoology: QL505+
Meadow beauty
  Botany: QK495.M514
Meadow ecology
  Biology: QH541.5.M4
Meadowfoam
  Botany: QK495.L73
Meadows
  Botany: QK938.M4
  Ecology: QH541.5.M4
  Zoology: QL115.5
Mealybugs
  Zoology: QL527.P83
Mean density of the earth: QB341
Mean field theory
  Statistical physics: QC174.85.M43
Meaning
  Philosophy of science: Q175.32.M43
Means, Analysis of: QA279+
Measles
  Microbiology: QR201.M43
Measles vaccine: QR189.5.M4
Measure
  Integral calculus: QA312+
Measure theory
  Mathematical physics: QC20.7.M43
  Quantum mechanics: QC174.17.M4

Mercury ores
  Mineralogy: QE390.2.M47
Mercury (Planet): QB611+
  Perturbations: QB371
  Transit: QB515
Mercury telluride
  Semiconductor physics:
    QC611.8.M38
Mercury thermometers: QC272
Mergers, Stellar: QB818.5
Meridian, Determination of: QB207
Meridian instruments
  Astronomical instruments: QB101
Meridians, Prime
  Astronomy: QB224
Merlucciidae: QL638.M4
Meropeidae: QL598.7.M4
Meropidae: QL696.C754
Merostomata: QL447.7
  Paleozoology: QE825+
Merothripidae: QL598.3.M47
Merumite
  Mineralogy: QE391.M45
Mesencephalon
  Neurophysiology: QP378+
Mesentery
  Anatomy: QL864
  Human anatomy: QM367
  Physiology: QP157
Mesitornithidae: QL696.G85
Mesoclimatology: QC981.7.M4
Mesogastropoda
  Paleozoology: QE809.M4
Mesomerism
  Physical chemistry: QD471
Mesometeorology: QC883.4+
Mesons
  Elementary particle physics:
    QC793.5.M42+
Mesopause
  Meteorology: QC881.2.M3
Mesoscopic phenomena
  Solid state physics: QC176.8.M46
Mesosphere
  Meteorology: QC881.2.M3
Mesotaeniaceae: QK569.M48
Mesoveliidae: QL523.M4
Mesozoa: QL391.M4
Mesozoic
  Paleobotany: QE921+
  Paleontology: QE731+
  Stratigraphy: QE675+
Messenger RNA
  Animal biochemistry: QP623.5.M47
Metabasite: QE475.M45
Metabolism
  Bacterial physiology: QR88+
  Biology: QH521
  Heart physiology: QP114.M48
  Physiology: QP171+
  Phytochemistry: QK881+
Metachandidae: QL561.M44,
  QL561.M44
Metal carbonyls
  Spectra: QC463.M38
Metal-insulator transitions
  Solid state physics: QC176.8.M48
Metal oxides
  Semiconductor physics: QC611.8.M4
Metal vapors
  Spectra: QC462.M47
Metallic oxides
  Magnetic materials: QC766.M4
  Spectra: QC464.M48
  Surface chemistry: QD509.M46
Metallic wood borers: QL596.B8
Metalloenzymes
  Animal biochemistry: QP601.7+
Metallogeny
  Mineralogy: QE364.2.M37
Metalloproteins
  Animal biochemistry: QP552.M46
Metallothionein
  Animal biochemistry: QP552.M47
Metals
  Analytical chemistry: QD132+
  Animal biochemistry: QP532
  Effect on plants: QK753.M47
  Effect on plants and animals:
    QH545.M45
  Geochemistry: QE516.M65
  Microbial degradation: QR135.5.M37
  Microbial metabolism: QR92.M45
  Spectra: QC462.M49

Microbiological assay
  Microbiology: QR69.M48
Microbiological chemistry: QR148
Microbiology: QR1+
Microbiology for nurses: QR46
Microbiology, Pharmaceutical: QR46.5
Microbiotheria: QL737.M43+
  Paleozoology: QE882.M35
Microbiotheriidae: QL737.M435
Microbodies
  Cytology: QH603.M35
Microbursts
  Meteorology: QC880.4.M52
Microcalorimeters: QC293.M5
Microcharmidae: QL458.72.M52
Microchemical analysis
  Analytical chemistry: QD79.M5
  Organic chemistry: QD272.M5
  Qualitative analysis: QD98.M5
  Quantitative analysis: QD117.M5
Microchemistry
  Quantitative analysis: QD117.M5
Microcirculation
  Physiology: QP106.6
Microclimatology
  Climatology: QC981.7.M5
  Ecology: QH543+
Microclusters
  Atomic physics: QC173.4.M48
Micrococcaceae: QR82.M5
Microcomputer workstations: QA76.525
Microdesmidae: QL638.M5
Microhylidae: QL668.E26
Microlensing
  Galaxies: QB857.5.G7
Microlocal analysis
  Mathematical physics: QC20.7.M53
Micromalthidae: QL596.M47
Micromechanics
  Solid state physics: QC176.8.M5
Micrometeorology: QC883.7+
Micrometers
  Astronomical instruments: QB113
  Physical instruments: QC102.5
Micromonosporaceae: QR82.M55
Microorganisms
  Cellulose: QR160
Microorganisms
  Development: QR73.4
  Evolution: QR13
  Plant products: QR160
  Recombination genetics: QH448+
Microorganisms in the animal body
  Microbiology: QR171.A1+
Microorganisms of amphibians: QR314
Microorganisms of animals: QR301+
Microorganisms of birds: QR311
Microorganisms of fishes: QR321
Microorganisms of insects: QR327
Microorganisms of invertebrates:
  QR325+
Microorganisms of mammals: QR303
Microorganisms of microorganisms:
  QR340+
Microorganisms of plants: QR351
Microorganisms of poikilotherms:
  QR330
Microorganisms of reptiles: QR315
Microorganisms of vertebrates:
  QR302+
Micropaleontology: QE719+
Micropeplidae: QL596.M5
Micropezidae: QL537.M43
Microphotometry
  Optics: QC391
Microphoton excitation microscopes:
  QH212.M84
Microphysics
  Atomic physics: QC173.4.M5
Microphysidae: QL523.M47
Micropipette techniques
  Cytology: QH585.5.M52
Micropolar elasticity
  Analytic mechanics: QA932
Microprobe analysis
  Biological research: QH324.9.M5
Microprogramming
  Digital computers: QA76.635
Micropterygidae: QL561.M48
Microsatellites
  Genetics: QH452.2
Microsauria
  Paleozoology: QE868.M53

Microscope specimen preparation: QH231+
Microscopic analysis
  Petrology: QE434
Microscopic anatomy
  Human histology: QM550+
Microscopic determinations
  Determinative mineralogy: QE369.M5
Microscopy
  Natural history: QH201+
  Plant anatomy: QK673
Microseisms
  Seismology: QE539.2.M5
Microsoft Excel (Computer file)
  Mathematical statistics: QA276.45.M53
Microsoft .NET
  Computer software: QA76.76.M52
Microsoft Network
  Data processing system: QA76.57.M52
Microsoft Visual Basic
  Programming languages: QA76.73.M53
Microsoft Visual Basic for applications
  Programming languages: QA76.73.M53
Microsoft Windows 7
  Computer software
    Operating systems: QA76.774.M43
Microsoft Windows Me
  Computer software
    Operating systems: QA76.774.M48
Microsoft Windows NT
  Computer software
    Operating systems: QA76.774.M53
Microsoft Windows Vista
  Computer software
    Operating systems: QA76.774.M56
Microsoft Windows XP
  Computer software
    Operating systems: QA76.774.M58
Microsomes
  Cytology: QH603.M4
Microspectrophotometry
  Cytology: QH585.5.M53
Microsporida: QL368.M5
Microsporidiosis
  Microbiology: QR201.M73
Microstigmatidae: QL458.42.M5
Microtechnique
  MIcroscopy: QH231+
  Plant anatomy: QK673
Microthyriaceae: QK623.M5
Microtomy: QH233
Microtrombidiidae: QL458.2.M53
Microtubules
  Cytology: QH603.M44
Microwave meteorology: QC972.6+
Microwave optics
  Electromagnetic theory: QC675.8
Microwave spectroscopy
  Analytical chemistry: QD96.M5
  Physics: QC454.M5
Microwaves
  Physiological effect: QP82.2.M5
  Plasma physics: QC718.5.M5
  Radio waves: QC677+
Micrurgy
  Microbiology: QR69.M5
Midbrain
  Neurophysiology: QP378+
Middle American killifishes: QL638.P788
Middle atmosphere
  Meteorology: QC881.2.M53
Middle Cretaceous
  Stratigraphy: QE687
Middle Jurassic
  Stratigraphy: QE683
Middle Triassic
  Stratigraphy: QE678
Middleware
  Computer software: QA76.76.M54
Midges
  Paleozoology: QE832.D6
  Zoology: QL537.C456
Mie scattering: QC427.8.M5
Migidae: QL458.42.M53
Migmatite: QE475.M5
Mignonette
  Botany: QK495.R4
Migration
  Animal behavior: QL754

Molecular rotation
  Physical chemistry: QD481
Molecular spectra
  Analytical chemistry: QD96.M65
Molecular spectroscopy
  Physics: QC454.M6
Molecular structure
  Physical chemistry: QD461
Molecular theory
  Physical chemistry: QD461
Molecular virology: QR389
Molecular weights
  Physical chemistry: QD463+
  Polymers: QD381.9.M64
Molecule models
  Physical chemistry: QD480
Molecules
  Statistical physics: QC175.16.M6
Moles (Animals)
  Anecdotes and stories: QL795.M57
  Zoology: QL737.S76
Molidae: QL638.M64
Molluginaceae: QK495.M6
Mollusca
  Paleozoology: QE801+
  Zoology: QL401+
Molossidae: QL737.C54
Molybdates
  Mineralogy: QE389.67
Molybdenite
  Mineralogy: QE391.M7
Molybdenum
  Chemical element: Q1 .M7
  Effect on plants: QK753.M6
  Effect on plants and animals: QH545.M6
Molybdenum enzymes
  Animal biochemistry: QP601.75.M64
Moments
  Elementary particle physics: QC793.3.S6
  Nuclear interactions: QC794.6.M6
Moments of inertia
  Analytic mechanics: QA839
Momentum, Angular
  Physical optics: QC446.3.A54
Momentum distributions
  Atomic physics: QC173.4.M67
Momotidae: QL696.C756
Monamine oxidase
  Animal biochemistry: QP603.M6
Monascaceae: QK623.M63
Monazite
  Mineralogy: QE391.M75
Mongooses
  Anecdotes and stories: QL795.M6
  Zoology: QL737.C235
Moniliaceae: QK625.M7
Moniliales: QK625.M74
Monimiaceae: QK495.M67
Monitor lizards
  Zoology: QL666.L29
Monitoring
  Ecology: QH541.15.M64
Monkeys
  Anecdotes and stories: QL795.M7
Monoblepharidaceae: QK621.M6
Monocanthidae: QL638.M645
Monocentridae: QL638.M65
Monoclinic systems (Crystallography): QD912
Monoclonal antibodies
  Immunology: QR186.85
Monocotyledons: QK495.A14
  Paleobotany: QE981
Monocytes
  Physiology: QP95.7
Monodactylidae: QL638.M653
Monodontidae: QL737.C433
Monoedidae: QL596.M53
Monognathidae: QL638.M654
Monomachidae: QL568.M6
Monommatidae: QL596.M55
Monomolecular films
  Surface chemistry: QD509.M65
Monooxygenases
  Animal biochemistry: QP603.M65
Monophlebidae: QL527.M37
Monoplacophora: QL430.15
  Paleozoology: QE805
Monotidae
  Paleozoology: QE812.M6
Monotomidae: QL596.M57

Morphology
  Myriapoda: QL449.9
  Neuroptera: QL514
  Odonata: QL520.4
  Orthoptera: QL509
  Plecoptera: QL530.4
  Porifera: QL374
  Protozoa: QL369
  Raphidioptera: QL514.95
  Reptiles: QL669
  Siphonaptera: QL599.8
  Strepsiptera: QL599.4
  Thysanoptera: QL598.4
  Trichoptera: QL519
  Worms: QL393
Morphotectonics: QE511.44
Mortality
  Birds: QL698.25
Mortierellaceae: QK621.M64
Mosaic viruses
  Virology: QR402
Mosaicism
  Genetics: QH445.7
Moschatel
  Botany: QK495.A178
Moschidae
  Zoology: QL737.U575
Mosquitoes
  Paleozoology: QE832.D6
  Zoology: QL536
Mössbauer effect: QC491
Mössbauer spectroscopy: QC491
  Analytical chemistry: QD96.M6
Mosses
  Botany: QK534+
  Paleobotany: QE959
Motacillidae: QL696.P252
Mothflies: QL537.P85
Mothman: QL89.2.M68
Moths
  Paleozoology: QE832.L5
  Zoology: QL541+
Motilin
  Animal biochemistry: QP572.M66
Motility
  Cells: QH647
  Microbiology: QR96
Motion
  Physics: QC133+
Motion in the line of sight
  Astronomy: QB857.5.M67
  Stellar spectroscopy: QB901
Motion of clouds: QC922+
Motion of gases
  Fluid mechanics: QC167.5+
Motion of planets: QB603.M6
Motion of surfaces
  Dynamics of a particle
    Analytic mechanics: QA855
Motion pictures
  Mathematics teaching aid: QA19.M6
Motion, Stellar: QB810+
Motions
  Kinematics: QA841+
Motivation
  Animals: QL781.3
  Neurophysiology: QP409
Motmots: QL696.C756
Mountain beavers: QL737.R626
Mountain bikes
  Effect on plants and animals:
    QH545.A42
Mountain biking
  Effect on plants and animals:
    QH545.A42
Mountain building: QE621+
Mountain climatology: QC993.6
Mountain ecology: QH541.5.M65
Mountain meteorology: QC993.6
Mountain winds: QC939.M8
Mountains
  Biogeography: QH87
  Ecology: QH541.5.M65
  Plant ecology: QK937
  Zoology: QL113
Mounting of microscope specimens:
  QH239
Mouse-tailed bats: QL737.C585
Mouth
  Anatomy: QL857
  Human anatomy: QM306
  Physiology: QP146+
Movement
  Biology: QH514

Mycotoxins
Animal biochemistry: QP632.M9
Myctophidae: QL638.M9
Myctophiformes: QL637.9.M93
Mydaidae: QL537.M93
Myelin
Animal biochemistry: QP752.M9
Myelin basic protein
Animal biochemistry: QP552.M88
Myelin proteins
Animal biochemistry: QP552.M88
Myidae: QL430.7.M9
Myiodactylidae: QL513.M86
Myliobatidae: QL638.85.M9
Mylonite: QE475.M95
Mymaridae: QL568.M94
Mymarommatidae: QL568.M944
Mymarothripidae: QL598.3.M9
Myobatrachidae: QL668.E2615
Myobiidae: QL458.2.M9
Myocardium
Physiology: QP113.2
Myocastoridae: QL737.R668
Myocoptidae: QL458.2.M93
Myodocopida: QL444.O85
Myogenesis
Embryology: QL979
Myohemoglobin
Animal biochemistry: QP552.M9
Myonueral junction
Physiology: QP369.5
Myoporaceae: QK495.M8
Myosin
Animal biochemistry: QP552.M93
Myriapoda: QL449+
Paleozoology: QE828+
Myricaceae: QK495.M83
Myrionemataceae: QK569.M87
Myristicaceae: QK495.M85
Myrmecobiidae: QL737.M335
Myrmecolacidae: QL599.3.M9
Myrmecophagidae: QL737.E24
Myrmecophilidae: QL508.M9
Myrmecophilism: QK924
Myrmeleontidae: QL513.M9
Myrmosidae: QL568.M97
Myrocongridae: QL638.M97
Myrothamnaceae: QK495.M86
Myrsinaceae: QK495.M87
Myrtaceae: QK495.M9
Myrtle
Botany: QK495.M9
Mysidacea: QL444.M35
Mysmenidae: QL458.42.M97
MySQL (Computer program language):
QA76.73.S67
Mystacinidae: QL737.C545
Mystacocarida: QL444.M9
Mysticeti: QL737.C42+
Mythicomyiidae: QL537.M98
Mytilidae: QL430.7.M95
Paleozoology: QE812.M94
Myxini: QL638.13+
Myxinidae: QL638.15.M9
Myxiniformes: QL638.14+
Myxococcaceae: QR82.M95
Myxomycetes
Botany: QK635.A1+
Myxophyceae: QR99.6+
Myxosporida: QL368.M8
Myxoviruses
Virology: QR404
Myzopodidae: QL737.C55

N

N stars: QB843.N12
Nabidae: QL523.N3
Nacellidae: QL430.5.N27
Nacreous clouds: QC921.43.N3
NAD (Coenzyme)
Animal biochemistry: QP625.N34
Naiadaceae: QK495.N3
Nails
Anatomy: QL942
Human anatomy: QM488
Naked singularities (Cosmology):
QB991.N34
Names
Planets: QB600.5
Nandidae: QL638.N25
Nannofossils
Paleontology: QE955

Neelidae: QL503.N4
Neenchelyidae: QL638.N3
Negative ions
  Electric discharge: QC702.7.N4
Negative refraction: QC426.8.N44
Neididae: QL523.N46
Neisseria infections
  Microbiology: QR201.N45
Neisseriaceae: QR82.N4
Nekton
  Aquatic biology: QH90.8.N44
  Marine biology: QH91.8.N37
Nelumbonaceae: QK495.N33
Nemaliales: QK569.N43
Nemastomataceae: QK569.N45
Nemastomatidae: QL458.52.N4
Nematistiidae: QL638.N33
Nematoda: QL391.N4
Nematode-destroying fungi:
  QK604.2.N45
Nematomorpha: QL391.N5
Nemertina: QL391.N6
Nemesiidae
  Zoology: QL458.42.N37
Nemestrinidae: QL537.N44
Nemichthyidae: QL638.N34
Nemipteridae: QL638.N347
Nemonychidae: QL596.N4
Nemopteridae: QL513.N4
Nemouridae: QL530.3.N4
Neobalaenidae: QL737.C427
Neobisiidae: QL458.62.N4
Neoceratiidae: QL638.N36
Neocortex
  Anatomy: QL938.N45
  Neurophysiology: QP383.12
Neodymium
  Chemical element: Q1 .N4
Neogene
  Paleobotany: QE928.5+
  Paleontology: QE738.5+
  Stratigraphy: QE693.5+
Neogeophilidae: QL449.55.N4
Neogregarinida: QL368.N4
Neolignathidae: QL570.3.N4
Neolobophoridae: QL510.3.N46
Neon
  Chemical element: Q1 .N5
Neopseustidae: QL561.N38
Neopterin
  Animal biochemistry: QP801.N44
Neoscopelidae: QL638.N38
Neostethidae: QL638.N387
Neotectonics: QE511.42
Neottiophilidae: QL537.N46
Nepenthaceae: QK495.N35
Nepheline syenite: QE462.N4
Nephilidae: QL458.42.N38
Nephridia
  Anatomy: QL872.5
Nephrite: QE391.A2
Nepticulidae: QL561.N4
Neptune (Planet): QB691+
  Perturbations: QB388
  Satellites and ring system: QB407
Neptunium
  Chemical element: Q1 .N7
Neriidae: QL537.N47
Neritidae: QL430.5.N5
  Paleozoology: QE809.N45
Nerthridae: QL523.N53
Nerve cells
  Anatomy: QL931
Nerve fibers
  Anatomy: QL931
Nerve growth factor
  Animal biochemistry: QP552.N36
Nerve proteins
  Animal biochemistry: QP552.N37
Nerve tissues
  Human histology: QM575
Nervous control of the heart
  Physiology: QP113.4
Nervous system
  Anatomy: QL921+
  Human anatomy: QM451+
  Human embryology: QM695.N45
  Invertebrates: QL935
  Physiology: QP361+
  Vertebrates: QL937
Nesiotinidae: QL540.3.N4
Nesogastridae: QL510.3.N48
Nessorhamphidae: QL638.N4

Nucleosidases
  Animal biochemistry: QP609.N8
Nucleosides
  Animal biochemistry: QP625.N88
Nucleosynthesis
  Nuclear astrophysics: QB464.3
Nucleotides
  Animal biochemistry: QP625.N89
  Microbial metabolism: QR92.N82
  Organic chemistry: QD436.N85
  Plant constituent: QK898.N83
Nucleus
  Cytology: QH595
Nuclides
  Elementary particle physics:
    QC793.5.N862+
Nucloidae
  Paleozoology: QE812.N8
Nuculanidae: QL430.7.N85
Nuculidae: QL430.7.N9
Nuda: QL380.5.N8+
Null models
  Ecology: QH541.15.N84
Numbat: QL737.M335
Number concept
  Animals: QL785.24
  Mathematics: QA141+
Number concept (Elementary):
  QA141.15
Number theory
  Algebra: QA241+
Numeration
  Mathematics: QA141+
Numeration systems
  Mathematics: QA141+
Numerical analysis: QA297+
Numerical approximation: QA297.5
Numerical calculating: QA71+
Numerical differentiation
  Numerical analysis: QA299
Numerical integration
  Numerical analysis: QA299.3+
Numerical simulation: QA298
Numerical solutions
  Theory of equations: QA218
Numididae: QL696.G258
Nurse sharks: QL638.95.G55
Nutation
  Plant movement: QK773
Nutation and precession
  Spherical astronomy: QB165
Nuthatches: QL696.P275
Nutmeg
  Botany: QK495.M85
Nutria: QL737.R668
Nutrient interactions
  Physiology: QP143.7
Nutrition
  Bacterial physiology: QR86
  Biology: QH519
  Physiology: QP141+
  Plant physiology: QK867+
Nutrition adaption
  Plants: QK915+
Nutritional aspects
  Immunology: QR182.2.N86
Nutritive matter
  Plants: QK746
Nyctaginaceae: QK495.N9
Nyctemeridae: QL561.N87
Nycteribiidae: QL537.N9
Nycteridae: QL737.C565
Nyctibiidae: QL696.C25
Nyctiboridae: QL505.7.N9
Nyctipithecidae: QL737.P957
Nymphaeaceae: QK495.N97
Nymphalidae: QL561.N9
Nymphidae: QL513.N9
Nymphomyiidae: QL537.N94
Nyssaceae: QK495.N975
Nyssonidae: QL568.N9

O

O stars: QB843.O12
Oak
  Botany: QK495.F14
Oarfishes: QL638.R4
Oberthuerellidae: QL568.O25
Object monitors
  Computer software: QA76.76.M54
Object-oriented methods
  Computer science: QA76.9.O35

Ordered algebraic structures
  Algebra: QA172+
Ordered groups
  Algebra: QA172.4
Ordered sets
  Algebra: QA171.48+
Ordinary differential equations: QA372
Ordovician
  Paleobotany: QE916.5
  Paleontology: QE726.2
  Stratigraphy: QE660
Ore minerals
  Mineralogy: QE390+
  Semiconductor physics:
    QC611.8.O68
Orectolobidae: QL638.95.O7
Orectolobiformes: QL638.94.O74
Oreohelicidae: QL430.5.O73
Oreosomatidae: QL638.O7
Ores
  Petrology: QE431.6.O7
Orexins
  Animal biochemistry: QP572.O74
Organic acid salts
  Mineralogy: QE389.7
Organic chemistry: QD241+
Organic chemistry, Physical: QD476
Organic compounds
  Meteorology: QC879.9.O73
Organic geochemistry: QE516.5
Organic photochemistry
  Organic compounds: QD275
Organic reaction mechanisms:
  QD502.5
Organic scintillators
  Radiation physics: QC476.77
Organic substances
  Animal biochemistry: QP550+
  Semiconductor physics: QC611.8.O7
Organic superconductors:
  QC611.98.O74
Organic synthesis: QD262
Organic thin films: QC176.9.O73
Organochlorine compounds
  Effect on plants and animals:
    QH545.O72
Organometallic chemistry
  Organic chemistry: QD410+
Organometallic compounds
  Effect on plants and animals:
    QH545.O74
  Organic chemistry: QD410+
  Spectra: QC463.O7
Organophosphorus compounds
  Effect on plants and animals:
    QH545.O76
  Spectra: QC463.O72
Organosilicon compounds
  Spectra: QC463.O73
Orgueil meteorite: QB756.O74
Oribatidae: QL458.2.O74
Orientation
  Animals: QL782.5
  Birds: QL698.85
Orientation in space
  Physiology: QP443
Origin
  Cosmic ray physics: QC485.8.O7
Origin of life
  Biology: QH325
Origin of planets: QB603.O74
Origin of solar system: QB503
Origin of the earth
  Astronomy: QB632
Oriolidae: QL696.P2585
Orion Nebula: QB855.9.O75
Ormyridae: QL568.O74
Orneodidae: QL561.A48
Ornithine
  Animal biochemistry: QP563.O7
Ornithine decarboxylase
  Animal biochemistry: QP613.O75
Ornithischia
  Paleozoology: QE862.O65
Ornithological illustration: QL674.4
Ornithological literature: QL672.5
Ornithorhynchidae: QL737.M72
Ornithosauria
  Paleozoology: QE862.P7
Orobanchaceae: QK495.O74
Orogeny: QE621+
Orothripidae: QL598.3.O7

INDEX

Ozone layer depletion
Meteorology: QC879.7+
Ozonization
Organic chemistry: QD281.O95
Ozonolysis
Organic chemistry: QD281.O95
Ozonosphere
Meteorology: QC881.2.O9

P

p-adic analysis
Mathematical physics: QC20.7.P23
p53 protein
Animal biochemistry: QP552.P25
Pacaranas: QL737.R646
Pacas: QL737.R623
Pachybolidae: QL449.65.P18
Pachycephalidae: QL696.P2595
Pachyneuridae: QL537.P3
Pachypodidae: QL596.P13
Packing
Algebra: QA166.7
Paddlefishes: QL638.P755
Padé approximant
Mathematical physics: QC20.7.P3
Paeoniaceae: QK495.P15
Paeromopidae: QL449.65.P22
Pain
Neurophysiology: QP401
Physiology: QP451.4
Painted snipes: QL696.C477
Paired and multiple comparisons
Mathematical statistics: QA278.4
Palacheite
Mineralogy: QE391.B75
Palaeonisciformes
Paleozoology: QE852.P3
Palaeosetidae: QL561.P17
Palaephatidae: QL561.P18
Paleoart: QE714.2
Paleobiogeography: QE721.2.P24
Paleobiology: QE719.8
Paleobiology, Evolutionary:
QE721.2.E85
Paleobotany: QE901+
Paleoceanography: QE39.5.P25
Paleocene
Paleobotany: QE927
Paleontology: QE736.8
Stratigraphy: QE692
Paleoclimatology
Meteorology: QC884+
Paleoecology
Geology: QE720+
Paleoecology, Evolutionary:
QE721.2.E87
Paleogene
Paleobotany: QE926.5+
Paleontology: QE736.5+
Stratigraphy: QE691.5+
Paleogeography: QE501.4.P3
Paleogeophysics
Geophysics: QC809.P3
Paleohydrology: QE39.5.P27
Paleolimnology: QE39.5.P3
Paleomagnetism
Geology: QE501.4.P35
Paleontological excavations:
QE721.2.P26
Paleontological illustration: QE714.2
Paleontology: QE701+
Paleontology as a profession: QE714.7
Paleopedology: QE473
Paleoseismology: QE539.2.P34
Paleotemperatures: QE721.2.P3
Paleoweathering
Geology: QE570
Paleozoic
Paleobotany: QE915+
Paleontology: QE725+
Stratigraphy: QE654+
Paleozoology: QE760.8+
Palingeniidae: QL505.3.P3
Palladium
Chemical element: Q1 .P4
Pallopteridae: QL537.P34
Palm
Botany: QK495.P17
Palm oil
Animal biochemistry: QP752.P35
Palmae: QK495.P17
Palmariaceae: QK569.P25
Palmchats: QL696.P2435

Palpigradi: QL458.55+
Palpigradida: QL458.55+
Palpimanidae: QL458.42.P34
Palygorskite
  Mineralogy: QE391.P34
Palynology
  Paleobotany: QE993+
  Perianth: QK658
Pamphagidae: QL508.P34
Pamphiliidae: QL568.P3
Panama-hat palm
  Botany: QK495.C975
Panchaetothripidae: QL598.3.P3
Panchloridae: QL505.7.P33
Pancreas
  Anatomy: QL866
  Human anatomy: QM353
  Physiology: QP188.P26
Pancreatic juice
  Physiology: QP195
Pandaceae: QK495.P175
Pandanaceae: QK495.P18
Pandas
  Anecdotes and stories: QL795.P18
Pandionidae: QL696.F36
Panesthiidae: QL505.7.P34
Pangaea: QE511.5
Pangamic acid
  Animal biochemistry: QP772.P3
Pangasiidae: QL638.P254
Pangolins: QL737.P5
Pannariaceae: QK585.P17
Panorpidae: QL598.7.P3
Pantethine
  Animal biochemistry: QP801.P28
Panthers
  Anecdotes and stories: QL795.P2
Pantodontidae: QL638.P258
Pantophthalmidae: QL537.P35
Pantopoda: QL447
Pantothenic acid
  Animal biochemistry: QP772.P35
Pantotheria
  Paleozoology: QE882.P3
Papain
  Animal biochemistry: QP609.P3
Papaveraceae: QK495.P22
Papaya
  Botany: QK495.C1997
Paper chromatography
  Analytical chemistry: QD79.C46
Paper work
  Mathematics teaching aid: QA19.P34
Papilionidae: QL561.P2
Papillomavirus diseases
  Microbiology: QR201.P26
Papillomavirus vaccines: QR189.5.P36
Papillomaviruses
  Virology: QR406+
Paracrinoidea
  Paleozoology: QE783.P3
Paradisaeidae: QL696.P26
Paradox
  Physics: QC6.4.P37
Paradoxornithidae: QL696.P2612
Paradoxsomatidae: QL449.65.P27
Paraffins
  Aliphatic compounds: QD305.H6
Paraganglia
  Neurophysiology: QP368.8
Paraganglia, Aortic
  Physiology: QP188.A6
Paragenesis
  Mineralogy: QE364.2.P3
Paraiulidae: QL449.65.P273
Paralepididae: QL638.P3
Paralichthyidae: QL638.P313
Parallax
  Astronomy: QB159
  Moon: QB583
Parallax, Annual
  Spherical astronomy: QB167
Parallax, Stellar: QB813
Parallel processing
  Digital computers: QA76.58
Parallel programming
  Digital computers: QA76.642
Parallel projection
  Descriptive geometry: QA502+
Paramagnetism
  Physics: QC762.9+
Paramos
  Botany: QK938.P3

Plasma spectroscopy
  Analytical chemistry: QD96.P62
Plasma transport
  Plasma physics: QC718.5.T7
Plasmasphere
  Geophysics: QC809.P5
Plasmids
  Genetics: QH452.6
  Microbiology: QR76.6
Plasmodiophoraceae: QK635.P6
Plasmodiophorales: QK635.P65
Plasmodiophorida: QL368.P55
Plasmodroma: QL368.A115
Plasmoids
  Plasma physics: QC718.5.P58
Plasmons
  Solid state physics: QC176.8.P55
Plastic embedding
  Human histology: QM556.5.P53
Plasticity
  Analytic mechanics: QA931+
  Crystallography: QD933
Plasticizers
  Spectra: QC463.P46
Plastoceridae: QL596.P5
Plastocyanin
  Plant constituent: QK898.P73
Platacanthomyidae: QL737.R666
Platanaceae: QK495.P72
Platanistidae: QL737.C436
Plataspidae: QL523.P57
Plate tectonics
  Geology: QE511.4+
Platelet activating factor
  Animal biochemistry: QP752.P62
Platelet-derived growth factor
  Animal biochemistry: QP552.P56
Platelets
  Immunology: QR185.8.P58
  Physiology: QP97+
Plates in sound vibrations: QC241
Platinum
  Chemical element: Q1 .P8
Platinum group
  Inorganic chemistry: QD172.P8
Platinum ores
  Mineralogy: QE390.2.P56
Platoridae: QL458.42.P6
Platycephalidae: QL638.P62
Platyceratidae
  Paleozoology: QE809.P5
Platycnemididae: QL520.3.P53
Platyctenea: QL380.5.T47
Platydesmidae: QL449.65.P42
Platygastridae: QL568.P55
Platygloeaceae: QK627.7
Platygloeales: QK627.7
Platyhelminthes: QL391.P7
Platylabiidae: QL510.3.P5
Platypezidae: QL537.P63
Platypodidae: QL596.P6
Platypsyllidae: QL596.P62
Platypus
  Zoology: QL737.M72
Platyrrhacidae: QL449.65.P427
Platystictidae: QL520.3.P58
Platystomatidae: QL537.P65
Platystrophiinae
  Paleozoology: QE797.P5
Platytroctidae: QL638.P63
Play behavior
  Animals: QL763.5
Pleasing lacewings: QL513.D5
Pleasure
  Neurophysiology: QP401
Plecoglossidae: QL638.P64
Plecoptera
  Paleozoology: QE832.P55
  Zoology: QL530+
Plectoptera
  Zoology: QL505+
Plectreuridae: QL458.42.P64
Pleidae: QL527.P6
Pleistocene
  Paleobotany: QE931.2
  Paleontology: QE741.2
  Stratigraphy: QE697+
Pleocomidae: QL596.P63
Pleomorphic fungi: QK604.2.P56
Pleosporaceae: QK623.P66
Pleosporales: QK623.P68
Plesiopidae: QL638.P648
Plesiosauria
  Paleozoology: QE862.P4

R

Red panda: QL737.C214
Redfieldiiformes
  Paleozoology: QE852.R4
Redlichiida
  Paleozoology: QE823.R4
Reduced gravity effects
  Polymers: QD381.9.R43
Reduced gravity environments
  Scientific research: Q180.55.R43
Reduced nicotinamide adenine dinucleotide dehydrogenase
  Animal biochemistry: QP603.R4
Reduction
  Chemistry: QD63.R4
  Organic chemistry: QD281.R4
Reduction of center of earth
  Astronomy: QB155+
Reduction, Star
  Spherical astronomy: QB168
Reductionism
  Philosophy of science: Q175.32.R47
  Physics: QC6.4.R43
Reductones
  Animal biochemistry: QP801.R4
Reduviidae: QL523.R4
Reefs
  Ecology: QH541.5.C7
Refactoring of software
  Computer software: QA76.76.R42
Reflectance spectroscopy
  Analytical chemistry: QD96.R4
  Physics: QC454.R4
Reflection
  Optics: QC425+
  Sound: QC233
Reflectivity
  Crystallography: QD941
Reflectometers: QC425.4
Reflexes
  Central nervous system: QP372+
Reflexes, Cardiogenic
  Physiology: QP114.C37
Reforestation
  Effect on plants and animals: QH545.R44
Refraction
  Optics: QC425.9+
Refraction
  Radar meteorology: QC973.8.R4
Refraction, Astronomical: QB155+
Refraction, Double
  Optics: QC426.8.D68
Refraction, Eye
  Physiology: QP477
Refractive indices
  Geometrical optics: QC387
Refractivity
  Crystallography: QD941
Refractometers: QC426.4
Regalecidae: QL638.R4
Regeneration
  Biology: QH499
  Heart physiology: QP114.R45
  Physiology: QP90.2
  Plant physiology: QK840
Regge trajectories
  Elementary particle physics: QC793.3.R4
Regional anatomy
  Human anatomy: QM531+
  Zoology: QL950.1+
Regression analysis
  Mathematical statistics: QA278.2
Regulation of respiration
  Physiology: QP123
Regulidae: QL696.P27
Reindeer
  Anecdotes and stories: QL795.R4
Reinforcement learning (Machine learning): Q325.6
Reintroduction, Plant: QK86.4
Rejuvenation
  Physiology: QP90
Relapsing fever
  Microbiology: QR201.R45
Relational calculus
  Mathematical physics: QC20.7.R38
Relative motions
  Kinematics: QA841+
Relativistic astrophysics: QB462.65
Relativistic effects
  Quantum chemistry: QD462.6.R42
Relativistic fluid dynamics: QA912
Relativistic kinematics: QA842

Relativistic mechanics: QA808.5
Relativistic thermodynamics: QC311.7
Relativistic wave mechanics:
  QC174.24.R4
Relativity physics: QC173.5+
Relativity (Statistical physics):
  QC175.36.R4
Relaxation
  Dielectrics: QC585.7.R4
  Gas dynamics: QC168.85.R45
  Nuclear magnetism: QC762.6.R44
Relaxation methods
  Mathematical physics: QC20.7.R4
  Numerical analysis: QA297.55
Relaxation phenomena
  Atomic physics: QC173.4.R44
  Quantum chemistry: QD462.6.R44
Relaxation spectroscopy
  Analytical chemistry: QD96.R44
Relaxin
  Animal biochemistry: QP572.R46
Reliability
  Computer software: QA76.76.R44
Relict plants
  Botany: QK86.7+
Remizidae: QL696.P272
Remnant vegetation conservation:
  QK86+
Remnant vegetation management:
  QK86+
Remoras
  Zoology: QL638.E2
Remote job entry
  Computer science: QA76.9.R45
Remote sensing
  Ecology: QH541.15.R4
  Freshwater biology: QH96.8.R34
  Geochemistry: QE515.5.R45
  Geology: QE33.2.R4
  Seismology: QE539.2.R45
  Structural geology: QE501.4.R45
  Volcanoes: QE527.55
Renin
  Animal biochemistry: QP609.R38
Rennin
  Animal biochemistry: QP609.R4
Renormalization
  Mathematical physics: QC20.7.R43
Renormalization theory
  Quantum mechanics: QC174.17.R46
Reoviruses
  Virology: QR414
Reparative processes
  Plant physiology: QK840
Replication
  Virology: QR470
Replication of DNA
  Animal biochemistry: QP624.5.R48
Reporter genes: QH447.8.R47
Representations of graphs: QA166.242
Representations of groups
  Algebra: QA176
Reproduction
  Bacterial physiology: QR86.5
  Biology (General): QH471+
  Birds: QL698.2
  Fishes: QL639.2
  Invertebrates: QL364.15
  Mammals: QL739.23
  Mollusca: QL431.3
  Physiology: QP251+
  Plant physiology: QK825+
  Reptiles and amphibians: QL669.3
Reproductive endocrinology: QP252+
Reproductive immunology
  Physiology: QP252.5
Reproductive interrelation
  Plant ecology: QK925+
Reproductive organs
  Anatomy: QL876+
  Human anatomy: QM401+
  Spermatophytes: QK652+
Reptile watching: QL645.6+
Reptiles
  Paleozoology: QE861+
  Zoology: QL665+
Reptiles and amphibians: QL640+
Requiem sharks: QL638.95.C3
Research
  Algebra: QA159+
    Group theory: QA174.62.C65
  Calculus: QA303.3
  Computer science: QA76.27+

Ribonucleases
  Animal biochemistry: QP609.R53
Ribonucleate nucleotidyltransferaes
  Animal biochemistry: QP606.R53
Ribonucleic acids
  Animal biochemistry: QP623+
  Organic chemistry: QD434
Ribonucleoside diphosphate reductase
  Animal biochemistry: QP603.R52
Ribosomes
  Cytology: QH603.R5
Ribs
  Human anatomy: QM113
Ricaniidae: QL527.R5
Ricciaceae: QK555.R5
Rice
  Nutrition: QP144.R53
Richardiidae: QL537.R5
Ricinidae: QL540.3.R5
Ricinoididae: QL458.67.R5
Ricinulei: QL458.65+
Ricinuleida: QL458.65+
Rickettsiaceae
  Microbiology: QR353.5.R5
Rickettsial diseases
  Microbiology: QR201.R59
Rickettsias
  Microbiology: QR353+
Ridiaschinidae: QL561.R53
Riebeckite
  Mineralogy: QE391.R5
Riemann surfaces: QA333+
Right whales: QL737.C423
Righteye flounders: QL638.P7
Rigid bodies
  Statics: QA831
Rigidity
  Discrete geometry: QA640.77
Ring breaking: QD281.R5
Ring enclosure: QD281.R5
Ring enlargement: QD281.R5
Ring formation
  Organic chemistry: QD281.R5
Ring-opening polymerization:
  QD281.R5
Ring system of Saturn: QB405
Ring-tailed phalangers
  Anecdotes and stories: QL795.R5
Rings of crystals
  Physical optics: QC445
Rings of planets: QB603.R55
Riodinidae: QL561.R56
Riparian areas in ecology:
  QH541.5.R52
Ripples, Cosmic: QB991.C64
Risk assessment
  Ecology: QH541.15.R57
Rissoidae: QL430.5.R57
Rivalry, Binocular
  Physiology: QP487.5
River dolphins
  Zoology: QL737.C436
River regulation
  Effect on plants and animals:
    QH545.R58
Riverweed
  Botany: QK495.P74
RNA
  Editing: QH450.25
RNA-ligand interactions
  Animal biochemistry: QP623.7+
RNA polymerases
  Animal biochemistry: QP606.R53
RNA viruses
  Structure: QR458
  Virology: QR395
Road ecology: QH541.5.R62
Roadrunners
  Zoology: QL696.C83
Roads
  Effect on birds: QL698.26
  Effect on plants and animals:
    QH545.R62
Roadside ecology: QH541.5.R62
Roatelos: QL696.G85
Robber frogs: QL668.E257
Robberflies: QL537.A85
Roccellaceae: QK585.R7
Rock-forming minerals: QE397
Rock-water interaction
  Petrology: QE431.6.W38
Rockets
  Meteorology: QC879.4+

Rockrose
  Botany: QK495.C5
Rocks
  Botany: QK938.R6
Rocks, Carbonate: QE471.15.C3
Rocks, Metamorphic: QE475.A2+
Rocks, Sedimentary: QE471+
Rocks, Ultrabasic: QE462.U4
Rockslides
  Geology: QE599+
Rocky Mountain spotted fever
  Microbiology: QR201.S65
Rodent bots: QL537.C8
Rodentia: QL737.R6+
  Paleozoology: QE882.R6
Rods in sound vibrations: QC241
Roentgen rays
  Physics: QC480.8+
Rolled-wing stoneflies: QL530.3.L49
Rollers (Birds): QL696.C73
Romaleidae
  Zoology: QL508.R65
Rondeletiidae: QL638.R65
Ronquils: QL638.B26
Root nodules
  Bacteriology: QR113
Root tubercles
  Plant anatomy: QK644
Roots
  Arithmetic: QA119
  Plant anatomy: QK644
  Theory of equations: QA212
Ropen: QL89.2.R67
Roproniidae: QL568.R6
Roridulaceae: QK495.R468
Rorquals: QL737.C424
Rosaceae: QK495.R78
Rosauridae: QL638.R68
Roscoelite
  Mineralogy: QE391.R7
Rose
  Botany: QK495.R78
Rosensteiniidae: QL458.2.R66
Rossby waves
  Meteorology: QC880.4.R6
Rostratulidae: QL696.C477
Rostroconchia
  Paleozoology: QE814
Rotating fluids
  Celestial mechanics: QB410
  Fluid dynamics: QA925
Rotation groups
  Quantum mechanics: QC174.17.R65
Rotation of crystals
  Crystallography: QD941
Rotation of the earth: QB633
Rotation of the moon: QB585
Rotation of the sun: QB523
Rotavirus infections
  Microbiology: QR201.R67
Rotifera: QL391.R8
Roulettes
  Infinitesimal geometry: QA623
Round fungus beetles: QL596.L35
Round Island boas: QL666.O633
Rounding
  Numerical analysis: QA297.65
Roundoff errors
  Numerical analysis: QA297.7
Roundworms: QL391.N4
Rove beetles: QL596.S75
Royal moths: QL561.C5
RR Lyrae stars: QB843.R72
Rubella vaccines: QR189.5.R8
Rubella viruses
  Virology: QR416.R8
Rubiaceae: QK495.R85
Rubidium
  Chemical element: Q1 .R3
Rubies
  Mineralogy: QE394.R8
Rudista
  Paleozoology: QE812.H573
Rumen
  Microbiology: QR171.R85
Running
  Physiology: QP310.R85
Ruppiaceae: QK495.R956
Rush
  Botany: QK495.J87
Russulaceae: QK629.R87
Rust flies: QL537.P83
Rust fungi: QK627.A1+

Saturn (Planet): QB671+
  Perturbations: QB384
  Satellites and ring systems: QB405
Saturniidae: QL561.S2
Satyridae: QL561.S3
Sauria: QL666.L2+
Sauries
  Zoology: QL638.S347
Saurischia
  Paleozoology: QE862.S3
Sauriurae
  Paleozoology: QE872.A8
Sauropterygia
  Paleozoology: QE862.S33
Saururaceae: QK495.S27
Savannas
  Ecology: QH541.5.P7
Saw sharks: QL638.95.P7
Sawfishes: QL638.77+
Sawflies: QL568.T3
Saxifragaceae: QK495.S3
Saxifrage
  Botany: QK495.S3
Saxitoxin
  Animal biochemistry: QP632.S27
SCA statistical system: QA276.45.S28
Scala (Computer program language):
  QA76.73.S28
Scalar field theory: QA433
Scalariidae: QL430.5.E6
Scales
  Anatomy: QL942
  Shoots: QK650
Scales (Weighing instruments): QC107
Scaling
  Quantum chemistry: QD462.6.S25
  Statistical physics: QC174.85.S34
Scaly-tailed squirrels: QL737.R624
Scandentia: QL737.S25+
  Paleozoology: QE882.S32
Scandium
  Chemical element: Q1 .S4
Scanning Auger electron microscopes:
  QH212.S24
Scanning electrochemical microscopes:
  QH212.S28
Scanning electron microscopes:
  QH212.S3
Scanning force microscopes:
  QH212.S32
Scanning probe microscopes:
  QH212.S33
Scanning systems
  Nuclear physics: QC787.S3
Scanning transmission electron
  microscopes: QH212.S34
Scanning tunneling microscopes:
  QH212.S35
Scapaniaceae: QK555.S34
Scapanorhynchidae: QL638.95.S3
Scaphidiidae: QL596.S28
Scaphiopodidae: QL668.E33
Scaphopoda: QL430.8
  Paleozoology: QE813
Scapolite
  Mineralogy: QE391.S28
Scarabaeidae: QL596.S3
Scarabs
  Zoology: QL596.S3
Scaridae: QL638.S3
Scarlatina
  Microbiology: QR201.S3
Scatophagidae: QL638.S32
Scatopsidae: QL537.S32
Scats (Fish): QL638.S32
Scattering
  Atomic physics: QC174.52.S32
  Electric discharge: QC702.7.S3
  Electric waves: QC665.S3
  Meteorological optics: QC976.S3
  Nuclear interactions: QC794.6.S3
  Optics: QC427+
  Radio waves: QC676.7.S3
  Sound waves: QC243.3.S3
  X-rays: QC482.S3
Scattering, Critical: QC427.8.C73
Scattering, Mie: QC427.8.M5
Scattering, Rayleigh: QC427.8.R3
Scattering theory
  Mathematical physics: QC20.7.S3
Scelionidae: QL568.S3
Scenedesmaceae: QK569.S32
Scenopinidae: QL537.S34

Spermatozoa
  Immunology: QR186.6.S64
Sphacelariaceae: QK569.S7
Sphaeriaceae: QK623.S73
Sphaeriales: QK623.S76
Sphaeriidae: QL430.7.S65, QL596.S65
Sphaeriodesmidae: QL449.65.S64
Sphaerioidaceae: QK625.S5
Sphaeritidae: QL596.S66
Sphaeroceridae: QL537.S7
Sphaerodactylidae: QL666.L245
Sphaerophoraceae: QK585.S64
Sphaeropsidaceae: QK625.S5
Sphaeropsidales: QK625.S6
Sphaerosepalaceae: QK495.S7455
Sphaerosomatidae: QL596.S68
Sphaerotheridae: QL449.65.S645
Sphagnaceae: QK539.S75
Sphalerite
  Mineralogy: QE391.S65
Sphecidae: QL568.S7
Sphene
  Mineralogy: QE391.S67
Spheniscidae: QL696.S473
Sphenisciformes: QL696.S47+
  Paleozoology: QE872.S4
Sphenocleaceae: QK495.S7456
Sphenodontidae: QL666.R48
Sphenophyllales
  Paleobotany: QE965
Sphenopsida
  Paleobotany: QE965
Spherical astronomy: QB140+
Spherical harmonics
  Mathematical physics: QC20.7.S645
Spherical projection
  Descriptive geometry: QA520
Spherical trigonometry: QA535
Sphincters
  Physiology: QP322
Sphindidae: QL596.S7
Sphingidae: QL561.S7
Sphingolipids
  Animal biochemistry: QP752.S6
Sphinx moths: QL561.S7
Sphyraenidae: QL638.S77
Sphyrnidae: QL638.95.S7
Spicebush
  Botany: QK495.C15
Spider beetles: QL596.A5
Spider mites: QL458.2.T4
Spider monkeys: QL737.P915
Spider wasps: QL568.P6
Spiderflower
  Botany: QK495.C198
Spiders
  General: QL451+
  Zoology: QL458.4+
Spiderwort
  Botany: QK495.C73
Spikefishes: QL638.T695
Spilites: QE462.S65
Spin
  Elementary particle physics:
    QC793.3.S6
Spin geometry: QA671.5
Spin glasses
  Solid state physics: QC176.8.S68
Spin labels
  Biological research: QH324.9.S62
Spin-lattice relaxation
  Nuclear magnetism: QC762.6.S64
Spin waves
  Nuclear magnetism: QC762.6.S65
Spinal cord
  Anatomy: QL938.S6
  Human anatomy: QM465
  Neurophysiology: QP371
Spinal nerves
  Neurophysiology: QP367
Spine muscles
  Physiology: QP330
Spinel
  Mineralogy: QE391.S68
Spinel group
  Inorganic chemistry: QD172.S6
Spines
  Plant ecology: QK923
  Shoots: QK650
Spinor analysis: QA433
  Mathematical physics: QC20.7.S65
Spinturnicidae: QL458.2.S75
Spiny eels: QL638.N58
Spiny-headed worms: QL391.A2

Spiny rats: QL737.R65
Spiral galaxies: QB858.42
Spiraxidae: QL430.5.S65
Spiriferidae
Paleozoology: QE797.S7
Spirillaceae: QR82.S6
Spirochaetaceae: QR82.S7
Spirostreptidae: QL449.65.S655
Spirotricha: QL368.A22
Spirulidae: QL430.3.S65
Spittlebugs
Zoology: QL527.C4
Splachnaceae: QK539.S76
Spleen
Anatomy: QL868
Human anatomy: QM371
Immunology: QR185.8.S65
Physiology: QP188.S7
Spline theory
Algebra: QA224
Spodumene
Mineralogy: QE391.S7
Spondylidae: QL430.7.S68
Sponges
Paleozoology: QE775
Zoology: QL370.7+
Spongillaflies: QL513.S65
Spongiphoridae: QL510.3.S66
Spontaneous mutation
Genetic mutation: QH464
Spookfishes: QL638.O657
Spoonbills: QL696.C585
Paleozoology: QE872.T5
Spores
Microbiology: QR79
Spores, Fossil: QE996
Sporidiales: QK627.8
Sporidiobolaceae: QK627.8
Sporozoa: QL368.A16
Spot tests
Analytical chemistry: QD98.S6
Spotted fever, Rocky Mountain
Microbiology: QR201.S65
Spread-winged damselflies:
QL520.3.L45
Spreadsheets
Chemistry: QD39.3.S67
Spring (Season)
Astronomy: QB637.5
Springhares: QL737.R672
Springs
Ecology: QH541.5.S65
Freshwater biology: QH99
Zoology: QL147
Springs, Hot
Geology: QE528
Springtails
Paleozoology: QE832.C63
Spriobolidae: QL449.65.S65
Spurge
Botany: QK495.E9
Sputtering
Solid state physics: QC176.8.S72
Spyware: QA76.76.S69
SQL (Computer program language):
QA76.73.S67
Squalidae: QL638.95.S84
Squaliformes: QL638.94.S75
Squall lines
Meteorology: QC880.4.S65
Squalls
Meteorology: QC880.4.S65
Squamata
Paleozoology: QE862.S65
Zoology: QL666.L19+
Square root: QA119
Tables: QA49
Squares and cubes
Tables: QA49
Squatinidae: QL638.95.S88
Squeezed light: QC446.3.S67
Squid
Laboratory manuals: QL813.S69
Squirrel monkeys: QL737.P925
Squirrelfishes: QL638.H64
Squirrels
Anecdotes and stories: QL795.S7
Zoology: QL737.R68
St. Johnswort
Botany: QK495.G87
Stability
DNA: QP624.5.S73
Mathematical physics: QC20.7.S68
Plasma physics: QC718.5.S7

Thuathe meteorite: QB756.T58
Thulium
  Chemical element: Q1 .T8
Thunderstorms: QC968+
Thurniaceae: QK495.T46
Thy-1 antigen
  Immunology: QR186.6.T48
Thyasidae: QL458.2.T5
Thyatiridae: QL561.T46
Thylacine: QL737.M336
  Anecdotes and stories: QL795.T47
Thylacinidae: QL737.M336
Thylacomyidae (Bilbies): QL737.M478
Thymelaeaceae: QK495.T48
Thymic hormones
  Animal biochemistry: QP572.T46
Thymus
  Immunology: QR185.8.T48
Thymus gland
  Anatomy: QL868
  Physiology: QP188.T5
Thynnidae: QL568.T4
Thyreophoridae: QL537.T49
Thyrididae: QL561.T48
Thyroglobulin
  Animal biochemistry: QP552.T5
Thyroid gland
  Anatomy: QL868
  Human anatomy: QM371
  Physiology: QP188.T54
Thyroid hormones
  Animal biochemistry: QP572.T5
Thyronines
  Animal biochemistry
    Hormones: QP572.T5
Thyroprotein
  Animal biochemistry: QP552.T55
Thyropteridae: QL737.C59
Thyrotropin
  Animal biochemistry: QP572.T55
Thyrotropin releasing factor
  Animal biochemistry: QP572.T56
Thyroxine
  Animal biochemistry: QP563.T5
    Hormones: QP572.T5
Thysanoptera
  Paleozoology: QE832.T5
Thysanoptera
  Zoology: QL598+
Thysanura: QL503.8.A1+
Tidal pool ecology: QH541.5.S35
Tidal pools
  Ecology: QH541.5.S35
Tide marshes
  Botany: QK938.S27
Tide theory
  Celestial mechanics: QB414+
Tidemarsh ecology: QH541.5.S24
Tidemarshes
  Ecology: QH541.5.S24
  Zoology: QL114
Tides, Theory of
  Celestial mechanics: QB414+
Tiger beetles: QL596.C56
Tiger moths: QL561.A8
Tigers
  Anecdotes and stories: QL795.T5
Tilefishes: QL638.B83
Tiliaceae: QK495.T5
Tiling
  Algebra: QA166.8
Tilletiaceae: QK628.T5
Tillite: QE471.15.T5
Tillodontia
  Paleozoology: QE882.C84
Timaliidae: QL696.P285
Timber beetles: QL596.L94
Time
  Philosophy of science: Q175.32.T56
  Practical astronomy: QB209+
Time dilatation (Relativity physics):
  QC173.59.T5
Time, Equation of
  Astronomy: QB217
Time, Finding the
  Astronomy: QB213
Time measuring instruments
  Astronomy: QB214
Time perception
  Physiology: QP445
Time-resolved spectroscopy
  Animal biochemistry: QP519.9.T59
Time reversal (Relativity physics):
  QC173.59.T53

Tropiduridae: QL666.L287
Tropisms
  Biology: QH514
Tropopause
  Meteorology: QC881.2.T75
Troposphere
  Meteorology: QC881.2.T75
Tropospheric radio wave propagation: QC973.4.T76
Tropospheric radio waves
  Radio meteorology: QC973.4.T76
Troupials: QL696.P2475
Trout
  Zoology: QL638.S2
Trout-perches: QL638.P468
TRP channels
  Animal biochemistry: QP552.T77
True bugs
  Paleozoology: QE832.H4
True starfish
  Paleozoology: QE783.A7
Trumpeters (Birds): QL696.G874
Trumpetfishes: QL638.A848
Truncatellidae: QL430.5.T78
Trunk
  Anatomy: QL950.3+
  Regional anatomy: QM540+
Trunk muscles
  Human anatomy: QM161
Trunks, Tree: QK646.7
Truth
  Philosophy of science: Q175.32.T78
Truth maintenance systems
  Artificial intelligence: Q338
Trypauchenidae: QL638.T95
Trypetheliaceae: QK585.T7
Trypetidae: QL537.T42
Trypoxylidae: QL568.T79
Trypsin
  Animal biochemistry: QP609.T7
Trypsinogen
  Animal biochemistry: QP609.T7
Tryptophan
  Animal biochemistry: QP562.T7
Tryptophan oxygenase
  Animal biochemistry: QP603.T78
Tuatara: QL666.R48
Tube-eyes: QL638.S88
Tuberaceae: QK623.T8
Tuberculariaceae: QK625.T8
Tuberculosis
  Microbiology: QR201.T6
Tuberculosis vaccines: QR189.5.T7+
Tubeshoulders: QL638.P63
Tubulidentata: QL737.T75+
  Paleozoology: QE882.T8
Tubulins
  Animal biochemistry: QP552.T82
Tucu-tucos: QL737.R642
Tuff
  Petrology: QE461+
Tuftsin
  Animal biochemistry: QP552.T83
Tugtupite
  Mineralogy: QE391.T85
Tularemia
  Microbiology: QR201.T8
Tulasnellaceae: QK629.T8
Tumbling flower beetles: QL596.M6
Tumor immunology: QR188.6
Tumor necrosis factor
  Immunology: QR185.8.T84
Tumors
  Microbiology: QR201.T84
Tuna
  Zoology: QL638.S35
Tundra ecology: QH541.5.T8
Tundras
  Botany: QK938.T8
  Ecology: QH541.5.T8
Tungidae: QL599.7.T8
Tungstates
  Mineralogy: QE389.67
Tungsten
  Chemical element: Q1 .W1
Tungsten ores
  Mineralogy: QE390.2.T85
Tunguska meteorite: QB756.T8
Tunicata
  Paleozoology: QE840.5
  Zoology: QL613
Tuning forks in sound vibrations: QC241

U

W

GPO U.S. GOVERNMENT PRINTING OFFICE: 2012–372–396/40015